solutions@syngres[illegible]

With more than 1,500,000 copies of our MCS[illegible] [illegible]sco study guides in print, we continue to look for ways we [illegible] the information needs of our readers. One way we do that is by listening.

Readers like yourself have been telling us they want an Internet-based service that would extend and enhance the value of our books. Based on reader feedback and our own strategic plan, we have created a Web site that we hope will exceed your expectations.

Solutions@syngress.com is an interactive treasure trove of useful information focusing on our book topics and related technologies. The site offers the following features:

- One-year warranty against content obsolescence due to vendor product upgrades. You can access online updates for any affected chapters.
- "Ask the Author"™ customer query forms that enable you to post questions to our authors and editors.
- Exclusive monthly mailings in which our experts provide answers to reader queries and clear explanations of complex material.
- Regularly updated links to sites specially selected by our editors for readers desiring additional reliable information on key topics.

Best of all, the book you're now holding is your key to this amazing site. Just go to **www.syngress.com/solutions**, and keep this book handy when you register to verify your purchase.

Thank you for giving us the opportunity to serve your needs. And be sure to let us know if there's anything else we can do to help you get the maximum value from your investment. We're listening.

www.syngress.com/solutions

SYNGRESS®

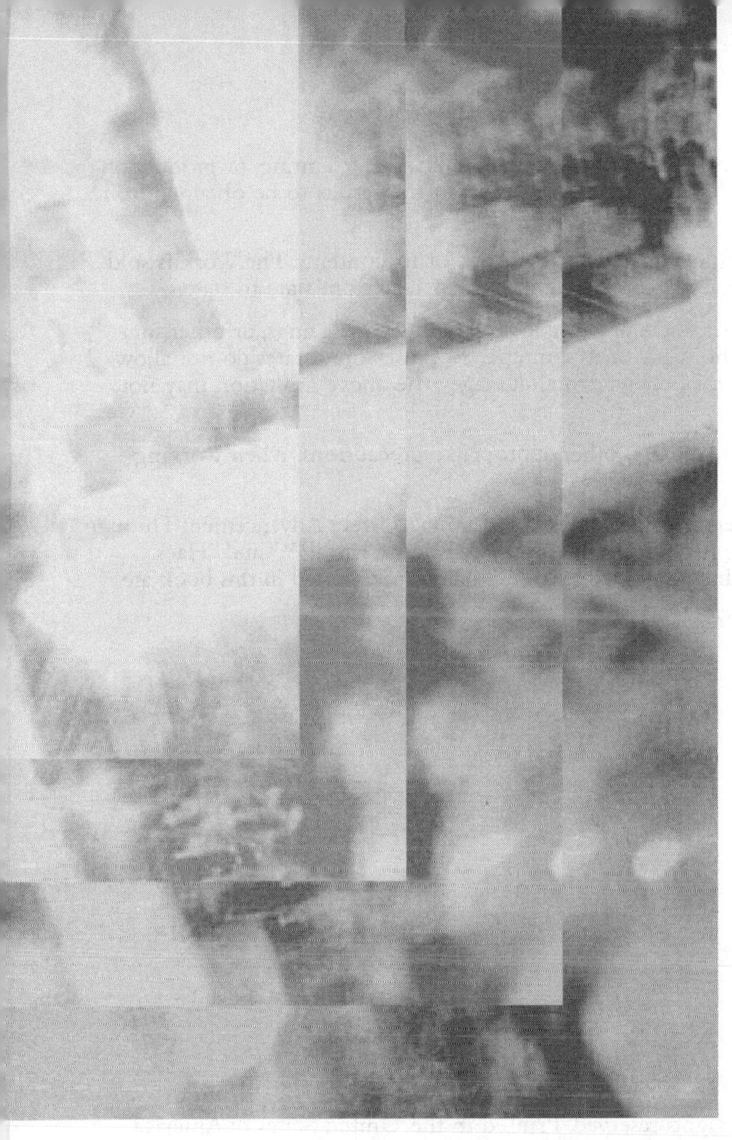

CONFIGURING
ISA SERVER 2000:
BUILDING FIREWALLS FOR WINDOWS 2000

SYNGRESS®

KEY	SERIAL NUMBER
001	NANFA94U53
002	MA3AEJDRF9
003	MKEA9UU2Q4
004	KT95QJFD95
005	ZPERJ7AT54
006	EK3ATZLCPE
007	5J6EMVCDAP
008	45SEJT9HSB
009	LDMA349F2G
010	XCFT678KM3

PUBLISHED BY
Syngress Publishing, Inc.
800 Hingham Street
Rockland, MA 02370

Configuring ISA Server 2000: Building Firewalls for Windows 2000

Printed in the United States of America

1 2 3 4 5 6 7 8 9 0

ISBN: 1-928994-29-6

Technical edit by: Martin Grasdal
Co-Publisher: Richard Kristof
Project Editor: Maribeth Corona-Evans
Copy edit by: Darlene Bordwell
Index by: Jennifer Coker
Page Layout and Art by: Shannon Tozier

Distributed by Publishers Group West

Acknowledgments

We would like to acknowledge the following people for their kindness and support in making this book possible.

Richard Kristof and Duncan Anderson of Global Knowledge, for their generous access to the IT industry's best courses, instructors and training facilities.

Ralph Troupe, Rhonda St. John, and the team at Callisma for their invaluable insight into the challenges of designing, deploying and supporting world-class enterprise networks.

Karen Cross, Lance Tilford, Meaghan Cunningham, Kim Wylie, Harry Kirchner, Bill Richter, Kevin Votel, and Brittin Clark of Publishers Group West for sharing their incredible marketing experience and expertise.

Mary Ging, Caroline Hird, Simon Beale, Caroline Wheeler, Victoria Fuller, Jonathan Bunkell, and Klaus Beran of Harcourt International for making certain that our vision remains worldwide in scope.

Anneke Baeten, Annabel Dent, and Laurie Giles of Harcourt Australia for all their help.

David Buckland, Wendi Wong, Daniel Loh, Marie Chieng, Lucy Chong, Leslie Lim, Audrey Gan, and Joseph Chan of Transquest Publishers for the enthusiasm with which they receive our books.

Kwon Sung June at Acorn Publishing for his support.

Ethan Atkin at Cranbury International for his help in expanding the Syngress program.

Joe Pisco, Helen Moyer, and the great folks at InterCity Press for all their help.

From Deb and Tom Shinder, Authors

As always, writing a book is a complex undertaking that involves many people in addition to the authors. This book was, in many ways, a special challenge. We were working with a brand new product, with new features, quirks, and—dare we say—a few bugs that had to be stepped on along the way.

A lot of blood, sweat, and tears (not to mention gallons and gallons of caffeine) went into the making of this book. Our goal was to create the definitive guide to Microsoft's ISA Server, a reference that can be consulted by network professionals as they roll out ISA on their production networks, a supplement to the formal study guides used by MCP/MCSE candidates in preparation for Exam 70-227, and an "interpreter" for those who find the sometimes overly technical jargon in the Microsoft documentation difficult to understand. It also serves as a record of our ongoing saga of discovery, frustration, confusion, and triumph as we worked with the product and struggled to master its intricacies.

There are many who contributed to the cause, without whose help the book could not have been written. We especially want to recognize and thank the following:

Martin Grasdal, of Brainbuzz.com, our technical editor. Although we moaned and groaned and cursed his name each time we received our chapters back with his many suggestions for wonderful improvements that would take days of work and add dozens of pages, the book would not be half as good (and perhaps not half as long) without his much-appreciated input.

Stephen Chetcuti, of isaserver.org, who provided encouragement, enthusiasm, and a forum in which we were able to promote both the product and this book, and get to know other ISA Server enthusiasts from all over the world.

Joern Wettern, of Wettern Network Solutions and Technical Lead in developing the Microsoft Official Curriculum for Course 2159A, Deploying and Managing Microsoft ISA Server 2000, who provided invaluable help and served as the "official word" on those perplexing questions that did not seem to have an answer.

Sean McCormick, of Brainbuzz.com, technical consultant/writer/Chief Executive Flunkie (CEF) and friend, who provided emotional and psychological support through the dark days (and nights!) when it seemed we might still be working on this book at the turn of the next century.

We also must thank literally dozens of participants in the Microsoft public ISA Server newsgroup and the discussion mailing list and message boards sponsored by isaserver.org. In particular, our gratitude goes to: Rob Macleod, Nathan Mercer, Jason Rigsbee, Trevor Miller, Slav Pidgorny (MVP), Ellis M. George, Jake Phuoc Trong Ha, Terry Poperszky, Vic S. Shahid, Tim Laird, Nathan Obert, Thomas Lee, John Munyan, Wes Noonan, Allistah, Eric Watkins, Rick Hardy, Tone Jarvis, Dean Wheeler, Stefan Heck, Charles Ferreira, Phillip Lyle, Sandro Gauci, Jim Wiggins, Regan Murphy, Nick Galea, Ronald Beekelaar, Russell Mangel, Hugo Caye, and Jeff Tabian. Our apologies for anyone we may have inadvertently left out.

All of the above were instrumental in the development of this book, but any errors or omissions lie solely on the heads of the authors. We have tried hard to make this manuscript as mistake-free as possible, but human nature being what it is, perfection is hard to achieve.

We want to send a very special message of thanks to Maribeth Corona-Evans, our editor. Her patience and understanding in the face of our weeping and wailing and gnashing of teeth has earned her a permanent place in our hearts.

And finally, to Andrew Williams, our publisher, whose e-mail queries regarding when the final chapters were going to be finished demonstrated the utmost in tact and diplomacy—even if undeserved on our part.

Dr. Thomas W. Shinder
Debra Littlejohn Shinder

Contributors

Thomas Shinder, M.D. (MCSE, MCP+I, MCT) is a technology trainer and consultant in the Dallas-Ft. Worth metroplex. He has consulted with major firms, including Xerox, Lucent Technologies, and FINA Oil, assisting in the development and implementation of IP-based communications strategies. Tom is a Windows 2000 editor for Brainbuzz.com and a Windows 2000 columnist for Swynk.com.

Tom attended medical school at the University of Illinois in Chicago and trained in neurology at the Oregon Health Sciences Center in Portland, Oregon. His fascination with interneuronal communication ultimately melded with his interest in internetworking and led him to focus on systems engineering. Tom and his wife, Debra Littlejohn Shinder, design elegant and cost-efficient solutions for small- and medium-sized businesses based on Windows NT/2000 platforms. Tom has contributed to several Syngress titles, including *Configuring Windows 2000 Server Security* (ISBN: 1-928994-02-4) and *Managing Windows 2000 Network Services* (ISBN: 1-928994-06-7), and is the co-author of *Troubleshooting Windows 2000 TCP/IP* (1-928994-11-3).

Debra Littlejohn Shinder (MCSE, MCT, MCP+I), is an independent technology trainer, author, and consultant who works in conjunction with her husband, Dr. Thomas Shinder, in the Dallas-Ft. Worth area. She has been an instructor in the Dallas County Community College District since 1992 and is the Webmaster for the cities of Seagoville and Sunnyvale, Texas.

Deb is a featured Windows 2000 columnist for Brainbuzz.com and a regular contributor to TechRepublic's TechProGuild. She and Tom have authored numerous online courses for DigitalThink (www.digitalthink.com) and have given presentations at technical conferences on Microsoft certification and Windows NT and 2000 topics. Deb is also the Series Editor for the Syngress/Osborne McGraw-Hill Windows 20000 MCSE study guides. She is a member of the Author's Guild, the IEEE IPv6 Task Force, and local professional organizations.

Deb and Tom met online and married in 1994. They opened a networking consulting business and developed the curriculum for the MCSE training program at Eastfield College before becoming full-time technology writers. Deb is the co-author of Syngress's *Troubleshooting Windows 2000 TCP/IP* (ISBN: 1-928994-11-3) and has contributed to *Managing Windows 2000 Network Services* (ISBN: 1-928994-06-7) and *Configuring Windows 2000 Server Security* (ISBN: 1-928994-02-4). She is the proud mother of two children. Daughter Kristen is stationed in Sardinia, Italy with the U.S. Navy and son Kristoffer will enter college this fall on a chess scholarship.

This book is dedicated to:

Our families, who believed in us and helped us to believe in ourselves: both Moms, Rich and D, and Kris and Kniki.

The friends and colleagues, many of whom we've never "met," with whom we work and talk and laugh and cry across the miles through the wonder of technology that allows us to building a meeting place in cyberspace.

We also dedicate this book to each other. It is a product of the partnership that is our marriage, our livelihood, and—we hope—our legacy.

DLS & TWS

Technical Editor

Martin Grasdal (MCSE+I, MCT, CNE, CNI, CTT, A+), Director of Cramsession Content at Brainbuzz.com, has worked in the computer industry for over eight years. He has been an MCT since 1995 and an MCSE since 1996. His training and networking experience covers a broad range of products, including NetWare, Lotus Notes, Windows NT and 2000, Exchange Server, IIS, and Proxy Server. Martin also works actively as a consultant. His recent consulting experience includes contract work for Microsoft as a Technical Contributor to the MCP Program on projects related to server technologies. Martin lives in Edmonton, Alberta, Canada, with his wife Cathy and their two sons.

Contents

Understand how ISA Server fits into .NET

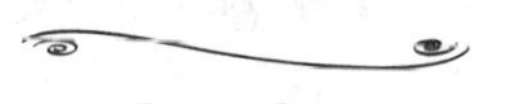

Just as Proxy Server was considered a member of the Microsoft BackOffice Family, ISA Server also belongs to a new Microsoft "family," the members of which are designed to work with Windows 2000 in an enterprise environment. This group of enterprise servers is now called the Microsoft.Net family, or simply ".Net" (pronounced dot-net) servers.

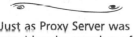

Find complete coverage of ISA Server in the Enterprise including hierarchical caching

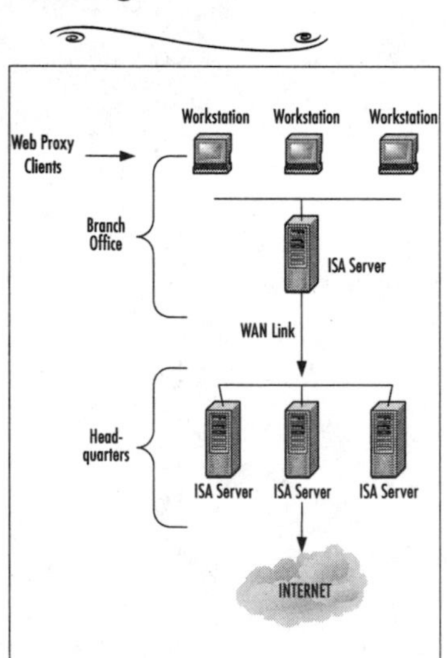

See how to incorporate ISA Server in your security plan

ISA Server's firewall function prevents unauthorized packets from entering your internal network. ISA also provides monitoring of intrusion attempts as well as allowing you to set alerts to notify you when intrusions occur. This chapter also covers system hardening, Secure Sockets Layer, SSL tunneling, and SSL bridging.

Understand the differences between Proxy Server 2.0 and ISA Server

- IPX/SPX is not supported.
- The Web Proxy Service listens on Port 8080 and Web proxy client implications.
- The Winsock client is not required on published servers.
- The Web cache is stored as a single file.
- There is no SOCKS service.
- The firewall client doesn't support 16-bit operating systems.
- There are incompatibilities between ISA and IIS on same machine.

Everything you need to manage ISA Server

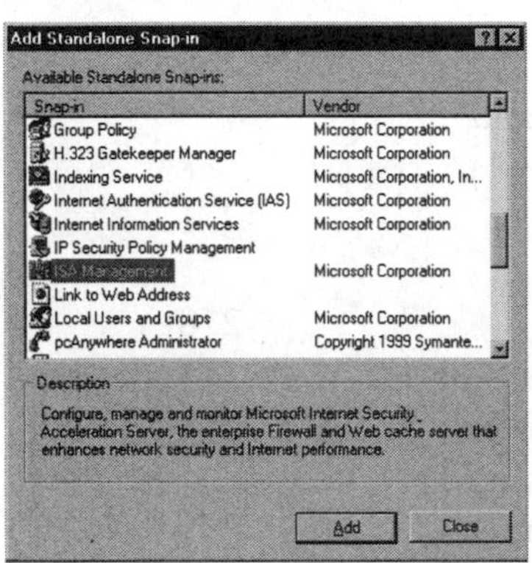

ISA Management can be added to a custom MMC.

Hundreds of security alerts, undocumented hints, and ISA Server mysteries make sure you don't miss a thing

Security Alert!

SecureNAT clients must be configured with the address of a DNS server that can resolve Internet names. You can use a DNS server located on the Internet (such as your ISP's DNS server), or you can configure an internal DNS server to use a forwarder on the Internet. Unlike the RRAS NAT Service, the ISA server does not perform DNS Proxy Services for the SecureNAT clients.

Answers all your questions about configuring outbound access

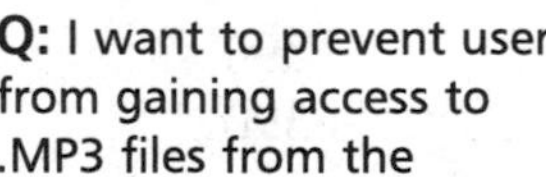

Q: I want to prevent users from gaining access to .MP3 files from the Napster site. Is there an easy way to do this?

A: Yes. Configure a site and content rule that prevents downloading of .MP3 files. If you are interested in blocking only .MP3 files, you can create a new content group in the Policy Elements node and then use this content group to create the site and content rule to limit the download of .MP3s.

Complete instructions for publishing content on a private network, including undocumented tips

You must configure a packet filter for the TZO client software to work correctly. Remember that all applications on the ISA server that require external network access require static packet filters. The packet filter settings are:

Filter type: Custom
IP protocol: TCP
Direction: Outbound
Local port: Dynamic
Remote port: Fixed Port
Remote port number: 21331

Master the Windows Messenger Service

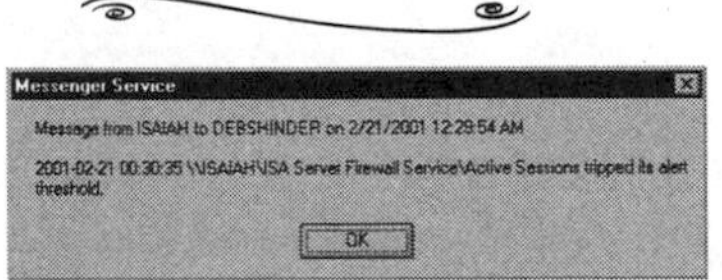

A Network Message Is Sent to the Specified Account When the Alert Is Triggered

Find step-by-step instructions for troubleshooting ISA Server

1. Information gathering
2. Analysis and planning
3. Implementation of a solution
4. Assessment of the effectiveness of the solution
5. Documentation of the incident

Introduction

—*Martin Grasdal, MCSE+I, MCT, CNE, CNI, CTT, A+*
Director, Cramsession Content, BrainBuzz.com

Security is a significant concern for any organization. If the organization has to have a presence on or a connection to the Internet, it will also have special needs to protect itself from unwanted intrusion and attacks from malicious and hostile sources.

The growth of the Internet has been accompanied by the growth in the numbers and sophistication of hackers and the tools available to them. As many organizations and home users who have a permanent connection to the Internet can attest, there is no shortage of people who want to scan ports or break into systems. The wide availability of inexpensive, high-bandwidth connections, such as cable modems and ADSL, has resulted in large increases in the number of people who are continuously connected to the Internet, thus increasing their risk for attack.

High-bandwidth connections have also made many forms of hacking a lot easier for more people. The wide availability of software designed to compromise the security of systems connected to the Internet is making the risks even greater. Malicious users do not now have to be particularly talented or knowledgeable to compromise systems that lack strong protection.

It is against this background that the market for firewall products has exploded. Five or ten years ago, there were relatively few players in the firewall market, and most of the products were expensive, some costing tens of thousands of dollars. Today, there are many firewall products on the market. In response to a real need, firewall products are widely used by almost every kind of user connected to the Internet, from home users to large corporations.

Internet Security and Acceleration Server (ISA Server) is Microsoft's latest entry into the firewall market. Its opening debut was impressive: within less than 30 days of its release in late 2000, it had already achieved ICSA Labs Certification for firewalls. For anyone familiar with ISA Server's predecessors, Proxy Server 1.0 and 2.0, they will recognize that ISA Server represents a significant improvement and advance on those products.

ISA Server shares most of the features and strengths of Proxy Server, but it also builds on them. The result is a scalable, enterprise-ready product that will be widely adopted by many corporations. Although easy to install, ISA Server is also a complex product that requires skill and knowledge to implement properly. It is also a very serious product that plays a critical role in your network infrastructure. ISA Server is not the kind of product you set up on your production network to play with or take lightly. Nor is it the kind of product that is necessarily easy to use or implement; it is certainly not the kind of product that is going to give you everything you want simply by virtue of having it installed and connected to your network.

One of the primary goals of *Configuring ISA Server 2000: Building Firewalls for Windows 2000* is to give readers information that will assist them in deploying and configuring ISA with the security and performance needs of their networks in mind.

Microsoft released Proxy Server 1.0 in November 1996. I first became familiar Proxy Server 1.0 in the late Fall of that year when I attended one of the first T-Preps (Trainer Preparation courses) on the product to qualify me to teach the official Microsoft course for it. There was a great deal of excitement in that classroom about the product. Here was a product that had some of the desirable characteristics of a firewall, such as circuit layer and application layer security, combined with the notable advantages of content caching.

At the time, the Winsock Proxy client seemed almost revolutionary. It worked extremely well in providing transparent access to Internet resources other than Web pages. And, the fact that you could, with some effort, configure Proxy Server 1.0 to act as an IPX to IP gateway seemed to make it a great solution for providing a comfortable level of security, if that was your primary concern.

However, it soon became apparent that the product had some way to go in order to win acceptance as a solution for securing networks. Although Proxy Server 1.0 did provide security at the circuit and application layer, it did not provide packet filtering, alerts, or the ability to provide detailed logs. Thus, it could not be considered a firewall product, even though it did provide a fair degree of protection on the perimeter of the network.

What Proxy Server 1.0 did provide that made it attractive to corporate users was its ability to provide content caching and to control access to Internet sites. With content caching, Proxy Server 1.0 was able to create savings on the use of bandwidth while making the apparent speed of Web access faster.

In 1996, good bandwidth to the Internet was relatively expensive. As a result, content caching became very attractive to many companies interested in keeping costs down. But, even in this area, Proxy Server 1.0 fell short for larger corporations because the content caching could not be distributed across multiple Proxy Servers and was not easily scalable.

To address the shortcomings of Proxy Server 1.0, Microsoft followed very quickly with Proxy Server 2.0 in 1997. Proxy Server 2.0 introduced many desirable features that were lacking in the original product. The product now included dynamic packet filtering. A very powerful means of protecting the network, dynamic packet filtering automatically opens ports for communication with the Internet only when communication has to take place. Administrators, in other words, did not have to manually open up static packet filters to allow access.

Proxy Server 2.0 also provided real-time alerts so that administrators could be notified when attempts to penetrate the network were made. SOCKS support was added so that non-Microsoft clients, such as Unix workstations that could not use the Winsock Proxy client, would not be limited to using CERN-compliant Web browsers for Internet access. Proxy Server 2.0 also introduced the ability to publish internal Web servers and to do server proxying. With this functionality, it was now possible to make most services running on your internal network available to users on the Internet.

Like its predecessor, Proxy Server 2.0 provided content caching. Here, Microsoft also made a number of significant improvements. Content caching was now scalable across multiple servers using either distributed or hierarchical caching. With distributed caching, administrators could create a content cache that was distributed in an array of multiple servers without duplicating any content among the caching servers. Caching arrays provided both fault tolerance and load balancing.

With hierarchical caching, administrators could connect proxy servers in a chain for content caching. Hierarchical caching was ideal for companies that had branch offices. If content could not be found in the cache of the local branch office Proxy Server, the request for content could be subsequently routed to the Proxy Server at the main office. Another significant improvement was the addition of active caching, which allowed the Proxy Server to automatically refresh commonly requested objects in the cache during periods when the server was relatively idle. This provided even better caching performance.

In spite of these improvements, Proxy Server 2.0 was not without its critics or its shortcomings. For one thing, server hosting was complicated and somewhat unreliable. To allow your internal Exchange Server, for example, to receive mail from the Internet, you had to install the Winsock Proxy client on the Exchange Server and then configure a WSPCFG.INI file with the proper settings that would "bind" a listening port for SMTP traffic on the external interface of the Proxy Server.

This created a configuration in which the Proxy Server would listen for SMTP requests on behalf of the internal Exchange server. It also required that a control channel be constantly maintained between the Exchange and the Proxy server. If the channel were lost for any reason, you would not be able to receive SMTP mail. In order to regain SMTP functionality after losing the control channel, the only solutions were to reinitialize services or reboot the computers. Although this kind of situation did not happen very often, it happened often enough to cause me to have some serious reservations about using Proxy Server 2.0 in large-scale deployments that required 7x24 SMTP functionality.

But, perhaps the most significant perceived shortcoming of Proxy Server 2.0 was its lack of ICSA Labs Certification for firewalls. Because Proxy Server 2.0 did not have ICSA Labs Certification, many people inferred that it could not, as a consequence, be considered a firewall or that it did not provide a high degree of protection. These inferences were perhaps unwarranted and unfair.

What prevented Proxy Server 2.0 from achieving the ICSA Labs Certification may have had little to do with the amount of security that it did or did not provide. Rather, the inability to achieve ICSA certification may have had more to do with the fact that proprietary client software, such as the Winsock Proxy client, was required to provide inbound and outbound traffic for some of the required services. The ICSA certification criteria are strict and explicit in this regard: no special or proprietary client software is allowed to provide inbound and outbound access for the required protocols, which include DNS, SMTP, HTTP(S), TELNET, and FTP.

The lack of ICSA Labs Certification no doubt hurt sales of Proxy Server 2.0. Many companies had policies in place that prevented them from even considering a firewall product unless it had ICSA certification. If you were to review newsgroup posts leading up to the release of ISA, you would find that one of the most common questions about ISA Server was whether it had ICSA certification.

ISA Server achieved the ICSA Labs Certification in January of 2001. The speed at which Microsoft was able to achieve ICSA certification was unusually fast. As a result of the ICSA certification and the fact that ISA Server is able to provide the same degree of security that people have come to expect from products that have had ICSA certification, ISA Server is likely to be adopted on a much wider scale than Proxy Server 2.0.

It should be noted, however, that in order to configure ISA Server to conform to the ICSA 3.0a criteria for firewall testing, you will have to do things like disable the Web Proxy service. You will find information in this book that will help you in configuring ISA Server so that you can reproduce the configuration that was required in order to pass the ICSA Labs criteria.

Anyone who has had even a cursory look at ISA Server will see that it is quite a different product from Proxy Server 2.0. Even though it shares many features in common with Proxy Server 2.0, such as the use of the dynamic packet filter and Caching Array Protocol (CARP) for distributed caching arrays, ISA Server introduces so many new features and improvements along with the new administrative interface that any similarities between the two products seem superficial.

One of the key differences is that ISA Server now comes in two editions, Standard and Enterprise. The Standard edition is a good, economical choice for smaller companies that have no need for caching arrays consisting of multiple servers, nor the need to control enterprise-wide array policies through Active Directory. Larger companies may wish to purchase the more expensive Enterprise edition in order to take advantage of the centralized policy administration that integration with Active Directory makes possible.

Another significant change and improvement is that ISA Server supports SecureNAT (Network Address Translation). This means that it is no longer necessary to install the Winsock Proxy client in order to use protocols other than HTTP(S) and FTP through the ISA Server. The result is that you no longer need to configure SOCKS to provide Internet access for your Macintosh and Unix clients.

You will find, as a consequence, that SOCKS support is significantly scaled back in ISA Server. Even though you no longer need to install the Firewall client in order to provide access to Internet resources, you may nonetheless want to install it in order to control outbound access by user and group name.

This book provides you with lots of information on the advantages and disadvantages of configuring your internal computers as SecureNAT or Firewall clients, and when it is appropriate to configure clients as either one or the other.

Providing access to internal Web servers and other services has also changed a great deal from Proxy Server 2.0. There are special wizards for publishing Web and Mail servers. Server Publishing is now accomplished through SecureNAT. Server Publishing no longer requires that you install the Winsock Proxy client on an internal server and configure a WSPCFG.INI file to bind the appropriate ports to the external interface of the ISA Server. However, ISA Server still supports this method of Server Publishing for backward compatibility and to provide a means for publishing applications that use secondary connections and for which you would otherwise require an application filter.

You will find that ISA Server comes with a number of application filters to handle inbound and outbound access for a number of protocols. It includes an application filter for handling FTP traffic. It also includes application filters for SMTP, HTTP redirection, DNS intrusion detection, Streaming Media, and H.323, among others.

ISA Server provides an H.323 Gatekeeper and Gateway to provide registration and calling services for H.323 compliant clients, such as Netmeeting. With the H.323 Gatekeeper and Gateway, Netmeeting clients can use full audio and video to communicate with one another on the internal network and on the Internet. Calls from the Internet can also be placed to internal Netmeeting clients that are registered with the Gatekeeper.

Understanding and configuring these components will challenge a number of administrators. This book provides some clear explanations and demonstrations of working configurations of the H.323 components. In fact, we found the H.323 functionality of ISA Server helpful in facilitating our own communication during the writing of this book.

Like Proxy Server 2.0, ISA Server supports VPNs. However, unlike its predecessor, ISA Server now makes it possible for internal clients to connect to VPN servers on the Internet. This will come as a welcome improvement to many. Another important improvement is the introduction of wizards to help step you through the creation of VPN configuration. If you want to create a demand-dial VPN connection with a remote ISA Server, for example, you will find that the VPN wizards do a superb job of making the setup straightforward. The ISA Server wizards are, in fact, a big improvement in comparison to the Routing and Remote Access wizards.

You will find that this book contains a good balance of explanations and practical walk-throughs that will step you through various configurations of ISA Server. Although many of the wizards, in particular the VPN wizards, greatly help to simply the administration and configuration of ISA Server, wizards are not always helpful for providing the conceptual background to what you are doing.

Wizards make it easy for you to accomplish the steps in a process that will result in a complete and successful configuration. But, often, people perform the steps as part of a sequence of individual steps, each of which appears in isolation and not as part of a contextual whole. It is helpful to know *why* you are performing a particular step and to place that step properly into the larger context of the goal. We hope that you find the many walk-throughs in this book do just that: provide explanations that will help to deepen your understanding of the product and that will make it easier for you to see your actions in the context of a wider whole.

In writing this book, the authors were always aware that both inexperienced and experienced administrators alike would read it. So, you will find that this book contains a good deal of background exposition on important topics, such as security. Chapter Three, for example, is entirely devoted to explaining important and relevant security concepts. Here you will learn what "Spoofing" is and what comprises a "Smurf" attack. Plus, the authors, one of whom has experience in law enforcement, discuss at length some of the security precautions you should take that go beyond the mere configuration of your ISA Server.

Protecting yourself against Social Engineering is important and should not be ignored, as the people at Versign discovered when they inadvertently gave Microsoft's digital certificates to an imposter. You will also find that the book provides some very good background information on concepts that are germane to firewall design and management. For example, the authors provide a thorough explanation of the Department of Defense TCP/IP and the OSI models in the context of firewalls. These explanations serve to help clarify some of the terms connected with firewalls, such as "circuit filtering" and "application filtering."

Installing and implementing ISA Server on your network is no trivial matter and should be undertaken only after careful and thoughtful consideration. Consequently, you will also find plenty of information in this book to help you deploy ISA Server so that your network will benefit from both the security and the performance improvements it provides. Because ISA Server is appropriate for both small and large networks, the book also provides information for planning to install ISA Server as a standalone server and as an Enterprise Array that requires either centralized or distributed administration.

The book's length is a reflection of the complexity of the product and the amount of detail we felt it necessary to provide. You will find that *Configuring ISA Server 2000: Building Firewalls for Windows 2000* is systematically organized and that it provides a thorough and detailed exploration of the product.

The first chapter begins by providing information on the features of ISA Server and then discusses its scalability as an enterprise product. This chapter also provides detailed information on Active Directory concepts. In the second chapter, we provide a detailed discussion of security concepts. This is followed by a chapter on planning for ISA Server, in which you will find information on both hardware and infrastructure considerations.

We recognize that you need to plan for a secure configuration for the Windows 2000 Server on which you will install ISA Server, so we provide detailed information for preparatory tasks such as disabling NetBIOS on your external interface to help ensure greater security of your server. We also provide information on the pros and cons of various disk configurations, such as RAID 5, information on the various types of de-militarized zones (DMZ's) you can deploy with ISA Server, and how ISA Server integrates with Active Directory.

In Chapter 5, we move to the nuts and bolts of installing ISA Server. You will notice that, like much of the content in this book, this chapter steps you through details of the process with thorough explanations of the meanings of the choices you make. From this point on, the book covers the setting up and configuration of the many features of ISA Server.

You will find information on how to publish services from a DMZ and from your internal network, how to configure logging and alerting, how to auto-configure clients, how to set up VPNs, how to set up routing, how to install digital certificates, and so on. In fact, you will find that this book steps you through the choices on practically every interface in ISA Server and provides useful information for helping you decide which configuration might be appropriate.

Although this book is comprehensive, we had to make decisions with regard to what information to emphasize and what examples to highlight. We have been working with the product since the early days of the beta and have been following newsgroup posts closely, leading up to the publication of this book. Consequently, you will find detailed information on how to set up Outlook Web Access in the discussion on Server Publishing. You will also find information on how to set up and configure DMZs. And, of course, you will also find plenty of troubleshooting information, based on our own experiences and those of others, to help guide you through any problems you may encounter.

Whether you are a newcomer to firewalls and proxy servers or have plenty of experience, we hope that you find *Configuring ISA Server 2000: Building Firewalls for Windows 2000* to be an important source of information for helping you plan, install, maintain, and troubleshoot ISA Server. I hope that you come away from this book as impressed as I was with the authors' very real and deep commitment to providing an authoritative, comprehensive, and solidly grounded reference book on ISA Server 2000.

Chapter 1

Introduction to Microsoft ISA Server

Solutions in this chapter:

- What Is ISA Server
- ISA Server Features Overview
- Who This Book Is For and What It Covers

☑ Summary

☑ Solutions Fast Track

☑ Frequently Asked Questions

What Is ISA Server?

The information technology (IT) world is full of acronyms; insiders refer to this vast maelstrom of initials as "alphabet soup." Sometimes it seems that there are so many acronyms—representing so many different concepts, products, components and protocols—that we've used up all the possible letter combinations and now we've started over. As you learn about this world, you'll find many instances in which the same acronym you had previously used in one context is now being used to describe something entirely different.

Hence, in this book, *ISA* has nothing to do with the Industry Standard Architecture (ISA) bus that long-time PC aficionados know and love (or at least know). Nor does it have anything to do with the Instrumentation, Systems, and Automation Society, an organization devoted to measurement and control technologies. Rather, ISA is yet another new server product from Microsoft (or more accurately, as you'll see, a new name for an improved version of a not-so-new product). This book will acquaint you with ISA Server's features and functionality.

In conjunction with the release of Microsoft's new business-oriented operating system, Windows 2000, the software company announced that it would be developing several new server products that would either provide new functionality in Windows 2000-based networks or provide enhancements to the functionality to add-on server products that were originally designed to run on Windows NT 4.0.

New versions of old standbys, such as Exchange 2000 and SQL Server 2000, were developed, with improved features and the ability to integrate with Active Directory. Brand-new products, such as the Microsoft Mobile Information 2001 Server and the Microsoft Application Center 2000 Server, were planned to take advantage of the latest trends in PC computing, such as wireless networking and the application service provider (ASP) explosion. Some of Microsoft's existing servers, such as SNA and Site Server, received new monikers like Host Integration Server and Commerce Server to reflect their updated features.

Another product that got a new name was Microsoft's Web-caching, filtering, and connection-sharing software package, Proxy Server. The Windows 2000-compatible version was code-named Comet in the development stages, but the final release was called Microsoft Internet Security and Acceleration Server 2000, or more simply, ISA Server (see Figure 1.1).

Figure 1.1 Microsoft's Internet Security and Acceleration Server 2000 Provides Features Similar to Those of MS Proxy Server—and More

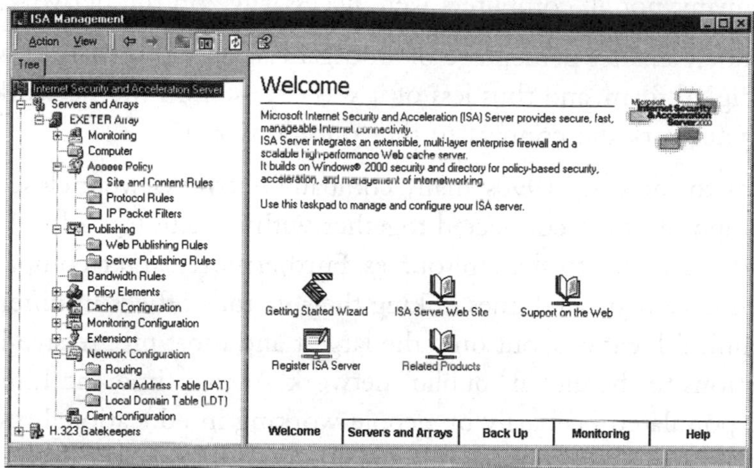

Why "Security and Acceleration" Server?

Internet Security and Acceleration. It sounds good, but what does it mean? Let's look at those two factors—security and acceleration—and the role each plays in ISA Server, as well as the reasons each is important to your network.

ISA (like Proxy Server before it) actually provides two very different sets of functionality. Consequently, some organizations use ISA primarily for its security function. For others, speeding up Web access via the acceleration function could be more important. Of course, many organizations benefit from both features.

Internet Security

In the early days of computer networking, security concerns were limited to government agencies that dealt with international secrets and large conglomerates subject to corporate espionage. The average small to medium-sized business did not place a high priority on security issues. Reasons for this lack of concern ranged from "We don't have anything on our computers that anyone would be interested in stealing" to "We already *have* a secure network—you have to type a password to log on."

Disinterest and naivety aside, most companies really *didn't* have as much need to concern themselves with security a few years ago as they do today. This increased need for security can be attributed to several factors:

- Computer and networking equipment were formerly more expensive and less widely available than they are today. Thus, even within a large company, not all computers were necessarily "on the network."
- A much smaller percentage of an organization's information was stored in digital form, and thus less of it was exposed on the network, even if that network did connect to the "outside world."
- Prior to the early 1990s, many company networks were closed systems. Computers were connected together within a site (on a local area network, or LAN) to share resources. Furthermore, larger companies might even have dedicated lines linking their various offices in different geographical locations, but only the largest and most progressive had connections to the global "public" network. At that time, the Internet was still populated primarily by people working in educational institutions and governmental entities. Companies that did use "the Net" often had only a dial-up connection, instead of being continuously connected. This made it more difficult for an outsider to penetrate the network.
- Because far fewer people had access to the Internet, there was less chance that anyone would have both the desire and the means to gain unauthorized access to a company's data, whether for profit, malevolent purposes, or "just for fun."
- Implementing a "firewall" (security protection) was often complex and expensive, requiring the purchase of new hardware and/or difficult-to-configure software.
- Far fewer statutory and other legal precedents held companies liable for intentionally disclosing confidential information by neglecting to secure their networks.

Changing Times Bring New Security Concerns

As technology enters the 21st century, more and more companies of all sizes, as well as home users and nonprofit organizations, have networked their computer systems to each other and to the worldwide Internet. This linkage gives computer users access to a tremendous wealth of information that they didn't have before and makes many of their jobs easier—but it also creates vulnerabilities.

Logic dictates that if the users of your LAN are able to access resources on computers all over the world, users of some of those computers might also be able to access yours. The connection is two-way, after all, and if you don't take steps to protect your internal network from intruders, it will be easy for a moderately knowledgeable hacker to read the files stored on your network servers, copy confidential data, and even implant viruses or erase your hard disks.

But it's not only *confidentiality* of information that is at stake. Some network administrators might not realize that security can be a concern even if the data on your network is not of a "top secret" nature. The *integrity* of your data is also crucial. A security solution focuses not only on keeping outsiders from accessing data that is private, but also on ensuring that important data is not destroyed or changed.

Designing & Planning...

Security Threats and Security Solutions

A comprehensive security solution must be able to address different types of security threats. Remember that several factors are involved in protecting your network from security threats. Your overall security plan should be designed to protect some or all of the following:

- Confidentiality of sensitive data
- Integrity of both sensitive and nonsensitive data
- Verification of the source or origin of data
- Network operability (protection from malicious destruction of system files via viruses or direct intrusion)

Security threats come in many "flavors," but they can be broadly divided into two categories: external threats and internal threats. For example, a denial-of-service (DoS) attack perpetuated by a hacker at a remote location is an external security threat. Accidental deletion of important files by a company employee on site is an internal threat. At first glance, it might seem that ISA Server protects you only from external threats—those that attempt to penetrate your LAN from the Internet. However, ISA also allows you to restrict outgoing network traffic, and in that way it offers protection from some (although certainly not all) internal security threats as well.

You should approach the process of developing an effective security solution for your corporate network as an exercise in problem solving. The problem is how to keep out the bad things (hackers, viruses), keep in the good things (sensitive data), allow users to access those parts of the outside world that they should (informational Web sites), and keep users out of the places they shouldn't go, at least on company time (porn sites, gaming sites, and general "time wasters"). It's a tall order.

Luckily, there is a product that can fill this order. The *proxy server* was originally designed as a solution to these problems. In the following section, we take a look at how proxies work and where ISA server fits in.

Proxy Servers Take Center Stage

Proxy servers have been around for quite a while. Despite its new, somewhat esoteric name, ISA Server *is* a proxy server, albeit a very full-featured one. The original meaning of *proxy* was "one who is authorized to act for another." Perhaps the most famous—or infamous—use of the word came about in relation to the practice of marriage by proxy, in which a substitute "stood in" for one of the parties, allowing a wedding ceremony to be performed even though the groom (or less commonly, the bride) was not physically present. Proxy weddings at one time were a popular way for a couple to get "hitched" while the groom was serving in the military.

Proxy servers are so named because they, like the hapless stand-in who says "I do" when it's really someone else who does, act as go-betweens to allow something to take place (in this case, network communications) between systems that must remain separate.

Proxy servers "stand in" between the computers on a LAN and those on the public network outside. Another good analogy is the gatekeeper who is stationed at the entrance to an estate to check all incoming visitors to ensure that they are on the list of invited guests. The proxy can actually hide the computers on the LAN from outsiders. Only the IP address of the proxy server is "visible" to others on the Internet; internal computers use private IP addresses (nonroutable over the Internet) that cannot be seen from the other side of the proxy.

In fact, a proxy can go further and function more like a prison guard, who not only makes certain that only authorized persons get in but also sees that only those who have permission go out. Just as the guard checks his list before letting anyone in or out, the proxy *filters* outgoing and incoming data according to predefined criteria. At this point, the proxy is behaving as a *firewall.*

Walls of Fire

ISA Server also performs the functions of a full-featured dedicated firewall. A firewall, of course, goes a bit further than just "standing in" for the local computers and hiding them from view on the global network. Firewalls are specifically designed to control access, preventing unauthorized data from entering the network and restricting how and what type of data can be sent out.

The firewall gets its name from the building industry. In commercial structures, it is common to build a barrier wall made of fireproof material between two areas of a building. This wall is designed to prevent fire from spreading from one part of the building to another.

Likewise, a network firewall acts as a barrier to prevent "bad data"—whether virus code or simply messages to or from unauthorized systems—from spreading from the outside network (usually the Internet) to the internal network and to prevent data packets of a particular type or to or from a particular user or computer from spreading from the LAN to the outside network.

NOTE

In choosing between firewall solutions, you will encounter two basic firewall design options. A firewall can be designed (1) to *permit* all packets to pass through unless they are expressly denied, or (2) to *deny* all packets unless they are expressly permitted. Obviously, the second method is more secure, but it can result in the denial of access that you wanted to allow. The first method is easier to implement but is also more easily penetrated or circumvented.

Firewalls can be implemented in different ways. Vendors offer a wide variety of firewall software packages that run on your gateway computer. Many vendors provide hardware firewall solutions, in which a separate device incorporates a computer system that runs special proprietary firewall software. Either way, the firewall program (or set of programs) generally works in conjunction with a router program or a Network Address Translation (NAT) program. These programs forward packets to the appropriate destination once they have been authorized to enter or leave the network. The firewall must also work with a proxy, which makes requests for Internet data and services on behalf of the internal computers.

The advantage of Microsoft's ISA Server is that it combines these components—proxy, NAT, and firewall—into one package. This makes it easier to deploy and administer than separate software programs and/or hardware devices.

In this book, we examine in depth ISA Server's firewall functionality as an important component in your overall network security plan.

Internet Acceleration

Although enhanced security is an important reason to implement ISA Server, it is not the only reason. ISA is not only an Internet security server; it is also an Internet *acceleration* server. What does that mean to you—and to your network? It means faster access to frequently viewed Web sites and less internetwork traffic. Although these benefits might not be as dramatic as ISA's security enhancements, they can save your organization both time and money.

Accelerated access and reduced outgoing traffic are achieved via ISA Server's *Web caching* functionality. Let's take a look at the meaning of this term.

It is common for many of the users on a network to access the same set of Web sites and for each individual user to access the same sites repeatedly. For example, if your company is a law firm, the attorneys and paralegals might often visit legal research sites or sites providing law dictionaries or lists of courts in a particular jurisdiction. In many cases, the content on specific pages will remain *static*—that is, once a judicial opinion for a case has been published on the Web site, it won't be changed. Your network users might need to return to that same page often because the opinion is relevant to many of the cases on which they work.

Popular Web browsers such as Microsoft Internet Explorer create a *cache* on each computer's local hard disk, where Web pages that have been accessed are stored. If you return to the same page again, using the same computer, it can be loaded from this location instead of having to download the page over the Internet (which is a slower process and uses the wide area network, or WAN, link bandwidth, often resulting in slower performance for all users who are sending or receiving data over the Internet connection).

This is good, as far as it goes. Yet, without ISA Server, the page will have to be downloaded in its entirety from the Internet each time someone accesses it from a different computer. Internet Explorer's Web cache is useful only for the single machine.

ISA Server provides faster Web performance to everyone in the organization. Web pages are cached, similarly to the way they're cached on the local machine by your Web browser, but on the ISA server. This means that even if you haven't accessed a page before, if someone else in your organization has accessed the page, a copy of it will be stored on the server. Because the server is on the LAN, to which you probably enjoy a connection speed of 10 Mbps to 100 Mbps, retrieving the page will be much faster than if you had to go out over a slower (typically 56 Kbps to 1.5 Mbps) WAN connection to get the page from its original location on the Internet.

NOTE

Web page caching is not, by any means, the only type of caching done by modern PCs. In fact, you'll encounter the word *caching* often, and you'll find that it means slightly different things depending on the context, but it always refers to some means of temporarily storing data, to speed up subsequent access to that data.

Caching occurs in hardware in the form of *cache memory,* which is special, very fast random access memory (RAM) that can be accessed more quickly than regular RAM. L1 and L2 cache are memory chips described by the *level* of closeness to the processor. A *disk cache* is an area set aside on the hard disk or in RAM that holds data recently read from the hard disk, so that it can be accessed quickly if needed again.

The Web caching that is performed by ISA Server in cache mode or integrated mode maintains a store of Web objects (HTML pages, graphics, sounds, and the like) that are frequently accessed. ISA does two types of Web caching: *forward caching*, which improves speed of access when internal users request Web objects from servers on the Internet, and *reverse caching,* which improves speed of access for external users who are accessing your internal Web servers. In addition, either forward or reverse caching can be of the *distributed caching* type. This means that the cached objects are spread across a server array to enhance performance and provide fault tolerance.

Because Web caching reduces Internet traffic, it can also reduce your bandwidth cost. This is particularly true if the organization's Internet connection uses a measured bandwidth method (for instance, satellite or other wireless solutions in which you must pay by the megabit for data downloaded).

The History of ISA: Microsoft Proxy Server

As we said earlier, ISA Server is really a new and improved version of a familiar product: Microsoft Proxy Server. The product has undergone an evolution since its debut as a solid but fairly generic proxy solution that lacked many of the impressive features that distinguish later versions.

In the Beginning: Proxy Server, Version 1.0

Microsoft released its first version of a proxy server in November 1996. It included some unique features such as Winsock proxy capability, which allowed for the use of applications that traditional proxy servers didn't support.

Unfortunately, though, version 1.0 suffered from some significant limitations that prevented it from becoming popular as a caching and security solution for large enterprise networks. One big drawback was the lack of redundancy. While its rivals, such as Netscape's proxy server, used distributed caching across multiple servers to provide fault tolerance, the first version of the Microsoft proxy did not include such a feature. The Microsoft proxy seemed better suited to smaller networks and perhaps to those in which its caching and security features were less mission critical.

Getting Better All the Time: Proxy Server, Version 2.0

The redundancy issue was addressed in Proxy Server, version 2. In fact, Microsoft surpassed Netscape's implementation by introducing the concept of proxy server *arrays.* An array is a group of two or more proxy servers that run as mirrors of one another and function as one entity, under a common name. With version 2, multiple proxies could be chained together for better load balancing, and Microsoft even developed a new protocol, called Cache Array Routing Protocol (CARP), for sharing data between proxy servers.

Undocumented ISA

CARP is a proprietary (Microsoft-only) protocol. It is used for management of multiple user Web requests across an array of proxy servers. The Internet Cache Protocol (ICP) is a similar protocol used by vendors of other proxy solutions (for example, Novell's Border Manager). Although the functionality of CARP and ICP are similar, they use different hashing algorithms. CARP offers some advantages over ICP, especially in terms of performance, because CARP does not exchange query messages between servers, as does ICP. In addition, CARP eliminates the problem of unnecessary redundancy of content on the servers in an array.

Automatic synchronization was added to propagate configuration changes to all the servers in an array. Caching capabilities were expanded to include support for both File Transfer Protocol (FTP) and HyperText Transfer Protocol (HTTP) caching. All these services were easily configured (see Figure 1.2).

Also new to version 2 was the *reverse proxy* feature, which allowed for publishing Web content from protected Web servers. Multiple Web sites could be published on a single proxy server, using multihoming support. In addition, version 2 included *reverse hosting* (in which the proxy server listens for and responds to incoming Web requests on behalf of multiple servers sitting behind it) and the ability to publish other services through *server binding.*

Figure 1.2 Proxy Server, Version 2, Offered Easy Configuration of New Features Such as Array Support

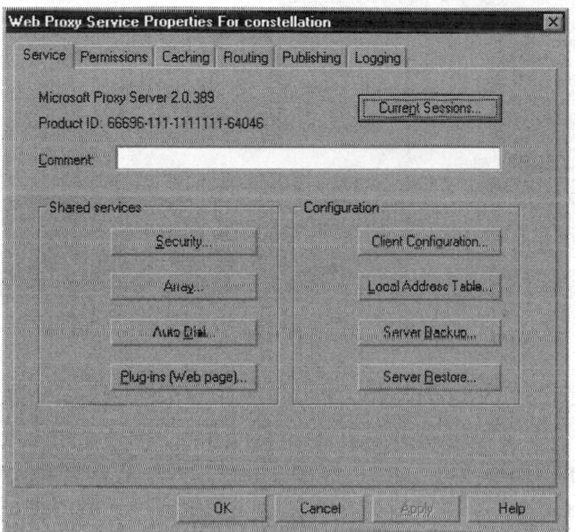

From the beginning, Microsoft's Proxy Server got high marks for ease of setup and configuration, compared with competing products. The second version also included the snap-in administration module for the Internet Information Server (IIS) 4.0 Microsoft Management Console (MMC), which gave administrators a convenient and powerful way to manage individual or multiple proxy servers (see Figure 1.3).

Proxy Server, version 2, earned accolades from network administrators and five-star ratings from reviewers, despite its relatively high price. It quickly became the standard against which other proxy software was measured, although IT professionals in hybrid network environments criticized the fact that Microsoft's proxy solution ran only on Windows NT Servers; some would like to see an implementation for UNIX machines.

A New Name for New and Improved Functionality: Proxy Server 3.0 (ISA Server)

The third—and thus far, the best—implementation of Microsoft's Proxy Server unfortunately still doesn't offer a version for UNIX, but it does include a number of enhancements that go beyond the definition of a proxy server, making it a full-fledged firewall solution in addition to its caching and acceleration abilities.

Figure 1.3 Microsoft Proxy Server, Version 2, Provided for Easy Administration Using the IIS MMC

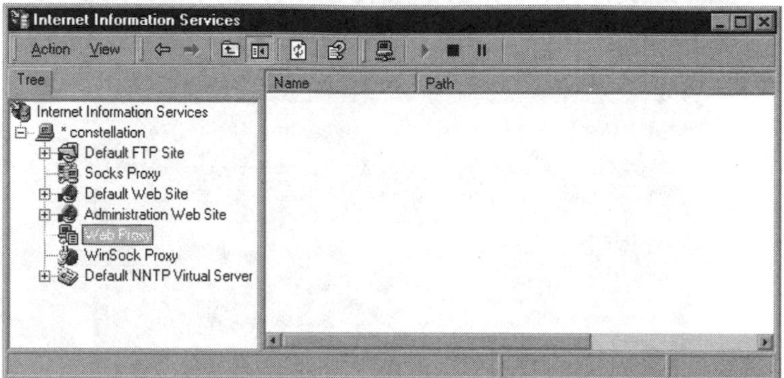

NOTE

What is or is not a firewall is a matter of contention within the network security community. All agree that firewalls are programs (or groups of programs) located at the gateway to a network and that protect the resources of that internal network from the outside. The National Institute of Standards and Technology (NIST), in SP-800-10, defines a firewall as an *approach* to security that helps implement a larger security policy by creating a perimeter defense through which all incoming and outgoing traffic must pass, thus controlling access to or from a protected network or site.

Some industry players use a broad definition of firewall that includes proxy servers. Under this premise, Microsoft marketed Proxy Server 2.0 as a firewall, but some security experts argued that it was not and that in order to meet the standard of "firewall," there must be more than just a router, bastion host, or other device(s) providing security to the network. These purists demand that to be considered a firewall, implementation must be policy-based.

In addition to its multilayer firewall functionality (packet filtering, circuit filtering, and application filtering), ISA Server offers such new or improved features as:

- **Integrated virtual private networking (VPN)** ISA Server can be used to set up either a remote access VPN between a client and gateway or a multiple member VPN tunnel from server to server.
- **Integration with Active Directory** ISA access policies and server configuration information are integrated with the Windows 2000 Active Directory for easier and more secure administration.
- **Intrusion detection** This exciting new feature can be set up to send you an alert if or when a particular type of attack is attempted against your network (for example, if an outsider attempts to scan your ports).
- **Support for Secure Network Address Translation (SecureNAT)** The extensible NAT architecture that is implemented by ISA provides a secure connection for clients that don't have the firewall client software installed, including Macintosh and UNIX clients and other non-Microsoft operating systems that are running Transmission Control Protocol/Internet Protocol (TCP/IP).
- **Bandwidth allocation** The amount of bandwidth allocated to a specific user, communication, client, or destination can be controlled by quality-of-service (QoS) rules that an administrator creates to optimize network traffic usage.
- **Secure server publishing** Internal servers can be made accessible to specific clients while the servers are protected from unauthorized access.
- **Enterprise management** ISA, like Windows 2000, was designed for greater scalability and more focus on the enterprise market than previous Microsoft products. ISA allows you to set enterprise-level policies as well as array-level policies, and management of ISA arrays is easily centralized.
- **Monitoring and report generation** ISA server allows you to monitor its performance and create detailed security and access logs and graphical reports. Report generation can be scheduled, and remote administration lets administrators keep tabs on the use and performance of the ISA server from an off-site location.
- **E-mail content screening** ISA Server provides for screening of e-mail content by keyword to allow administrators to implement and enforce strict security policies.
- **H.323 Gatekeeper functionality** This feature allows for use of videoconferencing software, such as Microsoft NetMeeting, through the proxy,

and NetMeeting directory functionality (replacing some of the functionality of ILS).

- **Enhanced software** This software can be used for streaming media, including live stream splitting, and caching of Windows Media content (when using Windows Media Server).

This is only a sampling of the many features offered by Microsoft's new Internet Security and Acceleration Server. Throughout this book, we expand on the functionality of the features listed and introduce you to other new features included in ISA Server.

Configuring & Implementing...

What Is the H.323 Standard?

H.323 is a standard of the International Telecommunications Union (ITU), which was approved in 1996 (version 2 was approved in 1998) to provide a foundation for audio, video, and data communications across IP-based networks such as the global Internet. Multimedia products and applications from different vendors that comply with H.323 can interoperate, allowing users to communicate with one another using, for example, different compliant videoconferencing programs, without worrying about compatibility issues.

H.323 is intended to be a standardized basis for network-based products for consumer, business, entertainment, and professional applications. The standard covers PC technologies and Standalone devices and supports both point-to-point and multipoint conferencing. It establishes standards (called *codecs*) for compressing and decompressing audio or video data streams, as well as for call setup and control protocols.

The H.323 standard is designed to be not only application-independent but also independent of network architecture and platform, ensuring the widest possible base of compatibility. For more information, see the excellent primer on the H.323 Series Standard at www.databeam.com/h323/h323primer.html.

Because H.323 is complex, uses multiple ports, and includes multiple User Datagram Protocol (UDP) steams, there is an inherent difficulty in constructing firewalls to allow H.323 application traffic. A good resource for information addressing the problems and implications of an H.323 proxy is located on the Intel developer's Web site at http://developer.intel.com/support/videophone/trial21/h323_wpr.htm.

ISA Server Options

Because one size doesn't necessarily fit all when it comes to networking solutions, Microsoft offers ISA Server in two different editions. Either of these editions can be installed in one of three different installation modes. In this section we take a brief look at the differences between the two editions and the three modes to assist you in making the correct choices for your network.

ISA Standard Edition

The ISA Server Standard Edition is appropriate for small business networks (or even sophisticated home networks) and for implementation on a departmental basis in larger organizations. This edition works well in a peer-to-peer (workgroup) environment; the Standard Edition is installed on a standalone Windows 2000 server and can use only local policies. It does not require Active Directory.

Nonetheless, the Standard Edition offers the same firewall functionality, Web caching capability, performance, ease of management, and extensibility as the Enterprise Edition. The Standard Edition will support a server with multiprocessor capability as long as it has no more than four processors.

NOTE

Windows 2000 operating systems can use *symmetric multiprocessing (SMP)* to take advantage of the performance benefits of machines that have more than one microprocessor installed. Windows 2000 Server supports up to four microprocessors, the same number supported by ISA Server Standard Edition. Enterprise Edition is designed to be installed on Windows 2000 Advanced Server (up to eight processors) or Datacenter Server (up to 32 processors).

Because it cannot be used as part of an array, the Standard Edition is more limited in terms of scalability. It supports hierarchical caching, as does the Enterprise Edition, but it does not support distributed caching. The ISA Standard Edition cannot store policy information in the Microsoft Active Directory, as Enterprise Edition does.

ISA Enterprise Edition

The ISA Enterprise Edition is designed for maximum scalability to the largest, high-traffic enterprise networks. Fault tolerance, centralized management, and multiple-level policy application are at the core of the Enterprise Edition's feature set.

Whereas the Standard Edition supports up to four processors, there is no limit on processor support in the Enterprise Edition. Perhaps more important, whereas ISA Standard Edition is a standalone server only, Enterprise Edition allows you to group ISA servers together in *arrays* to provide fault tolerance and distributed caching and spread the load of high network traffic across the group of machines. Response time for clients is improved, and if one server in the array goes down, you still maintain ISA functionality.

Enterprise Edition integrates fully with the Windows 2000 Active Directory, where its configuration and policy information are stored. Using Active Directory, enterprise-level policies can be defined and applied to one or multiple server arrays throughout the enterprise. This capability is referred to as *tiered policy*.

TIP

Tiered policy can be implemented only with the Enterprise Edition of ISA Server. Site and content rules, protocol rules, Web publishing rules, server publishing rules, and IP packet filters can be created at the array level and applied only to the servers in a particular array.

Site, content, and protocol rules can also be created and applied at the enterprise level so that all arrays in the enterprise network are affected by the policies. You can define at the enterprise level which arrays are authorized to publish servers. Enterprise policies can be used in conjunction with separate array policies, but array policy cannot override the enterprise policies. Thus, administrators of arrays can make policies defined at the enterprise level only *more* restrictive; the enterprise-level policy cannot permit what the array policy prohibits.

Of course, increased functionality comes at a price. Enterprise Edition is considerably more expensive than Standard Edition (by several thousand dollars). In determining which edition of ISA Server is most appropriate for your network, you should consider your specific needs and cost/performance factors.

Standalone versus Array Member

ISA Servers can be installed as individual standalone servers or, if you have the Enterprise Edition of the software, they can be installed as members of a server array. Enterprise Edition can also be installed as a standalone server, although it would be difficult to justify the much higher price of the software if you do not intend to use what is perhaps its most important additional feature.

Undocumented ISA

Although an array is usually thought of as a group of ISA servers, it is also possible to create an array with a single member. Why would you install your lone ISA server as an array member instead of a standalone machine? Because even with only one member, an array integrates with Active Directory, and you can apply enterprise policy to it. Additionally, if you add ISA servers in the future, they can be added to the array and utilize all the benefits of arrays.

Table 1.1 summarizes the characteristics of standalone ISA servers, contrasted with the characteristics of array members.

Table 1.1 Summary of Features of Standalone ISA Servers versus Array Members

Characteristics of Standalone ISA Servers	Characteristics of ISA Server Array Members
Does not require that Active Directory is installed on the network	Must be a member of an Active Directory domain
Can be installed in a Windows NT 4.0 domain (on a Windows 2000 member server)	Can be installed in a Windows 2000 domain only
Enterprise and array policies cannot be applied	Can use enterprise policies to set rules for all arrays in the enterprise as well as array policies that apply to a specific array (tiered policy)
Can be installed from either Standard or Enterprise Edition software	Requires Enterprise Edition software

A big advantage of joining multiple ISA servers in an array is the ability to manage them as one entity. All the servers in an array share the same configuration—that is, you only have to configure the array itself; the configuration is then applied to all its members. Because arrays provide for distributed caching capability, performance is enhanced as well.

Of course, all experienced network administrators are well aware of the importance of fault tolerance, which is the basis of server clustering. An ISA server array functions as a cluster of ISA servers; in the same way Windows 2000 clustering technology causes multiple Windows 2000 servers to act as one entity, so does the formation of an ISA array enable multiple ISA servers. Also similar to clustering, arrays allow for load balancing to spread server requests across the group of servers.

NOTE

All members of the same ISA server array are required to belong to the same Active Directory domain and to be members of the same Active Directory site. *Sites* are physical divisions of the network that consist of one or more TCP/IP subnets with a fast connection to one another. *Domains* are logical divisions of the network that consist of a group of computers sharing the same Active Directory database.

ISA Server Installation Modes

In addition to choosing between the two available editions of ISA Server, once you've made that decision, you must determine in which mode to install the software. There are three choices:

- Firewall mode
- Cache mode
- Integrated mode

In integrated mode, the firewall and caching modes are combined so that you get the benefits of both security and Web access acceleration in one package. When you choose to deploy ISA Server in only one mode or the other (firewall or cache), you should be aware that the feature set differs depending on the mode selected. Table 1.2 outlines the features that are available in either or both modes. Of course, in integrated mode, all features are available.

Table 1.2 ISA Server Mode Choice Effect on Available Features

Available in Firewall Mode	Available in Cache Mode	Available in Either Mode
Server publishing	Web caching service	Access policy (available only for HTTP in cache mode)
Virtual private networking (VPN)		Web publishing
Packet filtering		Real-time monitoring and alerts
Application filtering		Report generation

The Microsoft.Net Family of Enterprise Servers

Just as Proxy Server was considered a member of the Microsoft BackOffice Family, ISA Server also belongs to a new Microsoft "family," the members of which are designed to work with Windows 2000 in an enterprise environment. This group of enterprise servers is now called the Microsoft.Net family, or simply ".Net" (pronounced *dot-net*) servers.

The .Net enterprise servers are designed for large-scale, mission-critical performance in corporate networks that span multiple geographic locations. The enterprise servers focus on modern Web-based standards for interoperability with other platforms and networks. At the core of the .Net products is the Extensible Markup Language (XML), which is the latest cross-platform standard for sharing formatted data on the Internet, intranets, and elsewhere.

The .Net server products are designed with connectivity to the global network in mind. Just as Microsoft has built Internet integration into the latest versions of its productivity applications, such as the Office 2000 applications, the company sees the newest versions of its server products as part of a networking strategy that is tightly integrated with the Internet. Microsoft calls the enterprise servers comprising the .Net platform "enablers of the third generation of the Internet."

In addition to new Internet-integrated versions of previous products, Microsoft has introduced several new server products as part of the .Net family. In addition to ISA Server, the .Net enterprise servers include the following:

- **Application Center 2000** This "deployment and management tool" is designed to allow administrators to manage multiple servers and deploy Web-based applications more easily across an enterprise. It also includes monitoring and optimization tools that use a Web browser-based console interface.

- **BizTalk Server 2000** Microsoft describes BizTalk Server as a "business-to-business integration/enterprise application integration" product that allows users to exchange business documents among applications and span different platforms.
- **Host Integration Server 2000** A new incarnation of Systems Network Architecture (SNA), Host Integration Server (which inevitably will come to be called HIS; can HERS be far behind?) will allow seamless connectivity between legacy systems, such as IBM AS/400 mainframes, and the Internet, intranets, and Microsoft networks.
- **Microsoft Commerce Server** Another updated product with a new name, the server formerly known as Site Server has undergone a transformation designed to make it a more scalable e-commerce solution.
- **Exchange 2000** One of the few .Net servers to retain its previous name, Exchange 2000 is Microsoft's e-mail, messaging, and collaboration platform.
- **SQL Server 2000** Another familiar name, Microsoft's premier client/server database solution has been updated to scale to the enterprise and integrate smoothly with the Internet.

In addition to these products, Microsoft plans to release the following new .Net servers at some time during 2001:

- **"Tahoe" Server** This is the code name for a new server product that is designed to create an intranet portal that will allow indexing, searching, sharing, and publishing of information.
- **Mobile Information Server 2001** This new product will provide a platform for integration of mobile devices—cell phones, personal digital assistants (PDAs), handheld computers, and embedded systems—into the network. MIS, previously code-named Airstream, focuses on providing secure, reliable, real-time data services for mobile devices.

It is Microsoft's goal to offer, in the .Net family of servers, a group of products that can work individually or together to provide the full range of features needed in today's increasingly large and diversified network environments. ISA Server, as a full-fledged firewall solution and an Internet access acceleration solution, is positioned to play a leading role in that endeavor.

Configuring & Implementing...

What Is XML, and Why Is It Important?

XML is a *markup language* rather than a programming language. Markup languages generally use symbols or character sequences inserted into text documents to indicate the *formatting,* or how the document should look when displayed (for example, in a Web browser) or printed. These markup symbols are also called *tags.*

The most well-known markup language is HTML, the HyperText Markup Language, in which most Web documents are constructed. HTML is an SGML-based language. SGML, the Standard Generalized Markup Language, is a standard for how markup languages are specified. SGML is not itself a document markup language; it is a basis for standardization of markup languages. It is known as a *metalanguage* for this reason.

XML is also modeled on SGM, and is also a metalanguage. XML gives users a standardized way of describing data. XML differs from HTML in that the latter's tags merely describe how the data is to be displayed. For example, the HTML tag <b> indicates that the characters following it should be in bold type. In contrast, XML tags can describe the actual contents of the data. For example, the XML tag <zipcode> indicates that the characters following it constitute a postal ZIP code. Applications can then process this data as a ZIP code.

Many XML conventions will be familiar to readers who have worked with HTML. For example, a slash mark (/) is used to turn the tag off. That is, the ZIP code 75336 would be designated in XML as <zipcode> 75336 </zipcode>. XML and HTML can be (and are) used together in the same document. XML is called *extensible* because its markup symbols are unlimited; you can create your own tags to describe document content.

XML is important because, like HTML, it allows users to exchange data across platforms. It is not operating-system or network architecture dependent. Unlike HTML, it allows applications to process the data intelligently. For example, if you search HTML documents for the word *Rob*, you might get returns for pages pertaining to a man named Rob and pages instructing you on how to rob banks. With XML, *Rob* can be identified as a particular type of content using the <first-name> tag, and your search will be narrowed.

The Microsoft.Net server products are built on XML, so understanding its function is important to Windows 2000 enterprise-level administrators who will be integrating these products into their networks. For more articles and tutorials about XML, see www.xml.com.

The Role of ISA Server in the Network Environment

Because security and network performance—the two-pronged purpose of ISA Server—are so important in today's interconnected world, ISA Server plays a vital role in your overall network design. Of course, exactly how and where ISA will be implemented depends on the particulars of your network (including size), your security needs, and the type of business you do.

Possible scenarios include:

- ISA Server as a standalone firewall server to protect your small to medium-sized network from Internet intrusion
- ISA Server as part of an e-commerce solution to speed customer access to your Web site and provide security for financial transactions using X.509 certificates
- ISA Server as a Web-caching server to provide faster Web access to knowledge-based workers on your LAN
- An ISA Server array to distribute the load of client requests and provide fault tolerance
- ISA Server as an Internet connection-sharing solution
- ISA Server as a secure publishing solution to protect the Web servers on your LAN
- ISA Server as part of a perimeter network (DMZ) solution

Throughout this book, we examine the "whys" and the "how-tos" of using ISA Server in each of these scenarios.

An Overview of ISA Server Architecture

Because ISA Server provides several different functions, it is not surprising that its architecture is complex. The program's components work at various layers of the network communications models. The most popular of these models is, of course, the Open System Interconnection (OSI) model, developed by the International Organization for Standardization (ISO) as a way to graphically represent the network communication process. The OSI model consists of seven layers, as shown in Figure 1.4. Also shown in Figure 1.4 is the U.S. Department of Defense (DoD) model, developed prior to the OSI model in conjunction with the DoD's development of the TCP/IP protocol stack.

Figure 1.4 Comparison of the OSI and DoD Networking Models

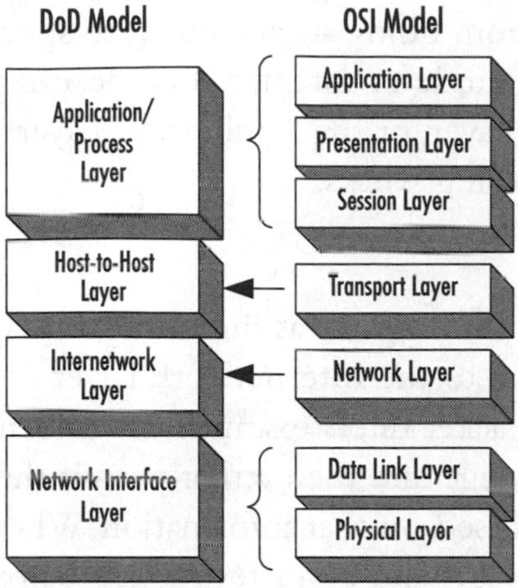

The models provide guidelines for vendors of networking products and developers of networking protocols and applications. Each layer in the model has specific roles and responsibilities in the communications process, as shown in Table 1.3.

Table 1.3 Functions of Each Layer of the Networking Models

OSI Model Layer	DoD Model Layer	Functionality
Application Layer	Application Layer	Interacts with the user applications
Presentation Layer	Application Layer	Manages data presentation and conversion issues such as compression and encryption
Session Layer	Host-to-Host Layer	Establishes and maintains communications channels (sessions)
Transport Layer	Host-to-Host Layer	Responsible for end-to-end integrity of data transmission
Network Layer	Internetwork Layer	Handles logical addressing and routing
Data Link Layer	Network Interface Layer	Responsible for establishing the link to pass data from one node to another
Physical Layer	Network Interface Layer	Manages placement of data onto the network media and taking it off at the other side

Layered Filtering

Firewall products support the filtering of messages to either allow data to pass through or prevent data from doing so, according to specified criteria. ISA Server, when installed in firewall mode or integrated mode, can perform filtering at the Packet Layer, the Circuit Layer, or the Application Layer. Let's look briefly at how each of these types of filtering works.

Packet Filtering

Packet filtering does most of its work at the Network Layer of the OSI networking model (equivalent to the Internetwork Layer of the DoD model), dealing with IP packets. Packet filters examine the information contained in the IP packet header of a message and then either permit the data to cross the firewall or reject the packet based on that information. When IP packet filtering is enabled, ISA Server intercepts and evaluates packets before passing them on to a higher level in the firewall or to an application filter.

The information that is used by the packet filter to make its decision includes the IP address of the source and/or destination computer(s) and the Transmission Control Protocol (TCP) or UDP port number. (The port numbers are in the Transport Layer header, so technically, although packet filtering generally operates at the Network Layer, it also processes some higher-layer information.) Packet filtering allows the data to proceed to the Transport Layer only if the packet-filtering rules allow it to do so.

Packet filtering lets you block packets that come from a particular Internet host or those that are destined for a particular service on your network (for example, the Web server or the Simple Mail Transfer Protocol, or SMTP, server).

TIP

Because ISA Server is designed as a security solution, by default enabling packet filtering causes exclusion of *all* packets coming into the LAN on the external network interface (the interface connected to the Internet)—unless a packet filter, access policy, or publishing rule exists that explicitly allows them. In fact, even if packet filtering is *not* enabled, ISA Server will not permit packets to enter the internal network unless you explicitly configure rules to permit access.

ISA Server provides administrators with flexibility in configuring packet filtering behavior. Two types of static IP packet filters can be configured:

- ***Allow* filters** You specify the packet types that should be allowed to pass through the firewall (either incoming or outgoing traffic). Other than the packet types you have specified, all packets will be prevented from crossing the firewall. For a service to "listen" (monitor traffic) on a particular port, you need to configure a packet filter to allow traffic on that port (unless the port is opened dynamically by a policy or publishing rule).
- ***Block* filters** You configure filters to explicitly block specified ports. Block filters are used in conjunction with allow filters to give you more flexibility and granularity of control over exactly what traffic will be permitted through the firewall.

Here is an example of how allow and block filters can be used together. You might need to generally allow traffic on a particular port; for instance, you could configure an allow filter to permit incoming e-mail traffic on port 110, which is the traditional port used by Post Office Protocol (POP) mail services. You could also configure block filters to keep mail from particular host machines, which are known to be sources of e-mail viruses or other unwanted network traffic, from crossing the firewall.

Dynamic packet filtering provides higher security because it opens the necessary port(s) only when required for communication to take place, then closes the port immediately after the communication ends.

NOTE

The criteria by which packet filters can be defined include (1) servers, (2) protocol, port, and direction (incoming or outgoing), (3) local host name or IP address, and (4) remote host name. Applying packet filters using each of these parameters is discussed more fully in Chapter 9, "Configuring ISA Server for Inbound Access."

Access and restrictions can often be accomplished by policy or publishing rules. In general, Microsoft recommends that rules be used instead of packet filters, when possible. This is because allowing access by packet filtering can create a security risk. When you use packet filtering to allow specified traffic to access the ISA server, the port associated with that traffic is opened *statically*. In other words, it remains open. Access policy and publishing rules must also open the necessary ports to let external traffic in, of course; the difference is that these methods open the ports *dynamically*, which means that the port does not open until a request arrives.

However, some situations require IP packet filtering in order to provide the needed access. In particular, the following situations will dictate that you must use packet filtering instead of policy and publishing rules:

- If you need to allow access to protocols other than the IP protocols handled by packet filters (TCP and UDP), you have to use packet filtering.
- If you use ISA Server to publish servers that reside within a demilitarized zone (DMZ), which is also referred to as a *screened subnet* or *perimeter network,* you have to use packet filters to allow access.
- If there are application programs or services running on the computer on which ISA Server is installed and that must "listen" to the Internet, packet filtering, rather than rules, is the appropriate choice.

It is important to note that packet filters cannot perform filtering based on anything that is contained in the data field of the packet, nor can it use the state of the communication channel to aid in making its decision to accept or reject the packet. If you need filtering decisions made on the basis of either of these, you need to use filtering that operates at a different layer (circuit or application filtering).

Circuit Filtering

Packet filtering is a widely used and understood concept for many network administrators, but *circuit filtering* might be less familiar to you. Microsoft's ISA Server documentation makes scant mention of it, and TechNet contains only a few references to it. In fact, circuit filtering seems to be "lumped in" with packet filtering in most discussions, as though the two were the same.

In fact, there is an important difference, but there's nothing mysterious or difficult to understand about it: Circuit filters simply operate at a higher layer of the OSI model, the Transport Layer (the Host-to-Host Layer in the DoD model). Circuit filters restrict access on the basis of host machines (not users) by processing the information found in the TCP and UDP packet headers. This allows you to create filters that would, for example, prohibit anyone using Computer A from using FTP to access files on Computer B.

When circuit filters are used, access control is based on TCP data streams or UDP datagrams. Circuit filters can act based on TCP and UDP status flags and sequencing information, in addition to source and destination addresses and port numbers.

NOTE

Circuit-level filtering applications are often called *circuit gateways.* Possibly the most famous (or infamous) circuit gateway application is SOCKS, which was originally designed to run on UNIX computers. SOCKS uses *sockets* to represent and keep track of individual connections. A SOCKS server handles requests from clients inside a firewall and either allows or rejects connection requests, based on the requested Internet destination or user identification.

The ISA firewall service works at the circuit level with most Internet applications and protocols, making them perform as though they were directly connected to the Internet. This is true both for clients that have the firewall client software installed and for those that don't (the latter are known as SecureNAT clients). If the firewall client is installed, Internet applications communicate using Winsock. For SecureNAT clients, it works a little differently. In this case, circuit-level filtering uses a SOCKS filter to forward requests from SOCKS 4.3 applications to the firewall service. See the discussion of SOCKS and Winsock later in this chapter for more details.

Circuit-level filtering allows you to inspect sessions rather than packets. A session is sometimes thought of as a connection, but actually a session can be made up of more than one connection. Sessions are established only in response to a user request, which adds to security.

Remember that circuit filters don't restrict access based on user information; they also cannot interpret the meanings of the packets. That is, they cannot distinguish between a GET command and a PUT command sent by an application program. To make this distinction, you'll have to use application filtering.

Application Filtering

At times, you might want to filter packets based on the information contained in the data itself. Packet filters and circuit filters don't use the contents of the data stream in making filtering decisions, but you *can* do this with application filtering.

An application filter operates at the top layer of the networking model, the (appropriately named) Application Layer. Application filters can use the packet header information but are also able to allow or reject packets on the basis of the data contents and the user information.

You can use application filtering to control access based on the identity of the user and/or based on the particular task the user is attempting to perform. With application filters, criteria can be set based on commands issued by the application. This means, for example, that you could restrict a particular user from downloading files to a specified computer, using FTP. At the same time, you could allow that user to upload files via FTP to that same computer. This is possible because different commands are issued depending on whether the user is retrieving files from the server or depositing them there.

NOTE

Firewalls that use circuit layer filtering and/or application layer filtering are sometimes said to be operating at the *proxy level.* You might hear these called circuit or application *gateways.* An advantage of proxy-level firewall functionality is that these gateways can be configured to require user-based authentication, whereas IP layer firewalls (packet filtering) cannot.

Many firewall experts consider application gateways the most secure of the filtering technologies. This is because the criteria they use for filtering cover a broader span than the other methods. For example, sometimes hackers write malicious programs that use the port address of an authorized application, such as port 53, which is the Domain Name System (DNS) address. A packet or circuit filter would not be able to recognize that the packet is not a valid DNS request or response and would allow it to pass through. An application filter, however, is able to examine the contents of the packet and determine that it should *not* be allowed.

Application filtering sounds like the perfect solution to all your security concerns, but it does have drawbacks. The biggest problem is that there must be a separate application gateway for every Internet service that you need to support. This makes for more configuration work; however, this weakness is also a strength that adds to the security of the firewall. Since a gateway for each service must be explicitly enabled, you won't accidentally allow services that pose a threat to your network.

Application filtering is the most sophisticated level of filtering performed by the firewall service and is especially useful in allowing you to protect your network against specific types of attacks such as malicious SMTP commands or attempts to penetrate your local DNS servers.

ISA Client Types

An important element in understanding the architecture of ISA Server is an understanding of the ISA client types. Three types of clients are supported by ISA Server:

- **Firewall clients** These are computers with the firewall client software installed and enabled.
- **SecureNAT clients** These are computers that are ISA server clients but do not have firewall client software installed.
- **Web proxy clients** This term refers to client Web applications that are configured to use ISA Server.

By definition, a SecureNAT client *cannot* also be a firewall client. On the other hand, both firewall clients and SecureNAT clients can also be Web proxy clients. The firewall client is the only client type that requires you to actually install client software on the client computer; however, you must configure the client machine's Web browser to make it a Web proxy client. Other significant differences between the three client types are illustrated in Table 1.4.

Table 1.4 Comparison Chart of ISA Client Types

Firewall Client	SecureNAT Client	Web Proxy Client
Supports Winsock applications	Requires application filters for multi-connection protocols	Supports the HTTP, HTTP-S, FTP, and gopher protocols
Only works on Windows operating systems	Works on all operating systems with TCP/IP installed	Works on all operating systems via Web browser
Supports user-level authentication	Does not support user-level authentication	Supports user-level authentication

We take a look at each client type and its characteristics in the following sections.

NOTE

When the ISA Server is installed in integrated mode, HTTP requests from SecureNAT clients are processed by ISA Server as though they were made by Web proxy clients. ISA uses an application filter to determine the nature of the request and then routes the request through the appropriate components.

Firewall Client

Those who are familiar with Microsoft Proxy Server will recognize the firewall client as an old component with a new name. ISA Server's firewall client is equivalent to the Winsock proxy client; it is used for applications such as RealAudio, Windows Media, IRC, Telnet, and any other Internet service that is written to the Winsock application programming interface (API).

The firewall client software can be installed on any 32-bit Windows operating system:

- Windows 95/98
- Windows Millennium Edition (ME)
- Windows NT 4.0
- Windows 2000
- Windows XP (Whistler)

These are the *only* operating systems that will run the ISA firewall client software. The firewall client is automatically enabled when installation is completed.

The process of installing the firewall client writes a log file on the computer on which the software is installed. This file has setup information that includes such useful items as which services were running during installation and what client applications were installed. The log file is helpful in troubleshooting any problems that you encounter during the installation process. Note that if you reinstall the firewall client software, the log file will be overwritten.

SECURITY ALERT!

The firewall client software should *not* be installed on the ISA Server computer.

Designing & Planning…

Understanding Winsock

Winsock is an Internet standard based on the Berkeley UNIX (BSD) Sockets API and adapted for use with Windows operating systems. Several different versions of Winsock are available. Like other APIs, Winsock makes it much easier for programmers to write applications without having to worry about the lower layers of the network communications process. WINSOCK.DLL is a *dynamic link library,* which is a collection of executable functions that are used by Internet applications to allow those programs to interact with the TCP/IP protocol stack.

This means that a developer can write an Internet application that is focused on the application programming details and let WINSOCK.DLL translate the program's commands to the TCP/IP stack. A *socket,* or a communications channel consisting of an IP address and a TCP or UDP port number, can be established between the communicating computers and data sent to that socket.

Winsock uses two types of sockets: those using TCP as a transport mechanism and those using UDP. TCP is a connection-oriented protocol, and TCP-based sockets are used more commonly than UDP ones. *Connection oriented* means that a one-to-one virtual connection is established before the data is sent, and acknowledgments are used to check that the data was delivered and arrived intact, so the transmission is more reliable. UDP is a *connectionless* protocol, and UDP sockets only deliver the data, they do not ensure the reliability of the transmission. UDP sockets are more vulnerable to error, but UDP is also faster because it doesn't have the high overhead of TCP's error checking and acknowledgments. UDP sockets are used in Winsock applications for real-time applications such as RealAudio because speed of transfer is important. Another advantage of UDP is that it can transmit the same data to multiple clients at a time, such as with Multicast GHOST.

For more information about Winsock, Winsock applications, Web sites, and mailing lists, see the WinSock-L site at http://papa.indstate.edu:8888/.

As mentioned, the firewall client software runs *Winsock* (short for "Windows Sockets") applications. Winsock is an API developers use to create Windows programs that communicate with other computers over a TCP/IP network. The firewall client uses the dynamic link library (DLL) that is used by the Winsock applications.

The firewall service on the ISA server intercepts Winsock API calls initiated by the clients and redirects those requests to the Internet computer to which they are addressed. The firewall service is acting as a "proxy" because it stands between the internal computer making the request and the external computer to which the request is made. The internal computer functions as though it were directly connected to the external host, but it is not. There are really two separate connections: The internal client is connected to the ISA Server, and the ISA Server is connected to the Internet. This allows the messages passing through the ISA firewall service to be secure.

The firewall client uses a local address table (LAT), which is installed to the hard disk of the client computer (in Program Files\Microsoft Firewall Client) when you install the firewall client software. The LAT file is named Msplat.txt. The LAT is used to determine whether a request made by a Winsock application is addressed to an internal computer or an external computer. If the LAT shows the destination address is one that is not on the local (internal) network, the request is sent to the firewall service on the ISA Server.

Computers "out there" on the Internet will not be able to see the IP addresses of any of the internal computers (firewall clients). Only the address of the ISA Server is visible on the external network.

TIP

The primary advantage of the firewall client is that it allows you to apply access policies to authenticated users rather than to computer IP addresses only. Users who are authenticated via NTLM or Kerberos can have specific rules, such as bandwidth limitations, applied to their user accounts. This is the best reason for using the firewall client instead of SecureNAT.

SecureNAT Client

If a computer is configured as a client to the ISA Server (by setting the default gateway in the computer's TCP/IP properties) and does not have the firewall client software installed, it will automatically be a SecureNAT client. Although these computers will not be able to benefit from all the features of ISA without the firewall software, they can still utilize most of its access control features. SecureNAT clients do not, however, support user-level authentication.

Configuring & Implementing...

Network Address Translation

NAT stands for Network Address Translation, a means of providing access to the Internet for the computers on an internal network that use IP addresses in the private addressing range. This is done by going through a computer called the *NAT host* that is running NAT software and has connections to both the internal network and the Internet. The NAT host maps the clients' Internet requests to a port number on an address translation table.

Numerous dedicated NAT programs, such as Sygate and NAT32, are available to provide this functionality. Windows 2000 has two address translation methods built into the operating system. Windows 2000 Professional includes Internet Connection Sharing (ICS); Windows 2000 Server includes both ICS and a more robust translation component that is called simply NAT and is installed and configured as a routing protocol in the Routing and Remote Access Service (RRAS) console.

ISA Server provides additional functionality over Windows 2000 NAT, allowing for application of ISA rules to the SecureNAT clients. Windows 2000 NAT does not have an authentication mechanism, but with ISA Server's NAT, policies regarding protocols, destination computers, and content type can be applied to the SecureNAT clients. ISA Server installs its own NAT editors for system security.

Important Note: You should *not* install the Windows 2000 NAT protocol through the RRAS console if you have ISA Server installed on the computer, because doing so will cause conflicts. You also should not install any third-party NAT editors. If NAT or ICS is installed on the server, remove it before installing ISA Server.

To read RFC 1631, which defines specifications for NAT, see http://community.roxen.com/developers/idocs/rfc/rfc1631.html.

SecureNAT clients can ping external addresses (those on the other side of the ISA Server), but firewall clients cannot. You do not have to install any special software on the clients to make them SecureNAT clients as you do for firewall clients. However, you need to configure the TCP/IP settings on the clients.

If your network setup is relatively simple (that is, if there are no routers between the client computers and the ISA Server), you should set the default gateway to the IP address of your ISA Server machine. The default gateway is the "way out" of the internal network; it is the address to which packets are sent if their destination address is not on the local subnet. Thus, all Internet traffic will go to the ISA Server machine, which will then forward the requests out over the Internet (assuming the packets are not rejected because of ISA's packet, circuit, or application filtering rules).

See Figure 1.5 for an example of how to set the default gateway settings on the SecureNAT client machines.

Figure 1.5 The Default Gateway on SecureNAT Clients Should Be Configured with the IP Address of the ISA Server on a Simple Network

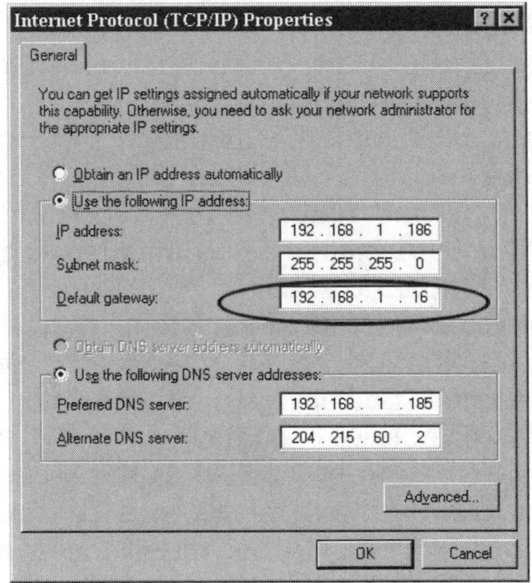

NOTE

The ISA Server will have two network interfaces and thus two IP addresses. The default gateway setting on the client should be the IP address of the ISA server's *internal* network address. Many administrators configure the computer or router acting as the default gateway with the first IP address on the subnet (for example, 192.168.1.1) or with a very high number address to help identify it more easily. However, this practice is merely a convention, not a requirement. The default gateway address can be any valid IP address on the subnet that is assigned to the internal interface of the device that forwards data out of the subnet.

You can either configure the SecureNAT clients' TCP/IP settings manually or use the Dynamic Host Configuration Protocol (DHCP) to assign the clients their IP addressing, subnet mask, and default gateway information. If you use DHCP, you should select the "Obtain an IP address automatically" check box on the TCP/IP Properties sheet.

If your network is larger and more complex and there are routers between the SecureNAT clients and the ISA Server, the default gateway settings on the clients will be configured with the IP address of the router on the local subnet. Then the router must be configured to route Internet traffic to ISA Server.

Other TCP/IP settings, such as the DNS server settings, depend on whether the clients will be requesting data from Internet servers only or will also be requesting data from internal servers. If the former, you can use the IP addresses of DNS servers on the Internet; otherwise, you should use a DNS server on the local network, configured to resolve both internal and external IP addresses.

NOTE

Another difference between a firewall client and a SecureNAT client is the responsibility for DNS host name resolution. The SecureNAT client is responsible for resolution of DNS hosts on the Internet; the firewall client is not.

Here is a step-by-step description of how SecureNAT works:

1. When a SecureNAT client sends a request (for example, when the Web browser software on the SecureNAT's client requests a Web page), it first is directed to the NAT driver on the NAT host machine. This is the component that records the request and information about the internal computer making the request to a table, then substitutes a public registered IP address (the address assigned to the ISA Server's external interface).
2. Next, the request goes to the firewall service. There it is examined against the firewall policies and then is filtered by whatever filters have been configured.
3. In the case of an HTTP request (for a Web page or other Web object), the request is redirected to the Web proxy service. If the requested Web object is already in the Web cache, it is returned to the client from there.

If it is not in the Web cache, the object is cached when it is returned from the Internet. Figure 1.6 provides a graphical illustration of the process.

Figure 1.6 The Steps of an HTTP Request from a SecureNAT Client Before It Is Sent Over the Internet

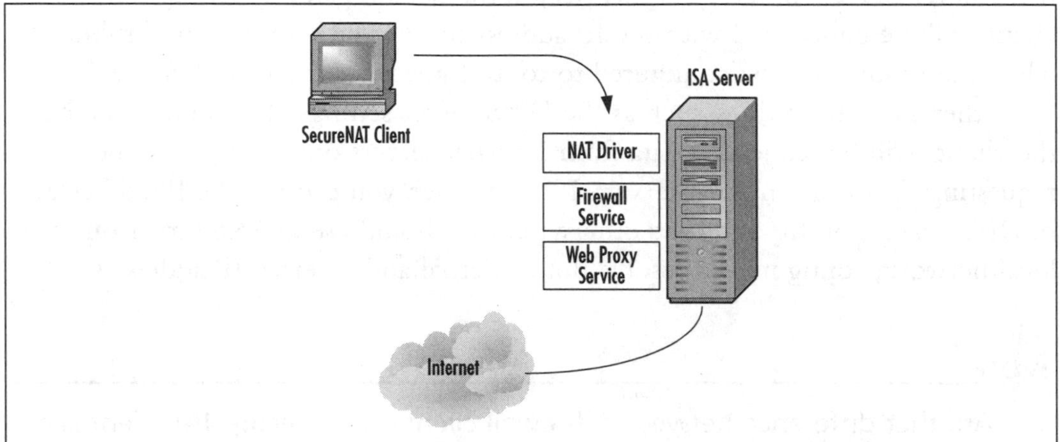

Security Alert!

It is important to note that ISA Server uses NAT and to understand the ramifications of this fact. Windows 2000 Internet Protocol Security (IPSec) is incompatible with NAT in transport mode. Thus it is not possible to use IPSec to secure packets end to end with an ISA implementation. On the other hand, you *can* create an IPSec tunnel using L2TP from the external interface of the ISA Server.

Web Proxy Client

As mentioned earlier, a computer can be a Web proxy client at the same time it is a firewall client or a SecureNAT client. The requirements for a Web proxy client are:

- The client must have a CERN-compatible Web browser installed.
- The Web browser must be configured to use the ISA server.

A request for Web objects sent from a Web proxy client is directed to the Web proxy service on the ISA Server. The Web proxy service determines whether the access is allowed and may retrieve the requested object from cache (if it is there) or cache the object when it is returned from the Internet. The Web browser must comply with the HTTP 1.1 standard.

There are two ways to configure the browser to use ISA Server's Web proxy. If the Web proxy client has the firewall client software installed, the Web browser settings can be configured automatically during the setup of the firewall client. If the client is not a firewall client, you can configure the browser settings to use the Web proxy service. If you're using Internet Explorer, you do so via the Tools | Internet Options | Connections setting. As shown in Figure 1.7, you have only to check a check box ("Use a proxy server") in the LAN Settings property sheet and enter the name of the ISA Server or array and a valid port number (such as 8080). The SecureNAT client uses the Web Proxy Service regardless of whether you have configured the CERN-compliant settings (see the Note) in the browser. Thus, you might wonder if these settings are unnecessary. They are necessary if you have an array and want routing requests to be resolved by the client before being sent to the ISA Server.

Figure 1.7 Configuring the Web Proxy Client by Modifying the Web Browser Settings to Use a Proxy Server

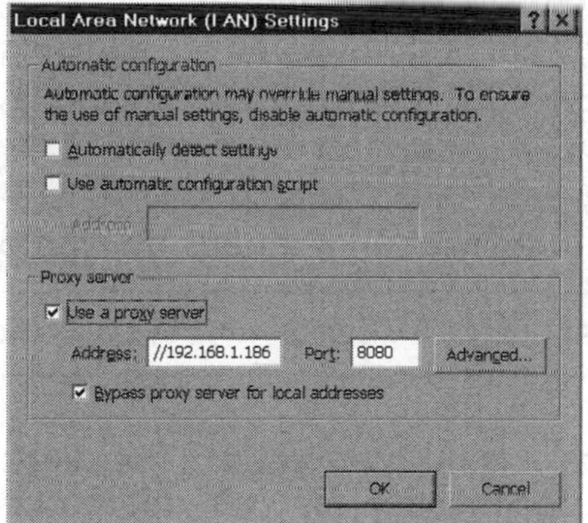

NOTE

CERN stands for Conseil Europeen pour le Recherche Nucleaire in French, or the European Laboratory for Particle Physics. What in the world does it have to do with your Web browser, you might ask? Although most of the laboratory's work is devoted to research in nuclear physics, CERN played a pivotal role in developing the World Wide Web and setting standards that resulted in the spectacular growth that made it the global forum it is today. The most popular Web browsers, including Microsoft Internet Explorer and Netscape Navigator and Communicator, are compatible with the CERN standards.

HTTP is the protocol that Web browsers use to communicate with Web servers to retrieve the Web objects they want to access. HTTP 1.1 is an improvement over the original version, which enhances performance and adds features such as support for persistent connections. More important, HTTP 1.1 adds security enhancements and caching specifications. The CERN Web site is located at http://cern.web.cern.ch/CERN/.

ISA Server Authentication

In order to gain access to a resource on your network, users must be *authenticated*; that is, their credentials must be checked to determine that they have the appropriate rights and permissions to access that object. In addition to Windows 2000 authentication required for access, when the user is attempting to access the resource over the Internet by going through an ISA Server in firewall or integrated mode that is protecting your network from outsiders, the user might also have to be authenticated by the ISA Server.

ISA provides different authentication options, depending on the type of client. Table 1.5 summarizes the authentication methods available for each client type.

Table 1.5 ISA Server Authentication Methods by Type of Client

Firewall Clients	SecureNAT Clients	Web Proxy Clients
Firewall client authentication is automatic; no configuration is required. The user credentials of the requesting user are employed.	There is no user-based authentication for SecureNAT clients. Access can be granted or denied based on sites, IP address, protocol, or time of day, but not based on user information.	The client authentication method can be configured. Client authentication is not required by default, but ISA can be configured to require that clients send authentication information. Authentication methods include basic, digest, integrated Windows authentication, or client certificate.

As shown in Table 1.5, there are four authentication methods to choose from when configuring settings for Web proxy clients:

- Basic authentication
- Digest authentication
- Integrated Windows authentication
- Client certificate authentication

These methods will be familiar to many administrators as the same authentication methods that are used by Internet Information Server (IIS) 5.0, Microsoft's Web server software that is included with Windows 2000. The authentication method(s) can be configured in the array's Properties sheet (see Figure 1.8).

Figure 1.8 Selecting the Authentication Method for an ISA Server Array

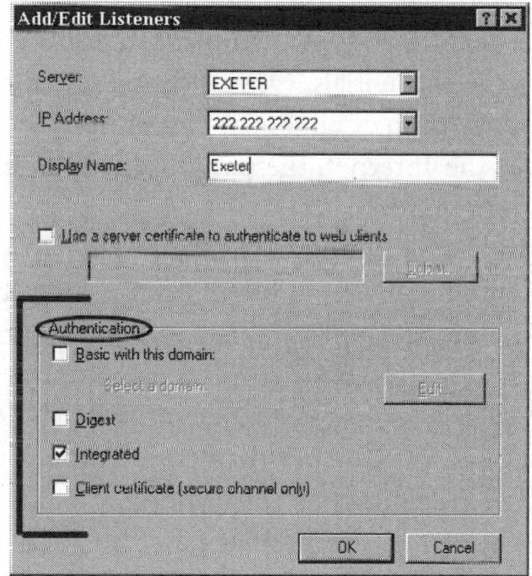

It is important to understand the differences between these methods and to choose the appropriate method, based on your network's desired level of security versus accessibility. It is also important to note that ISA Server can be configured to use multiple authentication methods.

SECURITY ALERT!

If the ISA Server is set up to use more than one authentication method, which one will it use? When a Web proxy client attempts to connect, the server and client negotiate to determine the method. The *most secure* method that is supported by both parties will be used.

Let's look at each of the authentication methods in a little more detail.

Basic Authentication

When you select the basic authentication option for the Web proxy client access, the user will be asked to provide a username and password before being allowed access. This information will be checked to confirm that there is a matching user account on the ISA Server or in a trusted domain.

Be aware that this information is sent in plain text; no encryption is used to protect the integrity of the credentials. Obviously, this method is more secure than requiring no authentication at all, but it can present a serious security risk because, as it travels over the Internet, the password is vulnerable to interception by a hacker using a packet sniffer.

The "up" side of basic authentication is that virtually all Web browsers support it, so compatibility isn't an issue. Basic authentication is actually a component of the HTTP protocol that Web browser software uses to communicate with Web servers.

Digest Authentication

Digest authentication goes a step further than basic authentication. Although the process is similar, the user credentials are *hashed* before being sent over the network. Hashing involves applying a mathematical calculation to the binary bits that make up the data being sent. This is a *one-way* process; that is, it is not possible to take the result of the calculation and reverse engineer it to come up with the original data (the username and password). This system, of course, adds a great deal more security to the transaction.

Other information is added to the user credentials when digest authentication is used. Besides just the name and password, data that identifies the user, the user's computer, and the domain to which the user belongs is added to the hash to prevent the possibility of *impersonation* of the user. In addition, the data is time-stamped so that a password that has been revoked or expired cannot be used. It's worth noting that the digest authentication method can be used only in Windows 2000 domains.

NOTE

The calculation that is performed by the hashing process is called the *hash algorithm.* The result of the hash is referred to as a *message digest.* For this reason, the authentication method that uses hashing is called *digest authentication*.

Integrated Windows Authentication

ISA Server can be configured to use Windows 2000 authentication, which is especially secure because the username and password don't have to be sent across the network at all. This eliminates the possibility of data interception in transit. Two protocols can be used when integrated Windows authentication is selected:

- **Kerberos v5** This is the default protocol for Windows 2000 domains.
- **Challenge/response** This is NT LAN Manager (NTLM) authentication.

UNDOCUMENTED ISA

ISA Server can use *pass-through authentication,* which is a means of passing the authentication information provided by the client to the server for which the message is destined. In other words, if a Web page were requested, the ISA server would pass the client's request on to the Web server. If the Web server responds that authentication is required, it also responds with the type of authentication type(s) it supports. This information goes back to the ISA server, which passes it back to the client. The client returns its authentication information to the ISA server, and once again ISA passes it through to the Web server. Although ISA supports pass-through authentication, it cannot use Kerberos for this purpose, only Challenge Handshake Authentication Protocol (CHAP).

Client Certificate Authentication

Finally, the Web proxy client can use Secure Sockets Layer (SSL) for authentication. This involves the use of a client certificate and a server certificate. The server first sends, in response to a client request, a server certificate that provides authentication of the server. If the server requests that the client authenticate itself, the client sends a client certificate to the server.

Certificates are digital "documents" that verify the identity of a client or server and that are issued by a *trusted third party* to which that identity has been satisfactorily proven. The trusted third party is called a *certification authority (CA)* and can be external (outside the organization) or internal. Windows 2000 Server provides the ability for companies to set up their own certification authorities to issue certificates internally. Certificates contain identifying information about the certificate holder.

If client certificate authentication is configured, the ISA Server identifies itself to the client as an SSL Web server by sending a certificate to the client. The ISA Server then requires that the client send a valid certificate before access will be granted.

The process of encrypting or decrypting client requests and then passing them to the Web server to which they are addressed is called *SSL bridging.* This process is used by the ISA Server when it initiates or ends an SSL connection.

When a client Web browser requests a Secure HTTP (S-HTTP) object (by default on port 8080, although if you have upgraded to ISA Server from Proxy Server 2.0, it will be 80 and can be any port you want to assign) through the ISA Server, a different process, called *SSL tunneling,* is used. In this scenario, the client creates a tunnel through the ISA Server directly to the Web server on which the requested object resides.

NOTE

SSL is an industry-standard protocol used on the Internet to secure messages by using a program layer that is between the HTTP (Application) layer and the TCP (Transport) layer. SSL was originally developed by Netscape for use in its Web browsers, but it is now supported by Microsoft Internet Explorer and most other Web application vendors. SSL uses public/private key encryption and digital certificates to provide security. SSL 3.0 is the current specification.

SSL's primary "competitor" is HTTP-S, which is an extension to HTTP. HTTP-S also uses encryption and digital certificates to provide secure Web transactions, but it operates at a higher level (the HTTP Application Layer) than SSL. Most modern browsers support both of these security methods.

ISA Server Features Overview

In this book, we look in detail at the security, acceleration, and Internet connection sharing features of ISA Server. Microsoft has ensured that ISA is packed with features to make it more usable than other comparable proxy solutions. The most important broad categories of features include:

- Firewall security features
- Web caching features
- Internet connection-sharing features
- Unified management features
- Extensible platform features

Let's look briefly at some of the specific features in each of these categories.

Firewall Security Features

The firewall functionality of ISA Server is a big focus of Microsoft's marketing efforts, and for good reason; *security* is the buzzword of the Internet industry today and will be at the top of most managers' priority lists for the foreseeable future. High-profile hack attacks, defacement of popular Web sites, denial-of-service attacks that bring down entire networks, e-mail viruses that threaten the integrity of user data—these are no longer merely topics of theoretical discussion or isolated incidents. The newspapers regularly feature network breaches that inconvenience thousands of people and cost companies millions of dollars.

The Certified Information Systems Security Professional (CISSP) designation is quickly becoming one of the IT industry's hottest certifications. Businesses are even hiring hackers to provide insight into the best way to protect networks from others like them. Even casual home computer users, who presumably have few if any trade secrets or confidential client files floating around on their systems, are concerned about security. Shareware or low-cost "personal firewall" software programs (such as ZoneAlarm, Gnat and Norton Internet Security 2000) are enjoying outstanding popularity.

Some might wonder why anyone would spend several hundred to several thousand dollars for ISA Server, given the number of free and inexpensive packages that are on the market. The answer is that Microsoft has built ISA Server to withstand the rigors of the business network and has loaded it with features that make the task of protecting your LAN easy and flexible.

NOTE

In addition to the CISSP (more information available at www.gocsi.com/cissp.htm), other professional certification programs for network security professionals are SANS GIAC (hwww.sans.org) tri-level certification and the Certified Internet Webmaster security professional certification (also called Master CIW Administrator certification).

Firewall Features Overview

A few of the firewall features integrated into ISA Server are shown in Table 1.6.

Table 1.6 ISA Server Firewall Security Features

Feature	Description
Multilayer filtering	ISA Server supports screening of network traffic at multiple layers of the networking model: packet, circuit, and application. Packet filtering can be either static or dynamic.
Stateful inspection	ISA examines traffic based on state and context information such as the protocol used and the state of the connection.
Intrusion detection	ISA provides the ability to issue an alert to the administrator or even take action (such as running a program or shutting down the server) if intrusion events are detected. Intrusion detection filters analyze traffic for specific intrusion types.
Email security	SMTP application filters can examine e-mail messages and accept or reject them based on the source, user, or domain. POP intrusion detection filters intercept POP traffic and check for POP buffer overflow attacks.
Web security	ISA Server lets you put your Web servers behind the firewall and "publish" the server to the Internet. This results in the incoming requests for Web objects going through the ISA Server, which impersonates the Web site by associating its own IP address with the Web server's DNS name.

Continued

Table 1.6 Continued

Feature	Description
Secure server publishing	ISA lets you use publishing rules to specify that certain servers on your LAN (such as your mail server) will be "published" to the Internet. ISA then "listens" for incoming requests addressed to that server and redirects the requests to the server.
Secure VPN	ISA Server allows secure virtual private networking connections to pass through the firewall so that a "tunnel" can be created through the Internet to connect a client to a private network that is also connected to the Internet.
System hardening (Security Configuration Wizard)	Like Windows 2000, ISA provides wizards to walk you through common tasks and make them easier. The Security Configuration Wizard lets you set a desired security level to lock down, or "harden," ISA Server to the degree that is appropriate for your organization's network.
Strong authentication	Authentication configuration is dependent on the client type. ISA supports NTLM and Kerberos authentication, client certificates and digests, and basic and anonymous Web authentication.
Streaming media splitting	ISA can split live media streams from the Internet and make the data available locally on a Windows Media Technology Server so that clients who subsequently request access do not use Internet bandwidth.

ISA Server's firewall features rival those of dedicated hardware-based firewall solutions. Here we examine some of these in more detail.

System Hardening

By including a friendly interface that allows you to perform *system hardening*, or a lockdown of the Windows 2000 operating system on which ISA Server is running, Microsoft has made it easy to configure security appropriate to your network's needs. One of the following security levels can be selected by running the ISA Server Security Configuration Wizard:

- **Secure** This is the best setting to use if the computer that is running ISA Server also has other server programs running on it (such as IIS, a mail server, or the like).
- **Limited Services** If ISA is set up to operate in integrated mode (as both a firewall and caching server), this setting is appropriate.
- **Dedicated** This setting is used when ISA is functioning as a dedicated firewall only and you have no other interactive applications running on the server machine.

Secure, Integrated VPN

One of ISA Server's star attractions is its smooth integration with virtual private networking. A VPN is established by creating a virtual "tunnel" through the Internet to communicate securely with a private network. With a VPN, you send data across a public network in a way that mimics a private, point-to-point connection.

For example, if your company has telecommuters who need to access the company network from their home computers, you can set this up in several ways. The traditional way is to set up a remote access server on the company LAN and have the telecommuters' use their modems to dial up the phone number of a line that is connected to a modem on the remote access services (RAS) server. This system allows the home user to log on to the company network and function as a remote node on the network. The user's connection is, in most practical ways, identical to that of the users who are on site at the company and whose computers are wired into the network via Ethernet cable. The biggest difference is in the data transfer speed; analog modems are limited to 56 Kbps (and actually do not generally reach that speed), whereas a typical Ethernet connection runs at either 10 Mbps or 100 Mbps.

This setup serves the purpose, but there are a couple of drawbacks:

- If you have more than one telecommuter who needs to connect to the company network simultaneously, your remote access server must have multiple modems (or a modem bank) and multiple telephone lines to accommodate the number of dial-in users you want to support.
- If the telecommuters live outside the local calling area (not an unusual occurrence), they have to pay long distance charges for the time they are dialed into the company RAS server. During business hours, this could add up to a costly proposition.

Luckily, there is another way to accomplish your objective—one that addresses both of these problems. If your company network is connected to the Internet via a dedicated Integrated Services Digital Network (ISDN) line or T-1 connection, as most business LANs are today, you can set up a VPN server on the network. Like the remote dial-up server, the VPN server accepts incoming calls, but it does not do so via a direct dial-up connection. Instead, the telecommuter dials up his or her Internet service provider (ISP) and establishes a connection to the Internet. Because both the telecommuter's computer and the company network are on the same global network, they can communicate with one another. Using a "tunneling" protocol, a virtual link is established in which communications are *encapsulated*. That is, one protocol (used for communication on your company LAN—this can be TCP/IP, IPX/SPX, or even NetBEUI) is hidden inside another during its travel across the Internet. Figure 1.9 presents an illustration of how this works.

Figure 1.9 A VPN Allows Establishment of a Secure Link to a Private Network Across the Public Internet

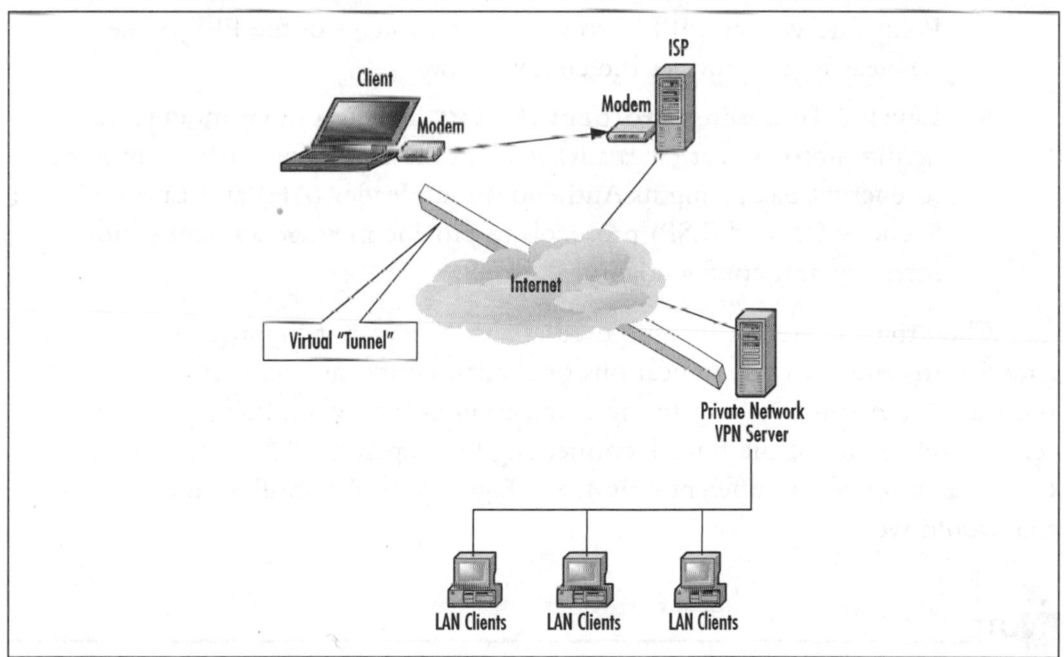

This solution overcomes both of the limitations of a dial-up connection:

- There is no need for multiple modems and telephone lines. The VPN server requires only one connection to the Internet. Separate *virtual ports* are created to accommodate multiple simultaneous connections.
- Because the remote users can dial up their local ISPs instead of dialing long distance to connect directly to the RAS server, the user will incur no long distance charges.

Windows 2000 includes the ability to function as a VPN server or client. The ISA Server is fully integrated with this VPN capability. You can run the VPN wizard on the ISA Server to easily create a virtual private networking connection, using one of the two tunneling technologies supported by Windows 2000:

- **Point-to-Point Tunneling Protocol (PPTP)** This is an industry standard that was also supported in Windows NT 4.0, which is an extension of the Point-to-Point Protocol (PPP) link protocol used to establish networking connections across a WAN link. PPTP uses Microsoft Point-to-Point Encryption (MPPE) to secure the contents of the PPP frame, whereas PPTP provides the encapsulation.
- **Layer 2 Tunneling Protocol (L2TP)** This is a more modern tunneling protocol that takes advantage of the IPSecurity (IPSec) protocol to encrypt data, using its Authentication Header (AH) and Encapsulating Security Payload (ESP) protocols to provide message authentication, integrity, and confidentiality.

When the ISA Server is configured as a VPN server, it supports secure gateway-to-gateway communications or client-to-gateway communications over the Internet. A gateway-to-gateway connection occurs when there is a VPN server at each end of the tunnel, connecting two separate LANs (for example, two branch offices in different cities). See Figure 1.10 for an illustration of how this would work.

NOTE

Windows 2000 users will be pleased to find that the VPN wizards included in ISA Server are significantly easier to configure than those that are part of the Windows 2000 operating system. It is rumored that the improvements in the ISA VPN wizards will be incorporated into Windows XP (code name Whistler), Microsoft's next operating system release.

Figure 1.10 An ISA Server Placed at Each End of the Tunnel to Provide VPN Between Two LANs

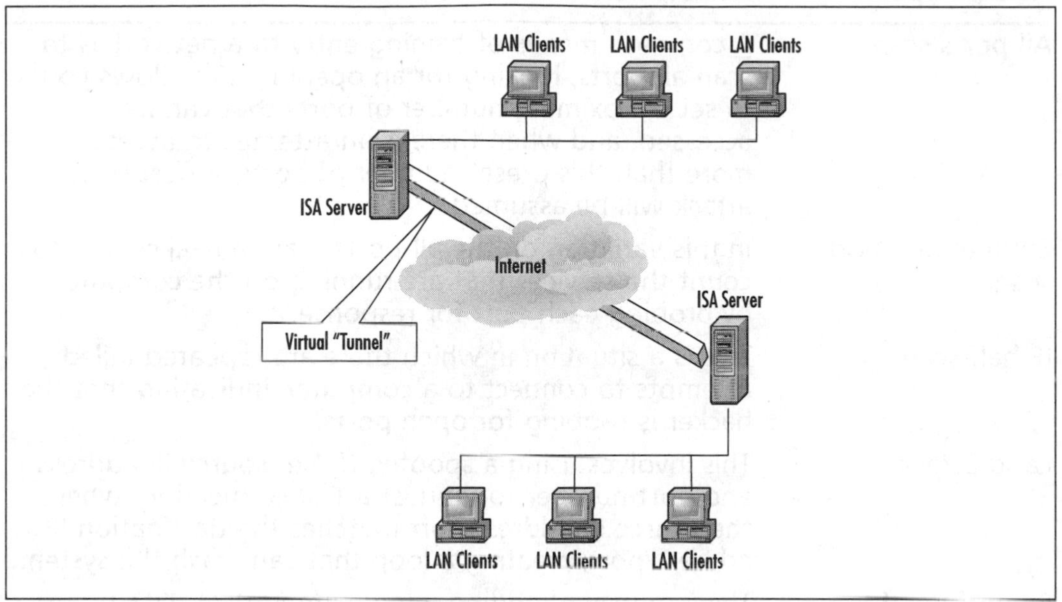

Integrated Intrusion Detection

An exciting feature of the ISA Server firewall service is the intrusion detection system that can actually recognize that an attack of a specific type is being attempted and can perform a predefined action when such an intrusion is identified. When ISA detects an attack, it can do one or more of the following:

- Send an e-mail message, send a network message, or page the administrator
- Write an event entry to the event log
- Run a previously specified program or script
- Stop the firewall service

Intrusion detection works at both the packet filtering and application filtering levels and can recognize many different common forms of network intrusion. Some of these forms are shown in Table 1.7.

Table 1.7 Common Intrusion Attacks Recognized by the ISA Firewall

Attack Type	Description
All-ports scan	A common means of gaining entry to a network is to scan all ports, looking for an opening. ISA allows you to set a maximum number of ports that can be accessed, and when there is an attempt to access more than this preset number of ports, a port scan attack will be assumed.
Enumerated port scan	In this variation on the all-ports scan, a hacker tries to count the services that are running on the computer by probing each port for response.
IP half-scan	This is a situation in which there are repeated failed attempts to connect to a computer, indicating that the hacker is probing for open ports.
Land attack	This involves using a spoofed (false) source IP address and port number to request a TCP connection, where the source IP address/port matches the destination IP address/port, creating a loop that can crash the system.
Ping of death	This is a way of adding a large amount of data to an Internet Control Message Protocol (ICMP) echo request/ping packet, causing a kernel buffer overflow that can crash the system.
UDP bomb	In this type of attack, the hacker sends an illegal UDP packet (one that has invalid values in certain header fields), which can cause some operating systems to crash.
Out-of-band attack	This is a type of denial-of-service attack that can cause the system to crash or lose network connectivity.

In addition to these, ISA Server includes a POP intrusion detection filter that analyzes POP mail traffic to guard against POP buffer overflows and a DNS intrusion detection filter that can be configured to look for DNS hostname overflow or length overflow attacks.

NOTE

Microsoft licensed the technology for its ISA Server intrusion detection mechanisms from Internet Security Systems (ISS), a leading vendor of network security services. For more information about ISS and its products and services, see www.iss.net.

Web Caching Features

ISA as a Web caching server also offers a plethora of features designed to speed Internet access for your organization while reducing WAN link bandwidth usage. In particular, ISA supports the following:

- **Smart caching** ISA not only caches Web sites that are accessed, it can also determine which sites are accessed most frequently and engage in "proactive" caching to refresh the contents of popular sites on a regular basis. Not only that, but ISA chooses a time when the network traffic load is light to retrieve the site from the Internet and load it into cache.
- **Scheduled caching** Perhaps you don't want to let ISA make the caching decisions for you, no matter how "smart" it might be. In that case, you can configure the ISA Server to download entire Web sites on a schedule that you configure. This ensures that your most accessed sites are refreshed when *you* want them to be refreshed.
- **Distributed caching** With the Enterprise Edition of ISA Server, the cached objects can be distributed across multiple ISA servers so that the entire load doesn't have to be borne by a single machine. This not only balances the traffic load, it also speeds client access to the cached objects.
- **Hierarchical caching** Enterprise Edition also allows for arrays of ISA Servers to be "chained" so that a hierarchy of caches is established and clients can access the cache that is nearest to them.

Security Alert!

In some ways, ISA's caching ability can be seen not only as a separate feature from its firewall functionality but almost as the antithesis of it. That is, it would seem that caching objects on a server would present a security risk. After all, the cache stores a copy of those pages and other objects that have been accessed; can't a busybody then just examine the cache and be privy to others' Web surfing habits?

Due to these security concerns, ISA builds in extra measures to prevent confidential information from being cached. For instance, if the pages you access require that you log in, ISA does not cache passwords or other forms of user authentication used on the Web. Neither does it cache *cookies,* which are files stored on a local disk to cause a client to send information to a Web server each time that client accesses the page.

Cookies allow you to personalize a Web page (for instance, to have the page "remember" your ZIP code so it can deliver the local weather news for your area). Encrypted objects (SSL and S-HTTP) are not cached, either.

Internet Connection-Sharing Features

Microsoft does not actually list connection sharing as one of ISA's features. However, a very common use of a proxy server is to allow computers on a LAN to access the Internet via a single modem or ISDN/DSL adapter and a single phone line, using one ISP account and requiring only one public registered IP address (either assigned permanently by the ISP or assigned dynamically by its DHCP server each time a dial-up connection is established to the ISP server).

ISA's NAT component provides this functionality. Certainly, if all you want to do is share an Internet connection, ISA Server could be considered a bit of "overkill." This is especially true considering the fact that Windows 2000 has a built-in NAT that will accomplish the same thing, without buying an additional program, and that the Windows 2000 NAT is easier to configure than an ISA Server. Windows 2000's "NAT Lite" (ICS) doesn't even require the server operating system; you can set up a Windows 2000 Professional machine as a NAT gateway for your LAN. In fact, even Windows 98 Second Edition (SE) includes this feature.

However, ISA's connection-sharing capability shouldn't be overlooked just because it is so basic. A shared connection does present certain security risks, especially if the connection that is being shared is an "always on" or dedicated connection, in which the local network is connected to the Internet 24 x 7 and the IP address remains the same. This is where ISA's firewall features come into play. Unlike a pure NAT solution, ISA gives you all the advantages of address translation and provides additional protection for the computers sharing the connection, all at the same time.

Unified Management Features

Microsoft designed ISA Server with the administrator in mind. That is obvious when you consider the more user-friendly interface and the handy wizards that are included to guide you through all the common setup and management tasks (see Figure 1.11).

Figure 1.11 ISA Server's Multitude of Built-In Wizards Are Designed to Ease Administration

ISA Server uses the Microsoft Management Console (MMC) that is the cornerstone of all Windows 2000 administrative tools (and was introduced with IIS 4.0 and Microsoft Proxy Server back when NT ruled the Windows networking roost).

Some of the management features offered by ISA include:

- **Integration with Active Directory** When using the Enterprise Edition of ISA Server, the software integrates tightly with the Windows 2000 directory services. User information, configuration information, and rules can be stored in the directory and managed through the Active Directory MMCs. Active Directory allows you to implement caching arrays, share the schema, and deploy access policies across an array or the entire enterprise.
- **Access control based on policy** The Policy wizards let you configure ISA Server to control access based on user and group information, the content of the data, the application, and/or the source and destination computers. Particular protocols can be allowed or rejected, ports can be opened or closed, and communication between specified computers can be blocked or permitted.
- **Management at multiple levels** *Multilevel management* simply refers to the ability to set policies at different levels; thus you can apply a policy broadly so that it affects the entire enterprise network or more narrowly

so that it affects only a particular array or arrays or just a single ISA Server.

- **Bandwidth allocation** The ability to prioritize bandwidth usage, based on groups, applications, sites, or content, using the Windows 2000 QoS features helps administrators keep costs down and optimize the overall performance of the network.
- **Remote management** Using either the ISA MMC or the Windows 2000 Terminal Services, you can perform management tasks on your ISA Server from a machine across the room or across the country. Remote management allows you to change settings or troubleshoot an ISA Server without being physically at its location.
- **Logging and reporting** An important part of any management plan, especially one pertaining to security issues, is documentation. ISA Server makes documentation easier by providing a robust logging and reporting function that will let you schedule reports, output the data to standard formats, and even send alerts to administrators, start or stop services, or run scripts to perform specified tasks when a predefined event occurs.

Figure 1.12 provides a view of the ISA MMC snap-in used to configure and administer ISA Server.

Figure 1.12 The ISA Security and Acceleration Functions Are Configured and Managed via the ISA Server MMC

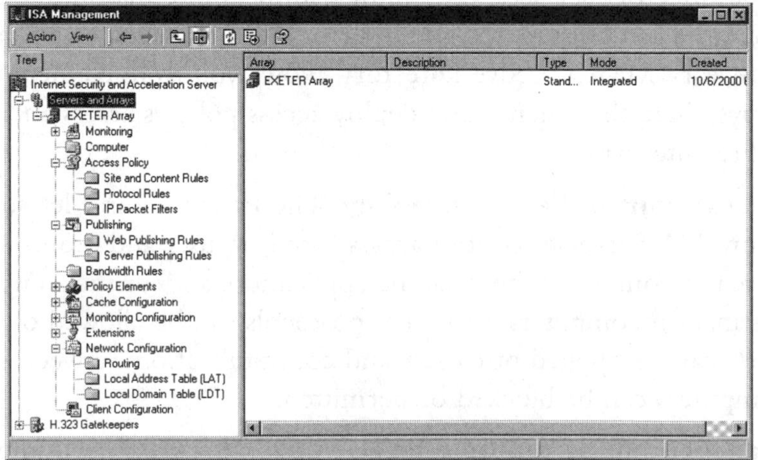

Extensible Platform Features

Microsoft is positioning ISA Server as an *extensible* platform, based on the fact that developers can add to its user interface with ISA Administrator COM objects. This can be done in one of two ways:

- Using Visual Basic or C++ programming
- Using scripting languages such as VBScript or JScript

Application developers are able to write add-ons for ISA that will expand its functionality. For example, they can add administrative tools, packet and application filters, NAT editors, and extensions to the user interface or the caching functionality.

Designing & Implementing

What Is COM?

COM stands for *Component Object Model,* which is an architecture that provides for a way that software components developed by different vendors can be combined together in applications. COM is a standard for constructing components that will interoperate; it can be used on a variety of platforms. COM works on Windows, Macintosh, and UNIX systems. It doesn't depend on a particular programming language, either. Any language that calls functions via pointers, from BASIC to C++, can be used to write components that comply with the COM standard.

A COM *object* is a bit of compiled code that provides a service to the rest of the system. Component objects access other COM objects through interface pointers rather than accessing them directly. In this context, an *interface* is a related group of functions. It is the binary standard clients and COM objects used to communicate.

The COM standard defines how applications *interoperate*. It is not concerned with how the individual applications are structured. On Microsoft operating systems, COM is implemented through a DLL.

For more information on COM and related technologies such as DCOM, COM+, and ActiveX, see www.microsoft.com/com/wpaper/.

Administrators who have some programming or scripting experience can use COM objects of ISA Server in scripts or VB applications to automate administration and configuration of ISA.

The ISA Server Software Developer's Kit (SDK) documentation for ISA Server can be found in the \SDK\Help\ folder of the installation CD. The file is Isasdk.chm. The SDK contains many step-by-step samples that you can use to construct additional filters, MMC snap-ins, reporting tools, and other administrative extensions.

ISA Server's extensibility features open the door to third-party software vendors to provide applications and extensions that enhance its functionality to provide virus protection, customized content filtering, and management tools. For example, LANguard, a leading Internet access control and intrusion detection tool, offers seamless integration with ISA and allows administrators to utilize all of LANguard's features into their ISA firewalls and manage and configure LANguard through the ISA MMC. This is only one of many independent vendor products that will be able to interoperate with ISA Server, thanks to its built-in extensibility features. A list of software manufacturers that have partnered with Microsoft to offer solutions that work with ISA Server is available on Microsoft's ISA Server Web site at http://channels.microsoft.com/isaserver/thirdparty/offerings.htm.

Who This Book Is For and What It Covers

Microsoft has targeted ISA Server for the enterprise market, and that notion is reflected in the company's stated audience profile for the exam: Candidates are expected to have at least a year of experience operating in a medium-sized to very large networking environment (defined as 200 to 26,000 or more users and multiple physical locations) where the Windows 2000 operating system is in use.

We know that some of our readers fit this description, and others don't. Our goal in writing this book is to provide value both to readers who are rolling out ISA Server in a large-scale network for mission-critical applications and those who are deploying it on a small home network to familiarize themselves with the product as they study for the exam.

If you're looking for specific scenarios that address your own situation or answers to troubleshooting problems that occur in your ISA deployment, we have tried to make it easy for you to find and flip to the section of this book that you need. We have put in numerous tips and tricks for dealing with ISA in the real world and provided references to give you more information about related topics that you could come across as you work with ISA. We have also attempted to provide context for comparing ISA Server to other, similar firewall and/or caching solutions.

If you're working through the book progressively in an attempt to understand the concepts behind ISA and learn the "how tos" of configuration and administration with the exam objectives in mind, we have laid out the book in a logical order that will allow you to master the new terminology and ideas first and then to proceed through the step-by-step "walk-through" exercises that will show you exactly how to perform the tasks involved in setting up, managing, and troubleshooting an ISA Server.

The remainder of this book covers the following topics in detail, based on our own experiences, trials, and tribulations with ISA Server:

- **Chapter 2: ISA Server in the Enterprise** First, we discuss how the enterprise network differs from the small business network and how this difference affects your ISA Server deployment plan. We look at ISA features that are specially designed for the enterprise, including multiserver arrays, distributed caching, and multiserver management. We also cover ISA licensing issues and how ISA can lower your total cost of operation (TCO).
- **Chapter 3: Security Concepts and Security Policies** This chapter begins with an overview of basic computer security concepts and a discussion of common Internet security threats and what can be done to protect against them. We discuss firewalls in general and ISA's firewall functionality in particular. You will learn about security policies, how Microsoft has improved security in Windows 2000, and how ISA Server fits into your overall network security plan.
- **Chapter 4: ISA Server Deployment Planning and Design** Before you get down to the nitty-gritty of deploying ISA Server in your production network, it is important to plan ahead and have your design goals firmly in mind. This chapter will take you through the process of evaluating your hardware and existing application software, your current network configuration, and determining the best way to incorporate ISA Server to accomplish the results you want without any nasty surprises.

- **Chapter 5: ISA Server Installation** The first step in deploying any new software product is installation, and when a product is as complex and feature-rich as ISA Server, installation issues are likely to need examination before you do a full-scale rollout. We first discuss planning and design issues and then get into the "nitty gritty" of how to install ISA Server on a Windows 2000 Server, how to migrate from Microsoft Proxy Server 2.0, and how to troubleshoot common installation problems.
- **Chapter 6: Managing ISA Server** This chapter introduces you to the Internet Security and Acceleration Server MMC snap-in. You'll learn how to create a custom MMC for managing ISA Server, how to navigate the MMC's interface, how to use the multiplicity of wizards built into ISA, and how the reporting and logging services can be used to monitor your ISA Server's performance and usage. You'll learn about remote administration, too.
- **Chapter 7: ISA Architecture and Client Configuration** An in-depth look at the ISA Server architecture provides a foundation for understanding the practicalities of administering the product. This chapter will also show you how to configure the three types of ISA clients: firewall, SecureNAT (S-NAT), and Web proxy.
- **Chapter 8: Configuring ISA Server for Outbound Access** Because Microsoft designed it to be a flexible solution that would work in diverse networking situations, ISA's configuration options can be overwhelming without guidance. We walk you through the process of configuring both the server and the clients as well as how to configure access policies and rules, Web caching, and secure publishing.
- **Chapter 9: Configuring the ISA Server for Inbound Access** The firewall function is likely to be ISA's most popular use, especially in an enterprise environment. Let's face it: Enhanced performance is nice, but security is vital in today's globally connected environment. This chapter focuses on the many firewall features of ISA, and we hold your hand as we lead you through the sometimes confusing forest of filtering options (at the packet, circuit, and application levels), traffic screening, security templates, intrusion detection, authentication methods, and different client types.

- **Chapter 10: Publishing Servers to the Internet** This chapter will look at the fine points of web and server publishing, and explore how you can use ISA Server to provide access to your internal servers, including web servers, Exchange mail servers, database servers and FTP servers, for Internet users. We will also discuss configuring a perimeter network (DMZ), and using Windows 2000 terminal services with ISA Server.
- **Chapter 11: Optimizing, Customizing, Integrating, and Backing Up ISA Server** This chapter provides insights into how you can get the best performance and the highest level of security out of your ISA Server solution and specifically looks at bandwidth priorities, scalability issues, and application support. This chapter gives you a look at some third-party software packages, developed in Microsoft's partnering programs, that are designed to integrate with ISA Server.
- **Chapter 12: Troubleshooting ISA Server** Regardless of how much work Microsoft put into developing a reliable, easy-to-implement solution and regardless of how much time you put into mastering all the nuances of ISA Server, Murphy's Law still applies: If something can go wrong, it will go wrong. Unfortunately, ISA Server gets no special dispensation from that law. In this last chapter, we attempt to anticipate some of the problems that could occur during your deployment of ISA and offer suggestions on how to deal with them. We also briefly address general troubleshooting procedures and help you approach your ISA problems in a way that will ensure a quick and relatively pain-free solution.

An understanding of the TCP/IP protocol stack is necessary to configuring and working with ISA Server. If you do not have previous networking experience, or come from a NetWare 4.x or earlier environment and need a good review of the concepts, see *Troubleshooting Windows 2000 TCP/IP*, by Deb and Tom Shinder (Syngress Publishing, 2000).

Summary

In this introductory chapter, we've discussed the features and the "three-pronged" functionality of ISA Server: as firewall, as caching (acceleration) server, and as Internet connection-sharing solution. ISA Server can provide all or some of these functions for your network, depending on your needs and how you configure the product.

ISA Server is an Internet connectivity solution that provides network address translation to allow the client computers on your LAN to connect to the Internet through the ISA Server, with no requirement that the internal computers have modems, phone lines, or separate public registered IP addresses. This saves your organization money—but, as they say in the commercials, that's not all. Because all the internal IP addresses get "translated" to a single public address, which is the only address visible to computers on the Internet, this system provides a measure of security to the computer on your local network and exposes only one computer—the ISA Server—to the "world outside."

But that's only the beginning of ISA's security features. ISA is a network security solution that provides full-fledged firewall functionality. As a highly configurable multilayer firewall, ISA performs filtering at the packet, circuit, and application levels, giving you a maximum number of options in deciding just how "locked down" you want your system and your network to be. Securing your network is made even easier by the ISA Server Security Configuration Wizard, which allows you to choose from three security levels, depending on the role ISA Server plays on your network.

However, as important as it might be, security is not the only benefit to be gained from using ISA Server. ISA is a Web performance solution that uses its caching ability to speed access to frequently visited Web sites for all your internal users. With reverse caching, ISA can also increase performance for user who access your internal Web servers from outside your network. This performance benefit comes at no cost in terms of security, because the firewall and caching functions can be used separately (firewall and caching modes) or in combination (integrated mode).

Although ISA Server offers a plethora of features, Microsoft had the forethought to ensure that its functionality could be expanded in the future. ISA is an open platform solution built on the Component Object Model (COM), a non-platform-dependent standard that allows developers to create extensions to expand ISA's capabilities, including management tools and additional filters. Third-party vendors can write (and already have written) software applications that interoperate with ISA Server and add to its functionality.

ISA Server is all this and more. As a member of the new .Net family of servers that form the foundation of Microsoft's Internet-centric approach to the 21st century, ISA Server offers network administrators a flexible, powerful solution to many of their networking dilemmas. Mastering ISA Server will not be easy, but it *will* be worth the effort.

Solutions Fast Track

What Is ISA Server?

☑ Internet Security and Acceleration (ISA) provides two very different sets of functionality. Consequently, some organizations use ISA primarily for its security function. For others, speeding up Web access via the acceleration function could be more important. Of course, many organizations benefit from both features.

☑ Proxy servers have been around for quite a while. Despite its new, somewhat esoteric name, ISA Server is a proxy server, albeit a very full-featured one.

☑ Proxy servers "stand in" between the computers on a LAN and those on the public network outside.

☑ ISA Server performs the functions of a full-featured dedicated firewall.

☑ The advantage of Microsoft's ISA Server is that it combines these components—proxy, NAT, and firewall—into one package. This makes it easier to deploy and administer than separate software programs and/or hardware devices.

☑ ISA is not only an Internet security server; it is also an Internet acceleration server. This means faster access to frequently viewed Web sites and less internetwork traffic.

☑ Because Web caching reduces Internet traffic, it can also reduce your bandwidth cost.

☑ H.323 is a standard of the International Telecommunications Union (ITU), which was approved in 1996 (version 2 was approved in 1998) to provide a foundation for audio, video, and data communications across IP-based networks such as the global Internet.

- ☑ The ISA Server Standard Edition is appropriate for small business networks (or even sophisticated home networks) and for implementation on a departmental basis in larger organizations.
- ☑ The ISA Enterprise Edition is designed for maximum scalability to the largest, high-traffic enterprise networks. Fault tolerance, centralized management, and multiple-level policy application are at the core of the Enterprise Edition's feature set.
- ☑ ISA Servers can be installed as individual standalone servers or, if you have the Enterprise Edition
- ☑ A big advantage of joining multiple ISA servers in an array is the ability to manage them as one entity.
- ☑ Just as Proxy Server was considered a member of the Microsoft BackOffice Family, ISA Server also belongs to a new Microsoft "family," the members of which are designed to work with Windows 2000 in an enterprise environment. This group of enterprise servers is now called the Microsoft.Net family, or simply ".Net" (pronounced dot-net) servers.
- ☑ It is Microsoft's goal to offer, in the .Net family of servers, a group of products that can work individually or together to provide the full range of features needed in today's increasingly large and diversified network environments.

  Firewall products support the filtering of messages to either allow data to pass through or prevent data from doing so, according to specified criteria.
- ☑ Packet filtering does most of its work at the Network Layer of the OSI networking model (equivalent to the Internetwork Layer of the DoD model), dealing with IP packets.
- ☑ Dynamic packet filtering provides higher security because it opens the necessary port(s) only when required for communication to take place, then closes the port immediately after the communication ends.
- ☑ Circuit filters restrict access on the basis of host machines (not users) by processing the information found in the TCP and UDP packet headers. This allows you to create filters that would, for example, prohibit anyone using Computer A from using FTP to access files on Computer B.

- ☑ The ISA firewall service works at the circuit level with most Internet applications and protocols, making them perform as though they were directly connected to the Internet.
- ☑ Application filtering is the most sophisticated level of filtering performed by the firewall service and is especially useful in allowing you to protect your network against specific types of attacks such as malicious SMTP commands or attempts to penetrate your local DNS servers.
- ☑ By definition, a SecureNAT client cannot also be a firewall client.
- ☑ The firewall service on the ISA server intercepts Winsock API calls initiated by the clients and redirects those requests to the Internet computer to which they are addressed.
- ☑ If a computer is configured as a client to the ISA Server (by setting the default gateway in the computer's TCP/IP properties) and does not have the firewall client software installed, it will automatically be a SecureNAT client.
- ☑ If your network is larger and more complex and there are routers between the SecureNAT clients and the ISA Server, the default gateway settings on the clients will be configured with the IP address of the router on the local subnet.
- ☑ Certificates are digital "documents" that verify the identity of a client or server and that are issued by a trusted third party to which that identity has been satisfactorily proven.

ISA Server Features Overview

- ☑ By including a friendly interface that allows you to perform system hardening, or a lockdown of the Windows 2000 operating system on which ISA Server is running, Microsoft has made it easy to configure security appropriate to your network's needs.
- ☑ One of ISA Server's star attractions is its smooth integration with virtual private networking. A VPN is established by creating a virtual "tunnel" through the Internet to communicate securely with a private network.
- ☑ When the ISA Server is configured as a VPN server, it supports secure gateway-to-gateway communications or client-to-gateway communications over the Internet.

- ☑ An exciting feature of the ISA Server firewall service is the intrusion detection system that can actually recognize that an attack of a specific type is being attempted and can perform a predefined action when such an intrusion is identified.
- ☑ ISA as a Web caching server also offers a plethora of features designed to speed Internet access for your organization while reducing WAN link bandwidth usage.
- ☑ ISA allows computers on a LAN to access the Internet via a single modem or ISDN/DSL adapter and a single phone line, using one ISP account and requiring only one public registered IP address (either assigned permanently by the ISP or assigned dynamically by its DHCP server each time a dial-up connection is established to the ISP server).
- ☑ ISA Server uses the Microsoft Management Console (MMC) that is the cornerstone of all Windows 2000 administrative tools (and was introduced with IIS 4.0 and Microsoft Proxy Server back when NT ruled the Windows networking roost).
- ☑ Microsoft is positioning ISA Server as an extensible platform, based on the fact that developers can add to its user interface with ISA Administrator COM objects.
- ☑ Administrators who have some programming or scripting experience can use COM objects of ISA Server in scripts or VB applications to automate administration and configuration of ISA.

Who This Book Is For and What It Covers

- ☑ Microsoft has targeted ISA Server for the enterprise market, and that notion is reflected in the company's stated audience profile for the exam: Candidates are expected to have at least a year of experience operating in a medium-sized to very large networking environment (defined as 200 to 26,000 or more users and multiple physical locations) where the Windows 2000 operating system is in use.
- ☑ If you're looking for specific scenarios that address your own situation or answers to troubleshooting problems that occur in your ISA deployment, we have tried to make it easy for you to find and flip to the section of this book that you need.

☑ An understanding of the TCP/IP protocol stack is necessary to configuring and working with ISA Server. If you do not have previous networking experience, or come from a NetWare 4.x or earlier environment and need a review of basic TCP/IP concepts, see *Troubleshooting Windows 2000 TCP/IP*, (Syngress Publishing, 2000).

Frequently Asked Questions

The following Frequently Asked Questions, answered by the authors of this book, are designed to both measure your understanding of the concepts presented in this chapter and to assist you with real-life implementation of these concepts. To have your questions about this chapter answered by the author, browse to **www.syngress.com/solutions** and click on the **"Ask the Author"** form.

Q: What client platforms are supported by ISA Server?

A: The ISA Server firewall client software supports 32-bit Windows client operating systems: Windows 95, 98, and ME, Windows NT, and Windows 2000. The firewall client adds user-level authentication as well as support for additional protocols. However, this is only an optional component. ISA Server can support virtually any client platform due to the SecureNAT transparency feature. Any CERN-compatible Web browser (including Netscape and Microsoft Internet Explorer) support ISA's HTTP client, and any client application that uses HTTP to access the Internet can be used with the HTTP application filter.

Q: Must I have a Windows 2000 Server to install ISA Server? Must I be running Active Directory to install ISA Server?

A: The answer to the first question is "Yes." ISA Server requires the Windows 2000 operating system; it will not run on Windows NT. However, you *can* use ISA Server on a standalone (member) Windows 2000 server that is part of a Windows NT domain. Although ISA Server integrates with Active Directory and takes advantage of its administrative and security features, Active Directory is *not* required for the Standard Edition of ISA Server. (Enterprise Edition does require Active Directory in order to implement arrays.)

Q: What does SecureNAT do?

A: NAT (Network Address Translation) is a means of providing Internet access to computers on an internal network using only one external (registered) public IP address. The NAT computer (which is connected to both the Internet and the internal network) maps client requests to a port (keeping this information in a mapping table) and passes them on to the external network. ISA uses address translation to pass traffic between internal computers and the Internet. SecureNAT intercepts traffic on the network and applies outbound firewall policies to it, with no need to install client software or configure browser settings.

Q: How is virtual private networking (VPN) used with ISA Server?

A: ISA Server has VPN wizards that assist you in configuring Windows 2000's built-in VPN services. A VPN connection can be made to the ISA server itself, or VPN connections can be initiated by the internal client computers behind the ISA server to VPN hosts on the Internet.

Q: What is reverse caching?

A: Reverse caching is often used in e-commerce solutions; it consists of putting a cache in front of a Web server or electronic transaction application, which allows Web managers to cache and distribute Web content. Because traditional Web caching is implemented by the Web clients, whereas this type of caching is implemented by the administrators of the Web servers, it is called *reverse caching*.

Q: Is it possible to upgrade from Microsoft Proxy Server to ISA Server?

A: Yes. Microsoft has provided an upgrade path for users running Proxy Server 2.0 on Windows 2000. Most of the Proxy Server rules, network settings, and configurations will be migrated to the ISA Server. If your Proxy Server 2.0 is running on a Windows NT 4.0 server, you must first upgrade the operating system to Windows 2000 Server before you can upgrade Proxy Server to ISA.

Q: Must I use both the firewall and the Web caching functions of ISA Server, or can I choose to use just one or the other?

A: If you do not need both functionalities, you can deploy ISA as a firewall only or as a caching server only. ISA Server can be installed in one of three modes:

firewall, cache, or integrated. In firewall mode, you are able to secure the network using filtering and you can publish your internal servers to share data securely with users over the Internet. In cache mode, you can use ISA's performance and acceleration features and conserve network bandwidth by storing commonly accessed Web pages on the ISA server. Integrated mode allows you to enjoy the "best of both worlds," with both firewall and caching functionalities.

Q: Can I run a mail or Web server behind my ISA Server?

A: Yes! With ISA Server's secure publishing feature, you can make your Web servers and mail servers accessible to users on the Internet without compromising the security of the internal network. When you publish your Web or mail servers to the Internet, you can configure publishing rules that ISA Server will use in allowing outside traffic to be forwarded to the internal servers. This allows you to protect your Web and e-mail servers from outside attack, yet the process is transparent to users.

Chapter 2

ISA Server in the Enterprise

Solutions in this chapter:

- Enterprise-Friendly Features
- Designing Enterprise Solutions
- Planning Multiserver Arrays
- Understanding ISA Server Licensing

☑ Summary

☑ Solutions Fast Track

☑ Frequently Asked Questions

Introduction

Now that you have been provided with an overview of ISA Server's functionality and features in the previous chapter, let's step back and take a look at the network environment Microsoft is targeting in its marketing of the product. Although ISA can provide many benefits to small and medium-sized businesses, it is in the *enterprise* that its superiority to Proxy Server 2.0 and competitors' products really shines.

This chapter examines the characteristics of the typical enterprise network that present special challenges and opportunities as well as the ISA features that make it appropriate for this type of large-scale networking.

Enterprise-Friendly Features

What makes the enterprise network different from networks of smaller organizations? At first glance, the difference might seem to be merely a matter of size, but it's really much more than that.

Traditionally, Microsoft's products were geared toward medium-sized and somewhat large business networks, but they did not scale as well to large, multi-location enterprise-level organizations (such as Microsoft itself has become). Over the past several years, however, the company has made a conscious effort to penetrate the enterprise market, and we have begun to see the Windows server operating systems replace or at least take their place beside the UNIX machines and mainframes that have served this market in the past.

What is an *enterprise network?* Generally, when we think of the term, we think of a large company network. An enterprise network is not just big; it's also diversified. Enterprise technologies provide ways to integrate the networking needs of an organization that has multiple divisions, functions, and/or physical locations. Microsoft defines an enterprise network as one that incorporates multiple subnets with routed LAN and WAN links.

The new .Net server family, which we discussed in Chapter 1, is a group of products specifically targeted for the enterprise, and ISA Server is one of its premier members.

In this chapter, we discuss the requirements for products that aspire to serve the enterprise market and the ways in which the many enterprise-friendly features built into ISA Server help it meet those requirements.

In the following sections, we look specifically at ISA's suitability for deployment in the enterprise in relation to these enterprise features:

- Reliability
- Scalability
- Multiprocessor support
- Network load balancing
- Clustering
- Distributed caching
- Total cost of ownership

After we address each of these topics, we discuss some general design principles for enterprise networking and how these principles apply to ISA Server solutions.

Reliability

If one requirement is—or should be—at the top of the list for an enterprise-level solution, it is reliability. In a large business network environment, access and security are not just desirable; they are mission critical. Loss of Internet connectivity could mean the consequent loss of hundreds or thousands of dollars or even more.

NOTE

Reliability is defined as a computer system's or device's likelihood to continue to function over a given period of time and under specified conditions. In the enterprise network, *reliability* refers to the dependability of mission-critical hardware and software—the likelihood that it will not fail at a time when such failure would create a loss of productivity or data.

The ability to create server arrays, which can be managed together as a single entity, is one of the features that provide fault tolerance, making ISA Server a highly reliable solution to your network's security and access acceleration needs. The monitoring and alerting features allow you to detect performance problems quickly and address them before your network users' productivity suffers. Remote management support provides a way for you to administer your ISA servers via Windows 2000 Terminal Services, using the MMC from a machine at a distant location or using Distributed Component Object Model (DCOM) command-line scripts. Because ISA Server runs on top of the Windows 2000 operating system, it benefits from the increased reliability and stability of Windows 2000's architecture.

Scalability

Scalability has become a favorite buzzword for both hardware and software manufacturers, and Microsoft is no exception. However, the word means different things to different people (and in different networking situations). Before we can meaningfully discuss ISA's scalability, we must define what it is that we're describing.

Scalability can be defined as the ability of a system (individual computer or network) to maintain or improve performance as size (of the application or network load) increases. Scalability is important because of the rapid growth experienced by many organizations and their networks.

Scalable software is that which can be used in small and medium-sized network environments but also *scales* to the large and very large network environment. In many cases, software that is designed to be scalable comes in different versions or editions, and this is true of ISA Server, which is available in both Standard and Enterprise editions.

Scalability requires that system throughput and overload characteristics be improved to function smoothly under the large and sometimes sporadic loads that are common to very large networks. Another aspect of scalability is ease of administration in the large network environment, including centralized administration of multiple servers.

A scalable product must support the advanced hardware used in the enterprise environment, including multiple processor machines (discussed in the next section) and those with large amounts of physical memory (RAM). It must be able to support large numbers of simultaneous users.

Scalability issues are often divided into three categories:

- Scaling *up*
- Scaling *out*
- Scaling *down*

Let's take a brief look at each.

Scaling Up

Scaling up generally refers to the addition of more resources (for example, memory, processors or disks). ISA Server supports scaling up through its ability to run on computers utilizing multiple processors and to take advantage of Windows 2000's support for symmetric multiprocessing (SMP), which is possible with both the Standard Edition and, to a greater extent, the Enterprise Edition.

Scaling Out

Scaling out refers to the ability to distribute resources across multiple computer systems so that higher performance is possible even though the requirements might be greater than the capability of a single system. ISA supports scaling out through its capability (using the Enterprise edition) of joining multiple ISA servers in arrays to distribute caching and the processing load for highest efficiency.

Scaling Down

Although we usually think of scalability in terms of growth, the phenomenon of downsizing has become a familiar specter on today's business landscape. There are times when *scaling down* can be beneficial to a business, and when this occurs, the network might have to be reconfigured to the smaller scale. Thus mission-critical applications' ability to scale down is as important as their ability to scale up. ISA Server's flexibility allows you to scale down if necessary and still retain the security and Internet acceleration benefits with no loss in functionality.

Multiprocessor Support

ISA's support for SMP is an important aspect of its scalability features. Windows 2000 Server can support up to four microprocessors out of the box and up to 32 processors in the OEM versions of Windows 2000 Data Center Server. (Advanced Server's SMP support falls in between, at eight processors.) Let's take a look at why SMP support is vital to enterprise-level products such as ISA.

The Advantages of Multiprocessing

A PC's microprocessor is the component that performs the calculations of binary information (ones and zeros) that make up the *machine language* used by the computer at the lowest levels. The microprocessor is a chip that responds to and processes the basic instructions on which the computer runs.

NOTE

Most programmers use high-level languages called *programming languages* (for example, C++ or Visual Basic) to write the instructions that make up computer applications or other programs. A *program* is simply a set of ordered operations, or sequence of instructions, for the computer to perform.

Assembly language is a lower-level language that converts the basic computer instructions into binary digits (*machine language).* In the early days of computing, programmers wrote programs in machine language, but it is much easier for programmers to use the high-level languages and then use a special program called a *compiler* to process the programming language and convert it to machine code.

The speed at which a computer can process data (by performing the necessary arithmetical calculations on the binary code) depends on the speed of its microprocessor. Processor speeds are measured in megahertz (MHz) or gigahertz (GHz); typical speeds of processors made by Intel (Pentium III, Celeron) and Advanced Micro Devices (K-6, Athlon, Duron) at the beginning of 2001 ranged from 500MHz to more than 1GHz (or 1000MHz).

NOTE

Multiprocessing hardware is more costly than single processing machines, so it is important to determine whether the benefits, in your particular networking situation, will be worth the extra expense. In order to justify the additional cost, the computer must be running applications or performing functions that are processor intensive.

Shared applications (client/server database engines such as Microsoft's SQL or e-mail servers such as Exchange) can benefit significantly from multiprocessing, whereas file and print servers could see little or no performance gain, since their tasks are more disk intensive. As a matter of fact, it is possible in this situation for the overall system performance to actually be *slowed* by adding processors, because there is overhead involved in the coordination and scheduling of the execution of the threads between the processors.

Processing speed can be increased by upgrading to a faster processor. Another way to increase processing speed if the computer's operating system and applications can take advantage of it is to add microprocessors, making it a multiprocessor machine. Of course, this step also requires a PC motherboard that allows for multiple processors.

When a machine has multiple processors installed and the operating system and software support multiprocessing, the calculations involved in processing can be performed simultaneously by two or more processors. There are several different types of multiprocessing: asymmetric multiprocessing (AMP), symmetric multiprocessing (SMP), and massively parallel processing (MPP). ISA Server, like Windows 2000, supports SMP.

Why Symmetric Multiprocessing?

AMP uses two (dual) or more processors, but typically one of the processors is dedicated to the work of the system, while the other processes user requests. Code is written so that specific executing threads will run on specific processors. In other implementations, one processor could be dedicated to processing of specific tasks such as video. An advantage of AMP is that it does not require that applications be written to be multiprocessor aware. However, increase in performance is not as great as with SMP because much of the processing power might be wasted. This is because the system rarely needs the processor all the time, so that processor could sit idle while the processor that is used for applications is overloaded.

With SMP, the load of all processing tasks, whether system or user applications, is spread across the processors equally. A thread to be executed will run on the first available CPU. This system fully utilizes the power of multiprocessing. SMP is sometimes referred to as *tightly coupled multiprocessing*, to differentiate it from MPP. With SMP, the processors share memory and the input/output (I/O) bus. A single copy of the operating system controls the multiple processors.

MPP uses a slightly different concept, in which each of multiple processors uses its own separate operating system and memory. MPP allows use of an extremely large number of processors (200 or more), all working on the same program via a coordinated interconnected arrangement of data paths that permits messages to be exchanged between the processors. An MPP system is sometimes called a *loosely coupled system*. MPP is often used for very large data warehousing applications but is significantly more expensive than SMP.

NOTE

The smallest units of executable code that are processed by a microprocessor are called *threads.* In order to take advantage of SMP hardware, an operating system must be *multithreaded,* which means that processes are broken into multiple threads, which can be processed separately. Modern operating systems that support multithreading (and thus multiprocessing), in addition to Windows 2000, include NetWare 4.0 and later and most UNIX variants.

In order to really benefit from SMP, the application(s) should also be written with multiprocessing in mind. Those that aren't can still run on a multiprocessor system but will not derive the performance benefits that are possible with SMP-aware applications. ISA Server was designed to take advantage of SMP.

Network Load-Balancing Support

Load balancing, as its name suggests, refers to spreading the burden, or *load,* of work across servers so that no one server is overloaded. Due to the redundancy involved, load balancing and fault tolerance go hand in hand. Load-balancing technologies make it much easier to add or remove servers without disrupting service to the network's users. Load balancing attempts to distribute network traffic or other tasks evenly between servers. Load balancing can be implemented as a software service (as Microsoft has done), implemented as a dedicated hardware device (as marketed by Cisco and RadWare), or integrated into routers or switches (such as those made by Alteon and ArrowPoint).

Microsoft first offered the Windows Load Balancing Service (WLBS) in Windows NT 4.0. The name has been changed to Network Load Balancing (NLB) in the Windows 2000 operating systems. NLB is included in Windows 2000 Advanced Server and Data Center Server. NLB is part of Microsoft's *clustering services,* the primary feature that distinguishes the Advanced Server product from the "plain old" Server operating system.

Microsoft's primary use of NLB is for Web services, but it is also supported for virtual private networking (VPN), streaming media (Windows Media Services), terminal services, and Microsoft's proxy services, which means ISA Server.

Clustering

What is a server *cluster?* Microsoft defines a cluster as a group of independent servers that are managed as a single system for higher availability, easier manageability, and greater scalability. The servers that make up a cluster must be connected together in a network and must run software that will allow them to work together, be managed as a single entity, and provide fail-over and recovery if one of the members of the cluster goes down.

The benefits of clustering are obvious:

- Fault tolerance is provided because the failure of one server will not impact the availability of the services or data to network users.
- Load balancing allows distributing the data or processing load across the multiple machines to enhance performance and prevent the overloading of a single server.
- Resources are easier to manage than would be true with multiple independent servers.
- Performance is enhanced when multiple machines share the processing load.

The ability to cluster servers is important in the Enterprise environment. Microsoft Cluster Server (MSCS), which was originally code-named Wolfpack, was built into the Enterprise Edition of Windows NT 4.0, and an enhanced version of MSCS is included in Windows 2000 Advanced and Data Center servers. However, MSCS isn't the only type of clustering supported by Microsoft.

If you're thinking the whole concept sounds suspiciously like an ISA server array, you're right. An array is really a special type of server cluster, which meets all the elements of Microsoft's definition of clustering technology. Microsoft even uses the term in some of its ISA documentation in referring to grouping servers into arrays. In fact, it is primarily this ability to cluster ISA servers (along with stronger SMP support) that distinguishes the Enterprise from the Standard edition of ISA.

Hierarchical and Distributed Caching

Another feature that is important to large networks and that is included in the Enterprise Edition is the ability to distribute the cache content across the members of an ISA Server array. Again, this capability offers two distinct advantages: enhanced performance and fault tolerance.

It is important to understand the difference between *hierarchical* caching and *distributed* caching.

NOTE

Distributed caching is supported only by the Enterprise Edition; *hierarchical caching* can be implemented using either the Standard or Enterprise edition (or both).

Hierarchical Caching

Hierarchical caching is accomplished by *chaining* individual ISA servers or arrays. A group of ISA servers is connected in a hierarchical (multilevel) arrangement in such a way that client requests are sent "upstream" through the hierarchy of servers until the cached object is found. Figure 2.1 illustrates a hierarchical cache arrangement (or ISA chain).

Figure 2.1 Hierarchical Caching Uses ISA Servers Arranged in a Multilevel Chain

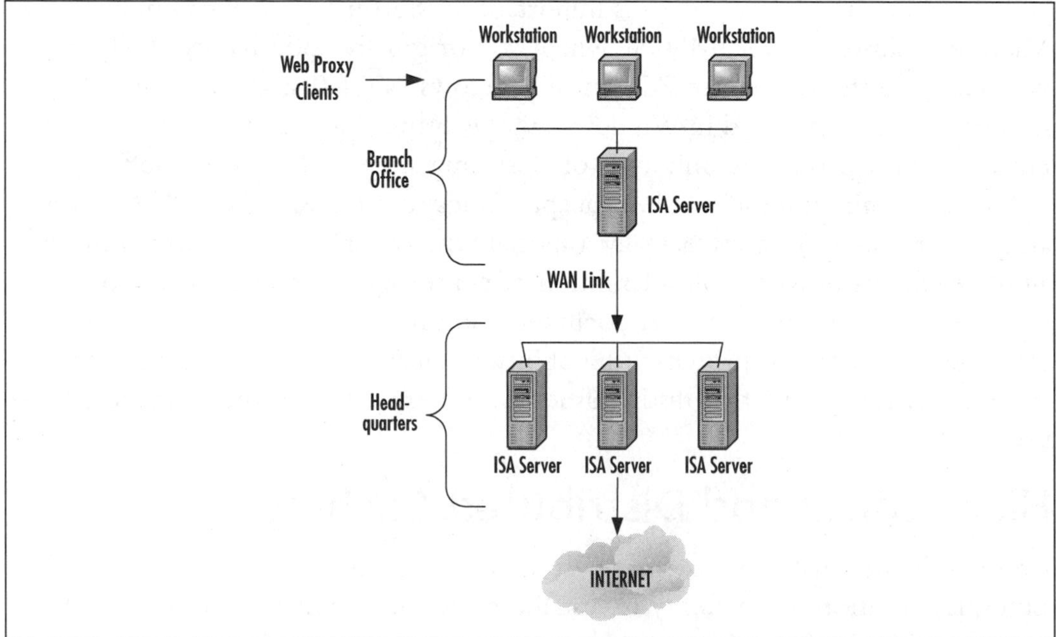

In the illustration, when a Web proxy client at the branch office makes a request for a Web object such as a Web page, that request first goes to the ISA server there on site. If the object is not found in the local ISA server's cache, it is then sent to the ISA array at the headquarters location. If the object is not found there, either, the request is finally sent to the Internet. Once the page is retrieved, the ISA servers at both the headquarters office and the branch office then cache it. If any of the Web proxy clients subsequently request the same object, it can be retrieved from the branch office ISA server's cache.

Distributed Caching

ISA Server uses Cache Array Routing Protocol (CARP) to allow multiple ISA servers to use a single logical cache. This process is called *distributed caching.* Objects can be physically stored on any member of the array.

Configuring & Implenting...

How CARP Works

When a request for a cached object is made, CARP determines the best path through the array using hash-based routing algorithms to determine to which cache a request should be sent. The text of the requested Uniform Resource Locator (URL) is subjected to a calculation formula that generates a large number from the text. Each URL that is subjected to this same formula generates a different number, but the numbers that are generated fall into a certain range.

Distribution across servers can be decided in a couple of ways. In one implementation, CARP splits the range (for this example, we will split it in two, but it can be split into more than two parts). Half the URLs are in the first range and half in the second. Now we have two caches, which are stored on two different machines. When a request is received, it is passed to one of the two caches. All requests for which the URLs generate a number that falls below the split mark are sent to Cache 1, and those that fall above it are sent to Cache 2, spreading the load evenly.

Microsoft's CARP implementation combines the hash result for each URL with the hash result for the name of each ISA server. The server-plus-URL combination that has the highest value becomes the owner of the cache.

The CARP algorithms operate on top of HTTP. If the requested object is not found in the cache, HTTP is used to request the object from the Internet.

CARP was designed to overcome some of the limitations of the Internet Cache Protocol (ICP). ICP provides for caching to be distributed across an array of proxy servers, but it works in a different way. ICP uses queries to locate the cached objects. This technique can generate a great deal of network traffic. A big problem with this method is that if you add more proxy servers to the array, the network traffic increases accordingly, so the scalability of this solution is limited.

CARP uses "queryless" distributed caching, which reduces the extra network traffic and thus conserves bandwidth. Using hash-based routing (see the "How CARP Works" sidebar), CARP can resolve requests in a single hop because the Web browser or downstream proxy "knows"—based on the number generated by the hash function—on which server in the array a particular URL is stored. An array membership list is used to determine the hash result range for each server in the array. The list is updated automatically, using a time-to-live (TTL) countdown.

Because the exact server on which the object is cached is known, there is no increase in network traffic if ISA servers are added to the array, making CARP a much more scalable solution than ICP. Adding servers to or removing servers from the array causes an automatic reassignment of URL cache ranges, which is transparent to users.

Another problem with ICP is that each proxy server adds objects from resolved requests to its own cache, so redundant copies of frequently requested objects proliferate on the array. Because CARP assigns cached objects to a specific ISA server within the array based on the result of the hash, there is no redundancy and disk space is conserved. All the servers truly do function as one logical cache.

NOTE

For more information about Microsoft's implementation of CARP, see the white paper on the Microsoft Web site at www.microsoft.com/proxy/guide/CarpWP.asp.

CARP distinguishes between hierarchical and distributed routing. With hierarchical routing, requests are forwarded from a single ISA server to an upstream array. *Distributed routing* refers to the resolution of requests that are received by one array, using another "peer" array member. The advantage of distributed routing is that downstream clients running legacy operating systems, which are unable to use CARP, can still benefit from it. The two routing methods can be combined. That is, a request might be routed to a fellow array member first (distributed routing) and if the cached object isn't found, it can then be forwarded to an upstream array (hierarchical routing).

Because CARP allows for more efficient routing of requests and conserves network bandwidth, it indirectly has a positive impact on the ISA servers' total cost of ownership (TCO), which we discuss in the next section.

Total Cost of Ownership

Reduction of TCO, or *total cost of ownership,* of computer and networking equipment and software is a priority for corporate managers today. Nowhere is this more true than in the enterprise environment. Because of the large number of machines deployed, even a small reduction in TCO per machine or user can result in a significant positive impact on the company's bottom line.

In recent years, businesses have come to realize that the initial costs of hardware and software are only a part of the expense involved in operating a computer network. Maintenance, user support, training, upgrades, and many other "hidden" costs contribute to the TCO.

NOTE

Some publications define TCO as total cost of *operations.* Either way, the meaning is the same: TCO refers to as complete an accounting as possible of all direct and indirect costs and benefits associated with owning and operating IT components.

TCO is calculated as a cost/benefit analysis, recognizing that greater benefits can offset higher costs and balancing initial investment against long-term expenses. TCO is compared with total benefits of ownership (TBO) to arrive at intelligent planning and purchasing decisions. For example:

- Paying a higher "ticket price" for equipment made with higher-quality components could result in lower TCO due to later reduction in costs of repairs and earlier replacement.
- A higher initial cost that includes free maintenance or a longer warranty period could reduce your overall TCO.

- Lower-priced software that has a steep learning curve, resulting in an extended loss of worker productivity and the need for more formal training, could create a higher TCO than a more user-friendly software package that carries a higher initial cost.
- The effect on the TCO of differences in software licensing agreements from different vendors should not be overlooked.

GartnerGroup, a well-respected IT industry think tank that provides research, advisory, and consulting services to many top organizations, is credited with developing the concept of TCO/TBO analysis. You can download the .PDF version of a report on minimizing TCO published by Gartner from www.netapp.com/tech_library/gartner_papers_tco.html.

Software packages are available to assist in calculating TCO. An example is *TCO Wizard (HMC),* shown in Figure 2.2. More information on this product is available at www.hmcintl.com/tcowizard.html.

Figure 2.2 Software Packages Such as TCO Wizard Help Network Administrators Assess TCO and TBO of IT Components

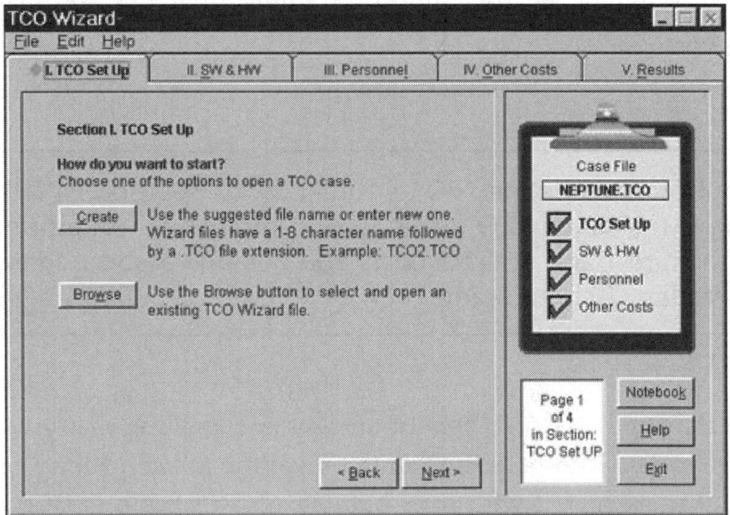

Some sources estimate that the TCO for the average business computer generally equals three to four times the purchase price of the machine.

These are just a few of the ways in which Microsoft has positioned ISA Server as an important part of your company's overall TCO reduction plan. In the next section, we look at some of the basic principles involved in designing an enterprise solution that incorporates ISA Server.

Designing & Planning...

How ISA Server Reduces TCO

ISA Server can lower the TCO for your company's systems in several ways.

ISA Server's address translation function does more than provide a way to implement security for the computers on your internal network; it also allows more cost-effective connectivity to the Internet for multiple computers on the LAN. Without a NAT solution, in order for your internal computers to access the Internet, you need to either deploy a routed solution, requiring registered public IP addresses for each computer (generally resulting in an additional cost from your ISP for the extra addresses), or attach separate modems and phone lines to each computer that needs Internet access, increasing costs (and lowering security) by a huge factor.

ISA Server's caching capabilities can impact TCO indirectly by speeding access to needed resources and thus increasing employee productivity.

ISA Server's ease of use (installation and configuration, based on wizards) saves money in terms of administrative time and the necessity for outside assistance.

ISA Server's security features can impact TCO in many ways: by preventing loss of valuable data and by reducing legal liability and lost productivity related to employee access to undesirable Web sites.

ISA Server's integration with other .Net products and with Windows 2000, as well as its use of the standardized MMC interface, reduce the learning curve and training time required for administrators to master the software.

ISA Server's extensible, open platform allows your in-house developers to build customized solutions, avoiding the extra cost of purchasing additional third-party software.

Designing Enterprise Solutions

According to a character created by author Ernest Hemingway, "The very rich are different from you and me." To this sentiment, another character responded, "Yes, they have more money."

Likewise, the enterprise network is very different from our typical business LAN—and it's not simply because it has more computers. The enterprise is different because its requirements (for reliability, for accessibility, for security) are different, because its priorities are different, and because its focus is often very different. In some ways, the enterprise network differs from a small or medium-sized company network as much as a primate differs from a single-celled organism. Not only are there more "pieces," but also, all those parts must interoperate in a way that benefits the overall entity.

General Enterprise Design Principles

Rarely (if ever) does an enterprise network spring to life fully formed. It is unlikely that a network architect will be called in to design a multisite, multifunction, million-user network from scratch. That's not the way large organizations come into being. Generally, businesses start small, as do their networks, and expand either gradually or rapidly, with the network sometimes scrambling to keep up. That's why many large networks are a hodgepodge of both technologies and IT philosophies; they were not so much planned as they "just grew that way."

This is unfortunate, because the solutions that work well in a small network environment might not be the best choices for the enterprise. In this section, we look at some characteristics of enterprise networks, define terms, identify common services and protocols, and discuss the best ways to ensure that our expanding networks grow gracefully—keeping in mind how our ISA Server deployment can help (or hinder) that growth process.

Enterprise Core Services and Protocols

The enterprise network, by definition, is diverse and runs multiple network services. The trend today is toward open standard Internet services such as HTTP (Web), FTP (file transfer), SMTP/POP/IMAP (e-mail), NNTP (news), and DNS (name resolution). This is in contrast to vendor-specific services (such as Novell's file and print sharing or Microsoft's Exchange 5.x directory services). These more generic cross-platform services can be thought of as the *core services* on the enterprise network.

You will recognize these protocols and services as part of the protocol suite that serves as the foundation for the Internet (and most of today's large networks): TCP/IP. The Internet Protocol, IP, is the basis for routing messages across vast internetworks; it is used by ISA Server in forwarding data to and from internal clients to hosts outside the LAN and in filtering traffic to determine whether it should be allowed to pass through the firewall. ISA Server is dependent on TCP/IP and cannot function without it.

NOTE

Most experienced Windows domain administrators will be familiar with the TCP/IP protocol suite and the functionality of its components. Readers who have worked exclusively with small, nonrouted, peer-to-peer LANs or in Novell NetWare environments might want to consult a resource such as *Troubleshooting Windows 2000 TCP/IP* (Syngress Publishing, 2000) for an overview of today's most popular protocol suite.

The Enterprise Networking Model

Many small businesses operate their networks as *workgroups,* in which all computers function as both client (requesting access to the resources of other computers) and server (sharing their resources with others), and some medium-sized organizations have networks that are collections of several workgroups. However, the enterprise network demands a different networking model: the *client/server* (sometimes called *server-based*) *model*, in which the processing load is distributed between the client computer and the server. For example, when you log on to a client/server network, the client computer sends the server a request to log on that includes information (user credentials), the server processes the data sent and returns results (in a Windows NT- or Windows 2000-based network, the results take the form of *access tokens*). In Windows networks, client/server networking is built on the concept of *domains.*

Domains are logical divisions of the network into *administrative and security boundaries.* A domain is a group of users, computers, and resources that are managed as an entity and that share a security accounts database so that users within a domain can (assuming that they have the appropriate access permissions) access the resources that are available in that domain.

Although small and medium-sized networks can often benefit from client/server networking as well, the logical and physical structure of the network is generally much simpler, and often a single domain is sufficient for the network's purposes. This is especially true of Windows 2000 networks.

Windows NT Domains versus Windows 2000 Domains

One of the major differences between Windows NT and Windows 2000 networks has to do with how and why domains are created and how they interoperate. Specifically, these differences relate to:

- Domain size limitations and the number of domains required in a network
- Flat versus hierarchical domain structures
- Trust relationships between domains
- Domain controller roles
- Administrative boundaries

In Windows NT 4.0 networks, there was a limit on the number of security objects (user accounts, group accounts, computer accounts) that could exist in a single domain. The security accounts management (SAM) database had to fit in RAM on the primary domain controller, so the number of domain objects was dependent on the amount of RAM installed. A general rule of thumb often suggested by Microsoft was around 40,000 security objects per domain. This limitation does not exist in Windows 2000. Security accounts information is stored in Active Directory, and domain implementations have been tested with millions of objects. This means that it is almost never necessary in a Windows 2000 environment to create separate domains because you have too large a number of accounts, as was often the case in the Windows NT environment.

Another difference between the two network types is the domain structure. NT domain-based networks use a flat structure. All domains are created at the same level and exist independently of one another. No trust relationships between domains exist by default; they must be explicitly created by the administrator. The namespace is flat also; the names of the domains on the network bear no "familial relationship" to one another.

Windows 2000 networks are built on the concept of domain *trees,* which are groups of domains that share a contiguous namespace. Each tree has a root domain, and those domains created under the root (at the second level) incorporate its name into their own. Additional levels can be added under this structure, all of which add their own unique "first names" to the "family name" created by those above them in the tree. This is, of course, the familiar Internet-standard DNS namespace, shown in Figure 2.3.

Multiple-domain trees can be joined into *forests*. The domains in separate trees have their own namespaces. See Figure 2.4.

All domains in a Windows 2000 domain tree share implicit, two-way transitive trust relationships with each other. Additionally, the root domains of all trees in a forest share implicit two-way transitive trusts, meaning that every domain in the forest automatically has a trust relationship with every other domain. There is no need for the administrators to create such trusts (although direct explicit trusts, called *shortcut trusts,* can be created to speed authentication through a complex multilevel domain tree).

Figure 2.3 The Windows 2000 Hierarchical Domain Structure: Domains in a Tree Share a Contiguous Namespace

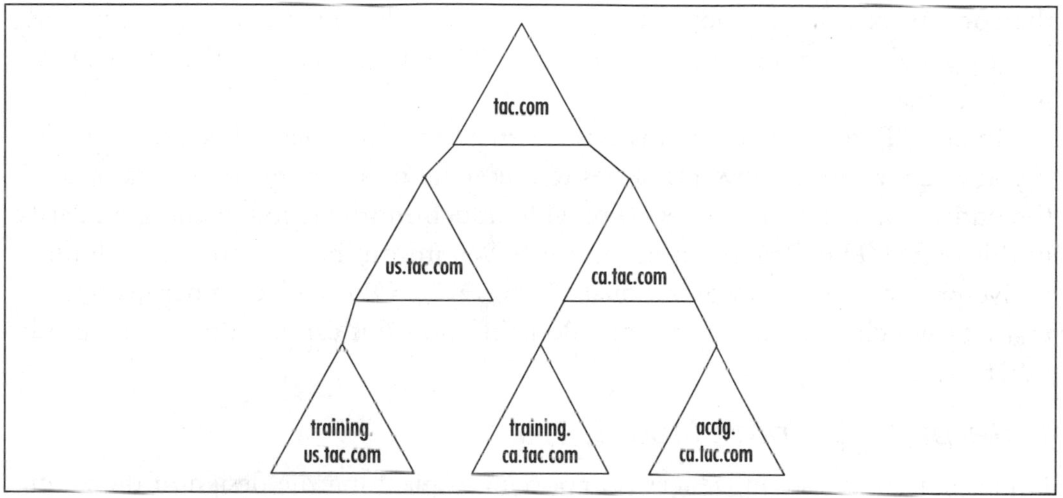

Figure 2.4 Multiple-Domain Trees Are Joined in Forests that Have a Noncontiguous Namespace

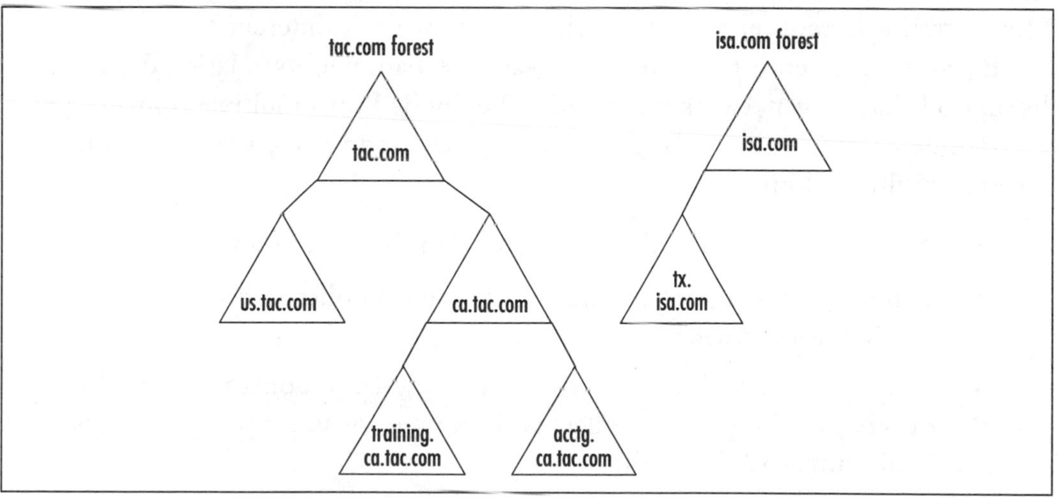

Another difference between the NT and Windows 2000 networks lies in the way *domain controllers* function. An NT domain must have one and only one *primary domain controller (PDC),* on which the master writable copy of the SAM

database is stored. Optional *backup domain controllers (BDCs),* of which there can be one or a large number, hold a replicated read-only copy of the SAM for authentication load-balancing and fault tolerance.

Windows 2000 networks can have multiple domain controllers, all of which have a writable copy of the Active Directory partition. Although there are five *single master operations* for which a single domain controller is designated as master, the concept of primary and backup domain controllers has been done away with. Most operations can be performed on any DC and replicated to the other DCs in the domain.

In an NT network, the domain is the smallest *administrative boundary.* That is, if you assign administrative privileges to a user, he or she is an administrator for the entire domain. Windows 2000 provides much more flexibility and granularity in this regard. The Delegation of Authority Wizard can be used to grant administrative privileges over Organizational Units (OUs). OUs are container objects, many of which can exist within one domain, and OUs can even be nested inside other OUs.

Enterprise Domain Models

Understanding these differences is important in planning the design of the enterprise network, although many organizations will, with Windows 2000, be able to reduce the number of domains—perhaps even able to achieve the single-domain network that Microsoft recommends as the best solution for many situations. However, this is another case in which the enterprise is different.

Because many enterprise networks span international boundaries, there is a likelihood that your network will need to be divided into multiple domains to accommodate differences in languages, currencies, and laws. Other reasons for creating multiple domains include:

- Need for decentralized administration or internal politics
- Differing domain policies (such as password policies) that must be applied domainwide
- Reduction of replication traffic (extremely large domains with a large number of domain controllers will create excessive replication traffic that could impact bandwidth)

The enterprise network can also incorporate multiple domain trees into a single forest. The most common occasion for doing so is when two independent companies join together (for instance, in a merger or acquisition) or when one company has two or more divisions that operate independently and under different names.

The mapping of your network's domain structure could affect how and where your ISA servers are deployed, and you will want to consider trust relationships between domains when determining where in the domain structure the ISA server(s) should be placed. We discuss placement options more fully later in this chapter.

Enterprise Technologies

Enterprise networks are, of course, not alone in their use of the global Internet. Businesses of all sizes, organizations of all types, and individual users of all persuasions are becoming more and more dependent on Internet connectivity as a routine part of everyday life.

However, a couple of related concepts are more common in the enterprise world than in other venues: *intranets* and *extranets*. Let's look at how these technologies fit into the design of the enterprise network.

The Intranet

An *intranet* in its simplest form is an internal, private Web. Businesses, especially large ones, have discovered the advantages of using Internet technologies such as HTTP to publish information for employees and provide a means for those within the organization to distribute information easily and inexpensively.

For example, training manuals, rules and regulations, internal telephone lists, commonly used forms, and a myriad of other companywide material can be published to a Website or as PDF files and easily accessed by anyone in the company. Personal information, such as human resources records and personnel evaluations, can be published to secured, password-restricted sites with access limited to the appropriate individuals. There are several advantages to such intranets:

- Information is accessed via a familiar (to most users) interface, the Web browser.
- If standard HTML is used, the information is accessible regardless of platform or operating system or a particular browser software.
- The cost of printing and disseminating reams of paper documents is reduced (users can print only those parts of the document that they need in hardcopy format).

- The HTML pages can be easily searched for keywords, and hypertext references can be included to make it easy to navigate to related information (such as definitions of terms).
- The space required for storing all those printed documents is reduced.
- The Web-based documents can be updated much more quickly and easily than printed documents.

Intranets are often connected to the Internet, and many companies provide VPN access so that employees can connect to the intranet from home or when on the road.

The Extranet

An *extranet* is similar to an intranet in that it is a private network using Internet technology. The difference is that whereas the intranet is made accessible to internal users (employees), the extranet is made accessible to selected external users (business partners, vendors, and customers). The same protocols used for the intranet (and the Internet) are the foundation of the extranet.

The VPN is a popular means of providing access to an extranet. This method allows users to tunnel through the public Internet to reach the private network. Another option is to have users dial directly into a remote access server; however, this option is more costly if extranet users are not within the local dialing area.

NOTE

It is common to use digital certificates to authenticate extranet users. An advantage of digital certificates for user authentication in the extranet environment is that they can either be issued by an external certification authority (CA), such as VeriSign, or your company can implement its own CA to issue certificates. Windows 2000 allows you to issue certificates outside your organization by setting up a standalone CA, or you can use an enterprise CA to issue certificates within the organization. For more information, see the Windows 2000 Server Help files.

The digital certificate contains the user's public key and other identification information. The International Telecommunications Union (ITU)'s X.509 is a widely used international standard for defining digital certificates.

Some examples of the uses of extranets include:

- Publishing wholesale catalogs for buyers
- Engaging in cooperative programs with other companies, such as joint training programs
- Publishing an "insider" newsletter exclusively for partners or customers
- Sharing confidential product development or research information with partners

Many enterprise-level networks combine a public Internet presence, an intranet for employees, and an extranet for outside partners and clients to most effectively utilize Web and related technologies.

Like an intranet, the extranet requires a security solution to keep the information private. This is where a firewall such as ISA Server comes in.

ISA Server Design Considerations

In the following sections, we address some of the most important factors involved in designing enterprise solutions with ISA Server:

- Network size and capacity planning
- User needs assessment
- ISA Server functionality
- ISA Server interoperability
- Administrative permissions
- ISA Server placement in the domain structure

Network Size and Capacity Planning

An important part of ISA design and deployment planning involves estimating the expected usage, based on number of users and usage patterns, in order to determine the number of ISA servers required. The number of users that a single ISA server can support depends on the function(s) it performs—firewall, caching, or both—as well as the capacity of the hardware on which ISA Server is installed.

For example, Microsoft documentation specifies that an ISA server deployed as a forward caching server (which maintains a centralized cache of Web objects that are requested frequently by your network users) can support 500 to 1000 users when installed on a Pentium III 550MHz machine with 256 MB of RAM and 10 GB of disk space allocated for caching. Microsoft states that if ISA is installed on a Pentium II 300MHz computer, the number of users supported for the same functionality drops to less than 500. When the number of users in this scenario exceeds 1000, you should upgrade the hardware or add another ISA Server computer.

If ISA is deployed in front of your network's Web server, publishing the Web server to the Internet, these numbers are different. In this case, Microsoft suggests that a Pentium II 300MHz machine can support up to 800 users. RAM requirements in this case are dependent on the size of the cacheable content being published, with enough RAM so that all this content can fit into memory.

Microsoft documentation says a rule of thumb is to add another ISA server (or, alternately, add another processor to the server if it supports SMP) for every 800 hits per second.

All these factors should be considered as you determine how many ISA servers will be installed on your network and how they will be grouped. As your number of users or hits increases, you might need to weigh the advantages of adding processors to your existing server against those of adding more ISA Server computers. See Table 2.1 for a quick comparison of these two solutions.

Table 2.1 Additional Processors versus Additional ISA Server Computers

	Advantages	Disadvantages
Adding processors	The purchase price of a processor is lower than that of a complete server computer.	If you have a single ISA server and it goes down, you have no fault tolerance.
Adding ISA Server computers	The more individual ISA servers you have, the more fault tolerance is built into your network.	The cost of additional complete computers is greater than the cost of processors only.

Of course, you have the option of adding processors only if your ISA Server machine's motherboard supports multiple processors.

A big advantage of installing additional ISA servers instead of merely adding processors to the existing server is the ability to group the multiple machines in arrays, providing the following benefits:

- Fault tolerance
- Scalability

- Load balancing
- Centralized management

Remember that the cost of adding computers or processors also includes licensing; we discuss ISA Server's licensing structure later in this chapter.

ISA Server Placement in the Domain Structure

Earlier in this chapter, we discussed Windows 2000 domain models. When you deploy ISA Server, one decision you must make is where, within the network's domain structure, the ISA server or servers will be placed.

If your network consists of a single domain, you have two choices: You can place the ISA server in the existing domain, or you can create a new domain in which to place it. If you opt for the latter, you also need to determine whether the new domain will be in the same domain tree or a different one. Finally, if you choose a different domain tree, you must decide whether that new tree will reside in the same forest as your existing domain tree or in a completely new and separate forest.

If you already have a multidomain network, your choices are similar but with an added layer of complexity. The most important consideration (and the reason that it matters in which domain your ISA servers "live" in the first place) is the trust relationships that exist between domains.

Remember that within a Windows 2000 forest, all domains effectively have a two-way trust relationship with all other domains. Some administrators recommend that the ISA servers be placed in their own domain in a separate forest, for added security. Since there are no implicit trusts between domains in different forests, you can create a one-way trust (with the domain in which the ISA servers reside trusting the domain where the user and client computer accounts are located). This structure allows functionality of your ISA servers without the risks inherent in the default two-way trusts that exist within a forest. (For example, if the ISA servers are in the same forest and the enterprise admin account is compromised, your ISA servers would be vulnerable.)

On the other hand (there is always another hand when you're trying to maintain balance on the fine line between accessibility and security), although that scenario will work with a relatively simple domain structure that has a single domain in each forest, administration becomes incredibly complex if your existing network has multiple domains at various levels in one or more domain trees. In that case, in order to provide ISA functionality to clients in all the domains, multiple explicit one-way trusts must be created and managed between the ISA Server domain and each of the other individual domains (see Figure 2.5).

Figure 2.5 Multiple Explicit One-Way Trusts between the ISA Domain and All Other Domains that Contain ISA Clients

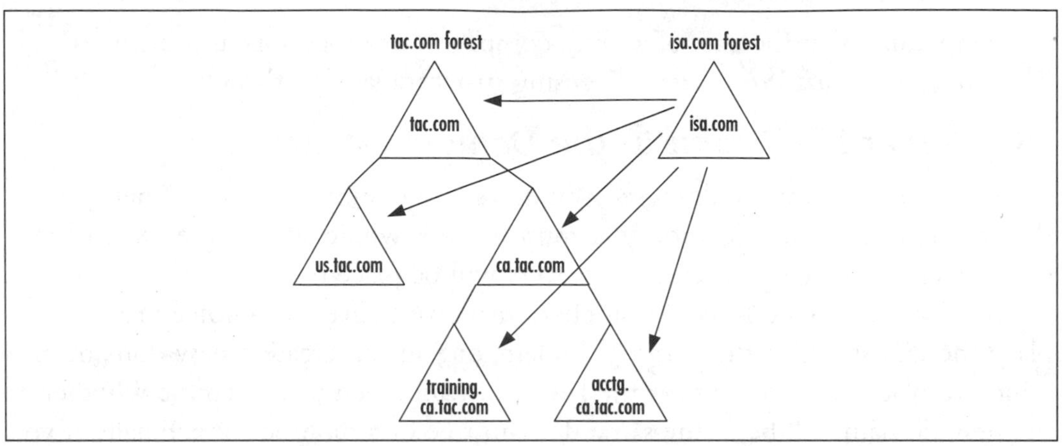

Ultimately, it's a trade-off. Placing the ISA servers in a separate forest does provide more security, but it also requires a higher cost in administrative time and effort.

What about placing the ISA servers in their own domain but in the same forest or tree as your existing domains? Is there any advantage to this solution? Regardless of where in the forest your ISA domain is placed, it still has an implicit two-way trust with the other domains in the forest, so you lose the security advantage of the one-way trust. One reason you might place the ISA servers in their own domain in the same forest is to create an administrative boundary. That is, if you want to assign a specific administrator or group to manage the ISA Servers, this is an option.

If we were working with an NT network, that would be a good reason to create a separate domain for the ISA Servers. However, because Windows 2000 provides for organizing resources into OUs and delegating administrative authority over individual OUs, you can place the ISA servers in an OU and assign administrative privileges to the selected users without giving them administrative control over the entire domain. However, keep in mind that the domain administrator will have administrative authority over all the OUs within the domain. Domain administrators don't have administrative authority outside their domains, however (unless that authority is granted by the administrator of the other domain), so this might factor into your decision as to whether or not to place the ISA servers in a separate domain or simply create an OU for them.

If your network is also divided into *sites,* which are physical divisions of the network as opposed to the logical divisions created by domains, bandwidth and performance issues could also come into play. If the ISA servers are located in a site that is separated from its clients by a slow WAN link, performance will be negatively impacted.

SECURITY ALERT!

Keep in mind that if you have multiple ISA servers that you want to join in arrays, all members of an array must belong to the same Windows 2000 domain *and* to the same Active Directory site.

There is no definitive right or wrong answer when it comes to where to place your ISA servers within the domain structure. Rather, you must evaluate your own priorities and determine which option works best in your particular network environment. Be aware that the complexity of the enterprise environment could be a factor in making this decision.

User Needs Assessment

An important step in planning the deployment of your ISA servers in the enterprise is assessing the needs of your users and determining what applications and services the internal clients require. Assessing your user needs will help you determine whether client computers should be configured as firewall clients, Web proxy clients, SecureNAT clients, or a combination of the three.

The checklist in Table 2.2 should help you assess your users' needs in terms of which client(s) should be deployed.

Table 2.2 Client Assessment Checklist

Assessment Question	Yes	No
Is ease of installation and configuration of client computers your top priority?	In this case, you can deploy SecureNAT clients, which require no installation of software and no complex configuration.	You might want to consider using the firewall client, which requires installation of client software, and/or the Web proxy client, which requires configuration of applications.

Continued

Table 2.2 Continued

Assessment Question	Yes	No
Do you plan to use the server publishing feature to make Web, e-mail, or other internal servers available to Internet users?	You might want to publish the internal servers as SecureNAT clients, using server publishing rules on the ISA server. This is much easier than publishing the internal servers as firewall clients.	You might want to use the firewall client for added security.
Is security your highest priority?	You might want to deploy firewall clients, allowing you to configure user-based access policy rules to allow access only for authenticated clients.	You might want to use the SecureNAT client, which is easier to set up and configure.

Other factors to consider when assessing user needs include:

- What types of applications do your users need to run? For example, if users are using Outlook Express to access Hotmail accounts, and the ISA Server is configured to require authentication, the request will fail.
- What other security needs do your users have? For example, IPSec in transport mode will not work with ISA's network address translation.
- Is there a need for such functionality as an incoming ping to internal clients? This option is not supported.
- Is there a need for internal clients to ping outside the LAN, to the other side of the ISA server? This works only with SecureNAT clients.
- Is there a need to control access by user account or group? With SecureNAT, you can control only by IP address, not by user or group. You need to use the firewall client to configure user-based policy rules.
- Do users need to use NetMeeting for conferencing? You might need to configure the H.323 gatekeeper in ISA and set the clients to use the gatekeeper.
- Do you need to improve the performance of internal clients' requests for Web objects? You should use the Web proxy client.

- Do you have non-Microsoft operating systems on the network and need to improve Web performance? You can use SecureNAT to pass requests transparently to the ISA Server firewall service and then on to the caching service.

ISA Server Functionality

In the enterprise environment, it is especially important that you consider the appropriate mode (firewall, caching, or integrated) in which each ISA server will be installed. All members of an array must run in the same mode.

Mode is selected during setup, so preplanning is essential. You will want to consider how the ISA servers will be used, what policies will be implemented, special needs such as VPN support, and the client types that will be installed.

Both the firewall and caching modes allow implementation of enterprise policy, but caching mode supports access policy only for HTTP. Both modes support Web publishing, but only the firewall mode supports server publishing. Packet and application filtering and VPN support are available only in firewall mode, but both firewall and caching modes support Web filters, real-time monitoring, alerts, and reports. Only Web proxy clients are supported in caching mode; all three client types (Web proxy, SecureNAT, and firewall clients) can be used with an ISA server running in firewall mode.

Table 2.3 provides a quick at-a-glance summary of the features supported by each mode.

Table 2.3 ISA Server Mode Functionality Comparison

ISA Functionality	Caching	Firewall	Integrated
Enterprise policy	X	X	X
Access policy	X (HTTP only)	X	X
Server publishing		X	X
Web publishing	X	X	X
Packet filtering		X	X
Application filtering		X	X
Web filters	X	X	X
Monitoring, alerts, and reports	X	X	X
VPN		X	X

Continued

Table 2.3 Continued

ISA Functionality	Caching	Firewall	Integrated
SecureNAT clients		X	X
Web Proxy clients	X	X	X
Firewall clients		X	X

Of course, in many cases you will want both the caching and firewall functionalities and will install your enterprise ISA servers and arrays in integrated mode.

ISA Server Interoperability

An enterprise network is a complex entity. Your network is likely to have in place existing security measures that could be affected by the deployment of ISA. You must also consider, as part of the planning process, how ISA Server will interoperate with various network services and other Internet-related software such as your Web server.

Here are some issues that need to be addressed as you determine how best to deploy ISA Server on your network:

- **Interoperation with Active Directory** This is dependent on whether ISA Server is installed as a standalone or an array member. If the former, its configuration information will be saved to the Registry on the ISA Server computer. However, configuration for ISA Server arrays is stored in Active Directory. This is the reason that arrays require a Windows 2000 domain (standalone ISA Servers can be installed on a Windows 2000 server in a Windows NT domain). The *enterprise initialization* is really just a fancy (or perhaps less scary) way of referring to modification of the Active Directory schema. The ISA schema information will be installed in your existing schema.

SECURITY ALERT!

Schema modifications are not to be taken lightly! Remember that a schema is shared by all domains in the forest, and once object classes or attributes have been added to the schema, they cannot be removed (although they can be deactivated).

- **Interoperation with IIS** The IIS 5.0 Web server is included with Windows 2000. It is possible to run IIS on the ISA Server (although it is not required). If you choose to do this, you can use the Web publishing rules to publish IIS to the Internet. However, you might need to do some "tweaking" of the IIS configuration. If ISA is listening for Web requests on port 80, IIS should be set up to use any currently unused port (for example, 81). IIS also should not use port 8080, the default port used by ISA for outbound Web requests. If you want IIS to listen on port 80, you could use packet filters to publish the Web server. The objective is to prevent port conflicts between ISA and IIS. Because of the potential for these problems, the ISA installation will stop the WWW publishing service. However, once you change the IIS ports, you can restart the service.
- **ISA impact on ICS or NAT** ISA provides address translation, so there is no use for Internet Connection Sharing or the Windows 2000 built-in NAT. If you have NAT configured in RRAS, the ISA Server installation will disable it and you will see an error in the system log (accessed via Event Viewer), as shown in Figure 2.6.

Figure 2.6 If NAT Is Configured, It Reports an Error in the System Log Stating NAT Was Unable to Start

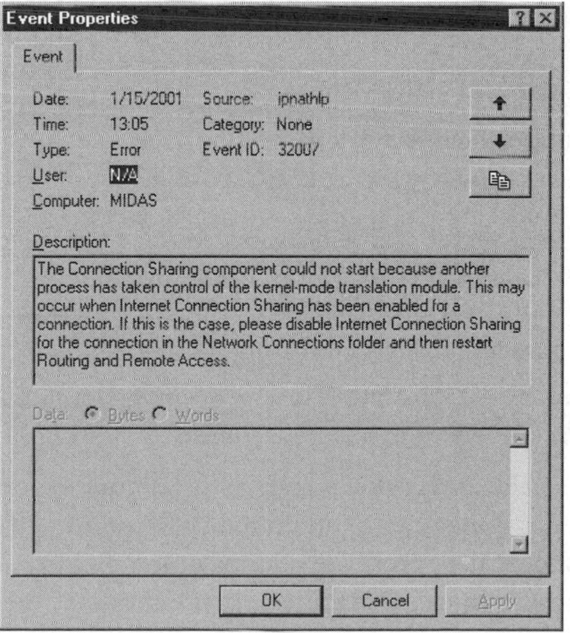

NOTE

Windows 2000 NAT recognizes that another process has taken over its address translation function, but it does not recognize that ISA Server is the culprit. Note that the error message suggests that the problem might be due to ICS being enabled on a network connection. This is *not* the case in this situation; it is ISA Server that is causing the error, not ICS.

Other interoperability issues include:

- **ISA Server interoperation with IPSec** As we have noted, IPSec will not work with ISA Server in transport mode, providing a secure end-to-end connection from a client on the internal network. However, IPSec *can* be enabled on the computer on which ISA Server is installed. If you do this, AH and ESP (IP protocols 50 and 51) will be controlled by the IPSec driver rather than by ISA's packet filter driver. This will ensure that the network allows only valid AH and ESP traffic.
- **Interoperation with RRAS** RRAS can coexist with ISA on the Windows 2000 Server computer, but ISA packet filtering will replace RRAS packet filtering (if you had the latter configured). The ISA Server will use dial-up entries that you have configured for use by RRAS.

Administrative Permissions

It is important to understand the role played by access permissions and to be aware of the permissions necessary to install, configure, and manage ISA Server:

- To install ISA Server as a standalone, you need an account that belongs to the local administrators group on the machine on which you are installing. If you are installing a standalone ISA server on a machine that belongs to a Windows 2000 domain, you can do so if you are a member of the domain administrators group (because domain admins are automatically members of the local administrators group).
- To initialize the enterprise, which must be done before you can install ISA Server as a member of an array in a Windows 2000 domain, you must belong to the enterprise admins group and the schema admins group (because initializing the enterprise modifies the Active Directory schema).

- By default, to install ISA Server as an array member (after the enterprise has already been initialized), you must be a domain admin of the domain in which the array is installed or an enterprise admin.
- To change enterprise policies for an array, you must be an enterprise admin; to change array policies, you must be a domain admin.

If you attempt to modify policies without the proper permissions, you will see the message shown in Figure 2.7.

Figure 2.7 Enterprise Policies Change Error Message

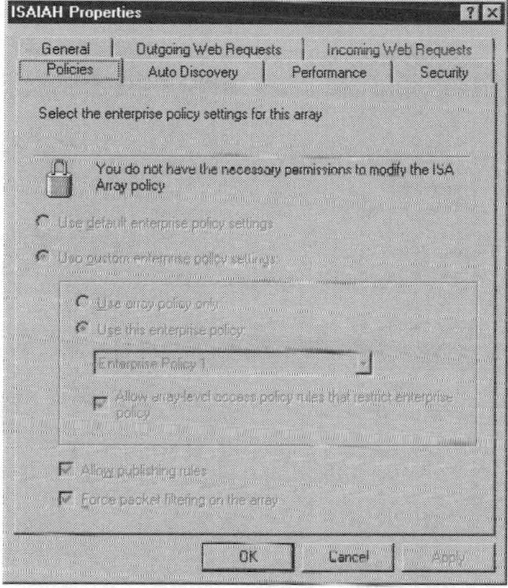

You can give additional users or groups permission to modify the array configuration. Simply right-click the array name in the left console tree of the ISA Management Console, select **Properties**, select the **Security** tab, and assign the Full Control permission to the user or group, as shown in Figure 2.8.

Permissions can be configured for a variety of ISA Server objects, including the following:

- **Enterprise policy settings** By default, enterprise admins have Full Control and all authenticated users have Read.
- **Enterprise policies** By default, enterprise admins have Full Control and all authenticated users have Read.
- **Arrays** By default, enterprise, domain and local admins have Full Control and all authenticated users have Read.

- **Sessions** By default, enterprise, domain, and local admins have Read Sessions Information and Stop Sessions; all authenticated users have Read Sessions Information.
- **Alerts** By default, enterprise, domain, and local admins have Read Alerts Information and Reset Alerts; all authenticated users have Read Alerts Information.
- **Gatekeeper** By default, enterprise, domain, and local admins have Full Control, Modify, and Read; all authenticated users have Read.

Figure 2.8 Assigning Permissions to Modify the Array Configuration to Users or Groups

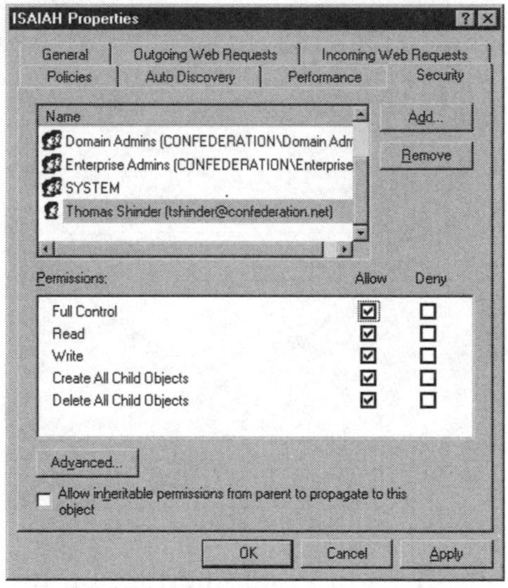

NOTE

The local system account has the same permissions as the enterprise admin accounts for each of the ISA objects listed.

In order to generate reports, a user must have the proper permissions. You need to enter the account credentials to generate a report. When you access the properties for a report job in the ISA Management Console, you need to enter the user account information on the **Credentials** tab for a user who has permissions to generate reports, as shown in Figure 2.9.

Figure 2.9 User Credentials Must Be Entered to Generate ISA Server Reports

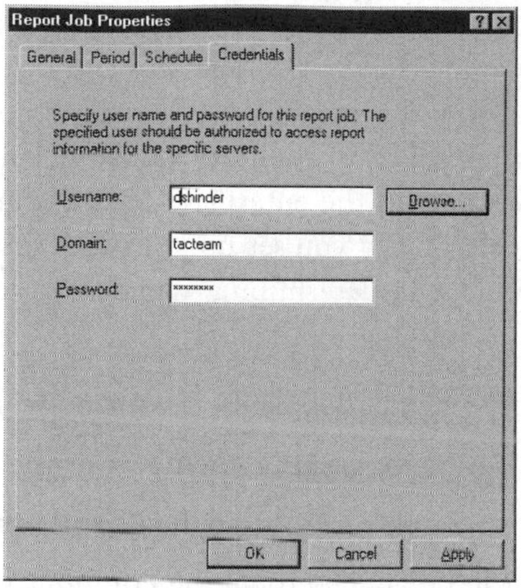

NOTE

In Chapter 9, in the section on "Monitoring, Alerts, and Reports," we look more closely at how to create and schedule a report job.

When generating reports for arrays, note that reports are generated on whichever server you used to configure the report job, but the logs on the other servers in the array must be accessed for the reports to be generated. This means that your user account must have permissions for creating reports on the other servers as well as the one on which you configure the report job.

To generate reports, by default you must be a member of the domain admins groups, be a member of the local administrators group on *every* ISA server in the array, or have permissions to access and launch the DCOM objects on every ISA server in the array.

NOTE

A thorough understanding of how permissions work is essential in effectively configuring, administering, and troubleshooting ISA Server.

Planning Multiserver Arrays

Arrays are appropriate for medium-sized and large networks, and in the enterprise environment, they offer many advantages. All the ISA servers in an array share the same configuration; this means that they can be managed as a single entity and provide fault tolerance, in addition to load balancing and distributed caching. In other words, many of the enterprise-level features we have discussed in this chapter are available only if you set up your ISA servers as array members.

Consult the following list in determining whether to install your ISA servers as array members:

- Active Directory must be installed on your network.
- One or more ISA Servers can be members of the array.
- A single enterprise policy can be applied to all arrays in the enterprise.
- Array policies can be applied to all the computers in an array.
- All array members must belong to the same Windows 2000 domain.
- All array members must belong to the same Active Directory site.
- All array members must be installed in the same mode.
- The same add-ins should be installed on all servers in the array.

TIP

If you install add-ins such as Web or application filters on an ISA server that is a member of an array, these add-ins are not automatically installed to the other array members. You must individually install the add-ins to each of the servers that belongs to the array.

Understanding Multiserver Management

Array members are managed as a single entity. By default, when you install the first member of the array, the array name is the same as the first member's name. To see the servers that are members of the array, open the **Computers** container in the left pane of the ISA Management Console, as shown in Figure 2.10.

Figure 2.10 The Array Members Appear in the Computers Folder

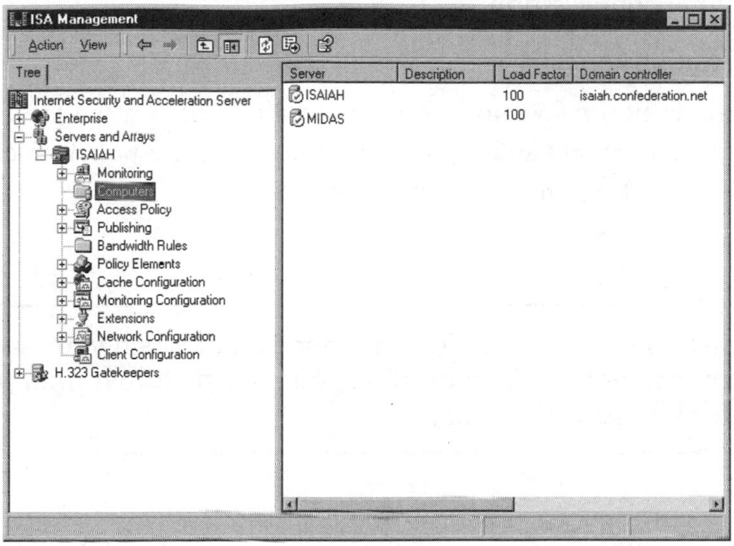

This centralized administrative model enhances security because all administrative duties can be performed from one computer. If there is a very large number of ISA servers in the array, the ability to apply the same configuration and policies to all array members at once can mean a tremendous saving in administrative time.

NOTE

In keeping with Microsoft's claim that ISA Server is infinitely scalable, it has placed no limitation on the number of ISA servers you can have in one array, as it did with Proxy Server 2.0.

Backing Up the Array Configuration Information

Array configuration information can be backed up using ISA Server's backup and restore feature. The backup function will save the following information:

- Access policy rules
- Publishing rules
- Policy elements

- Alerts information
- Caching configuration
- Array properties

This configuration information can be saved to a file on the local disk. The cache content, activity logs and reports, and the enterprise policy in effect are not saved when you back up the ISA configuration.

SECURITY ALERT!

For added security, Microsoft recommends that when you save configuration information to the local disk, you should store it on a partition that is formatted with NTFS.

Microsoft documentation recommends that you always back up the array configuration after making significant changes to your array, such as changing installation mode, cache size or location, or enterprise policy settings, and any time you add or remove a server to or from the array or change the name of a computer that is an array member.

Even if you have made none of these major changes, it's a good idea to back up your array configuration information on a regular basis, just as you back up any important data.

Backing up the configuration information is done via the ISA Management Console by right-clicking the array name in the left console pane and selecting **Back Up** from the context menu, as shown in Figure 2.11. You will be prompted to enter the path where you want to save the backup configuration information.

NOTE

Microsoft documentation states that the array configuration must be backed up to a location on the *local* computer, as was true of beta versions of the software. However, it is possible with the final release version to back up the information to a remote computer across the network and restore the configuration information from the remote location.

Figure 2.11 Use the ISA Management Console to Back Up Configuration Information

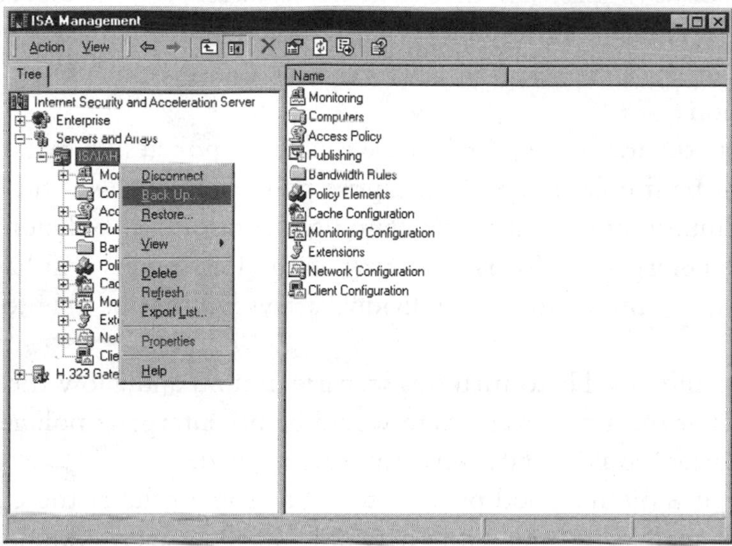

NOTE

If you have backed up array configuration information, it must be restored to the same array. You cannot restore the information to a different array or to a standalone ISA server. You also cannot restore backed-up array configuration information if the array is no longer using the same enterprise policy settings.

To restore the information, select the **Restore** option in the right context menu and select the location where the backed up configuration information is stored.

NOTE

The configuration information will be saved with the .BIF file extension.

Using Tiered Policy

The concept of *tiered policy* (another term for *multilevel policy*) is especially important to administrators working in the enterprise environment. Array policies and enterprise policies can be used together to create this layered approach to policy implementation.

Note that you are not required to use multilevel policies. In fact, in some cases, it might be simpler to apply enterprise policies only. This is the case if the enterprise administrators want to maintain tight control over policies for all ISA servers in the enterprise network. This way, all the ISA servers will have the same policies, and the administrators of individual arrays will not be able to set any rules.

It is also quite possible to turn this scenario around and allow the policy decisions to be set at the array level. There would be no enterprise policies applied, and array policies would dictate what rules are applied.

However, it is often a good practice to define some rules at the enterprise level that will apply across the entire network and allow array administrators to define further rules that may be appropriate only for their individual arrays. If you follow this course, it is important to be aware that array rules can only be *more restrictive* than enterprise rules, not the other way around. That is, if the enterprise policy imposes a restriction, array policies cannot circumvent that restriction—but the array policy *can* add more restrictions, which will be applied only to the ISA servers in that array.

UNDOCUMENTED ISA

In beta versions of ISA Server, you could change from array policy only to enterprise policy and vice versa. This is not possible in the final release of the product; you must now reinstall the software to make this switch.

Planning Policy Elements

Policy elements refer to properties of ISA policy rules, which can be created for your enterprise policy and for each array policy. The policy elements that you can define are:

- **Schedules** Define certain days/times that the rule will be in effect.

- **Bandwidth priorities** Allow you to assign priorities to individual connections that go through ISA Server, on a directional (outbound or inbound) basis.
- **Destination sets** Let you apply rules to specific destinations by computer name, IP address or IP range, and path (if applied to specific folders on a destination computer).
- **Client address sets** Allow you to apply rules to one or multiple client computers based on specified IP addresses.
- **Protocol definitions** Are used to create protocol rules or server publishing rules.
- **Content groups** Allow you to limit access to specific content based on file extensions or MIME type.
- **Dial-up entries** Specify how ISA Server will connect to the Internet.

Configuring & Implementing…

Configuring Content Groups

Content groups apply only to content that passes through the Web Proxy service; therefore, this category includes only content using the HTTP and FTP protocols.

Content groups don't do what the name might imply; that is, they don't allow you to apply rules based on keywords in the content of the data but rather based on the file type (or, in the case of data returned by a Web browser, the MIME type).

FTP content will be checked for file type, based on the file extension (for example, .DOC or .JPG). If a rule is found that applies to that content group, the rule will be processed. For example, you could create a rule that excludes all .EXE files.

HTTP content will be checked for either file type or MIME type, depending on the Web browser and how it returns header information. File type works the same as described for FTP content. Different MIME types are associated with different file name extensions by different Web server software. For example, if the Web server returning the content is

Continued

running IIS, the file extension .MNY is associated with MIME type *application/x-msmoney* and the file extension .EPS is associated with the MIME type *application/postscript*. As you might guess, the file extension .DOC is associated with the MIME type *application/msword.*

Note that content groups apply to HTTP but *not* to HTTPS (Secure HTTP). Also note that ISA Server includes several predefined content groups, including:

- Application
- Application data files
- Audio
- Compressed files
- Documents
- HTML documents
- Images
- Macro documents
- Text
- Video
- VRML

Understanding ISA Server Licensing

An important aspect of planning a deployment of ISA Server—or any other commercial software—in any network environment is understanding the licensing and pricing structure. Software licensing agreements have grown more complex, and the large number of machines (as well as the more complex configurations of those machines) in an enterprise network can make it even more difficult to accurately determine a vendor's licensing requirements.

Many experienced network administrators will be familiar with the licensing methods used by Microsoft for its server operating systems, Window NT and Windows 2000. In both cases, there are two options for licensing connections to the servers:

- Purchase of an individual Client Access License (CAL) for each client machine on the network, allowing it to access as many servers on the network as desired

- Purchase of a set number of licenses for each server, allowing that number of clients to connect simultaneously to that particular server

The first option is called *per-seat licensing* and is most cost effective in a network with multiple servers to which many clients need to connect. The second option is called *per-server licensing* and is preferred when there are only a few servers and all clients don't connect to the server at the same time.

Licensing for Microsoft Proxy Server 2.0 was simpler than this; in fact, it was the ultimate in simplicity: A license was required for each computer on which you wanted to install the Proxy Server software. Unfortunately, things get a little more complicated with ISA Server.

Processor-Based Licensing

ISA Server uses a processor-based licensing structure, which means that the cost of an ISA Server license is dependent on how many microprocessors are installed in the computer on which it runs. Thus, if the computers running ISA Server are using SMP, you must purchase a *processor license* for each CPU, and you must purchase additional licenses if you upgrade to SMP or add additional processors to an existing SMP machine.

The good news is that a processor license allows an unlimited number of users to access the ISA server. It does not matter whether these users connect from inside the LAN or WAN or from outside the firewall (across the Internet). There is no requirement to purchase CALs or Internet Connection Licenses. This is similar to the licensing scheme for IIS Web access on NT 4.0 Server or Windows 2000 Server.

Volume Licensing

Enterprise-level organizations often need multiple licenses. For example, if you will be setting up an ISA server array (or several), you need to purchase at least one license for each machine and, if some are multiprocessor machines, more than one. Volume licensing programs available through Microsoft can help to reduce the cost of deployment if your network requires multiple ISA Servers.

Upgrade Licensing

Cost per processor also differs depending on whether you purchase the Standard or the Enterprise edition and whether you qualify for the upgrade price or must purchase the full product.

You can purchase the upgrade if you are already a licensed user of a former Microsoft product or selected competitive products made by other vendors. Qualifying products include the following:

- Microsoft Proxy Server (version 1.0 or 2.0)
- Netscape Proxy Server
- Novell BorderManager for Windows NT
- Firewall-1 and VPN-1, from CheckPoint Software Technologies, Ltd.
- Axent Technologies' Raptor firewall
- Cisco Systems' Cache Engine and PIX firewall
- Inktomi Traffic Server
- CacheFlow, Inc.'s network caching appliances
- IBM's SecureWay firewall and WebSphere Cache
- Cobalt Cache/Cobalt Qube
- Network Appliance, Inc.'s NetCache Proxy Server

Standardized Licensing Model

Microsoft has announced that the processor-based licensing model used for ISA Server will also apply to other server products in the .Net family. The new licensing structure is intended to simplify and standardize the licensing process and was designed specifically with the e-commerce market in mind. In addition to ISA Server, other products that use per-processor licensing include Host Integration Server 2000, Commerce Server 2000, Application Center Server 2000, BizTalk Server 2000, and SQL Server 2000.

Summary

The enterprise network is not only bigger than other networks; it differs in other aspects as well. Planning an ISA Server deployment in a large, multilocation, high-traffic, multiuse environment is a challenge that requires careful and precise strategic planning.

ISA Server features that make this product enterprise-friendly include:

- Reliability
- Scalability
- Multiprocessor support
- Network load balancing
- Clustering
- Distributed caching
- Total cost of ownership

In planning your enterprise deployment, it is important for you to recognize the core protocols and services on which your network runs. In today's interconnected world, the vast majority of large networks are based on the TCP/IP protocol stack, and Windows 2000 domains require TCP/IP, as does ISA Server.

The physical and logical divisions of a Windows 2000 network consist of sites and domains, respectively. Domain structure differs in many ways from NT-based domains, and these differences include:

- Domain size limitations/number of domains required in a network
- Flat versus hierarchical domain structures
- The nature of the trust relationships between domains
- Domain controller roles
- Scope of administrative boundaries

An important step in planning the deployment of your ISA servers in the enterprise is assessing the needs of your users and determining what applications and services the internal clients will require. This, in turn, helps you determine how your ISA clients will be configured (as firewall, SecureNAT, or Web Proxy clients).

In the enterprise environment, it is especially important that you consider the appropriate mode (firewall, caching, or integrated) in which each ISA Server will be installed. All members of an array must run in the same mode.

An enterprise network is a complex entity. Your network is likely to have existing security measures in place that could be affected by the deployment of ISA. You must also consider, as part of the planning process, how ISA Server will interoperate with various network services and other Internet-related software such as your Web server.

Arrays are appropriate for medium-sized and large networks and, in the enterprise environment, offer many advantages. Array members are managed as a single entity. Array configuration information can be backed up using ISA Server's backup and restore feature.

An important aspect of planning a deployment of ISA Server—or any other commercial software—in any network environment is understanding the licensing and pricing structure. Microsoft uses a *per-processor* licensing model for ISA Server and other members of the .Net server family.

This chapter has provided an overview of some of the issues involved in planning an enterprise deployment of ISA Server. In the next chapter, we look at general Internet security concepts and how ISA fits into an overall security plan.

Solutions Fast Track

Enterprise-Friendly Features

- ☑ Over the past several years Microsoft has made a conscious effort to penetrate the enterprise market, and we have begun to see the Windows server operating systems replace or at least take their place beside the UNIX machines and mainframes that have served this market in the past.
- ☑ Enterprise technologies provide ways to integrate the networking needs of an organization that has multiple divisions, functions, and/or physical locations. Microsoft defines an enterprise network as one that incorporates multiple subnets with routed LAN and WAN links.
- ☑ In a large business network environment, access and security are not just desirable; they are mission critical.
- ☑ The ability to create server arrays, which can be managed together as a single entity, is one of the features that provide fault tolerance, making

ISA Server a highly reliable solution to your network's security and access acceleration needs.

- ☑ Scalability can be defined as the ability of a system (individual computer or network) to maintain or improve performance as size (of the application or network load) increases.
- ☑ Scaling up generally refers to the addition of more resources (for example, memory, processors or disks).
- ☑ Scaling out refers to the ability to distribute resources across multiple computer systems so that higher performance is possible even though the requirements might be greater than the capability of a single system.
- ☑ Windows 2000 Server can support up to four microprocessors out of the box and up to 32 processors in the OEM versions of Windows 2000 Data Center Server.
- ☑ The speed at which a computer can process data (by performing the necessary arithmetical calculations on the binary code) depends on the speed of its microprocessor.
- ☑ Load balancing refers to spreading the burden, or load, of work across servers so that no one server is overloaded.
- ☑ Microsoft defines a cluster as a group of independent servers that are managed as a single system for higher availability, easier manageability, and greater scalability.
- ☑ ISA Server uses Cache Array Routing Protocol (CARP) to allow multiple ISA servers to use a single logical cache. This process is called distributed caching.

Designing Enterprise Solutions

- ☑ The trend today is toward open standard Internet services such as HTTP (Web), FTP (file transfer), SMTP/POP/IMAP (e-mail), NNTP (news), and DNS (name resolution). This is in contrast to vendor-specific services (such as Novell's file and print sharing or Microsoft's Exchange 5.x directory services).
- ☑ ISA Server is dependent on TCP/IP and cannot function without it.

- ☑ In Windows NT 4.0 networks, there was a limit on the number of security objects (user accounts, group accounts, computer accounts) that could exist in a single domain.
- ☑ Windows 2000 networks are built on the concept of domain trees, which are groups of domains that share a contiguous namespace.
- ☑ All domains in a Windows 2000 domain tree share implicit, two-way transitive trust relationships with each other.
- ☑ An NT domain must have one and only one primary domain controller (PDC), on which the master writable copy of the SAM database is stored. Windows 2000 networks can have multiple domain controllers, all of which have a writable copy of the Active Directory partition.
- ☑ In an NT network, the domain is the smallest administrative boundary, but this is not true in a Windows 2000 network where administrative authority can be delegated at the OU level.
- ☑ Because many enterprise networks span international boundaries, there is a likelihood that your network will need to be divided into multiple domains to accommodate differences in languages, currencies, and laws.
- ☑ An intranet in its simplest form is an internal, private Web. Businesses, especially large ones, have discovered the advantages of using Internet technologies such as HTTP to publish information for employees and provide a means for those within the organization to distribute information easily and inexpensively.
- ☑ An extranet is similar to an intranet in that it is a private network using Internet technology. The difference is that whereas the intranet is made accessible to internal users (employees), the extranet is made accessible to selected external users (business partners, vendors, and customers).
- ☑ An important part of ISA design and deployment planning involves estimating the expected usage, based on number of users and usage patterns, in order to determine the number of ISA servers required.
- ☑ A big advantage of installing additional ISA servers instead of merely adding processors to the existing server is the ability to group the multiple machines in arrays.
- ☑ If you have multiple ISA servers that you want to join in arrays, all members of an array must belong to the same Windows 2000 domain and to the same Active Directory site.

☑ Both the firewall and caching modes allow implementation of enterprise policy, but caching mode supports access policy only for HTTP.

☑ To install ISA Server as a standalone, you need an account that belongs to the local administrators group on the machine on which you are installing.

Planning Multiserver Arrays

☑ Arrays are appropriate for medium-sized and large networks, and in the enterprise environment, they offer many advantages.

☑ Array configuration information can be backed up using ISA Server's backup and restore feature.

☑ Microsoft documentation recommends that you always back up the array configuration after making significant changes to your array, such as changing installation mode, cache size or location, or enterprise policy settings, and any time you add or remove a server to or from the array or change the name of a computer that is an array member.

☑ Policy elements refer to properties of ISA policy rules, which can be created for your enterprise policy and for each array policy.

Understanding ISA Server Licensing

☑ Many experience network administrators will be familiar with the licensing methods used by Microsoft for its server operating systems, Window NT and Windows 2000. In both cases, there are two options for licensing connections to the servers: 1. Purchase of an individual Client Access License (CAL) for each client machine on the network, allowing it to access as many servers on the network as desired. 2.Purchase of a set number of licenses for each server, allowing that number of clients to connect simultaneously to that particular server.

☑ ISA Server uses a processor-based licensing structure, which means that the cost of an ISA Server license is dependent on how many microprocessors are installed in the computer on which it runs.

☑ Enterprise-level organizations often need multiple licenses. For example, if you will be setting up an ISA server array (or several), you need to purchase at least one license for each machine and, if some are multiprocessor machines, more than one.

- ☑ Cost per processor also differs depending on whether you purchase the Standard or the Enterprise edition and whether you qualify for the upgrade price or must purchase the full product.
- ☑ Microsoft has announced that the processor-based licensing model used for ISA Server will also apply to other server products in the .Net family.

Frequently Asked Questions

The following Frequently Asked Questions, answered by the authors of this book, are designed to both measure your understanding of the concepts presented in this chapter and to assist you with real-life implementation of these concepts. To have your questions about this chapter answered by the author, browse to **www.syngress.com/solutions** and click on the **"Ask the Author"** form.

Q: Virtual private networking has become increasingly important to the enterprise network as the need to provide a means for employees, consultants, and partners to securely connect to the corporate network from a remote location has taken on a high priority in today's mobile world. ISA Server allows for VPN connections to the ISA server itself, but does it also allow VPN connections to be made by the internal client computers?

A: Yes. Not only does ISA Server provide for opening the PPTP call and receive ports so users on the outside network can create a VPN connection directly to the ISA server, but it also provides for users on the internal network, behind the ISA Server, to initiate VPN calls to establish a VPN between themselves and hosts on the Internet (or other network on the other side of the firewall). In fact, ISA Server includes VPN wizards that make setting up a virtual connection quick and easy.

Q: What sort of impact can we expect ISA Server to have on the network's performance?

A: Speed of access to Web pages and other Web objects should be noticeably improved. This results from ISA Server's caching capabilities. Using advanced features, such as hierarchical caching, which allow you to "chain" ISA servers or server arrays in a multilevel arrangement and cache pre-fetching and automated content download, ISA Server can significantly enhance performance from the user's point of view.

Q: I used the Enterprise Initialization Tool and installed the ISA schema to Active Directory. However, when I attempted to install ISA Server as an array member, I received an error message that the ISA Server schema has not been installed. What's the problem?

A: The information in Active Directory must be replicated to all the domain controllers in the domain, and this can take some time. You should wait until the changes have been replicated to the local domain controller, then you will be able to install ISA Server on the first array member to create the array.

Q: If I want to configure a content group that includes all file extensions, or all MIME types, must I enter each separately, or is there a way to do this easily?

A: You can use asterisks (*) as wildcard values if you are configuring the content group by specifying the MIME type. To do this, you would enter **application/*** to specify all application types. The asterisk must appear at the end of the MIME type following the slash mark (/). Unfortunately, wildcard values cannot be used when specifying file extensions.

Q: Who can create and modify the enterprise and array policies? Who can create arrays?

A: Enterprise administrators (members of the Enterprise Admin group) can change enterprise policy settings and create or modify enterprise policies. Members of the domain admins group in the root domain of the forest have enterprise admin permissions by default. To create or modify an array policy, you must be a member of the domain admins group for the domain in which the array is located or an enterprise admin. In order to create an array, the Active Directory schema must be modified first (this process is called *initializing the enterprise*). In order to run the enterprise initialization tool, which makes the schema modification, you must be a member of the enterprise admins group and the schema admins group.

Q: Can ISA Server be used in a Windows NT domain?

A: An ISA Server array can only be installed in a Windows 2000 domain. However, you can install an ISA Server as a standalone on a Windows 2000 server in a Windows NT domain. You can also provide Internet security to users and client computers that belong to an NT domain with an ISA Server array that is installed in a Windows 2000 domain, if you create a trust relationship between the Windows NT domain to which the users/clients belong and the Windows 2000 domain to which the ISA servers belong.

Chapter 3

Security Concepts and Security Policies

Solutions in this chapter:

- Security Overview
- Defining Basic Security Concepts
- Addressing Security Objectives
- Recognizing Network Security Threats
- Categorizing Security Solutions
- Designing a Comprehensive Security Plan
- Incorporating ISA Server in your Security Plan

☑ Summary

☑ Solutions Fast Track

☑ Frequently Asked Questions

Introduction

In this chapter, we look at the big picture: what we mean by network security in general and Internet security in particular—why it's necessary, how we can create a comprehensive security policy to protect our networks from unauthorized access, and where Microsoft's ISA Server fits into that picture.

Network security is a hot topic and is growing into a high-profile (and often highly paid) IT specialty area. Security-related Web sites such as AntiOnline (www.antionline.com), the Computer Network Security site (www.computernetworksecurity.com), and the Network Security Library (http://secinf.net/) are tremendously popular with savvy Internet users. Esoteric security measures such as biometric identification and authentication—formerly the province of science fiction writers and perhaps a few ultrasecretive government agencies—have become almost commonplace in corporate America.

Yet with all this focus on security, many organizations implement security measures in an almost haphazard way, with no well-considered plan for making all the parts fit together. Computer security involves many aspects of safekeeping, from protection of the physical equipment to protection of the electronic bits and bytes that make up the information that resides on the network.

In the next section, we provide a brief overview of what we mean by *security* in general and how the concept applies to your computer network.

NOTE

This chapter focuses on generic computer and Internet security concepts and the way to develop a comprehensive security plan for your organization. The last part of the chapter discusses how ISA Server fits into that security plan.

Security Overview

The term *computer security* encompasses many related but separate topics. These topics can be stated as security objectives:

- Control of physical accessibility to the computer(s) and/or network
- Prevention of accidental erasure, modification, or compromise of data

- Detection and prevention of intentional internal security breaches
- Detection and prevention of unauthorized external intrusions (hacking)

Network security solutions can be loosely divided into three categories: hardware, software, and human. This chapter provides an overview of basic security concepts, then examines all four security objectives and takes a look at each of the three categories of security solution.

It is important that you address each of the objectives in a comprehensive, documented *security policy*. At the end of the chapter, we focus on how to design a security policy for your organization and how to incorporate ISA Server as a part of your overall network security plan. Before we discuss these specifics, let's briefly review some basic security concepts and how they apply to computer networking.

Defining Basic Security Concepts

A generic dictionary definition of *security* (taken from the American Heritage Dictionary) is "freedom from risk or danger; safety." This definition is perhaps a little misleading when it comes to computer and networking security, because it implies a degree of protection that is inherently impossible to achieve in the modern connectivity-oriented computing environment.

For this reason, the same dictionary provides another definition specific to computer science: "The *level to which* a program or device is safe from unauthorized use" (emphasis added). Implicit in this definition is the caveat that the objectives of security and accessibility—the two top priorities on the minds of many network administrators—are, by their very nature, diametrically opposed. The more accessible your data, the less secure it is. Likewise, the more tightly you secure your data, the more you impede accessibility. Any security plan is an attempt to strike the proper balance between the two.

Speaking of dictionaries: At the end of this section you will find a list of some common terms that you are likely to encounter in the IT security field. As in any other specialty field, security professionals speak a language all their own, and understanding the concepts require that you learn the jargon.

Knowledge Is Power

The preceding heading is a famous hacker's motto (along with such other gems as "Information wants to be free" and the simplistic but ambitious "Hack the world!"). "Knowledge is power" is a truism that applies not only to people attempting to gain access to data they aren't supposed to see, but also to those who are trying to protect themselves from such intruders. The first step in winning any battle—and network security *is* a battle, a battle for the ownership and control of your computer files—is the same as it's always been: "Know thine enemy."

To protect your network resources from theft, damage, or unwanted exposure, you must understand who initiates these events, why they do it, and how they do it. This knowledge will make *you* powerful, too—and better able to prevent unauthorized intrusions into your network. The section "Preventing Unauthorized External Intrusions and Attacks" discusses the various motivations that drive network intruders and the types of people who make a practice of "breaking and entering" networks.

The very best place to learn is from hackers themselves. Even so, many network administrators and even some security specialists eschew the books and Web sites that are written to a hacker audience or from the hacker's point of view. This might be because they fear "guilt by association" or believe that they would be somehow lowering themselves to "hang out" with hackers. Although possibly based on high moral ground, this attitude is, strategically, a mistake. Whether you take a more formal route, such as the SANS GIAC or CISSP certification courses, or opt to learn on your own, you'll need to understand who the hackers are, what they do, and how and why they do it if you want to effectively protect your network from unwanted intrusions.

Think Like a Thief

It is well known in law enforcement circles that the best criminal investigators are those who are best able to "get inside the mind" of the lawbreaker. Network intrusion detectives will find that the same is true: to prevent your network from falling prey to hackers or to catch data thieves when they do get in requires you to be able to adopt a mindset emulating theirs.

This means learning to anticipate the intruder's actions. First, you must determine *what* needs to be protected, and to what degree. A wealthy person not only establishes a general security perimeter by building fences around his or her house and locking doors and windows, but the wise person also places the most valuable items in a wall or floor safe. This action provides multiple *layers* of protection.

Similarly, ISA Server can be an important layer of protection in your organization's security plan.

The Intrusion Triangle

Borrowing again from the law enforcement community, crime prevention specialists use a model called the Crime Triangle to explain that certain criteria must exist before a crime can occur. We can adapt this same triangle to network security: The same three criteria must exist before a network security breach can take place. The three "legs," or points of the triangle, are shown in Figure 3.1.

Figure 3.1 All Three Legs of the Crime Triangle Must Exist for Network Intrusion to Occur

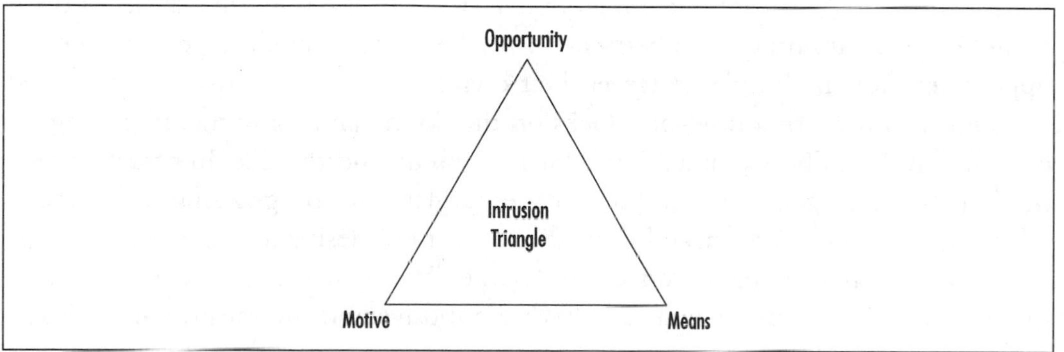

Let's look at each point individually:

- **Motive** An intruder must have a reason to want to breach the security of your network (even if the reason is "just for fun"); otherwise, he or she won't bother.
- **Means** An intruder must have the ability (either the programming knowledge or, in the case of "script kiddies," the intrusion software written by others), or he or she won't be able to breach your security.
- **Opportunity** An intruder must have the chance to enter the network due to flaws in your security plan, holes in a software program that open an avenue of access, or physical proximity to network components. If there is no opportunity to intrude, the would-be hacker will go elsewhere.

If you think about the three intrusion criteria for a moment, you'll see that there is really only one leg of the triangle over which you, as the network administrator or security specialist, have any control. It is unlikely that you can do much to remove the intruder's *motive*. The motive is likely to be built into the type of data you have on the network or even the personality of the intruder him- or herself. It is also not possible for you to prevent the intruder from having or obtaining the *means* to breach your security. Programming knowledge is freely available, and many experienced hackers out there are more than happy to help less sophisticated newcomers. The one thing that you *can* affect is the *opportunity* afforded (or not afforded) the hacker.

Removing Intrusion Opportunities

Crime prevention officers tell members of the community that they probably can't keep a potential burglar from wanting to steal, and they certainly can't keep the potential burglar from obtaining burglary tools or learning the "tricks of the trade." What community members *can* do is take away, as much as possible, the opportunity for the burglar to target their own homes.

This means putting dead-bolt locks on the doors (and using them); getting a big, loud, unfriendly dog; installing an alarm system, and the like. In other words, the homeowner's goal is not to prevent the burglar from burglarizing (that's the job of the police) but to make his or her home a less desirable target. Similarly, as a network "owner," your objective is to "harden" your own network so that all those hackers out there who already have the motive and the means will look for a more likely victim.

If you don't use them, the best and most expensive locks in the world won't keep intruders out of your house. And if those locks are difficult to use and cause you inconvenience in your everyday comings and goings, you probably *won't* use them—at least, not all the time. A poorly implemented network security system that is difficult to administer or that unduly inconveniences network users could end up similarly; eventually you will throw your hands up in frustration and just turn the darn thing off. And that will leave your network wide open to intruders.

It is not the job of the homeowners to prevent burglars from burglarizing—only to protect *themselves* from being victimized. Likewise, it is not the job of a network administrator or network security manager to keep hackers from hacking. You can only take steps to protect your network and its resources from those who "break and enter" networks for fun or profit.

A good network security system will help you easily remove the temptations (open ports, exploitable applications) and will be as transparent to your users as possible. ISA Server, when properly configured, meets these requirements—and more. We discuss the characteristics of a good network security system component further in the "Preventing Unauthorized External Intrusions and Attacks" section.

Security Terminology

Every industry has its own "language," the jargon that describes concepts and procedures peculiar to the field. Computer networking is infamous for the "technotalk" and the proliferation of acronyms that often mystify outsiders. Specialty areas within an industry often have their own brands of jargon, and the computer security subfield is no exception.

It is not possible to provide a complete glossary of security-related terms within the scope of this chapter, but in this section, we define some of the more common words and phrases that you might encounter as you begin to explore the fascinating world of computer security:

- **Attack** In the context of computer and network security, an *attack* is an attempt to access resources on a computer or a network without authorization or to bypass security measures that are in place.
- **Audit** To track security-related events, such as logging on to the system or network, accessing objects, or exercising user or group rights or privileges.
- **Breach** Successfully defeating security measures to gain access to data or resources without authorization, to make data or resources available to unauthorized persons, or to delete or alter computer files.
- **Brute force attack** An attempt to "crack" passwords by sequentially trying all possible combinations of characters until the right combination works to allow access.
- **Buffer** A holding area for data.
- **Buffer overflow** A way to crash a system by putting more data into a buffer than the buffer is able to hold.
- **Confidentiality of data** Ensuring that the contents of messages will be kept secret. See also *integrity of data.*
- **Cracker** A hacker who specializes in "cracking," or discovering, system passwords to gain access to computer systems without authorization. See also *hacker.*
- **Crash** Sudden failure of a computer system, that renders it unusable.
- **Denial-of-service (DoS) attack** A deliberate action that keeps a computer or network from functioning as intended (for example, preventing users from being able to log on to the network).

- **Distributed DoS attack** A type of DoS attack that uses intermediary systems, which are controlled by the attacker and from which the attack is launched, disguising its true origin.
- **Hacker** A person who spends time learning the details of computer programming and operating systems, how to test the limits of their capabilities, and where their vulnerabilities lie. See also *cracker.*
- **Integrity of data** Ensuring that data has not been modified or altered, that the data received is identical to the data that was sent.
- **Malicious code** A computer program or script that performs an action that intentionally damages a system or data, that performs another unauthorized purpose, or that provides unauthorized access to the system.
- **Penetration testing** Evaluating a system by attempting to circumvent the computer's or network's security measures.
- **Port scan** A means of determining the services that are running on a remote system, making that system vulnerable to penetration.
- **Reliability** The probability of a computer system or network continuing to perform in a satisfactory manner for a specific time period under normal operating conditions.
- **Risk** The probability that a specific security threat will be able to exploit a system vulnerability, resulting in damage, loss of data, or other undesired results.
- **Risk management** The process of identifying, controlling, and either minimizing or completely eliminating events that pose a threat to system reliability, data integrity, and data confidentiality.
- **Sniffer** A program that captures data as it travels across a network. Also called a *packet sniffer.*
- **Spoofing** Gaining access to a system or network using a forged IP address or other deceptive means.
- **Social engineering** Gaining unauthorized access to a system or network by subverting personnel (for example, posing as a member of the IT department to convince users to reveal their passwords).
- **Trusted Computer System Evaluation Criteria (TCSEC)** A system for evaluating the level of security of a system.

- **Technical vulnerability** A flaw or bug in the hardware or software components of a system that leave it vulnerable to security breach.
- **Trojan horse** A computer program that appears to perform a desirable function but contains hidden code that is intended to allow unauthorized collection, modification, or destruction of data.
- **Virus** A program that is introduced into a system or network for the purpose of performing an unauthorized action (which can vary from popping up a harmless message to destroying all data on the hard disk).
- **Vulnerability** A weakness in the hardware or software or the security plan that leaves a system or network open to threat of unauthorized access or damage or destruction of data.
- **Worm** A program that replicates itself, spreading from one machine to another across a network.

For definitions of many more security-related terms, see the following Web sites:

- InfoSec terminology (www.miora.com/articles/infosecterms.html#V)
- Security glossary (http://members.nbci.com/_XMCM/infosyssec/merged_glossary.html)

Once you are comfortable with network security terminology, you can begin to address the individual objectives that will assist you in realizing your goal of creating a secure network environment.

Addressing Security Objectives

If your security goal is to have complete control over the data that comes into and goes out of your networks, you must define objectives that will help you reach that goal. We listed some general security objectives related to computer networks—especially those connected to an outside internetwork such as the Internet—as controlling physical access, preventing accidental compromise of data, detecting and preventing intentional internal security breaches, and detecting and preventing unauthorized external intrusions. In the following sections, we examine each of these objectives in detail.

Controlling Physical Access

One of the most important and at the same time most overlooked aspects of a comprehensive network security plan is physical access control. This matter is often left up to facilities managers and plant security departments or outsourced to security guard companies. Network administrators concern themselves with sophisticated software and hardware solutions that prevent intruders from accessing internal computers remotely while doing nothing to protect the servers, routers, cable, and other physical components of the network from direct access.

SEURITY ALERT!

In far too many supposedly security-conscious organizations, computers are locked away from employees and visitors all day, only to be left open at night to the janitorial staff, who have keys to all offices. It is not at all uncommon for computer espionage experts to pose as members of cleaning crews to gain physical access to machines that hold sensitive data. This is a favorite ploy for several reasons:

- Cleaning services are often contracted out, and workers in the industry are often transient, so your company employees might not be easily aware of who is or isn't a legitimate member of the cleaning company staff.
- Cleaning is usually done late at night, when all or most company employees are gone, making it easier to surreptitiously steal data.
- The cleaning crew members are often paid little or no attention by company employees, who take their presence for granted and think nothing of their being in areas where the presence of others would normally be questioned.

Physically breaking into the server room and stealing the hard disk on which sensitive data resides might be a crude method of breaching security; nonetheless, it happens. In some organizations, it could be the easiest way to gain unauthorized access, especially for an intruder who has help "on the inside."

Physical Access Factors

It is beyond the scope of this book to go into great detail about how to physically secure your network, but it is important for you to make physical access control the "outer perimeter" of your security plan. This means:

- Controlling physical access to the servers
- Controlling physical access to networked workstations
- Controlling physical access to network devices
- Controlling physical access to the cable
- Being aware of security considerations with wireless media
- Being aware of security considerations related to portable computers
- Recognizing the security risk of allowing data to be printed
- Recognizing the security risks involving floppy disks, CDs, tapes, and other removable media

Let's look at the reason that each of these points is important and assess ways that you can implement a physical security plan that addresses all these factors.

Protecting the Servers

File servers on which sensitive data is stored and infrastructure servers that provide mission-critical services such as logon authentication and access control should be placed in a highly secure location. At a minimum, servers should be in a locked room to which only those who need to work directly with the servers have access. Keys should be distributed sparingly, and records should be kept of issuance and return.

If security needs are high due to the nature of the business or the nature of the data, access to the server room could be controlled by magnetic card, electronic locks requiring entry of a numerical code, or even biometric access control devices such as fingerprint or retinal scanners.

Other security measures include motion detectors or other alarm systems, activated during nonbusiness hours, and security cameras. A security guard or company should monitor these devices.

Keeping Workstations Secure

Many network security plans focus on the servers but ignore the risk posed by workstations that have network access to those servers. It is not uncommon for employees to leave their computers unsecured when they leave their offices for lunch or even when they leave for the evening. Often a workstation in the receptionist area is open to visitors who walk in off the street. If the receptionist manning the station must leave briefly, the computer—and the network to which it is connected—is vulnerable unless steps have been taken to ensure that it is secure.

A good security plan includes protection of all unmanned workstations. A secure client operating system such as Windows NT or Windows 2000 (unlike Windows 9x) requires an interactive logon with a valid account name and password in order to access the operating system. In addition, it allows a user to "lock" the workstation when he or she will be away from it, so someone else can't simply step up and start using the computer. Some degree of security can be provided for Windows 9x clients by using password-enabled screensavers, although savvy intruders can bypass this form of security by rebooting the computer.

Don't depend on access permissions and other software security methods alone to protect your network. If a potential intruder can gain physical access to a networked computer, he or she is that much closer to accessing your valuable data or introducing a virus onto your network.

Ensure that all workstation users adhere to a good password policy, as discussed in the section "Designing a Comprehensive Security Plan" later in this chapter.

Many modern PC cases come with some type of locking mechanism that will help prevent an unauthorized person from opening the case and stealing the hard disk. Locks are also available to prevent use of the floppy drive, to prevent copying of data to a diskette, or to prevent rebooting the computer with a floppy.

Protecting Network Devices

Hubs, routers, switches, and other network devices should be physically secured from unauthorized access. It is easy to forget that merely because a device doesn't have a monitor on which you can *see* data, that doesn't mean the data can't be captured or destroyed at that access point.

For example, a traditional Ethernet hub sends all data out every port on the hub. An intruder who has access to the hub can plug a packet-sniffing device (or a laptop computer with sniffer software) that operates in "promiscuous mode" (in which packets can be captured and read regardless of their source or destination) into a spare port and capture data sent to any computer on the segment, as shown in Figure 3.2.

NOTE

Packet sniffers are also called *protocol analyzers* or *network analyzers*. Sniffer and Sniffer Pro are two packet-sniffer products marketed by Network Associates.

Figure 3.2 An Intruder with Access to the Hub Can Easily Intercept Data

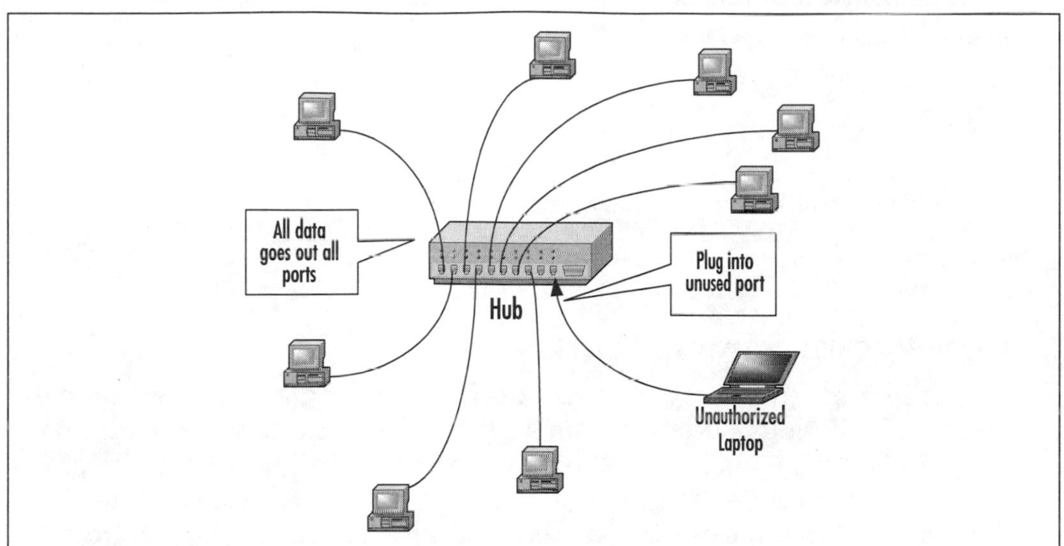

Although switches and routers are somewhat more secure than hubs, any device through which the data passes is a point of vulnerability. Replacing hubs with switches and routers makes it more difficult for an intruder to "sniff" on your network, but it is still possible to use techniques such as *Address Resolution Protocol (ARP) spoofing*. This technique is also sometimes called *router redirection*, in which nearby machines are redirected to forward traffic through an intruder's machine by sending ARP packets that contain the router's IP address mapped to the intruder's machine's Media Access Control (MAC) address. This results in other machines believing the intruder's machine is the router, so they send their traffic to it. A similar method uses ICMP router advertisement messages.

It is also possible, with certain switches, to overflow the address tables with multiple false MAC addresses or send a continuous flow of random garbage through the switch and trigger it to change from bridging mode to repeating mode. This means that all frames would be broadcast on all ports, giving the intruder the same opportunity to access the data that he or she would have with a regular hub. This practice is called *switch jamming*.

Finally, if the switch has a special monitor port designed to be used with a sniffer for legitimate (network troubleshooting) purposes, an intruder who has physical access to the switch can simply plug into this port and capture network data.

Due to the vulnerabilities described here, your network devices should be placed in a locked room or closet and protected in the same manner as your servers.

Designing & Planning…

How Packet Sniffers Work

Packet sniffer and protocol analyzer devices and programs are not used solely for nefarious purposes, although intruders use them to capture unencrypted data and clear-text passwords that will allow them to break into systems. Despite the fact that these devices can be used to "steal" data as it travels across the network, they are also invaluable troubleshooting tools for network administrators. The sniffer captures individual data packets and allows you to view and analyze the message contents and packet headers. This can be useful in diagnosing network communications problems and uncovering network bottlenecks that are impacting performance. Packet sniffers can also be turned against hackers and crackers and used to discover unauthorized intruders.

The most important part of the sniffer is the *capture driver*. This is the component that captures the network traffic, filters it (according to criteria set by the user), and stores the data in a buffer. The packets can then be analyzed and decoded to display the contents.

It is often possible to detect an unauthorized packet sniffer on the wire using a device called a *time domain reflectometer (TDR),* which sends a pulse down the cable and creates a graph of the reflections that are returned. Those who know how to read the graph can tell whether and where unauthorized devices are attached to the cable.

Other ways of detecting unauthorized connections include monitoring hub or switch lights, using Simple Network Monitoring Protocol (SNMP) managers that log connections and disconnections, or using one of the many tools designed for the specific purpose of detecting sniffers on the network. These include the following:

- Antisniff (www.l0pht.com/antisniff/)
- neped (www.apostols.org/projectz/neped/)
- Sentinel (www.packetfactory.net/Projects/sentinel/)

Continued

In addition, several techniques using PING, ARP, and DNS could help you catch unauthorized sniffers. The use of these techniques is beyond the scope of this book, but you can find instructions for using them (and much more excellent information on packet sniffing) at Robert Graham's Sniffing FAQ Web site, located at www.secinf.net/info/misc/sniffingfaq.html. You can even automate the sending of alerts (messages of notification to the administrator) when the presence of a packet sniffer is detected.

Securing the Cable

The next step in protecting your network data is to secure the cable across which it travels. Twisted-pair and coaxial cable are both vulnerable to data capture; an intruder who has access to the cable can tap into it and eavesdrop on messages sent across it. A number of companies make such "tapping" devices.

Fiber optic cable is more difficult to tap into because it does not produce electrical pulses but instead uses pulses of light to represent the 0s and 1s of binary data. It is possible, however, for a sophisticated intruder to use an optical splitter and tap into the signal on fiber optic media.

Compromise of security at the physical level is a special threat when network cables are not contained in one facility but span a distance between buildings. There is even a name for this risk: *manhole manipulation,* a term that refers to the easy access intruders often have to cabling that runs through underground conduits.

Cable taps can sometimes be detected using a TDR or optical TDR to measure the strength of the signal and determine where the tap is located.

Safely Going Wireless

Wireless media are becoming more and more popular as our society becomes more mobile. Many predict that wireless will be The Next Big Thing in networking during the first years of the new millennium.

Large companies such as Cisco Systems, Lucent Technologies, Sun Microsystems, and Microsoft have invested large amounts of talent and money in the wireless initiative. Wireless Internet access based on the Wireless Access Protocol (WAP) is common in Europe and beginning to catch on in the United States. Fixed wireless services are offered by communications giants such as AT&T and Sprint and companies such as Metricom (which offers the Ricochet wireless service).

Wireless networking offers several distinct advantages over traditional cabled networking. Laptop users can easily connect and disconnect as they travel, whether over long distances or from office to office. Workers in the field can maintain network communications in areas where there are no cables or phone lines. For professions such as policing, in which employees work from moving vehicles most of the time, wireless is the only way to stay connected to the department LAN. For telecommuters in rural areas where DSL and cable modem access are unavailable, wireless technologies such as satellites provide a broadband alternative to slow analog modems.

There are several different varieties of wireless networking:

- Radio (narrowband or spread spectrum)
- Satellite and microwave
- Laser and infrared

Despite the many benefits of these wireless technologies, they also present special problems, especially in the area of network security. Data traveling over wireless media is more vulnerable to interception than data over cabled media. Radio and microwave are known as *broadcast media*. Because the signals are transmitted across the airwaves, any receiver set to the correct frequency can easily eavesdrop on the communications. If security is a priority, any data sent via radio or microwave links should be encrypted.

NOTE

Laser signals are not as easy to intercept as radio and microwave signals; however, because laser is a line-of-sight technology, it is more limited in application—and lasers are much more sensitive to environmental factors such as weather.

Have Laptop, Will Travel

Portable computers—laptops, notebooks, and new fully functional handheld computers such as the Pocket PC and Palm machines—present their own security problems based on the very features that make them popular: their small size and mobility. Physical security for portable computers is especially important because it is so easy to steal the entire machine, data and all.

Luckily, a large number of companies make theft protection devices and security software for laptops. Locks and alarms are widely available, along with software programs that will disable the laptop's functionality if the device is stolen or even help track it down by causing the computer to "phone home" the first time the portable computer is attached to a modem (see Figure 3.3).

SECURITY ALERT!

One way to secure data on a stolen laptop or notebook computer is to encrypt the data on the disk. Windows 2000 provides the Encrypting File System (EFS) to encrypt data on NTFS partitions.

Figure 3.3 Tracking Programs Help Recover Stolen Portable Computers

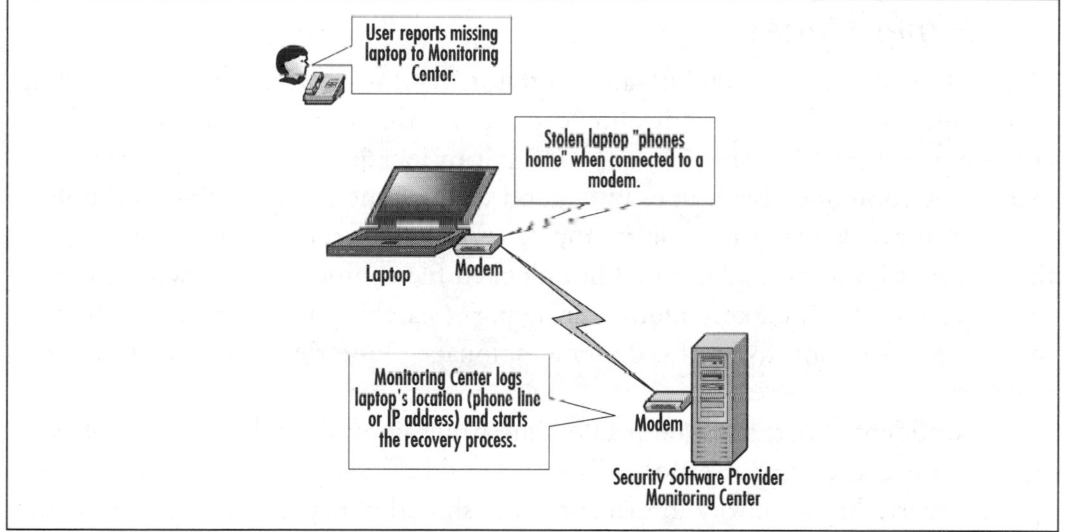

Some laptops come with removable hard disks. If you have highly sensitive data that must be accessed with your laptop, it's a good idea to store it on a removable disk (PC Card disks and those that plug into the parallel port are widely available) and encrypt it. Separate the disk from the computer when it is not in use.

NOTE

Theft recovery and tracking software for laptops includes Computrace (www.computrace.com) from Absolute Software Corporation, Alert PC (www.alertpc.com) from Eaglestar International, and Cyber Angel (www.sentryinc.com) from Computer Sentry Software. TrackIT (www.trackitcorp.com) is a hardware antitheft device for computer cases and other baggage.

The possibility of theft is not the only way in which laptops present a security risk. The threat to your network is that a data thief who is able to enter your premises might be able to plug a laptop into the network, crack passwords (or obtain a password via social engineering), and download data to the portable machine, which can then be easily carried away.

The Paper Chase

Network security specialists and administrators tend to concentrate on protecting data in electronic form, but you should recognize that intruders can also steal confidential digital information by printing it or locating a hard copy that was printed by someone else. It does little good to implement strong password policies and network access controls if employees can print sensitive material and then leave it lying on desks, stored in unlocked file cabinets, or thrown into an easily accessed trash basket. "Dumpster diving" (searching the trash for company secrets) is a common form of corporate espionage—one that, surprisingly, often yields results.

If confidential data must be printed, the paper copy should be kept as physically secure as the digital version. Disposal should require shredding, and in cases of particularly high-security information, the shredded paper can be mixed with water to create a pulp that is impossible to put back together again.

Removable Storage Risks

Yet another potential point of failure in your network security plan involves saving data to removable media. Floppy diskettes, Zip and Jaz disks, tapes, PC Cards, CDs, and DVDs containing sensitive data must be kept physically secured at all times.

Don't make the mistake of thinking that deleting the files on a disk, or even formatting the disk, completely erases the data; until it is overwritten, it is still there and can be retrieved using special software.

NOTE

The residual physical representation of data that has been "erased," from which that data can be reconstructed, is called *data remanence.* Methods used to prevent data remanence in high-security environments include degaussing, overwriting, and, in extreme cases, physical destruction of the media. *Degaussing* involves use of a device that generates a magnetic field to reduce the magnetic state of the media to zero, which restores it to an unrecorded state. Software (sometimes referred to as *file shredder* software) is available to overwrite all sectors of a disk with random bits in order to prevent recovery of the data. See http://packetstorm.securify.com/docs/rainbow-books/NCSC-TG-025.2.html for a detailed report on data remanence and the comparative merits of each solution.

Although removable media can present a security threat to the network, they can also play a part in your overall security plan. Removable disks (including fully bootable large-capacity hard disks installed in mobile "nesting" racks) can be removed from the computer and locked in a safe or removed from the premises to protect the data that is stored there.

Physical Security Summary

Ensuring a physically secure network environment is the first step in controlling access to your network's important data and system files, but it is only part of a good security plan. This is truer today than in the past because networks have more "ways in" than they once did. A medium-sized or large network can have multiple dial-in servers, virtual private network (VPN) servers, and a dedicated full-time Internet connection. Even a small network is likely to be connected to the Internet part of the time.

Virtual intruders never set foot on your organization's property and never touch your computers. They can access your network from across the street or from halfway across the world. But they can do as much damage as the thief who breaks into your company headquarters to steal or destroy your data—and they are much harder to catch. In the following sections, we examine specific network security risks and ways to prevent them.

Preventing Accidental Compromise of Data

The topic of network security might bring to mind a picture of evil corporate rivals determined to steal your company's most precious trade secrets or malevolent hackers bent on crashing your network and erasing all your data just for the sheer joy of it. Although these risks do exist, often the reality of network data loss is far less glamorous. A large proportion of erased, modified, or disclosed data is the result of the actions of employees or other authorized network personnel. Furthermore, a large percentage of *that* damage is the result of *accidental* compromise of the data.

Unintended errors in entering data or accessing network resources or carelessness in use of the computers and network can cause loss of data or crashing of individual computers, the server, and even the network. Your network security plan should address these unintended compromises, which can be just as disastrous as intentional breaches of security.

Know Your Users

To prevent accidental compromise of data, you should first know your users and their skill levels. Those with few technical skills should be given as little access as possible; allow them the access required to do their jobs, and no more. Too many network users have, in all innocence, destroyed or changed important files while attempting to clear space on their hard disks or troubleshoot a computer problem on their own.

Educate Your Users

Educating your users is one of the most important factors in eliminating or reducing such incidents. This does not necessarily mean upgrading the users' technical skills (although it can). Turning all your users into power users might not be cost effective or otherwise desirable. What *is* essential is to train all your network users in the proper procedures and rules of use for the network.

Every person who accesses your company network should be aware of your user policies and should agree to adhere to them. This includes notifying technical support personnel immediately of any hardware or software problems, refraining from installing any unauthorized software on their machines or downloading files from the Internet without authorization, and never dialing their personal ISPs or other networks or services from company machines without permission.

Control Your Users

In some cases, establishing clear-cut policies and making staffers and other users aware of them will be enough. In other cases, you will find that users are unable or unwilling to follow the rules, and you will have to take steps to enforce them—including locking down desktops with system or group policies and, with software such as ISA Server, implementing access rules and filtering to prevent unauthorized packets from being sent or received over the network.

Luckily, most users will at least attempt to comply with the rules. A more serious problem is the "insider" who is looking to intentionally breach network security. This person could be simply a maverick employee who doesn't like being told what to do, or he or she could be someone with a darker motive.

Preventing Intentional Internal Security Breaches

According to most computer security studies, as documented in RFC 2196, actual loss (in terms of money, productivity, computer reputation, and other tangible and intangible harm) is greater for internal security breaches than for those from the outside. Internal attackers are more dangerous for several reasons:

- They generally know more about the company, the network, the layout of the building(s), normal operating procedure, and other information that will make it easier for them to gain access without detection.
- They usually have at least some degree of legitimate access and might find it easy to discover passwords and holes in the current security system.
- They know what information is on the network and what actions will cause the most damage.

We discuss common motivations behind intentional security breaches, both internal and external, in the section, "Recognizing Network Security Threats." Preventing such problems begins with the same methods used to prevent unintentional compromises but goes a step further.

To a large extent, unintended breaches can be prevented through education. This obviously will not have the same effect on network users who intend to breach security as it has on "innocent" employees. The best way to prevent such breaches depends, in part, on the motivations of the employee(s) concerned.

Hiring and Human Resource Policies

In many cases, prevention starts with good human resources practices. That means that management should institute hiring policies aimed at recruiting people of good character. Background investigations should be conducted, especially for key positions that will have more than normal user network access.

The work environment should encourage high employee morale; in many cases, internal security breaches are committed as "revenge" by employees who feel underpaid, under-appreciated, or even mistreated. Employees who are enthusiastic about their jobs and feel valued by the organization will be much more likely to comply with company rules in general and network security policies in particular.

Another motivation for internal breaches is money. If your company engages in a highly competitive business, competitors could approach employees with lucrative offers for trade secrets or other confidential data. If you are in a field that is vulnerable to corporate espionage, your security policies should lean toward the *deny all access* model, in which access for a particular network user starts at nothing and access is added on the basis of the user's need to know.

SECURITY ALERT!

The "deny all access" policy model is one of two basic starting points in creating a security policy. The other is *allow all access,* in which all resources are open to a user unless there are specific reasons to deny access. Neither of these is "right" or "wrong," although the "deny all access" model is undisputedly more secure and the "allow all access" model is easier to implement. From which of these starting points you work depends on the *security philosophy* of your organization.

Detecting Internal Breaches

Implementing auditing will help you detect internal breaches of security by recording specified security events. You will be able to track when objects (such as files or folders) are accessed, what user account was used to access them, when users exercise user rights, and when users log on or off the computer or network. Modern network operating systems include built-in auditing functionality.

Auditing Security Events in Windows 2000

Like Windows NT, Windows 2000 provides for granular auditing of security-related events and records the information to a security log. The log can be viewed (by users with administrative privileges only) via the Windows Event Viewer.

Unlike Windows NT, Windows 2000 auditing is configured via *group policy*. Successful or failed access attempts, or both, can be audited. As shown in Figure 3.4, nine categories of events can be audited. Determining which categories of events to audit is the first step in setting audit policies. By default, no event categories are selected and no auditing takes place.

Figure 3.4 In Windows 2000, Audit Policies Are Configured via Group Policy Settings

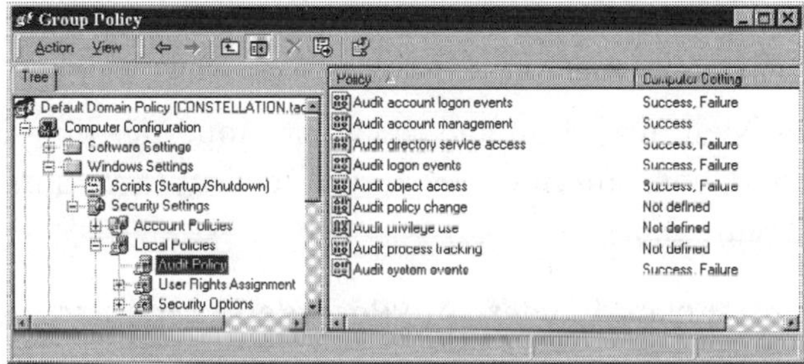

NOTE

You should audit only those events that are necessary to track to maintain your security policy. Auditing too many events (and access to too many objects) will have a negative impact on your computer's performance. Furthermore, many unnecessarily recorded events will make relevant events more difficult to find in the security log.

If you are auditing access to objects, you need to set auditing properties for the object to be audited. This is done in the object's Properties sheet using the Advanced button on the Security tab, as shown in Figure 3.5.

Figure 3.5 Auditing Set to Log Successful Attempts to Take Ownership of the Data Folder by Members of the Sales Group

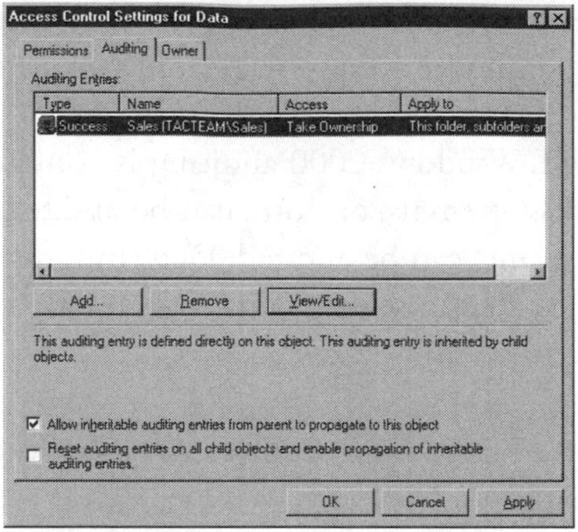

Viewing the Audit Log

Once auditing has been turned on and the audit properties have been set on objects to be audited, you can view a record of security events in the security log, as shown in Figure 3.6.

Figure 3.6 Security-Related Events Are Recorded in the Security Log, Displayed in Event Viewer

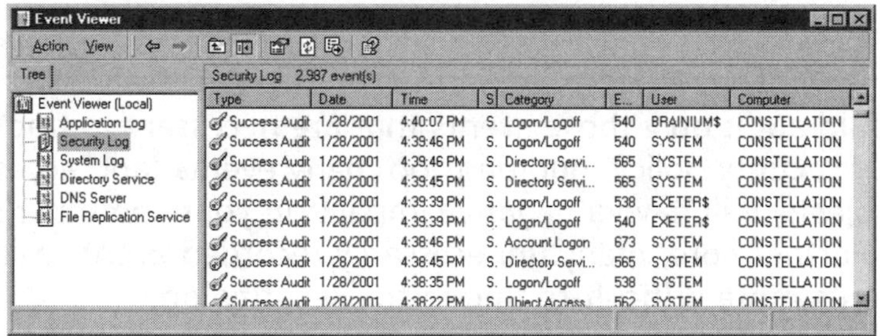

If you choose to audit many events or often-accessed objects, the security log can grow very large very quickly. You can set the security log's maximum size in kilobytes by configuring its Properties sheet in the Event Viewer (right-click Security Log and select Properties). You can also choose whether to overwrite previous events when the maximum size is reached or to require manual clearing of the log.

Preventing Intentional Internal Breaches

Firewalls are helpful in keeping basically compliant employees from accidentally (or out of ignorance of security considerations) visiting dangerous Web sites or sending specific types of packets outside the local network. However, firewalls are of more limited use in preventing intentional internal security breaches. Simply limiting user access to the external network cannot thwart insiders who are determined to destroy, modify, or copy your data. Because they have physical access, they can copy data to removable media or a portable computer (including tiny handheld machines) or perhaps even print it on paper and remove it from the premises that way. They could change the format of the data to disguise it, or they could upload files to Web-based data storage services.

In a high security environment, computers without floppy drives—or even completely diskless workstations—might be warranted. System or group policy can be applied to prevent users from installing software (such as that needed for a desktop computer to communicate with a Pocket PC or Palm Pilot). Cases can be locked; physical access to serial ports, USB ports, and other connection points can be covered so that removable media devices can't be attached.

Intentional internal breaches of security constitute a serious problem, and company policies should treat them as such.

Preventing Unauthorized External Intrusions and Attacks

External intrusions (or "hacking into the system") from outside the LAN have received a good deal of attention in the media and thus are the major concern of many companies when it comes to network security issues. In recent years, there have been a number of high-profile cases in which the Web servers of prominent organizations (such as Yahoo! and Microsoft) have been hacked. Attempts to penetrate sensitive government networks, such as the Pentagon's systems, occur on a regular basis. DDoS attacks—although not technically "intrusions" because only access to the system, not security of data, is affected—are still looked on as hacks by the media and the public, and these events make front-page news when they crash servers and prevent Internet users from accessing popular sites.

Psychological factors are involved as well. Internal breaches are usually seen by companies as personnel problems and are handled administratively. External breaches could seem more like a "violation" and are more often prosecuted in criminal actions. Because the external intruder could come from anywhere at any time, the sense of uncertainty and fear of the unknown could cause organizations to react in a much stronger way to this type of threat.

The good news about external intrusions is that the area(s) that must be controlled are much more focused. There are usually only a limited number of points of entry to the network from the outside. This is where a properly configured firewall can be invaluable, allowing authorized traffic into the network while keeping unauthorized traffic out. On the other hand, the popularity of firewalls ensures that dedicated hackers know how they work and spend a great deal of time and effort devising ways to defeat them.

Never depend on the firewall to provide 100-percent protection, even against outside intruders. Remember that in order to be effective, a security plan must be a multifaceted, multilayered one. We hope the firewall will keep intruders out of your network completely—but if they *do* get in, what is your contingency plan? How will you reduce the amount of damage they can do and protect your most sensitive or valuable data?

External Intruders with Internal Access

A special type of external intruder is the outsider who *physically* breaks into your facility to gain access to your network. Although not a true "insider" because he or she is not authorized to be there and does not have a valid account on the network, this person has many of the advantages of those discussed in the section on internal security breaches. Your security policy should take into account the threats posed by this "hybrid" type of intruder.

Tactical Planning

In dealing with network intruders, you should practice what police officers in defensive tactics training call *if/then thinking*. This means considering every possible outcome of a given situation and then asking yourself, "*If* this happens, *then* what could be done to protect us from the consequences?" The answers to these questions will form the basis of your security policy.

This tactic requires that you be able to plan your responses in detail, which means that you must think in specifics rather than generalities. Your security threat must be based in part on understanding the motivations of those initiating the attack and in part on the technical aspects of the type of attack that is initiated. In the next section, we discuss common intruder motivations and specific types of network attacks.

Recognizing Network Security Threats

In order to effectively protect your network, you must consider the following question: from *who* or *what* are you protecting it? In this section, we approach the answer to that question from two perspectives:

- **Who** Types of network intruders and their motivations
- **What** Types of network attacks and how they work

First we look at intruder motivations and classify the various types of people who have the skill and desire to hack into others' computers and networks.

Understanding Intruder Motivations

There are probably as many different specific motives as there are hackers, but we can break the most common intruder motivations into a few broad categories:

- **Recreation** Those who hack into networks "just for fun" or to prove their technical prowess; often young people or "antiestablishment" types.
- **Remuneration** People who invade the network for personal gain, such as those who attempt to transfer funds to their own bank accounts or erase records of their debts; "hackers for hire" who are paid by others to break into the network. Corporate espionage is included in this category.
- **Revenge** Dissatisfied customers, disgruntled former employees, angry competitors, or people who have a personal grudge against someone in the organization.

The scope of damage and extent of the intrusion is often—although by no means always—tied to the intruder's motivation.

Recreational Hackers

Teen hackers who hack primarily for the thrill of accomplishment often do little or no permanent damage, perhaps only leaving "I was here" messages to "stake their claims" and prove to their peers that they were able to penetrate your network's security.

There are more malevolent versions of the fun-seeking hacker, however. These are the cybervandals who get their kicks out of destroying as much of your data as possible or causing your systems to crash.

Profit-Motivated Hackers

Hackers who break into your network for remuneration of some kind—either directly or indirectly—are more dangerous. Because money is at stake, they are more motivated than other hackers to accomplish their objective. Furthermore, because many of them are "professionals" of a sort, their hacking techniques could be more sophisticated than those of the average teenage recreational hacker.

Monetary motivations include:

- Personal financial gain
- Third-party payment
- Corporate espionage

Those motivated by the last goal are almost always the most sophisticated and the most dangerous. Often *big* money is involved in theft of trade secrets. Corporate espionage agents could be employees who have been approached by your competitors and offered money or merchandise or even threatened with blackmail or physical harm.

In some instances, hackers working for competitors will go "undercover" and seek a job with your company in order to steal data that they can take back to their own organizations. To add insult to injury, these "stealth spies" are then paid by your company at the same time they're working against you to the benefit of your competitor.

There are also "professional" freelance corporate spies. They can be contacted and contracted to obtain your company secrets, or they might do it on their own and auction the data off to your competitors.

These corporate espionage agents are often highly skilled. They are technically savvy and intelligent enough to avoid being caught or detected. Fields that are especially vulnerable to the threat of corporate espionage include:

- Oil and energy
- Engineering
- Computer technology
- Research medicine
- Law

Any company that is on the verge of a breakthrough that could result in large monetary rewards or worldwide recognition, especially if the company's involvement is high profile, should be aware of the possibility of espionage and take steps to guard against it.

Vengeful Hackers

Hackers motivated by the desire for revenge are dangerous as well. Vengeance seeking is usually based on strong emotions, which means that these hackers could go all-out in their efforts to sabotage your network.

Examples of hackers or security saboteurs acting out of revenge include:

- Former employees who are bitter about being fired or laid off or who quit their jobs under unpleasant circumstances
- Current employees who feel mistreated by the company, especially those who are planning to leave soon
- Current employees who aim to sabotage the work of other employees due to internal political battles, rivalry over promotions, and the like
- Outsiders who have grudges against the company, such as dissatisfied customers or employees of competing companies who want to harm or embarrass the company
- Outsiders who have personal grudges against someone who works for the company, such as employees' former girlfriends or boyfriends, spouses going through a divorce, and other relationship-related problems

Luckily, the intruders in this category are generally less technically talented than those in the other two groups, and their emotional involvement could cause them to be careless and take outrageous chances, which makes them easier to catch.

Hybrid Hackers

Of course, the three categories of hacker can overlap in some cases. A recreational hacker who perceives himself as having been mistreated by an employer or in a personal relationship could use his otherwise benign hacking skills to impose "justice" for the wrongs done to him, or a vengeful ex-employee or ex-spouse might pay someone else to do the hacking.

It is beneficial to understand the common motivations of network intruders because, although we might not be able to predict which type of hacker will decide to attack our networks, we can recognize how each operates and take steps to protect our networks from all of them.

Even more important than the type of *hacker* in planning our security strategy, however, is the type of *attack*. In the next section, we examine specific types of network attacks and ways in which you can protect against them.

Classifying Specific Types of Attacks

The *attack type* refers to *how* an attacker gains entry to your computer or network and *what he does* once he has gained entry. In this section, we discuss some of the more common types of hack attacks, including:

- Social engineering attacks
- DoS attacks
- Scanning and spoofing
- Source routing and other protocol exploits
- Software and system exploits
- Trojans, viruses, and worms

When you have a basic understanding of how each type of attack works, you will be better armed to guard against them.

NOTE

In this chapter, we use the words *attacker, intruder,* or *hacker* to refer to a person who compromises the security of a network by gaining unauthorized access or who compromises the accessibility of a network by preventing authorized access.

Social Engineering Attacks

Unlike the other attack types, *social engineering* does not refer to a technological manipulation of computer hardware or software vulnerabilities and does not require much in the way of technical skills. Instead, this type of attack exploits *human* weaknesses—such as carelessness or the desire to be cooperative—to gain access to legitimate network credentials. The talents that are most useful to the intruder who relies on this technique are so-called "people skills," such as a charming or persuasive personality or a commanding, authoritative presence.

What Is Social Engineering?

Social engineering is defined as obtaining confidential information by means of human interaction (*Business Wire,* August 4, 1998). You can think of social engineering attackers as specialized con artists. They gain the trust of users (or even better, administrators) and then take advantage of the relationship to find out the user's account name and password, or they have the unsuspecting users log them on to the system. Because this type of attack is based on convincing a valid network user to "open the door," social engineering can successfully get an intruder into a network that is protected by high-security measures such as biometric scanners.

Social engineering is, in many cases, the easiest way to gain unauthorized access to a computer network. The social engineering competition at a Defcon annual hackers' convention in Las Vegas attracted hundreds of attendants eager to practice their manipulative techniques. Even hackers who are famous for their technical abilities know that *people* make up the biggest security vulnerability on most networks. Kevin Mitnick, convicted computer crimes felon and celebrity hacker extraordinaire, tells in his lectures how he used social engineering to gain access to systems during his hacking career.

NOTE

For more information on Mitnick's lectures, see "Mitnick Teaches Social Engineering," at www.zdnet.com/filters/printerfriendly/0,6061,2604480-2,00.html.

These "engineers" often pose as technical support personnel, either in-house or pretending to work for outside entities such as the telephone company, the Internet service provider, the network's hardware vendor, or even the government. They often contact their victims by phone, and they usually spin a complex and plausible tale of why they need the user to divulge his or her passwords or other information (such as the IP address of the user's machine or the computer name of the network's authentication server).

Protecting Your Network Against Social Engineers

Protecting against social engineering attacks is especially challenging. Adopting strongly worded policies that prohibit divulging passwords and other network information to anyone over the telephone and educating your users about the phenomenon are obvious steps you can take to reduce the likelihood of this type of security breach. Human nature being what it is, however, some users on every network will always be vulnerable to the social engineer's con game. A talented social engineer is a master at making users doubt their own doubts about his legitimacy.

The "wannabe" intruder could regale the user with woeful stories of the extra cost the company will incur if he spends extra time verifying his identity. He could pose as a member of the company's top management and take a stern approach, threatening the employee with disciplinary action or even loss of job if he doesn't get the user's cooperation. Or he might try to make the employee feel guilty by pretending to be a low-level employee who is just trying to do his job and who will be fired if he doesn't get access to the network and get the problem taken care of right away. A really good social engineer is patient and thorough. He will do his homework, and he will know enough about your company, or the organization he claims to represent, to be convincing.

Because social engineering is a human problem, not a technical problem, prevention must come primarily through education rather than technological solutions.

NOTE

For more information about social engineering and how to tell when someone is attempting to pull a social engineering scam, see the preview chapter "Everything You Wanted to Know about Social Engineering—But Were Afraid to Ask" at the Happy Hacker Web site, located at www.happyhacker.org/uberhacker/se.shtml.

Denial-of-Service Attacks

In February 2000, massive DoS attacks brought down several of the biggest Web sites, including Yahoo.com and Buy.com. DoS attacks are one of the most popular choices of Internet hackers who want to disrupt a network's operations. Although they do not destroy or steal data as some other types of attacks do, the objective of DoS attackers is to bring down the network, denying service to its legitimate users. DoS attacks are easy to initiate; software is readily available from hacker Web sites and *warez* newsgroups that will allow anyone to launch a DoS attack with little or no technical expertise.

NOTE

Warez is a term used by hackers and crackers to describe bootlegged software that has been "cracked" to remove copy protections and made available by software pirates on the Internet, or in its broader definition, to describe any illegally distributed software.

The purpose of a DoS attack is to render a network inaccessible by generating a type or amount of network traffic that will crash the servers, overwhelm the routers, or otherwise prevent the network's devices from functioning properly. Denial of service can be accomplished by tying up the server's resources—for example, by overwhelming the CPU and memory resources. In other cases, a particular user or machine can be the target of DoS attacks that hang up the client machine and require it to be rebooted.

NOTE

DoS attacks are sometimes referred to in the security community as *nuke attacks*.

Distributed Denial-of-Service Attack

Distributed DoS (DDoS) attacks use intermediary computers, called *agents,* on which programs called *zombies* have previously been surreptitiously installed. The hacker activates these zombie programs remotely, causing the intermediary computers (which can number in the hundreds or even thousands) to simultaneously launch the actual attack. Because the attack comes from the computers running the zombie programs, which could be on networks anywhere in the world, the hacker is able to conceal the true origin of the attack.

Examples of DDoS tools used by hackers are Tribe FloodNet (TFN), TFN2K, Trinoo, and Stacheldraht (German for *barbed wire*). Early versions of DDoS tools targeted UNIX and Solaris systems, but TFN2K can run on both UNIX and Windows systems.

Because DDoS attacks are so popular, many tools have been developed to help you detect, eliminate, and analyze DDoS software that might be installed on your network. The National Infrastructure Protection Center has recently announced one such tool to detect some types of DDoS programs on some systems. For more information, visit www.fbi.gov/nipc/trinoo.htm.

NOTE

An excellent article that provides details on how TFN, TFN2K, Trinoo, and Stacheldraht work is available on the NetworkMagazine.com Web site. You'll find the article, *Distributed Denial of Service Attacks,* at www.networkmagazine.com/article/NMG20000512S0041.

It is important to note that DDoS attacks pose a two-layer threat. Not only could your network be the target of a DoS attack that crashes your servers and prevents incoming and outgoing traffic, but your computers could be used as the "innocent middlemen" to launch a DoS attack against another network or site.

DNS DoS Attack

The *DNS DoS attack* exploits the difference in size between a DNS query and a DNS response, in which all the network's bandwidth is tied up by bogus DNS queries. The attacker uses the DNS servers as "amplifiers" to multiply the DNS traffic.

The attacker begins by sending small DNS queries to each DNS server, which contain the spoofed IP address of the intended victim (see "IP Spoofing" later in this chapter). The responses returned to the small queries are much larger in size, so if there are a large number of responses returned at the same time, the link will become congested and denial of service will take place.

One solution to this problem is for administrators to configure DNS servers to answer with a "refused" response, which is much smaller in size than a name resolution response, when they receive DNS queries from suspicious or unexpected sources.

NOTE

Detailed information on configuring DNS servers to prevent this problem is contained in the U.S. Department of Energy's Computer Incident Advisory Capability information bulletin J-063, available at www.ciac.org/ciac/bulletins/j-063.shtml.

SYN and LAND Attack

Synchronization request (SYN) attacks exploit the TCP "three-way handshake," the process by which a communications session is established between two computers. Because TCP (unlike UDP) is connection-oriented, a *session*, or direct one-to-one communication link, must be created prior to sending data. The client computer initiates the communication with the server (the computer that has the resources it wants to access).

The "handshake" includes the following steps:

1. The client machine sends a SYN segment.
2. The server sends an acknowledge (ACK) message and a SYN, which acknowledges the client machine's request that was sent in Step 1 and sends the client a synchronization request of its own. The client and server machines must synchronize each other's sequence numbers.
3. The client sends an ACK back to the server, acknowledging the server's request for synchronization. When the two machines have acknowledged each other's requests, the handshake has been successfully completed and a connection is established between the two computers. Figure 3.7 illustrates how the process works.

This is how the process normally works. A SYN attack uses this process to flood the system targeted as the victim of the attack with multiple SYN packets that have bad source IP addresses, which causes the system to respond with SYN/ACK messages. The problem comes in when the system, waiting for the ACK message from the client that normally comes in response to its SYN/ACK, puts the waiting SYN/ACK messages into a queue. This is a problem because the queue is limited in the number of messages it can handle. When the queue is full, all subsequent incoming SYN packets will be ignored. In order for a SYN/ACK to be removed from the queue, an ACK must be returned from the client or an interval timer must run out and terminate the three-way handshake process.

Figure 3.7 TCP Uses a "Three-Way Handshake" to Establish a Connection between Client and Server

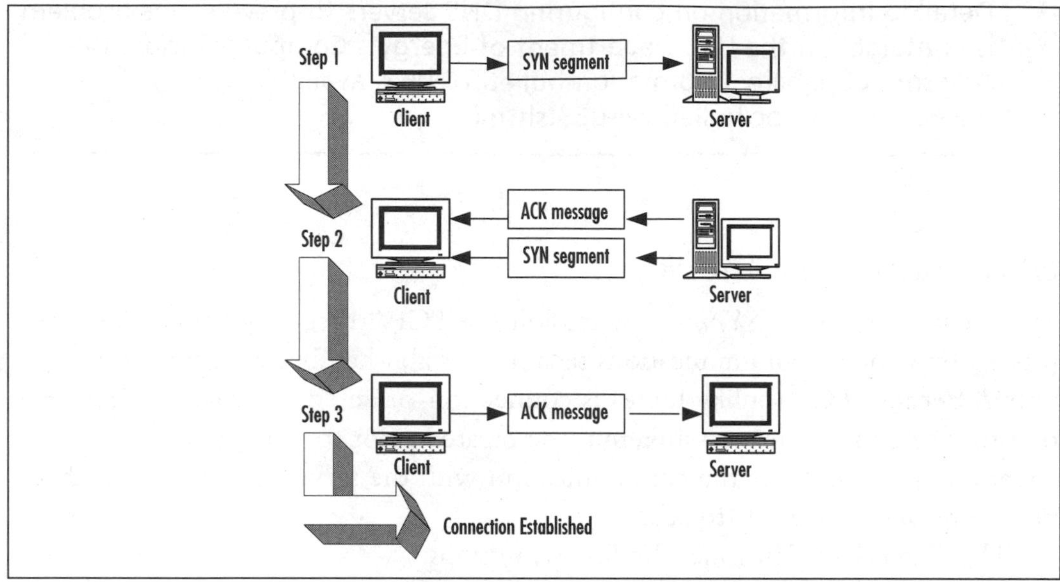

Because the source IP addresses for the SYN packets sent by the attacker are no good, the ACKs for which the server is waiting never come. The queue stays full, and there is no room for valid SYN requests to be processed. Thus service is denied to legitimate clients attempting to establish communications with the server.

The LAND attack is a variation on the SYN attack. In the LAND attack, instead of sending SYN packets with IP addresses that do not exist, the flood of SYN packets all have the same spoof IP address—that of the targeted computer.

The LAND attack can be prevented by filtering out incoming packets for which source IP addresses appear to be from computers on the internal network. ISA Server has preset intrusion detection functionality that allows you to detect attempted LAND attacks, and you can configure alerts to notify you when such an attack is detected.

Ping of Death

Another type of DoS attack that ISA Server can be set to specifically detect is the so-called *ping of death* (also known as the *large packet ping*). The ping-of-death attack is launched by creating an IP packet (sometimes referred to as a *killer packet*) larger than 65,536 bytes, which is the maximum allowed by the IP specification. This can cause the target system to crash, hang, or reboot. ISA allows you to specifically enable detection of ping-of-death attacks.

Teardrop

The *teardrop attack* works a little differently from the ping of death but with similar results. The teardrop program creates IP fragments, which are pieces of an IP packet into which an original packet can be divided as it travels through the Internet. The problem is that the offset fields on these fragments, which are supposed to indicate the portion (in bytes) of the original packet that is contained in the fragment, overlap.

For example, normally two fragments' offset fields might appear as shown here:

```
Fragment 1:   (offset) 100 - 300
Fragment 2:   (offset) 301 - 600
```

This indicates that the first fragment contains bytes 100 through 300 of the original packet, and the second fragment contains bytes 301 through 600.

Overlapping offset fields would appear something like this:

```
Fragment 1: (offset) 100 - 300
Fragment 2: (offset) 200 - 400
```

When the destination computer tries to reassemble these packets, it is unable to do so and could crash, hang, or reboot.

Variations on the teardrop include:

- NewTear
- Teardrop2
- SynDrop
- Boink

All these programs generate some sort of fragment overlap.

Ping or ICMP Flood

The *ping flood* or *ICMP flood* is a means of tying up a specific client machine. It is caused by an attacker sending a large number of ping packets (ICMP echo request packets) to the Winsock or dialer software. This action prevents the software from responding to server ping activity requests, which causes the server to eventually time out the connection. A symptom of a ping flood is a huge amount of modem activity, as indicated by the modem lights. This attack is also referred to as a *ping storm*.

The *fraggle attack* is related to the ping storm. Using a spoofed IP address (which is the address of the targeted victim), an attacker sends ping packets to a subnet, causing all computers on the subnet to respond to the spoofed address and flood it with echo reply messages.

NOTE

During the Kosovo crisis in Eastern Europe, the fraggle attack was frequently used by pro-Serbian hackers against U.S. and NATO sites to overload and bring down their networks.

You can use programs such as NetXray or other IP tracing software to record and display a log of the flood packets. Firewalls can be configured to block ping packets and prevent these attacks.

Smurf Attack

The *Smurf attack* is a form of "brute force" attack that uses the same method as the ping flood but that directs the flood of ICMP echo request packets at the network's router. The destination address of the ping packets is the broadcast address of the network, which causes the router to broadcast the packet to every computer on the network or segment. This can result in a very large amount of network traffic if there are many host computers, creating congestion that causes a denial of service to legitimate users.

NOTE

The broadcast address is normally represented by all 1s in the host ID. This means, for example, that on class C network 192.168.1.0, the broadcast address is 192.168.1.255 (255 in decimal represents 11111111 in binary), and in a class C network, the last or z octet represents the host ID. A message sent to the broadcast address is sent simultaneously to all hosts on the network.

In its most insidious form, the Smurf attack spoofs the source IP address of ping packet. Then both the network to which the packets are sent *and* the network of the spoofed source IP address become overwhelmed with traffic. The network to which the spoofed source address belongs is deluged with responses to the ping when all the hosts to which the ping was sent answer the echo request with an echo reply.

Smurf attacks can generally do more damage than some other forms of DoS, such as SYN floods. The SYN flood affects only the ability of other computers to establish a TCP connection to the flooded server, but a Smurf attack can bring an entire ISP down for minutes or hours. This is because a single attacker can easily send 40 to 50 ping packets per second, even using a slow modem connection. Because each packet is broadcast to every computer on the destination network, the number of responses per second is 40 to 50 times the number of computers on the network, which could be hundreds or thousands. This is enough data to congest even a T-1 link.

One way to prevent a Smurf attack from using your network as the broadcast target is to turn off the capability to transmit broadcast traffic on the router. Most routers allow you to turn off this option. To prevent your network from being the victim of the spoofed IP address, you need to configure your firewall to filter out incoming ping packets.

UNDOCUMENTED ISA

ISA Server filters ping packets on the external interface by default, returning a "request timed out" message if you attempt to ping the external interface.

UDP Bomb or Flood

An attacker can use the User Datagram Protocol (UDP) and one of several services that echo packets on receipt to create service-denying network congestion by generating a flood of UDP packets between two target systems. For example, the UDP chargen service on the first computer, which is a testing tool that generates a series of characters for every packet that it receives, sends packets to another system's UDP echo service, which echoes every character it receives. By exploiting these testing tools, an endless flow of echoes goes back and forth between the two systems, congesting the network. This is sometimes called a *UDP packet storm*.

In addition to port 7, the echo port, an attacker can use port 17, the quote-of-the-day service (quotd), or the daytime service on port 13. These services also echo packets they receive. UDP chargen is on port 19.

Disabling unnecessary UDP services on each computer (especially those mentioned) or using a firewall to filter those ports and services will protect you from this type of attack.

UDP Snork Attack

The *snork attack* is similar to the UDP bomb. It uses a UDP frame that has a source port of either 7 (echo) or 9 (chargen), with a destination port of 135 (Microsoft location service). The result is the same as that of the UDP bomb: a flood of unnecessary transmissions that can slow performance or crash the systems that are involved.

WinNuke: Windows Out-of-Band Attack

The *out-of-band (OOB) attack* is one that exploits a vulnerability in Microsoft networks, which is sometimes called the *Windows OOB bug*. The WinNuke program (and variations such as Sinnerz and Muerte) creates an OOB data transmission that crashes the machine to which it is sent. It works like this: A TCP/IP connection is established with the target IP address, using port 139 (the NetBIOS port). Then the program sends data using a flag called MSG_OOB (or Urgent) in the packet header. This flag instructs the computer's Winsock to send data called out-of-band data. On receipt, the targeted Windows server expects a pointer to the position in the packet where the Urgent data ends, with normal data following, but the OOB pointer in the packet created by WinNuke points to the end of the frame with no data following.

The Windows machine does not know how to handle this situation and will cease communicating on the network, and service will be denied to any users who subsequently attempt to communicate with it. A WinNuke attack usually requires a reboot of the affected system to reestablish network communications.

Windows 95 and NT 3.51 and 4.0 are vulnerable to WinNuke unless the fixes provided by Microsoft have been installed. Microsoft often releases these patches both as individual "hotfixes" and incorporated into subsequent service packs (for example, Windows NT 4.0's SP4 included the fix for the WinNuke exploit). Windows 98/ME and Windows 2000 are not vulnerable to WinNuke, but ISA Server allows you to enable detection of attempted OOB attacks.

Mail Bomb Attack

A *mail bomb* is a means of overwhelming a mail server, causing it to stop functioning and thus denying service to users. This is a relatively simple form of attack, accomplished by sending a massive quantity of e-mail to a specific user or system. Programs available on hacking sites on the Internet allow a user to easily launch a mail bomb attack, automatically sending floods of e-mail to a specified address while protecting the attacker's identity.

A variation on the mail bomb program automatically subscribes a targeted user to hundreds or thousands of high-volume Internet mailing lists, subsequently filling the user's mailbox and/or the mail server. Bombers call this attack *list linking.* Examples of these mail bomb programs include Unabomber, Extreme Mail, Avalanche, and Kaboom.

The solution to repeated mail bomb attacks is to block traffic from the originating network using packet filters. Unfortunately, this solution does not work with list linking, because the originator's address is obscured; the deluge of traffic comes from the mailing lists to which the victim has been subscribed.

Scanning and Spoofing

The term *scanner,* in the context of network security, refers to a software program that hackers use to remotely determine the TCP/UDP ports that are open on a given system and thus vulnerable to attack. Scanners are also used by administrators to detect vulnerabilities in their own systems in order to correct them before an intruder finds them. Network diagnostic tools such as the famous Security Administrator's Tool for Analyzing Networks (SATAN), a UNIX utility, include sophisticated port-scanning capabilities.

A good scanning program can locate a target computer on the Internet (one that is vulnerable to attack), determine the TCP/IP services running on the machine, and probe those services for security weaknesses.

NOTE

A common saying among hackers is, "A good port scanner is worth a thousand passwords."

Many scanning programs are available as freeware on the Internet. You can find an excellent resource for information about the history of scanning, how scanners work, and some popular scanning programs at www.ladysharrow.ndirect.co.uk/Maximum%20Security/scanners.htm.

Port Scanning

Port scanning refers to a means of locating "listening" TCP or UDP ports on a computer or router and obtaining as much information as possible about the device from the listening ports. TCP and UDP services and applications use a number of *well-known ports*, which are widely published. The hacker uses his knowledge of these commonly used ports to extrapolate information.

For example, Telnet normally uses port 23. If the hacker finds that port open and listening, he knows that Telnet is probably enabled on the machine. He can then try to infiltrate the system by, for example, guessing the appropriate password in a brute force attack.

There are a total of 65,535 TCP ports (and the same number of UDP ports); they are used for various services and applications. If a port is open, it responds when another computer attempts to contact it over the network. Port-scanning programs such as Nmap are used to determine which ports are open on a particular machine. The program sends packets for a wide variety of protocols and, by examining which messages receive responses and which don't, creates a map of the computer's listening ports.

Port scanning in itself does no harm to your network or system, but it provides hackers with information they can use to penetrate a network. Potential attackers use port scans in much the same way that a car thief might try the doors of parked vehicles to determine which ones are unlocked. Although this activity does not, in itself, constitute a serious offense, what the person conducting the scan does with the information can present a big problem.

NOTE

The intrusion and attack reporting center at www.doshelp.com/PC/trojanports.htm is an excellent resource for information on ports that should be closed, filtered, or monitored because they are commonly used for Trojan and intrusion programs.

IP Half-Scan Attack

Half scans (also called *half-open scans* or *FIN scans*) attempt to avoid detection by sending only initial or final packets rather than establishing a connection. A half scan starts the SYN/ACK process with a targeted computer but does not complete it. Software that conducts half scans, such as Jakal, is called a *stealth scanner.*

Configuring & Implementing...

Back to Basics: TCP/UDP Well-Known Ports

The official well-known port assignments are documented in RFC 1700, available on the Web at www.freesoft.org/CIE/RFC/1700/index.htm. The port assignments are made by the Internet Assigned Numbers Authority (IANA). In general, a service uses the same port number with UDP as with TCP, although there are some exceptions. The assigned ports were originally numbered from 0–255, but the numbers were later expanded to 0–1023.

Some of the most used well-known ports are:

- TCP/UDP port 20: FTP (data)
- TCP/UDP port 21: FTP (control)
- TCP/UDP port23: Telnet
- TCP/UDP port 25: SMTP
- TCP/UDP port 53: DNS
- TCP/UDP port 67: BOOTP server
- TCP/UDP port 68: BOOTP client
- TCP/UDP port 69: TFTP
- TCP/UDP port 80: HTTP
- TCP/UDP port 88: Kerberos
- TCP/UDP port 110: POP3
- TCP/UDP port 119: NNTP
- TCP/UDP port 137: NetBIOS name service
- TCP/UDP port 138: NetBIOS datagram service
- TCP/UDP port 139: NetBIOS session service
- TCP/UDP port 194: IRC
- TCP/UDP port 220: IMAPv3
- TCP/UDP port 389: LDAP

Ports 1024 to 65,535 are called *registered ports;* these numbers are not controlled by IANA and can be used by user processes or applications. However, that does not mean that they, too, are not vulnerable to attack. For example, port 1433 is used by SQL, which might be of interest to hackers.

Many port-scanning detectors are unable to detect half scans. ISA Server lists the IP half-scan option as part of its intrusion detection. However, Microsoft states in the Readme.htm file in the root directory of the ISA Server CD that the IP half-scan detection does not function as described in the ISA Server Help files. In fact, the IP half-scan alert actually notifies that an attempt was made to send TCP packets with invalid flags.

IP Spoofing

IP spoofing involves changing the packet headers of a message to indicate that it came from an IP address other than the true source. The spoofed address is normally a trusted port, which allows a hacker to get a message through a firewall or router that would otherwise be filtered out. Modern firewalls protect against IP spoofing.

Spoofing is used whenever it is beneficial for one machine to impersonate another. It is often used in combination with one of the other types of attacks. For example, a spoofed address is used in the SYN flood attack to create a "half-open" connection, in which the client never responds to the SYN/ACK message because the spoofed address is that of a computer that is down or doesn't exist. Spoofing is also used to hide the true IP address of the attacker in ping of death, teardrop, and other attacks.

IP spoofing can be prevented using source address verification on your router, if it is supported.

Source-Routing Attack

TCP/IP supports *source routing,* which is a means to permit the sender of network data to route the packets through a specific point on the network. There are two types of source routing:

- **Strict source routing** The sender of the data can specify the exact route (rarely used).
- **Loose source record route (LSRR)** The sender can specify certain routers (hops) through which the packet must pass.

The source route is option in the IP header that allows the sender to override routing decisions that are normally made by the routers between the source and destination machines. Source routing is used by network administrators to map the network or to troubleshoot routing and communications problems. It can also be used to force traffic through a route that will provide the best performance. Unfortunately, source routing can also be exploited by hackers.

If the system allows source routing, an intruder can use it to reach private internal addresses on the LAN that normally would not be reachable from the Internet, by routing the traffic through another machine that is reachable from both the Internet and the internal machine. Source routing can be disabled on most routers to prevent this type of attack.

Other Protocol Exploits

The attacks we have discussed so far involve exploiting some feature or weakness of the TCP/IP protocols. Hackers can also exploit vulnerabilities of other common protocols, such as HTTP, DNS, Common Gateway Interface (CGI), and other common protocols.

Active-X controls, JavaScript, and VBScript can be used to add animations or applets to Web sites, or even to HTML e-mail messages, but hackers can exploit these to write controls or scripts that allow them to remotely plant viruses, access data, or change or delete files on the hard disks of unaware users who visit the page and run the script. Both Web browsers and e-mail client programs that support HTML mail are vulnerable.

System and Software Exploits

System and software exploits allow hackers to take advantage of weaknesses of particular operating systems and applications (often called *bugs*). Like protocol exploits, they are used by intruders to gain unauthorized access to computers or networks or to crash or clog up the systems to deny service to others.

Common "bugs" can be categorized as follows:

- **Buffer overflows** Many common security holes are based on buffer overflow problems. Buffer overflows occur when the number of bytes or characters input exceeds the maximum number allowed by the programmer in writing the program.
- **Unexpected input** Programmers might not take steps to define what happens if invalid input (input that doesn't match program specifications) is entered. Such input could cause the program to crash or open up a way into the system.
- **System configuration bugs** These are not really "bugs" per se; rather, they are ways of configuring the operating system or software that leaves it vulnerable to penetration.

Popular software such as Microsoft's Internet Information Server (IIS), Internet Explorer (MSIE), and Outlook Express (MSOE) are frequent targets of hackers looking for software security holes that can be exploited.

Major operating system and software vendors regularly release security patches to fix exploitable bugs. It is very important for network administrators to stay up to date in applying these fixes and/or service packs to ensure that their systems are as secure as possible.

SECURITY ALERT!

Microsoft issues *security bulletins* and makes security patches available as part of TechNet. See the Web site at www.microsoft.com/technet/security/default.asp.

Trojans, Viruses, and Worms

Intruders who access your systems without authorization or inside attackers with malicious motives could plant various types of programs to cause damage to your network. There are three broad categories of *malicious code*:

- Trojans
- Viruses
- Worms

Let's take a brief look at each of these attack types.

Trojans

The name, short for *Trojan horse*, refers to a software program that appears to perform a useful function but in fact performs actions that the program user did not intend or was not aware of. Trojan horses are often written by hackers to circumvent the security of a system. Once the Trojan is installed, the hacker can exploit the security holes it creates to gain unauthorized access, or the Trojan program could perform some action such as:

- Deleting or modifying files
- Transmitting files across the network to the intruder
- Installing other programs or viruses

Basically, the Trojan can perform any action that the user has privileges and permissions to perform on the system. This means that a Trojan is especially dangerous if the unsuspecting user who installs it is an administrator and has access to the system files.

Trojans can be very cleverly disguised as innocuous programs, utilities, screensavers, or the like. A Trojan can also be installed by an executable script (JavaScript, a Java applet, Active-X control, etc.) on a Web site. Accessing the site can initiate the installation of the program if the Web browser is configured to allow scripts to run automatically.

Viruses

Viruses include any programs that are usually installed without the user's awareness and perform undesired actions (often harmful, although sometimes merely annoying). Viruses can also replicate themselves, infecting other systems by writing themselves to any floppy disk that is used in the computer or sending themselves across the network. Viruses are often distributed as attachments to e-mail or as macros in word processing documents. Some viruses activate immediately on installation; others lie dormant until a specific date or time or when a particular system event triggers them.

Viruses come in thousands of varieties. They can do anything from popping up a message that says "Hi!" to erasing the computer's entire hard disk. The proliferation of computer viruses has also led to the phenomenon of the *virus hoax,* which is a warning—generally circulated via e-mail or Web sites—about a virus that does not exist or that does not do what the warning claims it will do.

Real viruses, however, present a real threat to your network. Companies such as Symantec and McAfee make antivirus software that is aimed at detecting and removing virus programs. Because new viruses are created daily, it is important to download new *virus definition files,* which contain information required to detect each virus type, on a regular basis to ensure that your virus protection stays up to date.

Worms

A *worm* is a program that can travel across the network from one computer to another. Sometimes different parts of a worm run on different computers. Worms make multiple copies of themselves and spread throughout a network. The distinction between viruses and worms has become blurred. Originally the term *worm* was used to describe code that attacked multiuser systems (networks) and *virus* was used to describe programs that replicated on individual computers.

The primary purpose of the worm is to replicate. These programs were initially used for legitimate purposes in performing network management duties, but their ability to multiply quickly has been exploited by hackers who create malicious worms that replicate wildly and might also exploit operating system weaknesses and perform other harmful actions.

Categorizing Security Solutions

A multilayer security plan incorporates multiple security solutions. Security is not a "one size fits all" issue, so the options that work best for one organization are not necessarily the best choices for another. Security solutions can be generally broken down into two categories: hardware solutions and software solutions.

Hardware Security Solutions

Hardware security solutions come in the form of network devices. Firewalls, routers, even switches can function to provide a certain level of security. In general, these devices are dedicated computers themselves, running proprietary software.

Hardware-Based Firewalls

Packet filtering is the basis of the typical firewall. The functions performed by packet filters are similar to those performed by routers, and the languages used to program them are often based on router interface-type rule sets. Many firewall vendors provide hardware-based solutions. Some of the most popular hardware firewalls include the Cisco PIX firewall, SonicWall, the Webramp 1700, the Firebox from WatchGuard Technologies, and the OfficeConnect firewalls from 3COM.

Hardware solutions are available for networks of all sizes. For example, the 3Com products focus on small business and home office users, while the Cisco PIX comes in configurations that support up to 250,000 connections.

Hardware-based firewalls are often referred to as *firewall appliances.* A disadvantage of hardware-based firewalls is the proprietary nature of the software they run. Another disadvantage of many of these products, such as Cisco's highly respected PIX, is the high cost.

Other Hardware Security Devices

Other hardware-based components of your network security plan could include devices that provide extra security for authentication, such as:

- Smart card readers
- Fingerprint scanners
- Retinal scanners
- Voice analysis devices

These devices can be used in environments that require a high level of security for secure and reliable network authentication. Microsoft has acquired Biometric API (BAPI) technology from I/O Software and plans to incorporate support for biometric authentication devices into future versions of its operating systems. Windows 2000 already supports smart card authentication.

Software Security Solutions

Software security solutions cover a much broader range than hardware solutions. They include the security features built into network operating systems as well as additional security software made by Microsoft or third-party vendors.

Windows 2000 Security Features

Windows 2000 incorporates many new security features, any or all of which can be part of your overall network security plan. For example:

- Kerberos authentication
- Certificate services
- Encrypting File System (EFS)
- IP Security (IPSec)

Security Software

Microsoft and other vendors provide a wide range of security-related software programs. Software-based firewalls provide the same sort of functionality as hardware-based solutions but often at a lower price. Additionally, software-based firewalls run on familiar operating systems with easy-to-navigate user interfaces.

Firewall application programs such as ISA Server provide a great many security features. In addition to packet, circuit, and application filtering, ISA supports such features as SSL tunneling and bridging, which are discussed in the last section of this chapter, "Incorporating ISA Server into your Security Plan."

Designing a Comprehensive Security Plan

Now that you have some understanding of basic security concepts and terminology, general security objectives, common motivation of network intruders, various types of specific attacks and how they are used, and an overview of available hardware and software solutions, you can begin to design a comprehensive security policy for your organization.

A widely accepted method for developing your network security plan is laid out in RFC 2196, *Site Security Handbook,* and attributed to Fites, et al (1989). It consists of the following steps:

- Identify what you are trying to protect.
- Determine what you are trying to protect it from.
- Determine how likely the anticipated threats are.
- Implement measures that will protect your assets in a cost-effective manner.
- Review the process continually and make improvements each time a weakness is discovered.

NOTE

The entire text of RFC 2196, which provides many excellent suggestions that focus primarily on the implementation phase, can be found on the Web at www.faqs.org/rfcs/rfc2196.html.

It is important to understand that a security *plan* is not the same thing as a security *policy,* although the two words are sometimes used interchangeably. Your security policies (and there are likely to be many of them) grow out of your security plan. Think of policy as "law" or "rules," whereas the security plan is procedural; it lays out *how* the rules will be implemented.

Your security plan will generally address three different aspects of protecting your network:

- **Prevention** The measures that are implemented to keep your information from being modified, destroyed, or compromised.

- **Detection** The measures that are implemented to recognize when a security breach has occurred or has been attempted, and if possible, the origin of the breach.
- **Reaction** The measures that are implemented to recover from a security breach, to recover lost or altered data, to restore system or network operations, and to prevent future occurrences.

These can be divided into two types of actions: *proactive* and *reactive*. The first, prevention, is proactive because it takes place *before* any breach has occurred and involves actions that will, if successful, make further actions unnecessary. Unfortunately, our proactive measures don't always work. Reactive measures such as detection and reaction do, however, help us develop additional proactive measures that will prevent future intrusions.

Regardless of how good your prevention and detection methods, it is essential that you have in place a reaction plan in case attackers do get through your line of defense and damage your data or disrupt your network operations. As the old saying goes, "Hope for the best, and plan for the worst."

SECURITY ALERT!

For a concise commentary that is useful to keep in mind during security planning, see the Ten Immutable Laws of Security Administration on Microsoft's TechNet Web site at www.microsoft.com/technet/security/10salaws.asp.

Evaluating Security Needs

Before you can develop a security plan and policies for your organization, you must assess the security needs, which will generally be based on the following broad considerations:

- Type of business in which the organization engages
- Type of data that is stored on the network
- Type of connection(s) of the network to other networks
- Philosophy of the organization's management

Each of these factors will play a part in determining the level of security that is desirable or necessary for your network.

Assessing the Type of Business

Certain fields have inherently high security requirements. An obvious example is the military or other government agencies that deal with defense or national security issues. Private companies with government defense contracts also fall into this category. Others might be less obvious:

- Law firms, bound by law and ethics to protect client confidentiality
- Medical offices must protect patient records and confidentiality
- Law enforcement agencies, courts, and other governmental bodies
- Educational institutions that have student records stored on their networks
- Any company that gathers information from individuals or organizations under guarantee that the data will be kept confidential

The competitive nature of a business is also a consideration. In a field such as biogenetic research, which is a "hot" market in which new developments—any of which could involve huge profits for the company that patents the idea—occur on a daily basis, protecting trade secrets becomes vitally important.

Most businesses have *some* data of a confidential nature on the network's computer systems, but the security requirements in some fields are much higher than in others. The confidentiality needs of the business should be considered as you begin to develop your security plan.

Assessing the Type of Data

The second question to consider involves the type of data stored on your network and where it is stored. You could find that a higher level of security is needed in one department or division than another. You might, in fact, want to divide the network physically, into separate subnets, to allow better control of access to various parts of the company network independently.

Generally, payroll and human resource records (personnel files, insurance claim documents, and the like), company financial records (accounting documents, financial statements, tax documents), and a variety of other common business records need to be protected. Even in cases in which these documents are required to be made public, you will want to take steps to ensure that they can't be modified or destroyed. Remember that *data integrity* as well as *data confidentiality* are protected by a good security plan.

Assessing the Network Connections

Your network's exposure to outside intruders is another consideration in planning how security will be implemented on your network. A LAN that is self-contained and has no Internet connectivity nor any modems or other outside connections does not require the degree of protection (other than physical security) that is necessary when an intruder can take many avenues "in."

Dial-up modem connections merit special consideration. A dial-up connection is less open to intrusion than a full-time dedicated connection—both because it is connected to the outside for a shorter time period, reducing the window of opportunity for intrusion, and because it usually has a dynamic IP address, making it harder for an intruder to locate it on multiple occasions. This allows workstations on your network to have modems and phone lines can create a huge security risk.

If improperly configured, a computer with a dial-up connection to the Internet that is also cabled to the internal network can act as a router, allowing outside intruders to access not only the workstation connected to the modem but other computers on the LAN as well.

One reason for allowing modems at individual workstations is to allow users to dial up connections to other private networks. A more secure way to do this is to remove the modems and have the users establish a VPN connection with the other private network through the LAN's Internet connection.

The best security policy is to have as few connections from the internal network to the outside as possible and control access at those entry points (collectively called the *network perimeter*).

Assessing Management Philosophy

This last criterion is the most subjective but can have a tremendous influence on the security level that is appropriate for your organization. Most companies are based on one (or a combination of more than one) management model.

Understanding Management Models

Some companies institute a highly structured, formal management style. Employees are expected to respect a strict chain of command, and information is generally disseminated on a "need to know" basis. Governmental agencies, especially those that are law enforcement-related such as police departments and investigative agencies, often follow this philosophy. This model is sometimes referred to as the *paramilitary model*.

Other companies, particularly those in the IT industry and other fields that are subject to little state regulation, are built on the opposite premise: that all employees should have as much information and input as possible, that managers should function as "team leaders" rather than authoritarian supervisors, and that restrictions on employee actions should be imposed only when necessary for the efficiency and productivity of the organization. This is sometimes called the *one big happy family model.* Creativity is valued more than "going by the book," and job satisfaction is considered an important aspect of enhancing employee performance and productivity.

In business management circles, these two diametrically opposed models are called *Theory X* (traditional paramilitary style) and *Theory Y* (the modern, team-oriented approach). Although numerous other management models such as management by objective (MBO) and total quality management (TQM) have been popularized in recent years, each company's management style falls somewhere on the continuum between Theory X and Theory Y. The management model is based on the personal philosophies of the company's top decision makers regarding the relationship between management and employees.

An organization's management model can have a profound influence on what is or isn't acceptable in planning security for the network. A "deny all access" security policy that is viewed as appropriate in a Theory X organization could meet with so much resentment and employee dissatisfaction in a Theory Y company that it disrupts business operations. Always consider the company "atmosphere" as part of your security planning. If you have good reasons to implement strict security in a Theory Y atmosphere, realize that you will probably have to justify the restrictions to management and "sell" them to employees, whereas those same restrictions might be accepted without question in a more traditional organization.

Understanding Security Ratings

Security ratings could be of interest as you develop your company's security policy, although they are not likely to be important unless your organization works under government contract, requiring a specified level of security.

The U.S. government provides specifications for rating network security implementations in a publication often referred to as the *Orange Book,* formally called the *Department of Defense Trusted Computer System Evaluation Criteria,* or *TCSEC.* The *Red Book,* or *Trusted Network Interpretation of the TCSEC (TNI),* explains how the TCSEC evaluation criteria are applied to computer networks.

Other countries have security rating systems that work in a similar way. For example:

- CTPEC (Canada)
- AISEP (Australia)
- ITSEC (Western Europe)

To obtain a government contract in the United States, companies are often required to obtain a C2 rating. A C2 rating has several requirements:

- The operating system in use must be capable of tracking access to data, including both who accessed it and when it was accessed (as is done by the auditing function of Windows NT/2000).
- The users' access to objects must be subject to control (access permissions).
- Users must be uniquely identified on the system (via user account names and passwords).
- Security-related events must be trackable and permanently recorded for auditing (audit log).

In order to receive certification, a company must implement these requirements in particular ways. If your organization needs C2 rating for its systems, you should consult the National Computer Security Center (NCSC) publications to ensure that they meet all the requirements.

SECURITY ALERT!

The Department of Defense (DoD) Trusted Computer System Evaluation Criteria (the *Orange Book*) can be accessed online at www.radium.ncsc.mil/tpep/library/rainbow/5200.28-STD.html.

Legal Considerations

Another important step in preparing to design your network security plan is to consider legal aspects that could affect your network. It is a good idea to have a member of your company's legal department who specializes in computer law be involved in the development of your security plan and policies. If this is not possible, the written policies should be submitted for legal review before you put them into practice.

Designating Responsibility for Network Security

In any undertaking as complex as the development and implementation of a comprehensive corporate security plan and accompanying policies, it is vital that areas of responsibility be clearly designated.

Best practices dictate that no one person should have complete authority or control. Besides, in an enterprise-level network, it would be difficult for any single person to handle all facets of developing and implementing the security plan.

Responsibility for Developing the Security Plan and Policies

The initial creation of a good security plan requires a great deal of thought and effort. The policy will impact employees at all levels of the organization, and you should solicit input from as many representatives of different departments and job descriptions as is practical. An effective approach is to form a committee consisting of people from several areas of the organization to be involved in creating and reviewing the security plan and policies.

Your security planning committee might include some or all of the following:

- The network administrator and one or more assistant administrators
- The site's security administrator
- Heads of various company departments or their representatives
- Representatives of user groups that will be impacted by the security policies (for example, the secretarial staff, the data processing center, etc.)
- A member of the legal department who specializes in computer and technology law
- A member of the finance or budget department

Responsibility for Implementing and Enforcing the Security Plan and Policies

Security policies are generally implemented and enforced by network administrators and members of the IT staff. Job descriptions and policies should designate exactly who is responsible for the implementation of which parts of the plan. A clear-cut chain of command should specify whose decision prevails in case of conflict.

In some cases—such as physical penetration of the network—the company security staff will become involved. There should be written, clearly formulated policies that stipulate which department has responsibility for particular tasks in such situations.

The security plan should also address the procedures for reporting security breaches, both internally and if the police or other outside agencies are to be brought in (as well as who is responsible for or has the authority to call in outside agents).

One of the most important factors in a good security policy is that it must be enforceable. If the policy can be enforced through security tools, this method is preferred. If the policies must be enforced through reprimand or other actions against employees who violate them, there should be clearly worded, universally distributed written documentation indicating what constitutes a violation and the sanctions that will result, as well as who is responsible for imposing such sanctions.

Designing the Corporate Security Policy

The process of designing a good corporate network security policy will differ from organization to organization. However, common elements should be addressed, including (but not limited to) the following:

- Developing an effective password and authentication policy.
- Developing a privacy policy that sets forth reasonable expectations of privacy as to employees' e-mail, monitoring access to Web sites, access to users' directories and files, and so forth.
- Developing an accountability policy that defines responsibility in regard to security issues, including policies regarding users' obligation to report security violations and the process for doing so.
- A network use statement that defines users' responsibilities in regard to accessing network resources, protecting password confidentiality, reporting problems, and expectations as to availability of network resources.
- A disaster protection and recovery policy that specifies policies for fault tolerance, scheduling data backups and storing backed-up data, fail-over plans for critical systems, and other related matters.

It is beyond the scope of this chapter to provide detailed examples of all these elements. We do, however, address the first issue: how to go about developing an effective password policy and some of the factors that should be considered. The other policy areas should be addressed in similar depth and detail in your plan.

Developing an Effective Password Policy

In the networking world, passwords (in combination with user account names) are normally the "keys to the kingdom" that provide access to network resources and data. It might seem simplistic to say that your comprehensive security plan should include an effective password policy, but it is a basic component that is more difficult to implement than it might appear at first glance.

In order to be effective, your password policy must require users to select passwords that are difficult to "crack" yet easy for them to remember so that they don't commit the common security breach of writing the password on a sticky note that will end up stuck to the monitor or sitting prominently in the top desk drawer.

A good password policy is the first line of defense in protecting your network from intruders. Careless password practices (choosing common passwords such as "god" or "love" or the user's spouse's name; choosing short, all-alpha, one-case passwords, writing passwords down or sending them across the network in plain text) are like leaving your car doors unlocked with the keys in the ignition. Although some intruders might target a specific system, many others simply "browse" for a network that's easy to break into. Lack of a good password policy is an open invitation to them.

SECURITY ALERT!

Expensive, sophisticated firewalls and other strict security measures (short of biometric scanning devices that recognize fingerprints or retinal images) will not protect you if an intruder has knowledge of a valid username and password. It is particularly important to use strong passwords for administrative accounts.

Best practices for password creation require that you address the following:

- Password length and complexity
- Who creates the password?
- Forced changing of passwords

Let's discuss each of these considerations.

Password Length and Complexity

It's easy to define a "bad" password: It's one that can be easily guessed by someone other than the authorized user.

One way in which "crackers" (hackers who specialize in defeating passwords to break into systems) do their work is called the *brute force attack*. In this kind of attack, the cracker manually or, more often, using a script or specially written software program, simply tries every possible combination of characters until he or she finally hits on the right one. These programs can utilize huge dictionaries that contain many thousands of words and character combinations. Using this method, it is easier to guess a short password than a longer one because there are more possible combinations. For this reason, most security experts recommend that passwords have a minimum required length (for example, eight characters). Modern network operating systems such as Windows 2000 allow domain administrators to impose such rules so that if a user attempts to set a password that doesn't meet the minimum length requirement, the password change will be rejected.

Physical security is critical in thwarting brute force attacks, since they are more likely to succeed when the hacker has physical access to the machine than when they are launched across the network.

NOTE

In addition to the accounts assigned to individual users, services use accounts to perform their functions. Because the passwords on these service accounts are often static, they present a special point of vulnerability.

Who Creates the Password?

Network administrators might be tempted to institute a policy whereby they create all passwords and "issue" them to users. This method has the advantage of ensuring that all passwords meet the administrator's criteria in regard to length and complexity. However, it has a few big disadvantages as well:

- It places a heavy burden on administrators, who must handle all password changes and be responsible for letting users know what their passwords are. Of course, you would not want to notify the user of his or her password via e-mail or other insecure channels. In fact, the best way is to personally deliver the password information. In a large organization, this becomes particularly taxing if you have a policy requiring that passwords be changed on a regular basis (as you should; we discuss this rule in the next section).

- Users have more difficulty remembering passwords that they didn't choose themselves. This means that they are more likely to write the passwords down, resulting in security compromises. Otherwise, users might have to contact the administrator frequently to be reminded of their passwords.
- If the administrator creates all passwords, the administrator *knows* everyone's password. This might or might not be acceptable under your overall security policy. Some users (including management) could be uncomfortable with the idea that the administrator knows their passwords. Even though an administrator can generally access a user's account and/or files without knowing the password anyway, that fact is less obvious to users and thus of less concern.

Allowing users to create their own passwords within set parameters (length and complexity requirements) is usually the best option. The user is less likely to forget the password because he or she can create a complex password that is meaningless to anyone but the user.

For example, it would be difficult for others to guess the password "Mft2doSmis." It has 10 characters, combines alpha and numeric characters, and combines upper and lower case in a seemingly random manner. To the user, it would be easy to remember because it means "My favorite thing to do on Sunday morning is sleep."

Password Change Policy

Best practices dictate that users change their passwords at regular intervals and after any suspected security breach. Windows 2000 allows the administrator to set a maximum password age, forcing users to change their passwords at the end of the specified period (in days). Password expiration periods can be set from 1 to 999 days. The default is 42 days.

NOTE

Individual user accounts that need to keep the same passwords can be configured so that their passwords never expire. This configuration overrides the general password expiration setting.

Because it is the nature of most users to make their passwords as easy to remember as possible, you must institute policies to prevent the following practices, all of which can present security risks:

- Changing the password to a variation of the same password (for example, changing from Tag2mB to Tag3mB)
- Changing the password back and forth between two favored passwords each time a change is required (that is, changing from Tag2mB to VERoh9 and back again continuously)
- Changing the password to the same password (entering the same password for the new password as was already being used)

Administrators can use operating system features to prevent these practices. For example, in Windows 2000, you can configure the operating system to remember the user's password history so that up to a maximum of the last 24 passwords will be recorded. This way, the user will not be able to change the password to one that has been used during that time.

Summary of Best Password Practices

Keep these best practices in mind:

- Passwords should have a minimum of eight characters.
- Passwords should not be "dictionary" words.
- Passwords should consist of a mixture of alpha, numeric, and symbol characters.
- Passwords should be created by their users.
- Passwords should be easy for users to remember.
- Passwords should never be written down.
- Passwords should be changed on a regular basis.

- Passwords should be changed any time compromise is suspected.
- Password change policies should prevent users from making only slight changes.

Educating Network Users on Security Issues

The best security policies in the world will be ineffective if the network users are unaware of them or if the policies are so restrictive and place so many inconveniences on users that they go out of their way to attempt to circumvent them.

The security plan itself should contain a program for educating network users—not only regarding what the policies are but *why* they are important and how users benefit from them. Users should also be instructed in the best ways to comply with the policies and what to do if they are unable to comply or if they observe a deliberate violation of the policies on the part of other users.

If you involve users in the planning and policy-making stages, you will find it much easier to educate them and gain their support for the policies at the implementation and enforcement stages.

Incorporating ISA Server into Your Security Plan

ISA Server can be an important part of your overall security plan. In a sense, the rest of this book concerns itself with how to incorporate your ISA server(s) into the corporate security plan and how to use ISA Server to implement your security policies.

In the following sections, we look at just a few specific ways ISA can play an important role in creating the secure but accessible network environment that is right for your organization:

- ISA Server's role in intrusion detection
- Implementing a system-hardening plan with ISA
- Using SSL tunneling and bridging for secure Web communications

ISA Server Intrusion Detection

Microsoft has made it easy for you to configure ISA Server to protect against common intrusion types and notify you when such an attack is detected. In the

IP Packet Filters Properties sheet, on the Intrusion Detection tab, you can select one or more of the following attack types:

- Windows out-of-band attacks (also called *OOB* or *WinNuke*)
- LAND attacks (a variation on the SYN flood)
- Ping of death (also called the *killer packet*)
- IP half scan
- UDP bomb (also called *UDP flood* or *UDP packet storm*)
- Port scan

The Intrusion Detection Configuration sheet is shown in Figure 3.8.

Figure 3.8 Microsoft Includes Preconfigured Filters to Detect Common Intrusion Types

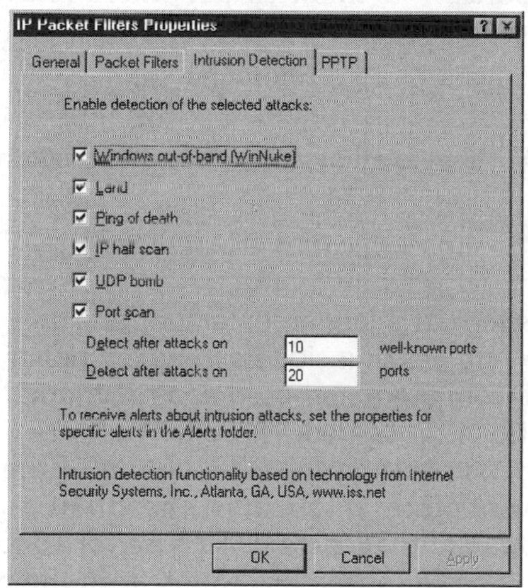

Third-party add-ons, such as GFI's LANguard and ISS's RealSecure, integrate with ISA Server to provide additional intrusion detection functionality. LANguard recognizes over 800 attack types and includes automatic downloading of updates to the attack database. RealSecure combines host-based and network-based intrusion detection in a single package and allows a variety of configurable responses to detected intrusions.

NOTE

For more information on third-party products, visit www.gfi.com (LANguard) and www.iss.net (RealSecure).

Implementing a System-Hardening Plan with ISA

The claims of expensive security specialists aside, it is not possible to "hack proof" your network—at least, not if you want to maintain accessibility for authorized users.

Although it might not be possible or even desirable to have *complete* security, it *is* possible—and important—to know exactly where your network's vulnerabilities lie. The AntiOnline Web site has a prominently displayed tagline: "Hackers know the weaknesses in your system. Shouldn't you?"

Every system that is accessible from the network has weaknesses. A number of third-party tools are available to allow you to test your system's vulnerabilities.

NOTE

Once again, let's look at a law enforcement analogy. Several years ago, in the wake of a number of incidents in which police officers had their own guns taken from them and used against them, the popularity of so-called "security holsters" soared. These holsters are made in such a way that there is a trick to getting the weapon out of the holster, which is intended to prevent officer disarmings. The intent is good; however, it soon became apparent that there was cause for concern when officers themselves were unable to free their guns from the holsters when they needed them. Soon police officials realized that, as in networking, the need for security must be weighed against the need for accessibility. The only completely secure holster is the one that keeps everyone—including the officer—from removing the gun. However, that isn't a very practical solution.

ISA Server's firewall function prevents unauthorized packets from entering your internal network. ISA also provides monitoring of intrusion attempts as well as allowing you to set alerts to notify you when intrusions occur (see Figure 3.9).

Figure 3.9 ISA Server Can Monitor Intrusions and Alert Administrators

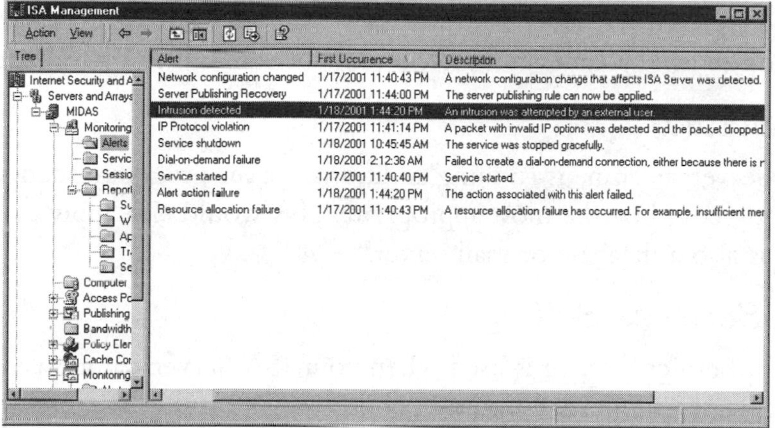

When an alert is triggered, one of several actions can be configured to occur. For example, an e-mail message can be sent to members of the Administrators group, an event can be logged to the event log, an application or script can be executed, or one or more ISA Server services can be stopped or started.

As you can see, ISA gives you several layers of security, similar to the layered home security scheme suggested by crime prevention experts. ISA's filtering features act like the locks that keep the "bad guys" out, and its monitoring and alerting features act like the burglar alarm system that lets you know when someone is trying to gain entry.

System-Hardening Goals and Guidelines

The goal of *system hardening* is to create as many barriers as possible to unauthorized persons who would try to access your network. A good system-hardening plan for your ISA Server deployment must take into consideration the security needs of your network and the configuration of the ISA Server computer (including the mode in which ISA is operating and the other applications that are running on the server).

Microsoft has included a wizard in ISA Server, called the System Hardening Wizard in beta versions but referred to in the final release as the Security Configuration Wizard. The wizard makes it easy for administrators to quickly apply a range of security settings to all servers in an array. The wizard provides predefined templates for three security levels from which you can select:

- Secure
- Limited Services
- Dedicated

Let's look at these settings and the circumstances in which each is appropriate.

Secure Setting

If the ISA Server machine is running additional server programs, such as IIS, the Secure setting could be the most appropriate. This would also apply to an ISA server that is also a database or mail server.

Limited Services Setting

The Limited Services setting is used when your ISA Server computer is operating in integrated mode, functioning as both firewall and caching server. There could be an additional firewall protecting the ISA server. Use this setting if the ISA Server is a domain controller.

Dedicated Setting

If the ISA Server machine is dedicated to the firewall function, running no other server applications, and not serving as a caching server, the Dedicated setting is generally the most appropriate. This is for a highly secure standalone firewall server.

Using the Security Configuration Wizard

The Security Configuration Wizard is accessed by right-clicking the computer name for which you want to configure security in the Computers folder, located in the left console pane of the ISA Management console. When you select Secure from the context menu, the Security Configuration Wizard will be invoked, as shown in Figure 3.10.

Chapter 9, "Configuring ISA Server for Inbound Access," walks through the steps of configuring your ISA Server's security settings with the wizard.

Hardening your system against intrusion is an important element in addressing the security objectives listed at the beginning of this chapter. In the next sections, we look at each of those objectives and how they all fit together as part of your network security plan.

Figure 3.10 System Hardening Can Be Done Quickly and Easily with the Security Configuration Wizard

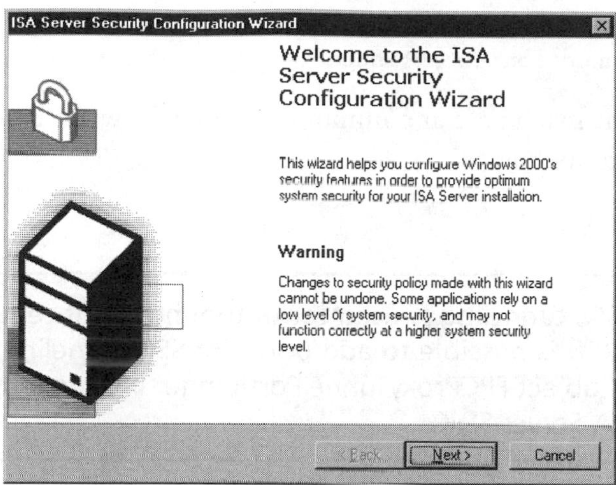

Using SSL Tunneling and Bridging

Secure Sockets Layer (SSL) is a protocol that can be used to manage the security of Internet communications. SSL operates between HTTP at the Application layer and TCP at the Transport layer. Although it was originally developed by Netscape for secure communications with their browser, SSL is now included in both Netscape Communicator and Microsoft Internet Explorer browser software. SSL uses public key encryption and digital certificates to ensure secure communications.

ISA Server can use SSL tunneling or bridging to provide secure communications between a client and a Web server when requests go through the ISA server.

SSL Tunneling

SSL tunneling allows a client computer to create a tunnel through the ISA server to a Web server whenever the browser on a client machine requests a secure HTTP object, thus allowing the client to connect to and communicate directly with the external Web server. The ISA server sends a connect request in the following format:

```
https://URL_name
```

Then the following request is sent to port 8080 on the ISA computer:

```
CONNECT URL_name:443 HTTP/1.1
```

The ISA machine connects to the destination Web server on port 443, and when the TCP connection has been established, the ISA server returns the following message:

```
HTTP/1.0 200 connection established
```

Now the client machine can communicate directly with the destination Web server using SSL tunneling.

TIP

By default, SSL tunneling is used for outbound client requests to ports 443 and 563. It is possible to add ports for SSL tunneling using the ISA Admin COM object FPCProxyTunnelPortRange. Instructions for doing so are in the ISA Server SDK.

SSL Bridging

Using *SSL bridging,* ISA Server can encrypt or decrypt requests from clients and forward the requests to a Web server. Unlike SSL tunneling, where the client communicates directly with the Web server, in a bridging situation the client establishes a connection with the ISA server, which then creates a connection to the Web server. This connection can be used for both outgoing and incoming requests, but it is more typically used in the publishing or reverse proxy situation, in which a client requests an HTTP or SSL object from an internal Web server. (When an internal client makes an HTTPS request on port 8080, SSL tunneling, rather than bridging, is used.) To use SSL bridging for outbound Web requests, the client's browser software must support secure communication with the Web proxy service.

In considering whether to use SSL on the internal network, you should consider the accompanying overhead and how it compares to alternate security methods such as IPSec.

SSL Bridging with Reverse Publishing

Here is an example of the steps used for SSL bridging with reverse publishing:

1. The external client makes an SSL request for a resource and makes an SSL connection to the ISA Server.
2. ISA Server and the external Web browser perform SSL negotiation.

3. ISA Server checks its cache for the requested object. If the object is in the cache, ISA Server returns it to the client.
4. If the object is not in the cache, ISA Server examines the Web publishing rule and sends the request to the internal Web server as an HTTP or SSL request. (If it is an SSL request, ISA Server must perform SSL negotiation again with internal Web server, which is a CPU-intensive operation.)
5. The Web server returns the object to the ISA server.
6. The ISA server returns the object to the client.

UNDOCUMENTED ISA

You can configure whether the ISA server will cache SSL objects. To do so, you must use the FPCWebRequestConfiguration COM object. Normally, cacheable Web objects are cached by the ISA server.

These steps represent only one possible SSL bridging scenario. Note that a great deal of encrypting and decrypting is going on to maintain the security of the object.

SSL Bridging with Incoming Web Requests

Let's look at how incoming Web requests are handled. First, the ISA server must be configured to listen for SSL requests on the port with which the external client will connect, as illustrated in Figure 3.11. By default, this is port 443. This is done by enabling SSL listeners on the Incoming Web Requests tab of the array's Properties sheet. You have the following options:

- Use the same listener configuration for all internal IP addresses
- Configure listeners individually per IP address

NOTE

If you want to use SSL for two different Web servers, you need to select the second choice and configure the listeners individually.

Figure 3.11 Configure the Array Properties to Enable and Configure SSL Listeners

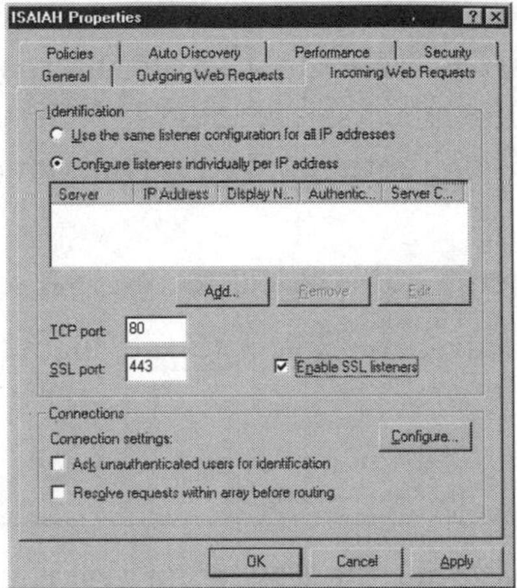

Additionally, a server certificate for Web requests must be specified. If you selected the first option, you can now edit the IP address properties. If you selected the second option, you might need to first add an IP address before you can configure its properties.

In either case, you then check the "Use a server certificate to authenticate to Web clients" check box and choose a certificate from the list.

NOTE

You will not be able to configure this option unless you have certificates installed on the ISA server. For this configuration to work properly, each internal Web server should be published on different public IP address and a server certificate mapped to each.

Now the incoming Web requests will be handled as follows:

1. The external client sends an HTTPS request for a Web object on the internal Web server.
2. ISA Server decrypts the request and terminates the SSL connection.
3. ISA Server sends the request to the Web server using HTTP, FTP, or SSL, depending on how the Web publishing rules are configured.

4. If the Web publishing rules specify HTTPS, ISA Server creates a new SSL connection with the Web server and sends the request to port 443, acting as an SSL client to the Web server.
5. The Web server must respond with a server-side certificate.
6. If the Web server is configured to require a certificate, the ISA server must respond with a client-side certificate.

SSL Bridging with Outgoing Web Requests

SSL tunneling is normally used for internal client requests of HTTPS objects from external servers. However, you can use routing rules to configure clients to use SSL bridging instead if the client supports secure communication directly with the ISA server (that is, if its browser or Web application supports SSL communications).

In this case, you configure the Outgoing Web Requests tab similarly to the way you configured incoming requests earlier, enabling SSL listening (on port by default) and enabling or selecting certificates.

NOTE

For more detailed instructions on configuring SSL tunneling and bridging in ISA Server, see Chapter 8, "Configuring ISA Server for Outbound Access," and Chapter 9, "Configuring ISA Server for Inbound Access."

Summary

This chapter covered a lot of ground. Even so, we barely went past the tip of the iceberg when it comes to computer, network, and Internet security issues. The chapter provided many excellent resources that you can consult for more details on the basic security concepts, specific security threats, and development of security plans and policies.

Although this chapter is a review for some readers, it is very important that before you deploy ISA Server as part of your overall security plan, you review that plan as a whole and ensure that you have addressed physical access factors, prevention of accidental data compromise, prevention of deliberate internal security breaches, and prevention and detection of unauthorized external intrusions.

To get the most out of ISA's features, you must be able to recognize the security threats to which your network is subject and understand a little about the motivations of typical intruders. It is not necessary that you *be* a hacker in order to prevent your network from hacking attempts, but it *will* benefit you to know something about how unscrupulous hackers think and how they do their dirty work.

You must be aware of the various types of attacks with which you could be confronted and understand how to protect your network from social engineering attacks, DoS attacks, scanning and spoofing, source routing and other protocol exploits, software and system exploits, and Trojans, viruses, and worms.

A number of hardware-based security solutions and even more software-based firewalls are on the market. You should have a basic understanding of the capabilities and limitations of each type and how ISA Server compares—in terms of features and cost—to some of the others. We think you will find that ISA Server offers an excellent value in comparison to competitive products, along with easy configurability and options to integrate third-party programs for even more functionality.

Your comprehensive security plan is integral to protecting your network from both internal and external threats. There is no "one size fits all" when it comes to corporate security plans and policies; yours should be based on the nature of the business in which your organization engages, the nature of the data stored on your network, the number and types of connections your network has to the "outside world," and your management's philosophy regarding organizational structure.

A good security plan is one that meets the needs of IT administration, company management, and network users. The best way to ensure that your security plan meets these criteria is to involve people from all levels of the organization in the planning process. Once you have a good, comprehensive security plan and corresponding policies worked out, you will be able to use ISA Server as an important element in your security plan, to implement and enforce those policies and provide monitoring, notification, and record keeping to document the successful functioning of your security plan. The following chapters show you how to do just that.

Solutions Fast Track

Security Overview

☑ Network security solutions can be loosely divided into three categories: hardware, software, and human.

Defining Basic Security Concepts

☑ To protect your network resources from theft, damage, or unwanted exposure, you must understand who initiates these events, why they do it, and how they do it.

☑ A good network security system will help you easily remove the temptations (open ports, exploitable applications) and will be as transparent to your users as possible. ISA Server, when properly configured, meets these requirements.

Addressing Security Objectives

☑ File servers on which sensitive data is stored and infrastructure servers that provide mission-critical services such as logon authentication and access control should be placed in a highly secure location. At a minimum, servers should be in a locked room to which only those who need to work directly with the servers have access. Keys should be distributed sparingly, and records should be kept of issuance and return.

☑ Don't depend on access permissions and other software security methods alone to protect your network. If a potential intruder can gain physical access to a networked computer, he or she is that much closer to accessing your valuable data or introducing a virus onto your network.

- ☑ Although switches and routers are somewhat more secure than hubs, any device through which the data passes is a point of vulnerability. Replacing hubs with switches and routers makes it more difficult for an intruder to "sniff" on your network, but it is still possible to use techniques such as *Address Resolution Protocol (ARP) spoofing*.
- ☑ Despite the many benefits of wireless technologies, they also present special problems, especially in the area of network security. Data traveling over wireless media is more vulnerable to interception than data over cabled media. Radio and microwave are known as *broadcast media*.
- ☑ According to most computer security studies, as documented in RFC 2196, actual loss (in terms of money, productivity, computer reputation, and other tangible and intangible harm) is greater for internal security breaches than for those from the outside.
- ☑ Like Windows NT, Windows 2000 provides for granular auditing of security-related events and records the information to a security log. The log can be viewed (by users with administrative privileges only) via the Windows Event Viewer.

Recognizing Network Security Threats

- ☑ There are probably as many different specific motives as there are hackers, but we can break the most common intruder motivations into a few broad categories: recreation, remuneration, revenge.
- ☑ In some instances, hackers working for competitors will go "undercover" and seek a job with your company in order to steal data that they can take back to their own organizations.
- ☑ Unlike the other attack types, *social engineering* does not refer to a technological manipulation of computer hardware or software vulnerabilities and does not require much in the way of technical skills. Instead, this type of attack exploits *human* weaknesses—such as carelessness or the desire to be cooperative—to gain access to legitimate network credentials.
- ☑ Because social engineering is a human problem, not a technical problem, prevention must come primarily through education rather than technological solutions.
- ☑ Although they do not destroy or steal data as some other types of attacks do, the objective of DoS attackers is to bring down the network,

denying service to its legitimate users. The purpose of a DoS attack is to render a network inaccessible by generating a type or amount of network traffic that will crash the servers, overwhelm the routers, or otherwise prevent the network's devices from functioning properly.

- ☑ *Distributed DoS (DDoS) attacks* use intermediary computers, called *agents,* on which programs called *zombies* have previously been surreptitiously installed. The hacker activates these zombie programs remotely, causing the intermediary computers (which can number in the hundreds or even thousands) to simultaneously launch the actual attack.
- ☑ The *DNS DoS attack* exploits the difference in size between a DNS query and a DNS response, in which all the network's bandwidth is tied up by bogus DNS queries. The attacker uses the DNS servers as "amplifiers" to multiply the DNS traffic.
- ☑ *Synchronization request (SYN) attacks* exploit the TCP "three-way handshake," the process by which a communications session is established between two computers. Because TCP (unlike UDP) is connection-oriented, a *session,* or direct one-to-one communication link, must be created prior to sending data. The client computer initiates the communication with the server (the computer that has the resources it wants to access).
- ☑ The ping-of-death attack is launched by creating an IP packet (sometimes referred to as a *killer packet*) larger than 65,536 bytes, which is the maximum allowed by the IP specification. This can cause the target system to crash, hang, or reboot. ISA allows you to specifically enable detection of ping-of-death attacks.
- ☑ A *worm* is a program that can travel across the network from one computer to another. Sometimes different parts of a worm run on different computers. Worms make multiple copies of themselves and spread throughout a network.

Categorizing Security Solutions

- ☑ Hardware security solutions come in the form of network devices. Firewalls, routers, even switches can function to provide a certain level of security.
- ☑ Hardware-based firewalls are often referred to as *firewall appliances.* A disadvantage of hardware-based firewalls is the proprietary nature of the

software they run. Another disadvantage of many of these products, such as Cisco's highly respected PIX, is the high cost.

- ☑ Software security solutions cover a much broader range than hardware solutions. They include the security features built into network operating systems as well as additional security software made by Microsoft or third-party vendors.

Designing a Comprehensive Security Plan

- ☑ A widely accepted method for developing your network security plan is laid out in RFC 2196, *Site Security Handbook,* and attributed to Fites, et al (1989).
- ☑ It is important to understand that a security *plan* is not the same thing as a security *policy,* although the two words are sometimes used interchangeably.
- ☑ A LAN that is self-contained and has no Internet connectivity nor any modems or other outside connections does not require the degree of protection (other than physical security) that is necessary when an intruder can take many avenues "in."
- ☑ The best security policy is to have as few connections from the internal network to the outside as possible and control access at those entry points (collectively called the *network perimeter*).
- ☑ An organization's management model can have a profound influence on what is or isn't acceptable in planning security for the network.
- ☑ The U.S. government provides specifications for rating network security implementations in a publication often referred to as the *Orange Book,* formally called the *Department of Defense Trusted Computer System Evaluation Criteria,* or *TCSEC.* The *Red Book,* or *Trusted Network Interpretation of the TCSEC (TNI),* explains how the TCSEC evaluation criteria are applied to computer networks.
- ☑ Best practices dictate that no one person should have complete authority or control. Besides, in an enterprise-level network, it would be difficult for any single person to handle all facets of developing and implementing the security plan.

- ☑ Best practices for password creation require that you address the following: password length and complexity, who creates the password, and forced changing of passwords.

Incorporating ISA Server in your Security Plan

- ☑ ISA Server's firewall function prevents unauthorized packets from entering your internal network. ISA also provides monitoring of intrusion attempts as well as allowing you to set alerts to notify you when intrusions occur.
- ☑ The goal of *system hardening* is to create as many barriers as possible to unauthorized persons who would try to access your network.
- ☑ *Secure Sockets Layer (SSL)* is a protocol that can be used to manage the security of Internet communications. SSL operates between HTTP at the Application layer and TCP at the Transport layer.
- ☑ *SSL tunneling* allows a client computer to create a tunnel through the ISA server to a Web server whenever the browser on a client machine requests a secure HTTP object, thus allowing the client to connect to and communicate directly with the external Web server.
- ☑ Using *SSL bridging,* ISA Server can encrypt or decrypt requests from clients and forward the requests to a Web server.

Frequently Asked Questions

The following Frequently Asked Questions, answered by the authors of this book, are designed to both measure your understanding of the concepts presented in this chapter and to assist you with real-life implementation of these concepts. To have your questions about this chapter answered by the author, browse to **www.syngress.com/solutions** and click on **"Ask the Author"** form.

Q: Does IP spoofing allow a hacker to communicate on the network anonymously?

A: Not really. IP spoofing makes the source address appear to be other than that of the original sender. However, responses to a message with a spoofed IP address go back to the spoofed address, not to the real address of the original sender. Hackers use spoofing in situations in which they do not need to receive a response. For example, a hacker can use a spoofed IP address to initiate a ping flood or a UDP flood. A hacker *cannot,* however, hide his identity by pretending to be someone else while engaging in two-way communications, because he will not receive the responses to his messages.

Q: The laws regarding import and export of cryptography to and from various countries are very confusing. Where can I find more information on this topic?

A: An excellent document, *International Law Crypto Survey*, provides information about laws and regulations pertaining to cryptography at the Bert-Jaap Koops homepage at http://cwis.kub.nl/~frw/people/koops/lawsurvy.htm.

Q: Why does SSL work with ISA Server (and Microsoft Proxy Server 2.0) when it does not work with some other proxy servers?

A: SSL regards Application layer proxies such as the CERN proxy server as "middlemen," and SSL was designed to prevent man-in-the-middle attacks. Because Microsoft Proxy Server and ISA Server use packet filtering, which operates at the Network layer, they can be configured to open a trusted, reserved port (443 for secure HTTP and 563 for secure NNTP) to allow SSL traffic to "tunnel" through the proxy.

Q: What is ingress filtering, and how can it be used to protect against network intrusions?

A: Ingress filtering is a method of preventing attackers in a particular network from perpetrating network intrusions and attacks using spoofed IP addresses that don't comply with the ingress-filtering rules. ISPs can use ingress filtering to prevent the use of forged source addresses that aren't in the range of legitimate prefixes. When ingress filtering is used, the origin of attempted intrusions can be traced to their actual source because a valid source address must be used. Information about ingress filtering is contained in RFC 2267, the text of which is available on the Web at http://info.internet.isi.edu/in-notes/rfc/files/rfc2267.txt.

Q: What solutions have been developed to provide better security over wireless LAN links?

A: Vendors such as 3Com have developed security solutions for wireless networks, including Layer 3 wireless tunneling that is easier to implement than earlier Layer 2 tunneling implementations. 3Com's SuperStack II Router 400 can be set up between the wired network infrastructure and the wireless clients, and the Microsoft Point to Point Encryption Protocol can be used to provide secure communications between the two. Other vendors offer similar solutions for securing wireless connections.

Q: What are smart cards, and how do they work?

A: A smart card is a device the size and shape of a credit card that is used to securely store public and private keys, passwords, and other types of personal information. A smart card reader is required to use the card. Smart cards can be used for access control to a physical site or for logon authentication to a computer network. Windows 2000 supports smart card authentication, using certificate-based cryptography. This feature provides for stronger security than a username/password logon alone because, in order to log on to the network, a user must have access to the card itself in addition to entering the correct user credentials. (In this case, the user enters a personal identification number, or PIN, instead of the username and password.) Smart cards can be an important part of a public key infrastructure (PKI) that provides security for Windows 2000 networks.

Q: How does IPSec protect data as it travels over the network?

A: IPSec is a set of protocols that are implemented at the Network layer (Layer 3) to encapsulate and encrypt data to prevent it from being read if it is intercepted while it travels across the network. Packet sniffers can be used to capture data in transit, and if the data is not encrypted, the contents of the packets can be read. The implementation of IPSec at the Network layer means that applications do not have to be IPSec-aware. (Security mechanisms implemented at higher layers, such as SSL, require that applications support the security method.) Unlike security that is implemented at a lower level, such as Link layer encryption, all links along the data path are protected, resulting in end-to-end security. All applications and services that utilize IP for transport can be secured with IPSec. Other protocols can be protected if the packets are encapsulated by IP.

Both computers in a transaction must support IPSec. IPSec uses ISAKMP to initiate security negotiations, and the two computers perform a key exchange and establish an ISAKMP security association, using a shared secret key. They can they negotiate the level of security that will be used for the data transmission. The IPSec driver on the sending computer signs outgoing packets for integrity and encrypts the packets for confidentiality. When the destination computer receives the packets, its IPSec driver checks the signature and decrypts the packets.

Windows 2000 IPSec uses the Authentication Header (AH) and the Encapsulating Security Payload (ESP) protocols to provide authentication, integrity, and confidentiality for the IPSec communication.

Chapter 4

ISA Server Deployment Planning and Design

Solutions in this chapter:

- ISA Deployment: Planning and Designing Issues
- Active Directory Implementation
- Mission-Critical Considerations
- Planning the Appropriate Installation Mode

☑ Summary

☑ Solutions Fast Track

☑ Frequently Asked Questions

Introduction

To this point, we've talked about general concepts as they relate to network security and enterprise design considerations. In this chapter, we start getting into the specifics of planning and implementing an ISA Server solution for your network.

Planning your ISA Server installation before actually performing it is absolutely critical. As with Windows 2000, the amount of thought and analysis you put into your design will help optimize ISA performance and will minimize the chance of making a substantial error that will adversely affect your security or access schemes.

ISA Deployment: Planning and Designing Issues

When you decide to put together an ISA Server solution for your organization, you should plan ahead. ISA Server is an integral part of your security configuration scheme, and you do not want to merely install the server and hope that everything works out right. Carpenters have an old saying: "Measure twice, cut once." If you thoroughly map out your design, you'll avoid pitfalls in your deployment and further down the line.

In this section, we focus on planning and design issues as they relate to the installation of ISA Server. The primary issues of concern are:

- Network and hardware specifications
- The edition of ISA Server to be installed
- The mode in which ISA Server will be installed
- Standalone versus array configurations
- Client configuration requirements
- ISA Server Internet connectivity

You should make firm decisions about each of these ISA Server design issues *before* you begin your installation. The conclusions you reach at this point will determine your choices when it comes time to install ISA Server.

Assessing Network and Hardware Requirements

Prior to installing ISA Server, you need to assess hardware requirements to meet the needs of your organization's ISA Server deployment plan. An organization that has 50 network clients and chooses to utilize only the Web proxy service will have very different requirements than an organization with 30,000 network clients that wants to avail itself of all the networking services ISA Server has to offer.

System Requirements

Whether you choose to install one or 100 ISA servers, each server must meet minimum hardware and software requirements. The minimum requirements for any ISA server—regardless of the role the machine might play on the network—are:

- Windows 2000 Server family operating system with Service Pack 1 or later installed
- A Pentium II or K7 (Athlon) Processor running at 300MHz or faster
- A minimum of 256 MB of RAM (Microsoft recommended)
- A minimum of 20 MB for the program files
- A minimum of 2 GB for the Web cache
- At least two network interfaces—one to the internal network and a second to an external network, such as the Internet or corporate backbone (the exception is an internal caching-only server)
- Partitions formatted as NTFS to store the program, log, and cache files
- A Windows 2000 Domain if Enterprise Policies will be implemented

Each of these components requires thoughtful consideration before implementing the ISA server on your network. Let's look at each one of them in more detail.

Software Requirements

ISA Server must be installed on a Windows 2000 Server family computer. It will not install on Windows NT 4.0 or Windows 2000 Professional. If you try to install ISA Server on a Windows 2000 Server machine that does not have Service Pack 1 installed, you will get an error message during the installation, informing you that you must first install the service pack before the installation routine can continue.

If you do not have Windows 2000 Service Pack 2 installed, you must install a pre-Service Pack 2 hotfix that is included on the CD-ROM. The file, q27586_w2k_sp2_x86_en.exe, is contained in a folder named *HotFix*. The hotfix will update several system files. Although doing so is not required, you should restart your machine after installing the hotfix.

ISA Server Standard Edition can be installed on any member of the Windows 2000 Server family. The Enterprise Edition of ISA Server must be installed on either Windows 2000 Advanced Server or Datacenter Server. Therefore, if you organization has only the "Server" version of Windows 2000, not the Advanced or Datacenter versions, you need to upgrade before installing ISA Enterprise Edition.

Processor Requirements

Processor requirements are somewhat flexible. It is rather unusual to see a production server in a corporate environment running at 300MHz or less; such a server would be rather long in the tooth at this point. If your servers are even a year old, it's unlikely that they are slower than 500MHz. Because the address translation and rule processing performed by ISA Server is processor intensive, you will benefit from a more powerful processor or multiple processors.

If you configure a large number of packet filters or content and site rules, you'll want to maximize the processor configuration on your server. If you don't plan to implement a lot of rules on the server and will use it primarily for Web caching, a 300MHz machine should present no problems. Table 4.1 will help you assess your processor requirements.

Table 4.1 ISA Server Processor Requirements

External Interface Data Rate	Processor Requirement	Type of Connection
Less than 10 Mb/second	Pentium II or K6-2 300MHz	ISDN, cable, or DSL
10 to 50 Mb/second	Pentium III or K7 500MHz	T3 or comparable
More than 50 Mb/second	Pentium III or K7 500MHz (Add a processor for each increment of 50 Mb/second.)	Very Fast

We have included AMD processor offerings along with the Intel specifications that Microsoft includes in its documentation. Microsoft still doesn't like to talk too much about AMD because of Microsoft's long association with Intel. However, AMD has closed the gap, and its K7/Athlon processors provide superior performance at lower cost. The only reservation you might have regarding the K7 series is its multiprocessor support. At this juncture, it might be wise to go with Intel when designing a multiprocessor solution.

Undocumented ISA

The rate-limiting factor when it comes to processor requirements can be boiled down to the number of rules per second that ISA Server needs to evaluate. An ISA server with a few rules but high throughput could have roughly the same requirements as a machine that has many rules but little throughput through its external interface. Note that we cannot make a decision based on throughput on the internal interface, because it is assumed that other types of traffic that are not processed by any ISA services could flow through this interface. Therefore, you can use the speed of the external interface as a guideline for the level of processor support your ISA server requires.

Multiprocessor Support

Keep in mind that ISA Server and Windows 2000 support multiprocessor system setups. If you are configuring the server as an integrated firewall and Web cache server, and if the server is performing any other duties (such as acting as a domain controller for a dedicated ISA Server domain), you'll want to strongly consider a multiprocessor machine. ISA Server has been certified as Windows 2000 compliant, and part of the certification process included its ability to take advantage of symmetric multiprocessing. Windows 2000 Server supports up to 4 processors. Windows 2000 Advanced Server supports up to 8 processor, and Windows 2000 Datacenter Server supports up to 32 processors.

The number of processors determines how much you'll pay for ISA Server, because the licensing fees are based on the number of processors on the server. Since the costs can increment outrageously for a multiprocessor machine, you should consider installing ISA Server on a system with a single processor, then carry out performance monitoring to aid you in making a cost/benefit analysis of a multiple-processor solution.

Table 4.2 contains the pricing structure for ISA Server at the time of this book's publication.

Table 4.2 ISA Server Price Estimates for Full and Upgrade Versions

ISA Server Version	Estimated Price	Upgrade Information
ISA Standard Version	$1499.00 per CPU	The following products qualify for upgrade: ■ Proxy Server 2.0 ■ Netscape Proxy Server ■ Novell Border Manager ■ Checkpoint Firewall-1 and VPN-1 ■ Axent Raptor ■ Inktomi Traffic Server ■ IBM Secure Way Firewall and Websphere cache ■ Cobalt cache, Cobalt Cube ■ Network Appliance NetCache
ISA Enterprise Version	$5999.00 per CPU	
ISA Standard Version—Upgrade	$749.00 per CPU	
ISA Enterprise Version—Upgrade	$2999.00 per CPU	

Note: All prices are in U.S. currency.

If you do not qualify for the upgrade, you should consider the cost of buying Proxy Server 2.0, which is very reasonably priced, and then upgrade your version of Proxy Server to ISA Server. This is especially sound advice if you intend to purchase the Enterprise Version of ISA Server. Open license and select license plans are also available; these can dramatically reduce costs. You'll have to call your local Microsoft representative for the details on these types of licensing.

RAM Configuration

Microsoft recommends that any ISA server you deploy should have at least 256 MB of RAM to take advantage of all the product's features. However, we have installed ISA Server on machines with 192 MB of RAM without difficulty, and it performed reasonably well in a limited laboratory environment. If you do choose to install ISA Server on machines with less than 256 MB of RAM, you should not run any other memory- or processor-intensive services on that machine and should limit such configurations to very small businesses.

NOTE

If you are "hardware challenged" and must use a minimal RAM configuration, you should dedicate the machine to ISA only and use it for no other services, not even file-sharing and Web services.

The NAT tables maintained by ISA Server are stored in RAM. Even in a large network, the NAT tables should not consume much memory. However, ISA Server offers a new feature as part of the Web proxy service: the ability to hold a large portion of the Web cache in RAM. This capability greatly improves cache performance, but you must have a large chunk of RAM to dedicate to the cache in order to realize these benefits.

Hardware designs that include less than 256 MB of RAM can experience bottlenecks in Web-caching performance. This is because the ISA Server Web-caching feature takes advantage of RAM to store the Web cache. When there isn't enough RAM to store a good portion of the Web cache in memory, the server must place the files in the disk-based cache. This results in URL retrieval times that are much longer than retrieval times from RAM cache.

The size of the Web cache you want to keep in RAM correlates with the number of users on your network. Table 4.3 provides some general guidelines regarding the relationship between number of users and RAM requirements.

Table 4.3 ISA Server RAM Requirements

Users Behind ISA Server	Total ISA Server RAM
Fewer than 250	192 MB (Microsoft states 128 MB)
250 to 2000	256 MB
More than 2000	256 MB plus an incremental increase of 256 MB for every 2000 users

Note that the Microsoft recommendation for fewer than 250 users correlates with our own recommendation for small, simple networks. However, we believe that the 128 MB lower limit is set too low. RAM prices are quite volatile, but they continue to fall with time. We recommend that you get as much RAM as your hardware budget allows. You will notice considerable improvement in Web cache if the amount of RAM in the machine exceeds the size of your Web cache.

Disk Space Considerations

The amount of disk space you allot to your ISA Server configuration can be quite variable. The space required for the program files will always be about 20 MB, which shouldn't be an issue on any mission-critical server on which you chose to install ISA Server. However, when you plan your disk space requirements, you must consider other important factors.

The most important issue is the amount of disk space you want to dedicate to the Web cache. Unlike that of Proxy Server 2.0, the ISA Server Web cache is stored in a single file. This single-file format is a lot more efficient than the file system-based storage used in Proxy Server 2.0.

The file system-based storage used in Proxy Server 2.0 also had some security problems because it allowed users with the appropriate permissions to easily view the contents of the cache by opening the individual files. The cache could also be indexed and searched for information that an organization might consider proprietary.

Even though SSL-protected pages were not cached on Proxy Server 2.0, most companies did not protect their internal network Web resources using SSL and used authentication-based access instead. Although access to internal Web servers was secured by requiring authentication, the contents of the interaction were cached and therefore could be made available to users without the users having to actually access the server itself.

The single-file storage system for the Web cache gets around this problem. The .CDAT file used to store cached objects on the ISA Server is a database file. You cannot open this file with a text editor or Web browser. However, you can use a tool on the ISA Server CD-ROM called CacheDir.exe to view the contents of the cache and key information about the cache file entries.

Another major advantage of the single-file storage system is that the cache file is not dynamically resized. If you set the cache for a particular drive to 100 MB, the .CDAT file will start as 100 MB and will not change. Performance gains are realized by avoiding processor cycles required to dynamically resize the file.

Cache Size Considerations

In the past, Microsoft recommended that you begin with a Web cache of at least 100 MB plus 0.5 MB for each user on the network. These figures were included with the Proxy Server 2.0 documentation. The nature of the Internet and how people interact with the Internet has changed radically since the release of Proxy Server 2.0, and therefore these minimal guidelines no longer apply. To fully realize the advantages of Web caching, you need to create a much larger Web cache.

Table 4.4 provides guidelines for configuring your Web cache. *These Web cache recommendations are extremely conservative*. Even in small networks, you should plan for a much larger Web cache.

Table 4.4 ISA Server Disk Space Requirements

Number of Users	Disk Space for Web Cache
Fewer than 250	2 GB to 4 GB
250 to 2000	10 GB
More than 2000	10 GB plus another 10 GB for every 2000 users

Undocumented ISA

The numbers given by Microsoft for disk space allocations are interesting because they represent disparate requirements per user, based on the number of users behind the ISA server. For example, suppose we have 200 users. Let's assume that we choose to use the top recommendation for that number of users, which is 4000 MB (4 GB). The number of MB per user is therefore 4000 MB/200 users, which turns out to be 20 MB per user. Now, if we have a network that has 2000 clients behind the ISA server, the number of MB per user is 10,000 MB (10 GB) ÷ 2000, which equals only 5 MB per user.

You need to plan for a larger amount of disk space per user in a larger environment because there will be a wider variation in the per-user statistics. The high-end users will typically throw your averages off and have a disproportional effect on your cache requirements. We therefore recommend that you plan for at least 20 MB per user, and if your hardware can support it, try for 50 MB per user.

Logging and Reporting

Another factor in determining ISA Server disk space requirements includes the log files and reports that will be stored on your ISA Server. The log files can grow very quickly, depending on the level of logging you have configured on your server. If you enable packet filtering and detailed Web proxy service logging, even a small network can easily generate log files in the range of 5 to 10 MB per day.

If you are working on larger networks, you can expect your log files to expand at the rate of 50 to 100 MB per day if you carry out detailed logging. It is a good idea to dedicate a partition of *at least 1 GB* to your log files if you plan to carry out even a moderate amount of logging. You might also want to compress the partition on which the log files are created. Since these are plain text files, you should be able to get a compression ratio of 4:1 or greater. Be aware that compression does require additional processor cycles and increases the amount of fragmentation on the drive. If your monitoring sessions indicate a potential processor bottleneck, you should not implement file compression.

You need a month's worth of log files to create many of the more interesting reports that ISA Server can generate. Furthermore, you might want to create reports spanning multiple months, in which case you need all the log files available on disk.

Network Interface Configuration

You should have at least two network interfaces if you plan to use the ISA server as a firewall. However, if you want to use the machine as a Web-caching server only, you can use a computer with a single, internal network interface.

If you configure multihomed computers, at least one of those interfaces will be directly connected to the Internet or to a network backbone. If you connect directly to the Internet, the interface can be an Ethernet connection (for example, to a DSL or cable modem), ISDN, or analog modem connection. For the internal network interface, you will likely use an Ethernet connection.

If you plan to use a perimeter network, that network can be connected to a third interface connected to the ISA Server. That interface will be considered an external interface and must be configured with public addresses on a different subnet from the external interface. Figure 4.1 shows the configuration of such a perimeter network.

NOTE

You can also configure a DMZ network between a pair of ISA servers. In this case, the DMZ network interface would be considered an internal interface for the ISA machine because an ISA machine must have at least one internal interface.

Figure 4.1 A Trihomed Server with a DMZ Network on the Third Interface

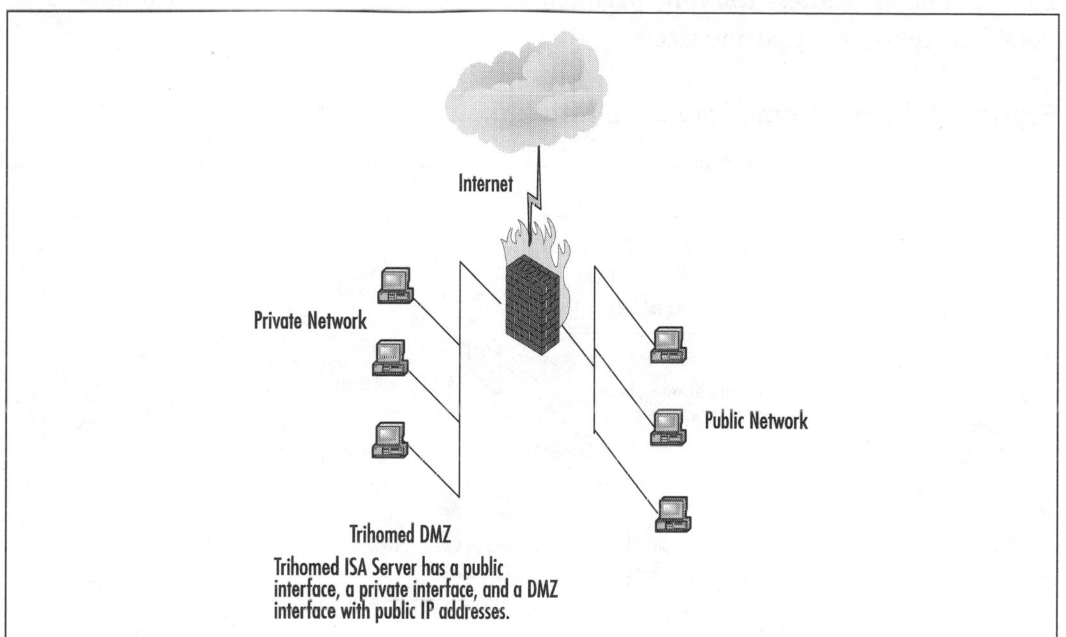

A perimeter network can also be configured to lie between a pair of ISA Servers. In this model, an ISA Server lies on the edge of the network with an interface directly connected to the Internet, while a second interface is connected to a perimeter network. The second ISA Server has one interface connected to the perimeter network; the second interface is connected to the internal network. Note that this intermediary network is a public network and should not be considered part of the internal network. Figure 4.2 shows what such an intermediary DMZ network configuration might look like.

The ISA server that acts only as a Web-caching server can get by with a single internal network interface. Network clients send their requests to the ISA Server's internal interface, and the ISA server forwards those requests to *its* gateway to the Internet. Responses from Internet servers are returned to the single-homed Web-caching server, which in turn returns data to the ISA clients. Figure 4.3 shows what such a single-homed network configuration might look like.

The TCP/IP configuration of the interfaces should be set up correctly before the ISA server is installed. The only interface that should have a default gateway is the external interface of the ISA server. If you have multiple external interfaces that connect to your ISP(s), you can put in gateways for each of those interfaces.

However, if you are using multihomed ISA servers in which one of the interfaces has a public IP address for your perimeter network, you should not configure a default gateway on that interface.

Figure 4.2 An Intermediary DMZ Network

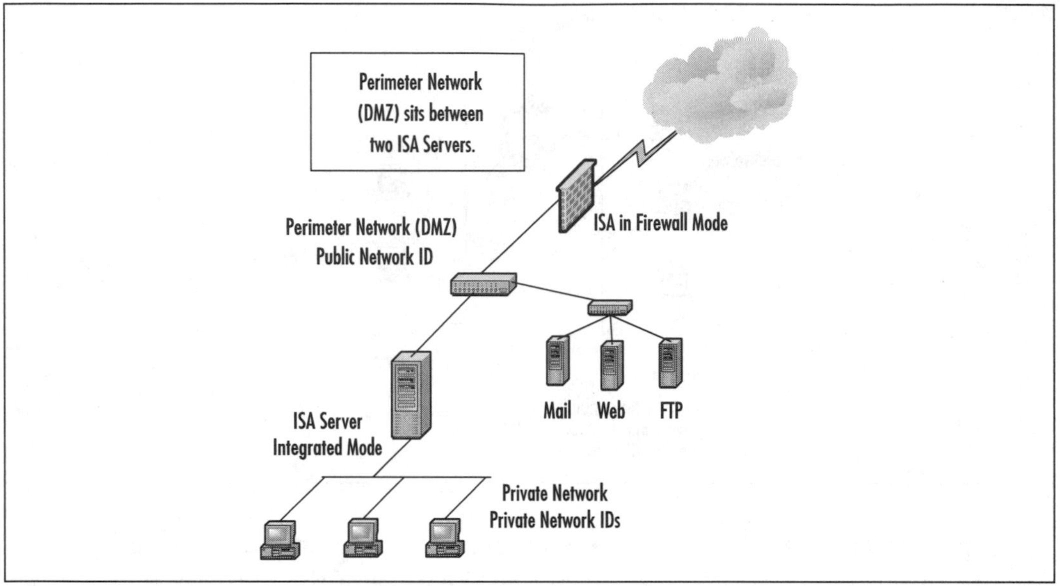

Figure 4.3 A Single-Homed Web-Caching-Only Server

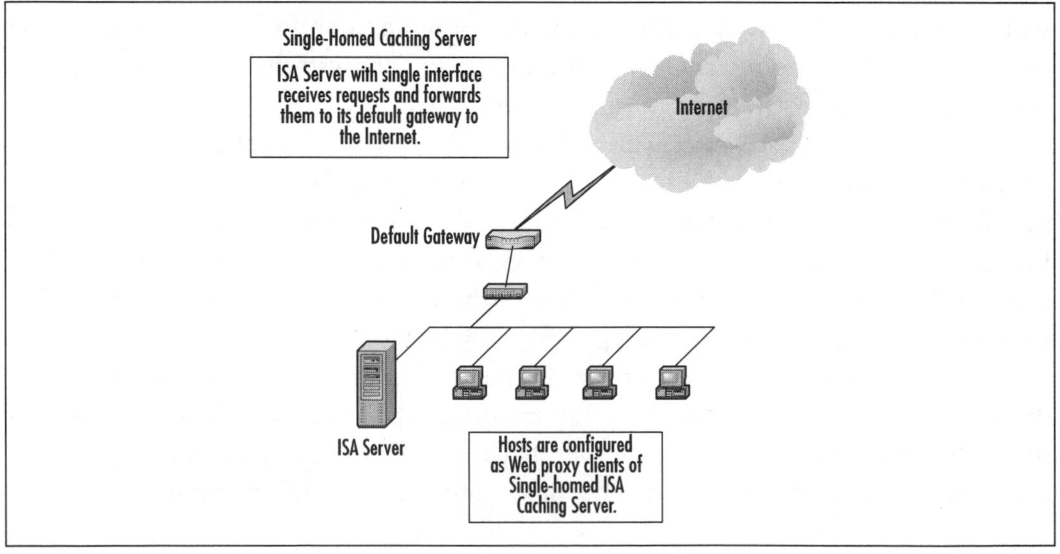

The DNS server addresses vary depending on the interface you are configuring. The interfaces connecting to your ISP need DNS entries that can resolve Internet names. These DNS server entries can be your ISP's DNS servers (which is the most typical arrangement), or you can configure the DNS entry to be any other server on the Internet that can resolve Internet addresses.

For your internal interfaces, configure the DNS entry to a server that can resolve the names of the computers on your internal network. It is critically important that you have your DNS infrastructure in place and that it is functional prior to implementing ISA Server, because inbound requests will use your internal DNS server to resolve requests for machines on the internal network.

Securing the Network Interfaces

ISA Server includes features such as packet filtering that will protect your external interface, but there are some general measures you should take in order to prevent potential security breaches.

NOTE

The File and Printer Sharing for Microsoft Networks option allows you to turn off or on the Microsoft *Server Service*. This Server Service allows you to create shares that are accessible to other server message block (SMB) clients on the network. The flip side of the Server Service is the *Workstation Service* or *Redirector*. The Redirector (technically, the SMB Redirector) allows a machine to be a client to a machine running the Server Service. When you turn off the Redirector, it will not be able to access SMB shares on a Microsoft network.

You should always disable file and print sharing for Microsoft networks on the external interface and even for the internal interface of the ISA computer. Due to the inherently insecure nature of the file-sharing protocol (SMB) used on Microsoft systems, you should never expose the file system to SMB access. The ISA server should be a device dedicated to firewall and/or Web-caching functions and should not be used as a file or network application server.

To disable file and print sharing on a particular interface:

1. Open the interface **Properties** dialog box.
2. Remove the check mark from the **File and Printer Sharing for Microsoft Networks** check box.

3. Remove the check mark from the **Client for Microsoft Networks** option.
4. If you are using a dial-up connection and it is up when you make the changes, hang up the connection and then redial for the new settings to take effect. Figure 4.4 shows what this process looks like.

Figure 4.4 Disabling File and Print Sharing on the External Interface

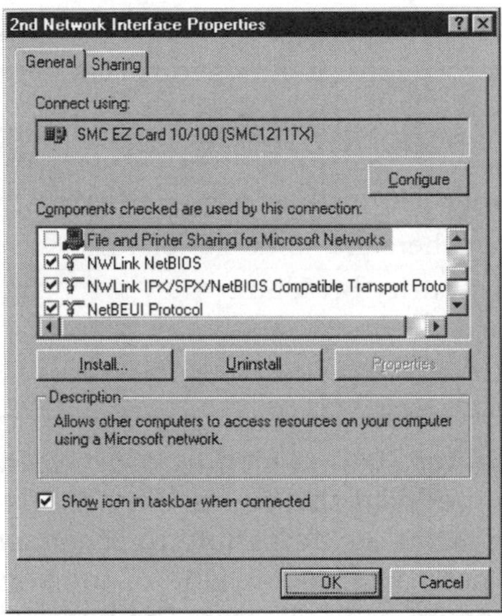

You should also disable the NetBIOS interface on the external interface. No machine on the Internet needs access to the ISA server via NetBIOS over TCP/IP; such access could provide an avenue for attackers to compromise your ISA server. To disable NetBIOS over TCP/IP:

1. Open the network interface **Properties** dialog box.
2. Click the **Advanced** button.
3. Click the **WINS** tab. You will see a screen like the one in Figure 4.5.

You might also want to disable NetBIOS on the internal interface. However, you must be careful about doing so, because certain services that you might want to enable, such as the Alerter service, remain dependent on NetBIOS to communicate with stations on the internal network.

Note that if your external interface is a dial-up connection such as an analog modem or ISDN terminal adapter, you will not be able to disable the NetBIOS interface via the methods described. In fact, if you go into the properties of the dial-up connection you've configured, you'll not even see the NetBIOS option buttons.

Figure 4.5 Disabling NetBIOS on the External Interface

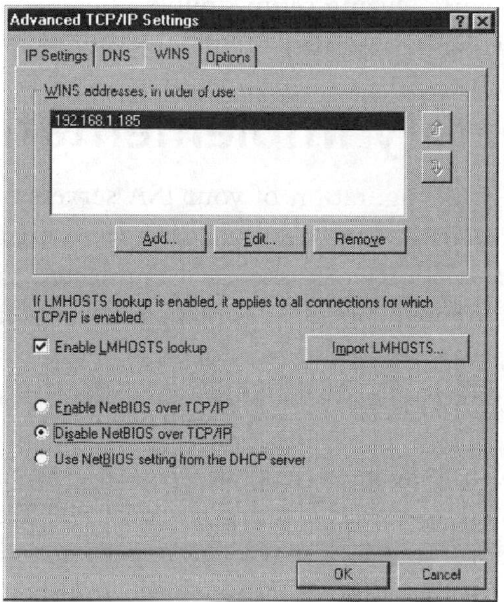

Keep in mind that a "dedicated" ISDN connection connects to its remote router in the same way that a "dial-up" connection does. The only configuration difference is that the dedicated connection will have a static IP address affixed to the external interface. Another thing to remember is that a dial-up connection can be configured only with a single IP address. ISA Server does not provide the address-pooling features that the Windows 2000 NAT Server provides.

Keep the External Interface Off the LAT

Although this is not an interface configuration option per se, it is related to the internal and external interfaces. The LAT is used by the ISA server's Firewall Service to determine which networks are internal and which are external. ISA Server does not apply policies to packets destined to an internal network location. If it receives such packets, it merely forwards them.

You will run into problems if the external interface on your ISA server is included in the LAT. If the external interface is seen by ISA Server as local, it assumes that any packets it receives on that interface are from internal network hosts, and it does not apply security policy to those packets. In addition, keep in mind that packet filtering is applied only to *external* interfaces on the ISA server. If the external interface is on the LAT, no packet filtering rules will apply.

Incorrectly configuring the LAT is a one of the quickest ways to completely disable security provided by ISA Server. Prior to installation, be sure to write down and confirm all the internal network IDs your organization uses so that the LAT is configured properly. During setup, double-check your selections when the LAT Configuration dialog box appears.

Active Directory Implementation

If you plan to centralize configuration of your ISA servers or you want to install an array of ISA servers, you need an Active Directory domain.

ISA servers that have all network interfaces connected to the internal network can safely be configured as members of an internal Active Directory domain. Since these servers are not at risk for Internet intrusion, you can focus security concerns on internal network threats that affect all servers on the internal network.

However, if you plan to keep an array of ISA servers on the edge of the network, you should strongly consider creating a domain dedicated to the ISA array itself. For security reasons, you do not want to expose your internal network's Active Directory and user accounts database to the Internet. To prevent such exposure, you can create a dedicated ISA Server domain to interface with the Internet.

This dedicated ISA Server domain should be in a different forest from your internal Active Directory domain. The ISA Server domain can then be configured to trust the internal AD domain but *without* a reciprocal trust. This is because you do not want your internal network to trust the accounts on the ISA Server domain. This setup helps minimize potential damage should an administrative account in the external domain become compromised.

This type of domain configuration is the ideal, but it might not fit the needs of organizations that have more than one domain as part of their internal networks. For example, if you have a root domain of isacorp.net and subdomains of west.isacorp.net and east.isacorp.net, and you then configure an external trust (also known as an *explicit trust*) from the ISA Server domain to the isacorp.net domain, you will run into problems with the lack of transitivity. The security accounts in the isacorp.net domain will be respected by the ISA Server domain, but the subdomains' accounts will not be trusted, because external trusts lack transitivity.

To solve this problem, you need to make the ISA domain a part of the same forest as the rest of your domains so that you can take advantage of trust transitivity. The ISA domain administrators do not have any automatic administrative privileges in the internal network domains. Just be sure *not* to delegate to ISA domain accounts any authority regarding resources in the internal network's domain.

NOTE

For a detailed discussion of the issue of ISA Server domain configurations, please refer to Chapter 2, "ISA Server in the Enterprise."

Mission-Critical Considerations

Your ISA Server installation is likely to be a cornerstone of your Internet access scheme. Some businesses literally live or die by their ability to connect to and work via the Internet. Even a few minutes of downtime can lead to thousands or even tens of thousands of lost dollars. Therefore, before implementing your plan, if Internet access is a mission-critical service for any part of your organization, you need to consider fault tolerance.

Four key areas of fault tolerance and mission-critical availability are:

- Hard disk fault tolerance
- Network fault tolerance
- Server fault tolerance
- Bastion host configuration

Here we look at each of these issues in turn.

Hard Disk Fault Tolerance

When considering disk fault-tolerance schemes, you need to pin down what it is that you want to accomplish. Right out of the box, Windows 2000 supports two forms of software-based disk fault tolerance:

- Mirrored volumes (mirror sets)
- RAID 5 volumes (stripe sets with parity)

Although Windows 2000 does include these methods of disk fault tolerance without requiring any added software or hardware, you might find that your situation requires a more high-performance solution. If you are implementing ISA Server in a large enterprise environment, you will find that the resource demands of software fault tolerance drain server resources to an unacceptable degree.

For high-load ISA Server environments, the better solution is hardware-based *Redundant Array of Independent Disks (RAID)*. In hardware-based RAID, the fault-tolerance mechanisms are built right into the hard disk controller and require no appreciable processor or memory overhead. We cover both software and hardware RAID implementations in this chapter.

TIP

Before you can implement mirrored volumes or RAID 5 volumes on a Windows 2000 server, you must convert the disks on which the volumes will reside to *dynamic* disks.

Mirrored Volumes (Mirror Sets)

Mirrored volumes provide a method to allow all data written to one volume to be automatically copied to a second volume. Mirrored-volume configurations allow for real-time fault tolerance for the data stored on a mirrored volume.

The best use of the mirrored-volume configuration is found when the boot and system files are on the primary member of the mirrored volume and then mirrored on a secondary member of the mirror set, with the secondary volume located on a different disk and controller. This configuration, in which the secondary member of the mirrored volume is located on a different disk and controller than the primary member, is known as *disk duplexing*. Figure 4.6 characterizes this sort of configuration.

NOTE

To the operating system, mirrored disks (both disks on the same controller) and duplexed disks (on different controllers) appear the same, and both are shown as mirrored volumes in the Windows 2000 disk management console. Duplexing is a hardware differentiation. Duplexing provides not only fault-tolerance benefits but also superior performance, since disk reads and writes can take place simultaneously across different controllers.

Figure 4.6 Mirrored Volumes Configured in a Duplex Arrangement

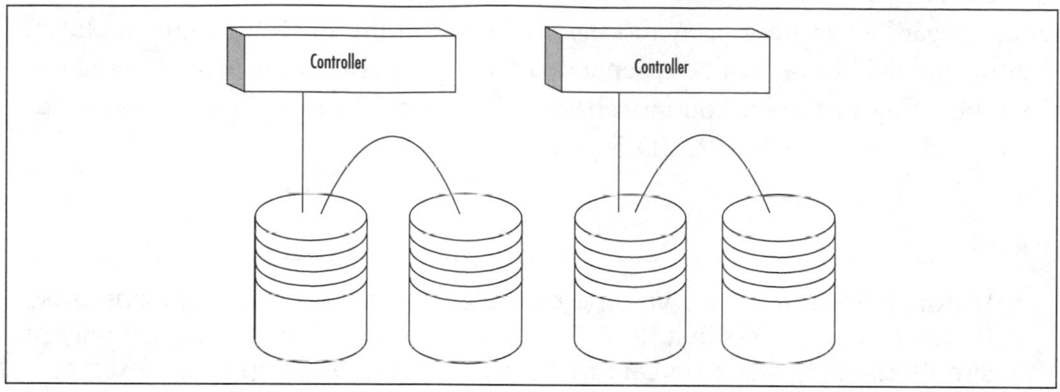

The primary member of the mirror set is the "live" part of the mirror set—the one that is actually being used by the user and operating system. However, everything that is copied or changed on the primary member is also updated on the secondary member of the mirror set. If the primary member should fail, the system will automatically fail-over and the secondary member of the mirror set will take over the duties once held by the primary member. There is no negative effect on performance. In fact, write performance should improve slightly because changes will not have to be written twice.

When either member of the mirror set fails, there will be no discernable change in terms of server availability and users will be totally unaware that any changes have taken place. However, you should configure some sort of notification mechanism so that an administrator is informed when a member of the mirror set fails so that it can be repaired quickly.

NOTE

Once a single member of the mirror set fails, there is no longer any fault tolerance until a new disk is configured as a secondary disk. Note that regardless of which disk fails, the remaining disk becomes the primary member and the new disk becomes the secondary member.

RAID 5 Volumes (Stripe Sets with Parity)

The other "out of the box" RAID solution that you can consider using in your ISA Server solution is the *RAID 5 volume*. RAID 5 volumes were known in the

Windows NT world as *stripe sets with parity*. Because parity information is stored in the RAID 5 volume, you have fault tolerance in the event of a single disk failure, regardless of how many disks are included in the RAID 5 volume. The data on the failed disk can be regenerated from the parity information stored on the other disks in the set. You must have a minimum of three physical disks (and up to 32 disks) to create a RAID 5 volume.

NOTE

Unfortunately, a RAID 5 volume can tolerate the failure of only one disk. If two or more disks in a RAID 5 volume should fail either sequentially or simultaneously, the data cannot be regenerated and you must restore the information stored on the array from backup.

The major advantage of a RAID 5 volume over a mirrored volume is speed. Striped volumes have faster read/write performance than mirrored volumes. However, one disadvantage of the RAID 5 volume is that you cannot place the system or boot files on such a volume. This is a limitation of the software implementation of RAID 5, because the operating system must be able to load and access the fault-tolerance disk driver (ftdisk.sys) before it can mount the volume. Since you must be able to access the system files to load the disk drivers, you cannot include the system files on a RAID 5 volume.

The primary disadvantage of a RAID 5 volume compared with a RAID 1 volume is a higher cost of entry. You can create a RAID 1 volume with a single pair of disks, whereas the RAID 5 volume requires at least three physical disks. This could be a factor for very small shops that are highly cost constrained.

However, RAID 5 has a couple of advantages over RAID 1 in that the total cost of a RAID 5 solution per megabyte is lower when more disks are added to the array. The amount of "unusable" disk space on a mirror set equals 50 percent of the total disk space dedicated to the set, whereas the space required for storing parity information on a RAID 5 array equals 1 ÷ *number_of_disks*. So, if you have a 10-disk array, you are only "wasting" one-tenth of your disk space for fault-tolerance information.

The second advantage of the RAID 5 array is the much larger volume size that can be created. The largest usable volume size on a RAID 1 array is equal to the size of one of the disks in the array. However, the size of a RAID 5 array is the sum of all the disks (up to 32) minus the fraction used for parity information.

Designing & Planning…

Cost Factors in Choosing a Disk Fault-Tolerance Scheme

Initial hardware cost for implementing a mirrored volume is less to implement than implementing a RAID 5 volume. This is because you must buy only two disks for a mirrored volume, but you must have a minimum of three disks for RAID 5.

However, the cost per megabyte of data is less for a RAID 5 configuration, and that cost decreases as the number of disks in the RAID array increases. For example, if you have three physical disks in the RAID 5 set, the equivalent of one physical disk (or one-third of the total disk space) is used for parity information, whereas the rest (two-thirds of the disk space) is available for data. If you increase that to 10 physical disks, only one-tenth of the total disk space must be used for storing the parity information and nine-tenths is available for storing your data.

Thus, over the long term, a RAID 5 volume is usually better in terms of pure cost effectiveness. You will want to weigh other factors, such as ease of recovery and need to provide fault tolerance for system and boot partitions, when selecting the best fault-tolerance method for your situation. Figure 4.7 characterizes a RAID 5 configuration.

Figure 4.7 A RAID 5 Volume

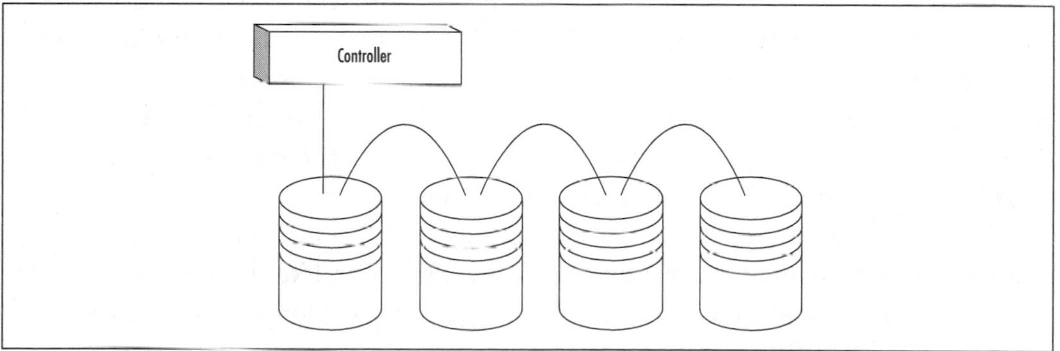

Optimizing a Software RAID Configuration

In your ISA Server configuration, you should include log files, cache files, and reports on the RAID 5 array. Doing so will significantly speed ISA server performance and allow for fault tolerance for these important files. *Keep in mind that your array is fault tolerant only when all disks are in working order.*

If a single disk in a RAID 5 fails, your array is no longer fault tolerant, and you need to replace the disk as soon as possible—not only for fault tolerance reasons, but also because the process of reconstructing the data from the parity information will slow performance significantly.

If you are running the Web proxy service's Web-caching feature, you want to be able to ensure the fastest read performance possible. This is because the Web cache is typically implemented to improve client-perceived performance. Write time to the cache isn't quite as important, since the Web-caching feature will store URLs in RAM for a certain period of time before writing them to cache. However, you do want to be able to retrieve cached Web objects as quickly as possible.

RAID 5, because it is striped, has better read performance than RAID 0; therefore, you should consider placing the cache files on a RAID 5 array if you require fault tolerance for your cache. In a production environment that is strapped for Internet bandwidth, you might consider this option. However, the Web cache itself is not generally a mission-critical component, and you might want to sacrifice fault tolerance for superior read performance. In this case, you should use the software-based RAID 0, or *striped volumes*. Although they do not provide fault tolerance, they do provide the best read performance of any RAID type.

The log files present a different set of requirements. If you plan to do extensive logging (which you would consider in a very secure environment), you need to place the log files on a volume that supports optimal *write* performance. Log files are read only occasionally, but they are written to constantly. Both RAID 1 and RAID 5 suffer from write latency because, in a RAID 1 configuration, the data must be written twice, and in a RAID 5 configuration, the parity information must be calculated and then written in addition to the data.

Unlike the situation with the Web cache, the log files are mission critical and do require placement on a fault-tolerant disk set. Given the choice between RAID 1 and 5, your best option is the mirror set.

Reports are rarely written and only occasionally accessed. Therefore, read/write performance is not a primary issue. However, like the log files, you do not want to lose these or you will have to recreate them. You can place these reports on either a RAID 1 or 5 volume.

Hardware-Based RAID

Although we have discussed fault-tolerant disk arrays in the context of the software-based schemes provided with Windows 2000 out of the box, you can also implement fault tolerance via hardware RAID controllers. Almost all organizations that require the highest level of fault tolerance and performance use hardware-based RAID.

There are many advantages to using hardware RAID controllers. These controllers allow you to mirror the boot and system partitions, because they are not dependent on the operating system initializing before fault-tolerance sets can be established. Furthermore, the hardware solutions are significantly faster on software-based RAID. A hardware implementation of RAID appears to the operating system as though the array were a single physical disk.

One type of hardware-based RAID that has gained widespread popularity is known either as RAID 10 or RAID 0+1. This RAID implementation creates a *striped volume* and then mirrors the striped volume to provide fault tolerance. This process gives you the best of both worlds: the performance of a striped volume and the fault tolerance of a mirror set.

For example, you could configure a three-disk set as part of a RAID 0 array. This set would be mirrored onto another three disks, so such an array would require a total of six disks. If any member of the RAID 0 array should fail, a corresponding disk from the mirror set would be brought into service. However, at this point you no longer have fault tolerance and you need to replace the disk as soon as possible.

More sophisticated (and expensive) RAID implementations allow you to keep "hot spares" online so that, in the event of a disk failure, a hot spare is introduced to the array automatically. Again, you have fault tolerance as long as you have one hot spare available. When there are no more spares, you need to add new disks.

Network Fault Tolerance

When implementing ISA Server, you must consider the level of availability you require for both your internal and external network interfaces. Your server configurations can be designed to be fully fault tolerant, but if your single interface to the Internet becomes unavailable, all your machine fault tolerance is moot.

The type of fault-tolerant configuration you design for your external interfaces depends on the type of interface and the arrangements you have with your Internet service provider (ISP). For example, if you have a single ISDN connection via a single account with your ISP, there's not much you can do with such a configuration, as is, to allow for any level of fail-over.

The ideal network fault-tolerance solution for your external interface is to have multiple ISA Servers participating in an enterprise array on the edge of your network. You would then configure routing rules so that, in the event of an interface failure, the request can first be resolved within the array and then forwarded to another server within the array if it needs to be sent to the Internet for retrieval.

UNDOCUMENTED ISA

The ability to configure ISA Server with routing rules in the event of an external interface failure is a powerful fault-tolerance mechanism built into ISA Server. However, this mechanism requires you to have made provisions for multiple connections to the Internet, which require purchasing and maintaining multiple access accounts.

Large organizations can more easily absorb the costs of multiple high-speed dedicated connections. If you are working in a smaller networking environment that is more sensitive to cost, you might consider an analog backup line in the event of failure of another low-cost solution such as cable, dial-up ISDN, or DSL.

Network load balancing, another important issue related to fault tolerance (as well as performance), is discussed in detail in Chapter 11, "Optimizing, Customizing, Integrating, and Backing Up ISA Server."

Server Fault Tolerance

There are several ways to ensure fault tolerance for ISA servers in the event of a server crash or the necessity of taking a server offline for maintenance or upgrade. The best way to provide for server fault tolerance is to take advantage of arrays of ISA servers when you deploy the Enterprise Edition. An ISA Server array is a collection of ISA servers that share the same configuration information and Web cache content. An array provides a high degree of fault tolerance; if a single server becomes unavailable, the other servers can take over to service requests for the downed ISA server.

NOTE

All members of an array share the same Web cache policies and can access each other's cached Web content. However, the contents of the cache do *not* mirror in any way the contents of other servers in the array. In addition, the cache location settings must be set on the individual servers. The cache location is not part of the cache configuration shared by the array. However, this setting doesn't happen automatically. If your clients are configured to access a certain ISA server and that server becomes unavailable, the client will not necessarily be able to access the next server in the array. In order to provide a measure of fault tolerance for client access, you must devise some scheme that will allow the clients to fail-over to another ISA server.

DNS Round Robin

One way you can accomplish server fault tolerance is to configure a *DNS round robin* on your network. In your DNS, you assign the same host name to the IP addresses of your respective ISA servers. That is, your ISA servers will each have the same fully qualified domain name.

If you are using Windows 2000 DNS servers, DNS round robin is enabled by default. However, you should never take it for granted that the settings on a particular server are at their defaults. To assess whether DNS round robin is available on your Windows 2000 DNS server:

1. Right-click the server name in the left pane of the DNS console.
2. Click **Properties**.
3. Click the **Advanced** tab. You will see the screen that appears in Figure 4.8. Make sure that "Enable round robin" is checked if you want to take advantage of the DNS round-robin feature.

With DNS round robin enabled, when a network client queries DNS, it receives the IP address of one of the ISA servers. If that server is not available, the network client receives an error message. When a subsequent request is made, the ISA client receives another IP address after the expiration of the time-out period of the DNS response it received earlier. Since these addresses are assigned randomly, there's a good chance that it will receive the IP address of a different ISA server (one that is still up and running).

For example, suppose we create three DNS round-robin entries for the host name *isaserver* in the *tacteam.net* domain. The entries would look something like this:

```
isaserver.tacteam.net    A    222.222.222.222
isaserver.tacteam.net    A    222.222.222.223
isaserver.tacteam.net    A    222.222.222.224
```

Figure 4.8 Configuring DNS Round Robin on a Windows 2000 DNS Server

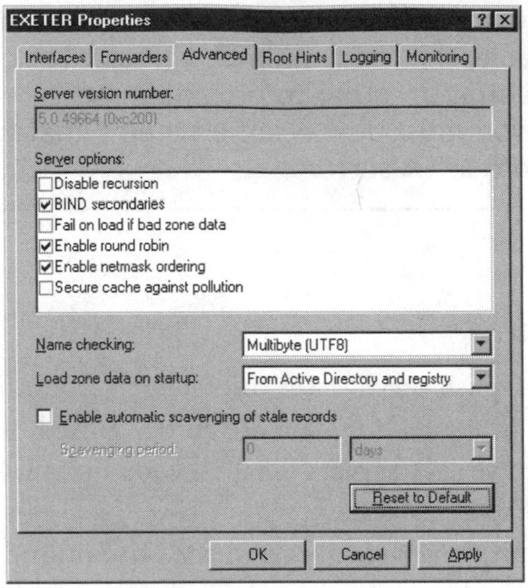

We also set the time-out for these records so that the DNS clients remove the entries from their DNS caches after 1 minute. If a client makes a request for *isaserver.tacteam.net* and receives the IP address 222.222.222.222 and that machine is down, and then the client makes another request 5 seconds later, the IP address will be retrieved from the DNS cache and the DNS server will not be queried again. However, if the request is made 90 seconds later, the entry will have timed out of the cache, and the DNS server will be queried again to resolve the name *isaserver.tacteam.net*.

However, DNS round robin has some notable disadvantages when it comes to fault tolerance. Because the rotation of the IP addresses sent to DNS clients is random, there's the chance that the DNS client will receive the same IP address it got before and therefore will have to wait for the Time to Live (TTL) on that entry to expire before attempting to get another IP address.

You can help minimize this problem by configuring very short TTLs on your round-robin entries in the DNS. However, doing so reduces the efficacy of the client-side DNS cache and could have a negative impact on network performance on a loaded network.

Another thing that complicates this scheme is that the Windows 2000 DNS clients are configured with the ability to "negatively cache" failed DNS requests. By default, the negative cache entry stays in effect for 5 minutes. This means that if an ISA client receives the IP address of the downed ISA server, it will remain a negative cache entry for 5 minutes and the client will not attempt to query the DNS server again until the negative cache entry has timed out.

NOTE

If you check Figure 4.8 again, you'll notice another option, "Enable netmask ordering." When this option is enabled, *local subnet priority* has precedence over random round-robin assignments. Local subnet prioritization allows the DNS server to compare address records with the source IP address of the DNS query. If a host record in the DNS is located on the same or similar network ID as the DNS client, that record will always be delivered to the client and the client will not receive a random record. This could be an issue if you have array members on different network IDs and clients on the same networks as the array members. If all array members have the same network ID, DNS round robin will be applied to hosts on the same network as the array members.

You can change the time-out period for the negative cache entries by configuring the registry. The key can be located at:

```
HKLM\System\CurrentControlSet\Services\Dnscache\Parameters
```

The value to configure is the NegativeCacheTime, which, by default, is configured for 300 seconds.

Bastion Host Configuration

A *bastion host* is a computer that has an interface with an untrusted network. In the context of ISA Server, that untrusted network is typically the Internet. The bastion host can lie with an interface directly connected to the Internet, or it can be placed on a perimeter network behind a router but in front of the internal network.

All traffic that moves between the Internet and your internal network should move through a bastion host, which is your ISA Server. It is the job of the bastion host to ensure that all packets sent to and received from the Internet are evaluated and assessed for their relevance and safety.

Because of the central role the bastion host computer plays in your Internet access scheme, it is important that the operating system is hardened and made as stable as possible. System hardening can be performed via the ISA Server Security

Configuration Wizard. This wizard applies security settings derived from a set of security templates that are installed with Windows 2000 Server family products.

In addition to applying strict security settings to the file system, registry, and applications, you need to review the services running on the bastion host computer. Each service running on your bastion host provides a possible target for an attacker to exploit. Common operating system and network services that are installed by default can provide avenues of opportunity for attackers. Some of these services include:

- The Browser Service
- The IIS Admin Service
- The Indexing Service
- The Remote Registry Service
- The SMTP Service

Many more potentially hazardous services are started by default on Windows 2000 Server family products. We cover the issues of system hardening and bastion host configuration in more detail in Chapter 9, "Configuring ISA Server for Inbound Access."

Planning the Appropriate Installation Mode

There are three types, or *modes*, of ISA Server installation. You must select one of the three modes when you install ISA. The selections are:

- Firewall mode
- Cache mode
- Integrated mode

The type of installation you choose determines which feature set will be available to you. Table 4.5 lists the features available in firewall and cache modes. *Integrated mode allows you to take advantages of both firewall and cache mode features.*

Table 4.5 Comparing Firewall and Cache Mode Features

ISA Server Feature	Firewall Mode	Cache Mode
SecureNat client support	Yes	Yes
Web proxy client support	Yes	Yes
Reports	Yes	Yes
Alerts	Yes	Yes
Real-time service monitoring	Yes	Yes
Web site filtering	Yes	Yes
Web server publishing	Yes	Yes
Enterprise policy	Yes	Yes
Access policy—HTTP	Yes	Yes
Access policy—all protocols	Yes	No
Non-Web server publishing	Yes	No
Packet filtering	Yes	No
Application filters	Yes	No
Web caching	No	Yes

When we take a closer look at this table, it is relatively easy to digest. Let's look at a few factors you'll want to consider in deciding which mode to deploy.

Installing in Firewall Mode

ISA servers support virtually all ISA Server features, with the exception of the Web cache. The Web-caching feature is very memory and processor intensive; therefore, it makes sense to exclude this feature from a server for which the primary purpose is to act as a firewall. A firewall should not run extra services in order to minimize the risk of exposure.

In addition, you want to be able to harness all the available system resources in order to process packet-filtering rules, protocol rules, and site and content rules as quickly as possible on your firewall.

Installing in Cache Mode

When you install the server in cache mode, you intend that server to work as a Web proxy server only. The Web proxy service supports the HTTP, HTTPS, FTP, and Gopher protocols. If you want to support only these protocols and take advantage of the Web-caching features, but you don't want to implement a full-fledged, policy-based firewall, the Web cache option is a good one.

Another reason that you might want to implement a caching-only server is that you already have a firewall in place. Many organizations already have powerful firewall solutions such as Cisco PIX, Checkpoint Software's Firewall-1, and many others. You might even want to consider this scenario when you are using a second ISA server for a firewall on the edge of your network. In this way, you can take advantage of the powerful Web-caching features included with ISA Server and have the protection of a sophisticated firewall.

SECURITY ALERT!

You should consider the Web proxy mode a minimalist configuration. In fact, if all you want is a Web-caching server, we strongly recommend that for security reasons, you do not place this server at the edge of your network. The cache mode configuration is secure to the extent that it allows you to use private IP addresses on your internal network, but it does not allow the firewall features required for a server that is located on the edge of the network.

A cache mode server is best placed on the internal network, in which case you can use a single interface or multiple interfaces. *Be sure that you implement some kind of firewall solution at the edge of your network to protect your internal computers from Internet intruders.*

Installing in Integrated Mode

The integrated mode ISA Server allows you to take advantage of all the features ISA Server has to offer. However, this configuration is probably best left to organizations that are testing ISA features or are cost contained and cannot bear the expense of purchasing separate caching servers and firewalls.

The reason you would prefer not to have both the Web-caching services and the firewall services running on the same computer keys back into our discussion of bastion hosts. The more services running on a single computer, the more avenues of attack are open to intruders. Although ISA Server was tested thoroughly prior to its release, you must remain aware that all security software has potential holes that can be exploited. An attacker cannot exploit a hole in the Web proxy services on your mission-critical firewall if the hole is not there.

One exception to this general rule is when the ISA server is placed between a departmental LAN and the corporate backbone. In this case, you might want to avail yourself of some of the firewall features while also taking advantage of the Web-caching features. This is a reasonable configuration because the corporate backbone is less vulnerable to the type of attacks seen on the open Internet.

Table 4.6 shows some common placement scenarios for each configuration.

Table 4.6 Recommended Roles for ISA Server Modes

ISA Server Mode	Location
Firewall	■ Edge of the network
	■ Server that interfaces with internal and DMZ networks
Cache	■ Single-homed or multihomed, with all interfaces connected to the internal network
	■ Interfaces on the internal network and a DMZ network; DMZ is protected by a firewall
Integrated	■ Test network
	■ Interface with corporate backbone

Prior to implementing your solution, be sure that all members of the network security team are aware of the implications of the various ISA Server modes. This is important when you are comparing the exposure and protection that each mode provides for the network.

Planning for a Standalone or an Array Configuration

ISA Server Enterprise Edition can be installed as either an array member or as a standalone server. There are many advantages to installing the server as an array member. These advantages include:

- The ability to implement enterprisewide array policies via Active Directory
- The ability to easily implement a common configuration for multiple ISA Server computers
- The option to expand the scope of a single ISA Server to multiple servers with a common configuration
- Fault tolerance

You must first prepare Active Directory prior to installing an ISA server as an array member. The procedure for preparing AD, called *enterprise initialization*, is accomplished via the installation wizard included on the ISA Server CD. If you like, you can manually run the ISA Enterprise initialization and install ISA Server at a later time. If you choose to install ISA Server in an array configuration, the Setup program will check to see if the schema has been properly modified before it allows you to continue.

Once the array member is installed, a single enterprise array policy can be implemented on any array in your organization. All array members are able to access configuration information, because array configuration settings are stored in Active Directory. This is a nice fault-tolerance method for your configuration because Active Directory is replicated throughout your AD domain controller network.

SECURITY ALERT!

You might want to implement an enterprise security policy before installing any members of an array. It would seem you could do this by creating the array first in the ISA MMC. However, our experience shows that although the array can be created, you cannot then join computers to an array that has no members.

Even if you plan to implement just a single ISA server, you should consider the possibility that you will want to expand your configuration in the future. If you choose the standalone ISA Server configuration and later decide to deploy an array of ISA servers, you will need to run the enterprise initialization. Then you can *promote* the standalone server to array member. In Chapter 5, we will walk through this process in step-by-step fashion.

NOTE

If you have the Standard Edition of ISA Server, you won't have the choice to deploy an array. The Standard Edition is a viable solution for small companies with relatively simple requirements, but it is not designed to scale to the needs of complex enterprise networks.

Planning ISA Client Configuration

A critical aspect of your ISA Server design is the ISA Server *client base* you expect to support. Proxy Server 2.0 supported what were known as the *Web proxy client, WinSock proxy client*, and *SOCKS proxy client*. The SOCKS service is no longer required, and the Winsock proxy client has changed its name.

The client types supported by ISA Server are:

- The firewall client
- The Web proxy client
- The SecureNat client

Each client type offers it own advantages and disadvantages. Let's examine the features and capabilities of each client type and assess how they fit into an overall ISA design scheme.

The Firewall Client

Network computers configured as Firewall Service clients are able to access all Winsock protocols. When applications on the firewall client send a request to a host on a network ID not contained on the LAT (typically the Internet), the firewall client software installed on the firewall client will intercept the request and forward it to the Firewall Service on the ISA server.

The primary advantage of a configuring machine as a firewall client is that you can control access to protocols, sites, and content on a per-user or per-group basis. This feature allows you more granular control over your access policies than you have compared with the SecureNat or Web proxy client. You cannot control access to specific protocols on a user or group basis with the SecureNat client, only via IP addresses, in a manner similar to the SOCKS Service in Proxy Server 2.0. The Web Proxy Service can be configured to require authentication, but you cannot limit access to the Web Proxy Service mediated protocols on a per-user or per-group basis.

Another significant advantage to the firewall client software is that it supports just about any application protocol it encounters. Some applications require that multiple connections be established between the client and the destination server. The Firewall Client supports these protocols; the NAT client might or might not be able to support them. However, since all NAT calls to the ISA server must be processed by the Firewall Service, almost all applications should be supported.

The disadvantage of configuring a host as a firewall client is that you must install the firewall client software. Not all operating systems support this software. The only operating systems that do support it are:

- Windows 95 OSR2
- Windows 98/ME
- Windows NT 4.0
- Windows 2000
- Windows XP (Whistler)

This represents a departure from the support offered by the firewall client's "older brother," the Winsock proxy client. The Winsock proxy client software included with Proxy Server 2.0 supported Win 3.x machines using a 16-bit client software installation. The firewall client software does not include a 16-bit client. Keep this in mind if you have the ill fortune of needing to support Windows 3.x machines.

Firewall Client Support for Windows 3.x Machines

If you must support Win 3.x machines, one workaround is to use the Winsock proxy client provided with Proxy Server 2.0. Of course, you must have a copy of Proxy Server 2.0 to implement this solution. The reason that you can do this is that the firewall client and the Winsock client are interchangeable in terms of their functionality.

For this reason, you do not need to install the firewall client on your machines that already have the Winsock proxy client installed. You can also use the firewall client software to connect to the Winsock proxy service on a Proxy Server 2.0 server. The Firewall Service on ISA Server is more sophisticated than the Winsock proxy service in Proxy Server 2.0, but the client side essentially works the same way.

Firewall Client Does Not Support IPX/SPX

Another feature that was supported by the old Winsock proxy client software was the IPX/SPX gateway. In Proxy Server 2.0, you could configure Winsock proxy clients to use the IPX/SPX protocol to gain access to the Internet via the Winsock Proxy Service. The Firewall Service does not provide this support. If you are still running IPX/SPX on your internal network, you'll have to take this factor into consideration.

In fact, prior to considering an ISA Server proxy solution, you need to convert your network to a TCP/IP-based infrastructure. This conversion is required in order to implement ISA Server, but there are many other compelling reasons to retire your IPX infrastructure. If yours has been a Novell shop for some time, you might need to retrain your administrators. The cost of investing in learning and implementing TCP/IP on your network will expand the possibilities of expansion for your network and allow you to more easily troubleshoot network problems because of the large number of tools available to investigate TCP/IP networks.

The Web Proxy Client

The Web Proxy Service provides access to a limited set of protocols:

- HTTP
- HTTPS (HTTP secured via SSL)
- FTP
- Gopher

Whereas we can safely dismiss Gopher from our consideration, the other protocols represent the bulk of typical Internet connectivity requirements for the majority of organizations that want to implement ISA Server solutions.

If all you require are these "Web" protocols, a Web proxy client/server configuration might best fit your organization. Even if you need to install the firewall client software to take advantage of other Winsock applications, you might still want to configure your machines as Web proxy clients due to a slight performance advantage you'll gain for Web access via HTTP 1.1 CERN-compliant browsers.

SECURITY ALERT!

Among the group of ISA Server application filters is the HTTP Redirector filter. If you configure this filter to redirect HTTP requests to the Web Proxy Service (so that firewall and SecureNat clients can take advantage of the Web cache), security information sent from the firewall client will be lost. This means that the firewall client might need to manually enter authentication information to access HTTP. You can circumvent this manual authentication process by making the firewall (and SecureNat) client a Web proxy client as well.

The Web proxy client has the advantage of not requiring installation of any dedicated client software and is compatible with all operating systems. If you have a browser that supports proxy client configuration, such as Internet Explorer, you can take direct advantage of the Web Proxy Service. You can even configure Netscape Navigator running on Linux to use the Web Proxy Service. The Web Proxy Service also supports user authentication, which gives it an advantage over the SecureNat client.

The SecureNat Client

SecureNat clients are the simplest type of ISA client to set up, because virtually no configuration is required. In order to create a SecureNat client, all you need to do is one or the other of these:

- Configure the client to use the ISA server as its default gateway.
- Point the SecureNat client to a gateway that will be able to route Internet-bound packets to an ISA server.

The SecureNat client is able to take advantage of the Web cache when the HTTP Redirector filter is enabled. However, even though the SecureNat client is able to utilize the Web cache portion of the Web Proxy Service, SecureNat clients cannot be authenticated against Active Directory or a server's local security accounts database. Access controls for SecureNat clients are implemented via IP addresses rather than user or group membership. If you want a SecureNat client to be authenticated before accessing "Web protocols," configure the SecureNat client as a Web proxy client.

Small organizations that do not have easy access to technical support assistance or those that do not want to install or configure client software will benefit most from the SecureNat client.

Assessing the Best Solution for Your Network

You should decide in advance what type of ISA client configuration you want to implement on your network before beginning the ISA Server rollout. Table 4.7 can be of some assistance when weighing your options.

Table 4.7 Comparing ISA Server Client Features

ISA Client Type	Best-Fit Scenarios
SecureNat client	■ Organization has a simple setup. ■ Organization has no technical support in house. ■ Organization wants to avoid client software installation. ■ Organization does not require user or group authorization to access resources. ■ Organization has non-Windows clients or non-CERN-compliant browsers. ■ Organization ants to publish servers on the internal network or on a DMZ segment.
Firewall client	■ Client software installation is not an issue. ■ Organization requires user- or group-based authentication for access control on a per-protocol basis. ■ Organization requires access to all Winsock protocols. ■ Organization has administrative support for client installation, policy configuration, and client/server troubleshooting.
Web proxy client	■ Organization requires only HTTP, HTTPS, FTP and Gopher access. ■ Organization uses HTTP 1.1 CERN-compliant browsers. ■ Organization does not require access to other Winsock protocols. ■ Organization requires authentication for Web protocols. ■ Organization does not want to configure a default gateway on network clients. ■ Organization has non-Windows clients.

Of course, you are not limited to implementing a single ISA client configuration. You can take advantage of various combinations of clients. For example, you can configure an ISA client as a Web proxy and firewall client to improve performance of Web protocol access, or you can configure a client to be a SecureNat and Web proxy client and take advantage of authentication for Web protocols.

The only mutually exclusive client configuration pair is the firewall client and the SecureNat client. That is because the firewall client will always be subject to the firewall client configuration parameters. The firewall client software will intercept all Winsock requests and forward them to the ISA server. This is in contrast to the SecureNat client, for which the native Winsock interface forwards packets to the machine's default gateway.

Internet Connectivity and DNS Considerations

ISA Server supports just about any interface you want to use to connect to the Internet. Your external interface can be:

- ISDN
- Analog
- DSL
- Cable
- T-Carrier
- X.25
- ATM

An important consideration is whether you want to implement a dedicated or a dial-up solution for Internet connectivity. The advantages of a dedicated connection are speed and reliability. The prime disadvantage of dedicated connections is often cost. However, even the cost of dedicated connections is coming down. In areas that support cable and DSL connections, you can have a dedicated connection to the Internet for well under $100 per month.

Level of Service

Consider the level of service you require before deciding on the type of connection you will use on the external interface. Many businesses seem almost hypnotized by the low prices and potential for high-speed access that DSL and cable connections offer. However, those businesses are often left grinding their teeth and cursing their providers later.

The problem lies in the fact that you are not guaranteed bandwidth or level of service with these types of connections. Although you typically purchase a certain level of service based on an agreement for minimum and maximum throughput, those numbers represent upper limits of service more often than they ever guarantee a minimum level of service. At this time, neither cable nor DSL should be considered reliable enough alternatives on which to base your corporate Internet solution. They are more "rich man's hobbies," to quote a well-heeled DSL engineer we know.

If your business requires a reliable and dedicated connection to the Internet, you are best served by using established technologies such as T-carrier and ISDN. Although the cost of these connections is much higher than the new kids on the block, you won't find yourself worrying about when your connection might become unavailable.

However, it is important to keep in mind that your bandwidth is guaranteed for a couple of router hops. You have no guarantees to bandwidth once your request leaves the control of your service provider. Therefore, although you should be watchful of your average sustainable bandwidth parameters, your primary concern is uptime.

Finally, when researching ISPs, look for a provider that will be able to grow with your organization. Your company might have modest needs for access at this time, but you hope to grow, and your Internet requirements will likely grow with you. You can avoid a significant amount of stress and strain if you can avoid having to move a large and complex Web site in the future when your ISP can no longer handle the traffic.

External Interface Configuration

Regardless of your connection method, you need to configure the external interface's IP configuration. Depending on the design of your Internet access solution, you might have a single IP address or multiple IP addresses bound to the external network interface. You can also choose to use multiple external interfaces. ISA Server does support multiple external interfaces as well as multiple IP addresses bound to a single interface. In fact, it does not even differentiate between them.

If you plan to provide Internet users with access to internal network resources, you will probably want to get one or more static IP addresses to bind to the external interface. If your organization is exceptionally sensitive to cost issues, you can get around the problem of using dedicated IP addresses by taking advantage of third-party dynamic DNS hosting.

Services such as Tzo.com allow you to have a dynamically assigned IP address register in your own domain name on their servers. If you have a cable, ISDN, or DSL configuration that uses DHCP, you can get around changing IP addresses using such a service. You can even create publishing rules that will allow you to register a single domain name and redirect requests to multiple servers on your internal network without having to enter individual Host (A) records on the Tzo.com DNS servers. Larger organizations will foot the cost of dedicated addresses if Internet users must have access to internal network resources.

NOTE

Many companies use ISDN to access the Internet. ISPs sell ISDN corporate packages that often include a higher level of service and support. They also provide a subnetted block of IP addresses for your internal servers. Although you would not want to run a busy Web presence via an ISDN connection, you can use multiple IP addresses and register different domain names to each one. However, you cannot do this with dial-up connections, which includes "dedicated" ISDN. The dial-up account interface only allows you to bind a single IP address to the ISDN terminal adapter.

When configuring the external interface, be sure to include the IP address, subnet mask, and default gateway (remote router) used by that interface. Do *not* configure any internal interface on the ISA server with a default gateway. Since the ISA Server services handle all requests coming into the internal interfaces, you do not need to have a gateway configured on the internal interface. Finally, do not configure the external interface to use DHCP unless your ISP explicitly gives you instructions to do so. For most ISA Server installations on the edge of a network, you will use dedicated IP addresses, so it would be rare to use DHCP.

DNS Issues

ISA Server supports Web publishing and server publishing. By publishing servers, you are able to offer Internet clients services on your internal network. ISA Server Publishing allows you to publish services such as HTTP, NNTP, SMTP, and POP mail to users on the Internet in a secure context.

Most users want to connect to your published network resources via a fully qualified domain name rather than an IP address. Therefore, you need to register one or more domain names to implement a fully functional publishing solution. Once you have obtained these domain names, you can have your ISP's DNS server host your domain database, or you can manage your own DNS servers. If you choose to manage your own DNS, you need to provide the IP addresses of at least two publicly available DNS servers.

After registering your domain names, you need to populate your DNS database with Host (A) address records. Typically, you'll add a record for host names such as "www," "ftp," "mail," and "news" for the Web, FTP, SMTP, and NNTP access, respectively. ISA allows you to publish servers on your internal network or on a perimeter network, so you can use just a single IP address on the external interface and access multiple servers hosting these services.

NOTE

When users connect to an Internet or intranet resource via a Winsock application, they typically do so using a *fully qualified domain name,* or *FQDN*. The FQDN is actually a combination of two names: a *host name* and a *domain name*.

For example, if you are managing the DNS for a domain such as *tacteam.net* and you have a host in that domain named *www*, the FQDN for that host is *www.tacteam.net.* An *unqualified* name would either not include the host name or, more frequently, would include an incomplete path for the domain name. If someone used the name *www.tacteam*, that would represent an unqualified request. Resolution of unqualified requests depends on the DNS client configuration of a particular machine.

For example, you have two machines on your internal network, one that will host your Web server and a second that will host your mail server. You have registered your domain name, *isaserver.net*. You have one external IP address: 222.222.222.222. In the DNS, you enter a Host (A) address record for *www.isaserver.net* and *mail.isaserver.net*. Both of these Host (A) records will point to 222.222.222.222. When a user types *www.isaserver.net* into his or her browser address bar, the user will be connected to 222.222.222.222 Port 80. The server-publishing rule will forward the request to the internal Web server. In the same fashion, when an SMTP application attempts to connect to *mail.isaserver.net*, it will connect to 222.222.222.222 Port 25. The ISA server will forward the request to your published internal mail server.

DNS planning is pivotal to a successful server-publishing scheme. You must configure multiple DNS zones to account for machines located on the internal and external domains. Because this is such an important topic, we cover DNS planning in Chapter 10.

Summary

In this chapter, we covered key planning and design considerations you should undertake before beginning your ISA Server rollout. We highly recommend that you put a good deal of time into the planning phase before you begin to roll out your ISA Server solution. If you know what you need to accomplish prior to the actual execution of your task, you minimize the chances of security breaches during the implementation phase of your plan.

We discussed important issues related to preparing the computer software and hardware for ISA Server. The base requirements for ISA Server are not extreme, but they do need to match the requirements for the level of service you expect ISA Server to provide. The more users who will access the server, the higher the hardware requirements.

You learned about important planning issues regarding network configuration and what to consider when planning your internal and external interfaces. You need to be sure that all interfaces on the ISA server computers are as free from potential security holes as possible, since the ISA server will likely be one of the primary gateways into your internal network.

Internet access for your organization is a mission-critical concern. Therefore, you need to ensure that a high level of fault tolerance is built into your ISA Server solution. We discussed some methods you can put into play when building a fault-tolerant ISA Server deployment.

Finally, we covered some basic issues regarding Internet access and DNS issues. The DNS configuration will be one of your most challenging planning issues, and it must be set up correctly to make internal resources accessible to external hosts and external resources accessible to internal hosts. We touched on some of those issues here and will expand on them in Chapter 10 of this book.

Solutions Fast Track

ISA Deployment: Planning and Designing Issues

☑ Prior to installing ISA Server, you need to assess hardware requirements to meet the needs of your organization's ISA Server deployment plan. An organization that has 50 network clients and chooses to utilize only the Web proxy service will have very different requirements than an organization with 30,000 network clients that wants to avail itself of all the networking services ISA Server has to offer.

- ☑ Whether you choose to install one or 100 ISA servers, each server must meet minimum hardware and software requirements.
- ☑ ISA Server must be installed on a Windows 2000 Server family computer.
- ☑ If you do not have Windows 2000 Service Pack 2 installed, you must install a pre-Service Pack 2 hotfix that is included on the CD-ROM.
- ☑ ISA Server and Windows 2000 support multiprocessor system setups.
- ☑ The number of processors determines how much you'll pay for ISA Server, because the licensing fees are based on the number of processors on the server.
- ☑ Microsoft recommends that any ISA server you deploy should have at least 256 MB of RAM to take advantage of all the product's features.
- ☑ The amount of disk space you allot to your ISA Server configuration can be quite variable. The space required for the program files will always be about 20 MB.
- ☑ You need to plan for a larger amount of disk space per user in a larger environment because there will be a wider variation in the per-user statistics.
- ☑ You should have at least two network interfaces if you plan to use the ISA server as a firewall.
- ☑ If you plan to use a perimeter network, that network can be connected to a third interface connected to the ISA Server.
- ☑ You should always disable file and print sharing for Microsoft networks on the external interface and even for the internal interface of the ISA computer.
- ☑ Incorrectly configuring the LAT is a one of the quickest ways to completely disable security provided by ISA Server.

Active Directory Implementation

- ☑ If you plan to centralize configuration of your ISA servers or you want to install an array of ISA servers, you need an Active Directory domain.
- ☑ ISA servers that have all network interfaces connected to the internal network can safely be configured as members of an internal Active Directory domain.

Mission-Critical Considerations

- ☑ *Mirrored volumes* provide a method to allow all data written to one volume to be automatically copied to a second volume. Mirrored-volume configurations allow for real-time fault tolerance for the data stored on a mirrored volume.
- ☑ The major advantage of a RAID 5 volume over a mirrored volume is speed.
- ☑ In your ISA Server configuration, you should include log files, cache files, and reports on the RAID 5 array. Doing so will significantly speed ISA server performance and allow for fault tolerance for these important files. *Keep in mind that your array is fault tolerant only when all disks are in working order.*
- ☑ More sophisticated (and expensive) RAID implementations allow you to keep "hot spares" online so that, in the event of a disk failure, a hot spare is introduced to the array automatically.
- ☑ The ideal network fault-tolerance solution for your external interface is to have multiple ISA Servers participating in an enterprise array on the edge of your network.
- ☑ The best way to provide for server fault tolerance is to take advantage of arrays of ISA servers when you deploy the Enterprise Edition.
- ☑ One way you can accomplish server fault tolerance is to configure a *DNS round robin* on your network. In your DNS, you assign the same host name to the IP addresses of your respective ISA servers.
- ☑ A *bastion host* is a computer that has an interface with an untrusted network. In the context of ISA Server, that untrusted network is typically the Internet.

Planning the Appropriate Installation Mode

- ☑ There are three types, or *modes*, of ISA Server installation: Firewall mode, cache mode, integrated mode.
- ☑ ISA servers support virtually all ISA Server features, with the exception of the Web cache.

- ☑ A cache mode server is best placed on the internal network, in which case you can use a single interface or multiple interfaces. *Be sure that you implement some kind of firewall solution at the edge of your network to protect your internal computers from Internet intruders.*
- ☑ ISA Server Enterprise Edition can be installed as either an array member or as a standalone server.
- ☑ A critical aspect of your ISA Server design is the ISA Server *client base* you expect to support. Proxy Server 2.0 supported what were known as the *Web proxy client, WinSock proxy client*, and *SOCKS proxy client*.
- ☑ Network computers configured as Firewall Service clients are able to access all Winsock protocols.
- ☑ SecureNat clients are the simplest type of ISA client to set up, because virtually no configuration is required.
- ☑ ISA Server supports Web publishing and server publishing. By publishing servers, you are able to offer Internet clients services on your internal network. ISA Server Publishing allows you to publish services such as HTTP, NNTP, SMTP, and POP mail to users on the Internet in a secure context.

Frequently Asked Questions

The following Frequently Asked Questions, answered by the authors of this book, are designed to both measure your understanding of the concepts presented in this chapter and to assist you with real-life implementation of these concepts. To have your questions about this chapter answered by the author, browse to **www.syngress.com/solutions** and click on the **"Ask the Author"** form.

Q: Can I install ISA Server on a Windows NT 4.0 server?

A: No. ISA Server can be installed only on a Windows 2000 Server family computer that has Service Pack 1 or later installed.

Q: Can I install ISA Server on a Windows 2000 server that is a member of a Windows NT 4.0 domain?

A: Yes. ISA Server can be installed on a Windows 2000 Server family computer that is a member of a Windows NT 4.0 domain. However, ISA Server must be installed as a standalone server and cannot be a member of an enterprise array. The Windows NT 4.0 SAM does not support storing the array configuration information. You must have an Active Directory domain in place, and the computer must be a member of an Active Directory domain in order to be an array member.

Q: Why should I dedicate a bunch of disk space to log files? Can't I just back them up and restore them when I want?

A: You should dedicate a fairly large amount of disk space for your log files because they can grow fairly quickly. If you want to create reports at the end of the month, you need at least the last month's worth of log files available on disk. You can also create reports based on the activity of several months, but those files need to be available on the server to create the reports.

If you dedicate disk space for log files spanning multiple months, the files will be handy in case you need to quickly create a report. You could restore these files from backup, but the backup might not be available on a timely basis for that impromptu meeting scheduled to start in an hour.

Q: I want to include an enterprise array that will interface with the Internet. How should I configure the domain memberships of these machines that sit on the edge of the network?

A: Whenever you expose an ISA server to the Internet, you need to separate the security context of that machine from your internal network. A standalone ISA server can be placed on a standalone server. However, if you implement an enterprise array and interface the array to the Internet, you should create a dedicated Active Directory domain for the ISA servers. After configuring a dedicated ISA domain, create a one-way trust so that the ISA domain trusts the internal domain. Do *not* configure the internal domain to trust the ISA domain.

The reason you want to allow the ISA domain to trust the internal domain is to ease management of the array. However, you might not want to choose this option and instead have no trust relationships between the domains. In that case, you can always use the Runas command to manage the ISA server in the external domain.

Q: How can I use a single interface on my caching-only server? I thought I needed two interfaces to run a proxy server.

A: A caching-only ISA server with a single interface is a simple configuration to set up and maintain. This server requires only a single interface on the internal network. The Web proxy clients are configured to use the single interface on the caching-only ISA server to send their requests.

When the caching-only server receives the requests, it checks its cache for the Web object. If the Web object is not located in the cache, the ISA server will forward the request to the Internet on behalf of the Web client. The caching-only server must be configured with a gateway that allows it to request objects on the Internet.

Q: I want to use ISA Server to connect a small real estate office to the Internet. They have about 35 clients and they use a dedicated ISDN connection. They do not have a dedicated support person, and they call me a couple times a month when there are problems. What is the best client configuration in this type of setup?

A: Since the office does not have onsite support personnel, it might be best to configure the machines in the office as SecureNat clients. You can simplify setup by installing a DHCP server and then configuring a scope that includes the ISA server's internal interface as the default gateway.

If you need to implement user- or group-based access controls, you won't be able to use the SecureNat client. If they want to control access to sites and content based on user or group membership, you'll have to configure the Web proxy clients or install the firewall client software.

Q: How should I configure the DNS settings on my internal and external interfaces?

A: We talk more about the details of DNS later in the book, but for now, you should set the DNS address for the external interface to a DNS server that can resolve Internet host names. Typically, although not always, this will be a DNS server run by your ISP. The internal DNS address should be set for a server on your internal network that can resolve the host names of machines that you are publishing to the Internet.

Q: I have multiple servers on my internal network that I would like to publish to the Internet. Do I have to create Host (A) records for each of these on the publicly available DNS server, or is there some why around this?

A: If your DNS is being managed by a third party, such as your ISP, you can ask that party to create a "wildcard" entry so that all requests that contain your domain name will be sent to the external interface of your ISA server. In this way, you can create publishing rules so that requests for defined host names are forwarded to specific servers on your internal network. We'll go over the details later in the book when we discuss server publishing.

Chapter 5

ISA Server Installation

Solutions for this chapter:

- Installing ISA Server on a Windows 2000 Server
- Performing the Installation
- Migrating from Microsoft Proxy Server 2.0

☑ Summary

☑ Solutions Fast Track

☑ Frequently Asked Questions

Introduction

ISA Server can provide the single network access point to the Internet for your network, or it can be implemented as one of several pieces of your network security infrastructure. Before installing ISA Server, you will need to perform a thorough review of your infrastructure. Once ISA Server's place in the system is decided, you can get to the work of installing ISA Server.

In this chapter, we will discuss how to prepare for the installation and then how to perform the actual installation. We will also take a look at the procedure you use to migrate from Proxy Server 2.0 so that you can make the upgrade as quick and as seamless as possible.

Installing ISA Server on a Windows 2000 Server

Installing ISA Server is a relatively simple matter, but you should know what to expect before you run the Installation Wizard. When you deploy ISA on a production network, it is very important that you complete and approve your ISA network design before beginning the installation.

Only a few important decisions must be made during the installation. The "hard stuff" comes *after* installation is complete.

Putting Together Your Flight Plan

To ensure that your installation goes smoothly, have the answers to the following questions before you begin:

- Where are the installation files?
- Do you have appropriate permissions to install ISA Server?
- What is the CD key, and where is the product license?
- Will the Active Directory Schema need to be updated?
- What server mode will you use?
- Where will you store the program files, log files, and Web cache?
- What are the network IDs for the hosts on your internal network?
- What ISA features do you want to include in your installation?
- Will you be creating or joining an array?

Let's look at these points in a little more detail before beginning the installation.

Installation Files and Permissions

The installation files for ISA Server can be accessed via the product CD-ROM or from a network installation share point. If you are installing from a share point, make sure that the Share and NTFS permissions at the source allow you to install the program.

You must be logged on with an account that has permission to install the program. If you are installing a standalone ISA Server, you must be a member of the Administrators group for that machine. If you want to install an enterprise array, you must be a member of the Domain Administrators group. If you have a multiple forest environment, you should be a member of the Enterprise Admins group, and if you are responsible for initializing Active Directory, you also have to be a member of the Schema Admins group.

Table 5.1 lists the required permissions for ISA Server installation.

Table 5.1 Permissions Required to Install ISA Server and Components

You Plan to Install	Permissions Required
Standalone ISA Server	Local Administrators Group (Domain Administrators are automatically placed in this group)
An array member	Domain Administrator
An enterprise array	Enterprise Admin
ISA schema update	Schema Admin

TIP

You must be a member of *all* the following groups to install the ISA schema to Active Directory: administrators group on the local computer, enterprise administrators group, and schema admins group.

CD Key and Product License

The *CD key* is located on the CD case. It is a 10-digit number. You might also find it on the product packaging. Be sure that you have the license readily available and that you photocopy it, scan it, and then put it in a safe place.

It is an important part of your fault-tolerance plan to have multiple copies of your product licenses and to store them in a safe location. Doing so will help you avert unfortunate fines should your company be the subject of an audit.

NOTE

The CD key is a 10-digit number. You will be requested to supply the CD key during the installation process.

Active Directory Considerations

If you plan to install an enterprise array, the machine onto which you install ISA Server must be a member of a domain. You also need to connect to a domain controller during the installation. Confirm network connectivity to a domain controller prior to beginning the installation.

As mentioned earlier, when you perform an enterprise initialization, you will be altering Active Directory so that it can store array configuration information. Remember that altering the schema is a one-way process. The only way to get back to where you were is to restore from backup.

Configuring & Implementing...

Verifying Domain Communications

You must be able to communicate with a domain controller in your domain via a secure channel before performing the enterprise initialization. This is not the same as being able to access a file share on the domain controller. To confirm a secure channel between your computer and a domain controller, use the Netdom utility included with the Windows 2000 Resource Kit. Use the following command:

```
netdom query /Verify server
```

You will get a screen print of the servers in your domain that have a verifiable secure channel. You can also use the netdiag utility to confirm the secure channel.

Server Mode

Decide in advance the server mode you will assign to the ISA server. The server modes are cache mode, firewall mode, and integrated mode. This decision should be made after conferring with your security group and determining exactly what function(s) this ISA server will perform on your network. The security implications of the modes are quite different; these implications need to be addressed prior to implementation.

Disk Location for ISA Server Files

Decide where you want to install the ISA Server program files. These files require only about 20 MB of disk space and do not incur much read/write activity, so you will be safe installing them to the default location, which is in the Program Files folder on the boot partition.

During installation, you need to decide where you want to place your Web cache files. It is best to place these on a RAID array, which must be formatted as NTFS. The RAID configuration should ensure the best performance possible. Refer to Chapter 4 for a detailed discussion regarding optimizing read/write access for the Web cache.

NOTE

Web cache files can be placed only on an NTFS partition or volume. In fact, when you configure the Web cache, either during installation or via the ISA Management console, you will not be given the opportunity to place the cache on FAT formatted drives.

Although you won't need to decide where to put your log files during installation, you should have your server configured so that you can adjust the configuration to put the logs on their own volume. Log files are written to much more than they are read. Therefore, after the installation is complete, you should move the log file location to a volume that has the fastest write access. See the discussion in Chapter 4 regarding optimal placement of log files.

NOTE

By default, the log files are placed on the boot partition, but after installation is complete, you will be able to change the location via the ISA Administration console. The exact path for the default location is <drive>:\Program Files\Microsoft ISA Server\ ISALogs.

Internal Network IDs and the Local Address Table

You will be asked to configure the local address table (LAT) during the installation routine. To prepare the LAT correctly, you need to know the network IDs in use inside your company. The LAT will be used to determine if requests should be sent directly to an internal server or if they should be subjected to ISA Server rules and policies.

It is paramount that you configure the LAT correctly because it defines the networks that are considered internal and those that are considered external. If for some reason an external network ID finds itself on the LAT, requests from that network ID will be treated as internal network clients and will not be subjected to the same access controls applied to external network hosts. This means that these external network hosts could have direct access to your internal network resources.

Optimal configuration of your LAT is based on the routing tables configured on your ISA servers. You'll have the option for ISA Server to configure the LAT based on the routing table on that server. The best way to have the LAT configured correctly and reliably is to have an accurate routing table on the machine. This can be done automatically via a routing protocol, such as RIP or OSPF, or you can create manual routing table entries via the Routing and Remote Access console GUI interface or via the ROUTE command. Refer to Chapter 4 for details on how to plan and create your routing table entries.

ISA Server Features Installation

A few services are labeled "add-in" services by the ISA Server installation routine. Before you begin the installation, you should determine whether you want to include these services:

- The H.323 Gatekeeper Service
- The H.323 Gatekeeper Administration Tool
- The Message Screener

The H.323 Gatekeeper allows multiple inbound and outbound calls using a program such as NetMeeting to conduct voice, video, and data sessions. The H.323 Administration tool allows you to administer the service. Thus, if you install the service, you should install the tool as well.

The Message Screener is a tool you use together with secure Mail Server publishing. The Message Screener tool allows you to check incoming mail for a number of elements, such as keywords. If you plan to implement secure Mail Server publishing, you should install this tool.

NOTE

If you plan to use the Message Screen tool, you need an installation of the IIS 5.0 SMTP Service to act as a relay. The IIS SMTP service is used to relay messages to your internal mail server.

NOTE

As part of the installation routine, the ISA Server Setup program will change the TCP/IP driver's dynamic port range to 65,535. (The effect takes place when the computer is rebooted after installing ISA Server.)

Performing the Installation

We are now at the point where we can start installing ISA Server. The following walkthrough goes through each step required to install ISA Server as a standalone server on a Windows 2000 Advanced Server computer. Later, we will perform the enterprise initialization and upgrade the standalone server to an array member.

Installing ISA Server: A Walkthrough

These are the steps for performing a typical installation of a standalone ISA server:

1. We begin the installation by placing the installation CD into the CD-ROM drive. The autorun begins and we are presented with the installation options screen (see Figure 5.1). Note that you have six options:

   - **Review Release Notes (the README file)** Select this option to read the latest information about ISA Server that did not make it into the Help files. It is highly recommend that you read these notes before beginning. If you don't want to read the notes right away, you should at least open the file and print it for reference. It contains important information that you must know before beginning the configuration phase of the ISA Server installation.
   - **Read Installation Guide** The installation guide is a pared-down version of the Help files. This guide focuses on the concepts that are important to planning, installation, and basic configuration of ISA Server. You should also print this file and read it at your leisure.
   - **Register ISA Server** Use this link to register your server online.
   - **Run ISA Server Enterprise Initialization** Use this link to prepare Active Directory for configuring an ISA Server array. We cover how to perform the enterprise initialization later in this chapter.
   - **Install ISA Server** This option begins the installation of ISA Server.
   - **Read About Migrating to ISA Server** This link opens a document that provides information about how to upgrade from Proxy Server 2.0 and Windows NT 4.0 installations that have Proxy Server 2.0 installed on them. We cover important migration issues in this chapter.

   For the purposes of this walkthrough, click the **Install ISA Server** option.

2. After beginning the installation, you will see the information screen shown in Figure 5.2, which informs you that you can install the product on only one server if you have only one license. Be aware of the licensing guidelines for ISA Server Standard Edition and Enterprise Edition.

Figure 5.1 The ISA Server Setup Dialog Box

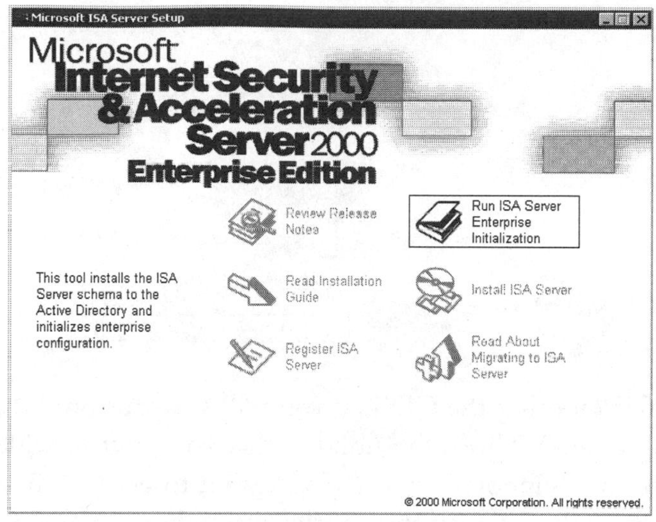

Figure 5.2 The Setup Welcome Screen

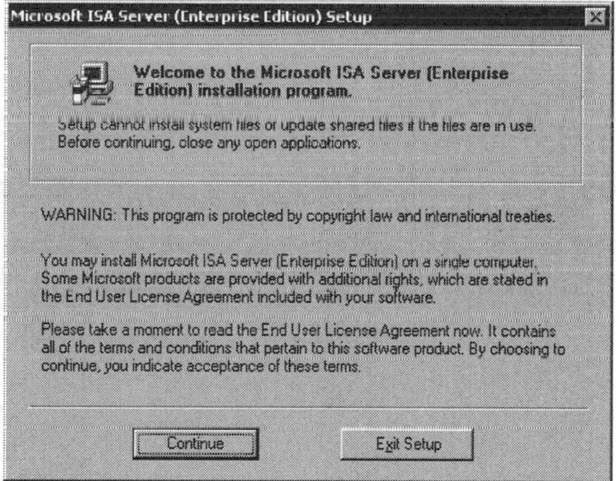

3. Now click **Continue**.
4. Enter your CD key (see Figure 5.3) and click **OK**. Notice that ISA Server uses the old CD key format, similar to that used by Proxy Server and different from the format used by other 2000 Series BackOffice server products (also known as .Net server products).

Figure 5.3 CD Key Dialog Box

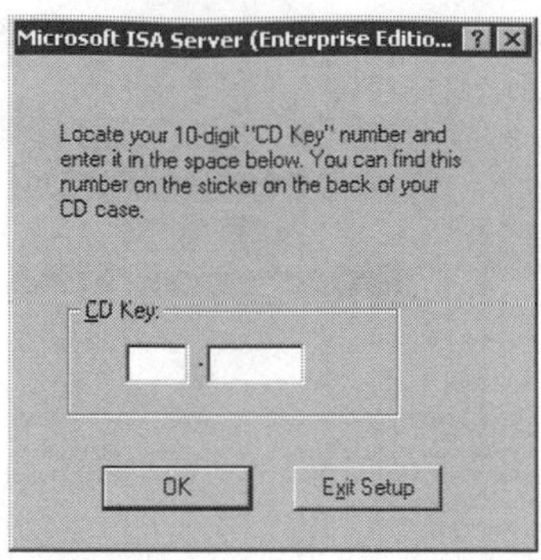

5. After entering the CD key, you will get your product ID number (see Figure 5.4). This is the number that you must provide to Microsoft Product Support Services if you want to get technical assistance from them. Take a screen shot of this dialog box, write down the product ID number, and put it in a safe place. Make multiple copies so that they're always available. The time that you won't be able to find your product ID is when you can't get your ISA Server started. Click **OK** to move to the next step.

Figure 5.4 The Product ID Dialog Box

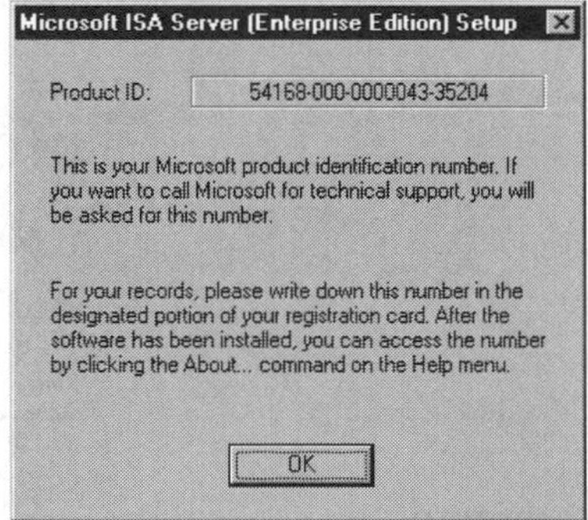

6. The ISA Server end-user license agreement (EULA) screen comes up (see Figure 5.5). You can scroll through the license agreement, or you can right-click the body of the license agreement text, click the **Select** All command, right-click again and select the **Copy** command, and copy the whole thing to Notepad to read it at your leisure. Click **I Agree** to continue the installation. (If you were to click **I Decline**, the installation would stop and you would be returned to the Desktop.)

Figure 5.5 The ISA Server End-User License Agreement

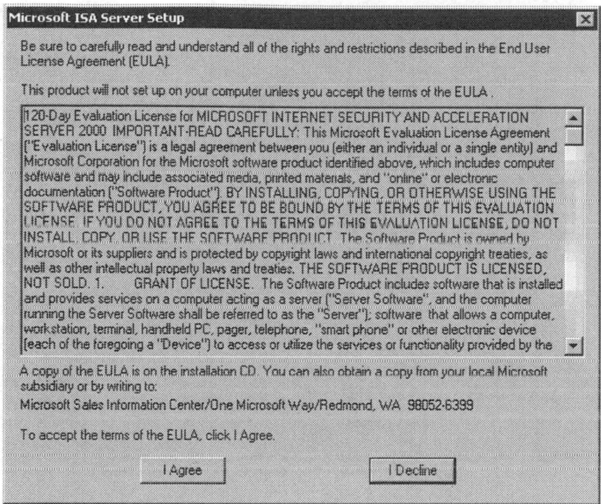

7. You now get to choose how you want to proceed with the installation (see Figure 5.6):
   - **Typical Installation** Install all the components on the boot partition. This option does not include the "add-on" products. The add-ons can be installed later if you choose not to install them at this time.
   - **Full Installation** The full installation includes all core program files and the add-on products. It installs these files to the boot partition.
   - **Custom Installation** The custom installation allows you to choose which optional components to install.
   - **Change Folder** The Change Folder button allows you to change the location of the core program files. If you do not want to install the program to the **Program Files** folder on the boot partition, click this button and change the location of the core program files. For this walkthrough, click the **Custom Installation** button.
8. When you select the custom installation, you get the dialog box shown in Figure 5.7, which allows you to choose the components to install. There are three options:
   - ISA Services
   - Add-in Services
   - Administration Tools

Figure 5.6 The ISA Server Installation Options Dialog Box

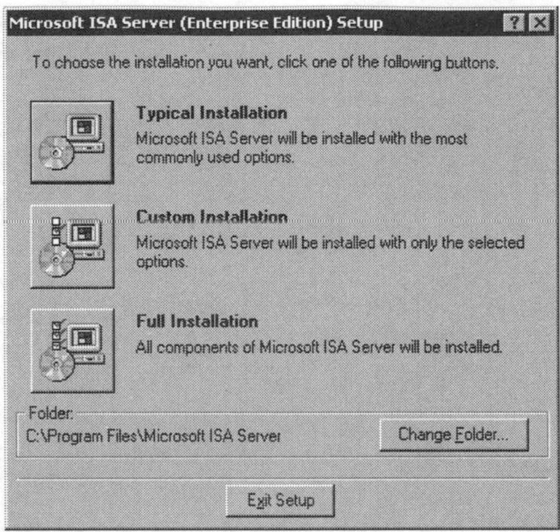

Figure 5.7 The Custom Installation Dialog Box

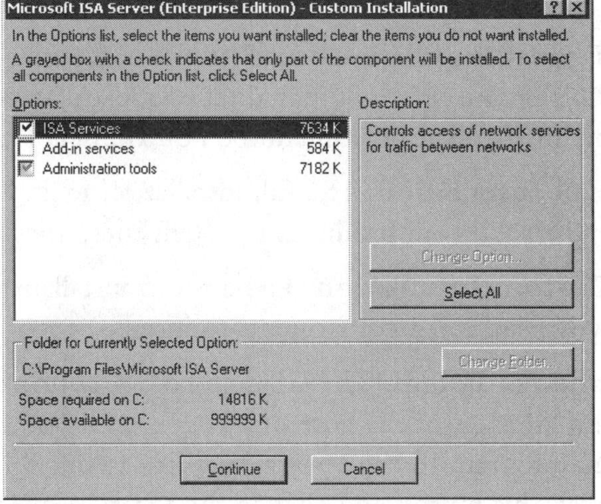

You *must* install the ISA Services. However, you can customize your selections for **Add-in services** and **Administration tools**. If you select **Add-in Services** and click the **Change Option** button, you will see the screen that appears in Figure 5.8.You have the choice of installing either or both the H.323 Gatekeeper Service and the Message screener. Now if you click the **Administrative Tools** option, you will see the options shown in Figure 5.9.

Figure 5.8 Add-in Services Change Option Dialog Box

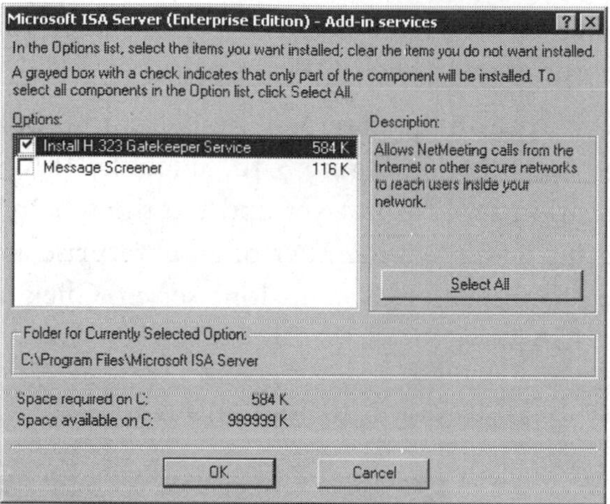

Figure 5.9 The Administrative Tools Options Dialog Box

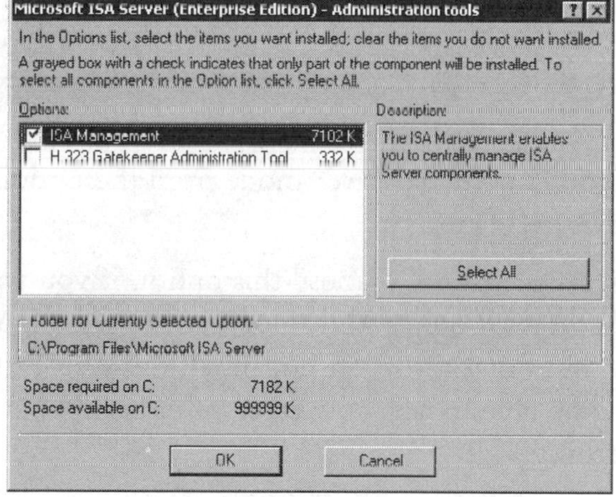

Here you have the choice of installing the **ISA Management** and/or the **H.323 Gatekeeper Administration Tool**. If you are installing the full product on the server, you will want to installation the administrative tools. In addition, you can choose to install only the administrative tools on a Windows 2000 Professional computer and administer any server or array in your organization.

If you choose to install the H.323 Gatekeeper administration tool, it will place a node in your ISA Management console that will allow you to configure the H.323 Gatekeeper service. In this walkthrough, select all the options and click **OK**.

9. We have not run the enterprise initialization tool yet, so we get the dialog box shown in Figure 5.10. Since the ISA Server Enterprise Initialization tool has not yet updated the schema, we are not able to install this server as a member of an enterprise array. However, we are allowed to install it as a standalone server. Click **Yes** to install a standalone ISA server.

Figure 5.10 Deciding to Join an Array

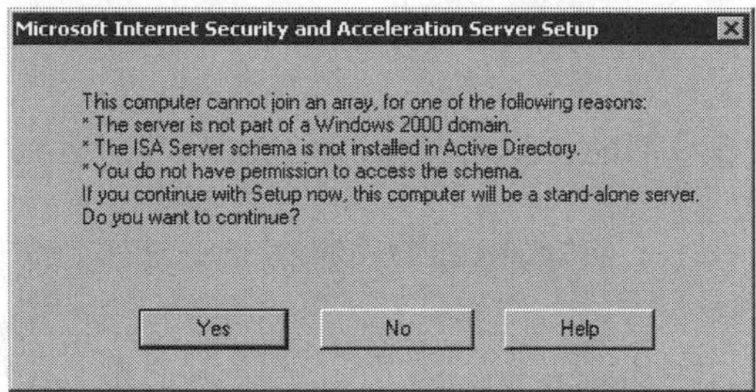

10. Here you choose the server mode from the options shown in Figure 5.11 and reviewed here:
    - **Firewall Mode** Choose this option if you want to install the server as a firewall only and do not want to use the Web proxy server. Keep in mind that if you do not install the Web Proxy Service, you will not be able to take advantage of either forward or reverse Web caching.
    - **Cache Mode** Choose this option if you want to use only "Web" protocols. Cache mode supports only HTTP, HTTPS, FTP, and Gopher. If you want to use other protocols such as SMTP for email or NNTP for newsgroups, you need to install either firewall mode or integrated mode. It is also recommended that you do not install a cache-mode-only server on the edge of your network, because the firewall features are especially important at the edge of the network.
    - **Integrated Mode** Choose this mode if you want to take advantage of all the features of ISA Server. You will be able to support all

Winsock applications and take advantage of the Web proxy server's Web caching feature.

Figure 5.11 Selecting the Server Installation Mode

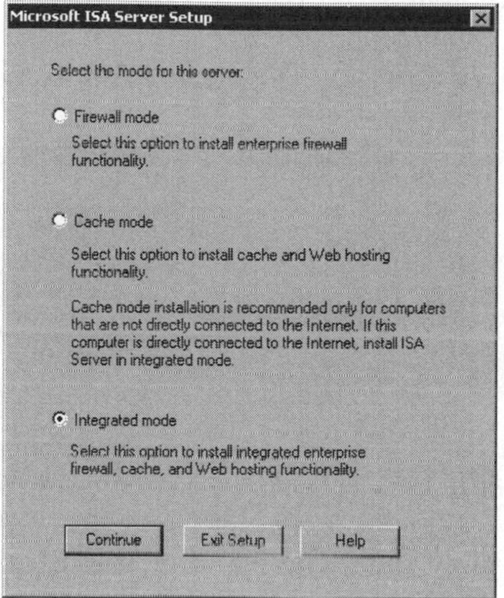

11. For this walkthrough, select **Integrated Mode** so that we can examine both the **Cache Mode** and the **Firewall Mode** components. After selecting the **Integrated Mode** option, click **Continue** to continue with the setup routine.
12. At this point, the ISA Server installation program will stop the IIS WWW service (W3SVC), as shown in Figure 5.12. However, the service will be restarted by the end of installation. It is important to understand the implications of running IIS on the same computer as ISA Server. On a multihomed machine, ISA Server uses TCP port 80 on the external interface to listen for incoming Web requests for servers that have been published using the Web Publishing Wizard. If you have a Web site or sites that are using port 80 on the ISA server's external interface, they will no longer respond to requests. You need to either change the port number for those Web sites or use the Web Publishing Wizard to publish them via the internal interface on an alternate port number.

    ISA Server listens for Web proxy server requests on port 8080 on the internal interface. This is a departure from the way Web proxy clients accessed the Proxy Server 2.0 Web Proxy Service, which they were able to access by connecting to port 80.

These changes point to an important fact: No component of ISA Server is dependent on IIS. In Proxy Server 2.0, the Web Proxy Service was an ISAPI plug-in to IIS; the management interface for the other services was dependent on IIS as well.

For this walkthrough, click **OK** to move on to the next step.

Figure 5.12 Warning Dialog Box About IIS Services

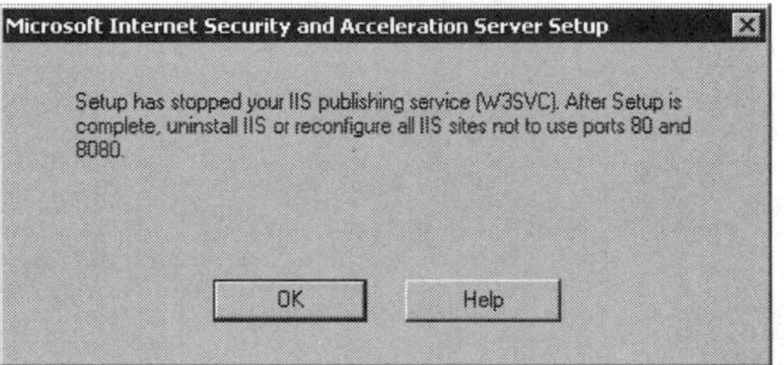

13. You now can configure the Web cache settings (see Figure 5.13). You are presented with a list of NTFS drives that can support the Web cache. You *must* place the cache on an NTFS drive. FAT partitions or volumes do not appear on the list. The default setting is to create a 100 MB Web cache file on the partition that has the most free disk space. After you enter the size of the cache, you must click the **Set** button. Refer to Chapter 4 for a discussion of optimal cache sizing.

    For this walkthrough, we configure a 100 MB cache on the E: drive. To move to the next step, click the **OK** button.

Figure 5.13 Configuring Web Cache Size

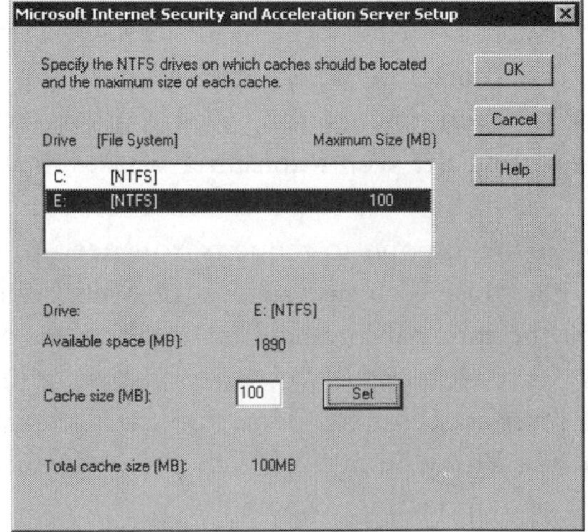

14. The LAT configuration dialog box (see Figure 5.14) appears and provides you a chance to configure the LAT during setup. If you choose not to configure the LAT at this time or if you change your mind regarding the configuration of the LAT, you can change the settings via the ISA Management console after the installation is complete. There are two ways that you can approach configuring the LAT. You can manually enter the start and end addresses in the **Edit** frame on the left side of the dialog box, or you can use the **Table** button:

    - When manually entering the information, you must include the entire range of your network IDs that are part of your internal network. Note that we have entered an illegal address for the start address for the LAT. This is OK and will not impair the functionality of the LAT.
    - If you choose to use the **Construct Table** button, the ISA Server will try to create the LAT for you based on the network ID of your internal interface(s). In addition to the network ID of your internal interface, it will also add the three private network ranges:

      192.168.0.0/24

      172.16.0.0/12

      10.0.0.0/8
    - If you choose to let ISA Server construct the table for you, you must be sure to check it over very carefully. If you have a network with multiple logical IP segments, you need to include all these segment IDs in your LAT. Otherwise, requests for those internal network clients will be subjected to the rules created for requests for external network requests.
    - Always make sure that your ISA server can route to all your internal networks properly. The way to accomplish this task is to configure routing table entries that accurately reflect the configuration of your internal network. By configuring the routing table appropriately, you will ensure reliable communications within your network and prevent problems with incorrect LAT entries that can compromise the security of your internal network.

    In this walkthrough, we have created an entry for our internal network ID, which falls within one of the private network address ranges. Click **OK** to continue to the next step.

Figure 5.14 Configuring the Local Address Table

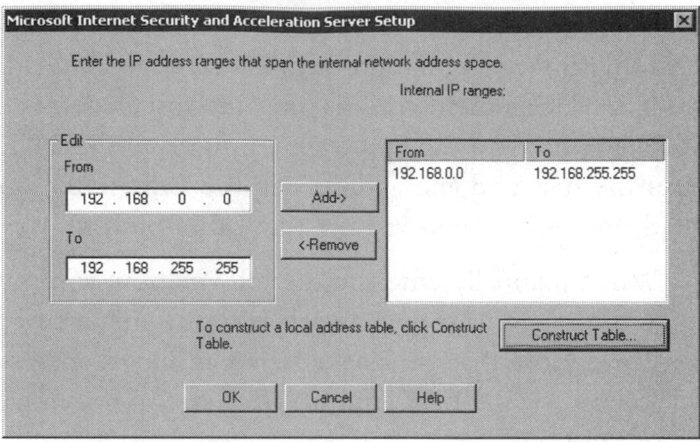

15. The installer copies the files to their target directories. After the file-copy phase is complete, you are offered the opportunity to have the Setup program open the ISA Management console and begin the **Getting Started Wizard** (see Figure 5.15). The wizard walks you through the configuration steps for ISA Server. We like to be obliging, so we'll click **OK** to allow the installation routine to start the wizard for us. However, we'll avoid the **Getting Started Wizard** because we're going to learn how to configure the server ourselves!

Figure 5.15 Launch the ISA Admin Tool Dialog Box

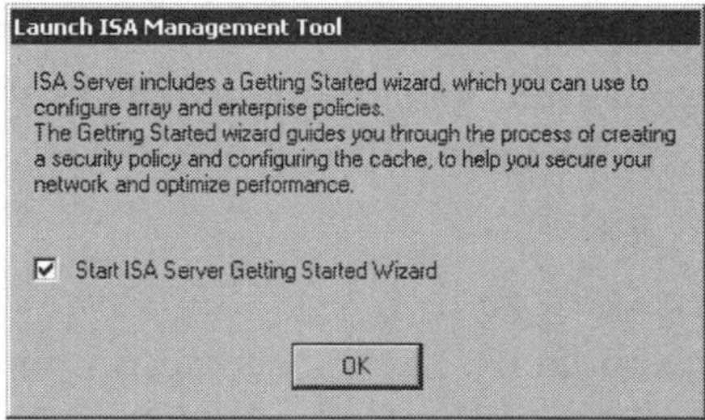

16. The **Getting Started** welcome screen (see Figure 5.16) is presented as the ISA Administration console is opened. You can use the wizard to help walk you through the steps of configuring the server. However, you should have a thorough understanding of ISA Server and all the implications of the settings you create *before* you work with the Getting Started Wizard. Once you have a firm understanding of ISA Server, the wizard can help you configure your server in an orderly fashion.

Figure 5.16 The ISA Server Management Console

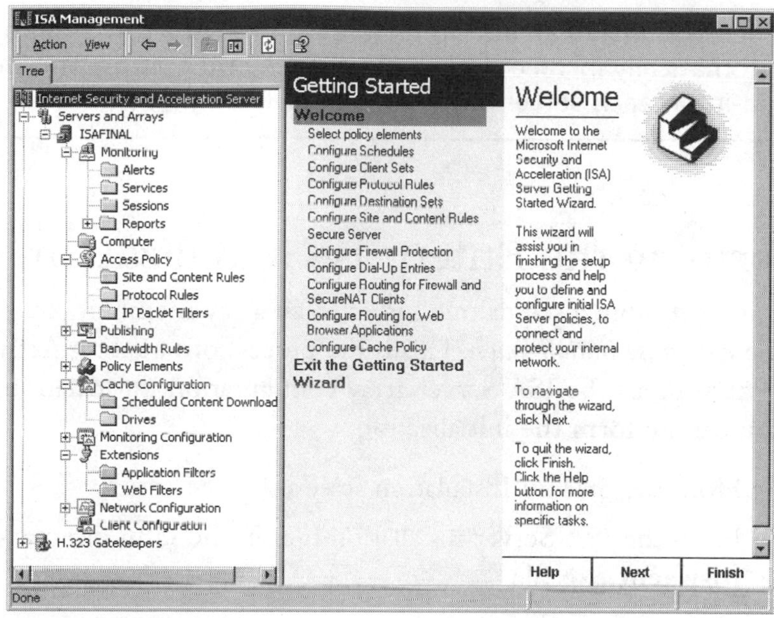

Upgrading a Standalone Server to an Array Member: A Walkthrough

In the first walkthrough, we installed the ISA Server as a standalone server. You might want to do this in your test lab while you're learning about the system, or you might like to put ISA Server into a limited production environment in order to get a better feel for how it fits into your organization. The chance is good that you'll like what you see, and later you'll want to take advantage of the additional features provided in an enterprise array configuration. The good news is that you don't have to reinstall ISA Server to make it an enterprise array member. You can *promote* the standalone server instead.

As we discussed earlier, you need to have a Windows 2000 domain deployed and available if you want to make the server a member of an enterprise array. The computer on which you want to perform the upgrade also needs to be a member of the Windows 2000 domain. If the machine is a member of a Windows NT 4.0 domain, the enterprise upgrade will not work, because the Windows NT 4.0 domain controller does not have the Active Directory in which to store the enterprise array configuration information.

NOTE

When you install an add-in feature on one server in an array, it is not automatically installed on all the servers in the array. You must install the add-in on each server in the array individually.

Performing the Enterprise Initialization

Before you promote a standalone server to an array member, you need to complete the *enterprise initialization*. This is the process of updating Active Directory so that it will support the ISA Server array configuration information. There are two ways you can perform the initialization:

- From the Startup Installation screen
- From the ISA Server installation files in the **i386** directory, run the **msisaent.exe** file

Both these methods walk you through the same process:

1. When you put the CD-ROM into the drive, the Autorun feature brings up a dialog box. You can also get it to run by clicking the isaautorun.exe file in the root of the installation files hierarchy.
2. To run the enterprise initialization, click the **Run ISA Server Enterprise Initialization** icon.
3. After starting the initialization process, you'll get a dialog box informing you that the Active Directory schema will be updated and that this is not a reversible process (see Figure 5.17). If you get an error message stating that the "the computer name is unacceptable," click **OK** to close the dialog box and restart the computer. The enterprise initialization will proceed normally after restarting. Click **Yes** to continue.
4. At this point, you need to decide how you want to apply enterprise policy (see Figure 5.18). Your choices are:
   - **Use Array Policy Only** When you choose to use Array Policy Only, an enterprise policy is created, but it will not be automatically applied to the array. You will have the opportunity to manually assign enterprise policy to the array after the initialization is completed by configuring it in the ISA Management console.

Figure 5.17 Warning About Irreversible Changes to the Active Directory

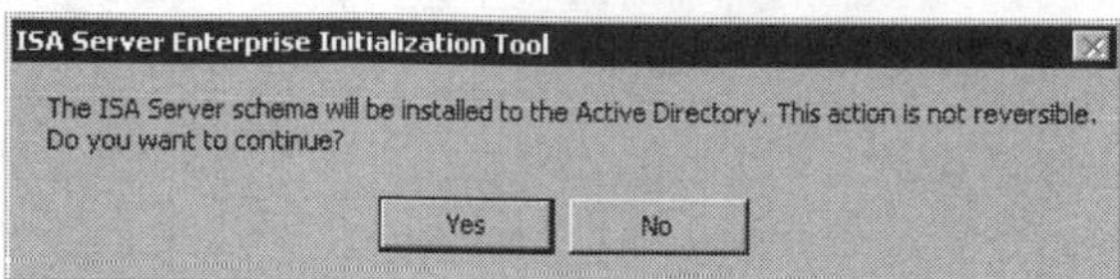

- **Use This Enterprise Policy** When you choose Use This Enterprise Policy, a default policy is created with the name Enterprise Policy 1. You can change the name if you want. If you select this option and do not select the Also Allow Array Policy option, any array policies are replaced by the enterprise policy. If you are thinking of choosing this option, be sure to back up your existing array policy prior to the enterprise initialization in the event that you want to restore the existing array policy (standalone policy as well) on the server.
- **Allow Array-Level Access Policy Rules That Restrict Enterprise Policy** If you choose this option, both the enterprise policy and the array policies will be applied. However, *array policies can only further limit the policies set for the enterprise*. What this means is that array policy cannot have any *allow rules*. The only allow rules are those determined by the enterprise policy.
- **Allow Publishing Rules** This option does exactly that. Publishing rules must be created on each server of an array separately, because the IP address(s) listening for requests for published servers will be different for each server. If you do not choose this option now, you can do so later after the enterprise is initialized and you promote the standalone server to an array.
- **Force Packet Filtering on the Array** This option enforces packet filtering on the array(s) to which this policy is applied. This forces packet filtering on each server in the array and cannot be overridden by array policy.

The default settings are displayed in Figure 5.18. We will allow array policy, allow publishing rules to be configured on the array, and force packet filtering. Then click **OK**. The schema is updated and shows the progression with a nice animated icon (see Figure 5.19).

Figure 5.18 Determining Policy

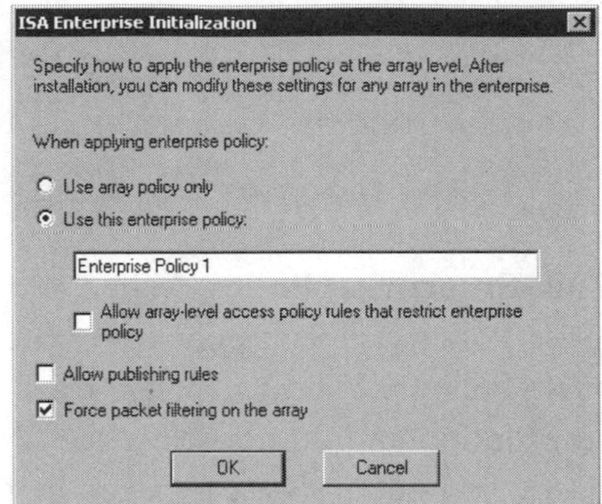

Figure 5.19 Initializing the Active Directory for ISA Server

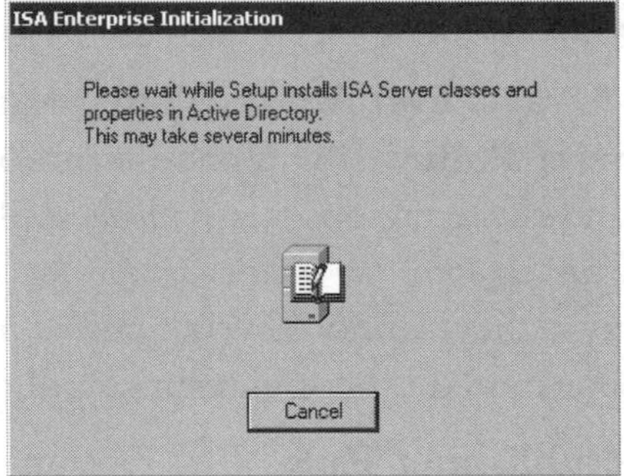

5. When the enterprise initialization is completed, you will see a dialog box informing you that everything worked (see Figure 5.20). If there were problems updating Active Directory, you will receive an error dialog box, and you will have to troubleshoot the problems with Active Directory and perhaps with connectivity. Note that if you have multiple domain controllers, you should wait before configuring ISA Server as an array member.

Figure 5.20 ISA Server Enterprise Initialization Tool Dialog Box

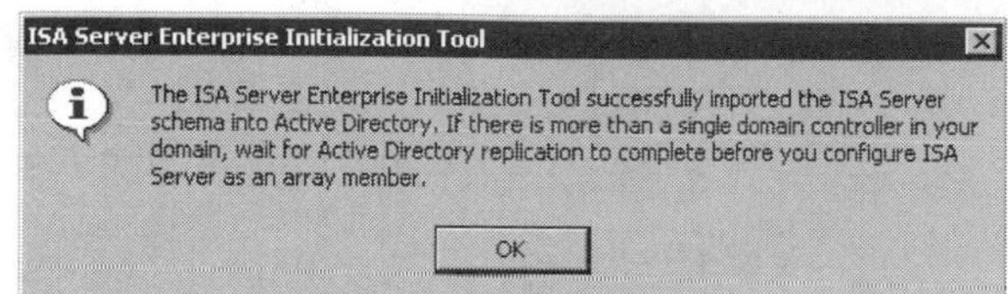

SECURITY ALERT!

We cannot stress too much the importance of the decision you make when deciding which policy or policies will be applied to the array. If you choose only to allow enterprise policies, *only* enterprise policies will be applied and you will *not* be able to create any array policies. If you do allow for array policies, remember *that you cannot create any allow rules in the array policy.* Array policies can *only restrict* the policies you set in the enterprise policy.

Backing Up a Configuration and Promoting a Standalone Server to an Array Member

After updating Active Directory to support your array, you can begin the process of promoting your standalone ISA server. Before promoting the server, confirm that you have connectivity with a domain controller in your Windows 2000 domain. You might also want to back up your configuration if you have not yet done so.

It's a good idea to back up your configuration when making changes of this kind. In fact, you should back up your standalone server or array configuration prior to making any changes to rules or filters. By backing up, you can easily roll back to a previous configuration that has worked for you. It is much easier, and much less error prone, to restore a backed-up configuration than to try to remember all the rules and configuration settings you made and hope that you enter them correctly a second time.

To back up an array or standalone configuration, perform the following steps:

1. Open the **ISA Management** console and right-click the name of your server or array (see Figure 5.21). Click the **Back Up** command.

Figure 5.21 Accessing the Back Up Command

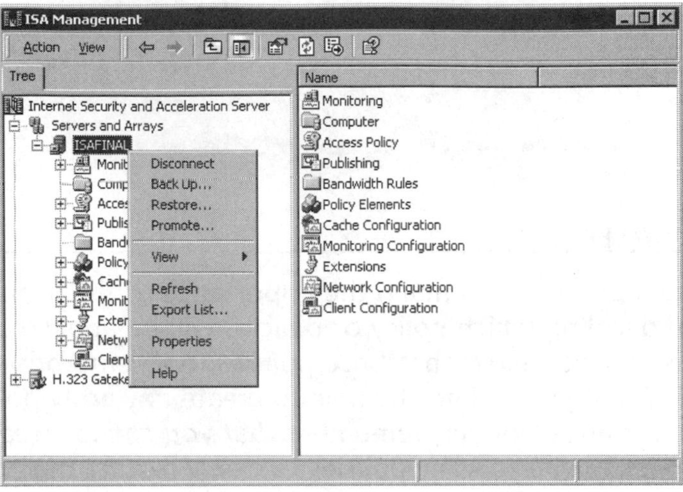

2. In the **Backup Array** dialog box, type the path where you can store the configuration backup file (see Figure 5.22). Be sure to include the name of the file to fully qualify the path. Then click **OK**.

Figure 5.22 The Backup Array Dialog Box

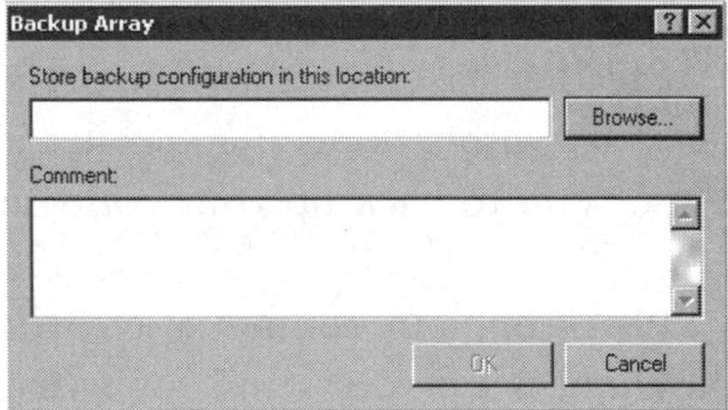

If the configuration backs up successfully, you will see a dialog box confirming that fact as seen in Figure 5.23. Note the warning in this dialog box. Although you have saved configuration settings specific to this array, it is not a complete backup of all system settings as they relate to ISA Server. This type of backup allows you to recover from errors you make in configuration settings in the **ISA Management** console, but it will not be enough to recover from a total system crash. For the purposes of disaster recovery, you should use the Windows Backup program or another backup program of your choice to back up the entire system, including the system state data. The system state data includes the registry, the COM+ Class Registration database, and the system boot files. It also includes the Certificate Services database if the machine is acting as a Certificate Server. If the computer is a domain controller, the system state will include the Active Directory database (ntds.dit) and Sysvol directory. See Chapter 11 for more details on backing up your ISA Server.

Figure 5.23 Confirmation of a Successful Backup

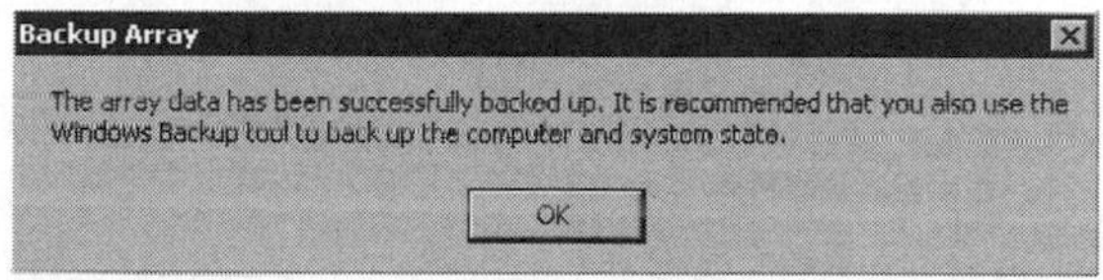

You can confirm the location of your backup files by opening Windows Explorer. Figure 5.24 shows these files in the root of the C: drive. Note that these are the names we chose for the backup files. The system does not provide a default name. However, the backup files for standalone servers will always have the .BIF file extension.

Figure 5.24 Backup Files Identified in the Root of Drive C:

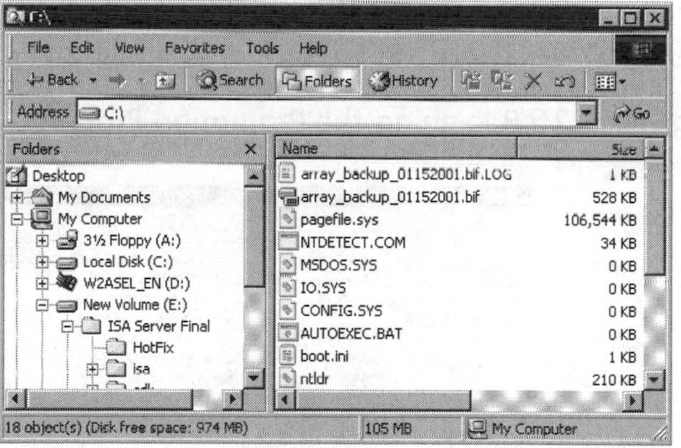

Now that we have backed up our standalone configuration, the next step is to back up the entire system. This way, we can roll back the system to a standalone server after the array promotion has been completed. There is no automatic mechanism for you to use to roll back from an array to a standalone server. You must restore from backup. After completing our backup duties, we can get to the process of promoting our server.

Before we begin the promotion sequence, right-click the name of the server and click **Properties**. The **Properties** show that the server is a standalone server in **Integrated** mode (see Figure 5.25). Note the tabs available when the server is a standalone server. There will be a new tab by the time we're done with this walkthrough.

Figure 5.25 The General Tab in the Server's Properties Dialog Box

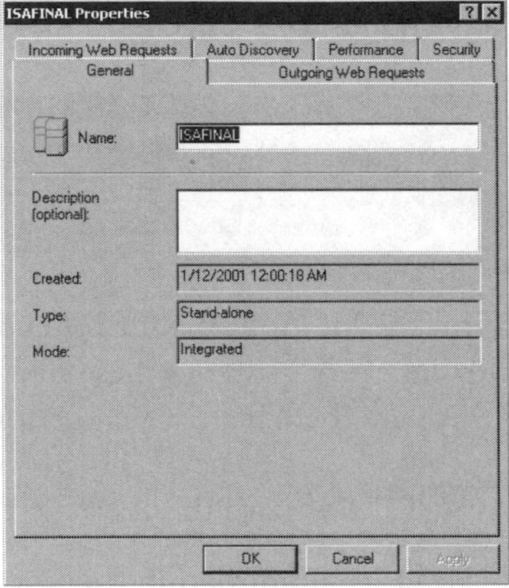

1. To begin the promotion, right-click the array node in the left pane, and then click the **Promote** command, as shown in Figure 5.26.

Figure 5.26 Beginning the Promotion Process

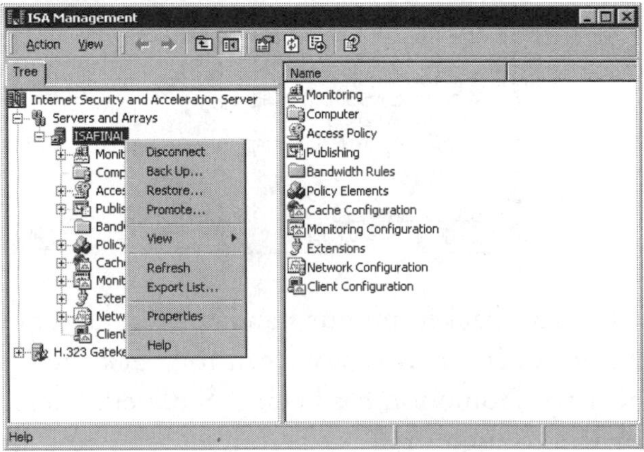

2. After clicking the **Promote** command, we get a dialog box that warns us that we can't go back to standalone server mode once the promotion to an array is completed (see Figure 5.27). Click **Yes** to continue the promotion.

Figure 5.27 Array Warning Dialog Box

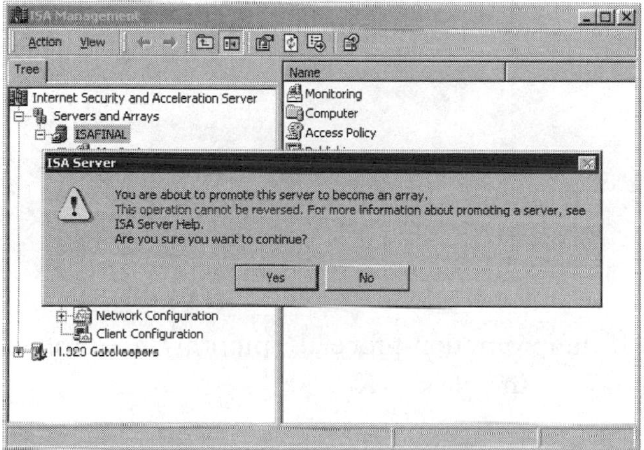

3. Before the promotion begins, you need to decide on the enterprise policy settings for the array (see Figure 5.28). We discussed the meaning of each of these choices earlier in this chapter. The default setting is **Use Default Enterprise Policy Settings**. However, for this walkthrough, choose **Use Custom Enterprise Policy Settings** and **Also Allow Array Policy**. The **Force Packet Filtering on the Array** option is also a default selection; select **Allow Publishing Rules to Be Created on the Array** as well. Then click **OK**.
4. The promotion begins (see Figure 5.29). Several things happen during the promotion, and you'll be informed of these events in the **Promoting Array** dialog box. The first step is **Converting Standalone Server to an Array**. The subsequent steps are:
   - Storing configuration in the Active Directory
   - Stopping all services
   - Committing changes
   - Restarting all services
   - Refreshing array list

Figure 5.28 Setting Enterprise Policy Settings

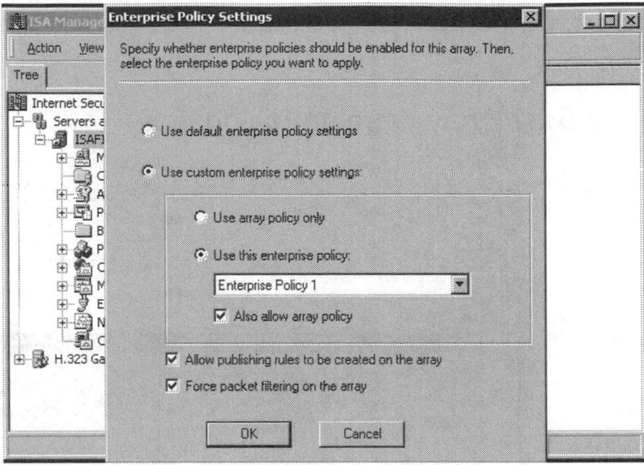

If the promotion proceeds smoothly, note the instructions in the dialog box and click **OK**.

Figure 5.29 The Promotion of the Standalone Server to an Array Begins

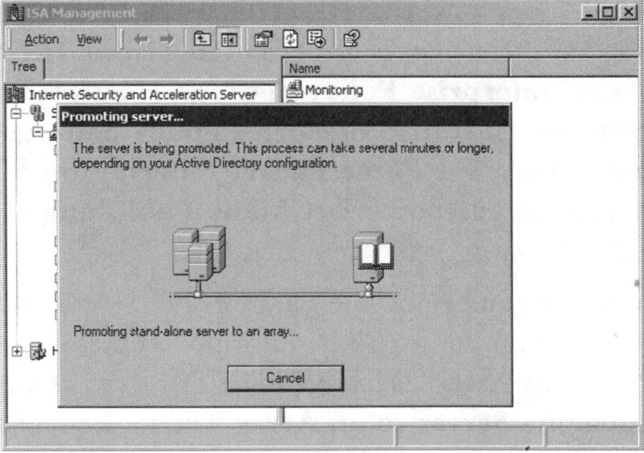

5. After clicking **OK**, you have to right-click the **Internet Security and Acceleration Server** node in the left pane of the **ISA Management** console and click the **Connect to** command. You then select the **Connect to Enterprise and Arrays** option button and click **OK**. Once connected, your console will have changed and look like what appears in Figure 5.30.

Figure 5.30 ISA Management Reflects After Promotion to Array Status

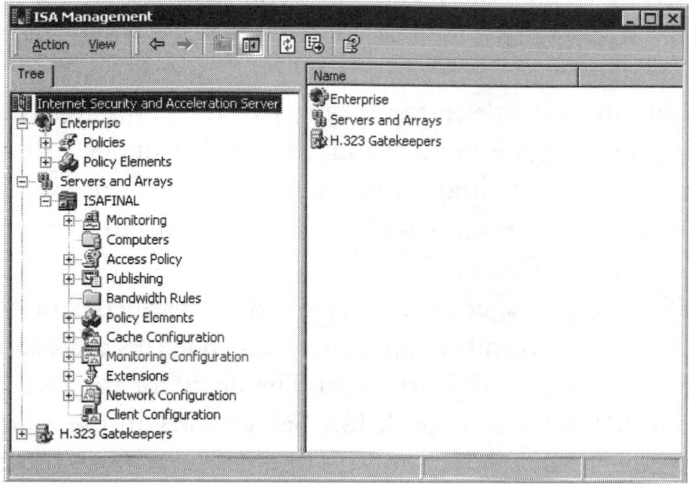

6. Right-click the array name and click **Properties**, and notice that there is a new tab in the dialog box, the **Policies** tab (see Figure 5.31). Note the options available.

Figure 5.31 ISAFINAL Policies Tab

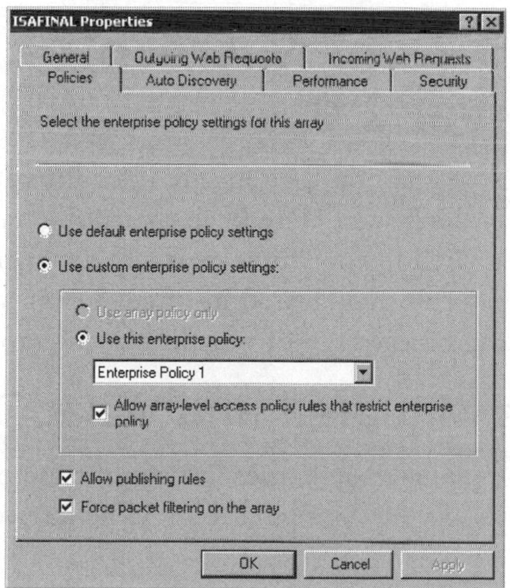

Changes Made After ISA Server Installation

As part of the installation routine, the ISA Server setup will change the TCP/IP driver's dynamic port range to 65,535. (The effect takes place when the computer is rebooted after installing.)

A number of additions are made in the Registry of the computer running ISA Server. Unfortunately, they are not all grouped together under a single registry key, so you'll have to hunt around for them. At this time none of the registry keys has been documented. However, as with most Microsoft products, this information will be available in the future.

After installing ISA, the ISA-specific counters will be installed. You can access these counters via the System Monitor applet, or you can access a preconfigured ISA System Monitor console via the Start menu. The entry for the ISA Management console is also found in the Microsoft ISA Server entry in the Start menu.

ISA Server has its own management console and does not snap into the Internet Services Manager console the way Proxy Server 2.0 does. You can create your own console that includes the ISA Management standalone snap-in along with other snap-ins. In this way you can streamline management by including snap-ins such as the ISA Management, Internet Services Manager, and other network- and Internet-related snap-ins to provide a central interface for your Internet and intranet-based solutions.

Migrating from Microsoft Proxy Server 2.0

If you work in an organization that already has a Proxy Server 2.0 installation in place, you probably don't want to redo all the configuration settings that you have so carefully applied to your three-year-old deployment. The good news is that just about every rule you created in Proxy Server 2.0 will be successfully migrated, depending on the type of migration you perform.

What Gets Migrated and What Doesn't

When you migrate your Proxy Server 2.0 configuration to Windows 2000, virtually all components of your configuration will be ferried over to ISA Server. These include:

- Proxy Server Domain Filters (ISA Server Rules)
- Proxy Server Network Settings (ISA Protocol Rules)

- Proxy Server Monitoring configuration (ISA Server Performance Monitor)
- Proxy Server Cache Configuration (ISA Cache Configuration)

All these elements will be brought over, depending on how you perform the migration in relation to your enterprise array configuration. The ways rules and other configuration elements are migrated depends on the user who performs the migration and the Enterprise Policy settings, if any, for that particular server or array.

Table 5.2 shows what happens during the migration from Proxy Server 2.0 to ISA Server when the enterprise array setting is set to Use Array Policy Only.

Table 5.2 The "Use Array Policy Only" Effect on Migration from Proxy Server 2.0

Enterprise Policy Setting	Enterprise Administrator Performing Upgrade	What Gets Migrated
Use Array Policy Only	Doesn't matter	All proxy server rules are migrated to the array policy

Note that when the enterprise policy is set to use the array policy only, it doesn't matter whether you are a domain admin or an enterprise admin. All the proxy server rules will be migrated to the array because, when only the local array policy is used, there are no interactions with the enterprise policy, so there's no impact on the permissions related to the enterprise policy and how it applies to a particular array.

Let's look at an example when the enterprise policy setting is configured to the Use Enterprise Policy Only setting (Table 5.3).

Table 5.3 The "Use Enterprise Policy Only" Effect on Migration from Proxy Server 2.0

Enterprise Policy Setting	Enterprise Administrator Performing Upgrade	What Gets Migrated
Use Enterprise Policy Only	Yes	All proxy server rules are migrated, and enterprise policy is set to Use Array Policy Only

Continued

Table 5.3 Continued

Enterprise Policy Setting	Enterprise Administrator Performing Upgrade	What Gets Migrated
Use Enterprise Policy Only	No	None of the Proxy Server rules are imported, and the new array uses the enterprise policy only

Note that when the user running the upgrade is an enterprise administrator, all the proxy server rules are migrated and the upgrade routine changes the enterprise policy to Use Array Policy Only to allow for the migration of the configuration settings from Proxy Server 2.0. It must do this in order to bring over the *allow rules* you have configured in Proxy Server 2.0.

This is not the case when the person performing the upgrade is *not* an enterprise administrator. Since the non-enterprise admin is not able to influence enterprise policy, none of the Proxy Server 2.0 rules will be imported. That's because the policy setting in this scenario is configured to use the enterprise policy only, and therefore the Setup program will not allow the domain admin or local admin security account to change the enterprise policy to Use Array Policy Only, if only temporarily for the upgrade process.

In the next scenario (see Table 5.4), we see what happens when the enterprise policy setting is configured to Use Enterprise and Array Policy.

Table 5.4 The "Use Enterprise and Array Policy" Effect on Migration from Proxy Server 2.0

Enterprise Policy Setting	Enterprise Administrator Permission	What Gets Migrated
Use Enterprise and Array Policy	Yes	All proxy server rules are migrated, and the enterprise policy configuration is set to Use Array Policy Only
Use Enterprise and Array Policy	No	Only deny rules are migrated to the array policy; allow rules are dropped

In this case, when the user performing the upgrade is an enterprise admin, the enterprise policy is changed to Use Array Policy Only so that the Proxy Server 2.0 rules can be migrated to the ISA array policy. You can then change the enterprise policy back to Use Enterprise and Array Policy after the migration is completed. Be sure to back up the migrated array policy after the upgrade and before the change policies settings to enterprise and array policy, because you won't be able to change back.

If the user performing the upgrade is not an enterprise admin, only deny rules are migrated. This puts you at a disadvantage in not migrating all your old settings and does not afford you the opportunity to use them in an array, should you decide *not* to use an enterprise policy.

NOTE

The "take home message" of this discussion is this: If you want the migration to go as smoothly and completely as possible, have a member of the enterprise admins group perform the upgrade. Otherwise, the chance of making errors and encountering unexpected results increases precipitously.

Functional Differences Between Proxy Server 2.0 and ISA Server

Proxy Server 2.0 and ISA Server have a good deal in common, but some of the things that you're used to doing in Proxy Server 2.0 are done a little differently with ISA Server. Some of the differences between the two include the following:

- IPX/SPX is *not* supported in ISA Server.
- The Web Proxy Service listens on Port 8080.
- The Winsock client is not required on published servers.
- The Web cache is stored as a single file.
- There is no SOCKS service.
- The firewall client doesn't support 16-bit operating systems.
- There are incompatibilities between ISA and IIS on same machine.

ISA Server Does Not Support IPX/SPX

Proxy Server 2.0 included the ability to access the Internet while network clients ran IPX/SPX as their transport protocol. This capability has not been extended to ISA Server. When Proxy Server 2.0 was released, Novell NetWare networks were not considered legacy. In order to successfully integrate into a mixed Windows NT/NetWare network, support for an IPX gateway was important. The versions of NetWare in use at that time required IPX/SPX.

However, NetWare's market share has profoundly diminished as Windows NT and now Windows 2000 have grown in popularity. Additionally, current versions of NetWare (5.0 and up) can run on pure IP. With the ascendance of TCP/IP as *the* networking protocol, Microsoft dropped IPX/SPX support in ISA Server.

If you are running Proxy Server 2.0 on an IPX network, you need to upgrade the networking infrastructure to support TCP/IP prior to installing ISA Server.

Web Proxy Service Users Port 8080

The Web Proxy Service in Proxy Server 2.0 listened for Web protocol requests on the server's internal interface port 80. It did so because the Web Proxy Service in Proxy Server 2.0 was actually an ISAPI plug-in to the WWW Service included with Internet Information Server, and the WWW service listened on Port 80. This made the Web Proxy Service dependent on the WWW service configuration. The Web Proxy Service included with ISA Server is not dependent on IIS or WWW Service configuration parameters.

ISA Server Web proxy clients need to send their requests to TCP port 8080 on the internal interface of the ISA server (by default). This does have some advantages, because the Autodiscovery mechanism uses TCP port 80 on the internal interface of the ISA server. It is important to note that you should not host a Web site on the external interface of the ISA server on TCP port 80, because the Web Proxy Service's Listener, which is used to listen for requests made for servers on the internal network which have been published, uses this port number. However, you do have the option of publishing a Web site hosted on any other available port on the internal interface if you need to run a Web site on the ISA Server

Because of this change in the Web Proxy Services internal listening port, you have to change either the default internal Web proxy listener port number or the configuration of the Web proxy clients to send requests to port 8080 on the ISA server.

SECURITY ALERT!

You cannot run Web sites off port 80 on the internal interface of the ISA server. Autodiscovery allows firewall and Web proxy clients to obtain valuable configuration information automatically. ISA Server allows firewall and Web proxy clients to obtain this information via port 80 on the internal interface.

However, our advice is to run no Web services on the ISA server and instead take advantage of publishing internal servers or providing Web services via a perimeter network. If you must use the ISA server to provide Web services, bind to the Web site an alternative port number that is not being used by any other services.

You can manually change this information on all the Web proxy clients, but that could be a time-consuming and administratively expensive proposition. A better approach is to configure your DNS and/or DHCP server to provide the address of the ISA server and then allow the ISA server to provide configuration information automatically to the network clients. We discuss in detail how to do this in Chapter 8, "Configuring ISA Server for Outbound Access."

Published Servers Do Not Require the WinSock Client

One of the sweetest features of ISA Server is that you do not need to configure servers that you want to publish to the Internet as Winsock proxy clients. In Proxy Server 2.0, you often had to monkey around with the wspcfg.ini settings on your published servers. Sometimes the configuration settings worked, but more often they didn't, at least not until after you spent an enormous amount of time trying to figure out what was wrong with your settings. To say the process wasn't very intuitive would be an understatement.

Kiss those frustrations goodbye. When you publish a DNS server, a mail server, or a database server with ISA, you do not need to configure tiresome text files and cross your fingers. The only requirement to make server publishing work correctly with ISA Server is that you configure the published servers to be secure NAT clients. Since setting up a secure NAT client is a no-brainer, you'll find the task of publishing internal servers to Internet clients easier than you ever imagined.

The Web Cache Is a Single File

Proxy Server 2.0 saved the Web cache to the file system. That meant you could easily collect tens of thousands of discrete files that needed to be managed by the NTFS file system.

Even though the NTFS file system is quite efficient, the large number of files did cause a perceptible performance hit for Web cache access times. The excessive number of files became even more problematic when you performed routine maintenance duties such as a nightly virus check, disk defragmentation, or searches of the hard disk for particular files.

ISA Server has solved this problem by saving the Web cache to a single file. The file is saved with the .CDAT file extension stored in a folder named url-cache. One .CDAT file is created on each drive you configured to store the Web cache. More than one .CDAT file can be created on a drive if your cache size is larger than 10 GB, since one .CDAT file is created for each 10 GB of cache file size. For example, if you created a cache file of 15 GB on drive D:, there would be one 10 GB .CDAT file and one 5 GB .CDAT file on that drive.

No More SOCKS Proxy Service

If you ran the SOCKS Proxy Service and configured access rules for SOCKS proxy clients on your Proxy Server 2.0, you won't be able to configure selective rules for those clients in ISA Server. This is because ISA Server does not have a SOCKS Proxy Service.

ISA does support SOCKS Version 4 clients via the SOCKS application filter. Machines that ran as SOCKS proxy clients in Proxy Server 2.0 must be configured as secure NAT clients when connecting to ISA Server. The SOCKS Application Filter intercepts the SOCKS requests on port 1080 and forwards the requests to the Internet.. You can control access for these clients as you would with any other secure NAT client.

Incompatibilities Between ISA and IIS on the Same Machine

Proxy Server 2.0 was highly integrated into IIS, so you did not have to worry about any potential incompatibilities between the two. However, you have to make some changes to your IIS configuration prior to upgrading a Proxy Server 2.0 installation to ISA Server.

When you upgrade from Proxy Server 2.0, you must take into consideration the IIS configuration. As discussed earlier, the best course of action is to not run

Web services on your ISA server and to uninstall IIS completely. However, you might not have this option.

If you must run a Web server from the same machine running ISA, make sure that no Web sites listen on port 80 of either the internal or external interface. As we said earlier, port 80 on the external interface is used by the Web Proxy Service Listener, and port 80 on the internal interface is used by the ISA Autoconfiguration publishing system.

Other IIS services could find themselves at issue with ISA Server if you plan on publishing internal servers to the Internet. If you want to publish internal mail servers, you cannot run the IIS SMTP Service on port 25 of the ISA server, because the publishing rule will use the external interface port 25 for publishing the internal SMTP server. In the same fashion, you cannot run the IIS NNTP Service on the external interface of the ISA server if you want to publish an internal NNTP site, because the published server needs to use the default port number for the service on the external interface, which is 119.

Undocumented ISA

When publishing internal servers to the Internet, you cannot configure ISA Server to remap ports. If a published server is configured to listen on a particular port number, the request will be forwarded to the same port number on the internal server. This setup prevents you from publishing internal servers by having them listen on alternate port numbers on the external interface. We cover this issue and other issues on server publishing in detail in Chapter 9, "Publishing Servers to the Internet."

An alternative is to change the listening ports on the IIS Services to an alternative number so that the published services can use the default port numbers. The changes to the listening ports can be made in the Internet Services Manager console.

Learn the ISA Server Vocabulary

If you are upgrading from Proxy Server 2.0 to ISA Server, you are probably already comfortable with the vocabulary of Proxy Server 2.0. It will be easier for you to make the transition if you learn the "new language" of ISA Server.

Table 5.5 includes some terms that mean the same thing in Proxy Server 2.0 and ISA Server.

Table 5.5 Translating Proxy Server 2.0 to ISA Server

Proxy Server Term	ISA Server Term
Web Proxy Service routing rules	Routing rules
Packet filters	Allow or block packet filters
Winsock permissions	Protocol rules
Publishing properties	Web publishing rules
Domain filters	Site and content rules

Upgrading Proxy 2.0 on the Windows 2000 Platform

Performing the actual migration from Proxy Server 2.0 to ISA Server is relatively easy. However, if you are going to install Proxy Server 2.0 directly onto a Windows 2000 machine, you must to use a special installation file called msp2wizi.exe that can be downloaded from the Microsoft Proxy Web site at www.microsoft.com/proxy.

However, there are a couple of things that you should do prior to beginning the migration:

- Back up your Proxy Server 2.0 settings.
- Stop all Proxy Server 2.0 services.

You should back up your Proxy Server 2.0 settings in case the ISA installation fails and you need to return to Proxy Server for some reason. You can back up the Proxy Server 2.0 configuration files from the Properties sheet of any of the Proxy Server 2.0 services. Perform the following actions to back up Proxy Server 2.0:

1. Start the Internet Services Manager.
2. Right-click one of the services, and click the **Properties** command. In the services' **Properties** dialog box, click the **Server Backup** button, as shown in Figure 5.32.
3. Type the complete path to the file that contains the backup information, as shown in Figure 5.33. Do not include the filename. The file will be saved with the name **MSP*.mpc**, where the wildcard will be replaced with the data. Click **OK**, and the text-based backup file will be saved to that location.

Figure 5.32 The Services Dialog Box

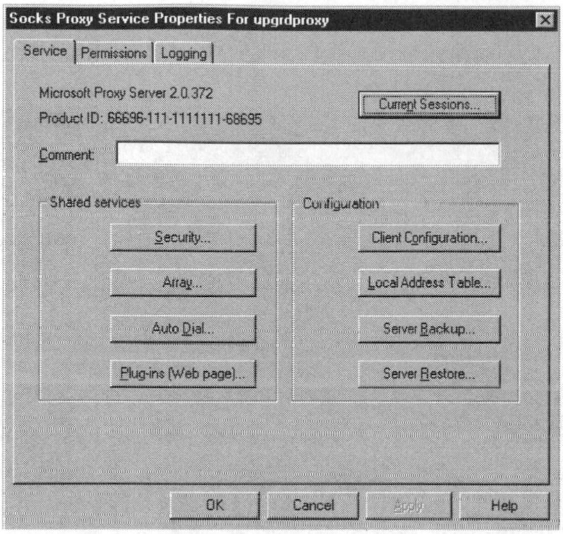

Figure 5.33 The Backup Dialog Box

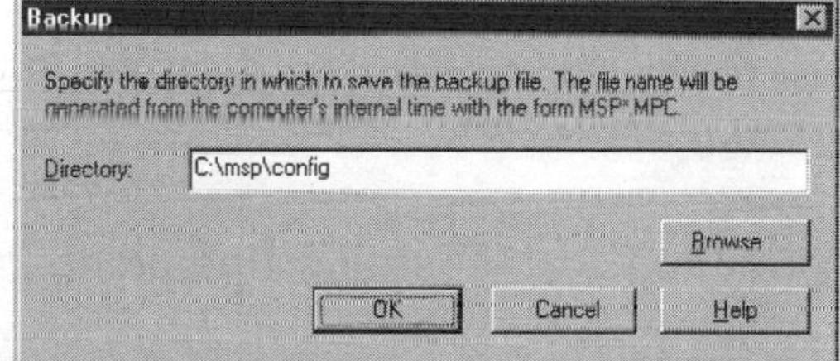

After the configuration, it's a good idea to copy the files to another location for safekeeping. You do not need to keep the backup on the same machine, because no utility will allow you to roll back from ISA Server to Proxy Server once the migration is completed. You would have to uninstall ISA Server and reinstall Proxy Server 2.0, then restore your settings from the backup.

You also need to stop all proxy server-related services prior to the migration. Type the following commands to stop the services:

```
net stop wspsrv
net stop mspadmin
net stop mailalrt
net stop w3svc
```

If everything works the way it's supposed to work, you should see something like the screen shown in Figure 5.34.

Figure 5.34 Stopping Proxy Server 2.0-Related Services

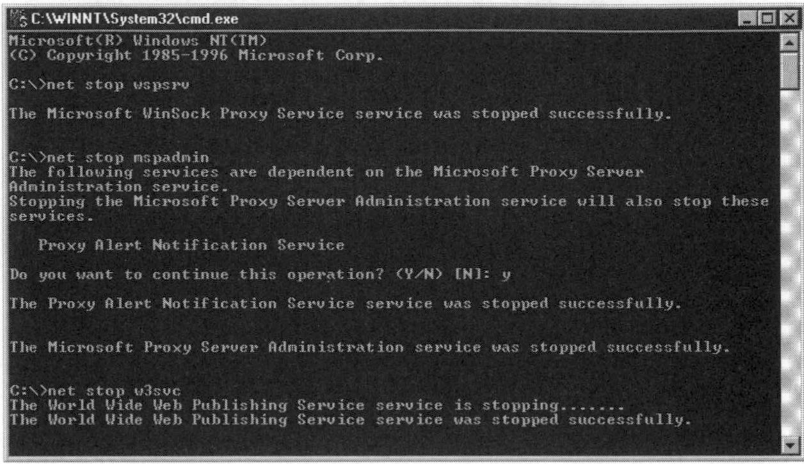

After stopping these services, you can begin the ISA Server installation process as we did earlier. Everything about the installation is the same, except for two dialog boxes related to the upgrade process itself. The first upgrade-related dialog box is displayed in Figure 5.35.

Figure 5.35 Information Box Regarding Upgrading Proxy Server

When the ISA Server installation routine detects that Proxy Server 2.0 was installed on the same machine, it will tell you that an older version of ISA Server

is on the machine. Well, this isn't *exactly* right, but you know what it's trying to say. When you are performing the upgrade, you want to install the files into the same folder.

Undocumented ISA

If you install the files into a different folder, you will be able to keep the original Proxy Server 2.0 files on your machine, although they won't be of much use to you because you can't run both Proxy Server 2.0 and ISA Server at the same time and you can't switch back and forth between the two.

The second upgrade-related dialog box is a little more accurate, as you see in Figure 5.36.

Figure 5.36 Proxy 2.0 Migration Dialog Box

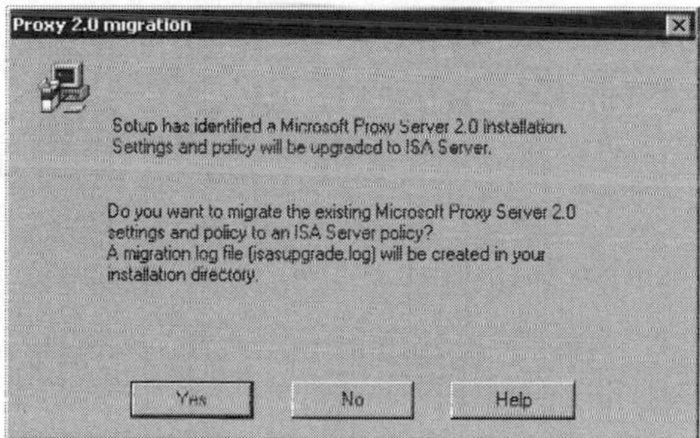

Since you want to migrate your Proxy Server 2.0 settings to the ISA Server, click **Yes** in this dialog box. If you want to install ISA Server without migrating your Proxy Server 2.0 settings, you can click **No** and the installation routine will ignore all settings from your old configuration. Keep in mind our earlier discussion regarding how the migration is affected by the group membership of the logged-on user and the enterprise policy settings.

Upgrading a Proxy 2.0 Installation on Windows NT 4.0

If you are planning to upgrade your Windows NT 4.0 Server that has Proxy Server 2.0 installed and then migrate your Proxy Server 2.0 settings to ISA Server, you'll need to know how to handle the upgrade to Windows 2000 while preserving your Proxy Server 2.0 settings.

If you are upgrading your Windows NT 4.0 Server with Proxy Server 2.0 installed, you are likely to run into one of two scenarios:

- You have planned the upgrade with the Proxy Server installation in mind.
- You forgot about Proxy Server and have already upgraded the Windows NT 4.0 machine to Windows 2000 without thinking about Proxy Server.

The following procedures will guide you in how to proceed in either situation.

A Planned Upgrade from Windows NT 4.0 Server to Windows 2000

The best way to approach an upgrade from Windows NT 4.0 to Windows 2000 is to plan the upgrade with Proxy Server 2.0 in mind. The following procedure will allow the upgrade from Windows NT 4.0 to Windows 2000 to go smoothly:

1. Use the Proxy Server configuration interface to back up your Proxy Server 2.0 settings as we did earlier in the chapter. To back up the Proxy Server 2.0 configuration, click the **Server Backup** button and select a location to store the proxy configuration files.
2. After backing up the Proxy Server 2.0 configuration, you need to uninstall the proxy server. Go to the **Start** menu, then to **Programs**, and then to **Microsoft Proxy Server**, and click the **Uninstall** command. During the uninstall process, be sure to leave the proxy server log files, Web cache, and backup configuration files in place. The Uninstall program will ask if you want to save these components.
3. Perform the upgrade of the Windows NT 4.0 Server to Windows 2000 Server or Advanced Server.

4. After the machine has been upgraded, confirm that the upgrade was successful by letting the machine run for a short shakedown period. If the installation is stable, install Microsoft Proxy Server 2.0.
5. Once Proxy Server is installed, use the **Server Restore** button in the **Proxy Server Properties** dialog box to restore your previous configuration. *You must remember the location where you stored the configuration files!*

The key to this approach is that you've backed up the Proxy Server 2.0 configuration, uninstalled Proxy Server 2.0, reinstalled Proxy Server 2.0 after the upgrade to Windows 2000, and then restored the old Proxy Server 2.0 configuration from the backup you made before the upgrade.

What If You Forgot About Proxy Server?

It is possible that when you upgraded your Windows 2000 Server, you forgot about Proxy Server or realized during the upgrade that Proxy Server was installed, but you thought that you'd get around to dealing with it after the Windows 2000 upgrade was completed. If you find yourself in this position, perform the following procedure:

1. Run the Update Wizard (msp2wizi.exe) that you downloaded from the Microsoft Web site. Be sure that the **Internet Information Server 5.0 Management** console is closed before you start the update.
2. During the installation process, you won't be given the option to update the existing Proxy Server installation. You need to perform a fresh installation. Be sure to choose the same installation locations that you did when you first installed Proxy Server 2.0 on the Windows NT 4.0 Server. If you place the files in the same location, your previous configuration *should* remain intact.

   Once the Microsoft Proxy Server 2.0 is installed on your Windows 2000 computer, you can access it via the **Administrative Tools** menu by clicking the **Internet Services Manager** command. You will see the **Internet Information Services** console as it appears in Figure 5.37.

After you have installed Proxy Server 2.0, there will be three new nodes in the left pane of the **Internet Information Services console**: the **Socks Proxy**, the **Web Proxy**, and the **WinSock Proxy**. To access the configuration of any of these proxy services, just right-click any one of them and click the **Properties** command.

Figure 5.37 The Internet Information Services Console

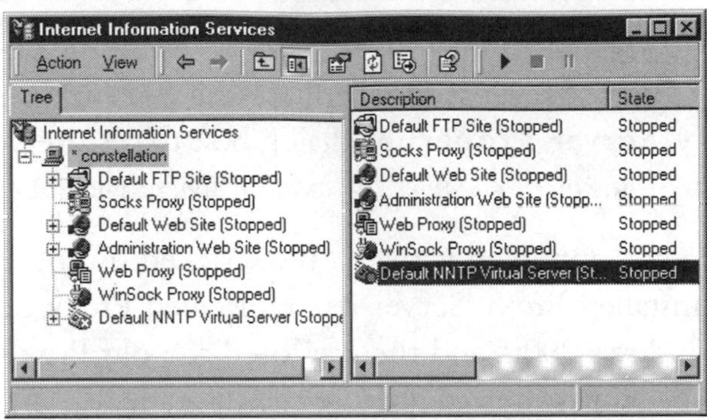

Realize that *all* upgrades place you in a delicate position. Even though everything should work correctly, long experience tells us that whatever can go wrong with an upgrade *will* go wrong. Even when an upgrade appears to be successful, rarely will the program work like a fresh installation.

Summary

In this chapter, we focused on issues related to planning and implementing the installation of ISA Server. We emphasized the critical importance of planning your ISA Server design before beginning the installation in order to prevent unexpected and potentially harmful results after the ISA Server installation is complete.

The following checklist will help guide you through the installation process:

- Check system requirements and ensure that you have the proper hardware and operating system.
- Review key concepts about ISA Server:
  - Firewall and security functions
  - Publishing
  - Caching
- Determine if you will install ISA Server as a standalone or array member.
- Determine the mode in which you will install ISA Server.
- Confirm that the routing table on the machine reflects the internal network infrastructure and contains all routes to networks within your internal network.
- Secure the network interfaces by disabling NetBIOS over TCP, the Microsoft client, and file and printer sharing for Microsoft networks.
- Confirm that no "stray" ports are opened by using the netstat –na command. This command lists ports that are connected or listening on your computer.
- Make the appropriate changes to your IIS installation, if you have one on your server. Either move the IIS services to another machine or make the port configuration changes, as discussed in this chapter.
- If you are installing in cache or integrated mode, verify that the computer has a Windows 2000 NTFS (NTFS 5.0) partition.
- If you are installing the first array member, initialize the enterprise.

- Review the installation process and ensure that you have all the necessary information (CD key, domain membership information) that will be requested during installation.
- Confirm connectivity to a domain controller if you are creating an enterprise array.
- Ensure that you have the appropriate permissions.
- Start the ISA Server Setup program.

The ISA Server installation process is a relatively straightforward one, but you can help prevent any unexpected problems during installation by proper planning—which includes backing up your Proxy Server 2.0 files if you are upgrading.

Solutions Fast Track

Installing ISA Server on a Windows 2000 Server

☑ The installation files for ISA Server can be accessed via the product CD-ROM or from a network installation share point. If you are installing from a share point, make sure that the Share and NTFS permissions at the source allow you to install the program.

☑ If you plan to install an enterprise array, the machine onto which you install ISA Server must be a member of a domain. You also need to connect to a domain controller during the installation.

☑ It is paramount that you configure the LAT correctly because it defines the networks that are considered internal and those that are considered external. If for some reason an external network ID finds itself on the LAT, requests from that network ID will be treated as internal network clients and will not be subjected to the same access controls applied to external network hosts.

☑ The H.323 Gatekeeper allows multiple inbound and outbound calls using a program such as NetMeeting to conduct voice, video, and data sessions.

Performing the Installation

- ☑ You *must* install the ISA Services. However, you can customize your selections for add-in services and administration tools.
- ☑ If you choose to install the H.323 Gatekeeper administration tool, it will place a node in your ISA Management console that will allow you to configure the H.323 Gatekeeper service.
- ☑ ISA Server listens for Web proxy server requests on port 8080 on the internal interface. This is a departure from the way Web proxy clients accessed the Proxy Server 2.0 Web Proxy Service, which they were able to access by connecting to port 80.
- ☑ You need to have Windows 2000 deployed and available if you want to make the server a member of an enterprise array.
- ☑ Before you promote a standalone server to an array member, you need to complete the *enterprise initialization*.
- ☑ ISA Server has its own management console and does not snap into the Internet Services Manager console the way Proxy Server 2.0 does. You can create your own console that includes the ISA Management standalone snap-in along with other snap-ins.

Migrating from Microsoft Proxy Server 2.0

- ☑ If you work in an organization that already has a Proxy Server 2.0 installation in place, you don't have to redo all the configuration settings that you have so carefully applied.
- ☑ When you migrate your Proxy Server 2.0 configuration to Windows 2000, virtually all components of your configuration will be ferried over to ISA Server.
- ☑ Proxy Server 2.0 included the ability to access the Internet while network clients ran IPX/SPX as their transport protocol. This capability has not been extended to ISA Server.
- ☑ If you are running Proxy Server 2.0 on an IPX network, you need to upgrade the networking infrastructure to support TCP/IP prior to installing ISA Server.

- ☑ The Web Proxy Service included with ISA Server is not dependent on IIS or WWW Service configuration parameters.
- ☑ ISA Server Web proxy clients need to send their requests to TCP port 8080 on the internal interface of the ISA server (by default).
- ☑ One of the sweetest features of ISA Server is that you do not need to configure servers that you want to publish to the Internet as Winsock proxy clients.
- ☑ Proxy Server 2.0 saved the Web cache to the file system. That meant you could easily collect thousands of files that needed to be managed by the NTFS file system. ISA Server saves the cache as one file.
- ☑ If you ran the SOCKS Proxy Service and configured access rules for SOCKS proxy clients on your Proxy Server 2.0, you won't be able to configure selective rules for those clients in ISA Server.
- ☑ If you must run a Web server from the same machine running ISA, make sure that no Web sites listen on port 80 of either the internal or external interface.
- ☑ Performing the actual migration from Proxy Server 2.0 to ISA Server is relatively easy. However, if you are going to install Proxy Server 2.0 directly onto a Windows 2000 machine, you must to use a special installation file called msp2wizi.exe that can be downloaded from the Microsoft Proxy Web site at www.microsoft.com/proxy.
- ☑ When the ISA Server installation routine detects that Proxy Server 2.0 was installed on the same machine, it will tell you that an older version of ISA Server is on the machine. Well, this isn't *exactly* right, but you know what it's trying to say. When you are performing the upgrade, you must install the files into the same folder.

Frequently Asked Questions

The following Frequently Asked Questions, answered by the authors of this book, are designed to both measure your understanding of the concepts presented in this chapter and to assist you with real-life implementation of these concepts. To have your questions about this chapter answered by the author, browse to **www.syngress.com/solutions** and click on the **"Ask the Author"** form.

Q: Must I install the schema to Active Directory each time I install an ISA server on my enterprise network?

A: No. The ISA schema has to be installed only once for the entire enterprise—when you install the first ISA server.

Q: If I decide I don't want the schema modified by the ISA installation, is there a way I can undo the addition of the new objects to the schema?

A: No. Active Directory does not allow you to delete schema objects once they have been added. (This rule applies to all schema modifications, not just those made by the ISA Server installation.) Object classes and attributes can be deactivated, but they cannot be removed. This is why it is critical that you first test ISA server in a controlled environment before committing yourself to changing your Active Directory structure to accommodate ISA Server.

Q: What are the advantages of installing a single ISA server as a lone member of an array instead of installing it as a standalone server?

A: If you anticipate that you might want to extend the ISA deployment to an array in the future, it will be easier to do so if you have installed your ISA server as a sole member of an array. With a lone array member, you can still configure enterprise policies and array policies separately. When you choose to add members to the array, the same array and enterprise policies will apply to the new members. Arrays offer several advantages: All the servers in the array share a common configuration and can be managed together, saving on administrative time. Enterprise policies can be applied to all the servers in an array, and having an array distributes the load across the multiple servers, increasing performance and providing fault tolerance.

Q: Do I *have* to install Active Directory on my network in order to create an array of ISA servers?

A: Yes. ISA Server array members can be installed only in a Windows 2000 domain. Promoting a Windows 2000 computer to domain controller to create a Windows 2000 domain installs Active Directory on the machine and deploys it on the network. In addition, an enterprise array requires Windows 2000 Advanced Server or Windows 2000 Datacenter center Server, and you must use the Enterprise Edition of ISA Server.

Q: Can ISA Server be installed in a Windows NT 4.0 domain?

A: Yes. Although ISA Server can be installed on only Windows 2000 Server machines, those machines can be member servers in Windows NT 4.0 domains or standalone servers. ISA Server must be installed as a standalone server in this environment; you cannot configure an array, because the configuration information will be stored in the local registry rather than in a centralized location (Active Directory).

Q: How do Active Directory sites affect installation of ISA Server arrays?

A: All members of an array must not only be members of the same Windows 2000 domain, they must also belong to the same Active Directory site. A *site* is a way of physically structuring the Windows 2000 network by joining well-connected subnets (those with a fast connection) into a grouping that is separated from other sites by slow WAN links. Domains can span multiple sites, and a site can include members of more than one domain.

Q: If I am installing a new ISA server as a member of an existing array, does it matter which mode I use?

A: Yes. If you install an ISA server as a member of an existing array, you should install it in the same mode (firewall, cache, or integrated) that the other members of the array are using. You should also install the same set of add-in features on each server in an array, to ensure the consistent functionality of all the servers.

Q: I have Macs on my network that use the SOCKS Proxy Service. Can I use ISA Server to support these clients?

A: Yes. Your Mac computers will be able to access the Internet via the ISA server. However, the ISA server does not have a SOCKS Service, as Proxy Server 2.0 had. Instead, configure your Mac clients as secure NAT clients and confirm that the SOCKS filter is enabled on the proxy server. By default, the SOCKS filter accepts requests on port 1080, but you can change that if you like from the ISA Server console.

Chapter 6

Managing ISA Server

Solutions in this chapter:

- Understanding Integrated Administration
- Performing Common Management Tasks
- Using Monitoring, Alerting, Logging, and Reporting Functions
- Understanding Remote Administration

☑ Summary

☑ Solutions Fast Track

☑ Frequently Asked Questions

Introduction

To *manage,* according to the *American Heritage Dictionary,* means "to direct or control." Effectively managing ISA Server means taking advantage of the tools Microsoft has provided to allow network administrators granular, fine-tuned control of the product's functionality and performance.

Flexibility, power, and features are important considerations in adopting any piece of software, especially an enterprise-level, mission-critical software package that is a vital part of your organization's security scheme. However, no matter how powerful and feature-rich a program, if its interface is not user friendly and it is difficult to configure and administer, you probably will not get the full benefits that it could offer.

In its efforts to make ISA Server as usable as it is powerful, Microsoft has equipped the product with the familiar Microsoft Management Console (MMC) interface used to give a standardized look and "feel" to all of Windows 2000's built-in administrative tools. The ISA management console is installed automatically as the interface to your ISA Server installation. It is also added to the list of standalone snap-in components that can be made part of a custom MMC.

In this chapter, we take a look at the ISA management console used to perform administration of ISA Server, the "how to's" of some specific management tasks, and ways of using the monitoring, alerting, logging, and reporting functionalities of ISA. We also discuss methods of administering your ISA Server or array from a remote location. Let's start by examining the concept of *integrated administration.*

Understanding Integrated Administration

You already know that an ISA Server or array can "wear more than one hat," or serve more than one function, on your network—as a firewall, as a caching server, or both. Unlike other solutions in which security and firewall functionality and caching and acceleration functionality require separate technologies, ISA's integrated administration enables you to manage both services using the same unified console and application of integrated policies.

An entire array of servers can be managed together as one entity. When the configuration of an array is changed, the desired modifications are made to every server in the array. Access policies and cache policies are all centrally managed. This system increases security as well, since it means that all configuration tasks can be performed at a single location.

Centralized administration is not limited to the array level. Enterprise policies can be used to control multiple arrays on your network. This integration allows an administrator to control all the ISA servers or server arrays in a large enterprise conveniently, even from a remote location.

In this section, you will learn to navigate the ISA Management Console, which is used to perform most management tasks, and you'll become familiar with the ISA Wizards that make common administrative duties easier by walking you through the process step by step.

The ISA Management Console

When you install ISA Server on a Windows 2000 server, the ISA Server selection will be added to the Programs menu with two selections, ISA Management and ISA Server Performance Monitor, as shown in Figure 6.1.

Figure 6.1 The ISA Management Programs Are Added to the Windows 2000 Programs Menu

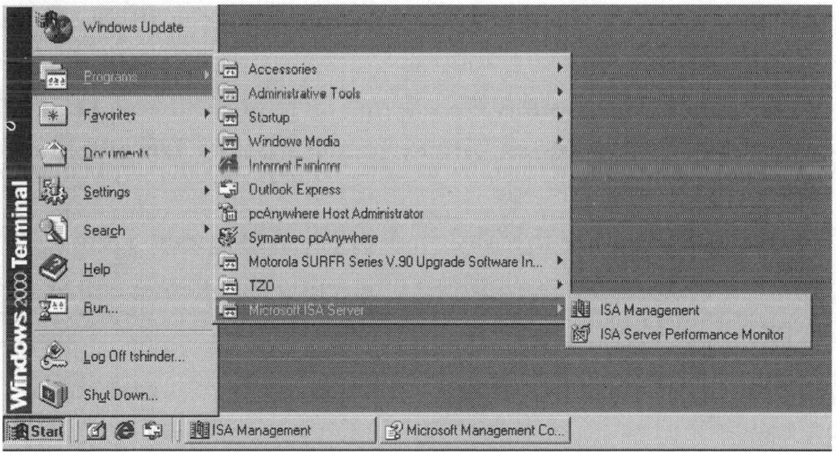

The console can also be opened by typing the full path for the msisa.msc file (for example, c:\Program Files\Microsoft ISA Server\msisa.msc) at the Run prompt or by navigating in Windows Explorer to the folder into which ISA Server was installed and double-clicking the msisa.msc icon.

The ISA Management Console is shown in Figure 6.2.

General procedures for working with the console are the same as with any MMC. You use the **View** menu at the top of the console to work with it. For example:

Figure 6.2 The ISA Management Console Allows You to Administer Your ISA Servers and Arrays

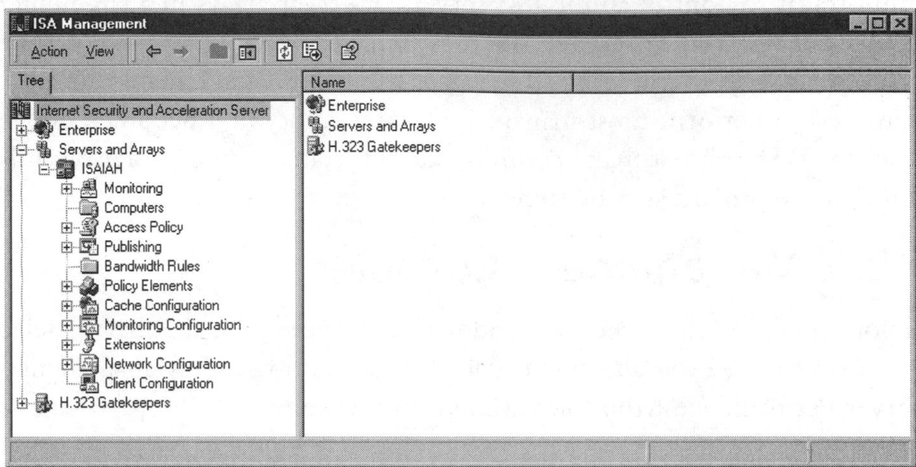

- You can choose the columns to be displayed in the right detail pane by selecting **View | Choose columns** and adding available columns to or removing them from the display.
- You can choose the display mode for the icons in the right detail pane by selecting **Large Icons**, **Small Icons**, **List**, or **Details** from the **View** menu.
- You can select either the **Taskpad** or the **Advanced** view.
- You can customize the console by selecting the elements that will be displayed or hidden.

A big advantage of the MMC interface is the ability to create custom MMCs that incorporate the specific snap-ins that you—or an assistant administrator to whom you delegate administrative duties—need to work with. The next section discusses how to add ISA Server management to a custom MMC.

Adding ISA Management to a Custom MMC

To create a custom MMC to which you can add whichever administrative tools you desire as snap-in modules, you first create an empty console by typing **mmc** at the Run prompt. The new empty console root window will be encapsulated in a larger window for which the menu bar includes the **Console**, **Window**, and **Help** menus. You can add ISA management by selecting **Add/Remove Snap-in** from the **Console** menu. When ISA Server is installed on the machine, the

ISA Management snap-in will be available to add to custom consoles, as shown in Figure 6.3.

Figure 6.3 ISA Management Can Be Added to a Custom MMC

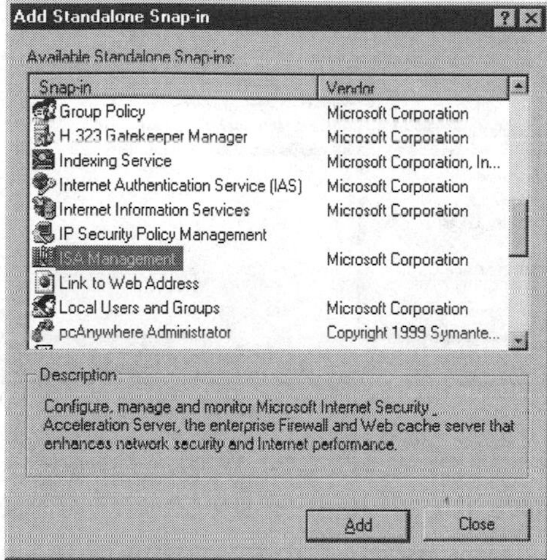

When you elect to add the ISA Management module, you will be asked to choose whether to connect to the local server, another standalone server, or the enterprise and arrays, as shown in Figure 6.4.

Figure 6.4 When Adding ISA to a Custom Console, You Must Choose from Three Connection Options

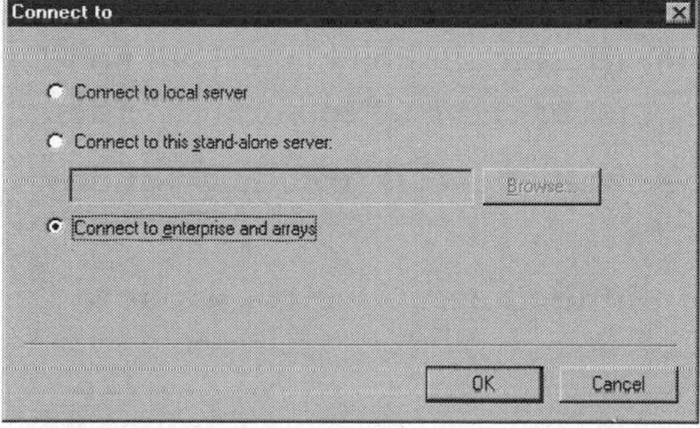

You will see the same console tree as in the preconfigured ISA Management tool. You can now add other snap-ins to allow you to perform a set of related administrative tasks, all from the same MMC. For example, in the MMC shown in Figure 6.5, you can manage your ISA Server array, the local Certification Authority, and IIS, all from the same custom console.

Figure 6.5 ISA Management Can Be One of Several Components in a Custom MMC

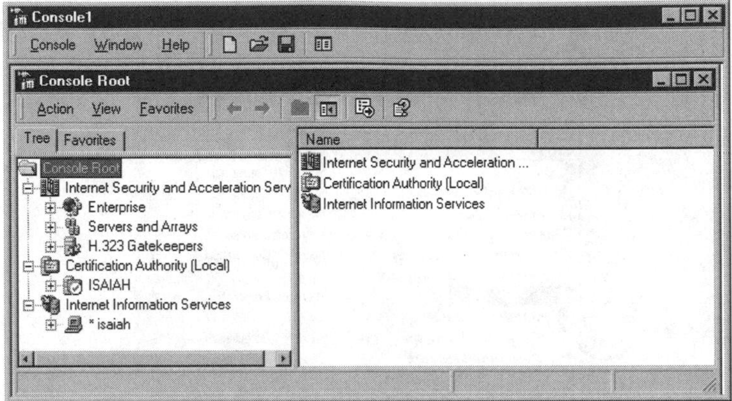

The custom console can now be saved with a unique name. By default, it will saved in the Administrative Tools folder in the Programs menu, in the profile of the currently logged-on administrator, and can subsequently be started from the **Start | Programs | Administrative Tools** menu.

Console Mode Options

Your custom console can be saved in one of four modes:

- **Author mode** Allows you to create new consoles or modify existing consoles.
- **User mode—full access** Provides full window management commands and full access to the console tree but prevents adding or removing snap-ins or changing console properties.
- **User mode—limited access, multiple window** Allows use of multiple windows.
- **User mode—limited access, single window** Limits access to a single window.

You specify the console mode by selecting **Options** from the **Console** menu. Regardless of the default mode in which the console is saved, it can be opened in author mode by typing the full MMC pathname with the **/a** switch at the **Run** prompt.

The Components of the ISA MMC

In this section, we look at the components of the ISA MMC and explain the function of each, including:

- The MMC window
- The menu bar
- The toolbar icons
- The console root and tree

First, we'll take a look at the MMC window.

The MMC Window

If you have created a custom console, you'll see a window within a window, as shown earlier in Figure 6.5. The outer window contains the main menu bar and the main toolbar common to all MMCs. The inner window is the *console window* and includes a menu bar, toolbar, description bar, and status bar. You can hide any of these elements by selecting **Customize** from the **View** menu and checking the check boxes of those elements you want displayed and unchecking those you want to hide, as shown in Figure 6.6.

Figure 6.6 You Can Select the MMC Elements You Wish to Display or Hide

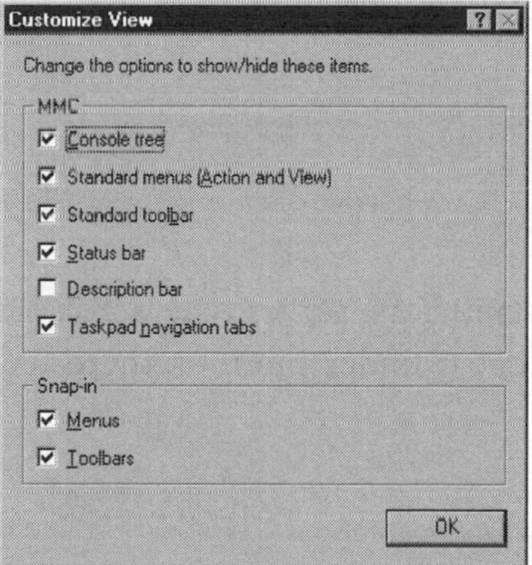

The console window of the ISA MMC contains a tab labeled **Tree**, which displays in the left console pane the hierarchy of your ISA management components. In the section "The Console Root and Tree," we look at these elements and how they are used in administering your ISA server or array.

The right console pane displays the details of the left pane element that is selected. For example, when you select **Policy Elements** in the left pane, those policy elements that appear under that container in the left console tree will be displayed in the right pane, as shown in Figure 6.7.

Figure 6.7 The Right Detail Pane Displays the Child Objects of the Selected Object in the Left Console Tree

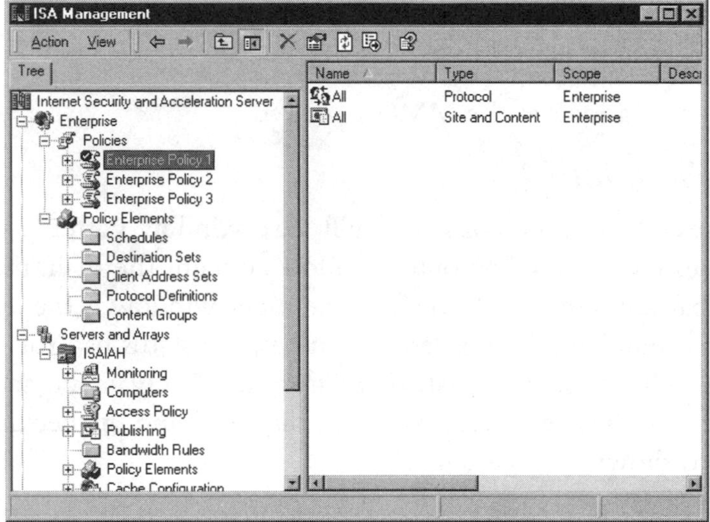

Note that in the figure, there are three containers under the root:

- Enterprise
- Servers and Arrays
- H.323 Gatekeepers

If the ISA server is a standalone server that is not a member of an array, only the last two objects will appear under the root; there will be no Enterprise object (as shown in Figure 6.8).

NOTE

The H.323 Gatekeepers object will appear here only if you specified that it be installed during the ISA Server installation process.

Figure 6.8 A Standalone ISA Server Has No Enterprise Object in the Left Pane

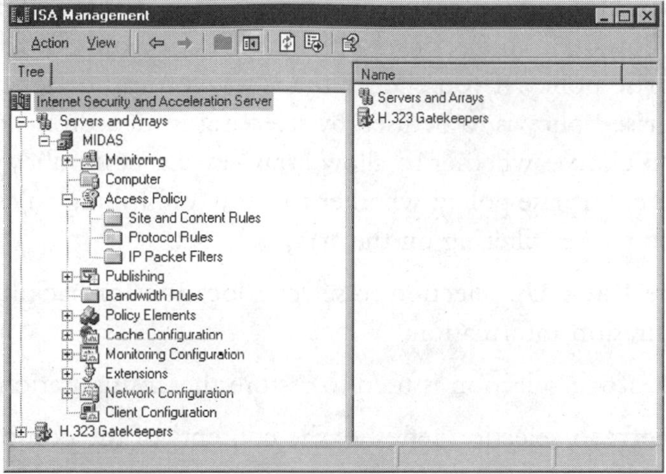

Observing the objects that appear in the left pane is one way to determine quickly, by a glance at the ISA MMC, whether the server is a standalone server or an array member.

The Menu Bar

The *menu bar* consists of two menus: **Action** and **View**. The contents of the **Action** menu depend on whether the ISA server is an array member and which object is highlighted in the console pane. The contents of the **Action** menu will be the same as the contents of the right context menu when you highlight the specified objects.

For example, the **Action** menu for an ISA server that belongs to an array provides the following options when the array or server object is highlighted:

- Set Defaults
- Back Up
- Restore
- Refresh
- Export List
- Properties
- Help

Let's take a quick look at each of these options:

- The **Set Defaults** selection on an ISA server that is a member of an array allows you to elect to use the array policy only or to use an Enterprise policy. If you choose the latter, you can designate which Enterprise policy is to be used by selecting from a drop-down box. You can also choose whether to allow array-level access policy rules that will restrict enterprise policy, whether to allow publishing rules, and whether to force packet filtering on the array.
- Use the **Back Up** selection to select a location for backing up the ISA configuration information.
- The **Restore** selection is used to restore the configuration from backup.
- The **Refresh** selection refreshes the contents of the console window.
- The **Export List** selection allows you to save the contents of the detail pane to a text file. You can choose from four formats: Text (tab delimited), Unicode Text (tab delimited), Text (Comma Delimited), and Unicode Text (Comma Delimited). The first two formats are saved with the .TXT extension; the last two are saved with the .CSV extension. The text files can be imported into a spreadsheet program such as Excel or a database program such as Access for data sorting and processing.
- The **Properties** selection allows you to set the security (DACL permissions) on the object and specify whether to allow inheritable permissions from the parent object to propagate to this one. The **Advanced** button allows you to edit permission entries, set auditing on the object, and view or change ownership of the object. These are the standard Windows 2000 access control settings.
- The **Help** selection invokes the ISA Help file, which is stored in the directory in which you installed ISA Server (**Program Files | Microsoft ISA Server** by default) as **ISA.CHM**.

If the ISA server you are managing is a standalone server instead of an array member, the **Action** menu will still include the **Refresh**, **Export List**, and **Help** selections, but it will include none of the others listed previously. It will have one additional selection, **Connect to.** This option is used to connect to another standalone server or to an enterprise or array, as shown in Figure 6.9. Note that you cannot connect to an array from a standalone server.

Figure 6.9 From a Standalone ISA Server, You Can Connect to Another Standalone Server

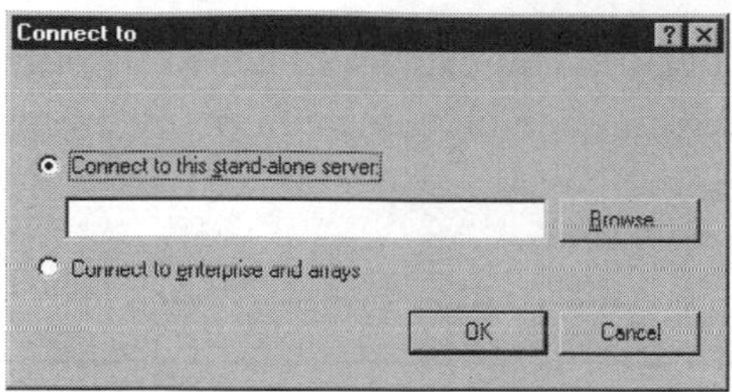

The **View** menu is identical for both standalone servers and array members. It contains the **Choose Columns** option that allows you to specify the column headers that will be displayed in the right detail pane. The choices available depend on which object you have highlighted in the left console tree. For example, if you have highlighted **Servers and Arrays** in the left pane, you will see a list of columns as shown in Figure 6.10.

Figure 6.10 You Can Choose the Columns to Display or Hide in the Right Detail Pane

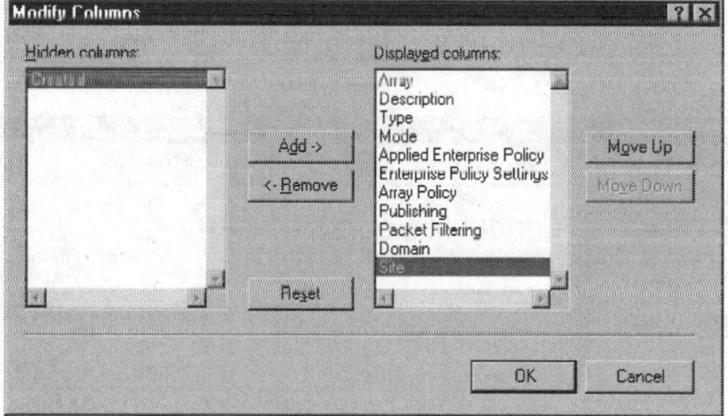

By default, all but one of the available columns is displayed. You can remove columns from the display by clicking the **Remove** button or add them by clicking **Add**. The **Reset** button will return the selection to the default setting.

You can select from the **View** menu the way you want the items in the right detail pane displayed, in keeping with the usual Windows Explorer views:

- Large icons
- Small icons

- List
- Detail

The Detail view is the default. You can also elect to use the Taskpad or Advanced view. The Taskpad view is the default, although many administrators are likely to opt for the Advanced view.

NOTE

The screenshots of the ISA Management Console in this book, except for those specifically illustrating the use of the Taskpad, are shown in the Advanced view.

The Taskpad view provides a more graphical interface for navigating the management options and configuring various elements of ISA Server. The Taskpad view uses a tabbed format that some administrators find more appealing than the standard detail pane. An example of the Taskpad view, with **Servers and Arrays** selected in the left pane, is shown in Figure 6.11.

Figure 6.11 The Taskpad View Provides a More Graphical, Tabbed Interface

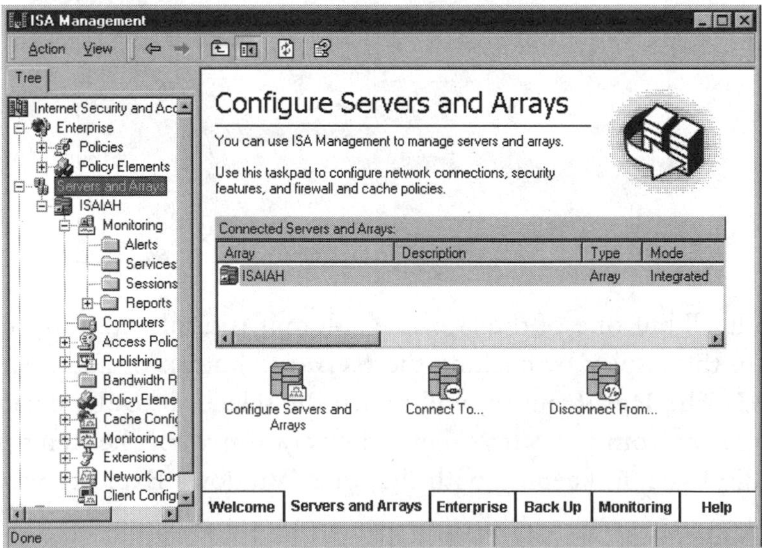

The same element selected (Servers and Arrays) with the Advanced view is shown in Figure 6.12. As you can see, the Taskpad view offers a more intuitive interface, whereas the Advanced view is simpler and less cluttered. Each administrator will make the choice of view based on personal preference.

Figure 6.12 The Advanced View Provides a Simpler, Less Cluttered, Less Intuitive Interface

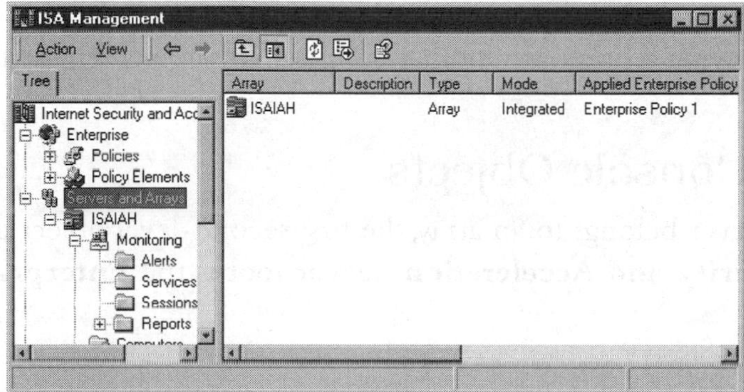

The last choice on the **View** menu is **Customize**, which allows you to customize the display by hiding certain MMC elements, as discussed earlier.

The Toolbar Icons

Seven icons appear on the ISA MMC main toolbar. These icons are standard navigation tools or items that mirror the functions of menu items. They include:

- **Back** and **Forward** buttons to return to previous locations in the console tree.
- The **Up One Level** button that takes the focus up a level in the console tree.
- The **Show/Hide Console Tree/Favorites** button that can be used to hide the left console pane, displaying only the right detail pane across the whole window.
- The **Refresh** button that, like the same choice on the **Action** menu, refreshes the display.
- The **Export List** button that performs the same function as the same selection on the **Action** menu.
- The **Help** button that invokes the ISA Server Help file.

Note that unlike the menu or toolbar for an application window, the MMC menu and toolbar cannot be customized.

The Console Root and Tree

The *console root* is the top-level object in the left pane of the ISA MMC. All objects under it are *child objects* of the root. Together, the root and its child objects make up the *console tree*. The console tree is the heart of the ISA management console, providing all the objects that can be configured.

In the following section, we look at each individual element of the ISA console tree.

The ISA Console Objects

If your ISA Server belongs to an array, the first second-level object under the **Internet Security and Acceleration Server** root is the **Enterprise** container.

NOTE

If you have worked with Windows 2000's Active Directory, you'll remember that a *container object* is an object in the tree inside of which other objects can reside.

The Enterprise Object

The **Enterprise** container holds two child container objects:

- Policies
- Policy Elements

The **Policies** object will hold any Enterprise policies that have been configured. By right-clicking an enterprise policy object in the left pane and selecting **Properties**, you can assign the policy to be explicitly applied to an array by checking the check box, as shown in Figure 6.13.

More information about the policy is shown in the right detail pane when you select the policy name in the left pane. As shown in Figure 6.14, this information includes the policy name, type, scope, action, protocol, schedule, source, destination, and content.

Figure 6.13 Enterprise Policies Are Explicitly Assigned to Arrays via the Arrays Tab on Their Properties Boxes

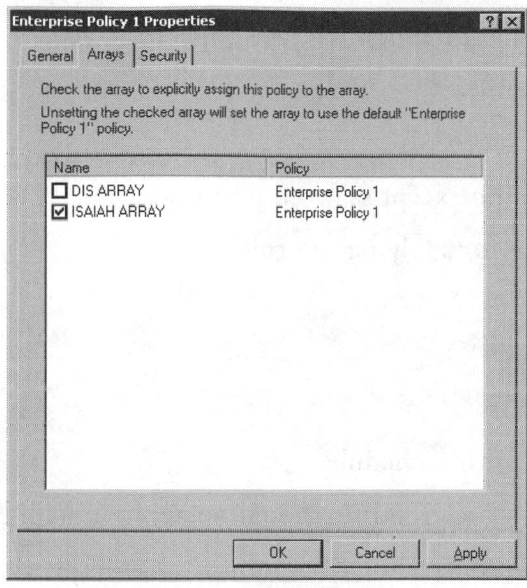

Figure 6.14 Information About Each Enterprise Policy Is Shown in the Right Detail Pane

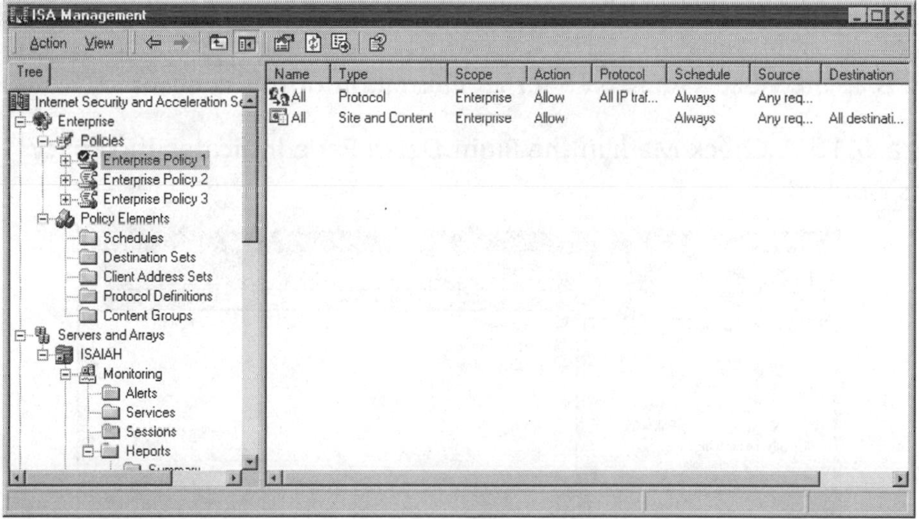

By right-clicking the policy row in the right detail pane and selecting **Properties**, you can configure the following:

- Enabling the policy
- The policy action (allow or deny requests)
- The protocol(s) to which the rule applies:
  - All IP traffic
  - Selected protocols
  - All IP traffic except selected protocols
- The schedule for applying the rule:
  - Always
  - Weekends
  - Work hours
  - A new, custom schedule
- Requests to which the rule should be applied:
  - Any request
  - Requests from specified client addresses
  - Requests from specified users and groups

You can determine which Enterprise policy has been applied by checking the icons in the right detail pane. The icon with a check mark indicates that the policy is applied. See Figure 6.15 for an illustration of this concept.

Figure 6.15 A Check Mark in the Right Detail Pane Indicates the Policy that Is Applied

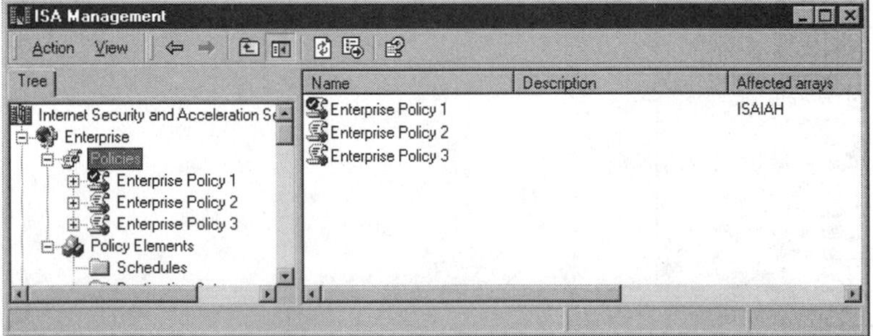

Note that in the figure, Enterprise Policy 1 displays the icon with the check mark and thus is the policy that is applied.

The enterprise **Policy Elements** container has five child objects:

- **Schedules** Specify when the rule will be in effect; can be applied to site and content rules, protocol rules, or bandwidth rules.
- **Destination Sets** One or more destinations (computer, IP address or IP range, path); can be applied to site and content rules, bandwidth rules, Web publishing rules, or routing rules.
- **Client Address Sets** One or more computers; can be applied to site and content rules, protocol rules, bandwidth rules, server publishing rules, or Web publishing rules.
- **Protocol Definitions** Used to create protocol rules or server publishing rules (inbound protocol definitions). Application filters can include protocol definitions as well.
- **Content Groups** Used to specify MIME types and filename extensions; apply only to HTTP and tunneled FTP traffic that goes through the Web proxy service.

The policy elements must be configured before the policies are configured. There are policy elements for both the enterprise policy and each array policy.

NOTE

Remember that when an enterprise policy is used in conjunction with array policies, the array policy can only impose further *restrictions*; it cannot be less restrictive than the enterprise policy.

When you use array and enterprise policies together, array-level rules can be applied to enterprise-level policy elements. This means that when you create a policy element at the enterprise level, it appears as a selection when you create a new rule at the array level. Let's look at how this works.

In Figure 6.16, you can see that we have created a custom schedule policy element at the enterprise level (displayed along with the two preconfigured schedule policy elements in the right detail pane).

Now if we go down to the array level (under the **Servers and Arrays** object) and, in the **Site and Content Rules** under **Access Policy**, we create a new rule, the wizard will walk us through the steps of creating our new rule. If

Figure 6.16 An Enterprise-Level Policy Element Named Custom Has Been Created

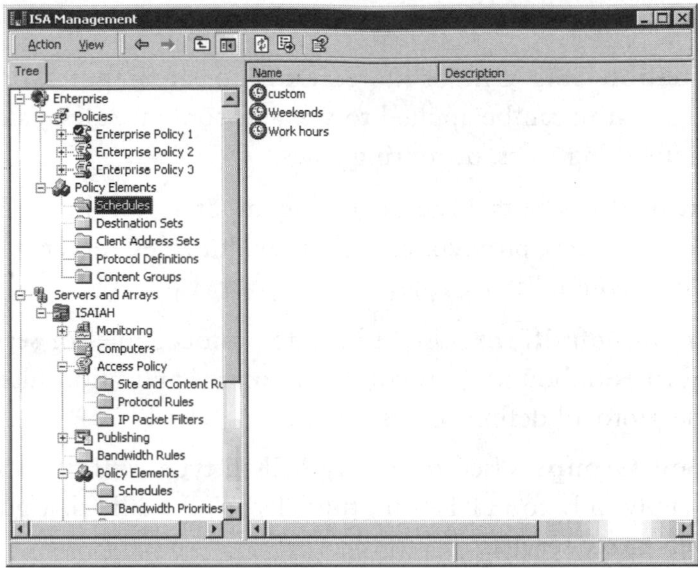

we choose to apply the rule based on time ("Deny access only at certain times"), we will find in the drop-down box of schedule policy elements the custom schedule that we created back at the enterprise level (see Figure 6.17).

Refer to Chapter 8 for details on configuring policy elements.

Figure 6.17 The Policy Element Created at the Enterprise Level Is Available to Be Applied to Rules at the Array Level

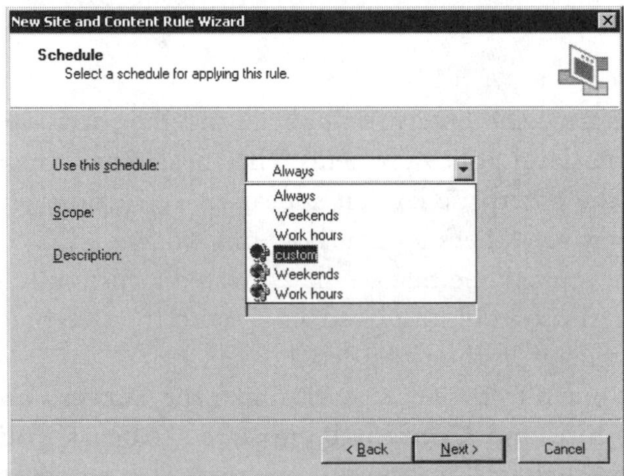

The Servers and Arrays Object

In the console tree, under **Servers and Arrays**, you will find a child object for each array, identified by the array name. By default, the array name is the same as the name of the first server that joins the array. However, you can change the array name (and you might want to do so, to avoid confusion) by right-clicking it, selecting **Properties**, and typing in the new array name, as shown in Figure 6.18.

Figure 6.18 You Can Change the Array Name to Avoid Confusion with a Server by the Same Name

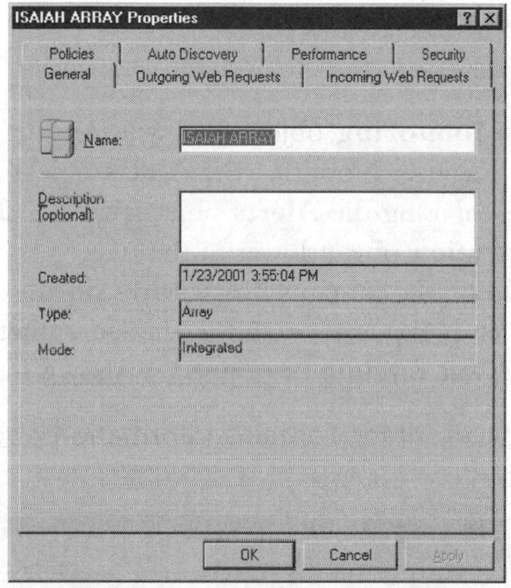

The array's Properties sheet also provides, on the **General** tab, information regarding the date and time the array was created and the mode in which its servers are installed (firewall, caching, or integrated).

The other tabs are used for configuration of outgoing and incoming Web requests, publication of autodiscovery information, and performance tuning (all of which are discussed in detail in Chapter 8) as well as incoming Web requests (discussed in Chapter 9), selection of enterprise policy settings for the array, and setting security permissions on the array object. (Object permissions are discussed later in this chapter, in the section titled "Performing Common Management Tasks.")

Under the Array object, you will see the following child objects:

- Monitoring
- Computers

- Access Policy
- Publishing
- Bandwidth Rules
- Policy Elements
- Cache Configuration
- Monitoring Configuration
- Extensions
- Network Configuration
- Client Configuration

If you expand the **Monitoring** object, you will see four folders: Alerts, Services, Sessions, and Reports. Note that the **Alerts** object is used to *view* alerts; they are actually *configured* using the **Alerts** object that is a child of the **Monitoring Configuration** object lower in the tree.

The **Services** child object contains ISA services on all servers in the array (the firewall service, Web proxy service, and scheduled content download service), indicating whether they are running or stopped, as shown in Figure 6.19.

Figure 6.19 The Services Folder Contains Information About ISA Services on All Servers in the Array

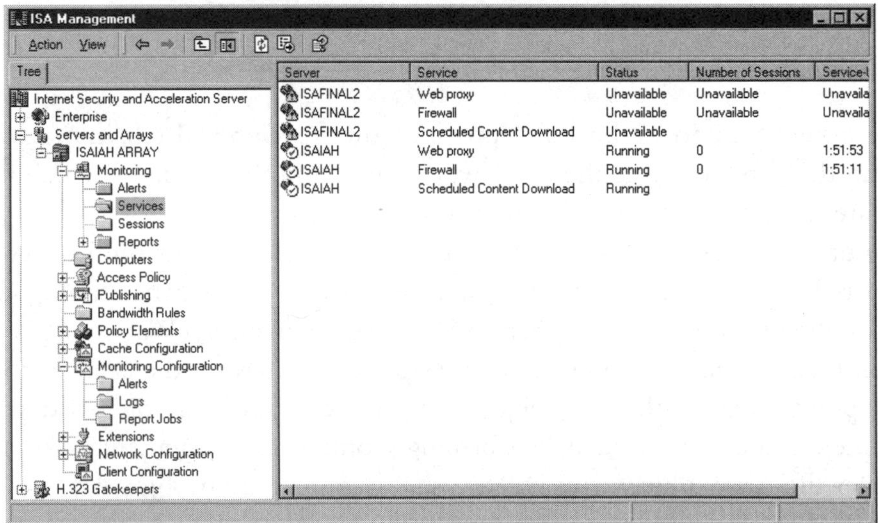

Note that, as shown in the figure, if a member of the array is offline, the status of its services will be displayed as "Unavailable."

The **Sessions** folder contains information about current sessions that are active for the Web proxy or firewall service, as shown in Figure 6.20.

Figure 6.20 Active Sessions Are Displayed in the Detail Pane When You Select the Sessions Folder

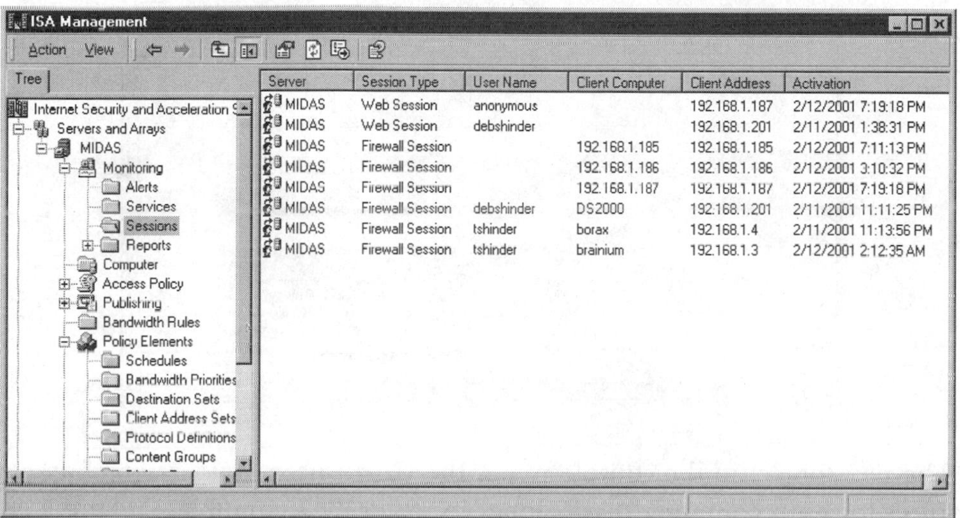

The **Reports** folder contains the results of report jobs that have been configured under the **Monitoring Configuration** object. These are further divided into five categories, or subfolders:

- Summary
- Web Usage
- Application Usage
- Traffic & Utilization
- Security

You can view a report by double-clicking it in the right detail pane (see Figure 6.21).

You will learn how to configure alerting, logging, and reporting later in this chapter, in the "Using Monitoring, Alerting, Logging, and Reporting Functions" section.

Figure 6.21 You Can View Reports by Double-Clicking the Report Name in the Right Detail Pane

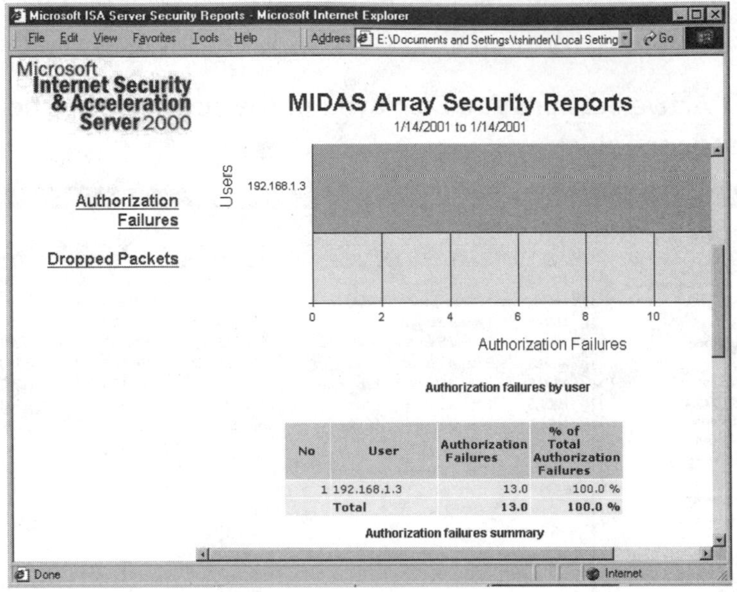

No	User	Authorization Failures	% of Total Authorization Failures
1	192.168.1.3	13.0	100.0 %
	Total	13.0	100.0 %

The next object in the console tree is the **Computers** folder, which contains an object for each computer that belongs to the array. By double-clicking a computer object in the right detail pane, you can display its Properties sheet, as shown in Figure 6.22.

Figure 6.22 Access the Properties Sheet for Each Array Member through the Computers Folder

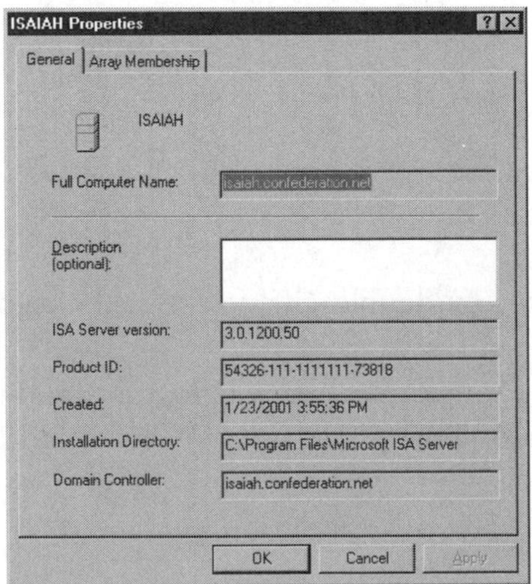

Undocumented ISA

Although the ISA Management Console allows you to change the name of an array, it does not support changing the name of an ISA Server computer.

In addition to general information such as the version number of ISA Server that is installed, the product ID, the date the ISA server was created, the installation directory path, and the domain controller, the Properties sheet has a tab labeled **Array Membership**. This tab shows the IP address used for intra-array communication and lets you specify the *load factor* for the server, which indicates its relative availability for caching in comparison to the other servers in the array. You can increase or decrease the load on a particular ISA server by increasing or decreasing the value in the load factor field. By default, this value is set to 100.

Configuring & Implementing...

Intra-Array Communication

The intra-array IP address information is typically the same address used by downstream clients and ISA servers to communicate with the server. Microsoft recommends that you not change this value, because it has to be replicated to all the other servers in the array. However, if you do need to change the address, you can do so by typing the new IP address into the box on the Array Membership tab.

The address that you use for intra-array communication must be configured to listen for requests on the same port as the address that is configured to listen for incoming Web requests. Otherwise, CARP will not function for incoming Web requests. This means you should set the incoming Web request properties for the array so that the same listener configuration is used for all IP addresses. Details of configuring CARP are discussed in Chapter 8.

Continuing down the console tree, you will find the **Access Policy** object, which has three subfolders:

- Site and Content Rules
- Protocol Rules
- IP Packet Filters

Configuration of these access policies, using a standalone ISA Server, as demonstrated in Chapter 8. If you have an array, you can create access policies at the enterprise level, the array level, or both. If the enterprise policy settings are configured to use enterprise policy only, you cannot add new rules at the array level. Conversely, if settings are configured to use array policy only, no enterprise policy will be applied to the array. If the enterprise administrator has configured settings for combined enterprise and array policy, an array policy will be added to the enterprise policy, with the enterprise policy overriding the array policy so that restrictions imposed by the enterprise policy will always apply. You can impose additional restrictions with the array policy but, as discussed previously, you cannot set an array policy that is less restrictive than the enterprise policy. If you configure settings to use enterprise policies only, you will not be able to use array policies without reinstalling ISA Server.

The next object in the tree is the **Publishing** object, containing two folders:

- Web Publishing Rules
- Server Publishing Rules

Configuration of these rules is discussed in Chapter 10, "Publishing Servers to the Internet." You can create a new rule of either type by right-clicking the appropriate folder and selecting **New** from the right context menu. This action invokes a wizard (see Figure 6.23), which will walk you through the steps required to create the new rule.

The **Bandwidth Rules** object is the next element in the console tree. Bandwidth rules let you specify which connections have priority over other connections. As with the creation of other rules, a New Bandwidth Rule Wizard assists you in creating bandwidth rules.

Policy elements come next in our journey down the left console pane. You will recognize most of these as the same as the policy elements available under the **Enterprise** object. However, there are two additional folders here: the Bandwidth Priorities element and the Dial-up Entries element. Configuration of these policy elements is discussed in Chapter 8.

Figure 6.23 New Web Publishing or Server Publishing Rules Are Created with a Wizard

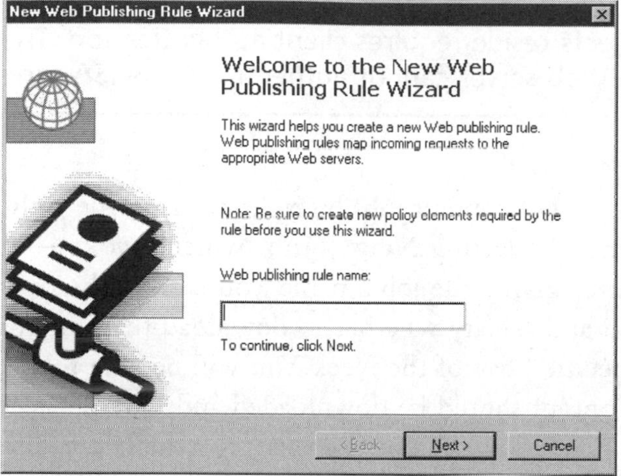

NOTE

Don't confuse bandwidth priority rules with bandwidth limitation. ISA Server rules do not limit the amount of bandwidth that can be used by a connection; they specify how the QoS packet-scheduling service should prioritize the use of multiple network connections.

Moving down the tree, we come to the **Cache Configuration** object. You will find two subfolders here:

- Scheduled Content Download
- Drives

The scheduled content service is **w3prefetch**, which lets you configure ISA to download cache content from specific URLs at specified times. This *prefetching* of regularly accessed pages speeds your users' access because the pages are already in the cache when users attempt to access them. For example, if users visit a particular news site daily, you could configure a scheduled download to occur on a daily basis so that the content in the cache would be updated each day.

NOTE

You cannot schedule a content download job if the Web server on which the Web objects reside requires client authentication. The job will fail because the Web server cannot authenticate the ISA server.

You create scheduled content jobs by right-clicking the **Scheduled Content Download** folder and selecting **New | Job**, which invokes—you guessed it!—another wizard. After giving the job a name, you can set the date and time to start the download and specify whether to download the content just once, daily, or weekly on a specified day of the week. You will be able to choose the URL from which the content should be downloaded and whether to download only content from the URL domain, not from sites to which it is linked. You also have the option of caching dynamic content, even when the HTTP cache control headers indicate they are not cacheable.

You can limit the depth of links to be cached as well. By default, there is no limit. You can also set a limit on the total number of objects to be cached, up to a maximum of 99,999.

When you have completed providing the information for the wizard, a summary of your selections will be presented, as shown in Figure 6.24.

Figure 6.24 The Scheduled Content Download Wizard Makes It Easy to Create a Job to Automatically Update the Cache of Specified URLs

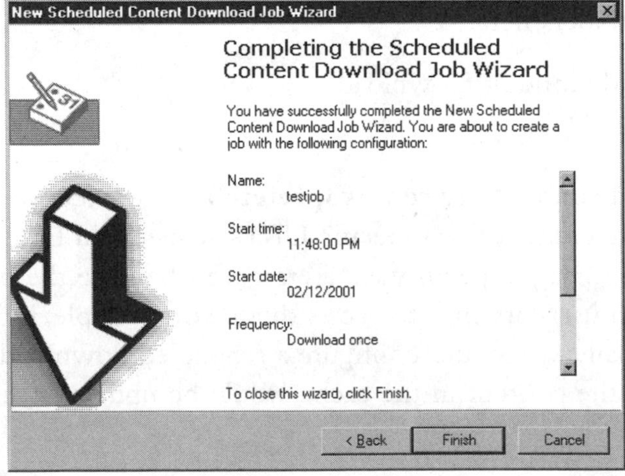

Now the job is displayed in the right detail pane along with other scheduled jobs, as shown in Figure 6.25.

Figure 6.25 Scheduled Content Download Jobs Appear in the Right Pane When the Folder Is Selected

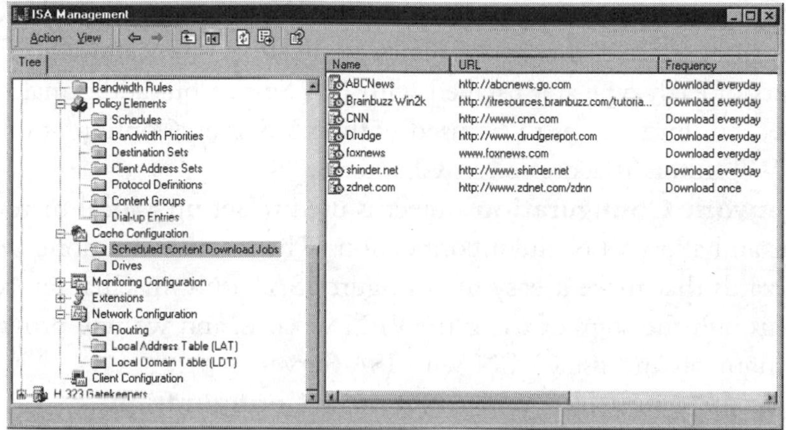

The **Drives** folder displays NTFS logical drives on the ISA servers in the array, provides information on the total amount of disk space and the amount of free space on each drive, and allows you to set a limit on the cache size, in megabytes, for each drive. Right-click the drive in the right detail pane to access the Properties sheet shown in Figure 6.26.

Figure 6.26 Configure the Amount of Disk Space on Each NTFS Drive to Be Allocated to the ISA Cache

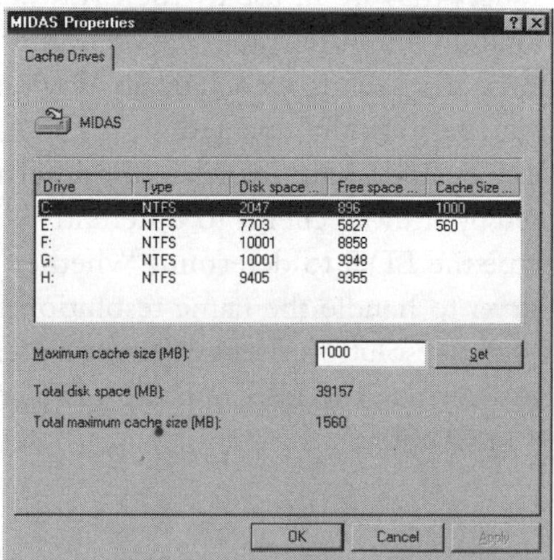

Continuing to move down the left console tree, you will see the **Monitoring Configuration** object that holds folders for Alerts, Logs, and Report Jobs. Later in this chapter, in the "Using Monitoring, Alerting, Logging and Reporting Functions" section, you will learn how to use each of these objects.

The next item in the tree is an object labeled **Extensions**. *Extensions* are filters that provide additional functionality for filtering applications and Web requests. Thus there are two types of filters: application filters and Web filters. Several filters of each type are installed with ISA Server, but additional filters can be developed by third parties to be used with ISA Server. Configuration of application and Web filters is addressed in Chapter 8.

The **Network Configuration** object is used to set up a local or remote ISA VPN server and allow VPN client connections. These setups are done with a series of wizards that make it easy to configure ISA VPNs. In Chapter 10, you will walk through the steps of using the VPN wizards, and we will provide some tips on configuring and using VPN with ISA Server.

There are three subfolders under **Network Configuration**:

- **Routing** Used to create and configure routing rules (using the Routing Rule Wizard).
- **Local Address Table (LAT)** Used to construct a local address table and to add entries to the existing LAT.
- **Local Domain Table (LDT)** Used to add new entries to the LDT.

Routing rules determine where Web proxy client requests are sent and apply to both incoming and outgoing Web requests. The *local address table* keeps track of the internal IP address ranges that are in use by the LAN behind the ISA server. ISA users the LAT to control communication between internal computers and those on external networks; the LAT is automatically downloaded to firewall clients, copies of which are periodically updated.

The *local domain table* lists all domain names in the internal network behind the ISA server and is used by firewall clients to differentiate between internal and external names. Clients use the LDT to determine whether to send a name resolution request to ISA Server to handle the name resolution for an external resource or to perform name resolution themselves for a local resource.

Configuration of routing rules, the LAT, and the LDT are all discussed in detail and demonstrated in Chapter 8.

Security Alert!

The LDT is not used by SecureNAT clients, which resolve both internal and external names via DNS and thus must have access to DNS servers.

As we move down the console tree, we next encounter the **Client Configuration** object. As shown in Figure 6.27, there are two configuration objects in the right detail pane: Web Browser and Firewall Client.

Figure 6.27 The Two Client Configuration Objects: Web Browser and Firewall Client

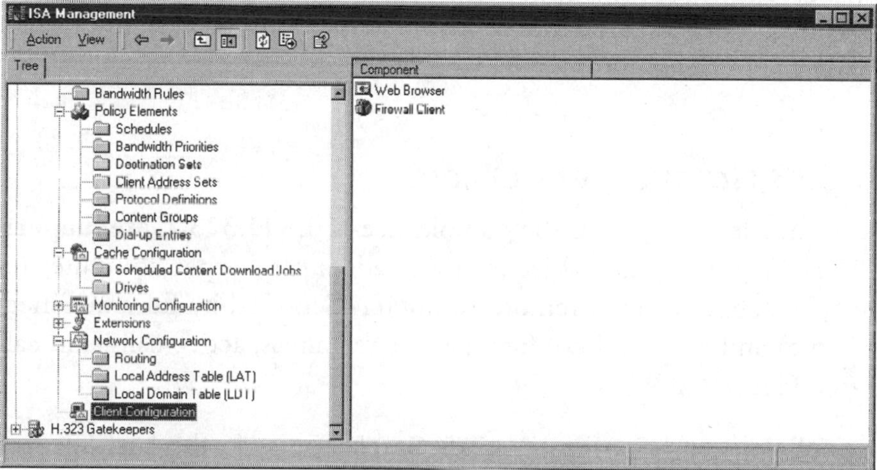

By double-clicking the configuration object name, you can access its Properties sheet, allowing you to view or change settings.

The *Web browser* Properties sheet allows you to choose whether to configure the Web browser during firewall client setup and whether to use automatic discovery and configuration. You can also choose to have the client bypass the proxy for local servers and/or directly access computers specified in the LDT, and you can specify the IP addresses, domain names, or computer names of specific computers that you want the client to be able to access directly, without going through ISA. You can also configure a backup route, designating how clients should access the Internet if the ISA server is unavailable. In Chapter 8, we walk through the steps involved in configuring the Web browser.

The Properties sheet for the *firewall client* is less complex. It allows you to specify whether the firewall client will connect to the ISA computer or array by name or IP address (and enter the DNS name or IP address of the ISA server to be used), and you can enable or disable autodiscovery in the firewall client. The Application Settings tab is used to add client configuration information for specific applications, if necessary.

Configuring application settings and thc entries that can be placed in configuration files for Winsock applications is discussed and demonstrated in Chapter 8.

SECURITY ALERT!

The default firewall client configuration works for the majority of Winsock applications, but in some cases, custom client configuration information needs to be stored in the Mspclnt.ini or Wspcfg.ini file.

The H.323 Gatekeepers Object

The last second-level object in the console tree is the **H.323 Gatekeepers** object. By right-clicking this object, you can add a gatekeeper computer (either on the local machine or on a remote computer identified by fully qualified domain name) and view and configure active terminals, active calls, and call routing (see Figure 6.28).

Figure 6.28 Add and Configure H.323 Gatekeepers via the Last Second-Level Object in the Console Tree

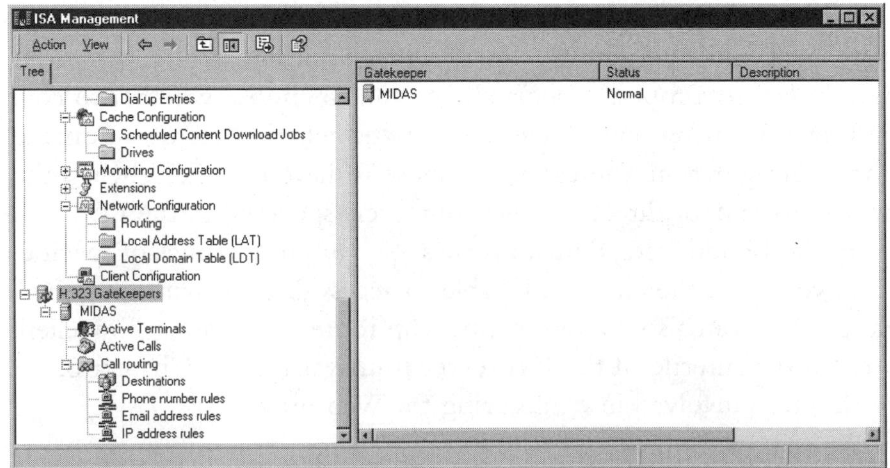

The H.323 Gatekeeper is used to allow clients to use NetMeeting and other H.323-compliant applications through the ISA server. The clients register a *well-known alias* (typically an e-mail address) with the gatekeeper, which allows others to contact them. The gatekeeper provides directory services and call routing for registered clients. All inbound calls to a well-known alias via these programs require registration with the gatekeeper. Outbound calls require clients to be registered only if they are using translation services; other outbound calls can be made without using the gatekeeper.

Configuration of the gatekeeper is discussed in great detail in Chapter 10.

Designing & Planning...

Understanding the H.32X Series Standards

The H.323 ITU standard for audio, video, and data communication across IP networks that do not provide QoS is part of a series of standards that all work to enable videoconferencing across disparate networks. The series is known collectively as the *H.32X standards*. H.320 provides specifications for using ISDN, and H.324 addresses the Public Switched Telephone Network (PSTN), also referred to in the industry as *POTS*, or *plain old telephone service*.

H.323 applies to both voice-only and full audio-videoconferencing. An advantage of the H.323 standard is that it allows communication over existing IP-based networks without any modifications to the network infrastructure. H.323 supports management of network bandwidth, allowing administrators to restrict the amount of bandwidth that can be used for conferencing or specify a maximum number of H.323 connections active on the network at any one time. H.323's support for multicasting also decreases bandwidth requirements. Platform independence means that users can communicate with one another using a variety of hardware platforms and operating systems.

The H.323 standard designates four major elements: terminals, gateways, gatekeepers, and multipoint control units (MCUs). The terminal is the endpoint for real-time two-way communication with another terminal or a gateway or MCU. H.323 terminals also must support H.245. The latter negotiates channel usage and capabilities. Gateways provide translation functions between the H.323 endpoints and other types of terminals. Gateways are optional components; if

Continued

both endpoints are on the same LAN, they are not needed. Gatekeepers function as the central point for call control services to registered endpoints in their zones. Gatekeepers provide address translation from terminal or gateway aliases to IP addresses. Gatekeepers can also manage bandwidth and route H.323 calls. A gatekeeper's *zone* refers to all the terminals, gateways, and MCUs that are managed by that gatekeeper. An MCU enables conferencing between multiple (three or more) endpoints (as opposed to simple one-to-one communication). The MCU is made up of two components: the multipoint controller (MC) and the multipoint processor (MP).

ISA Wizards

Following in the footsteps of Windows 2000, ISA Server provides a variety of wizards to assist you in setting up services, configuring features, and performing other common tasks. A wizard is a series of "friendly" dialog boxes that walk you through a process in a step-by-step fashion.

The Getting Started Wizard

The Getting Started Wizard is available when you start ISA Server after installing the ISA software. The wizard is designed to help you configure your initial array and enterprise policies. Steps include:

- Configuring enterprise policy settings and enterprise-level policy elements, protocol rules, and site and content rules (if you have installed an array rather than a standalone ISA server)
- Creating array-level policy elements, protocol rules, and site and content rules
- Setting the system security level
- Configuring packet filtering
- Configuring routing and chaining
- Creating a cache policy

Rules Wizards

After ISA Server is installed, you can create and configure new rules (routing rules, protocol rules, site and content rules) using the Rules Wizards that are invoked when you right-click the rule type under **Access Policy** or **Network Configuration** and select **New | Rule**.

One of the handiest aspects of the ISA wizards is the screen that appears after you finish entering the information requested by the wizard. This page summarizes the information you have entered, so you can double-check for accuracy *before* you click **Finish** to actually complete the process (see Figure 6.29).

Figure 6.29 The ISA Wizards Allow You to Check the Information Entered for Accuracy Before You Click Finish

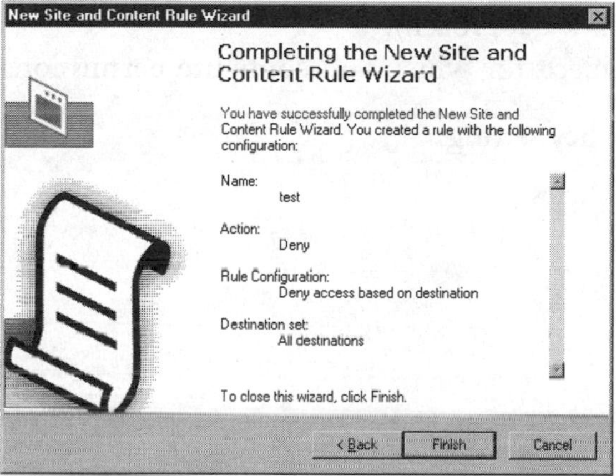

These rules wizards make it easy for you to create a new rule, but you can change the properties of the rule later by accessing the rule's Properties sheet; double-clicking the rule in the right detail pane to do so.

VPN Wizards

ISA includes three wizards to help you perform tasks related to setting up VPN connections:

- **The Local ISA VPN Wizard** Used for configuring the ISA server that will receive inbound VPN connections (the VPN server) or to set up the local ISA server to initiate VPN connections.
- **The Remote ISA VPN Wizard** Used to set up a remote ISA server to initiate or receive connections.
- **The Set Up Clients to ISA Server VPN Wizard** Enables roaming clients to connect to a VPN server.

In Chapter 10, you will learn how to use all three wizards and examine common scenarios in which each would be used.

Performing Common Management Tasks

In this section, we look at how to perform some common management tasks that are not covered in other sections or chapters of the book.

Configuring Object Permissions

ISA Server uses Windows 2000 discretionary access control lists (DACLs) to control access to objects and object properties. With Windows 2000, access is granted on a granular basis and can be granted to individual users or to groups (Microsoft's recommended approach).

The ISA Server objects for which you configure permissions are:

- Enterprise policy settings
- Enterprise policies
- Arrays
- Alerts
- Sessions
- The gatekeeper

Default Permissions

Depending on the type of object, certain permissions are assigned by default. You can view or change the object permissions by right-clicking on the object, selecting **Properties**, and selecting the **Security** tab, as shown in Figure 6.30.

The example in Figure 6.30 shows the permissions settings for the Array object. By default, the Administrator, Domain Admin, Enterprise Admin, and System accounts have full control, and the Authenticated Users group has read access. You can change the permissions or add other groups or individual user accounts in the same way you configure any NTFS permissions in Windows 2000.

Special Object Permissions

You will find that some ISA objects have special permissions, accessed by clicking the **Advanced** button and then selecting **View/Edit** for permissions. For example, the Sessions object has the **Read Sessions Information** and the **Stop Sessions** permissions. By default, authenticated users have the **Read Sessions Information** permission, whereas Administrators, Domain Admins and Enterprise Admins have full control, which encompasses both of these special

Figure 6.30 Set Permissions on Objects via the Security Tab on the Object's Properties Sheet

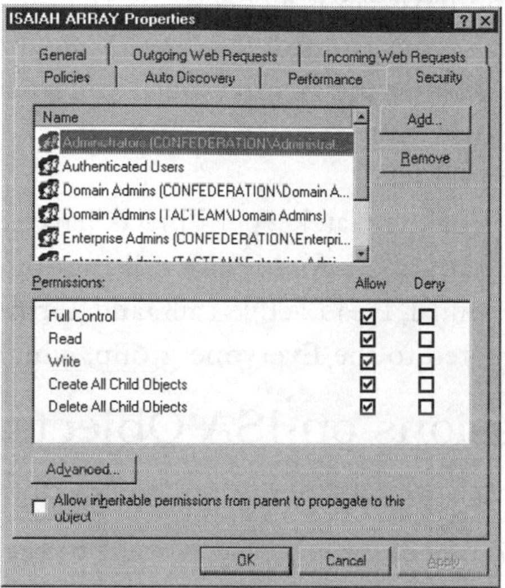

permissions. Likewise, the **Alerts** object has special **Read Alerts Information** and **Reset Alerts** permissions. Again, authenticated users have the first, and Administrators, Domain Admins, and Enterprise Admins have full control, encompassing both (see Figure 6.31).

Figure 6.31 Some ISA Objects Have Special Advanced Permissions Such as the Read Alerts Information and Reset Alerts Permissions for the Alerts Object

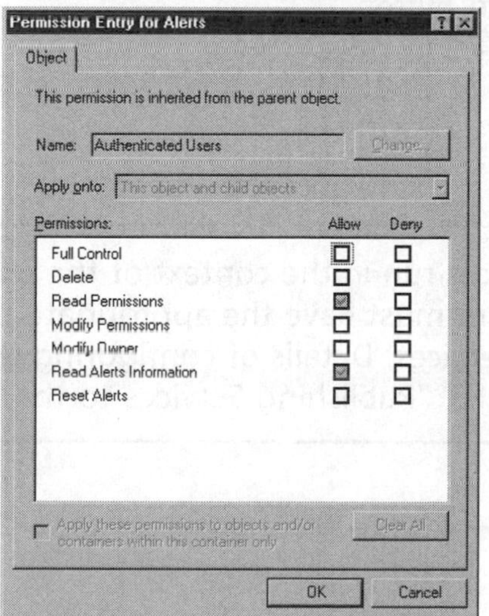

Permissions may be directly assigned to an object or they may be *inherited* from a parent object. Inheritance can be controlled by the administrator. At the bottom of an object's **Security** tab is a check box that, when checked, allows inheritable permissions to propagate to the object. You can prevent inheritance of special permissions by checking the **Apply these permissions to objects and/or containers within this container only** check box when you elect to view/edit advanced permissions.

Similarly, you'll find that the Gatekeeper objects have several special permissions, including Read call routing info, Modify call routing, Read terminals, Create static user, Unregister terminal, Read active calls, and Terminate call. By default, these permissions are granted to the Everyone group, which has full control.

Setting Permissions on ISA Objects

To set the standard and special permissions on an ISA object, follow these steps:

1. Right-click the object for which you want to set permissions.
2. Select **Properties** from the right context menu.
3. On the Properties sheet, select the **Security** tab.
4. Here you can change standard permissions and add or remove users and groups.
5. To set special permissions, click the **Advanced** button.
6. Select the user or group for which you want to modify special permissions, and click the **View/Edit** button or add a new user or group by clicking the **Add** button.
7. Allow or deny the desired permissions.

NOTE

All ISA Server services run in the context of the user account named Local System. This account must have the appropriate permissions and user rights to run the services. Details of configuring the gatekeeper are discussed in Chapter 10, "Publishing Services to the Internet."

Managing Array Membership

Installing the first ISA server that is made a member of an array creates the array. There are several requirements for doing this: You must be a member of the local Administrators, Enterprise Admins, and Schema Admins groups, because you must first initialize the enterprise (discussed in Chapter 5), which modifies the Active Directory schema.

Creating a New Array

Once an array has been created, you can create new arrays. Right-clicking the **Servers and Arrays** object in the left console pane and selecting **New | Array** invokes the New Array Wizard. (See Chapter 5 for a step-by-step description of the wizard.) You will be asked to supply information such as the site and domain name in which the new array will be located, as well as a name for the new array and the mode (caching, firewall, or integrated) in which the array will run.

NOTE

When you add an array to or remove an array from the enterprise, the information is written to the Active Directory and replicated to all domain controllers in the domain.

Adding and Removing Computers

You can remove a server from an array by right-clicking its name in the right detail pane when you highlight the **Computers** folder. Select **Delete**, and you will be prompted by the dialog box shown in Figure 6.32.

TIP

If a server was previously deleted from an array, you cannot use Add/Remove Programs in the Control Panel to uninstall ISA Server. Instead, you must use the rmisa.exe program on the ISA CD-ROM. Note that if you uninstall the only remaining computer in an array, the entire array will be removed.

Figure 6.32 Delete an ISA Server from an Array via the ISA Management Console

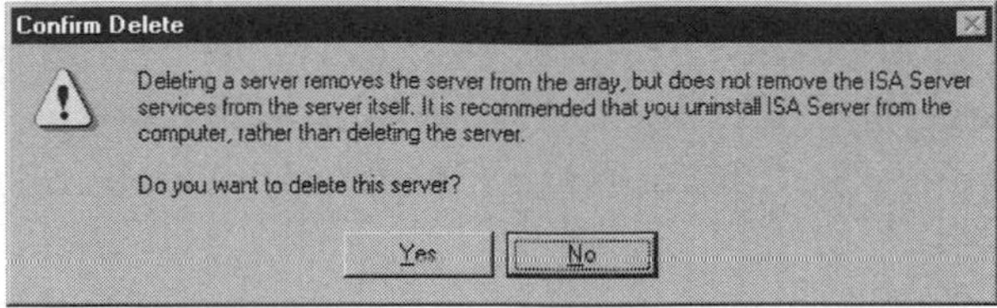

To join a server to an existing array, you must install (or reinstall) ISA Server. If the enterprise has been initialized, you can select which array the server will join (see Figure 6.33). When you install ISA as a member of an existing array, you must install it in the same mode as the other array members (caching, firewall, or integrated).

To move a server from one array to another, you must uninstall and reinstall ISA Server.

Figure 6.33 When You Install ISA Server, If the Enterprise Has Been Initialized, You Have the Option of Joining an Existing Array

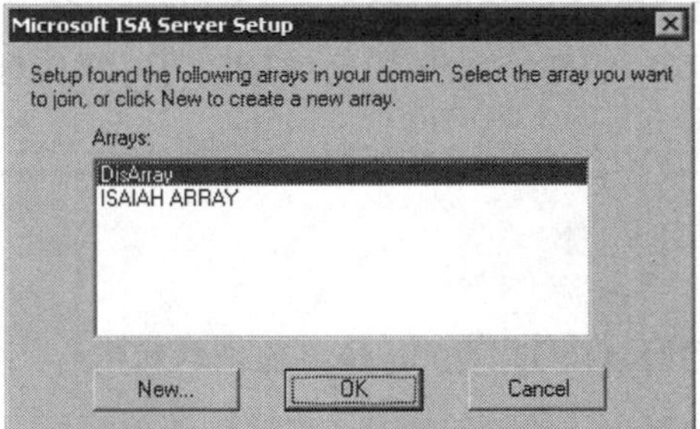

Promoting a Standalone ISA Server

A standalone ISA server cannot be joined to an existing array; however, after you have initialized the enterprise, you can *promote* a standalone server to create a new array of which the promoted server will be a member. To promote a standalone server and create a new array, right-click the server name in the left console pane, and select **Promote** from the context menu. You will see the message shown in Figure 6.34.

If you choose to promote the server, you will be asked to set global policy and choose how enterprise and array policies will be applied to the array. When you promote a standalone server to create an array, the configuration information for the array is stored in Active Directory.

Figure 6.34 Promoting a Standalone Server to Become an Array—An Operation that Cannot Be Reversed

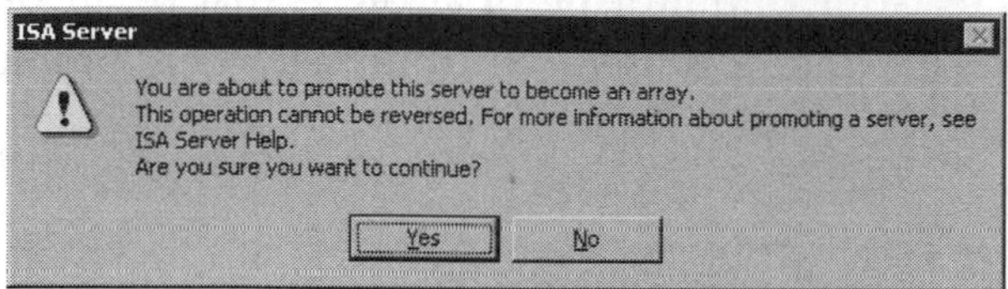

TIP

Once you promote the standalone server to become an array member, the action cannot be reversed. You can remove the server from the array, but doing so will *not* return it to standalone server status. ISA Server will have to be reinstalled.

Remember: Although a standalone ISA Server is not required to be a member of a Windows 2000 domain, an array member must be a domain member. Thus, in order to promote a standalone server to an array, the server must belong to a Windows 2000 domain.

NOTE

After you promote a standalone server to array status, you need to reconfigure the ISA Server object permissions.

Using Monitoring, Alerting, Logging, and Reporting Functions

In this section, we discuss how you can monitor ISA Server alerts and logging and generate reports using the ISA Management Console. Monitoring of performance, using the object counters in the ISA Performance Monitoring tool, is discussed in Chapter 11, "Optimizing, Customizing, Integrating, and Backing Up ISA Server."

Creating, Configuring, and Monitoring Alerts

ISA Server allows real-time monitoring of all alerts that occur on any of the servers in an array. This feature is useful in troubleshooting problems and assessing activity and usage.

Viewing Alerts

You can view the alerts by selecting **Monitoring | Alerts** under the Server or Array object and viewing the alerts in the right detail pane, as shown in Figure 6.35.

Figure 6.35 Viewing Alerts that Occurred on the ISA Server or Array

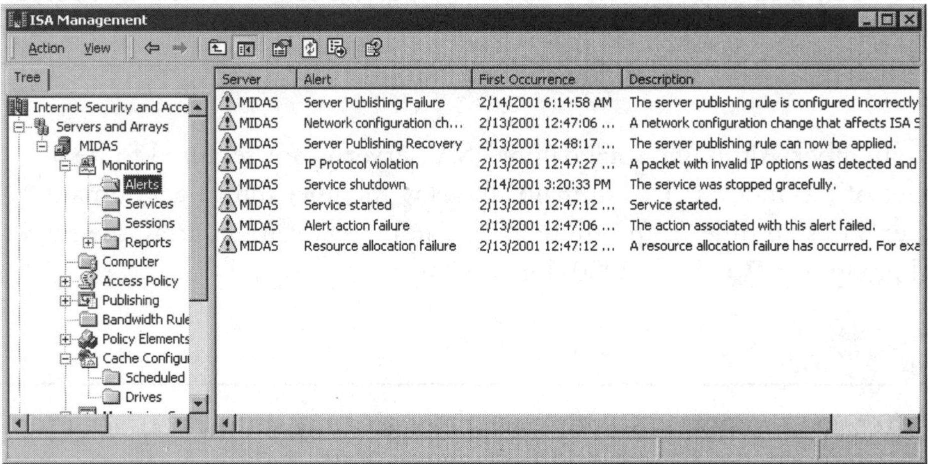

You will see, displayed in the detail pane, the server on which each event occurred, the alert type, the date and time of first occurrence, and a description of the event. Remember that this is where you *view* the alerts; they are configured using the **Alerts** object under the **Monitoring Configuration** object, further down in the tree.

Creating and Configuring Alerts

To create and configure a new alert, right-click the **Monitoring Configuration | Alerts** object, and select **New | Alert**. The New Alert Wizard will ask you for the following information:

- A name for the new alert
- An event or condition that will trigger the alert

- An action to be performed when the alert is triggered

Trigger Events

You can select from the following events to trigger the alert:

- Alert action failure
- Cache container initialization error
- Cache container recovery complete
- Cache file resize failure
- Cache initialization failure
- Cache restoration completed
- Cache write error
- Cached object ignored
- Client/server communication failure
- Component load failure
- Configuration error
- Dial-on-demand failure
- DNS intrusion
- Event log failure
- Intrusion detected
- Invalid dial-on-demand credentials
- Invalid ODBC log credentials
- IP packet dropped
- IP protocol violation
- IP spoofing
- Log failure
- Missing installation component
- Network configuration changed
- No available ports
- Operating system component conflict

- Oversize UDP packet
- POP intrusion
- Report summary generalization failure
- Resource allocation failure
- Routing (chaining) recovery
- Routing (chaining) failure
- RPC filter—connectivity changed
- Server publishing failure
- Server publishing recovery
- Service initialization failure
- Service not responding
- Service shutdown
- Service started
- SMTP filter event
- SOCKS configuration failure
- The server is not in the array's site
- Unregistered event
- Upstream chaining credentials
- WMT live stream-splitting failure

Additional Conditions

Some of these event triggers allow you to select an additional condition. For example, if you select intrusion detection as the event that will trigger the alert, you will also be asked to select whether the alert will be triggered by any intrusion or by a specific intrusion type (see Figure 6.36).

The ISA Server's alert service acts as an event filter, recognizing when events occur, determining whether configured conditions are met, and seeing that the chosen action(s) occurs in response.

Figure 6.36 Some Events Allow You to Specify Additional Conditions to Trigger the Alert

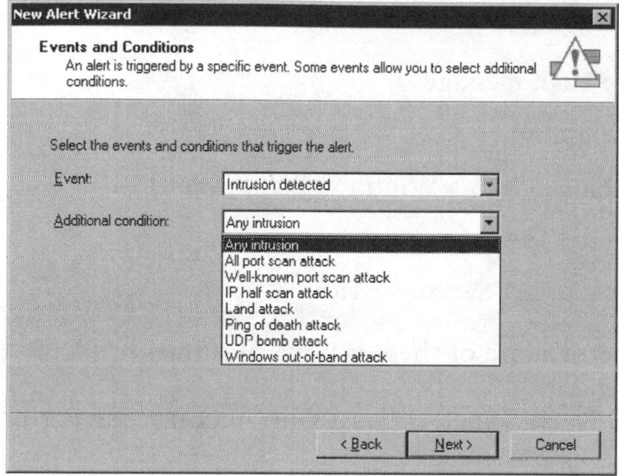

NOTE

You can configure the alert for the entire array, or you can limit the event to a specific server in the array.

Once configured, you can enable or disable an alert by checking or unchecking the **Enable** check box on the **General** tab of its Properties sheet. To do so, you can right-click the alert name in the detail pane when you have selected **Alerts** under **Monitoring Configuration**, and choose **Properties** in the right context menu.

Additional Configuration Specifications

You can also specify the following:

- Event frequency threshold (how many times per second the event must occur in order to issue an alert)
- Number of events that must occur in order to issue an alert
- Length of time to wait before issuing an alert a second or subsequent time

To set these specifications, right-click the alert you want to configure, and select **Properties**, then select the **Events** tab.

Actions to Be Performed When an Alert Is Triggered

You can choose from the following actions to be performed when a triggering event occurs and the conditions are met for issuing an alert:

- Send an e-mail message
- Run a program
- Report the event to a Windows 2000 event log
- Stop selected ISA Server services
- Start selected ISA Server services

You can select one or more of these actions, as shown in Figure 6.37.

Figure 6.37 You Must Select at Least One Action to Be Performed When an Alert Is Triggered

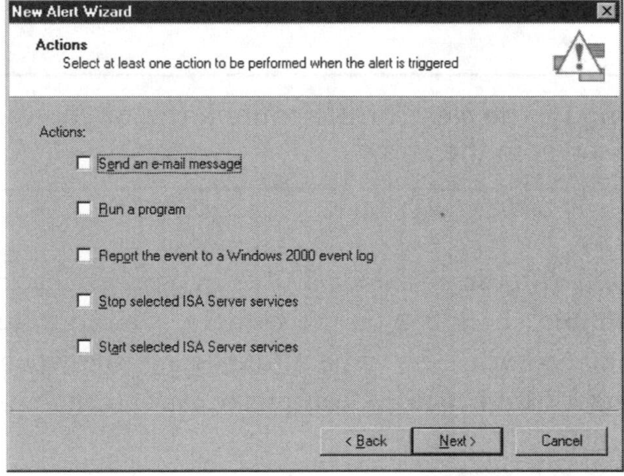

If you elect to send an e-mail message, you will be prompted to provide addressing information for sending the e-mail message, including the SMTP server and the From, To, and CC fields. You can send e-mail to multiple recipients by separating the addresses with semicolons in the To or CC field.

If you elect to run a program, you will be prompted to enter the path to the program you want to run. You also need to specify whether the credentials of the Local System account or a different user account should be used. If you choose the latter, you must enter the user account name and password. Otherwise, you must run the program in the context of the system account.

NOTE

If you want to send an e-mail message to a client using an external SMTP server (outside the local network) by specifying an external IP address, you need to create a static packet filter to allow the SMTP protocol. Another way to send a message to an external mailbox is to specify the internal IP address of an SMTP server on the local network that is capable of relaying to an external address.

If you elect to stop or start selected ISA Server services, you will be prompted to select the services that should be stopped or started. You can choose from one or more of the following: the firewall service, the scheduled content download, or the Web proxy service.

Refreshing the Display

The Alerts display is automatically refreshed on a periodic basis by default. (You will see the screen flicker when the display is updated.) You can force an immediate refresh or control the refresh rate by right-clicking the **Alerts** object under **Monitoring**. Select **Refresh** to immediately refresh the display, or select **Refresh Rate** to change the rate at which the display is updated. You can choose a high, normal, or low refresh rate. By default, this setting is Normal.

You can also elect to Pause the refresh if you do not want the display to be updated.

Event Messages

A number of event messages are related to ISA Server alerts. For example, message ID 14033 indicates that alert notification did not start and alerts are limited to event reporting. You will be advised to restart the ISA Server Control Service and to restart the firewall and Web proxy services because they are dependent on the Control Service.

A full listing of ISA event messages is available in the ISA Server Help files. (In the Help Index, search for Alerts, Alert event messages (list)). Event messages are discussed more fully in Chapter 12, "Troubleshooting ISA Server."

Monitoring Sessions

You can view the sessions that are active by selecting the **Sessions** object in the left console pane of the ISA MMC; information about current sessions will appear in the right detail pane, as shown in Figure 6.38.

Figure 6.38 View the Current Active Sessions in the Right Detail Pane of the ISA MMC

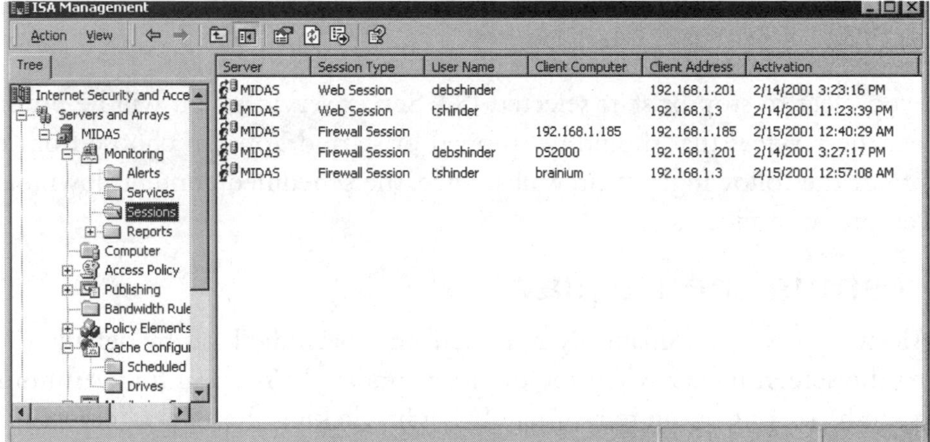

The Sessions display can be refreshed or the refresh rate set, in the same manner as that previously described for the Alerts display.

Session Information

Information available for each session includes:

- The server name
- The session type (Web or firewall)
- Username (for authenticated sessions; SecureNAT sessions are displayed as firewall sessions, with no username shown)
- Client computer (computer name for authenticated sessions or IP address for SecureNAT sessions)
- Client address
- Date and time of activation

NOTE

Web proxy sessions show the last minute of Web browser activity, even if the client is not browsing at the time you view the display.

Firewall sessions could be listed, even if no firewall clients are actually connected. The reason for this is that ISA shows a publishing server that is currently being published as a firewall session.

Disconnecting Sessions

You can disconnect a client session via the ISA Management Console. First, you must ensure that the **Advanced** option is checked in the **View** menu (by default, it is not).

To disconnect a session, right-click the session in the detail pane, and then from the right context menu, select **Abort Session**. This action disconnects the selected session, with no warning or notification to the client.

Using Logging

You can configure and generate logs in standard data formats for the following ISA Server components:

- Packet filters
- Firewall service
- Web proxy service

When your ISA servers belong to an array, logging is configured for the entire array, but log files are created on every ISA Server that is a member of the array. The logs can be created on a daily, weekly, monthly, or yearly basis and saved to a file or logged directly to a database.

Logging to a File

You can save ISA log data to a file in a directory that you specify. The files can be opened in a text editor or imported to a spreadsheet or database program.

Specifying a Log File Directory Location

There are two ways in which you can specify the directory to which the log file should be saved.

- **Save to a relative path** If you specify a relative path, the log will be saved in a folder named ISALogs in the ISA Server installation folder, which, by default, is named Microsoft ISA Server and is placed in the Program Files directory on the boot partition (the partition containing the system root folder in which the Windows 2000 operating system files reside, normally named WINNT).
- **Save to an absolute path** If you specify an absolute (full) path, that path must exist on every server that belongs to the array. If it does not, the ISA Server services will fail.

Selecting a Log File Format

When you choose to save ISA logs to a file, you can select one of the following formats:

- **W3C** Tab-delimited file that includes, along with the data itself, directives that describe the version, date, and logged fields (date and time are shown in GMT rather than local time). Unselected fields are not logged.
- **ISA** Comma-delimited file that contains only data. No directives are included, and all fields are always logged (unselected fields contain a dash to flag them as empty). Note that date and time in ISA format are shown in local time.

NOTE

Log files can be compressed to save disk space *if* they are saved on an NTFS-formatted partition. Microsoft recommends that you always store log files on an NTFS partition, which also allows you to configure NTFS permissions for the files.

Logging to a Database

A second way to save ISA log data is to log it to an Open Database Connectivity (ODBC) database. OBDC is a programming interface that allows various programs to access the data in systems using Structured Query Language (SQL). Programs use SQL to obtain information from or update information in a database, using command (query) language that allows users to locate, access, and insert data.

Database programs such as Access, dBase, and FoxPro support ODBC, and ODBC connectivity is provided by "back-end" client/server database solutions such as Microsoft SQL Server and Oracle.

In the context of this book, ODBC is a means for providing access, from an ODBC-compliant application such as Excel, to any data that is stored in an ODBC-compliant database server, such as SQL Server. The ODBC driver translates the application's queries into commands that can be understood by the target database application.

You can find a wealth of information about ODBC at the Microsoft Universal Data Access Web site at www.eu.microsoft.com/data.

NOTE

Logging to a database is unnecessary when you have SQL's Data Transformation Services (DTS) to move the data from the log files into database tables on a scheduled, automated basis. Logging to a database is not the best practice from a performance standpoint.

Using Scripts

Several sample scripts are included with ISA Server; you can use these scripts as templates to create log databases. Scripts for logging to a SQL database file are contained in the \ISA folder on the ISA Server CD-ROM. The script files include the following:

- **Pf.sql** Used to define the packet filter log table (PacketFilterLog).
- **W3proxy.sql** Used to define the Web proxy service log table (WebProxyLog).
- **Fwsrv.sql** Used to define the firewall service log table (FirewallLog).

Configuring ISA Server for Database Logging

After you create the log table(s), follow these steps to configure the ISA Server to use the data source name:

1. Select **Start | Programs | Administrative Tools | Data Sources (ODBC)** on the ISA server.
2. Select the **System DSN** tab. It is important to select the correct DSN, because choosing the wrong data source is a common mistake.

3. Click the **Add** button.
4. Select the applicable database driver in the Create New Data Source dialog box (for example, the Microsoft Access driver selected in Figure 6.39). You will be prompted for information needed to create the database.

Figure 6.39 Install the Appropriate ODBC Driver to Set Up a Data Source

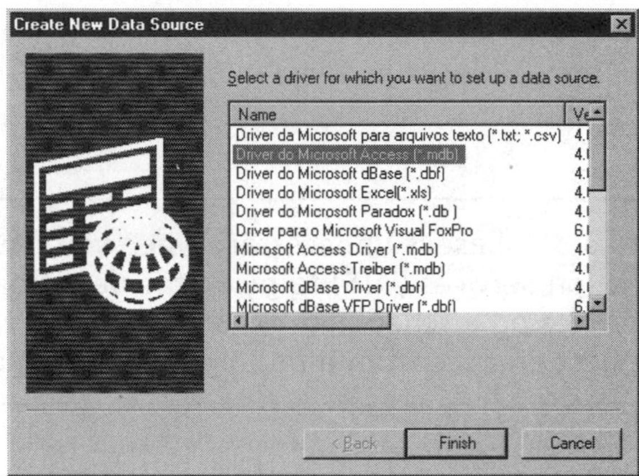

You will be required to enter a data source name, or DSN. Note that you cannot use spaces in the name. If you do so, the ISA Server services will stop.

Configuring Logging

To configure logging to either a file or a database, select **Logs** under the **Monitoring Configuration** object in the left console pane of the ISA MMC. The three ISA components for which logs can be generated (packet filters, firewall service, and Web proxy service) will appear in the right detail pane. Right-click the service for which you want to log data, and select **Properties**. You can configure logging using the Properties sheet, as shown in Figure 6.40.

Select whether to log to a file or a database, then configure the parameters for the selected option. If you log to an ODBC database, you need to set the user account and password to be used, and these must have the appropriate permissions.

Figure 6.40 Logging Is Configured via the Properties Sheet for the Service for Which Data Will Be Logged

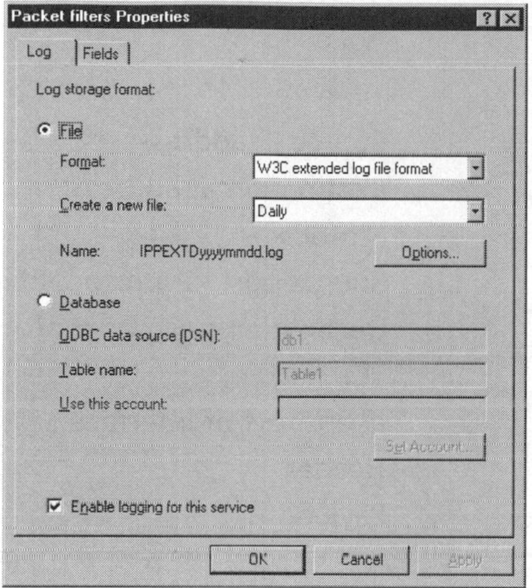

Logging Options

If you log to a file, you can access the Options configuration sheet by clicking the **Options** button. This allows you to specify the following:

- **Log file location** The default location is the ISALogs folder in the ISA Server installation folder, but you can type in the path or browse to another folder in which you want to save the log file.
- **Compress log files** Compression is enabled by default.
- **Limit the number of log files** The default is 7, but you can enter any number up to 999,999,999.

Selecting Fields to Be Logged

Click the **Fields** tab and select the fields that should be logged by checking the appropriate check boxes. For packet filter logging, you can choose to log the fields shown in Table 6.1. For firewall service logging, you can choose to log the fields shown in Table 6.2. For Web proxy service logging, fields available are generally the same as in Table 6.2, with the exceptions of the sessionid and connectionid fields.

Table 6.1 Log Field Options: Packet Filters

Field Name	Information in Field
PFlogDate	Date
PFlogTime	Time
SourceAddress	Source IP address
DestinationAddress	Destination IP address
Protocol	Protocol
Param#1	Source port, or protocol type if ICMP
Param#2	Destination port, or protocol code if ICMP
TcpFlags	TCP flags
Interface	IP address of interface
IPHeader	Header
Payload	Payload

Table 6.2 Log Field Options: Firewall Service

Field Name	Information in Field
c-ip	Client IP address
Cs-username	Client user account name
c-agent	Client agent
Sc-authenticated	Authorization status
Date	Date
Time	Time
s-svcname	Service name
s-computername	Computer name
Cs-referred	Referring server name
r-host	Destination host name
r-ip	Destination IP address
r-port	Destination port
Time-taken	Processing time
Cs-bytes	Number of bytes sent
Sc-bytes	Number of bytes received
Cs-protocol	Protocol name
Cs-transport	Transport used

Continued

Table 6.2 Continued

Field Name	Information in Field
s-operation	Operation
Cs-uri	Object name
Cs-mime-type	Object MIME
s-object-source	Object source
Sc-status	Result code
s-cache-info	Cache information
Rule#1	Rule #1
Rule#2	Rule #2
Sessionid	Session identification
Connectionid	Connection identification

Generating Reports

ISA Server's report functionality allows administrators to use the information recorded in the log files to create summary databases and combine relevant summary databases into a single report database. All of these databases are stored on the ISA Server's hard disk. Reports can be generated on a periodic basis and saved to a specified folder.

UNDOCUMENTED ISA

When you generate a report on an ISA server, it can be read only on that same computer. You cannot view it from another ISA Server computer's management console, even if the other server is in the same array.

Creating Report Jobs

You can create a report job by right-clicking **Report Jobs** under the **Monitoring Configuration** object, selecting **New**, and then selecting **Report Job**. This sequence displays the Report Job Properties sheet, shown in Figure 6.41.

Figure 6.41 A Name and Description for the Report Job Are Specified via the General Tab

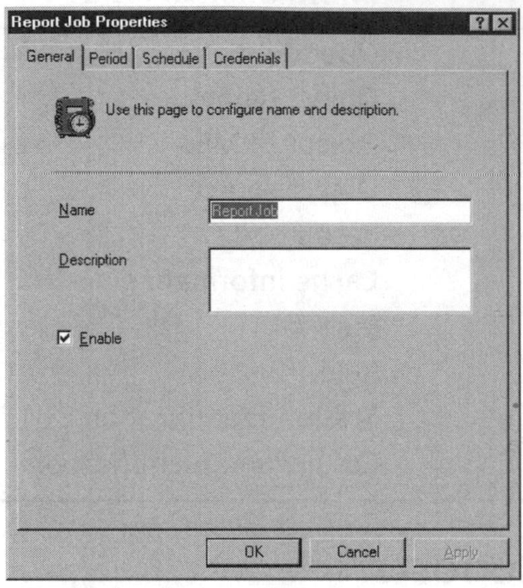

Configuring General Properties

On the **General** tab of the Properties sheet, you must specify a name for the report job. The default name is *Report Job.* The name must be unique; if it is not, you will receive a message from the ISA Report Generator informing you that the name already exists, and you will not be allowed to create the report job until you choose a new name. You can also provide a description of the job; this field is optional.

The report job is enabled by default when you create it. You can disable it later by accessing the Properties sheet (right-click on the report job name in the right detail pane) and unchecking the **Enabled** check box.

NOTE

The check box shown here enables reporting. You must also ensure that logging is enabled for the relevant ISA component(s), or there will be no meaningful data from which a report can be generated. A report job can still be created and a report will be generated, but it will contain no current data.

Configuring the Reporting Period

You can elect to have a report generated on a daily, weekly, monthly, or yearly basis or for a custom period. First, select a reporting period on the **Period** tab of the Properties sheet, shown in Figure 6.42. You also need to configure the **Schedule** tab, as shown in the next section, if you want the report to be generated on a recurring basis.

Figure 6.42 Configure the Reporting Interval by Selecting the Period Tab on the Properties Sheet

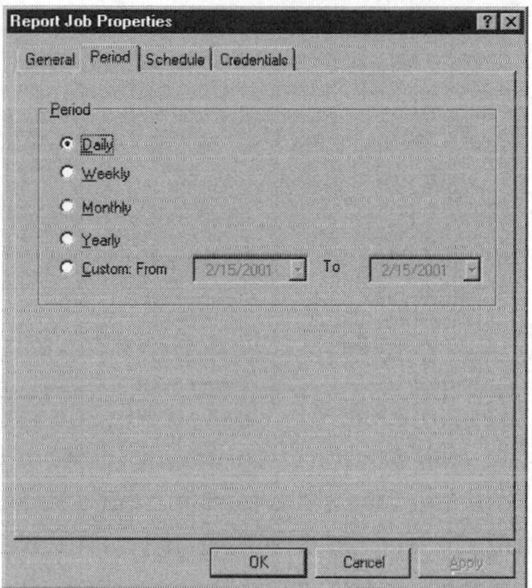

The report period configuration determines the period each report covers. The **Daily** option generates a report that covers the previous day's activity, the **Weekly** option covers the previous week's activity, and so forth. When you select the **Custom** option, you are prompted to choose a starting and ending date from a drop-down calendar.

Configuring the Reporting Schedule

Using the **Schedule** tab of the Properties sheet, you can specify when report generation should begin. By default, it is set to begin immediately on successful creation of the report job, but you can select a specific date and time using the drop-down boxes, as shown in Figure 6.43.

The **Schedule** tab is also used to specify the recurrence pattern for report generation. You can elect to have the report generated only one time or to recur every day, on specified days, or once per month on a specific day of the month.

Figure 6.43 The Schedule Tab Allows You to Set a Start Time and a Recurrence Pattern

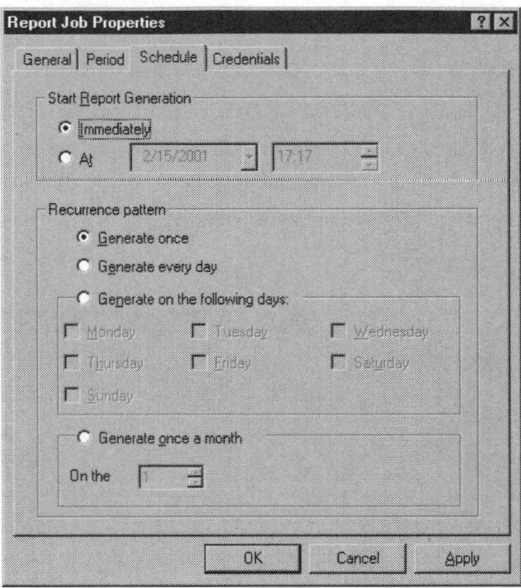

Configuring Report Job Credentials

You need to supply a username and password to run the report job. The user account must have permission to access report information for the server(s) relevant to the report job. You can create a report job on a local standalone ISA server without providing credentials. However, if you attempt to do so on a remote server or array, you will receive the message box shown in Figure 6.44, notifying you that you must provide credentials to run the job.

Figure 6.44 You Must Provide the Appropriate Credentials to Run a Report Job on a Remote Computer or Array

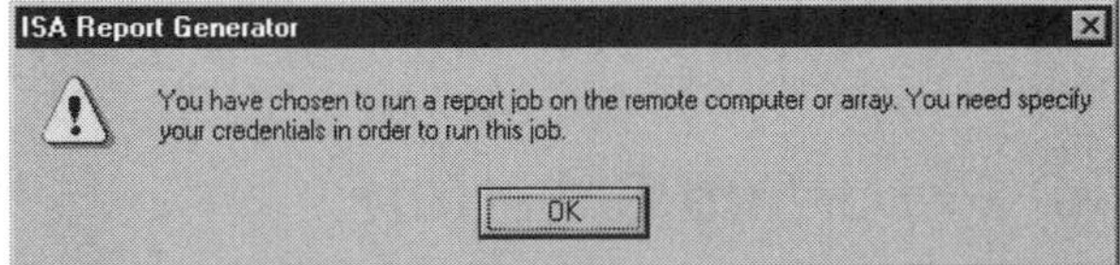

To provide credentials for running the report job, enter the user account name (or browse for it in the Directory by clicking the **Browse** button), the domain name to which the user account belongs, and the password on the **Credentials** tab of the properties box shown in Figure 6.45.

Figure 6.45 Enter a User Account Name, Domain, and Password to Run the Report Job

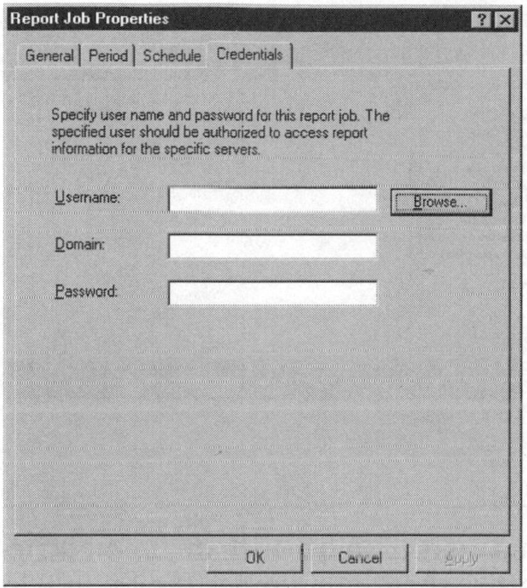

NOTE

The user account must have the proper permissions to run reports. By default, Domain Administrators have this permission, as does any user who is a member of the local Administrators group on *every* ISA server computer in the array.

Viewing Report Job Information

Once the report jobs have been created, they appear in the right detail pane when you select the **Report Jobs** folder, as shown in Figure 6.46.

The following information about each report job will be displayed:

- The name of the job
- The scheduled start date and time
- The next run time (if it is a recurring job)
- The ready status
- The result of the last attempt to run the job

Figure 6.46 Information About Each Configured Report Job Appears in the Right Detail Pane

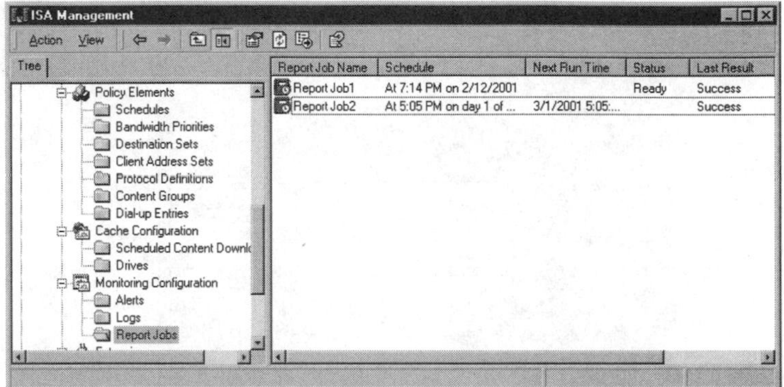

NOTE

When you select a start time other than "Immediately" on the Schedule tab of the Properties sheet, the time is shown in 24-hour clock format. However, in the detail pane, that information is shown in AM/PM format. Thus, if you choose 19:00 as the start time on the Schedule tab, it will be displayed in the detail pane as 7:00 PM.

You can go back and change the configuration properties of a report job by double-clicking it (or right-clicking it and selecting **Properties**) and accessing its Properties sheet.

Viewing Generated Reports

The reports themselves are accessed via the **Reports** folder under the **Monitoring** object near the top of the left console tree, as shown in Figure 6.47.

Note that all reports appear in the right detail pane when you select the **Reports** folder. You also see five categories of predefined reports sorted into the following folders:

- Summary reports
- Web usage reports
- Application usage reports
- Traffic and utilization reports
- Security reports

Figure 6.47 The Reports that Have Been Generated Are Accessed from the Reports Folder

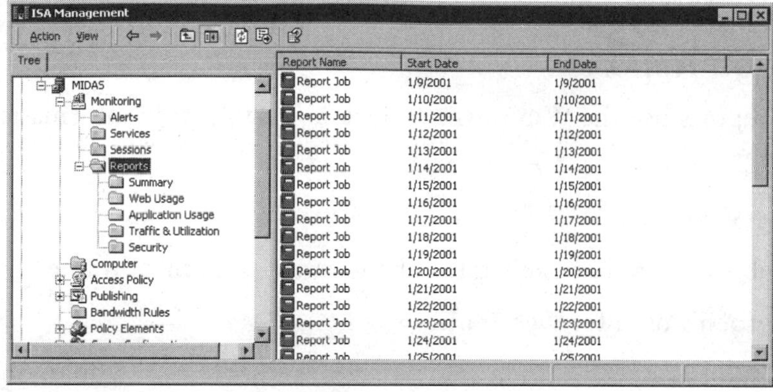

Reports are displayed in the Web browser and can be saved as .HTM (Web page) files. Let's take a look at what each of these includes.

Summary Reports

The summary reports network usage data that is sorted according to application. Network administrators can use these reports to plan or evaluate Internet connectivity issues. An example of a summary report for an array is shown in Figure 6.48.

Figure 6.48 Summary Reports Include Data from the Web Proxy and Firewall Service Logs Pertaining to Network Usage

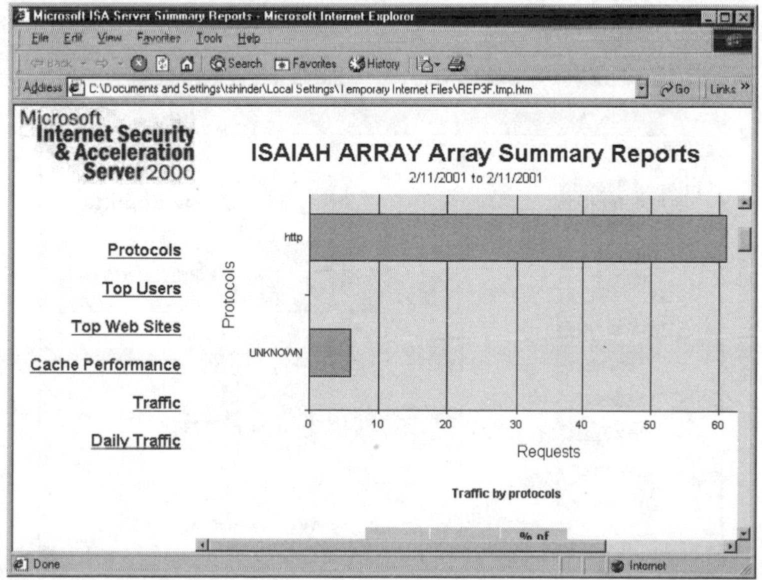

The information in the summary reports combines data collected from both the Web proxy service and firewall service logs. Logging for these services must be enabled to generate a meaningful summary report.

Web Usage Reports

Web usage reports use the Web proxy service logs to provide information about the following:

- Top Web users
- Web sites that have generated the greatest amount of traffic
- Protocols used for Web traffic
- Responses to HTTP requests (success, authorization failure, object not found, object moved, and other)
- Types of objects delivered by the ISA server (.DLL files, .HTML files, .EXE files, etc.)
- Web browser types used to connect to the Internet through the ISA server (browser name and version number)
- Operating systems used to access the Internet through ISA Server (Windows 2000, Windows NT 4.0, Windows 98, etc.)

An example of a Web usage report is shown in Figure 6.49.

Figure 6.49 Web Usage Reports Contain Information Collected from the Web Proxy Service Log Files

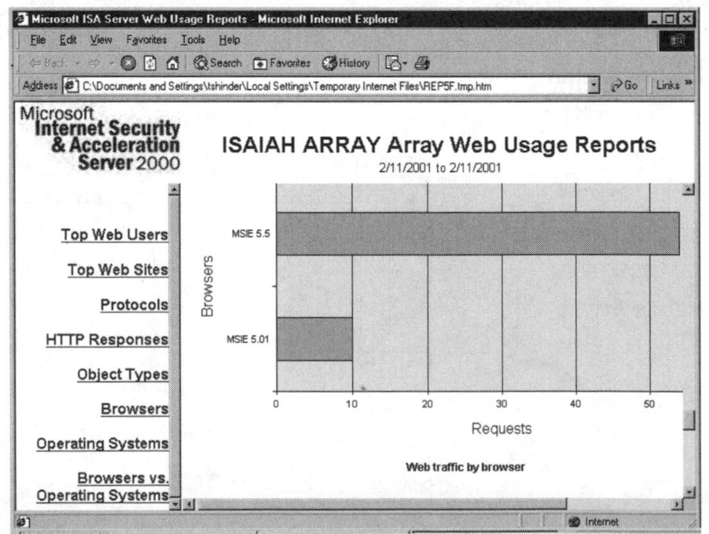

The Web usage reports can be used to evaluate how the Web is used in your organization, which could be useful to network administrators in planning for Internet connectivity and capacity and for managers setting policies to govern use of the Web.

Application Usage Reports

Application usage reports are based on the information collected by firewall service logging. The following information is provided:

- Communications protocols used for network traffic going through the ISA server
- Top application users (by IP address)
- Client applications that have generated the largest amount of network traffic during the report period
- Operating systems used on computers that have accessed the Internet
- Top destination computers (by IP address) with which internal users have communicated through the ISA Server

An example of an application usage report is shown in Figure 6.50.

Figure 6.50 Application Usage Reports Are Based on Information Collected in the Firewall Service Logs

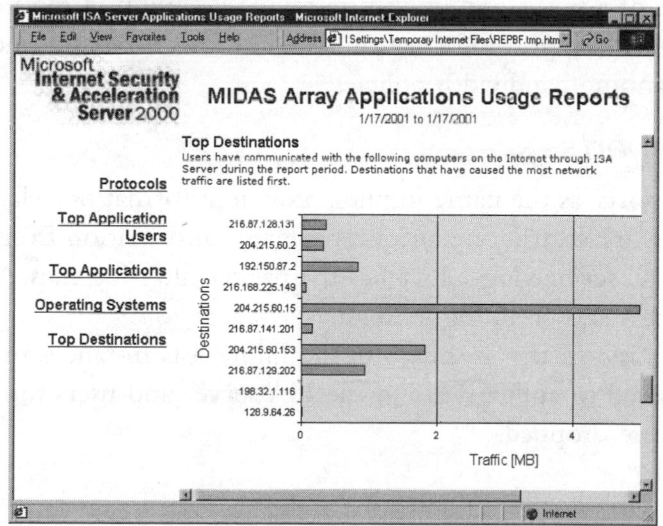

Application usage reports can help you plan for network and bandwidth capacity and determine the external network destinations that are creating the greatest amount of network traffic.

Traffic and Utilization Reports

The traffic and utilization reports use data from both the Web proxy and the firewall service logs to provide information such as the following:

- Communication protocols used
- Summary of traffic going through the ISA server, by date
- Cache performance data, showing the objects returned from the Internet, objects returned from cache with verification, objects returned from cache after verification that they had not changed, and objects returned from the Internet to update a file in cache
- Information on the peak number of simultaneous connections each day
- Information on the average request processing time each day
- Chart summarizing average network traffic flow through the ISA server each day
- Errors reported by ISA Server in attempting to communicate with other computers, broken into Web proxy and firewall service error categories.

An example of a traffic and utilization report is shown in Figure 6.51. The traffic and utilization report information is useful for monitoring network capacity and planning bandwidth policies.

Security Reports

The security reports, as the name implies, provide information related to possible breaches of network security. Security reports use information from the Web proxy and firewall service logs as well as the packet filter log files. An example of a security report is shown in Figure 6.52.

The security report that is shown in the figure lists instances in which users or computers failed to authenticate to the ISA server and users for whom network packets were dropped.

Figure 6.51 The Traffic and Utilization Reports Combine Information from the Web Proxy and Firewall Service Logs

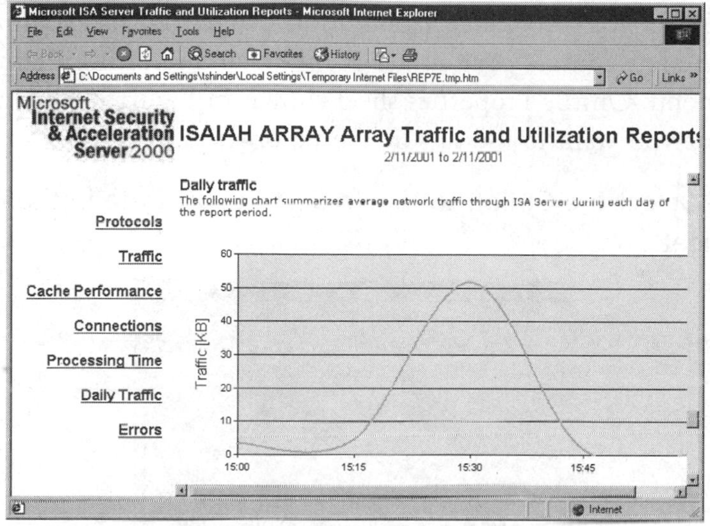

Figure 6.52 Security Reports Can List Authorization Failures and Other Security-Related Events Recorded in the Web Proxy Service, Firewall Service, and Packet Filter Logs

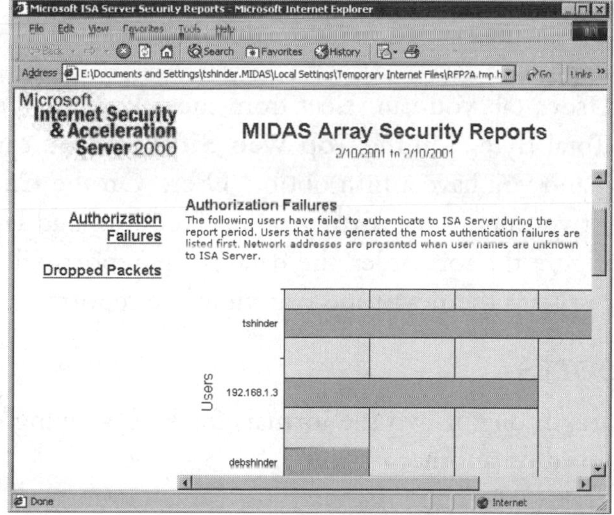

Configuring Sort Order for Report Data

You can determine the order in which report data is sorted by right-clicking the report type (Summary, Web Usage, Application Usage, Traffic & Utilization, and Security) in the left console pane under **Reports** and selecting **Properties** from the context menu. On the Properties sheet shown in Figure 6.53, you can select the option that you want to use to sort the report data.

Figure 6.53 Select the Option to Use to Sort Report Data in the Report Type Properties Sheet

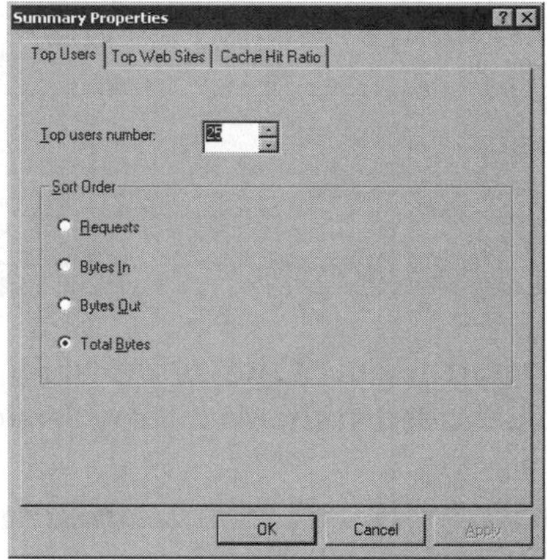

On the **Top Users** tab, you can select from the following: Requests, Bytes In, Bytes Out, or Total Bytes. On the **Top Web Sites** tab, you can sort by the same four options, and you have a fifth option: Users. On the **Cache Hit Ratio** tab, you have only two options for sorting order: Requests and Bytes.

After you configure the sort order, the data in the report will be sorted according to your criteria the next time you view the report.

Saving Reports

You can save reports in one of two file formats for later viewing or to a removable disk to be viewed on another machine.

Saving Reports in .HTM format

Reports can be saved as hypertext document files (.HTM) by selecting the report type under **Reports** in **Monitoring** in the left console pane, right-clicking the report name, and selecting **Save as** in the context menu.

Saving Reports in .XLS format

You can save a report as an Excel spreadsheet file (.XLS) by selecting **Reports** and right-clicking the report name in the right console pane, then selecting **Save as**.

Providing Information for Saving Reports

To save as .HTM, you access the report from the applicable report type folder; to save as .XLS, you access the report from the **Reports** folder. Either way, you will be asked to select a location in which to save the file and to enter a filename (the default filename is the name of the report displayed in the right detail pane).

UNDOCUMENTED ISA

In order to save the report in .XLS format, you must have Excel installed on the ISA server computer. Otherwise, this choice will not appear as an option.

Configuring the Location for Saving the Summary Database

You can specify the location in which the daily and monthly summaries database is to be stored. Right-click **Report Jobs** in the left console pane under **Monitoring Configuration**, and select **Properties** in the right context menu.

On the **Log Summaries** tab, shown in Figure 6.54, check the box to enable daily and monthly summaries.

Figure 6.54 Set a Location for Saving Daily and Monthly Summaries and Specify the Number of Each that Should Be Saved

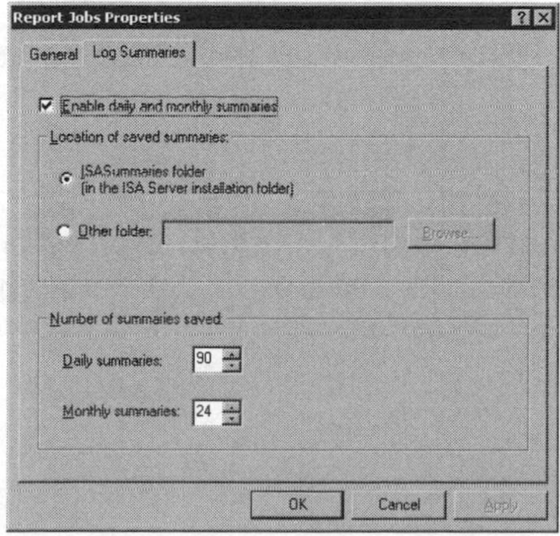

You can set the location for saving the summary database. You have two options:

- Save the summaries in the ISA Summaries subdirectory, in the directory to which ISA Server is installed on the local computer (this is the default).
- Save the summaries in a different location by choosing **Other folder** and typing a path or browsing for a folder by clicking the **Browse** button.

You can also specify how many daily summaries and how many monthly summaries are to be saved. You can specify a minimum of 35 and a maximum of 999 daily summaries and a minimum of 13 and a maximum of 999 monthly summaries. Summary files are saved with the .ILS extension (see Figure 6.55).

Figure 6.55 Summary Files Are Saved by Default in the ISASummaries Folder with an .ILS File Extension

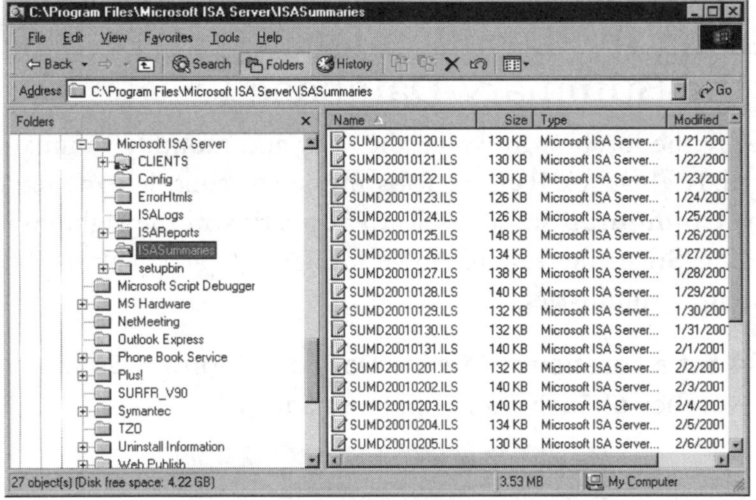

NOTE

The ISALogs, ISAReports, and ISASummaries directories are located on each server in the array in the Microsoft ISA Server installation folder.

Understanding Remote Administration

In this section of the chapter, we explore how you can administer an ISA server or array from a remote location, either using the ISA Management Console on a remote computer or by setting up the ISA server as a terminal server and connecting to it via the terminal server client software. Remote administration allows you to perform management tasks and configure components for your ISA server or array when you are not at the same site as an ISA server computer.

You can connect to the network via a WAN link by dialing in to the remote access server or by connecting across the Internet through a VPN. Once the connection to the local network is established, you can remotely manage a standalone ISA server, an array, or the enterprise.

Installing the ISA Management Console

You can install ISA Management on a Windows 2000 Server that is not running ISA Server or on a Windows 2000 Professional computer. This is done as part of the setup process when you run the ISA Server installation CD.

NOTE

ISA Server or the ISA Management tools can also be installed on computers running Windows XP/Whistler, the next version of the Windows operating system.

When you run the setup program, select **Custom installation**, and check only the **Administration Tools** check box, as shown in Figure 6.56.

After you install the Administration tools, ISA Server Management is accessible through the **Programs** menu on the remote computer. You can then connect to an ISA server or an array that is in the same domain or a domain with which a trust relationship exists.

Managing a Remote Standalone Computer

To manage a standalone ISA server remotely, open the ISA Management Console and right-click the root object in the left pane (Internet Security and Acceleration Server). Select **Connect to** from the context menu, and type the name of the standalone server that you want to manage in the box, as shown in Figure 6.57, or click the **Browse** button to find a computer in the directory.

Figure 6.56 To Install ISA Management on a Computer from Which You Want to Administer ISA, Select Custom Installation, and Check the Administration Tools Check Box

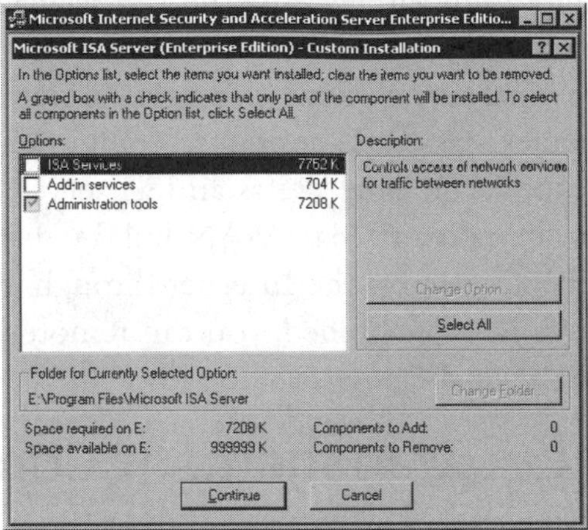

Figure 6.57 To Manage an ISA Server Remotely, You Must First Connect to It

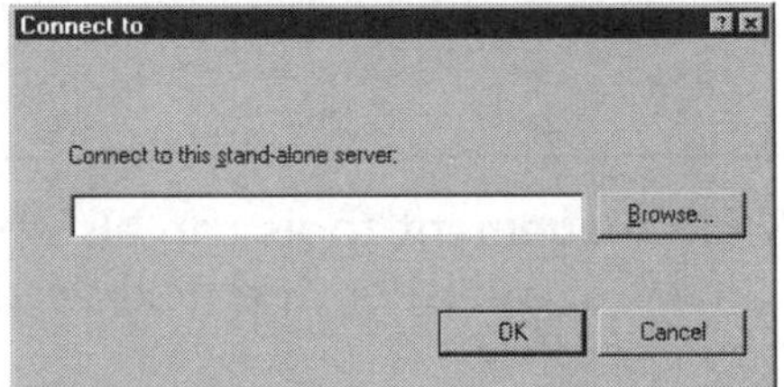

Undocumented ISA

You must be a member of the Administrators or Server Operators group on the remote computer that you want to manage.

After you are successfully connected to the remote ISA server, the ISA objects for that server appear in the Management Console, and you can administer the server as though you were logged on to it locally.

Remotely Managing an Array or Enterprise

To manage an ISA server that is an array member from a remote location, you must choose to manage the enterprise. In this case, in the **Connect to** dialog box, select the **Connect to enterprise and arrays** radio button, as shown in Figure 6.58.

Figure 6.58 To Manage an Array Remotely, Choose "Connect to Enterprise and Arrays"

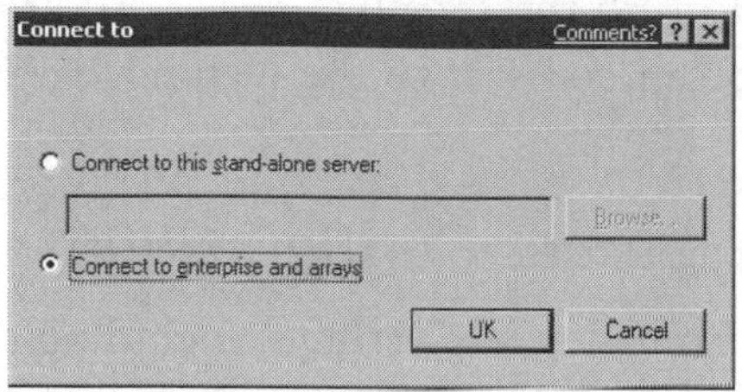

You will be connected to the array and can administer it from the management console as though you were logged on locally to an ISA server belonging to the array.

Using Terminal Services for Remote Management of ISA

Another way to remotely administer your ISA servers and arrays without installing the ISA Management tools on the computer from which you want to manage ISA is to use Windows 2000 Terminal Services.

Windows 2000 Server family products (Server, Advanced Server, and Datacenter Server) include terminal services as a Windows component. Terminal Services provide remote access to a server desktop, using thin client technology that serves as a terminal emulator. Processing is done on the server, so terminal services client software can be installed on low-powered machines running older operating systems such as Windows 3.x. With the Citrix metaframe client software, you can even connect to a Windows 2000 terminal server from a machine running MS-DOS, UNIX, or Macintosh.

Terminal Services is the solution for remotely administering your ISA Server if you need to do so from machines running these operating systems.

Installing Terminal Services on the ISA Server

Windows 2000 Terminal Services are installed from the **Add/Remove Programs** applet in Control Panel as a Windows component.

Terminal Server Mode

Terminal Services can be deployed in one of two modes: application server or remote administration. Application server mode is used to provide users a Windows 2000 desktop and applications via "thin-client" computing. By default, when you install Terminal Services, they are deployed in remote administration mode.

You should run Terminal Services in remote administration mode on the ISA Server. This does not require Terminal Services client licenses and allows only two concurrent connections to the terminal server. Additionally, only members of the Administrators group can connect to the terminal server in remote administration mode.

Terminal Services Server Configuration

You can configure the terminal server settings, including selection of the mode in which the Terminal Services will run, using the Terminal Services Configuration tool. This tool is installed in the **Start | Programs | Administrative Tools** menu when you install Terminal Services on the server. See Figure 6.59.

Figure 6.59 The Terminal Server Settings Are Configured via the Terminal Services Configuration Tool

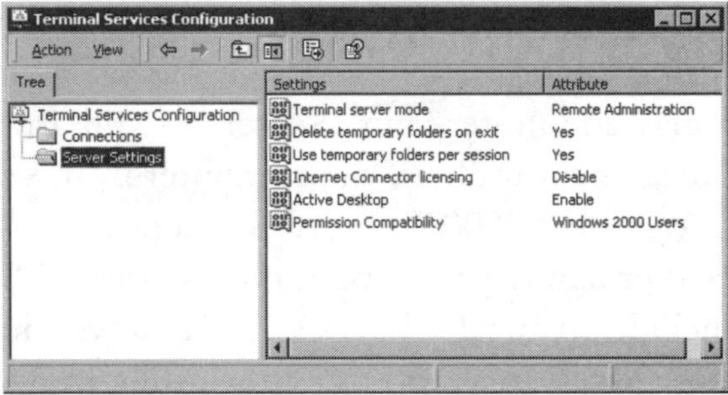

Another tool that is installed with Terminal Services on the server is the Terminal Services Manager, which is used to view and manage client connections to the terminal server, as shown in Figure 6.60.

Figure 6.60 Use the Terminal Services Manager to View and Manage Client Sessions

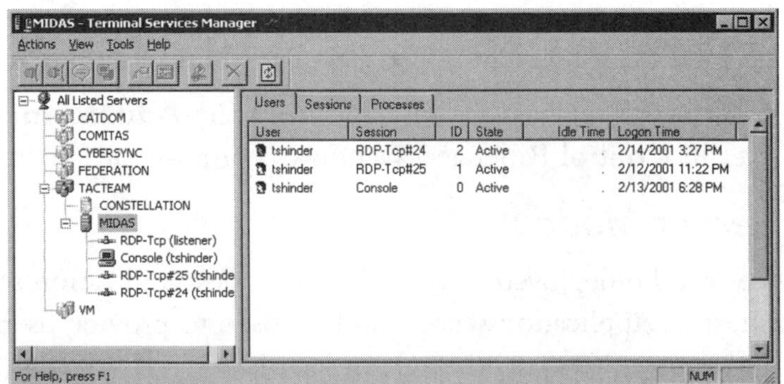

A terminal server can be accessed from any other computer on the network running the terminal client software, including dial-in or VPN clients.

Installing Terminal Services Client Software

You can create installation disks containing the Terminal Services client software by running the Terminal Services Client Creator program on the terminal server. The 16-bit client installation program for Windows 3.x requires four floppy disks; the 32-bit client installation program for Windows 9x/2000 computers requires only two floppy disks.

Run the appropriate client installation program to install the Terminal Services client to the computer(s) from which you want to access the ISA Server running Terminal Services.

Creating a Connection Shortcut with the Client Connection Manager

Once the services are installed, you can access the Microsoft Terminal Services Client through the **Start | Programs** menu. The Client Connection Manager, shown in Figure 6.61, is used to create a new connection to the ISA Server/terminal server.

Figure 6.61 Use the Client Connection Manager to Create a Connection to a Terminal Server

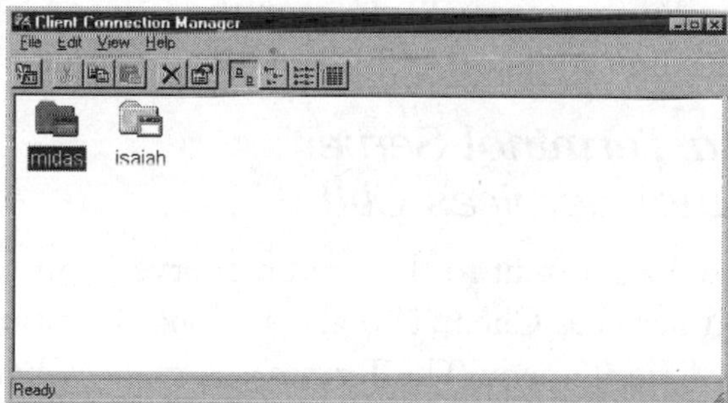

To create a new connection to a terminal server, select **File | New Connection**. This sequence starts the Client Connection Wizard, which creates a shortcut for connecting to the ISA Server/terminal server. You will be asked to provide a name for the connection and to enter the name or IP address of the terminal server, as shown in Figure 6.62.

The wizard allows you to specify the user account name and password to use in logging on to the server. You can leave this blank if you want and type in the credentials each time you connect. If you enter the information, you will not have to provide it when you log on to a terminal session. You can also choose the screen resolution at which the terminal window should run, or you can elect to have the terminal connection displayed full screen instead of in a window. You can also choose to enable data compression and/or to cache frequently used bitmaps to speed access, and you can specify a program path to run a program automatically when you connect to the terminal server.

Figure 6.62 The Client Connection Wizard Creates a Shortcut to the Terminal Server

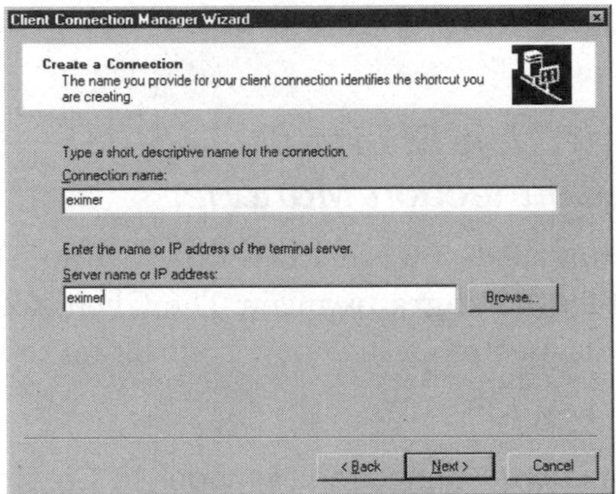

The new connection shortcut will appear in the Client Connection Manager Wizard, and you can connect to the terminal server by double-clicking it.

Connecting to a Terminal Server with the Terminal Services Client

If you have not created a shortcut to the terminal server, you can still connect to it, using the Terminal Services Client, also accessed via the **Start | Programs | Terminal Services Client** menu. The Terminal Services Client is shown in Figure 6.63.

You can type a terminal server name into the Server field, even if you have not created a shortcut connection to it using the Client Connection Manager. You can also use the Terminal Services Client when you want to connect to a terminal server using a screen resolution or other parameters that are different from those specified in the shortcut connection. Just type in or select the terminal server to which you want to connect, and click the **Connect** button.

Figure 6.63 You Can Use the Terminal Services Client to Connect to a Terminal Server

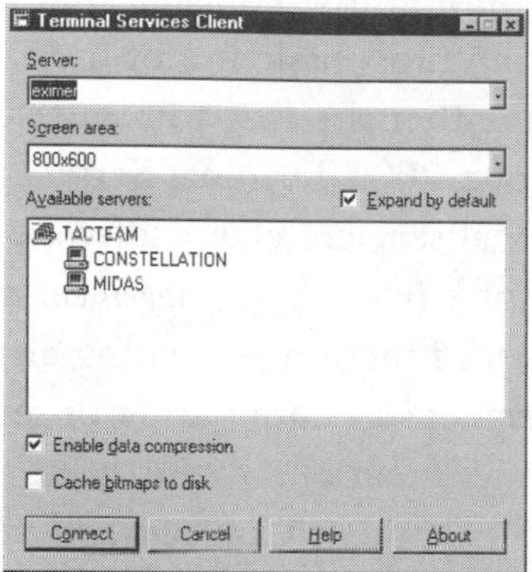

Using the Terminal Desktop

Once your connection to the terminal server is established, you will see the server desktop, as shown in Figure 6.64.

If the terminal server is an ISA Server, you can now open the ISA Management tool and perform all administrative tasks as you would if you were sitting at the ISA server.

Figure 6.64 Use the Terminal Server Desktop to Remotely Administer the ISA Server

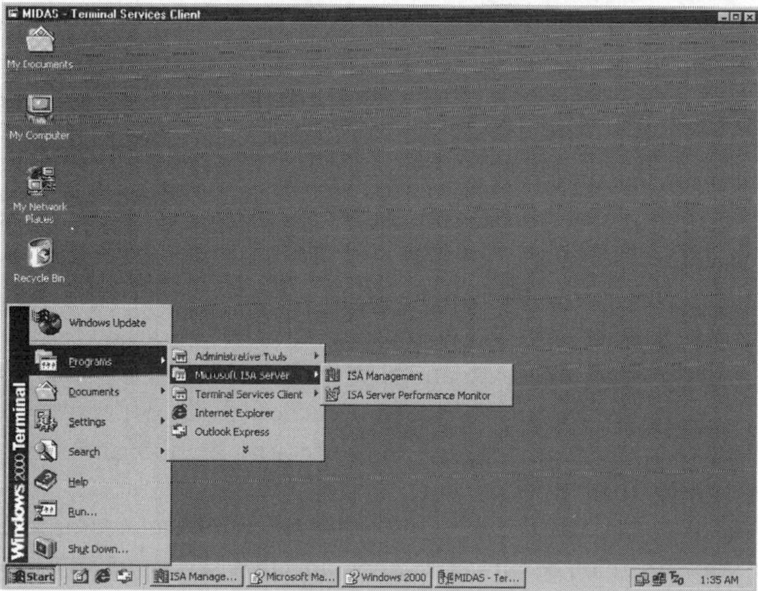

Summary

This chapter has taken you through the concepts and practices involved in managing an ISA server—from the most basic use of the ISA MMC and wizards to remote administration, using either the ISA administrative tools on a non-ISA computer or running Windows 2000 Terminal Services on the ISA Server and connecting to it using terminal services client software on a remote machine.

You learned that Microsoft's *integrated management* concept allows you to administer both of ISA Server's functions—caching and firewall—from a common interface and to manage an entire array of servers as one entity. You can even administer multiple arrays in an enterprise, from one centralized location.

We explored the ISA Management Console, and you learned to create a custom MMC and add the ISA Management snap-in for more convenient administration and easier delegation of selected administrative duties.

We examined each component of the ISA MMC, starting with the menu bar and main toolbar, describing the function of each icon or button and then looking at the console root and tree. You learned about each object in the left console pane and how to use the information in the right detail pane when various left-pane objects are selected.

Next, we looked at the many wizards provided with ISA Server to make configuration and creation of new objects simpler. Specifically, we addressed the Getting Started Wizard that helps you with the initial setup of your ISA Server; the Rules Wizards that walks you through the process of creating new routing, protocol, or site and content rules; and the three VPN wizards that assist you in performing tasks related to setting up virtual private networking connections.

You learned to perform some common management tasks such as configuring permissions on an ISA object and managing array membership. Then we delved into the intricacies of using the monitoring, alerting, logging, and reporting functions of ISA. You learned to set up trigger events and conditions for issuing an alert and how to monitor and disconnect user sessions. We discussed logging of information relating to three ISA Server components: packet filters, the firewall service, and the Web proxy service. You learned that you can save log information to a file or to an ODBC database, and we showed you how to enable and configure logging. Next, you learned about generating reports from the data collected in the log files, how to create a report job, and how to view and save the reports that are generated.

Finally, we discussed remote administration of an ISA server or array, and you learned that you can manage either a standalone ISA server or an array or enterprise in one of two ways: by installing the ISA Management tools on a non-ISA Server computer and using the ISA MMC to connect, or by installing Windows 2000 Terminal Services on your ISA server, making it a terminal server and connecting to it from another computer on the network that is running the Terminal Services Client software.

Much of the material covered in this chapter provides a foundation for the detailed discussions and instructions in Chapters 8 and 9, in which you will learn the step-by-step processes for configuring your ISA server for outbound access and configuring the ISA firewall and other inbound access issues.

Solutions Fast Track

Understanding Integrated Administration

☑ An entire array of servers can be managed together as one entity. When the configuration of an array is changed, the desired modifications are made to every server in the array.

☑ When you install ISA Server on a Windows 2000 server, the ISA Server selection will be added to the Programs menu with two selections, ISA Management and ISA Server Performance Monitor.

☑ If you have worked with Windows 2000's Active Directory, you'll remember that a *container object* is an object in the tree inside of which other objects can reside.

☑ When you use array and enterprise policies together, array-level rules can be applied to enterprise-level policy elements. This means that when you create a policy element at the enterprise level, it appears as a selection when you create a new rule at the array level.

☑ *Routing rules* determine where Web proxy client requests are sent and apply to both incoming and outgoing Web requests.

☑ The H.323 Gatekeeper is used to allow clients to use NetMeeting and other H.323-compliant applications through the ISA server.

Performing Common Management Tasks

☑ ISA Server uses Windows 2000 discretionary access control lists (DACLs) to control access to objects and object properties.

☑ When you add an array to or remove an array from the enterprise, the information is written to the Active Directory and replicated to all domain controllers in the domain.

☑ A standalone ISA server cannot be joined to an existing array; however, after you have initialized the enterprise, you can *promote* a standalone server to create a new array of which the promoted server will be a member.

Using Monitoring, Alerting, Logging, and Reporting Functions

☑ ISA Server allows real-time monitoring of all alerts that occur on any of the servers in an array.

☑ The ISA Server's alert service acts as an event filter, recognizing when events occur, determining whether configured conditions are met, and seeing that the chosen action(s) occurs in response.

☑ When your ISA servers belong to an array, logging is configured for the entire array, but log files are created on every ISA Server that is a member of the array.

Understanding Remote Administration

☑ You can connect to the network via a WAN link by dialing in to the remote access server or by connecting across the Internet through a VPN. Once the connection to the local network is established, you can remotely manage a standalone ISA server, an array, or the enterprise.

☑ Windows 2000 Server family products (Server, Advanced Server, and Datacenter Server) include terminal services as a Windows component.

☑ Terminal Services can be deployed in one of two modes: application server or remote administration.

☑ You can create installation disks containing the Terminal Services client software by running the Terminal Services Client Creator program on the terminal server.

Frequently Asked Questions

The following Frequently Asked Questions, answered by the authors of this book, are designed to both measure your understanding of the concepts presented in this chapter and to assist you with real-life implementation of these concepts. To have your questions about this chapter answered by the author, browse to **www.syngress.com/solutions** and click on the **"Ask the Author"** form.

Q: Can the ISA Management console be used to change the names of ISA servers and arrays?

A: Yes and no—or more accurately, no and yes. You can change the name of an ISA array by right-clicking the array name in the left console pane, selecting **Properties**, and typing a new name in the Name field on the **General** tab. However, ISA does not support changing the name of ISA server computers. You will find that when you right-click a computer name in the **Computers** folder and select **Properties**, you are unable to change the name in the Full Computer Name field, nor can you change any of the computer information on this tab other than that in the optional Description field.

Q: What is the difference between enterprise policies and array policies, and when is each used?

A: The enterprise administrator decides whether and how the enterprise policy is applied to arrays in the enterprise. The administrator can specify that enterprise policy will be applied only at the array level, meaning that no new rules can be added at the array level—only the enterprise policy rules will be applied. Alternately, the administrator can specify that both enterprise and array policies will be applied. The array policy in this case will actually be added to the enterprise policy. This means that additional rules/restrictions can be imposed at the array level, beyond those in the enterprise policy. However, the array policy cannot be *less* restrictive than the enterprise policy. Finally, the third option for an enterprise admin is to elect for array policies only to be applied. This means that no enterprise policy will be applied to the array. The array policy can be as restrictive or permissive as desired.

Q: At what level are publishing rules and packet-filtering rules created?

A: Publishing rules must be created at the array level; they cannot be created at the enterprise level. Similarly, packet filtering cannot be enabled at the enterprise level; you must do it at the array level. However, the confusion comes in because the enterprise admin can specify whether an array is allowed to publish servers and whether to force packet filtering at the array level. (The enterprise admin can also choose to allow array administrators to make the decision as to whether packet filtering should be available at the array level.)

Q: Can I move an ISA server that is an array member to a different domain or Active Directory site?

A: All array members must reside in both the same Windows 2000 domain and the same Active Directory site. It is possible to move a Windows 2000 server to a different domain or site; however, if the server is running ISA Server and is a member of an array, you cannot move it to a domain or site that will separate it from other array members. If you do, the ISA Server services will not function properly.

Q: Why am I unable to generate reports when I have permissions on the ISA Server to which I am logged on?

A: In order to create a report job and generate reports on ISA servers that are members of an array, you must have the appropriate permissions to access and use the reporting mechanism on *all* the servers in the array. You should be able to generate reports if you are a member of the Domain Admins group, if you are a member of the local Administrators group on *every* ISA server in the array, or if your account has permission to access and launch DCOM objects on *every* ISA server in the array.

Chapter 7

ISA Architecture and Client Configuration

Solutions in this chapter:

- **Understanding ISA Server Architecture**
- **Installing and Configuring ISA Server Clients**

☑ **Summary**

☑ **Solutions Fast Track**

☑ **Frequently Asked Questions**

Introduction

In this chapter we start getting into the "nuts and bolts" of ISA Server. We begin our configuration foray with a deep exploration into the setup involved in secure outbound access from your internal network. *Secure outbound access* allows you to control the material that internal users and applications can access via your Internet connection and provides you a granular method to control who can access particular sites, content, and protocols and when they can access these elements.

The ability to control outbound access is critical to your network security scheme. In the past, corporations allowed almost unfettered access to Internet resources and didn't exhibit much concern about what their employees were "doing" on the Internet. Managers assumed that users would limit themselves to viewing content directly related to their jobs and that they would refrain from accessing Web sites that were "recreational" in nature.

Many companies have been burned by these early policies. Unrestricted access to the Internet invites abuse of the network infrastructure. Here are some examples of the ways in which a company can get into trouble by not limiting Internet access:

- Network bandwidth saturation due to file-sharing applications such as Napster.
- Legal ramifications from employees visiting objectionable Web sites, such as pornography sites. Other employees could inadvertently (or perhaps purposely) view this content on the offending user's computer and try to capitalize on what they claim to be a hostile work environment.
- Users accessing sports, entertainment, and multimedia sites. These sites allow employees to waste time, which reduces overall productivity.
- Personal Web servers configured on user workstations. Users can set up personal Web servers on their workstation and use tunneling techniques to allow them to distribute illegal material such as child pornography and *warez* (bootlegged software).

These are just a few reasons that you need to exert strict control over the sites users can access over the Internet. Controlling outbound access is the first prong in your security configuration. The second prong, controlling inbound access, is discussed in the Chapter 9.

This chapter focuses on the implementation of outbound access control and gives examples of real-world situations and how you would configure ISA Server to meet the requirements of particular outbound access problems. It also includes many step-by-step walkthroughs. You can perform these walkthroughs on your own test bed and confirm them by performing your own proof-of-concept configurations.

Now let's focus on the first two pieces of the outbound access control plan:

- The ISA Server architecture
- How to install and configure the various ISA Server clients

We begin the discussion by reviewing the ISA Server architecture. You need a thorough understanding of the ISA Server architecture in order to appreciate the mechanisms that underlie the security schemes you plan to implement via ISA. After this discussion, we'll proceed with a discussion of installing and configuring the various ISA Server client types.

Understanding ISA Server Architecture

If you have experience with Proxy Server 2.0, you'll recall that it was built on three basic services: the Web Proxy Service, the Winsock Proxy Service, and the SOCKS Proxy Service. The Web proxy server and the SOCKS Proxy Service were implemented together within the Web Proxy Service, which provided access to Web protocols for Web proxy clients and SOCKS clients. The Web Proxy Service was implemented as an Internet Server Application Programming Interface (ISAPI) plug-in to the Internet Information Server's WWW Service. The Winsock Proxy Service provided Internet access for Winsock applications on machines that ran the Winsock Proxy client software. Together, these three services provided the proxy and firewall functionality of Proxy Server 2.0.

The architecture of ISA Server is somewhat different. The four components that form the foundation of the ISA Server are:

- The Web Proxy Service
- The Firewall Service
- The Network Address Translation Protocol driver
- The Scheduled Content Download Service

The Web Proxy Service

The Web Proxy Service (w3proxy.exe) provides and controls access to the Web protocols, which are Application layer protocols. These include:

- HTTP
- HTTPS (SSL secured HTTP)
- FTP
- Gopher

These are the only protocols processed by the Web Proxy Service. When the Web Proxy Service receives a request, the service assesses whether there are site/content rules and protocol rules that allow access and, if so, whether those rules require authentication. If access is allowed, the Web Proxy Service replaces the source header with the IP address of the external interface of ISA Server and changes the source port number to a dynamically assigned value. The destination server sends its response to the IP address and dynamically opened port number, and finally ISA Server forwards the response to the source of the request via its internal interface.

NOTE

Site and content rules are used to determine the network clients or users/groups that can access particular sites and servers on the Internet. *Protocol rules* are used to determine the protocols clients can access through the ISA Server. We will talk about these rules in detail in Chapter 8 when we discuss configuring outbound access.

The Web Proxy Service is implemented as the **w3proxy.exe** file. You can start and stop the service via the **net start w3proxy.exe** and the **net stop w3proxy.exe** commands. The Web Proxy Service in ISA Server is *not* dependent on the Internet Information Server's WWW Service. In fact, it is recommended that you do not install IIS on the same machine as ISA Server unless you have a special need, such as wanting to use the SMTP Message Screener application.

If you have been using Microsoft Proxy Server 2.0, this restriction might seem somewhat unusual, since Proxy Server 2.0 required IIS to be installed *prior* to installing the Proxy Server. ISA Server definitely does not share this dependence. However, ISA Server does have its own form of WWW service that listens for HTTP requests. In fact, plug-ins known as *Web filters* are ISAPI extensions that connect to ISA Server.

One of the advantages of the Web Proxy Service is that the Web proxy client is platform independent. You do not need to install any Microsoft-specific or proprietary applications on a computer in order to take advantage of the Web Proxy Service. The only requirement is that the Web Proxy client application be CERN compliant.

NOTE

Many students ask how to tell whether their applications are CERN compliant. In general, CERN-compliant applications are Web browsers. The best and only way to make this assessment is to find the configuration interface for the application and enter the IP address and appropriate port number for your ISA server's Internal Web Proxy Service listener port. If the application is able to access Internet resources, it is CERN compliant. Virtually every Web browser available in the last three or four years is CERN compliant. The only exception to this rule might be the America Online (AOL) proprietary browser.

The Web Proxy Service is also responsible for the *Web cache,* which provides a mechanism that allows content retrieved from the Internet to be stored on the ISA server. Once the content has been accessed from the Web and placed in cache, subsequent requests for the same content can be retrieved from cache rather than being fetched from the Internet server again.

After a client on the internal network makes a request for an Internet object (such as a Web page), the data is returned by the Internet server, placed in the Web cache, and then returned to the computer that made the initial request. A time-to-live (TTL) is placed on the object, and if another request for the same Internet object is made before the object's TTL has expired, it is returned to the requesting host from the Web cache instead of being retrieved a second time from the Internet server. This system helps reduce the amount of traffic on the external interface and therefore increases the bandwidth available to requests for new objects.

We discuss the Web-caching features of ISA Server in detail in Chapter 8.

The Firewall Service

The Firewall Service (fwsrv.exe) provides the same functionality to network clients as the Winsock Proxy Service did in Proxy Server 2.0. This service allows virtually all Winsock applications to access the Internet without those applications needing to be aware of the Firewall Service. This lack of awareness is expressed by the fact that you do not need to configure any of your Winsock programs to use the Firewall Service. As far as the programs are concerned, they are directly connected to the Internet.

Examples of Winsock protocols supported by the Firewall Service are SMTP, NNTP, IRC, Telnet, RDP, and many others. The Firewall Service is available to these Winsock protocols if you install ISA Server in either integrated or firewall mode and after you install the firewall client software.

The primary drawback of the Firewall Service is that you must install special firewall client software to take advantage of the service. The firewall client software can be installed on any 32-bit Windows operating system; it does not support Windows 3.1. The Winsock Proxy Client software provided with Proxy Server 2.0 is compatible with ISA Server's Firewall Service. Therefore, even though there is no native support for 16-bit Windows for the Firewall client, the Winsock Proxy Client program does have a 16-bit version and therefore allows you to access the Firewall Service.

NOTE

Even though there is a workaround for Windows 3.11 network clients, there is no such workaround for other platforms, such as DOS, Macintosh, and UNIX (including the Linux variant). Although there is no native support for all the features of the Firewall Service for these non-Windows clients, we'll see later how they are still able to take advantage of some of the Firewall Service's features.

How the Firewall Service Works

The firewall client installs a special version of the Windows Sockets (Winsock) interface. The Winsock interface is a Session layer interface and is implemented as an API. TCP/IP-based applications written to the Winsock interface send their network bound requests to the firewall client's version of Winsock.

If the firewall client assesses that a request is bound for a machine that is not located on the internal network (in other words, the destination address is not on the LAT), the firewall client version of the Winsock interface captures the request and forwards it to the Firewall Service on the ISA server. If the request is for a local resource (the destination address is on the LAT), the request is passed to the native Winsock interface and sent directly to the destination host. This reduces load on the ISA Server because it does not need to process requests for local hosts that are on internal, trusted networks.

The firewall client software captures Winsock API calls and forwards them to the Firewall Service via the Firewall Service's *control channel*. This control channel serves several purposes:

- It is used to deliver the LAT to the client on a periodic basis (every 6 hours by default, as determined by the mspclnt.ini file setting).
- It is used to map port numbers for requests made by the firewall client so that the firewall client and server can negotiate the client's source port and the ISA server's destination port for the initial request, before it is forwarded by the ISA server.
- It is used to send UDP-based Application layer protocol messages, such as DNS requests.
- Autoconfiguration information is sent to the firewall client via the control channel.

It is important to note that the control channel is *not* used to transfer data to and from the firewall client and the ISA server. It is used to communicate important information such as name resolution queries and the LAT, but it is not used for actual data transfer. It is analogous to the FTP client/server relationship, wherein the FTP client connects to the FTP server's port 21 to establish a control channel. No actual data transfer takes place through port 21, but important information about how to handle data transfers does take place through the FTP control channel. The same applies to the firewall client/server relationship.

Control channel messages that can fit inside a single UDP packet, such as DNS requests and port negotiations, are sent to and received from UDP port 1745 on the ISA server. Control messages that do not fit inside a single UDP packet, such as the LAT, are sent to and received from TCP port 1745 on the ISA server.

Like the Web Proxy Service, the Firewall Service works in tandem with the Network Address Translation Protocol driver.

The Network Address Translation Protocol Driver

The Network Address Translation (NAT) Protocol driver allows network clients on a network that uses a private IP addressing scheme to access the Internet. The private network IDs are defined in RFC 1597. The following are the IP address ranges for the private network IDs:

- 10.0.0.1–10.255.255.254/8
- 172.16.0.1–172.31.255.254/12
- 192.168.0.1–192.168.255.254/16

These address ranges are reserved for use on private internal networks and are not valid on the Internet. Internet routers will not route to clients with these network IDs, and packets with a source or destination address that includes an IP address in one of these ranges will not be routed on the Internet. Since these addresses are of no use on the Internet, they are available to everyone, without concern for duplicate IP addresses on nonrelated networks.

These private network IDs are convenient because you do not need to worry about registering them with anyone, but they present a problem. How will these computers with private IP addresses access Internet resources? A host with a source IP address in the private network range can send a message to a destination Internet server, but when the Internet server responds to the request, if it does so at all, the request cannot be routed back to the source.

SECURITY ALERT!

Many firewall products, including ISA Server, provide mechanisms for intrusion detection. Some of the things an intrusion detection system looks for are inbound requests that contain a source IP address in the private network range. This type of request indicates an invalid request and likely a spoofed packet. This technique can be utilized by attackers to compromise your systems.

To solve the problem of Internet access for private network hosts, Windows 2000 provides the Network Address Translation Protocol, or NAT. This protocol allows private network clients to send requests to the NAT server rather then directly to the Internet host.

The NAT server changes the header on the packet, changes the source address to its external interface, and changes the source port to a dynamically assigned port number. The Internet server sends its response to the NAT server's external interface. Then the NAT server checks its NAT table to see what internal host made the initial request. If the NAT table contains an entry that corresponds to the response it received from the Internet server, the NAT Server forwards the response to the internal private network host via its internal interface.

ISA Server takes advantage of the NAT Protocol driver included with Windows 2000 and extends its functionality so that it is able to work with the other ISA Server services. Note that you cannot run both the Routing and Remote Access Server NAT Protocol implementation *and* ISA Server on the same machine.

NOTE

Microsoft documentation warns that you should not run both RRAS NAT and ISA Server on the same machine. However, if you install ISA Server on a machine that already has RRAS enabled, the ISA Server installation routine will disable the RRAS NAT Protocol. At this point, you would assume that since the RRAS NAT Protocol has been disabled, there won't be any problems. However, we have observed unpredictable behavior on ISA servers that have the RRAS NAT Protocol installed. We strongly recommend that you delete the RRAS NAT Protocol before you install ISA Server. For more installation information, see Chapter 5.

The Scheduled Content Download Service

The Scheduled Content Download Service provides ISA Server a mechanism to automatically download Web content from sites you want to have available on the ISA server before a user actually makes a request for the content. This service can increase the available bandwidth on the external interface during peak hours and provide a fault-tolerance mechanism in the event that a mission-critical site becomes unavailable when users need to access content.

For example, suppose you have a relationship with a vendor that updates its component prices once a day and puts those prices on its partnering Web site. Your users normally access this information during business hours when they need to provide quotes for material and services. What if access to the partner's site went down during work hours? Any data that had not already been accessed by a user that day would not be in the Web proxy cache, resulting in a delay in processing a request and potential loss of sales. However, if you configured the content to be downloaded early that morning, the entire site would be available in cache, and business could proceed as usual.

This service is executed as the **w3prefch.exe** process and can be observed in the Task Manager. Requests for Web content are done under the context of the local system account. This service is integrated with the Web Proxy Service; therefore, if you have installed ISA Server in firewall mode only, the service won't be available to you.

ISA Server Services Interactions

The Web Proxy Service, the Firewall Service, and the NAT Protocol driver all work very closely together and can be tightly integrated. This integration provides a way for all network clients to take advantage of the features provided by all ISA Server services.

All requests, regardless of whether they are from SecureNAT, firewall, or Web proxy clients, must pass though the ISA server's packet filters. All requests are passed through the packet-filtering rules to assess whether they should be passed on to other ISA Server services. If a packet filter rule is configured to drop a particular request, the request is dropped immediately. This makes good sense, since the amount of processing time required to evaluate the packet filters is less demanding than that required to process the Application layer protocol rules. After passing the packet filter test, the request can be passed on to its respective service.

Requests from SecureNAT and firewall clients are always passed to the Firewall Service. Requests coming from SecureNAT clients are first intercepted by the NAT Protocol driver and then passed to the Firewall Service. Requests originating from firewall clients are passed directly to the Firewall Service.

The fate of these requests after they reach the Firewall Service depends on how you have the HTTP Redirector Filter configured on your ISA Server computer. By default, the HTTP Redirector Filter is enabled. When enabled, the default behavior of this filter is to redirect HTTP requests to the Web Proxy Service. When these HTTP requests are redirected to the Web Proxy Service, NAT and firewall clients are able to take advantage of the Web cache. This is a new feature; in Proxy Server 2.0, Winsock proxy clients never had access to the Web cache. Only Web proxy clients had access to the Web Proxy Service's Web cache.

Note that in order for the HTTP Redirector Filter to perform these actions, both the Firewall Services *and* the Winsock Proxy Services must be available. In order for both of these services to be available, you must have installed ISA Server in integrated mode.

We cover the HTTP Redirector Filter in detail in Chapter 8.

NOTE

It is interesting to note that requests issued from a Web proxy client to a Web proxy server are always HTTP requests. This includes both HTTP and FTP requests issued from the Web browser. The FTP (and Gopher) requests are encapsulated inside an HTTP **GET** or **POST** command. The requests are unwrapped when they arrive at the ISA Server to expose the underlying protocol. Because of this encapsulation of FTP requests, FTP communications can also take advantage of the Web Proxy service's Web Cache.

Non-HTTP requests sent by firewall clients to the Firewall Service (and NAT clients, because all NAT communications must pass through the Firewall Service) can also be subjected to a number of possible *Application layer filters.* Some of the built-in Application layer filters include:

- The SMTP filter
- The FTP filter
- The POP3 filter
- The H.323 filter

The Application layer filters can make decisions on whether or not to forward a request. For example, you might configure the SMTP Filter to reject mail messages that contain a certain keyword, such as AOL or Napster. Even if the request had been allowed by packet filters, site and content, and protocol rules, it would be rejected by the Application filter.

HTTP requests issued by a Web proxy client, or a SecureNAT or firewall client with the HTTP redirector enabled, can also be subjected to a custom set of Application layer filters known collectively as *Web filters.* No Web filters are provided with ISA Server. Web filters are installed by third-party applications. One example of an application that installs Web filters is GFI's LANGuard product. This product allows you to configure the Web filter to examine the data contained in HTTP messages. You can configure the Web filter to delete or quarantine data based on keywords.

We'll spend more time with the Application filters provided with ISA Server later in Chapter 8. Now, let's take a look at the specifics of the various ISA Server client setups and configurations.

Configuration Changes and ISA Server Services Restarts

Many configuration changes you make on the ISA Server computer will require that you restart one or more ISA Server services. Typically, the ISA Server Control Service (isactrl) detects these changes and informs you that a service needs to be restarted. For example, if you want to change the authentication settings for outbound Web requests, you'll see the dialog box shown in Figure 7.1 after effecting the change.

Figure 7.1 ISA Server Warning that a Service Must Be Restarted

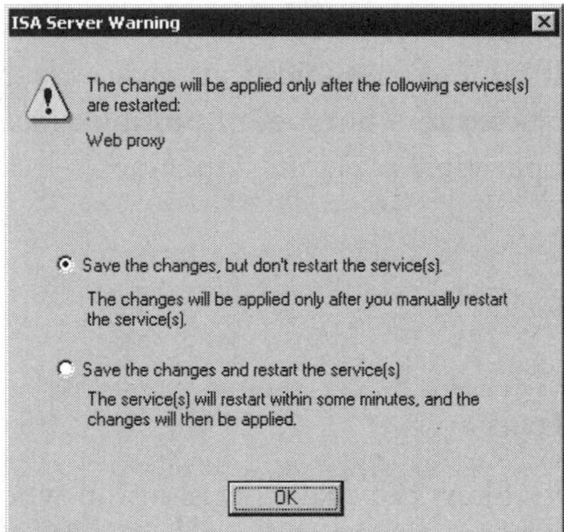

You'll have the choice of having ISA Server restart the service automatically or saving the change and restarting the service manually at a later time. You might not want to restart a particular service during work hours, because when the service is restarted, all current sessions are disconnected. This could make a top-level executive very upset if she was in the process of downloading an .MP3 file that she's been trying to download for months.

A record of the service restart appears both in the Event Viewer and in the ISA Server Alerts node in the left pane, as shown in Figure 7.2. Table 7.1 shows changes that require particular services to be restarted.

Figure 7.2 The Alerts Node Informs that a Service Has Started

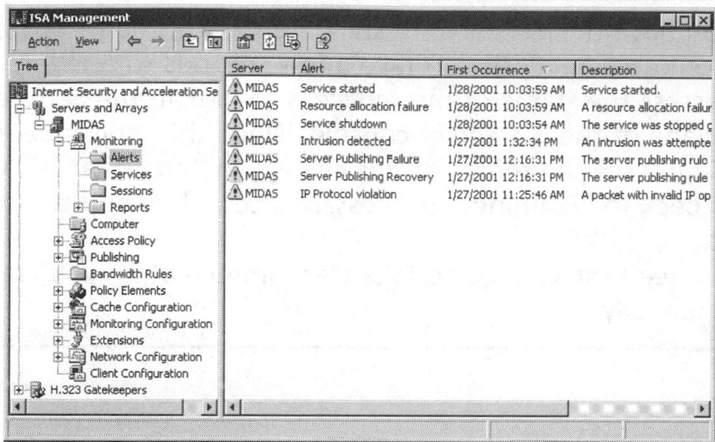

Table 7.1 Restarting ISA Server Services After Configuration Changes

Change Made	Service that Must Be Restarted
Updating an SSL certificate	Web Proxy
Adding/removing services from array	Web Proxy
Changes to Web filters	Web Proxy
Changing Web proxy listener configuration	Web Proxy
Changing Web cache parameters	Web Proxy
Manual change of mspclnt.ini file*	Firewall Service
Changing any application filter settings	Firewall Service
Enabling or disabling packet filtering	Firewall and Web Proxy Service
Enabling or disabling a network adapter*	Firewall and Web Proxy Service
Changing IP address on a network adapter*	Firewall and Web Proxy Service
Changing routing table entries*	Firewall and Web Proxy Service
Changing the LAT*	Firewall and Web Proxy Service
Changing the gatekeeper's network interface*	H.323 Gatekeeper Service

* You will not be informed that you need to change these settings, and the changes might or might not be reported by ISA Server Alerts or the Event Viewer. You must stop and restart the respective ISA Server Service manually when making these changes.

Undocumented ISA

When you have the ISA Server restart the service, the restart does not take place immediately. It can take a few seconds to a few minutes. One way to assess the status of the service is to look in the Services node in the left pane of the ISA Server console. When the service begins to restart, you'll see the service status change to "unavailable"; when it changes back to "Running," the restart is complete and the changes are in effect.

If you need the change to take place immediately, you can restart the service manually.

Installing and Configuring ISA Server Clients

This section reviews the various ISA Server client installation and configuration options. As you'll see, some of the client configurations are extremely simple to set up, and some of them can be relatively complex. The ISA Server client types are:

- The SecureNAT client
- The Firewall client
- The Web proxy client

Let's begin with the SecureNAT client.

The SecureNAT Client

The SecureNAT service provides virtually transparent proxy services for your network clients. The SecureNAT client requires no extra software to be installed on your computers. The SecureNAT client is supported by all operating systems and therefore isn't limited to Microsoft Windows family products. So, if you have a mix of UNIX, Mac, Windows, and other operating systems that need access to the Internet, the SecureNAT client is for you.

A SecureNAT client is created when you change the default gateway of a machine to an address that will route Internet requests to the internal interface of the ISA server. You might or might not need to restart the computer after making the change in the default gateway address. For example, if the client is a Windows

2000 machine, you do not need to restart the computer. However, any other Windows-based client needs to be restarted in order to take advantage of the new default gateway settings.

There are two types of networks on which you'll deploy a SecureNAT client:

- Simple networks
- Not-simple networks

SecureNAT Clients on Simple Networks

A *simple network* can be defined as one that has a single internal network segment and logical network ID. With this setup, the SecureNAT clients are on the same network ID as the internal interface of the ISA server. On simple networks, you configure the SecureNAT client to use the internal interface of the ISA server as its default gateway. Figure 7.3 depicts a simple network setup.

Figure 7.3 A Simple Network Setup

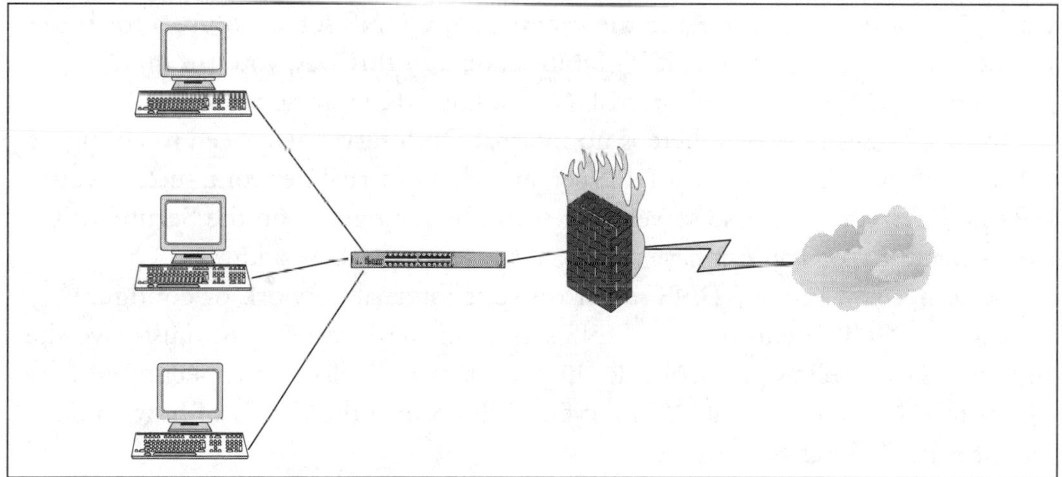

There are two ways to configure network clients with the right default gateway. The hard way is to physically go to each machine and manually make the change. The easy way is to configure a DHCP server to deliver the default gateway address to the client automatically.

Name resolution for network clients on a simple network is an important issue that you must address. Typically, such simple networks will not have a dedicated DNS server at their disposal, and in most cases you will not need one, unless the simple network has a Windows 2000 domain controller installed.

NOTE

If you're installing ISA Server in a simple network scenario, it's often the case that other Internet connection-sharing methods have already been put into effect. These include Internet Connection Sharing (ICS) and the RRAS NAT. In these scenarios, ICS or the Windows 2000 NAT Service might have been providing IP addressing via their DHCP Allocator Services. When ISA Server is installed on the same computer, it disables ICS or NAT, including the DHCP Allocator. A DHCP Server needs to be installed to replace these services.

If the latter is true, the Windows 2000 domain controller can also host a DNS server that is configured to use a forwarder on the Internet (typically, your ISP's DNS server). SecureNAT clients can be configured to query that DNS server to resolve Internet names. An even better solution is to configure the internal DNS server to use a caching-only forwarder that is also located on the internal network. You would then configure the caching-only DNS server to use a forwarder on the Internet (such as your ISP's DNS server). In this way, you can quickly build up the DNS cache and speed DNS lookups on your network.

In those cases in which there is no internal DNS server, you need to configure the SecureNAT clients to use a DNS server on an external network, such as your ISP's DNS server. The DNS server address can be configured on the SecureNAT clients manually, or you can have a DHCP server assign these addresses.

Whether you install a DNS server on your internal network or configure your SecureNAT clients to use a DNS server on the Internet, you must have site and content as well as protocol rules in place that will allow your SecureNAT clients to query an external DNS server. We'll go into the details of how to do this later in Chapter 8.

SecureNAT Clients on "Not-Simple" Networks

We thought about defining a *not-simple network* as a complex network, but that wouldn't have been entirely accurate. A "not-simple" network is one that has more than a single logical network ID. Such networks need at least one router separating the SecureNAT clients from the internal interface of the ISA server, as depicted in Figure 7.4.

When you have routers separating the SecureNAT clients from the internal interface of the ISA server, you must configure the routing infrastructure in such as manner that packets not destined for a location on the internal network are sent to the internal interface of the ISA server. You must also ensure that your routers are not configured to drop packets destined for external networks.

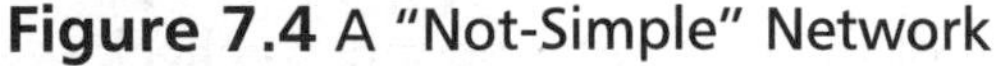

Figure 7.4 A "Not-Simple" Network

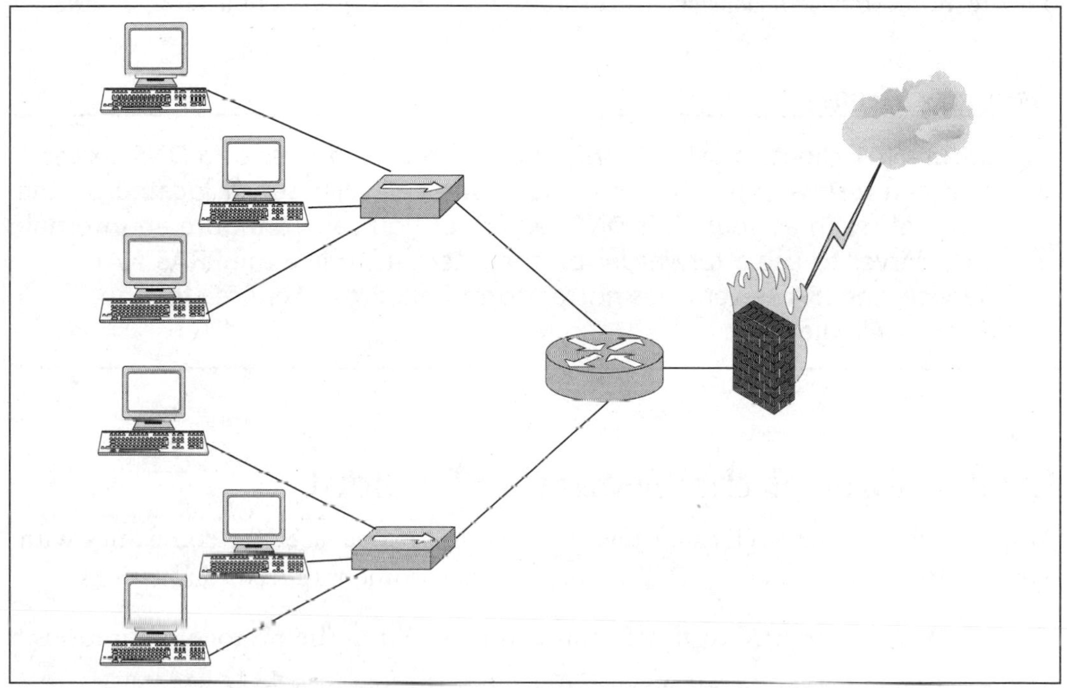

A routed environment will have an impact on where you place DHCP and DNS servers. For DHCP Server, you options are to:

- Place a DHCP server on each segment.
- Use a single DHCP server, configure superscopes, and deploy DHCP relay agents.
- Enable BOOTP forwarding and configure helper addresses on your routers.

If you choose to implement a single, centralized DHCP server, you must configure multiple scopes to service all network IDs that have DHCP clients. To support this configuration, you can place multiple network interface cards (NICs) on the DHCP server, each with an IP address bound to it that can listen for DHCP requests from each network ID. This isn't the best solution, because it requires you to add hardware that really isn't necessary. A better solution is to configure a superscope that includes all the scopes configured on the DHCP server.

DNS server placement isn't quite as messy. Unlike DHCP messages, DNS queries are not broadcast based. If your network is sufficiently complex, you still need to plan placement of DNS servers to minimize DNS name query latency and maximize availability. For a detailed discussion of these subjects, be sure to check out our book *Troubleshooting Windows 2000 TCP/IP* (Syngress Publishing, 2000).

SECURITY ALERT!

SecureNAT clients must be configured with the address of a DNS server that can resolve Internet names. You can use a DNS server located on the Internet (such as your ISP's DNS server), or you can configure an internal DNS server to use a forwarder on the Internet. Unlike the RRAS NAT Service, the ISA server does not perform DNS Proxy Services for the SecureNAT clients.

Limitations of the SecureNAT Client

Although the SecureNAT client might appear to be a panacea for companies with hybrid networks, the SecureNAT client does have some important limitations:

- Access is limited to those protocols included in the protocol definitions.
- SecureNAT requires Application filters for complex protocols.
- There is no user- or group-based authentication for network access.

The SecureNAT client depends on existing protocol definitions in order to access Internet applications on remote hosts. This is the case even if you have created a "wide-open" access policy in which all protocols are open to all clients to all destinations. If you are working with complex protocols that require opening "back channels," you need Application filters to help support SecureNAT clients.

Perhaps the biggest limitation of the SecureNAT client is that it cannot take advantage of user- or group-based access controls. For example, you might want to prevent Internet access to a group called Temporary Employees. The SecureNAT client will not support access control based on this group because it does not send any authentication information to the ISA server. This includes SecureNAT client requests for HTTP and FTP resources that go through the HTTP redirector filter.

Undocumented ISA

The access control limitations of the SecureNAT client are a complicating factor if you decide to allow outbound PPTP calls from your internal network. ISA Server supports outbound calls to PPTP Server from SecureNAT clients only. Since SecureNAT doesn't support user or group authentication, you cannot implement access control over these VPN connections based on users or groups.

Access controls for SecureNAT clients are similar to those available to the SOCKS client in Proxy Server 2.0. Access can be limited based on client address sets, which are collections of IP addresses. Therefore, if you want to exercise anything like granular access control on SecureNAT clients, you should physically group users together so that they belong to the same IP subnets or contiguous ranges of IP addresses.

Logging of client activity is another problem for the SecureNAT client. If you need to log information about user and group activity via the ISA server, you're out of luck with the SecureNAT client. You still get the source IP address, but security auditing based on IP address doesn't hold up to scrutiny as well as that based on user account, because it is the responsibility of the user to keep his or her account name and password confidential.

Security Alert!

Many network administrators have a difficult time expressing to their users how important it is to keep their account information confidential. Users often share passwords with one another in order to "help a friend" or even if someone simply asks for the password over the phone. Part of your corporate security policy must include training users in security awareness. One way to drive this point home is to let users know about the current acceptable use policy and that repercussions of violating the acceptable use policy are based on user account. Of course, if you configure your clients as simple SecureNAT clients, you won't have this stick to hold over your users.

Manually Configuring the SecureNAT Client

Configuring the SecureNAT client is quite easy. All you need to do is configure the appropriate default gateway. On a Windows 2000 client, you would go through the following procedure:

1. Right-click the **My Network Places** applet on the Desktop and click **Properties**.
2. In the **Network and Dial-up Connections** window, right-click the **LAN interface** and click **Properties**.
3. In the **Properties** dialog box, double-click **Internet Protocol (TCP/IP)**.
4. In the **Default Gateway** text box, enter the IP address of the internal interface of the ISA server or to a router that can route outbound Internet requests to the internal interface of the ISA server (see Figure 7.5).

Figure 7.5 The Internet Protocol (TCP/IP) Properties General Tab

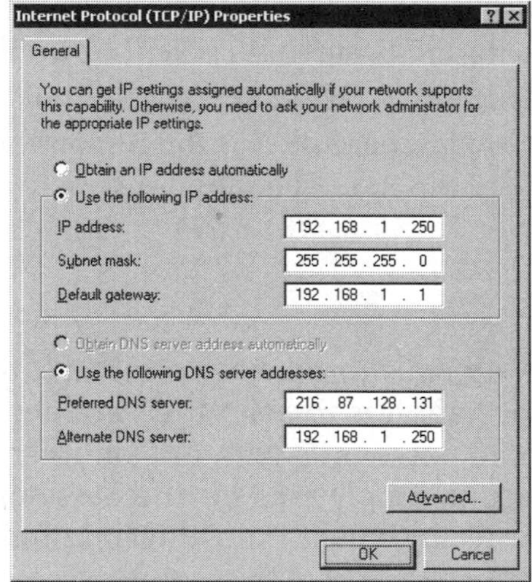

That's all there is to it. You might need to restart the computer, depending on the client operating system. To quickly test your configuration, open your browser and type in your favorite URL. Or if you prefer, you can ping your least favorite Internet host. If you typed in the correct IP address for your default gateway, you should be able to retrieve your Web page and receive echo replies from your ping.

NOTE

In order to ping an external client, the ISA Server must be configured to allow IP Routing. If IP Routing is not enabled, ping requests will fail. While the SecureNAT client does support pinging external Web sites, you must be sure that you can resolve the name of the site if you ping by host name.

Configuring the SecureNAT Client via DHCP

If you want to configure the SecureNAT client via DHCP, perform these steps:

1. Install a DHCP server on your network that is accessible to your SecureNAT client computer, either through broadcast or relay.
2. Configure a DHCP scope for each network ID that has SecureNAT clients.
3. Configure scope option **003 Router** and enter the IP address for the appropriate default gateway, as shown in Figure 7.6. Click **OK**.

Figure 7.6 The Scope Options General Tab

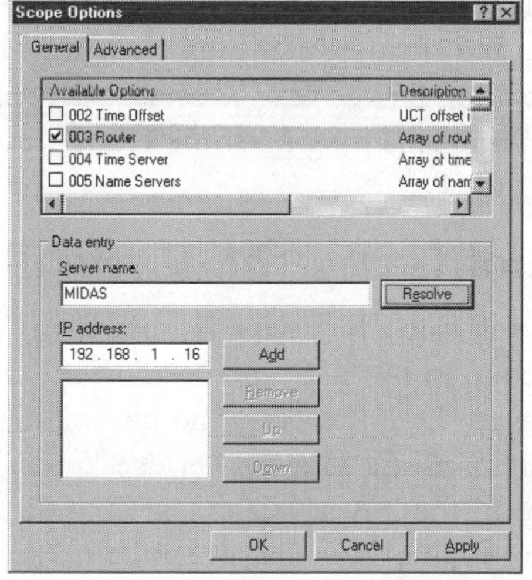

4. Restart the DHCP Server service, and either restart the DHCP/SecureNAT client or issue the ipconfig /renew command, depending on the client operating system.

The Firewall Client

ISA Server comes with firewall client software that you can install on 32-bit Windows-based computers:

- Windows 95/98/ME
- Windows NT 4.0
- Windows 2000
- Windows XP (Whistler)

The firewall client installation files are installed in a local directory on the ISA server in the path:

```
<drive_letter>:\Program Files\Microsoft ISA Server\CLIENTS
```

The drive letter is determined by the drive you selected to install the ISA Server application files.

The folder containing the firewall client software is automatically shared and can be accessed over the network via either a universal naming convention (UNC) path or a Web page. The UNC path to the firewall client installation file is located at:

```
\\<ISA_server_name>\mspclnt\setup.exe
```

The firewall client installation file can also be accessed via a Web page, but the Web installation information files must be manually moved to a directory in the Internet Information Server WWW service accessible hierarchy. We'll talk about the details of implementing both the UNC- and Web-based installations later.

Advantages of Using the Firewall Client

The firewall client software allows you to implement user- or group-based access control. This is in contrast to the SecureNAT client, for which you do not have authenticated access to the ISA server. The Firewall Service identifies users who are accessing resources via the Firewall Service. You can see the usernames in the active sessions listed in the ISA Management console, as shown in Figure 7.7.

Note that in this figure, there are several active firewall sessions, although only two have usernames appended. The reason is that SecureNAT client sessions also go through the Firewall Service. Therefore, machines that show up without a username in an active firewall session are SecureNAT clients.

Figure 7.7 Identifying a User-Based Firewall Session

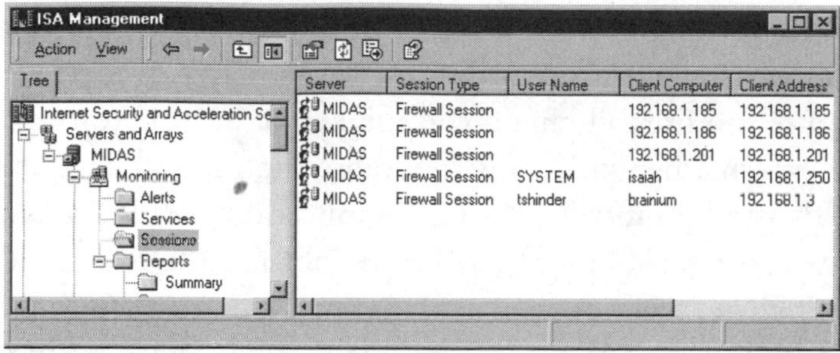

UNDOCUMENTED ISA

In Figure 7.7, the user SYSTEM has established a firewall session. The reason for this is that the server named Isaiah has been configured as a backup route for HTTP connections.

The log files include usernames when you implement the firewall client. In this way, you can identify users who are accessing particular sites at particular times. As we mentioned earlier, this can be a great convenience when you are building a security and access control report for management. We examine examples of how user information is included in log files and reports in Chapter 6, Managing ISA Server.

Disadvantages of Using the Firewall Client

Installing the firewall client software does confer some major advantages, but there are limitations associated with this software. The biggest problem is that only a subset of Windows-based clients are supported by the firewall client. In addition, the firewall client software does not support Windows 3.x clients. However, you can get around this limitation if you have the Proxy Server 2.0 Winsock client installed on the Windows 3.x machines.

If you have Mac, UNIX, or other non-Microsoft operating systems on the network, you will not be able to install the firewall client and therefore will not be able to take advantage of the complete range of protocols provided by the firewall client. Furthermore, user- and group-based authentication is available only to firewall clients. You'll have to carefully consider how important these features are to you. If they are important, your only option is to upgrade your client operating systems so that you can install the firewall client.

The exception to this rule occurs if you configure the Web browsers on the non-Microsoft clients to be Web proxy clients. A Web proxy client can be forced to send authentication information to the ISA Server. We'll go into this in detail in Chapter 8 in the discussion on outbound access.

When you use the firewall client, you might not be able to ping computers located on the external network. This is because the firewall client supports only UDP- and TCP-based protocols. The ping application uses ICMP messages to send its requests and replies. Since ICMP does not use UDP or TCP as a transport, the firewall client will not convey these messages. You see the same situation with outbound PPTP requests, which support the Generic Routing Encapsulation (GRE) Protocol, or IP Protocol ID 47.

Note that we said that the firewall client *might* not be able to ping remote hosts. This is because if you configure your computer with a default gateway that routes to the internal interface of the ISA server (and the ISA server is configured to allow IP routing), non-TCP/non-UDP protocols such as ICMP or GRE can be sent via SecureNAT. However, in your production environment, you should not configure your firewall clients with a default gateway.

NOTE

Even though we gave an example of configuring a default gateway on a firewall client to support ICMP messages and allow outbound ping requests and inbound replies, this does not mean that the client is both a SecureNAT and a firewall client. In fact, a computer cannot be both a firewall client and a SecureNAT client, because Winsock applications that use TCP and UDP still send their requests via the firewall client Winsock .DLLs. You can confirm this by creating a Winsock connection on your firewall client while having a default gateway configured. You will see the firewall session appear in the monitoring console on the ISA server.

You should not configure servers that are published to the Internet to use the firewall client. This is not a limitation of the firewall client itself, but rather an inconvenience. Published servers should be configured as SecureNAT clients; otherwise, you will have to configure a wspcfg.ini file, which can be somewhat more painful than setting up a SecureNAT client.

However, there could be some circumstances in which a published server needs the firewall client installed. For example, you might run a server application that requires an Application filter to manage connections, but you don't have such a filter installed on the ISA server. In such a case, you could get around the problem by configuring a wspcfg.ini file on the server running the firewall client.

Undocumented ISA

If you want to disable the firewall client software, you do not need to restart the computer on a Windows 2000 client. You might need to restart on other operating systems. If you do not restart the computer, you need to close any applications that have open Winsock connections. Similarly, if you want to enable the firewall client software again after you have manually disabled it, you can do that without having to restart the computer as well (at least on a Windows 2000 client machine).

DNS Configuration Issues for Firewall Clients

One of the most common troubleshooting issues we've seen arise in ISA Server deployments relates to DNS client and server configuration. In order to get your firewall client working correctly, you need to have your DNS infrastructure plan mapped out.

The firewall client can be configured without a DNS server address listed in its TCP/IP Properties sheet. In other words, the firewall client does not need to be configured to use a DNS server. The firewall client takes advantage of the DNS proxy features provided by ISA Server. The firewall client sends DNS name query requests over the control channel to the ISA server, and the ISA server resolves the name and send the answer to the firewall client over the control channel.

ISA Server can perform the name resolution for the firewall client for all Internet name requests using the DNS server configured on the external interface of the ISA server. The ISA server will send a DNS query to the DNS server configured on the external interface, receive the answer, and forward that answer to the firewall client.

This configuration has some significant limitations. If you need to resolve fully qualified domain names (FQDNs) on your internal network, you will not be able to do so, because the DNS server used by the external interface of the ISA server is unlikely to have any information about your internal host-naming scheme. When you try to connect to an internal host by its FQDN, the request fails.

NOTE

Internal networks with multiple domains are likely to have hosts with the same host name and most likely the same NetBIOS name. There are many good reasons for avoiding a schism in host and NetBIOS naming schemes. However, a Windows 2000 network with multiple domains is just one example of when such schisms could be required and thus an internal DNS Server sine qua non.

One way around this problem is to install and configure a WINS server on your internal network. When you use a Winsock application, it can take advantage of a WINS server to resolve the host name portion of the FQDN to an IP address and therefore connect to an internal client via the host name portion only. However, if you have multiple domains on your internal network, there is a good chance that you have multiple machines with the same host name, such as *www* and *mail*. Even if you configured DNS servers to forward names for which they are not authoritative to a WINS server, it still would not work because of the NetBIOS name duplication issue.

The preferred solution to the host name resolution quandary for firewall clients is to install a DNS server on the internal network and allow that machine to resolve Internet names for these clients. There are a couple of ways to configure the DNS server to do this. One is to allow the internal DNS server to complete recursion by performing its own iterative queries to Internet DNS servers. The second, and better, option is to configure the DNS server to use a forwarder. The DNS forwarder can resolve the Internet names and return this information to the internal DNS server. The forwarder allows for a higher level of security because you can configure the firewall to allow DNS communications only between your internal DNS server and the forwarder. An even better solution is to place a caching-only DNS server on a DMZ segment and configure the caching-only DNS server to use a forwarder on the Internet. Then you would configure the internal DNS server to allow DNS messages only between itself and the caching-only server on the DMZ.

One last component of the firewall client name resolution puzzle is the local domain table (LDT). The LDT is used to determine if a name is located on the local network. If the destination is contained in the LDT, the firewall client will use a local DNS server (if it is configured to use one) to resolve the name. If the name is not in the LDT, it will allow the ISA server to resolve the name. We will spend more time discussing the LDT in Chapter 8.

Deploying the Firewall Client

As we discussed earlier, the firewall client setup routine can be accessed via:

- A UNC path
- A URL
- Automatically via Windows 2000 Active Directory Software Distribution

Let's go through the steps involved with each type of installation.

Manual Installation of the Firewall Client via a UNC Path

You can access and install the firewall client setup routine by performing the following steps:

1. Open the **Run** command, and type into the text box **\\<ISA_Server_Name>\mspclnt\setup.exe**. See Figure 7.8.

Figure 7.8 The Run Dialog Box

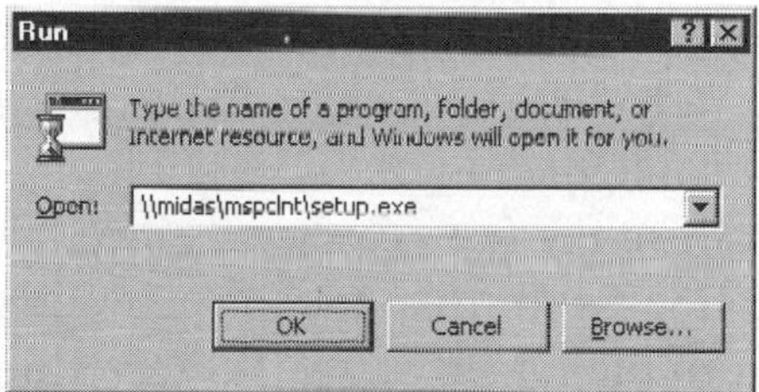

2. The Microsoft Firewall Client Installation Wizard will begin with a Welcome screen. Click **Next** to move forward.
3. The next page will display the Destination Folder options, as shown in Figure 7.9. If you want to change the installation folder, you can click the **Change** button. If you want to check how much space you have available on each of your local drives, you can click the **Space** button. Click **Next** to move forward in the wizard.
4. The Ready to Install the Program page appears. Click the **Install** button to start the installation. When the installation completes, you'll be presented with the Install Wizard Completed page. Click the **Finish** button to complete the installation of the firewall client software.
5. You will be asked to restart the computer after the software is installed. Restart the computer, and the firewall client will be installed and enabled.

Figure 7.9 The Destination Folder Options

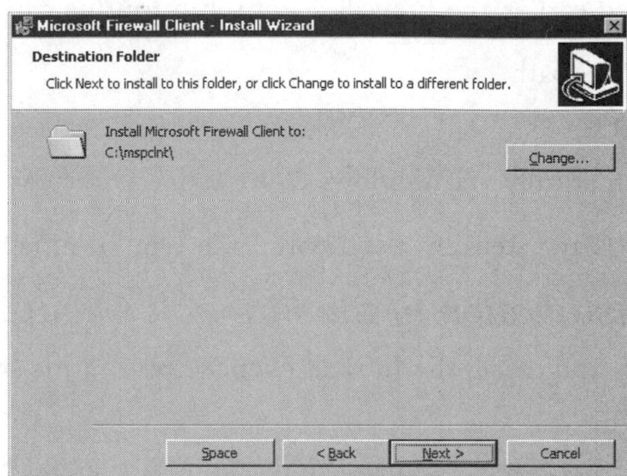

Manual Installation of a Firewall Client via URL

Users can access the installation files via their Web browsers by typing in a URL and clicking the appropriate link. However, in order to do this, you must configure the directory to be accessible via a Web browser. There are several ways you can handle this configuration.

First, you could share the firewall client source files located on ISA Server that are available to IIS. If you make the folder available to the IIS hierarchy, the users could connect to the folder via the IIS server on the ISA Server machine. There are security issues with this approach, and you don't really need the extra traffic on the internal interface of the ISA server. In addition, if you can at all get away with it, you shouldn't even have IIS installed on the ISA server. The optimal configuration for your firewall is to have all unnecessary services removed from the ISA server, and IIS is definitely not necessary.

A slightly safer approach would be to run IIS on the ISA server but create a virtual directory that contains the firewall client installation files located on another machine. But this approach also has the drawbacks of generating needless traffic on the internal interface of the ISA Server and requiring you to run IIS on the ISA server.

The best thing to do is to copy the installation files from the ISA server to another server on the network that runs IIS or any other Web server you like. Once the files are copied, you can configure the Web server on that machine to serve up the installation files. This process allows you to remove IIS from the ISA Server machine and reduces the traffic related to installing the firewall client.

The following example shows you how to configure the CLIENTS directory on the ISA server so that it is available to the local IIS server. You would follow the same procedure for making the installation files available on any other machine that has IIS installed. If you are using another Web server, follow the instructions as appropriate for your version:

1. At the ISA Server, find the directory that contains the firewall client installation files. You should find them at <drive_letter>:\Program Files\Microsoft ISA Server\CLIENTS.
2. Right-click the **CLIENTS** folder, and click the **Properties** command. Then click the **Web Sharing** tab, as shown in Figure 7.10.

Figure 7.10 The Web Sharing Tab

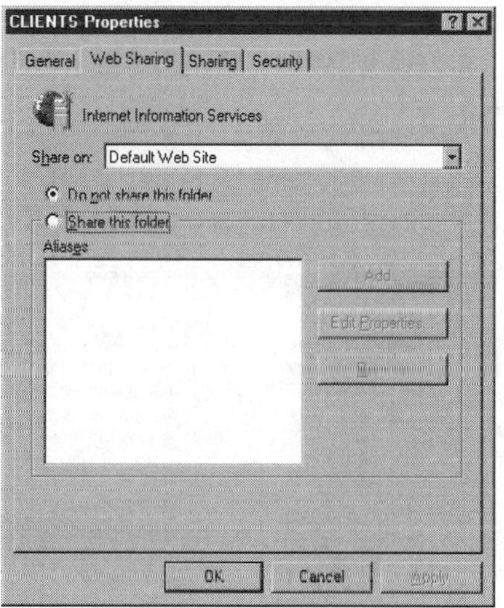

3. Click the option button for **Share this folder**. You will see the **Edit Alias** dialog box, shown in Figure 7.11.
4. In the **Edit Alias** dialog box, ensure that the **Read** permission is checked. Do not allow anyone to write to the folder. Allow **Scripts** to be executed. You can also change the name of the virtual directory in the **Alias** text box. Click **OK,** then click **OK** again.
5. From the **Administrative Tools** menu, open the **Internet Information Services** console. You should see the virtual directory for this folder listed in the left pane, as shown in Figure 7.12.

Figure 7.11 The Edit Alias Dialog Box

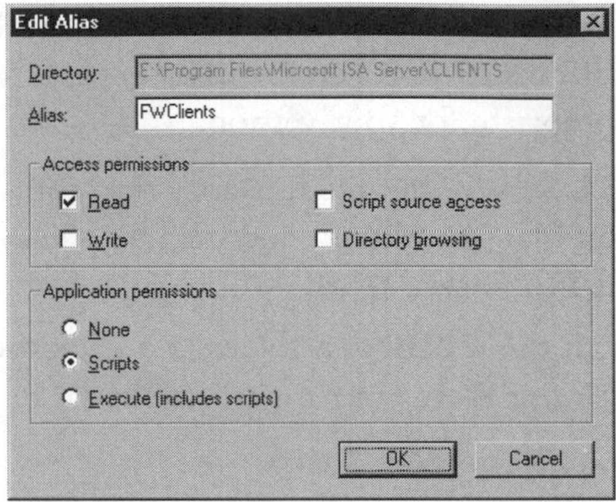

Figure 7.12 The Internet Information Services Console

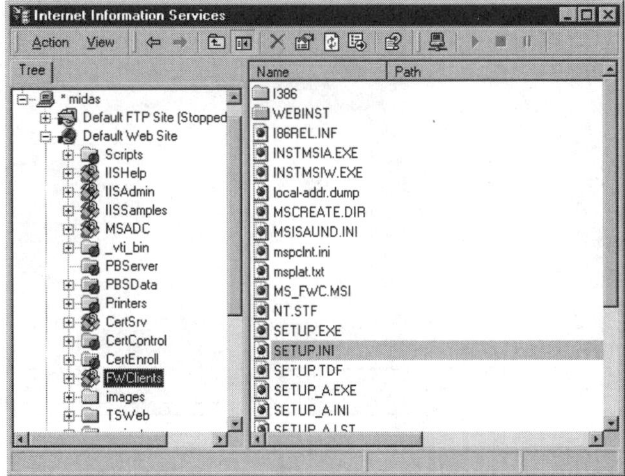

6. Go to a client onto which you need to install the firewall client. Open Internet Explorer, and type in the URL http://<server_**name>/ <virtual_directory_name>/webisnt** and press **Enter**.
7. The ISA Server Client Installation for Microsoft ISA Server 2000 Web page will appear, as shown in Figure 7.13. To install the firewall client software, click the link, and the installation process will begin. The installation will proceed in the same manner as it did in the previous exercise.

Figure 7.13 The ISA Client Installation Page

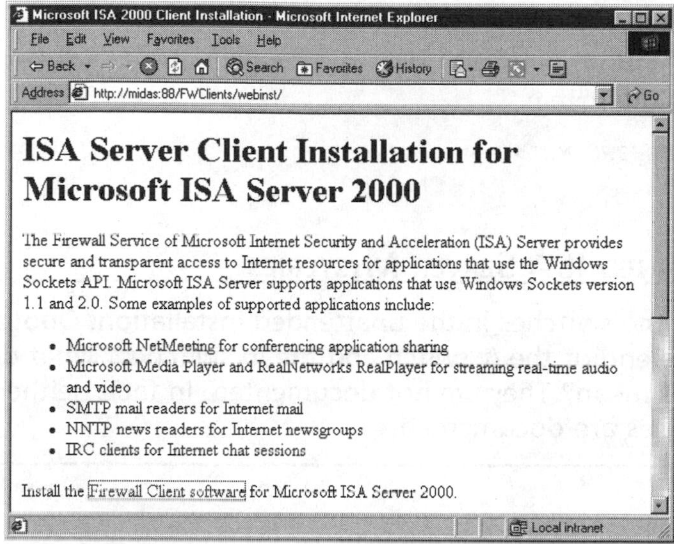

Command-Line Parameters for a Scripted Installation

If you prefer a scripted installation, you can use the command-line parameters shown in Figure 7.14.

Figure 7.14 Command-Line Parameters for Client Setup

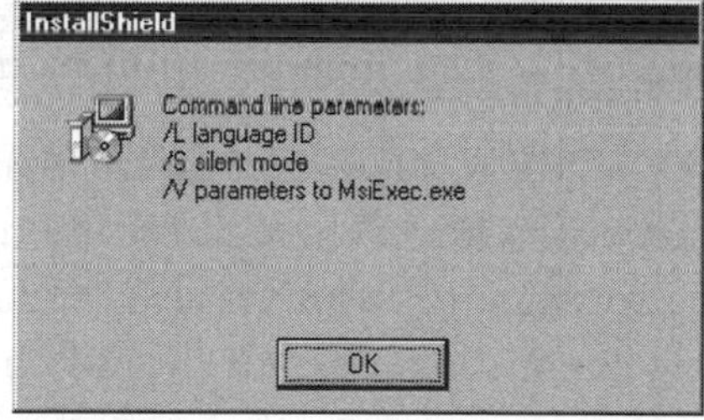

The parameters for a command-line or scripted setup are:

```
/L Language ID
/S Silent Mode
/V parameters for MsiExec.exe
```

For complete information on the MsiExec.exe command-line parameters, check out article Q230781 at Microsoft TechNet's site, www.microsoft.com/technet.

If you want to perform a silent, unattended installation, use the following command-line string:

```
<Path_to_MS_FWC.MSI>\setup/v"/qn"
```

Unexplained ISA Server Mysteries

Note the switches in the unattended installation. Quote marks are used at the end of the /v switch and the /n switches. What do these quote marks mean? They are not documented. In fact, neither the /q nor the /n switches are documented.

Automatic Installation

In a company with 250,000 desktops, you probably don't want to manually install them all yourself. You could script the installation using a logon script, but this doesn't provide automatic application management. A better solution is to take advantage of the Active Directory Software Deployment and Management feature. To make this feature work, you need an Active Directory domain and the computers and users need to be members of an Active Directory domain.

Using the software deployment tools included with Windows 2000 Group Policy, you can either assign or publish an application to users and/or computers:

- **Assign software** When you assign software, that software will be installed on the network client. There are some minor differences between assigning software to users versus computers. However, in the case of the firewall client software, you should choose to assign the software to users in your domain.
- **Publish software** When you publish software, that software is made available to uses via the Add/Remove Programs applet in the Control Panel.

When you use the software deployment tools in the Windows 2000 Group Policy objects, you'll typically have an organizational unit (OU) or a set of OUs to which you will make the software available.

Undocumented ISA

Note that we recommend that you assign the firewall client software to users rather than computers. The reason for this preference is that if you assign the firewall client software to a computer, the installation begins before the logon dialog box appears, and there is a significant delay before the log on dialog appears. This delay could be so long that users will call the Help Desk complaining of the problem. If you want to assign the firewall client software to computers, you should do it over the weekend and restart all the computers so that the software has time to install before anyone tries to log on.

Let's go over the steps for assigning and publishing Software. We'll start with assigning software to *computers*.

Assigning Software to Computers

In this exercise we'll see how to go about assigning software to computers in an OU:

1. Open the Active Directory Users and Computers console from the Administrative Tools menu.
2. Right-click the OU to which you want to assign the software, and click **Properties**.
3. In the OU's **Properties** dialog box, click the **Group Policy** tab. Click the topmost Group Policy Object (GPO) in the list, and then click **Edit**.
4. Expand the **Computer Configuration** and **User Configuration** nodes in the left pane. Next, expand the **Software Settings** nodes.
5. Under the **Computer Configuration\Software Settings** node, right-click the **Software installation** node, click **New**, and then click **Package**, as shown in the Figure 7.15.
6. The **Open** dialog box appears. Drill down to the network location where the shared firewall client installation files are located. Note that you can copy these files to another server on your network if you want to avoid the traffic on the internal interface of your ISA server. Once you get to the shared folder, select the **MS_FWC.MSI** file, and click the **Open** button.

Figure 7.15 Beginning to Create a New Package in Software Installation

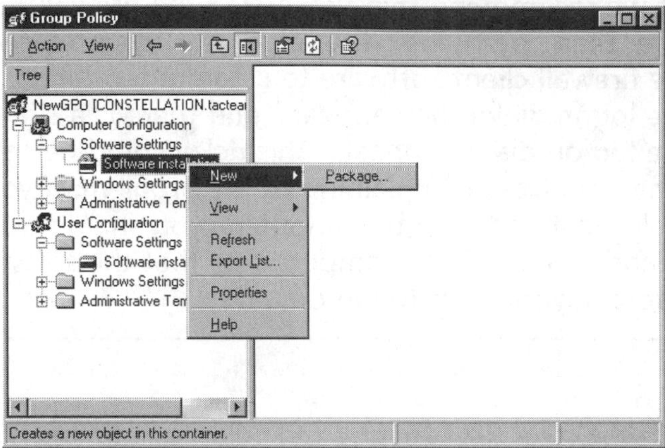

7. The **Deploy Software** dialog box will appear, as it does in Figure 7.16. Select the **Assigned** option button, and click **OK**.

Figure 7.16 The Deploy Software Dialog Box

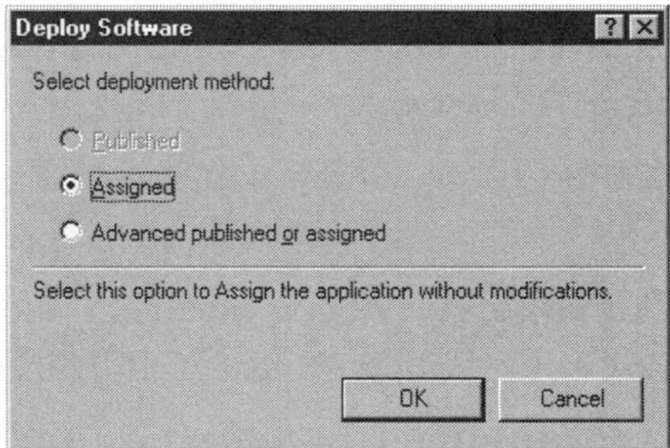

8. The package will appear in the right pane of the GPO and will be applied to all computers within the OU without user intervention.

Publishing Software to Users

In this walkthrough, we'll see how to publish software to users.

1. Open the **Active Directory Users and Computers** console via the **Administrative Tools** menu. Right-click the OU to which you want to publish the software. Right-click that OU, and click **Properties**.
2. Click the **Group Policy** tab, then click the topmost GPO, and click the **Edit** button to open the GPO for editing.

3. Expand the **User Configuration** node in the left pane, and then expand the **Software installation** node and right-click it. Click the **New** command, then click the **Package** command.
4. Drill down to the location of the installation files in the same way you did in the last walkthrough. Click the **MS_FWC.MSI** file, and click the **Open** button. The **Deploy Software** dialog box appears, as shown in Figure 7.17.

Figure 7.17 The Deploy Software Dialog Box

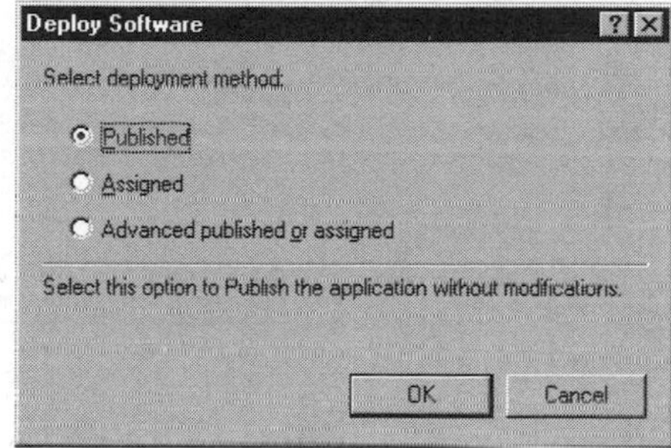

5. In the **Deploy Software** dialog box, select the **Published** option button, and then click **OK**. The **Microsoft Firewall Client** will now appear in the right pane of the GPO console.
6. After completing the software installation steps, log on as a user in that OU, and open the **Add/Remove Programs** applet from the **Control Panel**. Click the **Add New Programs** button in the left pane, and you should see the program advertised as in Figure 7.18.

Configuring the Firewall Client

You can begin to configure the firewall client via the graphical user interface (GUI). You will notice after installation of the firewall client that there is a new icon in the system tray; this icon should look like an electrical plug with a green, up-pointing arrow. If there is a red, down-pointing arrow, the firewall client has not connected to the Firewall Service on the ISA server.

You can enter the configuration interface either through the Firewall Client icon in the Control Panel, or you can right-click the Firewall Client icon in the tray and click the **Configure** command. Either method will present you with the dialog box shown in Figure 7.19.

Figure 7.18 The Published Application Appears in the Add/Remove Programs Applet

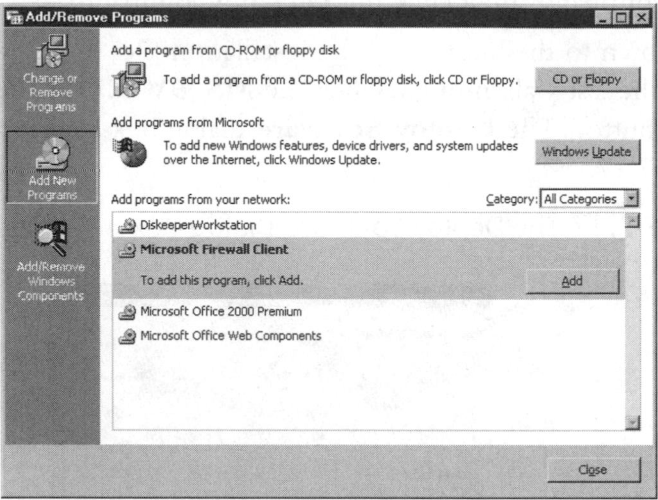

Figure 7.19 The Firewall Client Options Dialog Box

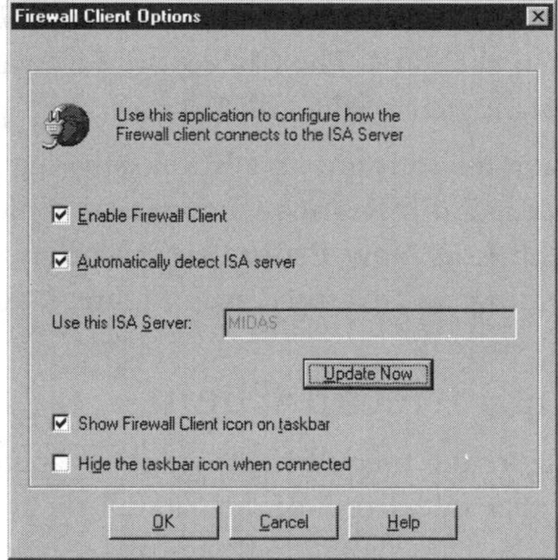

The **Enable Firewall Client** check box is used to enable and disable the firewall client software.

The **Automatically detect ISA server** check box allows the firewall client to use DHCPINFORM messages to query a DNS server to find the ISA server to which it can connect. We'll talk more about how to configure this setup later in the chapter.

The **Use this ISA Server** text box allows you to manually enter the name of the ISA server to which you want the firewall client to connect. You can also enter an IP address instead of a name. Note that this option is not available if you select the **Automatically detect ISA Server** option.

The **Show Firewall Client icon on taskbar** check box determines whether or not the firewall client icon will appear in the system tray. The **Hide the taskbar icon when connected** hides the taskbar icon when the firewall client successfully connects to the ISA server's Firewall Service. The icon will appear with a red downward-pointing arrow if the connection is lost.

Automating the Configuration of the Firewall Client

In a widespread deployment scenario, you might want to automate the configuration of the firewall client software. The firewall client supports a process known as *autodiscovery,* in which the firewall client is able to query either a DHCP server via a DHCPINFORM message or directly query a DNS server via a DNS query for the name wpad.<domain_name>.

The following network client operating systems support firewall client autodiscovery:

- Windows 2000
- Windows 98/ME
- Windows XP (Whistler)

Note that neither Windows 95 nor Windows NT is included on this list.

Configuring DHCP to Support Firewall Client Autodiscovery

If you will have your clients use a DHCP server for the autodiscovery process, make sure that the client can contact the DHCP server. All DHCP messages are broadcast messages. This includes the DHCPINFORM message used by the firewall client to query the DHCP server:

1. Open the **DHCP** console via the **Administrative Tools** menu on your Windows 2000 server. Note that you do not need to use a Windows 2000 DHCP server to enable autodiscovery. However, you must be able to configure the appropriate DHCP option as outlined in these steps.

2. Make sure that a scope is configured for each network ID for which there are firewall clients. Note that the firewall clients *need to be DHCP clients* to use this method. Expand the scope that you want to configure to support the wpad entry that will be used by the firewall client for autoconfiguration. If you plan to implement this on multiple scopes, you should consider making this a server option rather than a scope option.
3. In the left pane, right-click your DHCP server's name, and then click the **Set Predefined Options** command. Click the **Add** button. You should see something like the screen that appears in Figure 7.20.

Figure 7.20 Adding a DHCP Option to Support Autodiscovery

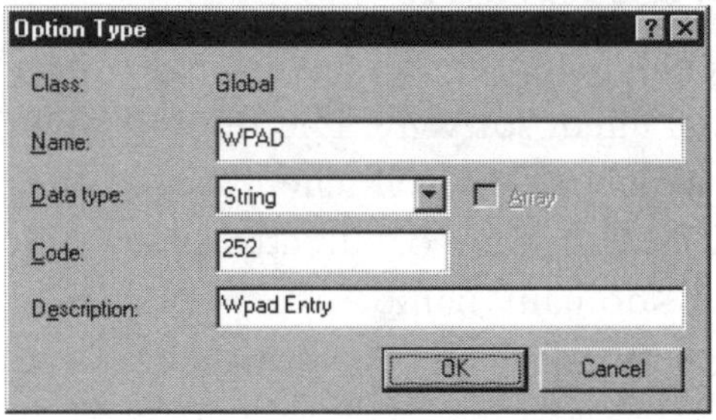

Option Type

Class: Global

Name: WPAD

Data type: String ☐ Array

Code: 252

Description: Wpad Entry

OK Cancel

4. In the **Option Type** dialog box, type in the following information:

```
Name: WPAD
Code: 252
Data Type: String
```

5. Then click **OK**.
6 In the **Predefined Options and Values** dialog box, type in the string value **http://ISA_Server_Name:Autodiscovery_Port_Number/Wpad.dat**. Your dialog box should look like the one in Figure 7.21. The Autodiscovery Port Number is the one defined in the server settings. The default port number of publishing autodiscovery information is port 80. We'll talk later in this chapter about how to change this value.
7. Click **OK** to make this new DHCP option available for assignment.
8. In the left pane of the **DHCP** console, right-click the **Scope Options** node under the scope of interest, then click the **Configure Options** command.

Figure 7.21 The Predefined Options and Values Dialog Box

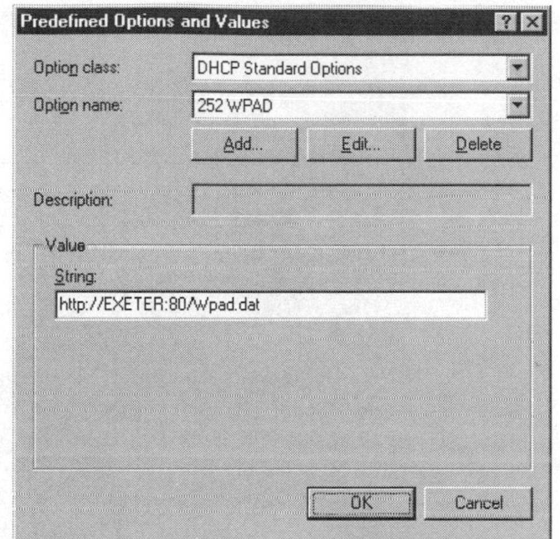

9. On the **General** tab, scroll down the list of DHCP options until you get to **252 WPAD**. Put a checkmark in the check box for this option, then click **OK**. The new option should appear in the right pane as a new scope option.

Now firewall clients from the network ID matching the scope will receive the URL from the DHCP server and will be able to obtain autoconfiguration information from the ISA server.

Configuring DNS for Automatic Firewall Client Discovery

You can configure DNS to provide autodiscovery information to your firewall clients. When configuring DNS for firewall clients, the ISA server must listen on port 80 for autodiscovery requests:

1. Open the **DNS** console via the **Administrative Tools** menu.
2. Expand the server name, and then expand the **Forward Lookup Zones** node in the left pane. Right-click the domain in which your ISA server belongs, and click **New Alias**.
3. In the **New Resource Record** dialog box, type **wpad** in the **Alias name** text box, and type in the FQDN for the ISA server in the **Fully qualified name for target host** text box. Your entry should look like Figure 7.22. Be sure to include the trailing periods. Then click **OK**.

Figure 7.22 Configuring a CNAME Record for Autodiscovery

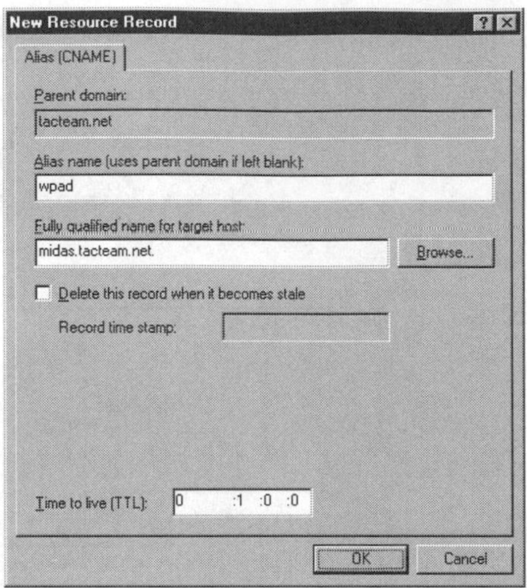

4. From the command prompt of the DNS server, type the command **nslookup wpad.<your_domain_name>** and press **Enter**. The wpad CNAME entry should resolve to your ISA server, as shown in Figure 7.23.

Figure 7.23 Resolving the Wpad Entry via DNS

NOTE

Firewall clients that use DNS to resolve the name of the wpad alias must be configured to query a DNS server on the internal network. You will not be able to use the DNS server configured on the external interface of the ISA server to query the DNS server on your internal network that contains the entry for your wpad CNAME record. A possible exception to this rule occurs if you publish your internal DNS server to be accessible to Internet hosts.

There are a couple of problems associated with using DNS for the wpad entry. First, you must use port 80 on the ISA server to publish autodiscovery information. If you use DHCP, you can configure autodiscovery to be published on any port number. Another issue with using DNS is that you must configure a wpad entry for each ISA Server client domain. If you have firewall clients in multiple domains, you need to create the wpad entry in each of those domains.

The most compelling reason to use DHCP, rather than DNS, when configuring your wpad entries is that DCHP allows you a more granular approach to assigning your ISA servers to the network clients. The DNS solution allows you to assign only a single ISA server to an entire domain. Many Windows 2000 domains are distributed over a wide area that can include multiple sites. It is unlikely that a multisite network will want all network clients to use the same ISA server, especially if you plan to take advantage of Web proxy chaining. When you use DHCP to configure your wpad entries, you can create different entries on a per-scope or per-server basis. This capability allows you to control, on a network ID basis, which ISA server is used for network clients.

Configuring Autodiscovery during Client Setup

You can ensure that firewall clients use the autodiscovery mechanism during setup by configuring the appropriate parameters in the **Firewall Client Properties** client configuration dialog box. Follow these steps to enable autoconfiguration at setup:

1. Open the **ISA Server Management** console, then expand the **Servers and Arrays** node in the left pane. Expand the Server name node, then click the **Client Configuration** node.
2. Double-click the **Firewall Client** entry in the right pane. You will see a screen like the one in Figure 7.24.
3. Enter either the DNS name or the IP address that the firewall clients will configure themselves with during setup. If you want to enable autodiscovery on these clients, simply place a checkmark in the check box for **Enable ISA Firewall automatic discovery in Firewall Client**. Then click **OK**.

After performing these steps, the clients will configure themselves to use the ISA server that you have configured in this dialog box.

Figure 7.24 The Firewall Client Properties General Tab

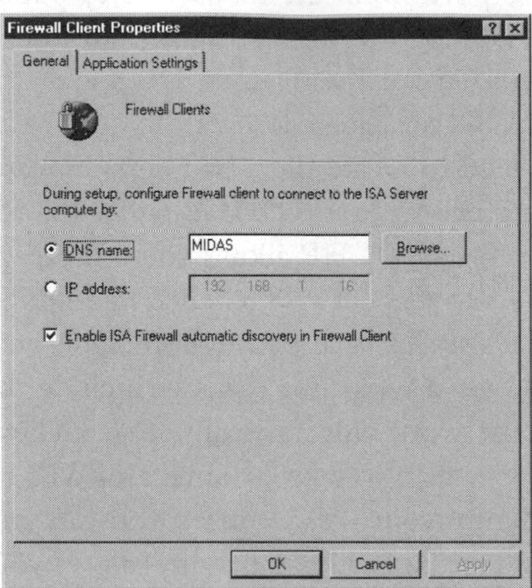

UNDOCUMENTED ISA

When you look at the dialog box used to automatically configure the firewall client during setup, do you notice something odd? You are given the choice to configure the firewall client to a particular server by DNS or by IP address. You are also given the option to enable automatic discovery. However, you do not have a choice to *only* allow automatic discovery. If you select the **DNS name** option button, you must put a name in the text box. If you choose IP address, you have the option of leaving it blank. What if you want the client to use just autodiscovery and not use either the DNS name or the IP address?

The answer is related to how the firewall client uses the autodiscovery information. The wpad entry only tells the firewall client what ISA server to query for more information. It does *not* tell the firewall client what ISA server it should use to connect to the Firewall Service.

For example, if you put in the IP address 0.0.0.0, the firewall client will query the DHCP or DNS server to get the address of the machine that contains the autodiscovery information. Once the firewall client connects to the address listed in the wpad entry in DNS or DHCP, it obtains the address 0.0.0.0, as configured in this dialog box. Since this address is bogus, the client will not be able to connect to the Firewall Service on the ISA server, even though it was able to connect to the ISA server to obtain the autodiscovery information. The reason is that the ISA server sent to the firewall client the information you configured in this dialog box.

When you select the **Enable ISA Firewall automatic discovery in Firewall Client** option, it configures the firewall client, during the setup of the firewall client software, to use autodiscovery. If you do not select this option, the firewall client software uses the address configured in this dialog box during setup, but it is not able to use autodiscovery unless you manually select this option after setup has completed. Disabling this function *does not* prevent a client manually configured to use autodiscovery from using this feature.

Automatically Configure the Firewall Client's Web Browser

The Web browser on the firewall client can be set up automatically when the firewall client is installed. The following steps determine firewall client browser configuration:

1. Open the **ISA Management** console, expand the **Servers and Arrays** node in the left pane, and then expand the Server name. Click the **Client Configuration** node.
2. Double-click the **Web Browser** entry in the right pane. You should see what appears in Figure 7.25.

Figure 7.25 The Web Browser Properties Dialog Box

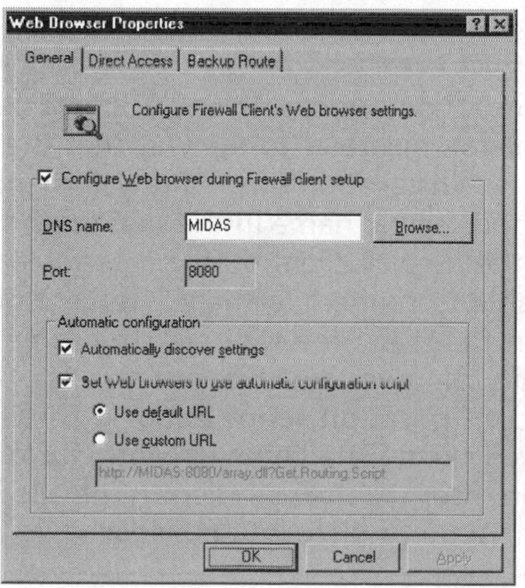

3. Place a checkmark in the check box **Configure Web browser during Firewall client setup** to have the browser configured automatically when the firewall client is installed.
4. Enter the DNS name of the ISA server in the text box for **DNS name**. You can also use the **Browse** button to find the name of the ISA server. Note that the **Port** entry defaults to 8080 and is not configurable via this interface. That is because the listener for outbound HTTP requests is configured in the **Outbound Listening** page of the Server Properties dialog box. If you change the port number of the outbound listener, that new port number will be reflected here as well.
5. In the **Automatic Configuration** frame, you can configure whether you want the client browsers to **Automatically discover settings**. When you enable the browser to automatically discover settings, the client can be moved from location to location and query either a DNS or DHCP server and find the ISA server to which to connect. You can also enable the client to take advantage of the automatic configuration script by enabling the **Set Web browsers to use automatic configuration script**. When the browser is set to use the autoconfiguration script, it will be able to take advantage of the distributed Web cache, which will reduce the number of hops required to access a cached Web page. We'll talk more about this issue in the "Web Proxy Cache" section of Chapter 8.

NOTE

All the configuration options on the **General** page of the **Web Browser Properties** dialog box refer to the way that the Web browser is configured during the installation of the firewall client software. For example, if you put a bogus server name in the **DNS name** text box, the Web browser on the firewall client during setup will use this invalid name and will not be able to connect to the ISA server unless you manually change the setting in the Web browser itself. The same is true for the **Automatically discover settings** and the **Set Web browsers to use automatic configuration script** options. These options are applied during firewall client installation only and have no effect on the browser configuration after the firewall client is installed. Contrast this with the firewall client settings discussed previously.

6. Click the Direct Access tab. You will see a screen similar to the one in Figure 7.26.

Figure 7.26 The Direct Access Tab

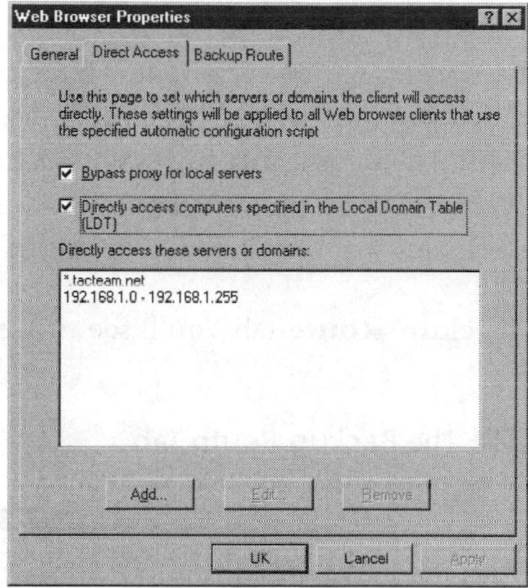

7. On the **Direct Access** tab, configure the IP addresses and/or domain name to which you want the Web proxy clients to directly connect without having to go through the ISA server.

   Now, you might be wondering why you have to do this, since the LAT is used to determine which hosts are local and which are remote. The reason is that the Web proxy client does not check the LAT before issuing requests, because Web proxy client requests do not get passed through the firewall client Winsock .DLLs. For this reason, you should configure the Web proxy client to bypass the ISA server when connecting to local hosts. This bypass will reduce the amount of traffic on your ISA server's internal interface.

   When you select the **Bypass proxy for local servers** option, any destinations that contain a dotted address format are treated as remote, unless you add them to the list of **Directly access these servers or domains** by clicking the **Add** button. For example, http://shinder would be treated as local, but http://shinder.tacteam.net would be treated as remote, even if these URLs both represented the same machine on the internal network. When the firewall client determines that an address is remote, the DNS query is sent to the ISA server for name resolution, which is accomplished through the ISA server's DNS proxy feature. When the firewall client determines that the address is local, the DNS query will be passed to the preferred DNS server configured on the firewall client TCP/IP Properties dialog box.

Because Windows 2000 environments are increasingly dependent on DNS for name resolution in the internal network, its is important that you add the domain names for all your internal domains to the list, so that name resolution for internal resources does not fail.

The **Directly access computers specified in the Local Domain Table (LDT)** option allows you to directly access machines located in domains that are included in the LDT.

8. Click the **Backup Route** tab. You'll see the screen that appears in Figure 7.27.

Figure 7.27 The Backup Route Tab

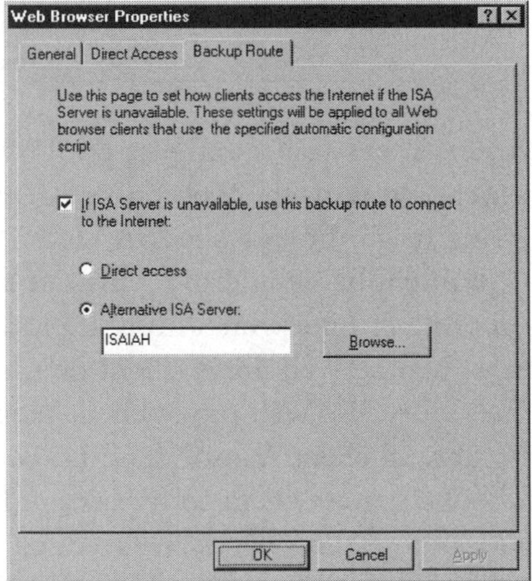

9. The **Backup Route** page allows you to configure the autoconfiguration script to tell the Web proxy client what to do when the Web Proxy Service on the ISA server is not available. The **Direct Access** option tells the Web proxy client to attempt to directly access the Web object. Of course, if the Web proxy client does not have a method, such as a modem, to directly access the resource, it won't work.

If you choose to redirect the request to an **Alternative ISA Server**, type in the name or IP address of another ISA server. If the Web Proxy Service on this ISA server becomes unavailable, the Web proxy client request will be forwarded to the ISA server configured here.

NOTE

Configuring a backup route for Web proxy clients allows you another measure of fault tolerance for your Web access solution. Since the requests from the Web proxy clients are automatically redirected to another machine when the connection becomes unavailable, users should not notice anything amiss. When you configure another ISA server as a backup, you must configure the outbound listener on the backup server to listen for requests on port 80. You must also stop all other services that might be running on port 80, such as the WWW service on an IIS Server installation on the same machine or the autodiscovery publishing information. You can run these other services, but you must change the port numbers they use to provide their services.

The reason that you must use port 80 on the backup machine is that when the Web proxy client "fails over" to the backup machine, it is *not* configured as a Web proxy client to the backup machine. Therefore, rather than sending the requests to the default ISA server Web Proxy Service port 8080, the client sends requests to port 80, as it would any other "normal" browser request. Keep this caveat in mind if you plan to use the backup machine as a primary gateway for other Web proxy clients on your network.

Firewall Service Client Configuration Files

When a machine is configured as a firewall client, two files are installed on the client computer that are used by the firewall client software:

- Mspclnt.ini
- Msplat.txt

Both of these files are created on the ISA server and copied to the firewall client via the control channel. The contents of these configuration files are determined by the choices you've made in the **Client Configuration** node at the ISA server.

The Mspclnt.ini File

The master copy of this file is located in the CLIENTS folder in the ISA Server folder hierarchy on the ISA server. You can also access this file via the default share created on the ISA server: \\<ISA_Server_name>\mspclnt. The initial copy of the file on the firewall client is located at \Program Files\Microsoft Firewall Client\internal_setup.

You should *not* directly edit this file unless there are configuration changes you need to make that cannot be done through the ISA Management console. Any changes to the file are made on the ISA server, and then the file is downloaded to the firewall client over the control channel on a periodic basis (by default, every 6 hours). You can view the file on either the ISA server or on the local machine, using any text editor. For example, here are the contents of the author's mspclnt.ini file:

```
;
; This file should not be edited.
; Changes to the client configuration should only be made using ISA
Management.
;
[Common]
WWW-Proxy=MIDAS
Set Browsers to use Proxy=1
Set Browsers to use Auto Config=1
Set Browsers to use Auto Detect=1
AutoDetect ISA Servers=1
WebProxyPort=8080
Configuration Url=http://MIDAS:8080/array.dll?Get.Routing.Script
Port=1745
ServerVersion=11
Configuration Refresh Time (Hours)=6
Re-check Inaccessible Server Time (Minutes)=10
Refresh Give Up Time (Minutes)=15
Inaccessible Servers Give Up Time (Minutes)=2
LocalDomains=.tacteam.net
[Servers Ip Addresses]
Name=MIDAS
```

```
[Master Config]
Path1=\\MIDAS\mspclnt\
[inetinfo]
Disable=1
[icq]
RemoteBindUdpPorts=0
ServerBindTcpPorts=0,1025-5000
NameResolutionForLocalHost=P
[Internal]
scp=9,10,11
[svchost]
Disable=1
[rvplayer]
RemoteBindUdpPorts=6970-7170
LocalBindTcpPorts=7070
[outlook]
Disable=0
[mapisp32]
Disable=0
[winlogon]
Disable=1
[wspsrv]
Disable=1
[w3proxy]
Disable=1
[services]
Disable=1
[spoolss]
Disable=1
[exchng32]
Disable=0
[net2fone]
ServerBindTcpPorts=0
[kernel32]
Disable=1
```

```
[realplay]
RemoteBindUdpPorts=6970-7170
LocalBindTcpPorts=7070
[rpcss]
Disable=1
[lsass]
Disable=1
[raplayer]
RemoteBindUdpPorts=6970-7170
LocalBindTcpPorts=7070
```

We can't go over all these settings here, but some of them are of interest. Note the settings in the [Common] section. This section provides some key values that determine how the firewall client interacts with the Firewall Service on the ISA server. One interesting value that cannot be changed via the GUI is:

```
Configuration Refresh Time (Hours)=6
```

This value determines how often the client downloads the mspclnt.ini file. You can edit the file to change the refresh interval.

If you would like a complete listing of all the entries in this file, check out the ISA Server Help File. Open the Help File and click the **Search** tab. In the text box, type **mspclnt.ini**. You should see four responses, of which the third-ranking entry gives you the information you need. The title of the section is "Configuring Firewall Client Settings."

The Msplat.txt File

The msplat.txt file contains the entries you've configured in the LAT. The file is stored on the ISA server and copied to the firewall clients periodically via the control channel. Again, you should not manually edit this file. Limit your configuration of this file via the ISA Server Management interface.

If you open the msplat.txt file in a text editor, it will look something like this:

```
10.0.0.0        10.255.255.255
169.254.0.0     169.254.255.255
172.16.0.0      172.31.255.255
192.168.0.0     192.168.255.255
192.168.1.0     192.168.1.255
192.168.10.0    192.168.10.255
```

```
224.0.0.0       255.255.255.254
127.255.255.255
```

Of course, your configuration could be different. Note that the file contains either ranges of IP addresses or single IP addresses, followed by a hard return. If you enter a single computer's IP address, the first and second entries on the line will have the same address.

The LAT is copied over to the firewall clients on a regular basis (6 hours, by default), and any changes you make to this file (on the client side) will be overwritten during the next refresh. If you want to create a custom LAT for a particular client, you must create a locallat.txt file.

If you need to include computers that you want to be treated as local, even though they are not included in the ISA server's copy of the LAT, you can create the locallat.txt file. The firewall client software evaluates the entries in *both* the msplat.txt *and* the locallat.txt files in order to determine whether a request is for a trusted host or an untrusted host. Perform the following steps to create a locallat.txt file:

1. Open **notepad.exe** or another text editor.
2. Save the Open file as **locallat**. Make sure that the file is saved as locallat.txt.
3. If you want to include a range of computers, type in the first IP address, then a space, and then the final IP address in the range. If you want to include a single computer, put the same IP in twice, separated by a space.
4. Make sure that the file is in the same folder as the msplat.txt file.

The Wspcfg.ini File

There could be some applications you want the firewall client to support that require special configuration changes. In order to achieve this end, you can create a wspcfg.ini file. This file is almost exclusively used to publishing servers located on the internal network and was used extensively in Proxy Server 2.0 environments for server publishing.

ISA Server allows you to publish servers by configuring them as SecureNAT clients, therefore virtually obviating the need to set up the published servers as firewall (Winsock) clients. Because the published servers are not configured as Winsock (firewall) clients, there is no need to configure a wspcfg.ini file to support server publishing.

However, not all protocols are supported for the SecureNAT client. Complex protocols that require multiple back-channels and that do not have an intelligent application filter on the ISA server to help them require more support than the SecureNAT client can provide. Protocols that imbed IP addresses and port numbers in the Application layer cannot be supported by SecureNAT clients, and it might be easier to configure a wspcfg.ini file for a firewall client than to build your own application filter. You need to configure these servers as firewall clients and configure a custom wspcfg.ini file for them.

It is beyond the scope of this book to cover the issue of configuring the wspcfg.ini files, because in ISA Server the SecureNAT client configuration supports virtually all configurations for widely used Internet services published to the Internet. However, if you do run into an unusual situation, you can write to the authors of this book at solutions@syngress.com, and we will be happy to address your specialized questions via e-mail and the book's Web site.

The Web Proxy Client

A Web proxy client is a CERN-compliant Web browser or other application that can be configured to send requests to the Web Proxy Service on the ISA server. Web proxy clients are not dependent on being configured as SecureNAT clients, nor are they dependent on the firewall client software. If all you require is access to the "Web protocols" (HTTP, HTTPS, FTP, and Gopher) and you can configure the browser independently of any other network configuration on that machine.

Like the SecureNAT client, the Web proxy client is platform independent. As long as the browser is CERN compliant, it can be configured as a Web proxy client.

Like the firewall client, the Web proxy client is able to send user information to the Web Proxy Service, which can be used for user- or group-based access controls. If you want to support authenticated access to Web protocols only, you do not need to install the firewall client; the Web proxy client will be able to send credentials to the Web Proxy Service. The advantage to doing this is that you acquire access control and the ability to identify per user utilization statistics, since the username will appear in the Web Proxy Service's log files.

Why You Should Configure the Web Proxy Client

Even if your computer is set up as a SecureNAT or firewall client, there is another major advantage to configuring your machines as Web proxy clients, and this relates to authentication issues.

The problem with authentication relates to how the SecureNAT and firewall clients are connected to the Web Proxy Service via the HTTP redirector filter. As we discussed earlier, when SecureNAT and firewall client computers send HTTP requests, the requests *could* be intercepted by the HTTP redirector filter and passed to the Web Proxy Service. The default behavior of the HTTP redirector filter is to pass these requests to the Web Proxy Service.

The problem with forwarding SecureNAT and firewall client requests to the Web Proxy Service is that information about the user, which could be used for authentication by the Web Proxy Service, is lost in the process of passing it up from the Firewall Service to the Web Proxy Service (remember that SecureNAT client requests always pass through the Firewall Service, too).

When an HTTP request is stripped of its credentials and passed to the Web Proxy Service, several things can happen. First, if *no protocol and site/content rule* allows for *anonymous access*, the request will fail. In fact, it will fail and you won't have any idea why it failed, because the Web Proxy Service *will not* ask for credentials. It'll simply tell you that the page is forbidden.

Later, when we configure protocol and site/content rules, you'll see that there is no option to configure "anonymous" access. In the context of protocol and site/content rules, anonymous access is synonymous with *all requests*. So, if you do not have a protocol rule and a site/content rule *somewhere* that allows for all users to access *both* the HTTP protocol *and* a particular site, the request will fail.

NOTE

This represents a departure from how protocol and site/content rules are normally processed. As you'll see later, **Deny** rules are normally processed before **Allow** rules. However, in the special situation of HTTP requests that are passed up from the Firewall Service to the Web Proxy Service, the rules engine seeks a rule that allows for anonymous connections before denying the request.

However, let's suppose that we've got a protocol rule that allows everyone to access the HTTP protocol and that we also have decided to leave alone the default site/content rule, which allows everyone to access all sites and content at all times. Given this scenario, the Web Proxy Service will accept the request that has been stripped of its credentials.

However, we're not entirely out of the woods yet. This is because the Web Proxy Service can be configured to force authentication. If you force authentication for nonauthenticated Web Proxy Service requests, the request will fail. This is in spite of the fact that the rules engine allowed the request. The bottom line is that you should configure your browsers as Web proxy clients.

DNS Considerations for the Web Proxy Client

DNS issues for the Web proxy client are similar to those confronted with the firewall client. The ISA server can perform DNS proxy services for the Web proxy client when Internet names need to be resolved. However, if you need to resolve local names, you must configure the Web proxy client with the address of an internal DNS server that can resolve these names.

Configuring the Web Proxy Client

You will get the best functionality, and best Web experience, if you use Internet Explorer 5.0 or later. Although the Web Proxy Service supports all CERN-compliant browsers, most Web sites are optimized for the Microsoft Internet Explorer. With this in mind, let's go through the configuration of the Web proxy client for Internet Explorer 5.0/5.5:

1. Open Internet Explorer and click the **Tools** menu, then click **Internet Options**.
2. Click the **Connections** tab. You should see something like Figure 7.28. Note the **Dial-up settings** frame. This is a list of dial-up networking connections that are configured on this computer. Typically, you would not have any dial-up connections on a corporate network, because modem connections within the network are a very bad thing and represent a major security hole. However, if you work in an environment that allows this sort of thing, you will see connections like those shown here.
3. Typically, you select the option to **Never dial a connection**. However, if you want to allow the clients to use a direct connection to the Internet as a backup route, you can select the **Dial whenever a network connection is not present** option. This choice allows the Web proxy client to initiate a dial-up connection when the Web Proxy Service on the ISA server is unavailable. Now click the **LAN Settings** button.
4. The LAN Settings page appears in Figure 7.29.

Figure 7.28 The Connections Tab in Internet Explorer

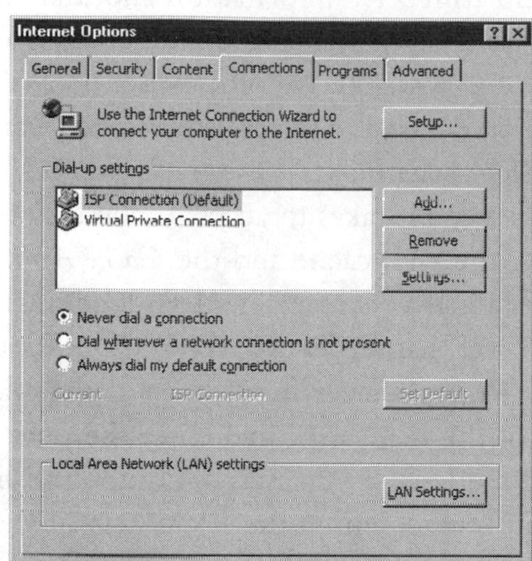

Figure 7.29 The LAN Settings Dialog Box

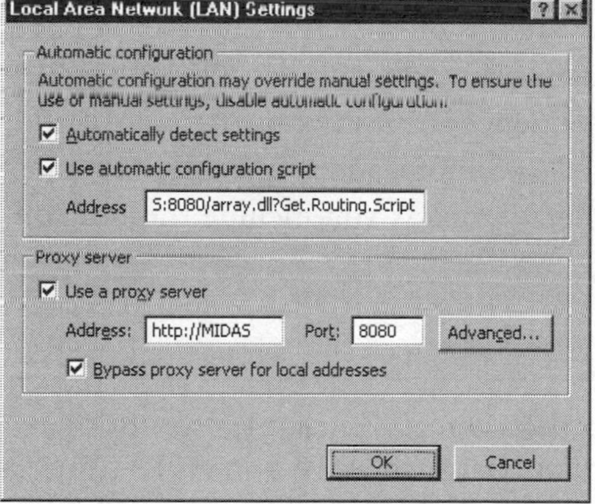

5. On the **Local Area Network (LAN) Settings** page, you make the specific configuration changes required for the Web Proxy client:

   The **Automatically detect settings** option allows the Web proxy client to query a DNS or DHCP server to find the address of the ISA server and obtain configuration information. The configuration information includes only the port number to use to access the Web Proxy Service. It does *not* include other information, such as the address for the automatic configuration script.

The **Use automatic configuration script** option allows the Web proxy client to receive information about an array. The autoconfiguration script is a key player in the fault-tolerance and load-balancing features provided with the Web Proxy Service. When the Web proxy client is configured to use the script, it can take advantage of ISA Server's *distributed caching* scheme via *hierarchical routing*. This scheme significantly reduces the time it takes to access cached Web objects. We'll talk more about how the Web cache and the *Cache Array Routing Protocol (CARP)* works later in this chapter. The default address for this script is http://<server_name>:8080/array.dll?Get.Routing.Script.

In the **Proxy server** frame, type in the address (including the **http://**) of the ISA server and enter the port number of the listener for outbound requests. By default, the outbound listener is port 8080. The address can include either the IP address or the host name of the ISA server. If you use the host name, be sure that the Web proxy client is able to resolve this name.

Enable the **Bypass proxy server for local addresses** to conserve bandwidth on the internal interface of the ISA server. Remember, the Web proxy client does not interact with the Firewall Service and thus has no awareness of the LAT. Local addresses are configured via the **ISA Management** interface in the **Client Configuration** node. Remember the consequences of using this option. All addresses that contain "dots" are treated as remote, and the Web proxy client sends all such requests to the ISA server, unless you include the domain suffixes in the LDT.

NOTE

Configuring the Web proxy client also improves performance for Web requests. This is because HTTP and HTTP tunneled FTP requests do not have to be sent to the Firewall Service and then through the HTTP redirector filter before processing by the Web Proxy Service.

Autodiscovery and Client Configuration

We have already talked quite a bit about the autodiscovery options available to the Web proxy client. We actually work with two mechanisms when we automate the Web proxy client setup:

- Autodiscovery
- Autoconfiguration

When the Web proxy client is configured to support autodiscovery, it can take advantage of a wpad entry contained in either a DHCP or DNS server. The Web proxy client queries the DNS or DHCP server for the wpad entry and receives the address of the ISA server it should contact to obtain autoconfiguration information. Note that both the firewall client and the Web proxy client can take advantage of the same wpad entries.

It is worth noting that if you want to use the DHCP wpad entry, you must be using Internet Explorer 5.0 or later, and your system must be a Windows 2000 system configured as a DHCP client. If your system specifications do not fit these parameters, you should configure the wpad entry in the DNS.

Another problem with the DHCP wpad entry occurs when a Web proxy client that is also configured as a DHCP client attempts to query a DHCP server for the wpad entry, but the entry does not exist. If there is no wpad entry, the Web proxy client will fail. When a Web proxy client is connected to such networks, you should disable autodiscovery in the browser configuration.

Once the Web proxy client obtains the address of the ISA server, it sends a request to the ISA server for configuration information. To configure the ISA server to support such queries, perform the following steps:

1. In the **ISA Management** console, expand **Servers and Arrays**. Right-click your server name, and click **Properties**.
2. Click the **Auto Discovery** tab. You will see the screen that appears in Figure 7.30.
3. Here you can view, and change, the port used on internal interface for autodiscovery requests. The default setting is port 80. You can change the port number if you like. However, do not make this change with the intent of publishing a Web site on port 80 of the ISA server's internal interface, because it will not work. To allow the ISA server to publish autoconfiguration information to clients that have discovered it via a wpad entry, place a checkmark in the check box for **Publish automatic discovery information**.

Figure 7.30 The Auto Discovery Tab in the Server Properties Dialog Box

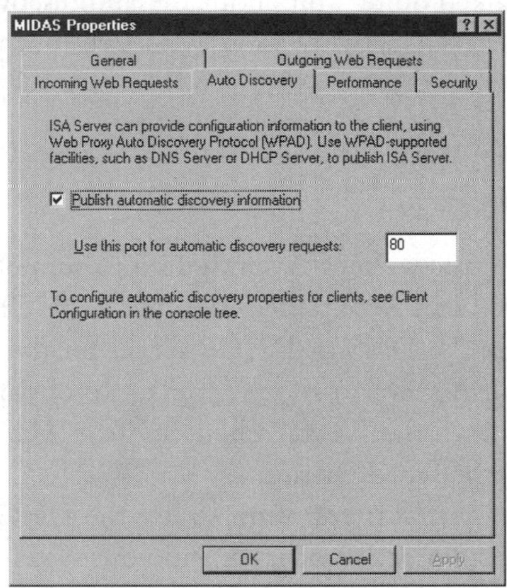

4. After enabling autodiscovery, you can configure the information that is sent to the Web proxy clients. This is done via the **Client Configuration** node in the **ISA Management** console. Double-click the **Web Browser** entry in the right pane. Note that only the configuration parameters on the **Direct Access** and **Backup Route** pages will be delivered to the autodiscovery Web proxy clients. The entries on the **General** tab apply to Web proxy clients that are configured during the setup of the firewall client software.

NOTE

You can configure the Web proxy client to use *both* autodiscovery and manual configuration entries. This approach is useful in the event that the autodiscovery process fails. If the Web proxy client cannot find an ISA server via autodiscovery, it can fall back on the manual entry.

Summary

In this chapter we covered ISA Server architecture and the setup and configuration of ISA Server clients. We saw how the ISA Server architecture is made up of the Web Proxy Service, the Firewall Service, the NAT Protocol driver, and the Content Download Service.

The Web Proxy Service allows CERN-compliant applications (typically, browsers) to access "Web protocols" through this service. The Web protocols include HTTP, HTTPS (SSL-protected HTTP), FTP, and Gopher. The Web Proxy Service in ISA Server is independent of Internet Information Server, which is a departure from the way the Web Proxy Service was implemented in Proxy Server 2.0. Web browsers configured as Web proxy clients send their requests to the Web Proxy Service through HTTP only. FTP and Gopher requests sent by the browser are tunneled HTTP requests. The default port on which the Web Proxy Service listens is port 8080. Requests to the Web Proxy Service can be authenticated, and access controls based on authentication information can be implemented for the Web Proxy Service and the protocols it supports.

The Firewall Service provides access to all Winsock protocols. These TCP- or UDP-based protocols are unaware of the fact that they are sending their requests to the Firewall Service and act as though they are directly connected to the Internet. The Firewall Service requires that its clients have firewall client software installed, which limits its utility. Some advantages of the Firewall Service are its ability to control access via users or groups because authentication information is sent to the Firewall Service and its ability to handle complex protocols. The Firewall Service communicates important connection and service management information through the Firewall Service control channel. The firewall client uses a dynamic port to connect to the Firewall Service's control port UDP or TCP 1745, dependent on the size of the messages being transferred.

The NAT Protocol driver allows clients from all operating systems to access Internet resources through the ISA server. The ISA Server NAT Protocol allows any network client to access the Internet as long as the default gateway of that client is configured so that requests destined for the Internet are routed to the internal interface of the ISA server. The NAT Protocol driver sends messages it receives from SecureNAT clients to the Firewall Service so that these requests can be sent through the ISA Server rules engine.

The Web proxy client is any CERN-compliant application that is configured to communicate with the Web Proxy Service on the ISA server. All operating systems support Web browsers that can be configured as Web proxy clients. To configure a browser as a Web proxy client, you must enter the configuration interface for the application and point it to the host name or IP address of the ISA server's interface IP address and the ISA server's outgoing Web requests listening port, which is port 8080 by default. Some Web proxy clients can be configured to automatically configure themselves based on wpad information contained on a DHCP or DNS server. Web proxy clients can take advantage of the redundancy and load-balancing features of the Cache Array Routing Protocol (CARP) through an autoconfiguration script. When Web proxy clients are configured to use the autoconfiguration script, they can take advantage of CARP's distributed caching via hierarchical routing.

The firewall client connects to the ISA server's Firewall Service through special firewall client software installed on Window-based computers supported by the firewall client software provided with ISA server. The firewall client can take advantage of complex protocols without requiring complex protocol definition configuration or Application filters. The firewall client can be automatically configured during software setup to connect to the appropriate ISA server and to have its browser configured automatically during the firewall client software installation. Like the Web proxy client, the firewall client can take advantage of wpad entries in a DNS or DHCP server to obtain the address of the ISA server that can provide it autoconfiguration information. Unlike the limited autoconfiguration information provided to a Web proxy client, the autoconfiguration information provided to the firewall client includes a rich amount of data about how the firewall client software and the Web browser on the firewall client should be configured.

The SecureNAT client is any computer, with any operating system, that has its default gateway set to an IP address that can route to the internal interface of the ISA server. On a simple network, the SecureNAT client has it default gateway set to the internal interface of the ISA server. On more complex or routed networks, the SecureNAT client has a default gateway set to a router interface that can route Internet-bound requests to the internal interface of the ISA server. The primary disadvantage of using the SecureNAT client is that it cannot pass authentication information to the ISA server, and therefore you cannot configure access controls based on user or group information.

Solutions Fast Track

Understanding ISA Server Architecture

- ☑ Proxy Server 2.0 was built on three basic services: the Web Proxy Service, the Winsock Proxy Service, and the SOCKS Proxy Service.
- ☑ The four components that form the foundation of the ISA Server are: the Web Proxy Service, the Firewall Service, the Network Address Translation Protocol driver, and the Scheduled Content Download Service.
- ☑ The Web Proxy Service (w3proxy.exe) provides and controls access to the Web protocols, which are Application layer protocols.
- ☑ The Web Proxy Service is implemented as the w3proxy.exe file. You can start and stop the service via the net start w3proxy.exe and the net stop w3proxy.exe commands.
- ☑ The Web Proxy Service is also responsible for the Web cache, which provides a mechanism that allows content retrieved from the Internet to be stored on the ISA server.
- ☑ The Firewall Service (fwsrv.exe) provides the same functionality to network clients as the Winsock Proxy Service did in Proxy Server 2.0.
- ☑ The firewall client installs a special version of the Windows Sockets (Winsock) interface. The Winsock interface is a Session layer interface and is implemented as an API.
- ☑ The firewall client software captures Winsock API calls and forwards them to the Firewall Service via the Firewall Service's control channel.
- ☑ The Network Address Translation (NAT) Protocol driver allows network clients on a network that uses a private IP addressing scheme to access the Internet.
- ☑ To solve the problem of Internet access for private network hosts, Windows 2000 provides the Network Address Translation Protocol, or NAT. This protocol allows private network clients to send requests to the NAT server rather then directly to the Internet host.

- ☑ ISA Server takes advantage of the NAT Protocol driver included with Windows 2000 and extends its functionality so that it is able to work with the other ISA Server services.
- ☑ The Scheduled Content Download Service provides ISA Server a mechanism to automatically download Web content from sites you want to have available on the ISA server before a user actually makes a request for thc content.
- ☑ All requests, regardless of whether they are from SecureNAT, firewall, or Web proxy clients, must pass though the ISA server's packet filters.
- ☑ HTTP requests issued by a Web proxy client, or a SecureNAT or firewall client with the HTTP redirector enabled, can also be subjected to a custom set of Application layer filters known collectively as Web filters.

Installing and Configuring ISA Server Clients

- ☑ The SecureNAT service provides virtually transparent proxy services for your network clients.
- ☑ Whether you install a DNS server on your internal network or configure your SecureNAT clients to use a DNS server on the Internet, you must have site and content as well as protocol rules in place that will allow your SecureNAT clients to query an external DNS server.
- ☑ If you choose to implement a single, centralized DHCP server, you must configure multiple scopes to service all network IDs that have DHCP clients.
- ☑ In order to ping an external client, the ISA Server must be configured to allow IP Routing.
- ☑ The firewall client installation file can also be accessed via a Web page, but the Web installation information files must be manually moved to a directory in the Internet Information Server WWW service accessible hierarchy.
- ☑ If you have Mac, UNIX, or other non-Microsoft operating systems on the network, you will not be able to install the firewall client and therefore will not be able to take advantage of the complete range of protocols provided by the firewall client.

☑ You should not configure servers that are published to the Internet to use the firewall client.

☑ When you use the software deployment tools in the Windows 2000 Group Policy objects, you'll typically have an organizational unit (OU) or a set of OUs to which you will make the software available.

☑ The firewall client supports a process known as autodiscovery, in which the firewall client is able to query either a DHCP server via a DHCPINFORM message or directly query a DNS server via a DNS query for the name wpad.<domain_name>.

☑ The most compelling reason to use DHCP, rather than DNS, when configuring your wpad entries is that DCHP allows you a more granular approach to assigning your ISA servers to the network clients.

☑ ISA Server allows you to publish servers by configuring them as SecureNAT clients, therefore virtually obviating the need to set up the published servers as firewall (Winsock) clients.

☑ A Web proxy client is a CERN-compliant Web browser or other application that can be configured to send requests to the Web Proxy Service on the ISA server.

☑ When the Web proxy client is configured to support autodiscovery, it can take advantage of a wpad entry contained in either a DHCP or DNS server.

Frequently Asked Questions

The following Frequently Asked Questions, answered by the authors of this book, are designed to both measure your understanding of the concepts presented in this chapter and to assist you with real-life implementation of these concepts. To have your questions about this chapter answered by the author, browse to **www.syngress.com/solutions** and click on the **"Ask the Author"** form.

Q: Do I have to install Internet Information Server to use the Web Proxy Service, as I did with Proxy Server 2.0?

A: No. Unlike Proxy Server 2.0, you do not need to install IIS in order to take advantage of the Web Proxy Service on ISA Server. In fact, it is recommended that you do *not* install IIS on the same machine as ISA Server.

Q: How do I know if my Web browser is CERN compliant?

A: The best way for you to determine whether or not your browser is CERN compliant is to configure it to use the Web Proxy Service. You can do this by configuring it to use port 8080 on the internal interface of the ISA server. If it works, it is CERN compliant. If it does not work, it is not CERN compliant. Almost all browsers released in the last three to four years are CERN compliant and will work with the ISA Server Web Proxy Service.

Q: Do I have to install the firewall client? I am concerned that if I install the firewall client software, my existing network applications will not work correctly.

A: You do not have to install the firewall client software. You can still access the Internet through the ISA server if you configure your clients as SecureNAT clients. However, you lose out on some of the convenience that the firewall client offers, and you also lose authentication information that would allow you to configure access control based on users or groups. Do not worry about the firewall client software breaking your existing applications. We had the same concern with the Proxy Server 2.0 software, but the firewall client software doesn't break anything, and it is easy to disable or remove if you decide that you do not want to use it.

Q: I've read a lot of books on Proxy Server 2.0, and it is always said that the control channel uses UDP 1745. What makes you think that it also uses TCP 1745?

A: Much of the research we did for this book included network-monitoring sessions that were used to determine ISA Server protocol behavior. We noticed that if we stopped and started the firewall service, the LAT was being transferred from the ISA server's internal interface's TCP port 1745 to the firewall clients. UDP is still used for communications that can fit inside a single UDP packet. Larger control messages use TCP instead of UDP.

Q: Can I run RRAS and ISA Server on the same machine? Also, can I run the RRAS NAT service at the same time I run ISA Server?

A: You should not run the RRAS NAT Protocol on the same machine as ISA Server. Even though ISA Server will disable the RRAS NAT Protocol, we have seen many difficult-to-explain errors when the NAT Protocol was still installed. You should delete it from the RRAS Service. The RRAS Service will run on the ISA server and is used by the ISA server, especially when you want to configure VPN connections.

Q: Sometimes when I make a change, it doesn't seem to work. But then when I come back to the computer later, things suddenly work. What is causing this?

A: If the change you've made requires the service to restart and you let the ISA server restart the service for you, it could take a few seconds to a few minutes for the service to complete the restart purpose. If you need the change to take effect sooner, tell the ISA server that will you restart the service yourself.

Q: Before using ISA Server, I used the RRAS NAT Service. Now my computer seems to be dropping off the network and not receiving IP addresses. What might be the problem?

A: Unlike the RRAS NAT Protocol, ISA Server does not include a DHCP allocator. If you want to automatically assign addresses to ISA Server clients, you need to install a DHCP server.

Q: I want to run programs like Napster and various Internet games on my ISA Server clients. I do not want to install the firewall client. However, it seems that these things work only with the firewall client installed. What can I do about this?

A: Napster and various Internet games required complex protocol connections that require primary connections and often multiple secondary connections. The easiest way to handle these is to use the firewall client. If you use the SecureNAT client, you might have to configure multiple protocol definitions to make them work correctly.

Q: When I use the firewall client, I can connect to mail servers on the Internet from my internal computers, but if I use the SecureNAT client, it does not work. I would rather not use the firewall client software, but I can't connect to mail servers on the Internet without it. Is there anything I can do about this?

A: The problem is likely due to the DNS configuration of your SecureNAT clients. The reason that you are able to access your mail servers when the firewall client is installed is that the Firewall Service is able to take advantage of DNS proxy via the Firewall Service. The Firewall Service resolves the name for the firewall client and returns that address to it. The SecureNAT client must have a DNS server address configured on it or it will not be able to resolve Internet names.

Chapter 8

Configuring ISA Server for Outbound Access

Solutions in this chapter:

- Configuring the Server for Outbound Access
- Network Configuration Settings
- Creating Secure Outbound Access Policy
- Configuring Application Filters That Affect Outbound Access
- Understanding and Configuring the Web Proxy Cache

☑ Summary

☑ Solutions Fast Track

☑ Frequently Asked Questions

Introduction

In this chapter we focus on ISA Server configuration issues that have their primary influence on outbound access and outbound access control. Although we often think of a firewall as something to prevent external intruders from accessing internal resources, just as much havoc can result if we fail to control what internal users can access on the Internet.

The major issues we tackle in this chapter include:

- Configuring ISA Server for outbound access
- Understanding and configuring the Network Configuration settings
- Creating a secure outbound access policy
- Configuring the application filters that affect primarily outbound access
- Understanding and configuring the Web proxy cache

Once you have a firm grasp on these issues, you will be able to configure a secure outbound access policy and ISA Server configuration.

Configuring the Server for Outbound Access

Several elements determine how outbound requests for Internet resources are handled. These elements can be broken down roughly into two groups:

- Outbound Web protocol requests
- Outbound "everything else"

The "everything else" includes Winsock application requests that are not wrapped in HTTP headers. Both SecureNAT and firewall clients issue Winsock application requests. Outbound access control for these clients centers around configuring protocol rules.

Outbound requests from Web proxy clients are handled a little differently, since they do not have to be run through the Firewall Service. However, they are still bound by protocol rules. You can configure how outbound Web protocol requests are handled on the internal interface of the ISA Server via the Server's Properties sheet.

Note that this is a departure from how things were done in Proxy Server 2.0. With Proxy Server, you configured Web protocol access controls and Winsock access controls through different configuration dialog boxes. In ISA Server, those dialog boxes are consolidated, and Web and Winsock protocols are now configured through the same interface.

Configuring Listeners for Outbound Web Requests

To access the configuration dialog box for **Outgoing Web Requests**, perform the following steps:

1. Expand the **Servers and Arrays** node in the left pane of the **ISA Management** console. Right-click your server or array, and click **Properties**.
2. Click the **Outgoing Web Requests** tab. You will see something like what appears in Figure 8.1.

Figure 8.1 The Outgoing Web Requests Tab on the Server Properties Sheet

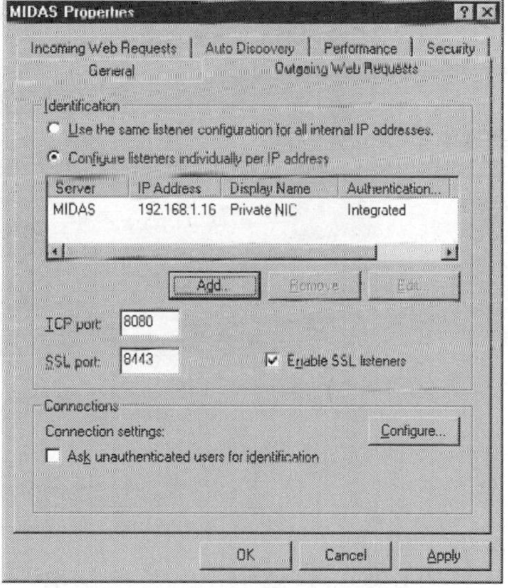

3. In the **Identification** frame, you have the option to configure the Outgoing Web Requests Listener for the Web Proxy Service to **Use the same listener configuration for all internal IP addresses**, or you can **Configure listeners individually per IP address**.

Your decision to use the same listener configuration rather than separate listener configurations for each IP address is determined by the type of authentication you want to require to access Web content via a particular listener. If you wanted to apply the same authentication requirements for *all* outgoing Web requests, you would choose to apply the same configuration to all IP addresses. If you need a more granular control over the type of authentication accepted for each listener, you should configure listeners individually.

Note that even though you can configure each listener to accept a different method of authentication, the decision to *require* authentication is a *global* configuration option. You *do not* have the choice to require authentication on one listener and not require authentication on another listener.

To add an Outgoing Web Requests Listener, click the Add button. You'll see something like Figure 8.2.

Figure 8.2 Adding a Listener for Outgoing Web Requests

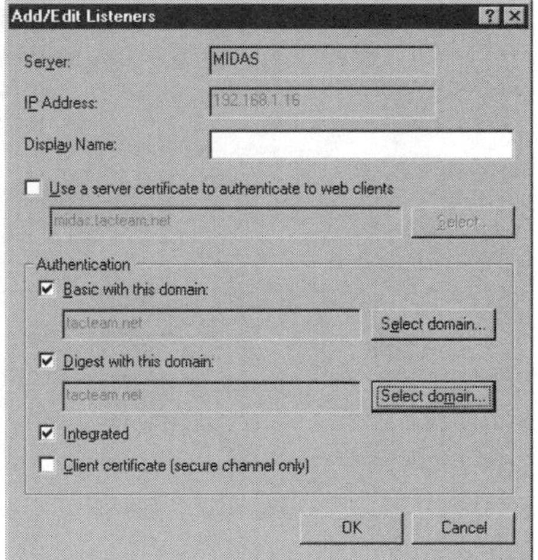

4. When you add a new listener for outgoing Web requests, you select the **Server**, which will likely be the server on which you are configuring the listener; the IP address that is associated with this listener; and the type of authentication you want to enable for this listener.

   You can also configure the listener to use a server certificate to authenticate it to internal Web clients. This allows SSL connections between the Web proxy client on the internal network and the ISA Server's internal interface.

5. In Figure 8.1, note the **TCP port** text box. This box defines the port number listening for Web proxy client requests. You can change this number to any port you like, but be sure that no other service is running on that port. You can determine whether or not another service is bound to that port by running the **netstat –na** command from the command prompt. If the **netstat** command shows that another service is listening on that port, you need to choose an alternate port assignment. The default port number for outbound Web requests is TCP 8080. We advise you to leave this value as it is, if possible.
6. If you want internal clients to connect to the listener via SSL, you must **Enable SSL Listeners** and include a port number. Note that the default port number is 8443. You should not change this port number. Furthermore, if you enable SSL on a listener, you must have a certificate installed on that listener. Note that Port 8443 is the port number to which browsers configured as *Web proxy clients* send their SSL connection requests. If the browser is not a Web proxy client, it does not send SSL requests to this port number. The non-Web proxy client browser doesn't need to send requests to this port number; because it is not a Web proxy client, it will not be able to authenticate with the Web proxy service.
7. In the **Connections** frame, decide whether you want to *force* authentication for Web proxy requests by selecting the **Ask unauthenticated users for identification**. Recall the effect this option has on SecureNAT or firewall clients that are not also configured as Web proxy clients: Their Web protocol requests fail. If this option is checked and a Web proxy client issues a request, the user will be presented with an authentication dialog box if there is no protocol and site/content rule allowing the request to be passed for anonymous requests.

   Also note that if you choose to use basic authentication, it will call up the logon dialog box. When integrated authentication is selected, credentials are passed transparently and the user will not need to enter credential information.

   When you click the **Configure** button, you see the screen that appears in Figure 8.3. Here you configure the number of simultaneous outgoing connections you want to allow to the Web Proxy Service. The timeout interval for dormant connections can be set here as well. Limiting the maximum number of connections can have the effect of improving the performance for users who are able to make a connection, albeit at the expense of users who are not able to connect. If you do limit the number of connections, be sure to configure the timeout to a low number so that people do not wait a long time for user connections to time out before they can get access to the ISA server.

Figure 8.3 The Connection Settings Dialog Box

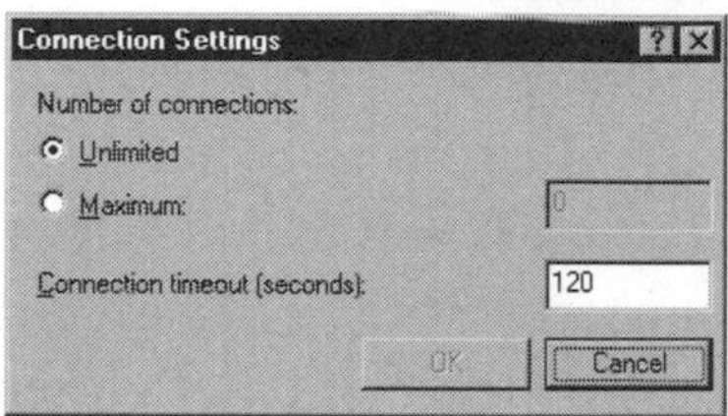

Server Performance

You can configure the amount of server memory and other resources dedicated to servicing Web requests via the **Performance** page. If you click the **Performance** tab on the server's **Properties** sheet, you see the screen that appears in Figure 8.4.

Figure 8.4 The Web Proxy Service Performance Page

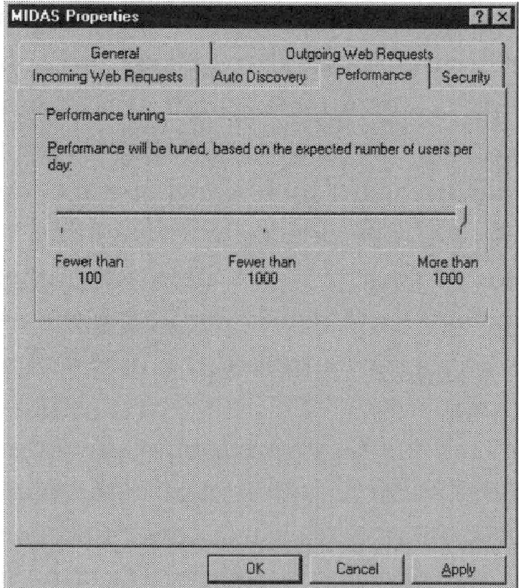

When you configure the **Performance tuning** slider bar to support more users per day, you dedicate more of the system resources to the ISA Server services. These resources can include memory and thread pools. Note that saying you have more users than you actually do will not improve performance. In this instance, you will be wasting server resources that can be used by other system processes.

Network Configuration Settings

ISA Server network configuration settings that influence outbound access controls include the following:

- Routing SecureNAT and firewall client requests
- Routing Web Proxy Service requests
- Passing outbound PPTP requests from internal clients
- The local address table (LAT)
- The local domain table (LDT)

Each of these influences how outbound requests are processed. We'll start with how SecureNAT and firewall client requests are routed in what are known as *firewall chains*.

Firewall Chaining: Routing SecureNAT and Firewall Client Requests

ISA Server provides a great deal of flexibility in terms of how client requests are routed. Rather than being limited to using the default connection on the ISA server, you can tell the ISA server to send specific requests via customized routes. When firewall clients send their requests to the ISA server, the requests can be routed directly to the Internet via the *primary connection* on the ISA server, or you can configure the Firewall Service on the ISA server to forward the request to another ISA server. The question is then, why would you want to do this? The immediate answer is because you can. However, that answer won't be very satisfying when you are trying to explain the rationale for your network infrastructure design to the network security committee.

One reason you might want to forward firewall client requests is that you want to partition the routing of firewall client and SecureNAT client requests from requests made by Web proxy clients. You might want to configure all the computers to use the same ISA server to make the initial connection, but once the connection is made, the Web proxy client requests would go to that server, and the firewall client requests would be routed to another server. In this way, Winsock application requests (such as SMTP, POP3, and NNTP requests) could reach the Internet via a different computer than the requests made by Web proxy clients.

The rationale for doing this might involve the fact that most Web requests do not require a high level of security, since typically a tiny percentage of Web connections are made via HTTPS (SSL-secured HTTP). Therefore, you could forward the Winsock (firewall client and SecureNAT client) requests to another ISA server that has a more "hardened" configuration.

Another reason to route firewall client and SecureNAT client requests separately is to apportion bandwidth between these clients and the Web proxy clients across two separate servers and their associated connections to the Internet.

The most common reason to configure firewall client routing is to support *chaining* of firewall client requests to upstream ISA servers. For example, you might have a branch office in Pasadena, Texas, and a main office in Dallas. When firewall client computers send a request to the ISA server located in Pasadena, you want the ISA server to forward the requests to the Dallas office, because the Internet access point for the organization is located in Dallas. In this example, the ISA server might use a VPN interface to connect to the upstream ISA server. This prevents users in the Pasadena office from accessing content from the Internet directly, and content must be accessed via the upstream ISA server in Dallas.

Unfortunately, you cannot configure granular Firewall Service routing rules the way that you can for the Web Proxy Service. For example, it would be nice to configure a firewall routing/chaining rule so that when your users made a request to sites such as Napster, you could selectively redirect those protocol requests to a server that has a 14.4Kbps modem connection.

Configuring Firewall and SecureNAT Client Routing

To configure the way that firewall and SecureNAT client requests are routed, perform the following steps:

1. In the **ISA Management** console, expand the **Servers and Arrays** node, then expand your server or array. Right-click the **Network Configuration** node, and click **Properties**. You will see the screen that appears in Figure 8.5.

Figure 8.5 The Firewall Chaining Dialog Box

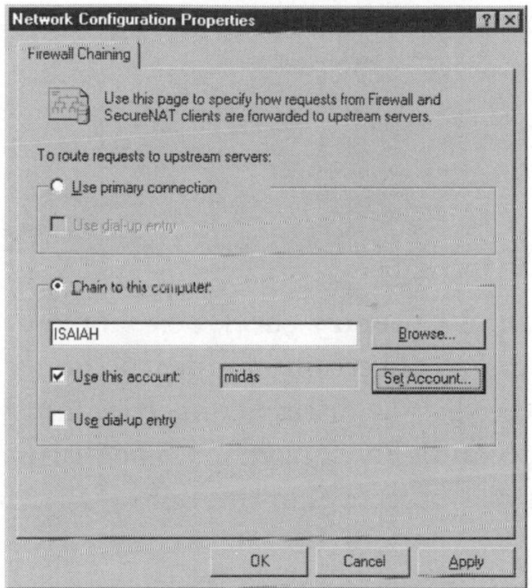

2. The **Use primary connection** option button is the default setting. When this option is selected, firewall client and SecureNAT client requests are sent out the external interface of the ISA server that receives the request. If you are using a dial-up connection on the ISA server, you *must* select the **Use dial-up entry** check box if you want the connection to automatically dial when a firewall client or SecureNAT client request arrives at the ISA server.
3. The **Chain to this computer** option button configures the ISA server to forward firewall client and SecureNAT client requests to another ISA server. Type in the name of the upstream ISA server in the text box, or you can look for the machine on your network via the **Browse** button.
4. The **Use this account** check box should be checked if you need this ISA server to pass credentials to the upstream ISA server. To set the credentials, click the **Set Account** button. You will see the screen that appears in Figure 8.6.
5. Enter the **User** in the text box, then enter the password and confirm the password in the **Password** and **Confirm Password** dialog boxes. *Do not enter credentials from your ISP in this dialog box. These are domain or server accounts.* Then click **OK**.

Figure 8.6 The Set Account Dialog Box

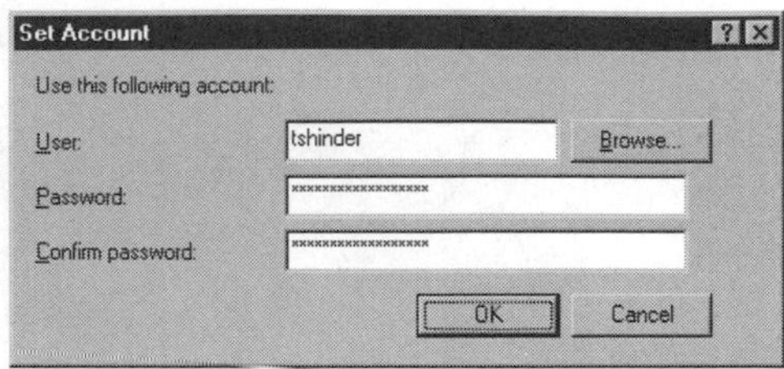

6. The **Use dial-up entry** check box should be checked if the ISA Server needs to dial a connection in order to connect to the upstream ISA server. Note that the dial-up connection can be either a direct dial-up connection or a VPN connection. The dial-up entry must be included in the list of dial-up entries in the **Policy Elements** on that ISA server.

SECURITY ALERT!

When you enable firewall chaining and the upstream server for firewall and SecureNAT clients is different from the server configured to route Web proxy requests, requests for Web objects from SecureNAT and firewall clients will be sent to the upstream server configured in the Firewall Chaining configuration dialog box. The requests are forwarded *before* the HTTP Redirector Filter has a change to "get at" them. We discuss the HTTP Redirector in more detail later in this chapter.

Authentication and Firewall Chaining

If you have enabled firewall chaining so that firewall client requests are passed from one ISA server to another, you address the issue of authentication for the firewall client computers. If a firewall client sends its ISA server a request that requires authentication, it will pass this authentication information to the upstream server to which the ISA server is configured to forward firewall client requests.

At times, the upstream ISA server might not be able to identify or confirm the credentials of the downstream ISA server firewall client. You'll see this happen if the upstream ISA server belongs to a domain that has no trust relationship with the firewall client that issued the initial request.

To handle this situation, configure the downstream ISA server to "stand in" for the firewall client by sending credentials that the upstream ISA server will recognize. This task is accomplished by setting an account for the downstream ISA server to use when "impersonating" the downstream firewall client computer. You configured these credentials in Steps 4 and 5 in the last walk-though we did.

For example, what if we don't add any authentication information in the dialog boxes seen in Steps 4 and 5? The ISA server will send the user's credentials. However, if we specify an account on the downstream server, that information will be sent *instead of* the user credentials. This option is useful in situations in which there are no trusts or when you want simplified account management for an entire branch office.

NOTE

The authentication we are referring to here is authentication against the ISA server itself. The ISA server can be configured to require authentication before allowing outbound requests. We are *not* referring to authentication information that might be sent to a destination server on the Internet.

Routing Web Proxy Client Requests

Your options to configure how Web proxy client requests are routed through the ISA server are a great deal wider than your options via the firewall chaining configuration we've just talked about. By taking advantage of Web proxy routing rules, you can forward Web proxy requests to another ISA server or directly to the Internet, or you can redirect requests to another Web site. Furthermore, these decisions can be made based on the URL included in the initial request. In addition, you can use Web proxy routing rules to determine how content is cached.

In order to understand the capabilities of these Web proxy routing features, let's go over a couple of examples.

Suppose you have figured out from analyzing the logs that a couple of Web sites consume a large amount of bandwidth on the external interface of your ISA server. Users need access to these Web sites to download fixes, patches, and third-party utilities and demo programs in order to provide services to your clients. The problem is that these downloads absorb a great percentage of bandwidth on the external interface of the single ISA server you have installed at this time. Web pages load very slowly; email messages are retrieved and sent very slowly, too.

To solve this problem, create a *destination set* (a concept we'll discuss later in this chapter) that includes the Web sites responsible for the heaviest downloads. Then when the primary ISA server's Web Proxy Service gets a request for one of these sites, it can redirect the request to another ISA server in your company. The external interface of the alternate ISA server can bear the brunt of the heavy download traffic. It would be nice to be able to configure such Web proxy routing rules to apply to selective client address sets or specific users or groups, but you can't do that with ISA server.

Another example of what you can do is redirect requests for certain sites. If users try to access an unproductive site or domain, such as aol.com, you can configure a routing rule to redirect the request to a URL that includes your appropriate use policy on your corporate home page.

Web proxy routing rules allow you to restrict the pages that are cached on the ISA server. For example, users might have to connect to a partner Web site where the information changes frequently throughout the day. You would prefer that your users not have to press the F5 key to manually refresh their browsers. You can configure a routing rule to prevent caching of that site's content and to access the site directly whenever a request is made.

The most common application of routing rules is to support *Web proxy chaining*. Web proxy chains can connect ISA servers located at different sites or LAN segments in a hierarchical fashion so that downstream ISA servers can take advantage of the cache contents of upstream ISA servers.

Configuring a Web Proxy Service Routing Rule

Before configuring a new routing rule, it's worth mentioning that when ISA Server is installed, a default routing rule is created. This rule is called *Default rule* and it has the order number of *Last*. This order number is important because routing rules are represented as a hierarchical list and are evaluated according to the order that you've set. A single request might match several different routing rules, but the rule highest on the list determines how the request is processed.

To create a new routing rule, follow these steps:

1. Open the **ISA Management** console, expand **Servers and Arrays**, and expand your server or array name. Now expand the **Network Configuration** node, and click the **Routing node**. You will see the current list of routing rules in the right pane of the console.
2. Right-click the **Routing node**, and click the **New** and then the **Rule** commands. This sequence will open the **New Routing Rule Wizard**. On the first page, enter the name of the routing rule, and click **Next**.

3. On the **Destination Sets** page, click the down arrow on the drop-down list box for **Apply this rule to**. You'll see the options as they appear in Figure 8.7.

   A *destination set* determines what computers or set of computers or sites should be included in this rule. Destination sets are created independently of routing rules via the **Policy Elements** node. Note that you have a number of options in terms of how the routing rule is applied. In this example, select the **Specified destination set**, and click **Next**.

Figure 8.7 The Destination Sets Page

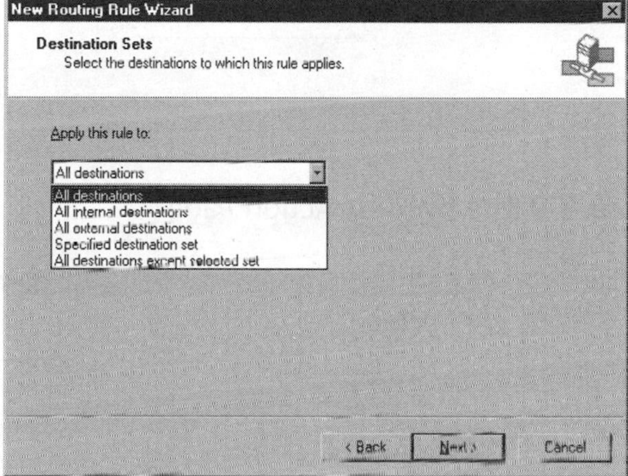

4. After you click the **Specified destination set** option, the dialog box changes so that you can select the destination set to which you want this routing rule applied. The change in the page is reflected in Figure 8.8.
5. In this scenario, we've created a destination set to apply to the aol.com domain. Select the **AOL Website** destination set, and then click **Next**.
6. On the **Request Action** page, decide how you want requests for this destination set processed. Figure 8.9 shows your options.

   Your options are to:

   - **Retrieve them directly from specified destination** This option allows the ISA server to send the request to the default interface on the ISA server that receives the request. Note that this does not imply that the request will bypass the Web Proxy or Firewall Services. It simply sets the request to be handled by the local server to retrieve the page directly, without redirection.

Figure 8.8 The Destination Sets Page After the Rule to Apply Is Selected

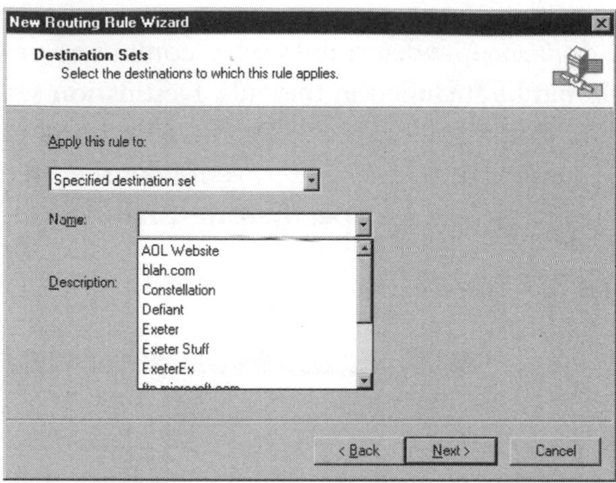

Figure 8.9 The Request Action Page

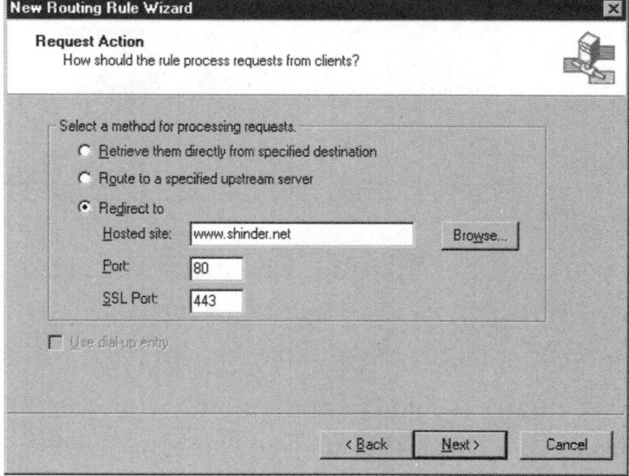

- **Route to a specified upstream server** This option allows you to forward the request to another ISA server for retrieval. When you select this option, you are configuring a proxy chain for this route. The upstream ISA server will obtain the Web object, put it in its cache, and then return the object to this ISA server, which will put it in its cache and return the object to the host that issued the initial request.

- **Redirect to** You can have the ISA server redirect the request to another site by typing in the server name in the **Hosted site** text box. You can also change the port number to which the request is sent. There is no default entry. In this case, we've entered the www.shinder.net site and told it to forward the request to port 80 on that Web server. You must also include the SSL port. In this case, configure it to use the default SSL port 443.

  Note that we don't use SSL port 8443, because that is the port used by Web proxy clients to send authentication information to the Web Proxy Service. In this case, the ISA server forwards the requests to a destination Web server that uses the standard SSL port 443, not to another ISA server in the role of a Web proxy client.

7. Now click **Next**. On the **Cache Retrieval Configuration** page, specify how the rule searches the cache and what to do if the requested object is not contained in the cache. Figure 8.10 shows this page.

Figure 8.10 The Cache Retrieval Configuration Page

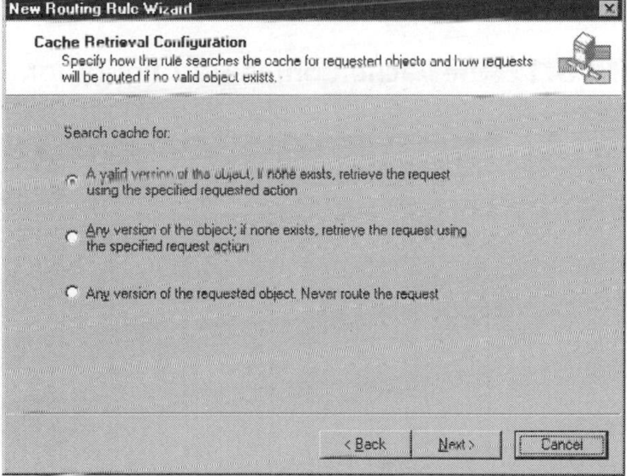

Under **Search cache for:** you have the following options:

- **A valid version of the object; if none exists, retrieve the request using the specified requested action** A valid version of an object in the Web cache is an object whose TTL has not expired. If you choose this option and a request comes in for an object whose TTL has expired, the request will be routed directly to the Internet or to an upstream ISA server.

- **Any version of the object; if none exists, retrieve the request using the specified request action** If you choose this option, expired objects will be returned to the user. This increases the chance that an outdated version of a page will be returned to the user, but it decreases the amount of bandwidth consumed on the external interface. If no version of the object exists in cache, the request will be forwarded to an upstream Web server or directly to the Internet.
- **Any version of the requested object. Never route the request** If you select this option, the ISA server will search the cache for the requested object. If it is in there, it will be returned. It the object isn't in the cache, the client will receive an error related to the object not being found.

  For this walk-through, select **Any version of the object...** to save bandwidth on the external interface. Then click **Next**.

8. In the **Cache Content Configuration** page, specify whether the retrieved object should be entered into the ISA server's Web cache. This page is shown in Figure 8.11.

Figure 8.11 The Cache Content Configuration Page

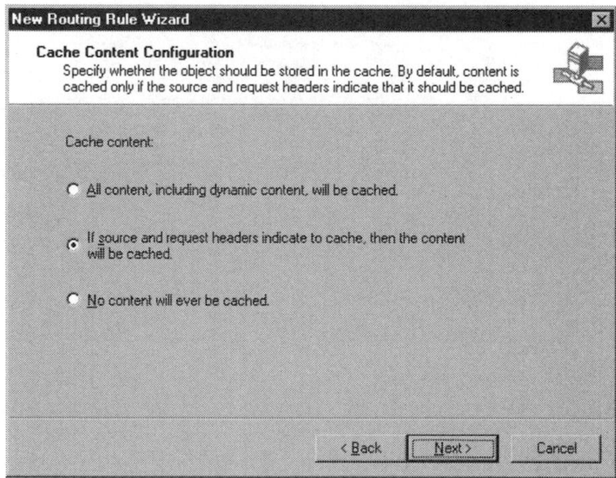

Your options are to **Cache content**:

- **All content, including dynamic content, will be cached** Choose this option if you want to ignore header information returned by Web pages that indicate whether or not content should be cached. This includes caching content on dynamic pages that include a question mark (?) in the URL.

- **If source and request headers indicate to cache, then the content will be cached** Choose this option if you want to cache content that the Web server wants to be cached. This information is contained in HTTP response headers. With this option, you won't cache dynamic content.
- **No content will ever be cached** Choose this option if you want to cache no content obtained via this routing rule. Note that this option is used to control content that is not cached on the ISA server. In Proxy Server 2.0, you had to configure cache filters. In ISA Server, you create destination sets and then create routing rules to inform the server that it should not cache content from sites included in that particular destination set.

  In this walk-through, select the option to cache content if the headers indicate to do so. Then click **Next**.

9. The last page of the wizard allows you to review your choices. If everything looks correct, click **Finish**. You can use the **Back** button to change your choices.

After the rule is completed, you can access the properties of the rule by double-clicking the rule or by right-clicking it and clicking the **Properties** command. After doing this, you'll see the screen that appears in Figure 8.12.

Figure 8.12 The Routing Rule Properties Dialog Box

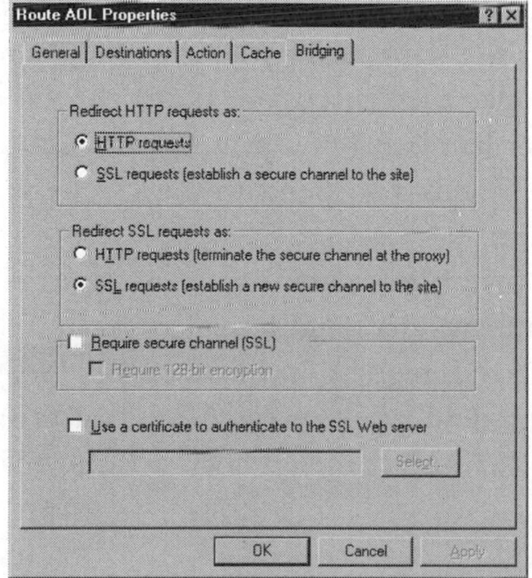

The tabs include **General**, **Destinations**, **Action**, **Caching**, and **Bridging**. The first four contain the same information you provided the wizard. However, the **Bridging** tab allows you to further refine how the request is routed. On the **Bridging** tab, you can decide how the requests will be forwarded.

The **Redirect HTTP requests as** frame contains the options:

- HTTP requests
- SSL requests

The **HTTP requests** option forwards HTTP requests as unsecured HTTP requests. If you choose the **SSL requests** option, the ISA server will establish an SSL channel with the destination server and send and receive with that server via SSL. You use this option when routing inbound requests to an internal Web server. For example, an Internet user makes a connection with the ISA server to access content on an internal Web site. You might want to redirect the HTTP request made to the ISA server to the internal Web server as an SSL request.

The **Redirect SSL requests as** frame includes the options:

- HTTP requests (terminate the secure channel at the proxy)
- SSL requests (establish a new secure channel to the site)

The **HTTP requests (terminate the secure channel at the proxy)** option allows the ISA server communicating with the client via SSL to forward the request as a plain HTTP request. Note that this is more useful when configuring a routing rule for inbound requests from the Internet than when routing outbound requests from the internal network to an external server.

While you want to protect certain communications via SSL as they move through the Internet, you don't typically require that communications be as secure once they reach a network under your control. By redirecting inbound SSL requests as HTTP once they enter your network, you can reduce the processor load. On the other hand, there's not much sense in taking outbound SSL-protected sessions made by internal clients to the ISA server and then forwarding them as unprotected requests.

The **SSL requests (establish a new secure channel to the site)** option allows the ISA server to forward a request made over an SSL channel to the internal Web server as an SSL request. In this case, the ISA server will establish a new SSL session with the destination server. Note that this is not the same as SSL tunneling, in which the ISA server merely forwards the SSL requests to a destination Web server.

The **Require secure channel (SSL)** option requires that the client enter HTTPS in the browser to access any URL described by the routing rule. If you don't select the box, you can use either HTTP or HTTPS. Selecting this box in the **Bridging** tab for the routing rule would require that the client establish an HTTPS connection when it tried to connect to the destination described by the rule. Another way to think about how this option is used with a routing rule is that this is like publishing but in a reverse sense. Selecting this box would eliminate some choices because you must use HTTPS.

You can check the **Use a certificate to authenticate to the SSL Web server** check box if you want the ISA server to able to authenticate itself with the destination site to which the request is being routed. When this option is checked, the **Select** button becomes available, and you can select the certificate you want to apply. Note that this certificate is a *client* certificate that the ISA server will present to identify itself to an upstream server.

Routing to a Linux Squid Server

Many administrators already have other proxy servers in place but would like to take advantage of the outbound access control features of ISA Server. One example of this situation is an organization that wants to use an ISA server downstream from a Linux Squid proxy server.

You can route Web proxy requests sent from clients to an ISA server to a Squid server and take advantage of the access controls configured on the ISA server. When the request arrives at the ISA server, it will be sent through the rules engine, and if there is a site and content and a protocol rule that allows the request, the ISA server will route the Web proxy request to the upstream Squid server. When the upstream Squid server retrieves the Web object, it will be returned to the ISA server, and the ISA server will put the object in its Web cache before returning it to the client that issued the request.

The only disadvantage to routing to an upstream Squid proxy versus routing to an upstream ISA server is that you cannot take advantage of hierarchical routing. With an upstream Squid proxy, the downstream ISA server cannot take advantage of the Autoconfiguration script that would allow the downstream ISA server to resolve requests within an upstream Squid CARP array in the same way it can with an ISA server array. We'll go over this issue in more detail when we cover upstream routing to an ISA server.

To route to an upstream squid Server, perform the following steps:

1. Open the **ISA Management** console, expand the **Servers and Arrays** node, and then expand the **Network Configuration** node. Right-click the **Routing** node, click **New**, and then click **Rule**.
2. In the **Welcome** page, type in the name of the rule—something like **Upstream Squid**—then click **Next**.
3. On the **Destination Sets** page, select **All destinations** in the **Apply this rule to** drop-down list box, then click **Next**.
4. In the **Request Action** dialog box, select the option to **Route to a specified upstream server**. If you must use a dial-up connection, be sure to place a check mark in the check box for **Use dial-up entry**, and then click **Next**.
5. On the **Primary Routing** page, you'll see something like Figure 8.13.

Figure 8.13 The Primary Routing Page

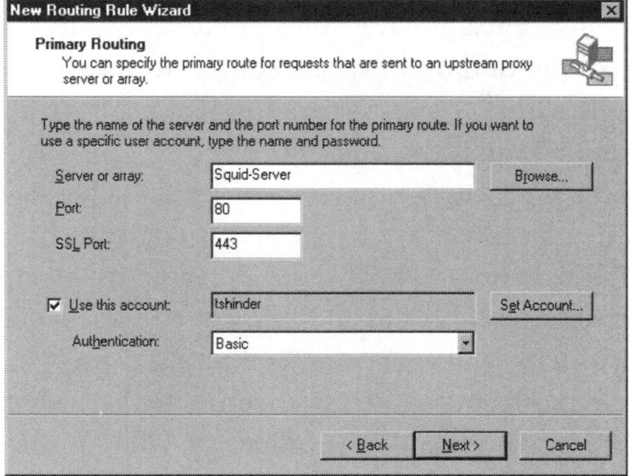

Type in the appropriate information for the name of the **Server or array**, the **Port** number and the **SSL Port** number to which you want the requests routed on the Squid server. If your upstream server listens on different ports, you should change them here.

If you require authentication on the Squid server, be sure to configure the account and the password by clicking the **Set Account** button and entering that information. For **Authentication**, you'll have to use **Basic** because the Linux box does not support integrated Windows authentication.

6. On the **Backup Routing** page, you can configure a path to use if the Squid server is not available. We'll talk more about backup configuration in the Web proxy chaining discussion that follows.
7. On the **Cache Retrieval Configuration** page, make the selection that fits your caching requirements.
8. On the **Cache Content Configuration** page, make the selection that fits your requirements.
9. Click **Finish** and the Routing Rule is complete.

Configuring ISA Web Proxy Chaining

Web proxy chaining allows you to extend the benefits of the ISA server's Web proxy cache to all members of an organization. It also allows you to bring the Web proxy cache closer to users that need access to cached Web objects. This makes the cache available to users in different departments in the same organization or located in remote offices.

A Web proxy chain allows ISA servers throughout an organization to take advantage of the contents of the Web cache of other ISA servers in the organization. By chaining ISA servers in this fashion, you can reduce the amount of bandwidth consumed on a corporate backbone or on WAN links that connect various sites. These WAN links can also include VPN connections.

Proxy Chaining Example 1: Chaining through a WAN

Suppose your main office is in Dallas. You also have remote offices in Abilene and Galveston. There are 2500 computers in the main office, 1500 computers in the Galveston office, and 400 computers in the Abilene office. You would like to maximize the potential of the ISA Server Web cache for all users in your organization and improve your users' Web experience as much as possible.

Each office has a dedicated connection to the Internet. The Abilene office has a dedicated 128Kbps basic rate interface (BRI) ISDN modem connection to the Galveston office, the Galveston office has a 256Kbps Frame Relay connection to the Dallas office, and the Dallas office has a 1.5Mbps T1 connection to the Internet. You want all Internet Web traffic to exit and enter the main office's link to the Internet. This creates a single point of access for Web traffic in your organization, greatly simplifying your ability to monitor access and implement access control.

To optimize the Web caching scheme for your organization, you can configure the smallest office (Abilene) to route Web requests to the ISA server in the Galveston office. You can then configure the Galveston ISA server to route Web requests to the Dallas office. The Dallas office would then route requests directly to the Internet.

Note that we can also make each link in the Web proxy chain fault tolerant. If any of the dedicated links that connect the sites becomes unavailable, you can configure *backup routes* that the ISA server can use to access Internet resources. In this scenario, where we are using dedicated links to connect the offices, we might want to install a second device, such as a modem, to provide a backup route for Internet access.

To see what happens when we create such as chain, let's examine what happens when someone at the Abilene office makes a request for a Web page. A user on that network sends a request for the Web page, and that request is sent to the ISA server at the edge of the user's network. The Abilene ISA server checks its Web proxy cache to see if it contains the object. If it does contain the object, it returns the object to the user without generating any WAN traffic. If it does not contain the object, the ISA server will route the request to the Galveston office.

Once the request arrives to the Galveston ISA server, that ISA server checks its own Web proxy cache for the requested object. If the object is located in its cache, it returns the object to the Abilene ISA server without generating any WAN traffic on its Frame Relay link to Dallas. The Abilene ISA server then puts the object in its own cache and then returns it to the user who made the request. If the object is not contained in the Galveston ISA server's cache, the server forwards the request to the Dallas ISA server.

The Dallas ISA server checks its cache. If the object is contained in cache, it returns it to the Galveston ISA server without generating any traffic on the T1 link to the Internet. The Galveston ISA server then puts the object into its cache. Then the Galveston ISA server returns the object to the Abilene ISA server, which puts the object in its cache, and then it returns the object to the host that made the initial request.

If the Dallas ISA server does not contain the object in its cache, it fetches it from the Internet server and returns it along that same path, with each ISA server in the return path placing the object in its own cache before returning it.

You can see in this example that a single request at the end of the chain has the potential of placing the object on all ISA servers in the chain. So, if another user at any location in the network needs to access the same object, it will be on the ISA server located closest to that user. This method saves bandwidth on all interfaces in the proxy chain. Note that the rationale of configuring the chain with the smallest number of users at the end of the chain reduces the probability of generating traffic on the central Internet link at the Dallas office.

Note that if any of the links between the offices fails, a backup route can be configured on the ISA servers in the chain so that a request can still be serviced.

Proxy Chaining Example 2: Chaining within a LAN

Another way to take advantage of the benefits of Web proxy chaining is to use it in an environment that has a number of departmental or area-specific LANs that are connected to a busy network backbone. By placing an ISA server on the edge of each of the LAN segments, you can reduce the amount of traffic on the backbone as well as on the Internet connection itself.

For example, suppose you are responsible for a small college's network. One of the backbone segments connects three college dorms and the recreation center to the Internet. You would like to reduce the amount of traffic on the Internet link as well as the amount of traffic over the network backbone, especially in light of the fact that the students like to use NetMeeting to call students in other dorms as well as in the recreation center. There is also quite a bit of audio/visual traffic coming in from the Internet in the form of streaming media, with students often accessing the same online concert simultaneously.

You can place an ISA server on the edge of each network segment that connects to the backbone and another ISA server that connects the backbone to the Internet. Then you configure the segment ISA servers to route Web requests to the ISA server (or array)on the edge of the campus network. In this way, the segment ISA server cache is searched first, and only if the object isn't found in the cache is the request sent over the backbone to the campus ISA server or array. If that ISA server has the object in cache, it returns it to the ISA server on the segment backbone.

In actual practice, the ISA server at the edge of the campus network needs a measure of fault tolerance; therefore, you would configure it as an enterprise array. When you configure the segment-level ISA servers to route requests to the enterprise array, you can also configure them to take advantage of the Autoconfiguration script. When the segment ISA servers use the Autoconfiguration script, they can identify which ISA server in the array will contain the cached object and directly retrieve the object for that server. In addition, the script will inform the segment ISA servers when one of the array members is unavailable. Therefore, there is fault tolerance as well as load balancing in this type of routing solution.

Configuring Routing for ISA Server Chains

Configuring the routing rule for ISA server chains is similar to configuration for the Squid routing rule, except this time we are able to take advantage of the Autoconfiguration script. Perform the following steps to create a link in an ISA server chain.

1. Open the **ISA Management** console, expand the **Servers and Arrays** node, and then expand the **Network Configuration** node. Right-click the **Routing** node, click **New**, and then click **Rule**.
2. On the **Welcome** page, type in the name of the rule—something like **Upstream ISA Server**—then click **Next**.
3. On the **Destination Sets** page, select **All destinations** in the **Apply this rule to** drop-down list box, then click **Next**.
4. In the **Request Action** dialog box, select the option to **Route to a specified upstream server**. If you use a dial-up connection, be sure to place a check mark in the check box for **Use dial-up entry**, then click **Next**.
5. On the **Primary Routing** page, type in the **Server or array** name. The default port number is **8080** and the default SSL port is **8443**. Do not change these values unless you change the Outgoing Web Requests Listener configuration on the upstream ISA server. Figure 8.14 shows these settings. If the upstream ISA server is configured to require authentication for outbound Web Proxy Service access, you must configure an account by checking the **Use this account** check box and clicking the **Set Account** button. Click **Next**.

NOTE

Remember that earlier in the chapter we were talking about configuring backup routes and how you had to change the outbound Web proxy listener to use port 80? That was because the client using the backup route was no longer a Web proxy client and was not sending requests to the backup route server's port 8080; it was sending them to port 80. In the present case of configuring an ISA server as a member of an ISA server chain, the downstream ISA server is acting as a *Web proxy client* to the upstream ISA server. Therefore, it needs to send its requests to port 8080 on the upstream ISA server's Web Proxy Service.

Figure 8.14 The Primary Routing Page

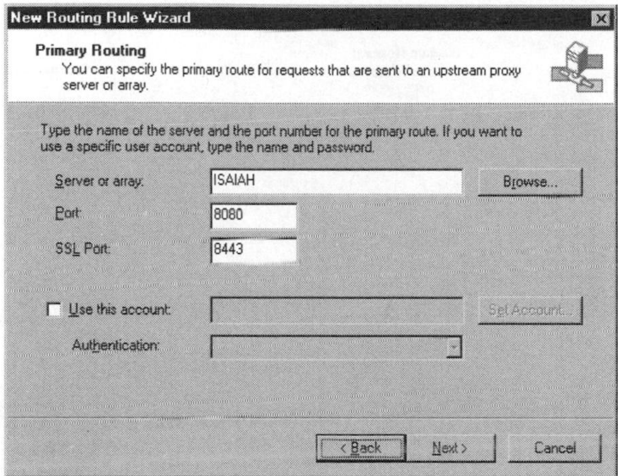

6. On the **Backup Routing** page (Figure 8.15), you are presented with the following options:

   - **Ignore requests** If the primary route is unavailable, the request will be dropped. Select this option to prevent the ISA server from trying other methods to access the Internet if the upstream ISA server is not available.
   - **Retrieve requests directly from specified destination** If the upstream server is not available, you can configure the ISA server to attempt to access the Web object directly. If you have a dial-up entry on the computer, you can configure ISA Server to use the dial-up entry for its backup route.
   - **Route requests to an upstream server** This option allows the ISA server to route the request to an alternate upstream proxy server in the event that the upstream ISA server for the primary route becomes unavailable. Note that this option will send requests to port 8080 on the alternate ISA server, since it is still a Web proxy client. When you make this selection, the next page will allow you to configure the name/address and port numbers for the upstream ISA server.

7. Click **Next**.
8. Select the appropriate option on the **Cache Retrieval** page, and click **Next**.

Figure 8.15 The Backup Routing Page

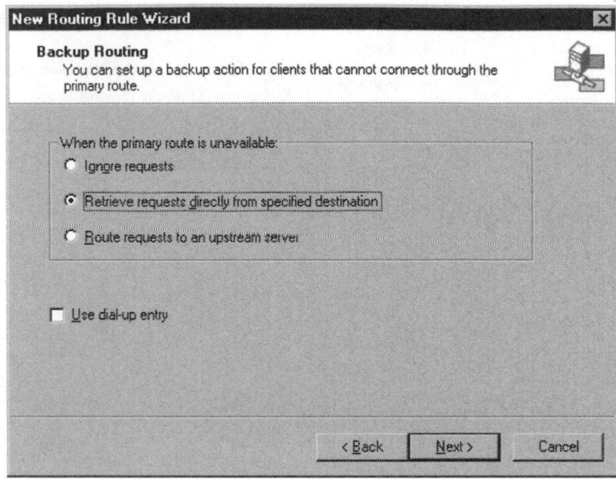

9. Select the appropriate option on the **Cache Content Configuration** page, and click **Next**.
10. Confirm your settings, and click **Finish**.

Outbound PPTP Requests

ISA Server supports outbound PPTP sessions between an internal network client behind an ISA server and a PPTP server located on an external network. This is a new feature, something you could not do with Proxy Server 2.0. However, there is a limitation to this feature. It is available *only* to SecureNAT clients. It will *not* work if the computer is set up as a firewall client only. In addition, remember that although ISA supports PPTP clients behind the firewall, it does not support L2TP/IPSec clients. This is due to issues with address translation and IPSec security negotiation.

To allow PPTP through the ISA server, perform the following steps:

1. Open the **ISA Management** console, expand **Servers and Arrays**, and then expand **Access Policy**. Right-click the **IP Packet Filters** node, and click **Properties**.
2. Click the **PPTP** tab. You will see the screen that appears in Figure 8.16.
3. Place a check mark in the check box for **PPTP through ISA firewall**. Click **OK**, and the clients will now be able to access PPTP VPN servers through the ISA server.

Figure 8.16 The PPTP Tab in the Packet Filters Properties Dialog Box

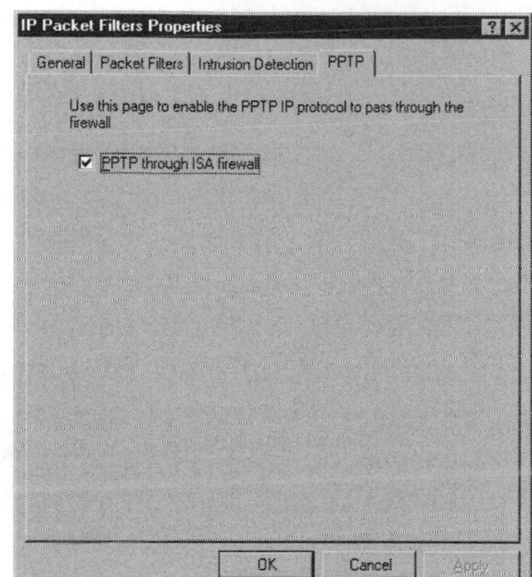

After enabling PPTP through the firewall, a new IP packet filter is created. You can click the **IP Packet Filters** node in the left pane and find the **SecureNAT PPTP** packet filter in the right pane. This packet filter opens up a predefined **PPTP call** filter. The PPTP call filter allows IP Protocol Number 47 (for GRE packets) to move outbound and inbound through the external interface of the ISA server.

This filter is available to *all* SecureNAT clients on your internal network and allows calls to any PPTP VPN server. However, one of the big problems with allowing outbound PPTP is that you cannot control access to what user or group, or even what machine, has access to outbound PPTP. This is because PPTP is not a TCP- or UDP-based protocol. Access controls can be placed only on protocols that use TCP or UDP.

Security Alert!

It is important to reiterate this point: You cannot exert any outbound access control over PPTP communications leaving the network if you enable the PPTP filter on the ISA server.

We investigate packet filters and how to configure them in more detail in Chapter 9.

The Local Address Table

The ISA server uses the *local address table (LAT)* to define the IP addresses that are internal and those that are external. Another way of thinking about the LAT is that it defines which networks are trusted and which networks are not trusted. Trusted network clients can be contacted directly. Hosts on untrusted networks must be contacted through the ISA server, and access rules will be applied to those requests.

One thing that the LAT does *not* allow you to do is configure what might be called an internal "DMZ" network where the hosts are located on the internal network. In such an internal DMZ, the hosts are located on the internal network but are treated as untrusted hosts that must be accessed through the ISA server's rules engine. With ISA Server, you must configure a DMZ or perimeter network segment as an untrusted network and then control access as you would for any other external network resource.

It is the Firewall Service that uses the LAT to make decisions regarding what is and what is not a trusted network. Firewall clients download a copy of the LAT on a periodic basis—every six hours, by default—and use the LAT entries to assess what requests should be sent to the ISA server and what requests should be sent directly to an internal computer on the local network. If the IP address of the destination host does not match an IP address on the LAT, the request is sent to the Firewall Service on the ISA server. Because of the LAT, you do not need to configure a default gateway on your firewall client computers.

SecureNAT clients do not download a copy of the LAT. This makes sense when you realize that a SecureNAT client is configured with a default gateway that routes requests to remote networks to the internal interface of the ISA server. If the SecureNAT client needs to contact a computer on the internal network, it does not need to check the LAT, because routing decisions are made by intervening routers rather than by the client itself.

Web proxy clients also do not download a copy of the LAT; they are configured to send *all* HTTP requests to a particular ISA server. Because Web proxy clients are preconfigured to send their requests to a specific server, they do not need to make routing decisions, because the ISA server makes those decisions for them. An exception to this rule occurs when a name without "dots" is typed in for the server in the URL. In this case, the Web proxy client treats the request as local and does not send it to the Web Proxy Service on the ISA server. Note that you can also configure the browser to treat "dotted" addresses as internal.

Configuring the LAT

The LAT can be configured during ISA Server setup or after ISA Server setup has been completed. It is a best practice to configure the LAT during setup and make configuration changes only after setup is complete.

You should always configure a meaningful and accurate routing table before installing ISA Server and creating the LAT. The ISA server must have a routing table that reflects the routed infrastructure of your internal network. The machine must know how to reach each network ID on your internal network. When a client from network ID 192.168.15.0/24 sends a request to the internal interface of the ISA server on network ID 192.168.1.0/24, the ISA server must know how to return the answer it receives from the Internet server to the requesting client. This can be accomplished only by configuring a correct routing table.

An incorrectly configured LAT will prevent ISA clients from being able to access Internet resources and could create a security risk. If an external address is inadvertently included in the LAT, any requests coming from such a host will be considered as arriving from a trusted network and will not be exposed to the same scrutiny as requests from an external network client.

If you haven't configured your LAT during setup or if you would like to redefine your LAT, perform the following steps:

1. Open the **ISA Management** console, expand **Servers and Arrays**, and expand the **Network Configuration** node in the left pane. Right click the **Local Address Table (LAT)** node, and click the **Construct LAT** command. The **Construct LAT** dialog box appears (Figure 8.17).

Figure 8.17 The Construct LAT Dialog Box

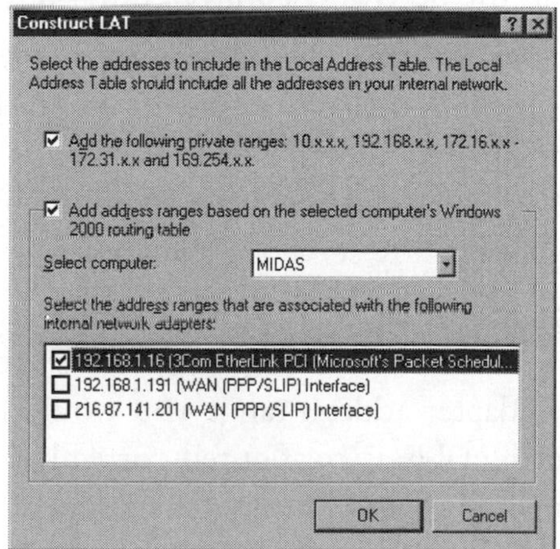

You are presented with the following options:

- **Add the following private ranges: 10.x.x.x, 192.168.x.x, 172.16.x.x-172.31.x.x and 169.254.x.x** This option automatically adds to the LAT all addresses contained within the private network ID address space. Although this is convenient, you might want to avoid using this option. One reason you might not want to include all private network IDs on the LAT is that a network backbone might be located on a private network ID. When you connect ISA servers at the edge of network segments that also have private network IDs, both the backbone and the departmental/local segment will seem to the ISA server as interfaces on an internal, and therefore trusted, network. This would undo any security plans you have in mind in terms of access control for each segment with a border ISA server. An even more compelling reason applies when you connect to an extranet through a VPN. You do not want the private network ID of the remote network in your LAT.
- **Add address ranges based on the selected computer's Windows 2000 routing table** This is the preferred method for configuring the LAT. ISA Server will examine the routing table on the ISA server and then automatically create the LAT based on those entries. This is the most reliable and least error-prone method of configuring the LAT. However, remember to include private network IDs for hosts that might connect to your network through a VPN connection in a gateway-to-gateway setup. You will need to include the private network ID address range(s) that will be used by those on the networks connected to yours in the VPN.

2. The **Select computer** drop-down list box allows you to select which computer's routing table you want to use in the construction of the LAT. Remember, in an array, all the array members share the same LAT. Each server should have the same routing table configuration; therefore, you could choose any server in the array.
3. The **Select the address ranges that are associated with the following internal network adapters** selection box allows you to choose the adapter address range you would like to include in the LAT. If your routing table is configured correctly it should not make any difference, since there will already be an entry for that adapter's network ID. Although this address is included in the routing table, you must make

a selection or the **OK** button will not become available. After you make your choices and click **OK**, this fact is confirmed in the following dialog box (Figure 8.18). As this dialog box states, the LAT is based on the routing table because we made that choice. All other choices are superfluous.

Figure 8.18 Confirmation Dialog Box after Constructing the LAT

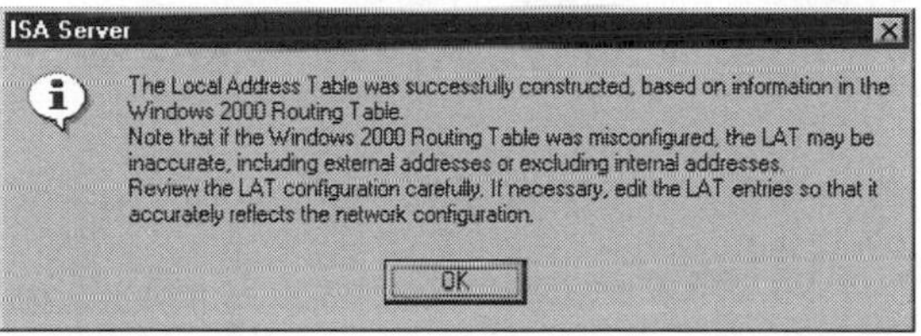

Before leaving this subject, let's take a look at how to build a routing table for the ISA Server.

Building the Routing Table

ISA Server uses the routing table to assess where to send packets based on their destination network IDs. The machine looks at the header for the destination IP address and then checks to see if it has a route for that address. There must be an established route for each network ID to which the internal interface needs to send packets, because the internal interface is not configured with a default gateway address. Therefore, the ISA server has only the routing table to assist it to get the packet to the internal address.

NOTE

The reason that you cannot configure the internal interface with a default gateway is that routers, including the Windows 2000 router, support a single gateway address for network ID 0.0.0.0. Since you must have a default gateway on the external interface to send packets to a router that knows how to route Internet-bound packets, you do not have the option, nor do you need one, of setting a default gateway on another interface. For this reason, you must configure a routing table so that packets can be intelligently routed to network IDs on your internal network.

While you can use the Routing and Remote Access console's GUI interface to construct a routing table, you might not want or need to enable RRAS. In our opinion, it is best if you construct the routing table from the command line. This obviates the need to enable RRAS. Let's use a simple three-segment internal network as an example. A single ISA server is configured with an ISDN 128Kbps BRI terminal adapter for its external interface and an Ethernet 10/100 connection for its internal interface. The internal interface's IP address is 192.168.1.1. Two dual-homed Windows 2000 servers act as routers on the internal network.

Router1 has these IP addresses:

192.168.1.185/24

192.168.10.1/24

Router2 has these IP addresses:

192.168.1.250/24

192.168.9.1/24

In order to configure the routing table, we need to manually configure routes to network IDs 192.168.9.0/24 and 192.168.10.0/24. We do not need to configure a route to network ID 192.168.1.0/24, because that network is directly connected to the internal interface.

To add a new route, use the following syntax:

```
route add [destination network ID] MASK [destination network subnet
mask] [gateway address] METRIC [metric value] IF [interface number]
```

Most of these comments are self-explanatory, but you might not be acquainted with the **IF** entry. The **IF**, or *Interface Number,* allows you to control the interface a particular route should use to send the packet. This control is helpful if you do not want the router to make its own determination of the best route to take and could slightly increase performance. In our example of dual-homed machines, there's no compelling reason to use this entry.

To allow our ISA server to route to network ID 192.168.9.0/24, we would enter the following at the command line:

```
route add 192.168.9.0 MASK 255.255.255.0 192.168.1.250
```

and then press **Enter**. After you press **Enter**, you will be returned to the command prompt and will not be informed that the route is correct. However, you will receive an error message if you configure a route to an interface that is not local to the adapter forwarding the packet.

To route to network ID 192.168.10.0, you would enter the following at the command line:

```
route add 192.168.10.0 MASK 255.255.255.0 192.168.1.185
```

and press **Enter**. To confirm the entries in the routing table, you can use the **route print** command.

One last but important thing: These routes will work perfectly until you restart the computer. After you restart, the routes will disappear because we did not use the *persistent* switch. To ensure that your routes survive a restart, make sure to include the **–p** switch. For this switch, the command begins **route add –p**.

NOTE

Routing table entries are stored in memory unless you use the –p switch to create a permanent route. Permanent routing table entries are stored in the registry.

Configuring the Local Domain Table

The *local domain table (LDT)* contains a list of local domains that is downloaded by firewall clients on a regular basis. The purpose of the LDT is to help the firewall client computer assess whether it should resolve a name or allow the ISA server to resolve the name for it.

UNDOCUMENTED ISA SERVER

If the LAT is stored in a file called msplat.txt, you might expect the LDT to be stored in a file called something like mspldt.txt—but you would be wrong. The fact is, you won't find that file anywhere on your hard disks. The LDT entries are included in the mspclnt.ini file.

For example, if we have ***.tacteam.net** in our local domain table, all name resolution requests for hosts in this domain will be sent by the firewall client to a DNS server that it is configured to use in the TCP/IP Properties dialog box. If the firewall client needs to resolve another domain name, such as **woodmaster.com**, the firewall client would check its local copy of the LDT, see that this is not an internal domain, and allow the ISA server to resolve the name for it.

The LDT solves a problem related to using FQDNs to access resources on the internal network. For example, if we had not included the *.tacteam.net entry in the LDT and then sent a request for *exeter.tacteam.net* for name resolution, the firewall client software would assume that since the request had "dots" in it, the request must be for an external server, and therefore the ISA server would be tasked to resolve the name. However, since we made an entry in the LDT, the firewall client software lets the client computer take over the name resolution duties and allows the name resolution request to be sent to its preferred DNS server.

To configure an entry in the LDT, perform the following steps:

1. Open the **ISA Management** console, expand **Servers and Arrays**, and then expand **Network Configuration**. Right-click the **Local Domain Table** node in the left pane, click the **New** command, and then click **LDT Entry**. You will see the screen that appears in Figure 8.19.

Figure 8.19 The New LDT Entry Dialog Box

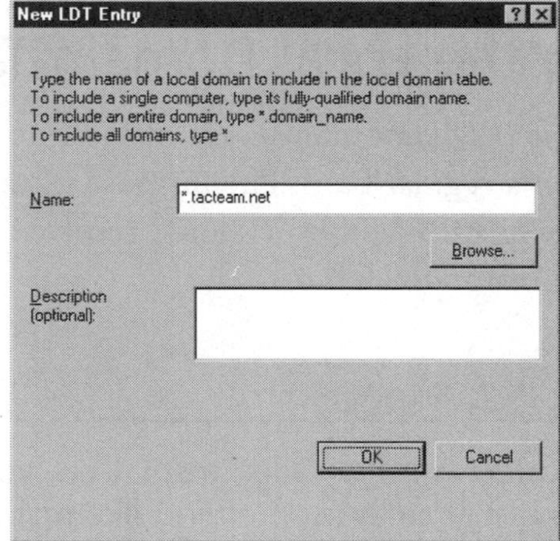

2. In the **Name** text box, type the name of a computer or include an entire domain, using the * as a wildcard to include all the computers in the domain. Click **OK** to complete the entry.

UNDOCUMENTED ISA SERVER

We just told you what the LDT is supposed to do. However, there's a little more to the story. From our testing, we find that when a firewall client computer is configured with a DNS server that is able to resolve Internet names, it will not use the ISA server to perform DNS Proxy at any time. We have confirmed this finding using Network Monitor. The only times the firewall client will use the ISA server to perform DNS Proxy occurs when the firewall client does not have a DNS server address configured in its TCP/IP settings or when the DNS server on the internal network is not able to resolve the Internet host name.

Creating Secure Outbound Access Policy

Microsoft ISA Server uses rules to determine the level of access allowed for Internet resources. Rules are also used to determine the level of external network client access to internal resources (through Web and server publishing rules) and resources contained on perimeter networks (through packet filters). Using the ISA Server rules, you can attain a high level of control over both inbound and outbound access.

ISA Server rules involved with outbound access are grouped into *access policies*. There are three categories of access policy:

- Site and content rules
- Protocol rules
- IP packet filters

Site and content rules are used to determine the sites (computers or domains) that can be accessed through the ISA server. They are also used to control the content that can be accessed via HTTP. A schedule can be applied to these rules that will assign the day and time when the rule is in effect. In order to access sites and content on the Internet, there must be a site and content rule that allows access. ISA Server includes a default site and content rule that allows access to all sites and all content at all times. You must create new site and content rules and disable the default to obtain more granular control.

Protocol rules determine the protocols that are available for both inbound and outbound access. Protocol rules will be used to determine outbound access, since you'll use publishing rules to determine inbound access policy, although both take advantage of protocol definitions. These rules determine the protocols and port numbers that are available to internal users, groups, or computers. In order for you to use a particular protocol to access Internet resources, a protocol rule must be in place to allow such access.

ISA Server always checks that there is *both* a site and content rule and a protocol rule that allows access to a external resource before access is granted. The availability of access policy rules depends on the type of ISA Server installation. Table 8.1 shows the relationships.

Table 8.1 Access Policies and Installation Types

Rule Type	Firewall Mode	Cache Mode	Integrated Mode
Site and content rules	Yes	Yes	Yes
Protocol rules	Yes	Web protocols only*	Yes

* The Web protocols include HTTP, HTTPS, FTP, and Gopher.

IP packet filters are used to control inbound and outbound access on the external interface of the ISA server. Typically, you will not use packet filters to control access to external resources by internal network clients; instead, you will use protocol rules. The advantage of using rules rather than packet filters is that protocol rules allow dynamic opening and closing of ports on the external interface.

Packet filters allow you to statically open or close a port on the external interface of the ISA server. When you deny access to particular port by using static packet filters, that port is not available, even if you wanted to use a protocol rule to allow access to it. In a sense, you could say that packet filters override configuration changes made by protocol rules. Packet filters are discussed in more detail in Chapter 9.

Access policies determine what, where, and when content can be accessed; other policies determine *how* the content is accessed. These policies include:

- Bandwidth rules
- Routing and chaining rules

Bandwidth rules allow you to shape the traffic moving through the ISA server. They allow you to indirectly assign the amount of bandwidth available to a particular connection type. This feature takes advantage of the Windows 2000 QoS packet scheduling service.

Routing and chaining rules determine where requests will be sent for further processing. You can use these rules to control the routing of Winsock application traffic, configure proxy chains, or control the content that is cached on the ISA server. Routing and chaining rule configuration depends on the ISA server installation mode. Table 8.2 details the specifics.

Table 8.2 Routing and Chaining Rules by Installation Type

Rule Type	Firewall Mode	Cache Mode	Integrated Mode
Routing rules	No	Yes	Yes
Firewall chaining	Yes	No	Yes

A last group of rules, called *publishing rules,* determines the level of external client access to internal network resources. We cover these rules in detail in Chapter 10.

The foundation of access policies are the *policy elements*. Before you even begin to create rules, you need to configure the policy elements that are used to create the rules. Therefore, we begin our discussion of the details of rules creation by delving into policy elements. After learning about policy elements, we can get to the business of creating protocol and site and content rules.

Creating and Configuring Policy Elements

Before creating rules, you must have the elements in place that are used to configure the rules. These policy elements include:

- Schedules
- Bandwidth priorities
- Destination sets
- Client address sets
- Protocol definitions
- Content groups
- Dial-up entries

Policies allow the use of different policy elements. You could create access policies "on the fly," but chances are that you will have to go back and create a policy element if you don't plan your policies in advance. When you plan your policies in advance, you will know which policy elements need to be created and you'll configure them before creating an access policy rule.

Let's go through the policy elements now and see what they entail and how to configure each one of them.

Dial-up Entries

If you use a dial-up connection for your external interface, you must configure a connection in the **Dial-up Entries** node. This dial-up entry is used in your Web proxy routing and firewall chaining rules. The dial-up entry allows ISA server to demand-dial a connection when it receives a request for an external resource.

Dial-up entries are based on connections that have already been configured in the **Network and Dial-up Connections** window. These connections are sometimes referred to as *connectoids*. You must create the connectoid before you create the dial-up entry. Because ISA Server uses Dial-up Networking connectoids, you lose some of the functionality you would have if they were configurable via the Routing and Remote Access Service.

NOTE

In order for the dial-up entry to dial on demand, you *must* put a check mark in the check box for **Use dial-up entry** in the Routing Rule Configuration dialog box for either the Web proxy routing rule or the firewall chaining routing rule.

For example, when a demand-dial connection is created in RRAS and used together with the RRAS NAT Service, you can create a pool of public IP addresses and create one-to-one mappings with servers on the internal network. This feature effectively lets you bind multiple IP addresses to the external interface of a dial-up adapter. Being able to bind multiple IP addresses to the external adapter greatly increases the flexibility you have in configuring things such as server publishing rules.

You cannot do this with ISA Server due to its dependence on the Dial-up Networking connectoids. In fact, you are limited to using a *single IP address* on the external interface when using dial-up connections. Even so-called "dedicated"

ISDN BRI connections, which must be configured as dial-up connectoids to establish the link, suffer from the problem.

UNDOCUMENTED ISA SERVER

Many DSL providers require that a protocol called Point-to-Point Protocol Over Ethernet (PPPoE) be used to establish the PPP link to their networks before the connection becomes functional. Note that this is not a limitation of DSL but an ISP implementation issue. This means that PPPoE DSL connections, which purport to be dedicated, suffer from the same limitation of using DUN connectoids as ISDN and other dial-up connections. These connections are able to assign a single IP address to their external adapter, whereas non-PPPoE DSL connections are able to bind multiple IP addresses.

Dial-up Entries for Arrays

Configuring dial-up entries for arrays is somewhat circuitous. The reason is that each member of an array must have the same dial-up entries configured, and each dial-up entry must be configured to use connectoids with the *same name*. You might wonder, how is ISAServer1 possibly going to use a dial-up connection configured on ISAServer2? These are two different machines using two different lines to connect to the Internet.

The answer is, it can't. The trick to making this work is to configure on *each ISA server* connectoids that have the *same name*. Although you create a connectoid called ISP_connection on each server in the array, each connectoid can be configured with different dial-up numbers and account information. In this way, each member of the array can have the same dial-up entries and use connectoids with the same names. This allows each machine to use its own dial-up connection to the Internet.

NOTE

Connectoids can be created to connect the ISA server to your ISP or to another ISA server via a direct dial-up link.

Creating Dial-up Entries

To create dial-up entries, perform the following steps:

1. Open the **Network and Dial-up Connections** window and use the **Make New Connection** wizard to create your connectoid.
2. After the connectoid is created, open the **ISA Management** console, expand **Servers and Arrays**, and expand **Policy Elements**. Right-click **Dial-up Entries**, and click the **Dial-up Entry**. Your screen will look something like Figure 8.20.

Figure 8.20 The New Dial-up Entry Dialog Box

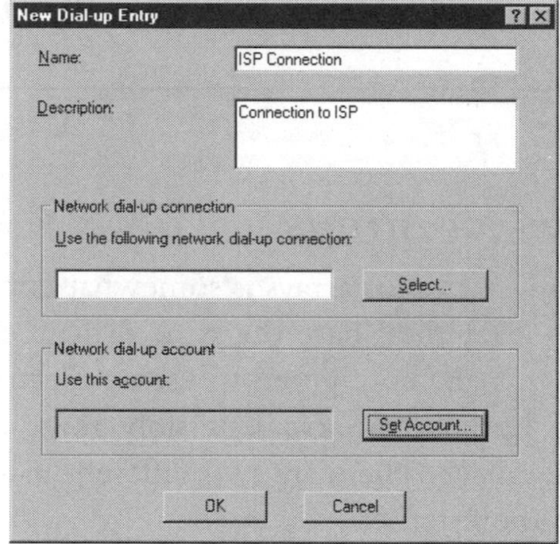

The **Name** text box defines the name of the dial-up entry. Keep in mind that this is *not* the name of the connectoid but the name of the dial-up entry used by ISA Server. If you are using an array, this dial-up entry will appear in *each* member of the array. The **Description** text box provides an optional field for you to describe what this dial-up entry is about.

In the **Network dial-up connection** frame, you can enter the name of the connectoid that the dial-up entry will use to establish the connection. If you can't recall the name, click the **Select** button and it will display all the connectoids that have been configured on that machine.

3. After choosing your connectoid, you need to configure dial-up credentials. Click the **Set Account** button and you'll see the screen that appears in Figure 8.21.

Figure 8.21 The Set Account Dialog Box

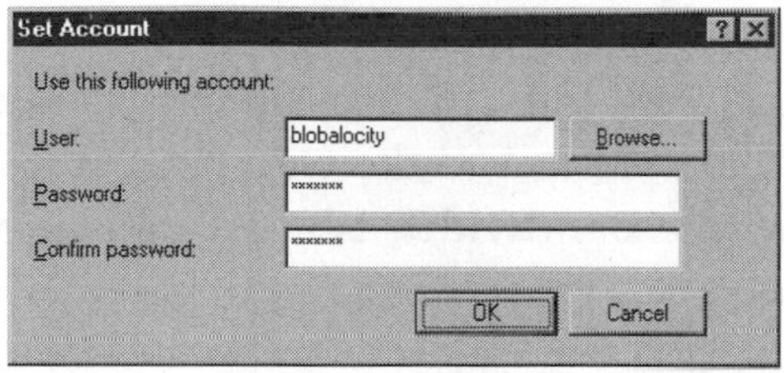

Enter the user account name in the **User** text box, and then type in the password and confirm the password. Note that the **Browse** button will allow you to browse for user accounts on the local computer and those in trusted domains. This capability is useful if you are calling another ISA Server computer but it is *not* to be used if you are calling an ISP.

If you do not configure the proper credentials, the ISA server will not able to autodial the connectoid when an outbound request arrives at the ISA server.

4. When the configuration of the dial-up entry is complete, you should see the screen that appears in Figure 8.22. Click **OK** to complete the entry.

Figure 8.22 The Completed New Dial-up Entry Box

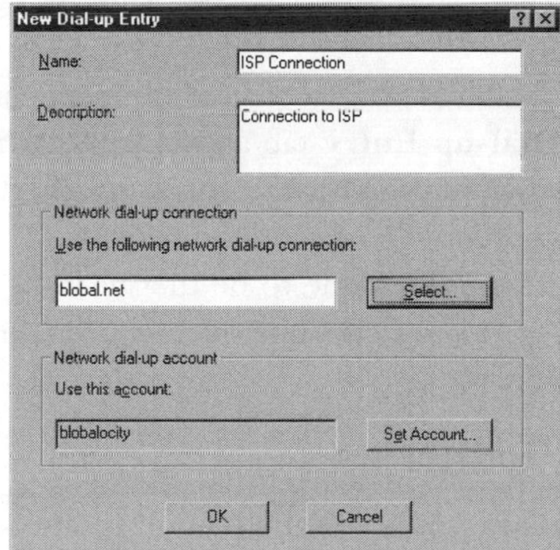

5. The dial-up entry will show up in the right pane. If you have only a single entry, it will automatically be configured as the **Active Entry**. If you have multiple dial-up entries, you can right-click the entry in the

right pane and click the **Set as Active Entry** command to make another dial-up entry the active one. *Only the active dial-up entry will be used to establish a connection.*

You can right-click the dial-up entry and click the **Properties** command to make changes to the entry after it has been configured. Figure 8.23 shows the **Bandwidth** tab of the **Properties** dialog box of one of the entries.

Figure 8.23 The Dial-up Connection Dialog Box

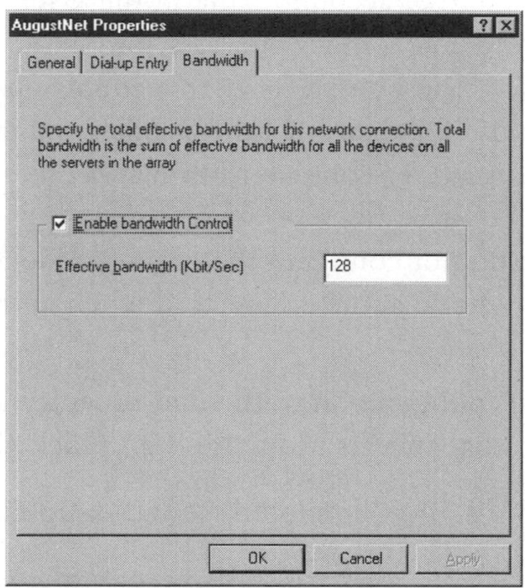

The **General** tab allows you to change the name and description for the dial-up entry. The **Dial-up Entry** tab allows you to change the connectoid and user account and password used for the entry. Finally, the **Bandwidth tab** allows you to enable and configure bandwidth control.

You should configure this value to be the speed of your external connection, because it is used by QoS to determine bandwidth allocation when bandwidth rules are implemented.

Bandwidth Priorities

Bandwidth priorities allow you to define communications to give prioritized bandwidth to different types of communications. These bandwidth priorities can be applied to bandwidth rules and allow a stratified access scheme based on account, protocol, IP address, schedule, or content. These priorities are used by the QoS Packet Scheduler to determine which communications have a larger slice of the available bandwidth. Bandwidth priorities allow ISA Server to allocate different percentages of bandwidth to different types of communications, as you define by bandwidth priorities.

Priorities are configured separately for inbound and outbound bandwidth. For each direction, you can configure a priority value between 1 and 200, with the higher value having the higher priority. Note that these priorities are based on a relative weighting rather than absolute bandwidth. The available bandwidth is apportioned based on the relative weightings of the requests. You cannot set aside or set a specific limit on the absolute bandwidth assigned to a particular communication.

You can design your bandwidth priorities in a number of ways. One approach is to create high, medium, and low priorities, as outlined in Table 8.3.

Table 8.3 Bandwidth Priority Configurations

Priority	Inbound	Outbound
Highest	200	200
Medium	100	100
Lowest	50	50

Bandwidth rules can then be created around these priorities. The priorities can be configured to have even finer gradations if you require them. For example, you might want to create priorities that go between these values, such as "High" and "Low" that would fit between the priorities in the table. ISA Server creates a default bandwidth priority. This priority level is applied to requests without a defined priority. Note that the default values are 100 for inbound and outbound requests. You might consider lowering these values, depending on the priority scheme you have developed. The default bandwidth priority will be applied to the default bandwidth rule. Bandwidth priorities are used in bandwidth rules to assign a specific user, group, or protocol to a bandwidth "pool" assigned to that priority.

For example, look at Figure 8.24. In this example, there are active connections by users, groups, or protocols that have been assigned to the **Default bandwidth priority** and the **Highest priority**. The QoS mechanism divides the available bandwidth among these two priorities. All connections assigned to the **Default bandwidth priority** share the bandwidth assigned to that priority, and all connections assigned to the **Highest bandwidth priority** share the bandwidth assigned to that priority.

Figure 8.24 Bandwidth Priorities in Action

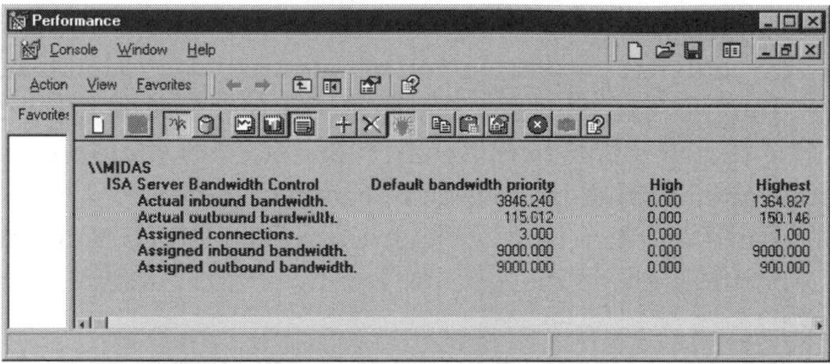

Now, what happens if a connection assigned to the High bandwidth priority is established? Look at Figure 8.25 to see what happens.

Figure 8.25 Changing Bandwidth Apportionment

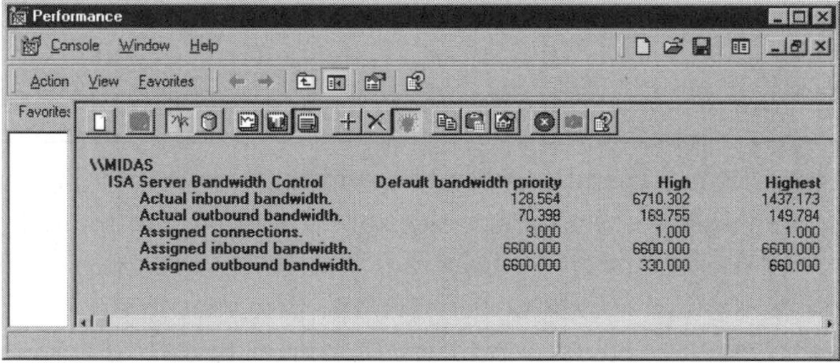

Notice how the total amount of bandwidth is reallocated because a connection assigned to the High bandwidth priority is established. Note that the total amount of bandwidth is divided among the priorities that have *active,* or assigned, connections. It's important to realize that although not all the allocated bandwidth for the **Highest** and **Default** bandwidth priorities is being utilized, connections using the **High** priority are limited to 6600bps inbound. Note that while the latest reading is 6710.302, the connections assigned to the High bandwidth priority all must share the 6600bps inbound bandwidth, with only very slight variations at any point in time.

Creating Bandwidth Priorities

Follow these steps to create bandwidth priorities:

1. Open the **ISA Management** console, expand **Servers and Arrays**, and then expand **Policy Elements**. Right-click **Bandwidth Priorities** and **New**, and then click **Bandwidth Priority**. You will see the dialog box that appears in Figure 8.26.

Figure 8.26 The New Bandwidth Priority Dialog Box

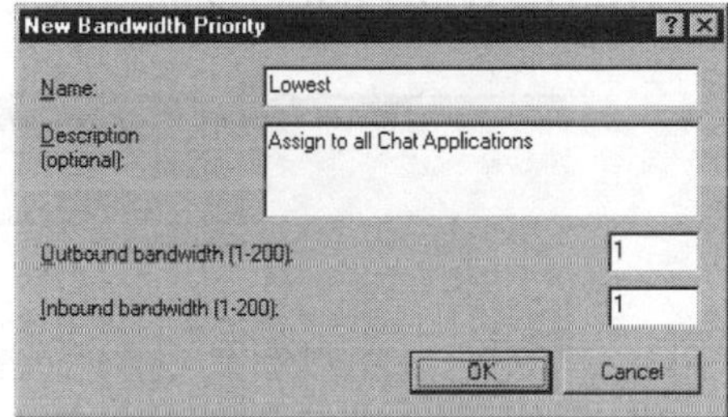

2. This dialog box is straightforward. Enter the name of the bandwidth priority, an optional description, and an outbound bandwidth and an inbound bandwidth in the appropriate text boxes. Click **OK** and the bandwidth priority is set and can be used in creating bandwidth rules.

Schedules

The **Schedules** policy element allows you to create various schedules that you can apply to:

- Site and content rules
- Protocol rules
- Bandwidth rules

ISA Server comes preconfigured with two schedules:

- **Weekends** All day Saturday and Sunday.
- **Work Hours** Monday through Friday, 9:00 AM to 5:00 PM.

You can create custom schedules to meet the needs of your organization. For example, you might want to create a schedule that applies to other shifts such as "swing shift" and "graveyard shift." You could then apply these schedules to workers who work those shifts.

Creating Schedules

To create a new schedule, perform the following steps:

1. Open the **ISA Management** console, expand **Servers and Arrays**, and then expand **Policy Elements**. Right-click **Schedules**, click **New**, and then click **Schedule**. You will see the screen that appears in Figure 8.27.

Figure 8.27 The New Schedule Dialog Box

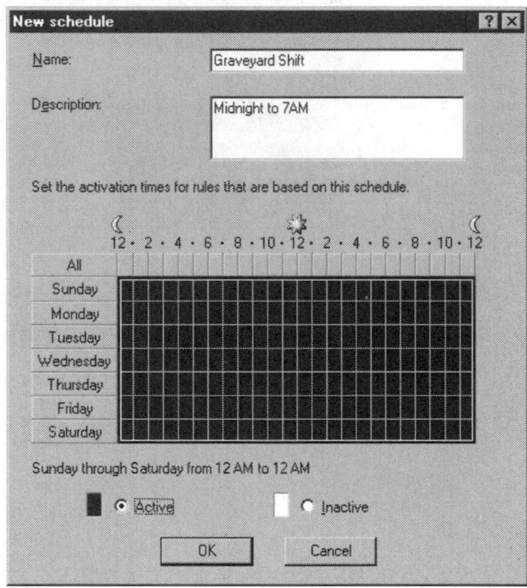

2. The default has all days and times active. We would like to limit our example schedule **Graveyard Shift** to be active Monday through Friday from 12:00 AM to 7:00 AM. To create this schedule, click the **All** button on the calendar, and then click the **Inactive** option button. This sequence clears the blue from the boxes and makes them white.
3. Now drag and select from **Monday 12AM** across to **Monday 7AM** and then down to **Friday 7AM**. After making the selection, click the **Active** option button. Your dialog box should like Figure 8.28.
4. Notice that the extent of the schedule is listed underneath the selected boxes. Click **OK** to complete the new schedule.

Figure 8.28 Creating a New Schedule

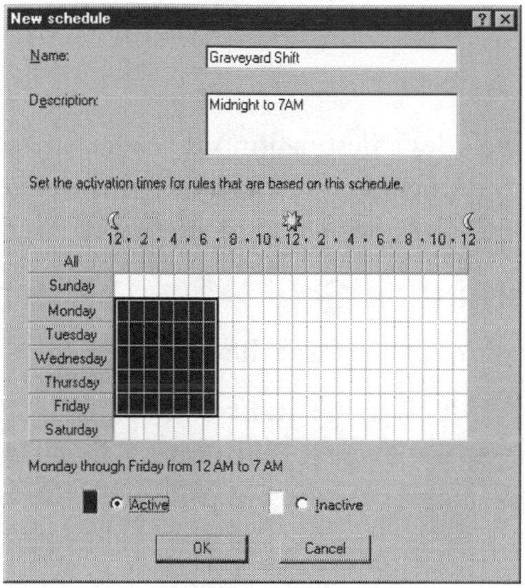

Destination Sets

Destination sets allow you to create rules that are based on a particular destination. A destination can be defined by an IP address, a group of IP addresses, a computer name, a fully qualified domain name, an entire domain, or a subfolder on a computer within a domain. You can include a path in the destination set to include folders located at a specific destination.

Destination sets can be included in the following policies:

- Site and content rules
- Bandwidth rules
- Web publishing rules
- Routing rules

For clients behind the ISA Server, destination sets are defined for external hosts. In this way, you can use destination sets in policy rules to control outbound access. Destination sets can also be defined for inbound requests. In this case, a destination set would represent a FQDN of a server that you intend to publish.

When creating destination sets that include a path, the following rules apply:

- To include a specific directory, specify the path **/dir**.
- To include all the files in the directory, specify the path **/dir/***.

- To include a specific file in the directory, specify the path **/dir/Filename**.
- All computers in a domain can be specified using an * as a wildcard, such as *.tacteam.net.

When a rule includes a destination set, the rule can state that all computers in the destination set are included or that all destinations *except* those in the destination set are included. This allows you to fine-tune your outbound access control.

Creating Destination Sets

To create a destination set, perform the following steps:

1. Open the **ISA Management** console, expand **Servers and Arrays**, and then expand **Policy Elements**. Right-click **Destination Sets**, then click **New**, and then click **Set**. You'll see the screen that appears in Figure 8.29.

   Figure 8.29 The New Destination Set Dialog Box

2. In the **Name** text box, type in the name of the destination set. Type an optional description in the **Description (optional)** text box. The **Include these destinations** box contains the destinations you want included in this destination set.

   To add a new destination to be included in this set, click the **Add** button. Since this destination set is aimed at all Microsoft-run sites, we might want to include all the machines in other Microsoft domains, such as the msn.com domain. Later, we can create a bandwidth rule that gives high priority to all Microsoft domains.

3. After clicking the **Add** button, you'll see the screen that appears in Figure 8.30. Since we want to add all hosts in the msn.com domain, we use the * as a wildcard and then the domain name. Click **OK** to add the destination. Note that if you want to block all content in a particular domain, you *do not* need to designate a path. Just use a wildcard entry for the host name portion of the FQDN and include the destination set in a site and content rule.

Figure 8.30 The Add/Edit Destination Dialog Box

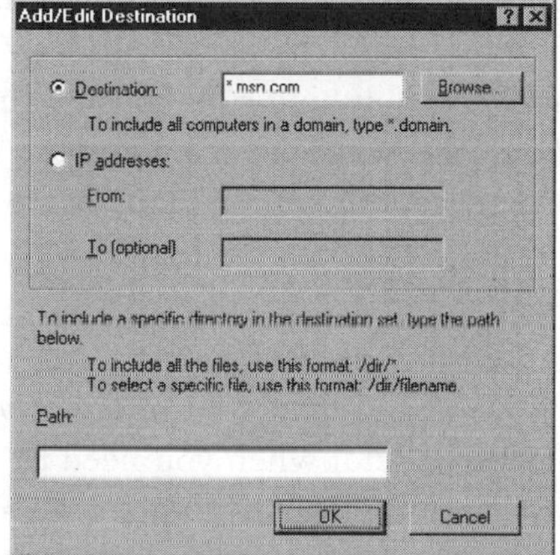

Creating Destination Sets for Incoming Requests

When creating destination sets for incoming requests, you want to include a FQDN that resolves to an IP address on the external interface of the ISA server. You do *not* want to include in your destination set the name of the *internal* server, because that name has no meaning for external clients. Destination sets created for inbound access are seen from the perspective of the external users that are using public DNS servers to access your sites.

For example, you want to publish an internal Web server so that hosts on the Internet can access it via a FQDN. The first thing you need to do is make sure a DNS record on a publicly available DNS server is entered for your host and mapped to an external interface on the ISA server. Then you would configure a destination set for this FQDN.

For example, let's say that you want to publish a server with the FQDN of www.funtimes.org. First you need a public DNS entry that maps to the external interface of the ISA server. Then you would configure a destination set for www.funtimes.org via the **Add/Edit Destination** dialog box. Finally, you use this destination set to create a Web publishing rule.

Another example of how to use destination sets is demonstrated by taking advantage of the **path** feature in the **Add/Edit Destination** dialog box. For example, you have a DNS entry for www.mybusiness.com that points to the external interface of your ISA server. You have published an internal server named **WebServer1** and all inbound requests to www.mybusiness.com are forwarded to **WebServer1**.

However, you want all inbound requests for www.mybusiness.com/catalog forwarded to another server, **WebServer2**. When the request is sent to **WebServer2**, you want the request sent to the **catalog** folder on that server.

This is accomplished by using a destination set that includes a path statement. In this example, you would enter the path **/catalog/** in the destination set. When you create the Web publishing rule, you use this destination set and have the request redirected to the **WebServer2**. Thus, the path option allows you a great deal of flexibility in how incoming requests are forwarded.

Client Address Sets

Client address sets are the flip side of destination sets. You can group clients together by *IP address ranges* and then control access via these client address sets. Client address sets are very useful when you need to control outbound access for SecureNAT clients. SecureNAT clients do not send authentication information to the ISA server, and so client address sets are your alternative to user/group access control. The limitation of this approach is that you must group your network clients in a way to make your client address sets manageable.

Client address sets are also useful if you want to limit inbound access. For example, you might publish a Web site that you only want partners to be able to access. You know that the partner uses a single gateway for all its outbound HTTP requests and that this gateway has a single static IP address. You can create a client address set that includes only this IP address and then allow access to your published Web site to these clients only.

Another example in which client address sets might be useful occurs when you want to publish an internal database server that is available to a Web server or a group of Web servers on your perimeter network. When you limit access to just the Web servers on your perimeter network, you allow the servers to communicate with the internal database server while protecting the database server from connections initiated by Internet users.

Creating Client Address Sets

To create a client address set, perform the following steps:

1. Open the **ISA Management** console, expand **Servers and Arrays**, and then expand **Policy Elements**. Right-click **Client Address Sets**, then click **New**, and then click **Set**. You'll see the screen that appears in Figure 8.31.

Figure 8.31 The Client Set Dialog Box

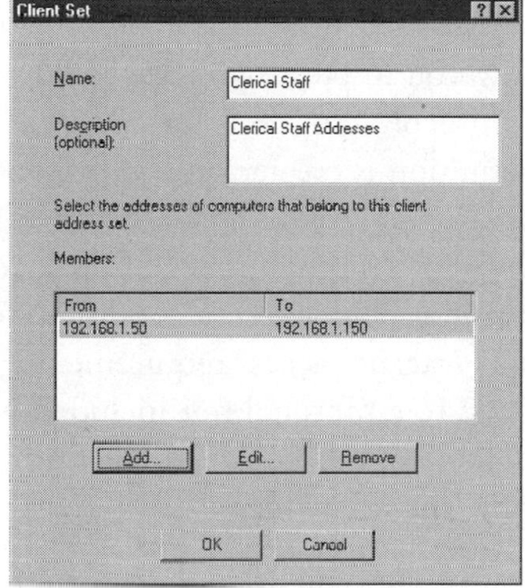

2. In the **Name** text box, type in the name for the client address set. In the **Description (optional)** box, type an optional description for this client address set. To add a new address set, click the **Add** button; to change an existing set, click the **Edit** button.
3. When you click the **Add** button, you'll see the screen that appears in Figure 8.32.

Figure 8.32 The Add/Edit IP Address Dialog Box

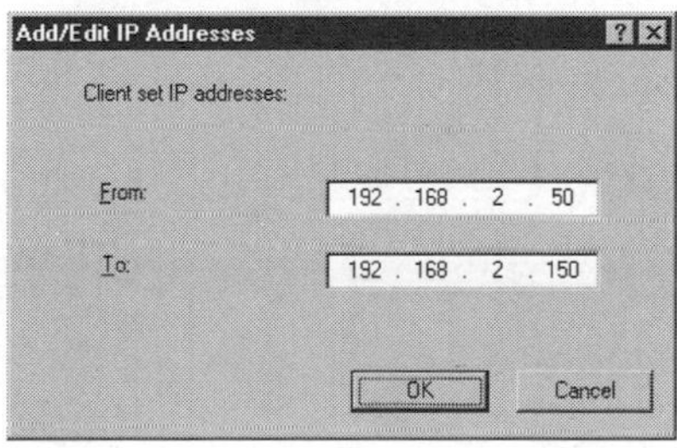

4. Enter the first IP address in the range in the **From** text box and the last IP address in the range in the **To** text box. Click **OK** to complete the action. You can include multiple ranges of IP addresses in a single address set. This allows you to include computers that are located in noncontiguous address ranges in a single client address set.

Protocol Definitions

Protocol definitions allow you to create policies based on Application layer protocols. You can create protocol definitions for any TCP/UDP-based protocol. After the protocol definition is created, you can then implement polices based on that protocol.

ISA Server comes with a large number of protocol definitions. These built-in protocol definitions cannot be deleted or modified. You can use these definitions for virtually all of your Internet access requirements.

If you require access to a protocol not included with ISA Server, you can create your own protocol definition. When creating your own protocol definition, you need to know the following:

- The direction of the request
- The Transport layer protocol (TCP or UDP)
- The inbound or outbound port number for the primary connection
- Secondary connections that need to be established, if any

Let's look at a popular example. ISA Server does not include a protocol definition that allows a SecureNAT client to connect to Napster. In order to allow the SecureNAT client to connect with the Napster client software to the servers on the Napster network, you need to create the following protocol definition:

Primary Connection:

Port Number: 8875

Protocol Type: TCP

Direction: Outbound

Secondary Connections:

6688-6699	TCP	Inbound
8888	TCP	Outbound

When the Napster client connects to the Napster servers, it needs to first establish a connection on the server's port 8875. After the initial outbound connection, the Napster server needs to establish new inbound connections in the range of 6688–6699 to the ISA Server, and the Napster client also needs to create a second outbound connection, after the first is established, to port 8888 on the Napster server. In order for ISA Server to manage all these connections, we need to create a protocol rule that includes both the primary and secondary connections.

NOTE

To complete the configuration of Napster for the SecureNAT client, you need to enable the Napster client software to use the SOCKS4 protocol and point it to the IP address on the ISA server's internal interface on the default SOCKS listening port 1080. Make sure that the SOCKS filter is enabled. Be aware that if you have the firewall client installed, you do not need to create a protocol definition, because the firewall client software will be able to manage these secondary connections automatically.

Protocol definitions are especially important to SecureNAT clients because these clients only have access to protocols included in the protocol definitions and do not have the ability to communicate to the Firewall Service the requirements that application protocol might require. These means that if you configure an outbound access policy allowing *all* protocols, SecureNAT clients can take advantages of all *defined* protocols. This is in contrast to the firewall client that can access virtually *any* Winsock protocol, whether or not a protocol definition exists.

User-defined protocol definitions can be modified or deleted. However, if you spend a lot of time creating protocol definitions, you might want to simply keep them. They won't be used and they won't leave any ports open or available unless you configure a rule that uses the particular protocol (including rules that allow *all* protocols).

Protocol Definitions and Application Filters

Application filters can install their own protocol definitions, and some application filters use protocol definitions included with ISA Server. You might or might not be able to delete the protocol definitions that come with the application filter. The only way to actually know is to check the protocol definition you want to delete. If the **DELETE** command is available, then you can delete the protocol definition.

However, if you disable an application filter, some of its associated protocol definitions may become unavailable, and you won't be able to use them in protocol rules. You can tell which protocol definitions are created by application filters by looking at the **Defined By** column in the right pane of the **ISA Management** console (Figure 8.33).

Figure 8.33 Viewing Protocol Definitions

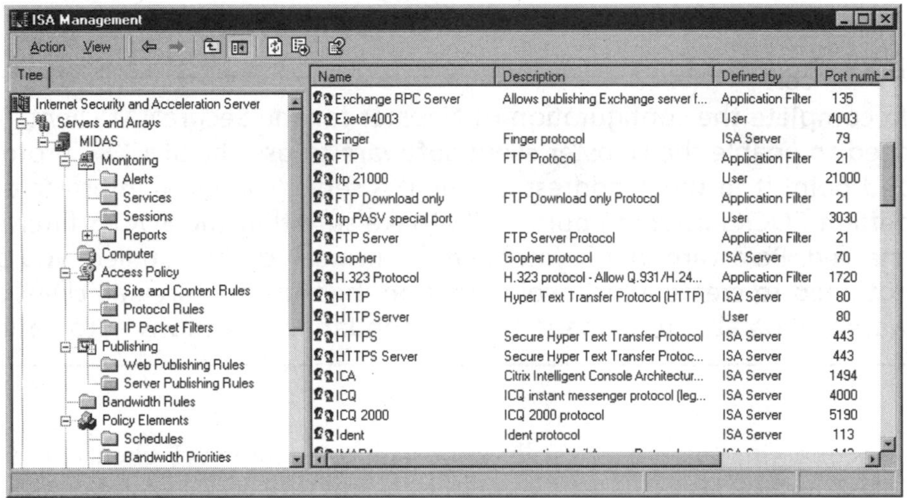

You'll notice some protocols that require multiple connections, such as FTP, do not require you to actually configure the "back channels" (inbound secondary connections) required for such a connection. Let's consider how the FTP protocol works to get a better appreciation for what the FTP application filter can do.

When a client sends out a request to an FTP server, that request is sent to the FTP server's port 21, which is the FTP control channel. Commands from the FTP client are sent to the FTP server's control channel. When the FTP client wants to download a file or list files and directories on the FTP server, it sends a PORT command to the FTP server, telling the FTP server the IP address and port number it should use to open a new connection back to the FTP client to receive the data.

Since the FTP client can't be reached directly from the FTP server, the ISA server must "listen in" on this conversation so that it can be ready to open a port to which the FTP server can send data. Note that the ISA server must be aware of the conversation taking place on the control channel so that it can expect a new inbound connection request from the FTP server's port 20 (the FTP server's data channel) to the port number it is assigned to receive the data and forward it to the internal FTP client.

You can test this for yourself by disabling the FTP application filter. This disabling will break your FTP client's ability to connect to an FTP server using the PORT command. On the other hand, if you are connecting to an FTP server with a PASV mode FTP client, the ISA server does not need to be aware of any new inbound connections, since the FTP client establishes all new connections. The built-in FTP protocol definitions allow PASV FTP clients to establish a connection and download files from an FTP server.

To see a complete list of the built-in protocol definitions, open the ISA Server **Help** file, click the **Search** tab, and type in **protocol definitions**. The top-ranked article will be **configuring protocol definitions**. This article contains the list of all built-in protocol definitions.

Creating a Protocol Definition: Supporting Terminal Services Publishing

You might want to publish an internal terminal server so that users on the Internet can access the internal terminal server via the external interface of the ISA server. In order to publish the terminal server, you must have a protocol definition in place. Since there is no built-in Terminal Services protocol definition, you need to create one.

To create the Terminal Services protocol definition, perform the following steps:

1. Open the **ISA Management** console, expand **Servers and Arrays**, and then expand **Policy Elements**. Right-click **Protocol Definitions**, then click **New**, and then click **Definition**.
2. This sequence starts the **New Protocol Definition Wizard**. Type in a name for the protocol definition. In this example, we'll call it RDP. Then click **Next**. This takes you to the Primary Connection Page, as seen in Figure 8.34.
3. Type in the port number you want the primary connection to use in the **Port number** text box. In this case, we'll put in port **3389**, which is the server port used by Terminal Services. For the **Protocol type**, select **TCP**; for the direction, select **Inbound** so that external clients can send inbound requests to access the terminal server. You do not need to configure an outbound protocol definition, because the ISA server will automatically open a dynamic response port. Click **Next**.

Figure 8.34 The Primary Connection Page

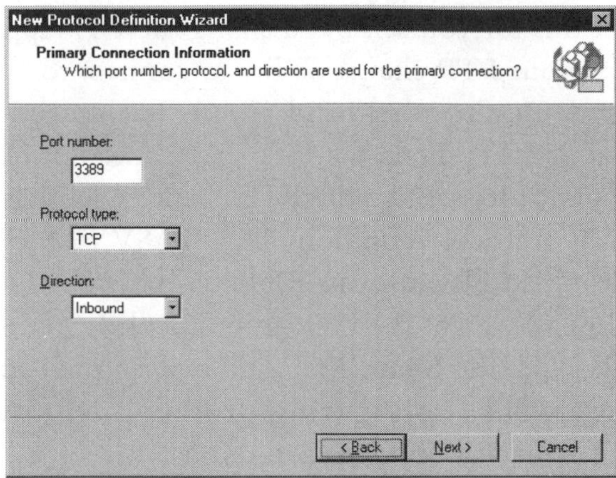

4. On the **Secondary Connections** page, you can configure any secondary connections that are required by the protocol. In this case, we do not need any secondary connections, so we can click **Next**.
5. The last page allows you to review your configuration. If everything looks right, click **Finish**.

NOTE

If you want to publish a terminal server, you cannot run a terminal server on the ISA server without making some configuration changes to the external port number used by the terminal server running on the ISA server. We'll go into this situation in more detail in Chapter 10, where we discuss publishing services.

Content Groups

Content groups allow you to control outbound access based on content contained in Web pages or FTP sites. You can create rules based on your content groups to limit access to selected content as defined in your groups. ISA Server comes with several predefined content groups that you can use right out of the box. Note that controlling access to content via content groups is available only for content accessed via HTTP or FTP that is tunneled inside HTTP requests.

Content groups are actually a collection of MIME types or file extensions. When FTP content is requested, ISA Server checks the file extension on the requested object. If there is a rule that contains this content that allows access, the file can be downloaded via FTP. If there is no access rule, access to the file is denied. Note that the default site and content rule allows access to all sites and content.

NOTE

Remember that rules limiting FTP access based on file extension information contained in content groups are only applied to FTP requests tunneled inside HTTP requests. This tunneled FTP access is performed by Web proxy clients. If you use a dedicated FTP program or the Windows 2000 command line FTP program, the requests are sent as non-tunneled FTP requests and are not subject to content rules.

A request for content from Web servers works a little differently. When a browser makes a request for a Web page, the ISA server retrieves the information from the Web site and then examines the content as it is returned from the server. There must be an allow rule for all content being retrieved. If there is no allow rule or if there is a deny rule for a certain MIME type or file extension of an object returned by the Web server, the content will be rejected and only the allowed content will be returned to the browser making the request.

Content groups included with ISA Server include:

- Application
- Application data files
- Audio
- Compressed files
- Documents
- HTML documents
- Images
- Macro documents
- Text
- Video
- VRML

Each of these content groups contains MIME types or file extensions that relate to the content group name. For example, if you wanted to create a rule to prevent a group of users from accessing video and audio data, you could create a site and content rule that applies to all sites and deny access to **Video** and **Audio** content groups.

To view a list of all the MIME types and file extensions, check the **Help** file for ISA Server. Click the **Search** tab and type in **Configuring Content Groups**, then click the **List Topics** button. The third-ranked listing will contain the correct article, **Configuring Content Groups**.

Viewing Content Groups

To view the MIME type and file extensions included in a content group, perform the following steps:

1. Open the **ISA Management** console, expand **Servers and Arrays**, and then expand **Policy Elements**. Click **Content Groups**, and then double-click one of the groups. In this example, we'll open the **Images** content group. You'll see the screen that appears in Figure 8.35.

Figure 8.35 The Images Properties Dialog Box

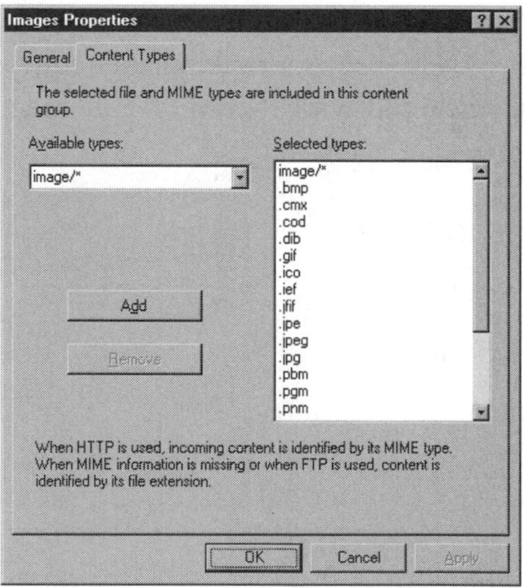

2. The **Selected type** box shows the MIME types and file extensions that are included in the group. You can always add more MIME types or file extensions by clicking the down arrow in the **Available types** drop-down list box, selecting a type, and then clicking the **Add** button.

Creating a New Content Group

If none of the built-in content groups fits your needs, you can create your own. For example, suppose you just want to prevent users from downloading or listening to .MP3 and .WAV files via HTTP, but you still want them to have access to all other sound formats (note that this will also prevent downloading .MP3 files via Napster). You can do this by creating your own group.

To create a content group, perform the following steps:

1. Open the **ISA Management** console, expand **Servers and Arrays**, and then expand **Policy Elements**. Right-click **Content Groups**, then click **New**, and then click **Content Group**. You will see the screen that appears in Figure 8.36.

Figure 8.36 The New Content Group Dialog Box

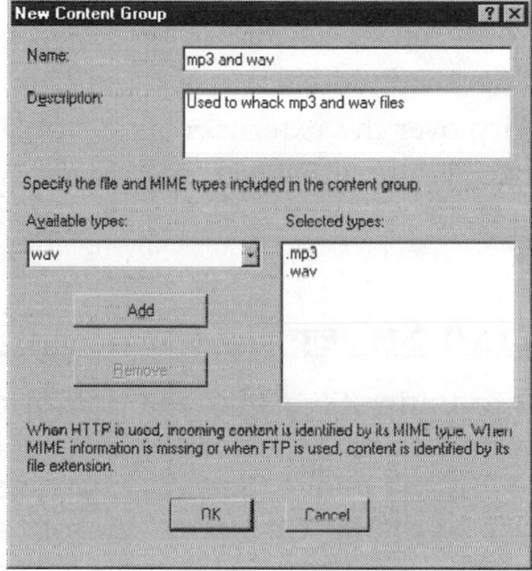

2. To populate the new group, you can click the down arrow for the **Available types** drop-down list box, or you can type in the MIME type or file extension and then click the **Add** button. This will add the type to the **Selected types** box. Click **OK** and the new group will be available for use.

Creating Rules Based on Policy Elements

After creating your policy elements, you are ready to create rules based on them. The policies will allow you to control what users can access on external networks, when they can access it, and at what time of day. Your access policies form the core of your outbound access scheme.

In contrast to the large number of policy elements, there are only four categories of access policy:

- Bandwidth rules
- Site and content rules
- Protocol rules
- IP packet filters

Bandwidth rules are somewhat different from the other access policies because these policies determine the performance of a particular connection rather than allowing or denying a connection. The other policy types are used to determine whether an internal host can access a resource.

Bandwidth Rules

Bandwidth rules build on the bandwidth priorities you created when configuring policy elements. Using bandwidth rules, you can determine which clients and protocols have priority over the external connection's available bandwidth. Users and protocols that have a higher priority will be allocated more of the available bandwidth than users and protocols with lower priorities.

Undocumented ISA Server

It is important to understand that you do not assign a hard-coded amount of bandwidth to a particular protocol or user/group. Rather, you assign a priority to the connection. You can see this dynamic assignment take place by using the **Performance** console and adding **ISA Server Bandwidth Control** counters. When you observe these counters in real time, you will see bandwidth dynamically assigned to the various bandwidth priorities.

To get a better idea of how we can use bandwidth rules, let's create one. In this example, suppose that in spite of your recommendations, the management wants to allow the AOL Instant Messenger (AIM) to be used during work hours. Your external connection is already maxed out, and one thing you don't need is AOLers jamming up what bandwidth you have left. In order to keep the peace and allow business-related activity to continue without interference from the AIM traffic, you have decided to configure a bandwidth rule to minimize the bandwidth allocated to AIM traffic.

Creating a Bandwidth Rule

To create this bandwidth rule, perform the following steps:

1. Open the **ISA Management** console, expand **Servers and Arrays**, and then right-click **Bandwidth Rules**. Click **New** and then **Rule**.
2. On the first page of the **New Bandwidth Rule Wizard**, type in the name of the rule. In this example, we'll call it **Whack AIM**. Then click **Next**.
3. On the **Protocols** page, you decide what protocols to which the rule should be applied. When you click the down arrow, you will see the screen that appears in Figure 8.37.

Figure 8.37 The Protocols Page

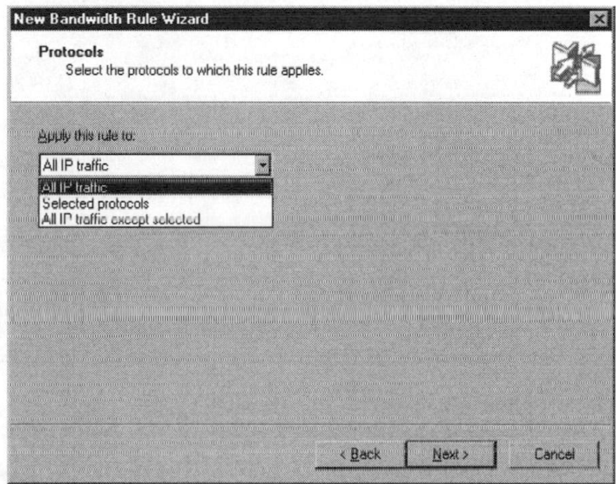

Your options are to apply the rule to:

- All IP traffic
- Selected protocols
- All IP traffic except selected

The **All IP Traffic** option doesn't allow you much granularity. In practice, it allows you to replace the default scheduling priority with a new custom rule that applies a new default scheduling priority, since it is applied to all protocols. The **Selected protocols** option allows you granular control over the protocols to which the bandwidth rule will be applied. The **All IP traffic except selected** allows you to apply the rule to all protocols except those protocols you want to except from the rule.

In this example, we'll choose the **Selected protocols** option.

4. After you make the selection, the **Protocols** window appears and offers you a list of protocols from which to choose. This list is derived from the list of protocol definitions contained in the policy elements node.

   For this example, place a check mark in the check box for **AOL Instant Messenger**, and then click **Next** (Figure 8.38).

Figure 8.38 Choosing Protocols

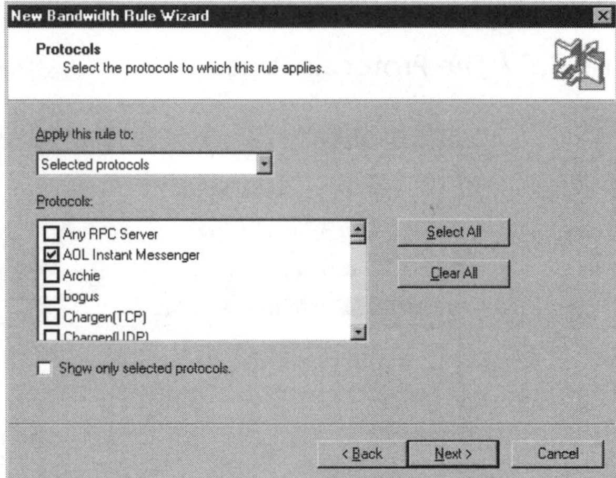

5. You now see what appears in Figure 8.39. After selecting the protocol, choose when you want the bandwidth rule to apply. Since bandwidth issues are most pressing during work hours, place the most severe restrictions on AIM access during this time. When you click the down arrow on the **Use this schedule** box, you have these options to apply this rule:

   - Always
   - Weekends
   - Work hours
   - Custom (Custom options appear only have you create custom Schedule policy elements.)

   Select the **Work hours** option, and then click **Next**.

Figure 8.39 The Schedule Page

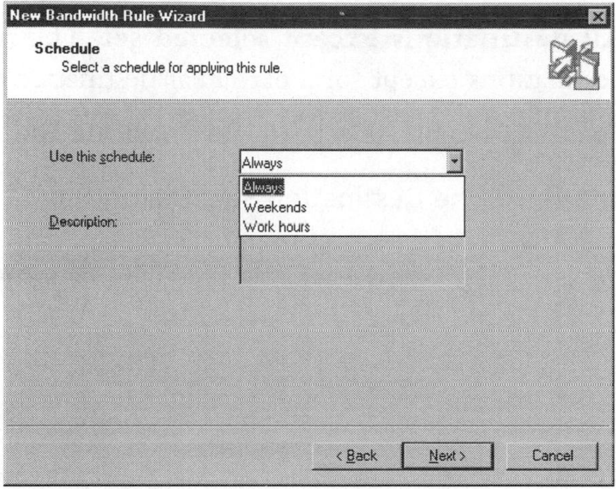

6. On the **Client Type** page, select the clients you want this rule applied to. The options are:
   - **Any request** The rule will be applied to all requests for this protocol.
   - **Specific computers (client address sets)** The rule will be applied only to requests from clients that belong to a particular client address set. Remember, client address sets are helpful when you are using the SecureNAT clients.
   - **Specific users and groups** The rule will be applied to specific users or groups. You can use this option if you have deployed the firewall client software, which allows user/group-based access controls.

   For this example, select **Any request**, then click **Next**.
7. On the **Destination Sets** page, you can choose the destination to which this bandwidth rule is applied. This allows you to set bandwidth priorities on a per-site basis. When you click the down arrow in the **Apply this rule to** box, you will see the screen that appears in Figure 8.40.

   You have the choice to apply this rule to:
   - **All destinations** The rule is applied to all destinations.
   - **All internal destinations** The rule is applied to all destinations listed in the LAT or LDT.
   - **All external destinations** The rule is applied to all destinations not listed in the LAT or LDT.

- **Specified destination set** The rule is applied to destinations included in a specific destination set.
- **All destinations except selected set** The rule is applied to all destinations except for a particular destination set.

  For this example, select **All destinations** and click **Next**.

Figure 8.40 The Destination Sets Dialog Box

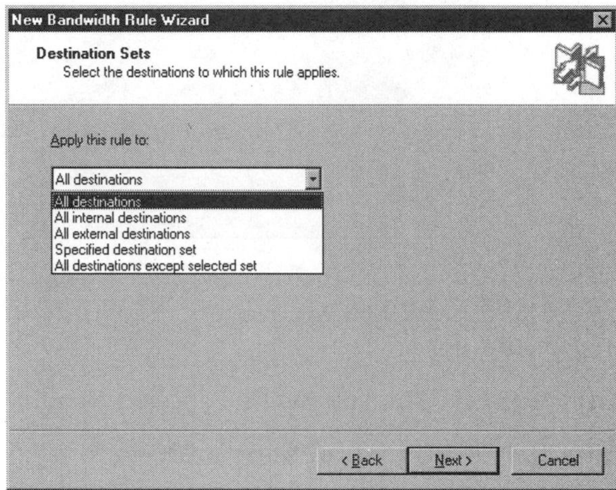

8. On the **Content Groups** page, you decide if the rule should be applied to any specific content. The only content that will be affected is content located at the site(s) included in the destination set for this rule. Your decision here *does not* apply to all sites, just the selected one (unless you have selected **All destinations**). Remember, this applies only to *HTTP content*—in other words, content that is accessed via HTTP or HTTP tunneled FTP.

   For this example, choose **All content groups**, and click **Next**.
9. On the **Bandwidth Priority** page, you will see something like what appears in Figure 8.41.

   On this page you have the options to:
   - **Use default scheduling priority** Choose this option to use the default scheduling priority you configured in the **Bandwidth Priorities** section of **Protocol Elements**.
   - **Custom** Choose this option to use one of the custom bandwidth priorities you created earlier.

Figure 8.41 The Bandwidth Priority Page

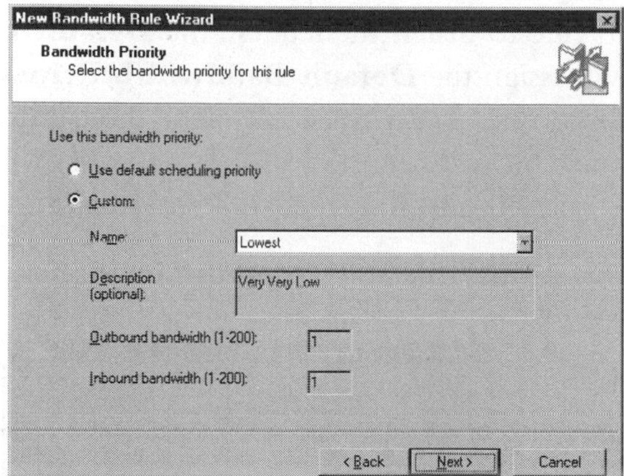

For this example, select the **Lowest** bandwidth priority, which is one we created earlier. Note that the dialog box provides information regarding the **Outbound** and **Inbound** bandwidth settings. After you choose the bandwidth priority, click **Next**.

10. On the last page of the wizard, you can inspect the settings and confirm that they are correct. Click **Finish** to complete the wizard.

Managing Bandwidth Rules

After creating a bandwidth rule, you can change any of the choices you made in the wizard by right-clicking the rule and then clicking the **Properties** command. After doing so, you will see the screen that appears in Figure 8.42. Note on the **Protocol** tab that you can choose to see only the selected protocol or all the protocol definitions on this ISA server. If you need to see them all in order to add another protocol definition to this bandwidth rule, remove the check mark from the check box for **Show only selected protocols**.

A nice feature of the **Protocol** tab is that you can click the **New** button and create a new protocol definition from there. If you click the **New** button, you will see the **New Protocol** dialog box, where you can create a new protocol definition (Figure 8.43).

Bandwidth rules are an *ordered* list. When ISA Server receives a request, it works its way from the top of the list downward, searching for a rule that matches the parameters contained within the request. The first rule to match the request will be used to determine the priority assigned to the communication.

Even though there might be other rules on the list that assign a different bandwidth priority, only the first one is applied.

If there is no rule to match the request, the **Default rule** is applied. The **Default rule** will assign the **Default Bandwidth Priority** to all requests without a matching rule. If you want to change the bandwidth priority assigned to the default rule, you will need to make the change in the **Default bandwidth priority** entry in the **Bandwidth Priorities** node.

Figure 8.42 The Bandwidth Rule Properties Dialog Box

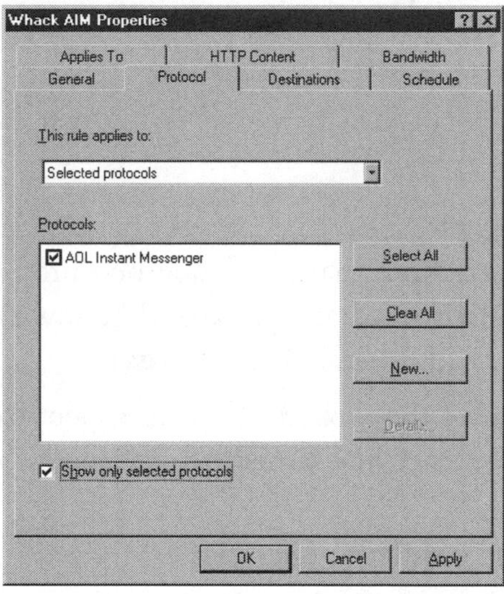

Figure 8.43 The New Protocol Dialog Box

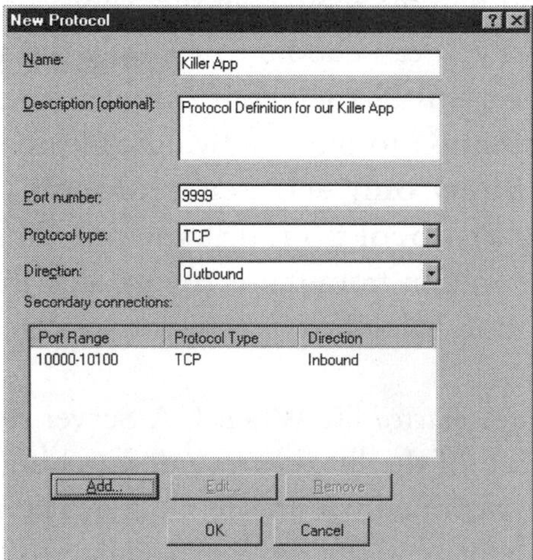

Site and Content Rules

Site and content rules allow you to control access to sites as defined by the destination sets that you've created. For any destination set or combination of destination sets, you can limit access to the entire content of the destination or to specific content elements as defined by your content groups. Site and content rules also allow you to limit access based on the day of the week and/or time of day.

So that you can get a better feel on how to use site and content rules, let's walk through the process of creating one. In this example, we'll see how to create a site and content rule that blocks access to graphics files on the aol.com Web site during office hours. We have decided to block access to graphics because a number of employees have been looking at the personal ads, and we have discovered that they look only at the ads with pictures.

Creating a Site and Content Rule

To create a site and content rule, perform the following steps:

1. Open the **ISA Management** console, expand **Servers and Arrays**, expand your server or array, and then expand **Access Policy**. Right-click **Site and Content Rules**, click **New**, and then click **Rule**.
2. On the first page of the **New Site and Content Rule Wizard**, type in the name of the site and content rule. For this example, name it **Block AOL Gfx**. Then click **Next**.
3. On the **Rule Action** page, you'll see the screen shown in Figure 8.44.

Figure 8.44 The Rule Action Page

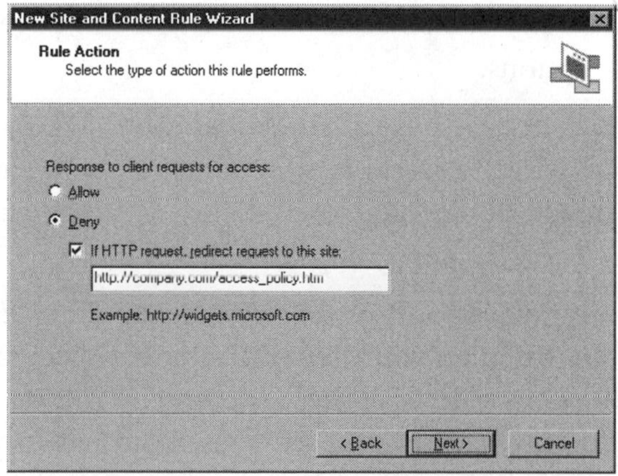

The options you have are:

- **Allow** If you choose the Allow option, you explicitly allow access to the site. You need to explicitly create allow rules only when you have disabled the default site and content rule that allows access to all content on all sites at all times. If you disable the default site and content rule, you need to create allow rules for all sites and content that you want your uses to be able to access.
- **Deny** The Deny option allows you to deny access to specific destinations based on destination sets, schedules, and content groups. You also have the option to redirect the request to another Web page if the user attempts to access a forbidden site by placing a check mark in the check box for **If HTTP request, redirect request to this site**. Note that this option is available only for HTTP requests, not for other protocols that access the site.

We highly recommend that you configure a page to redirect denied requests. Some issues in implementing site and content rules *may* require to you configure this option.

If you do choose to redirect, make sure that the user has access to the redirected page. The easiest way to do this is to redirect the user to a page located on the internal network. Otherwise, you might have to create one or more site and content rules to allow access to the redirected pages.

Select the **Deny** option, and then click **Next**.

4. On the **Rule Configuration** page, you'll see the screen that appears in Figure 8.45. The options on the **Rule Configuration** page allow you to specify whether you want the rule to apply to destinations, schedules, clients, or any combination of these. On this page you have the following options:

   - **Deny access based on destination** When you select this option, you can deny access to sites contained in a particular destination set. You will not be able to configure any other limitations, such as day/time or user/group restrictions.
   - **Deny access only at certain times** This option allows you to deny access based on your **Schedules** policy elements. This is a "catch-all" setting that affects all sites and content. You do not have the option of specifying a destination set or users/groups to which to apply a rule made with this option. Be careful in using this option.

Figure 8.45 The Rule Configuration Page

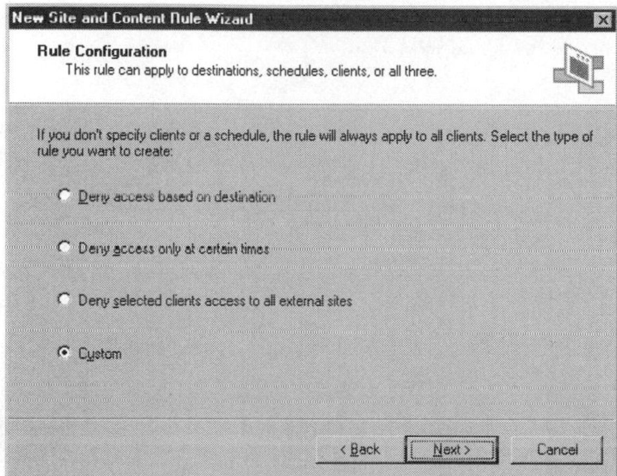

- **Deny selected clients access to all external sites** This option allows you to deny access to all external sites (those not contained in the LAT or LDT), based on client address sets or specific users/groups. A rule based on this option can also apply to all requests.
- **Custom** The custom option allows you to apply the rules to specific destination sets, schedules, client address sets, or users/groups and content groups. This option allows you the greatest number of options in creating a site or content rule.

For this example, select the **Custom** option button, and then click **Next**.

5. On the destination set page, you will see something that looks like Figure 8.46. We have selected the **Specified destination set option** and selected the **AOL domain** destination set for this rule. Note that when you create your destination sets, it's a good idea to include in the description the actual destinations in the description text box so that you can tell what destinations are represented by the set.

   After choosing the destination set, click **Next**.
6. On the **Schedule** page, you select the schedule policy element you want applied to the rule. In this case, we want the rule to apply to **Work Hours**, so select that rule and click **Next**.

Figure 8.46 The Destination Sets Page

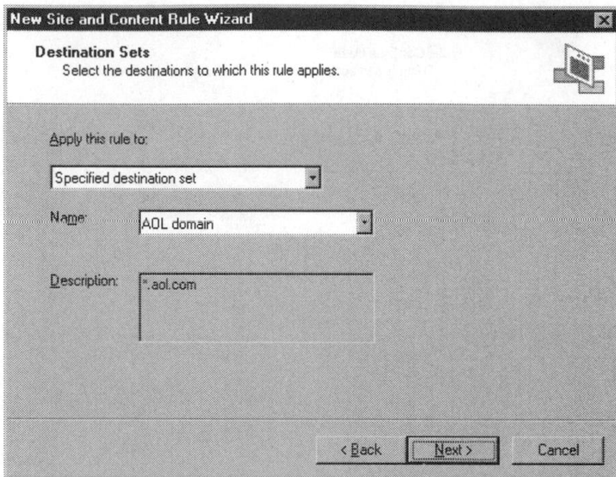

7. On the **Client Type** page, you have the following options:
   - **Any Request** Choose this option when you want the rule applied to all requests arriving to the ISA server.
   - **Specific computers (client address sets)** This option allows this rule to be applied only to clients defined in a client address set. This is useful when your network clients are configured as SecureNAT clients.
   - **Specific users and groups** You can apply the rule so that it limits only specific users and groups by selecting this option. In order for the rule to apply to users and groups, you need to be running either Web proxy or firewall clients, depending on the protocol, to pass authentication information to the ISA server. Note that Web proxy and firewall clients handle authentication for Web requests a bit differently. Check out the discussion on the HTTP Redirector later in this chapter.

   For this example, select **Any Request**, and click **Next**.
8. On the **Content Types** page, you'll see the screen that appears in Figure 8.47.

   Your options are:
   - **Any content type** When you select this option, all content included in the selected destination sets will be denied. Choose this

option if you don't want clients to access any type of content via HTTP.

- **Only the following content types** This option gives you more granular control over the type of HTTP content the users can access. Rather than denying all content for a particular destination set, you can limit only certain elements from being downloaded. In this example, we want to prevent the users from accessing any graphics files, but still allow them to access other content on the AOL domain. To do this, check the **Images** content group. This will prevent graphical elements from being downloaded while allowing all other content. Click **Next**.

Figure 8.47 The Content Groups Page

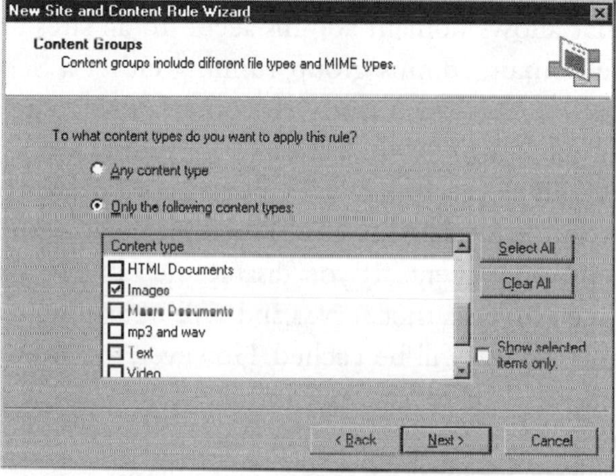

9. On the last page, you can confirm your choices. If all looks well, click **Finish**.

Managing Site and Content Rules

Site and content rules are not ordered. No particular rule has precedence over another site and content rule. That means that if a user or group has multiple site and content rules applying to them, their access could be considered cumulative. ISA Server searches the list of site and content rules until it finds one that matches the request.

In order to access a site and its contents, *there must be an allow rule* that permits access. In addition to a site and content rule, *there must be a protocol rule* that allows access. *Only* when there is both a site and content rule *and* a protocol rule will a request be allowed. Although site and content rules are not ordered, the *deny* rules are processed before the *allow* rules. Similar to NTFS permissions, if a user has one rule that allows him access and another that denies access, the deny rule will be applied and the user, group, or client address will not be allowed access.

Site and Content Rules, Web Requests, and SecureNAT/Firewall Clients

Remember that when firewall client and SecureNAT client computers attempt to access Web protocols, no credentials will be passed through the HTTP redirector filter. Therefore, if you decide to disable the default site and content rule, and create allow rules based on user/group information, your Web requests will fail for SecureNAT and firewall clients.

For example, suppose we disable the default site and content rule. Then we create a rule that allows domain admins access to all sites and all content. When a member of the domain admins group, running either a SecureNAT or firewall client computer, attempts to access Web content, the access attempt fails because the HTTP request is sent through the HTTP redirector. When the request passes through the HTTP redirector, all user credentials are lost. In order to get around this problem, you can disable the HTTP redirector, or you can configure the Web browsers as Web proxy clients. If you disable the HTTP redirector, requests will be sent directly to the Internet server and will not be sent to the Web Proxy Service, and no content will be cached. However, the firewall client credentials will be sent and are used for access control.

When configuring site and content rules, you have to decide on your security philosophy. The default site and content rule allows access to all sites at all times. This is an open approach that simplifies your access policy because it assumes that you want to allow access to all sites and content *except* for a relatively small selection of prohibited material.

Special Processing for Destination Sets That Include Paths

Recall during our discussion of destination sets we mentioned you could create sets that included just a subset of a site. For example, you might not want to apply access rules to the entire microsoft.com domain. However, you would like to control access to the subdirectory www.microsoft.com/downloads folder within the Microsoft site. You can do this by creating a destination set for www.microsoft.com and then include the path statement **/downloads/*** . This allows you to create rules to apply to all content in the downloads directory of the www.microsoft.com site.

Path statements in destination sets are processed a little differently, depending on the type of client that makes that request. The results differ depending on whether you use SecureNAT, firewall client, or Web proxy client. Table 8.4 shows how ISA Server handles requests from different ISA Server clients.

Table 8.4 Path Processing by Client and Protocol

Protocol	Web Proxy Client	SecureNAT Client	Firewall Client
FTP	Yes	No	No
HTTP	Yes	Sort of*	Sort of*
HTTPS	No	No	No

*SecureNAT and firewall client computers can process path statements in destination sets if the requests move through the HTTP redirector filter. If the filter is disabled, the path entries are ignored.

The content of Table 8.4 can be boiled down into two basic observations:

- If the request passes through the Web Proxy Service, the path will be processed.
- If an SSL request is made to a destination with a path statement, the path statement will never be processed.

Keep in mind that the Web Proxy Service handles all HTTP requests if the HTTP redirector is enabled and in its default configuration. This includes HTTP and FTP requests tunneled inside an HTTP request. That's why the Web Proxy Service is able to process FTP requests. Note that if a request does not support path processing, ISA Server ignores all destinations referred to in the entry with the path statement. However, the entire rule is not ignored.

For example, suppose you created a destination set that included the following entries:

www.sawhorse.net

www.potus.net/flotus

After creating the destination set, you create a site and content rule that *denies* access to the sites contained in this destination set. What would happen when you tried to access the sites contained in this destination set using NNTP? First, ask yourself if NNTP supports path processing. When you look at Table 8.4, you can see that NNTP is not contained in the table and therefore does not support path processing. What do you think will happen when you try to access sites contained in this destination set via your newsreader? When you try to access www.potus.net/flotus via your newsreader, you will be able to access the site. The reason is that NNTP does not support path processing, so it ignores the entry for the entire site and allows access (assuming that the default site and content rule is active and allows access to all sites that are not denied). When you try to access www.sawhorse.net via your newsreader, the request will be *denied*. Why? Because www.sawhorse.net does not have a path statement. Therefore, the destination is processed and the deny rule is applied.

SSL requests represent a special case when it comes to destination sets. If a site and content rule denies access to a destination set that includes a site with a path statement, such as www.microsoft.com/memberdownload, and the site is accessed via SSL, not only will the subdirectory be denied but the entire www.microsoft.com site will be denied. Be very wary of denying access to a destination set that includes a path if you expect to access any other area of that site.

Protocol Rules

Protocol rules determine the TCP/UDP protocols that network clients can access. Protocol rules can be configured to allow primary connections for either inbound or outbound requests. Protocol rules that have primary inbound connections are called *server protocols* because they can be used by server publishing rules.

By default, clients are not able to access any protocols, because ISA Server does not include a default protocol rule. Although site and content rules include a default rule that allows access to all sites and content to make administration easier, ISA Server increases the default level of security by disallowing access to all protocols until you create rules to allow access.

Protocol rules apply to all ISA Server clients. This includes SecureNAT, firewall client, and Web proxy clients. Even if you have configured your browser to be a Web proxy client, there still must be a protocol rule in place to allow the client to access the HTTP protocol. If there is no protocol rule that allows access to HTTP, the Web proxy client will be presented with a pop-up a dialog box asking for credentials. In spite of entering the correct credentials, you will not be able to access HTTP content and the request will be denied.

Protocol Rules Depend on Protocol Definitions

Protocol rules depend on the protocol definitions located in the **Protocol Definitions** node in the **ISA Management** console. A protocol definition must exist before you create a rule influencing access to any particular protocol. This is especially important for SecureNAT clients because if you create a protocol rule that allows access to all IP traffic, *only the protocols that have protocol definitions* will be available to SecureNAT clients. If there is no protocol definition, there will be no access for the SecureNAT client. This is in spite of the SecureNAT client having access to "all protocols."

If a protocol requires secondary connections, a SecureNAT client will need an application filter to allow it to access that protocol. Firewall clients do not require applications filters to support protocols with secondary connections because the firewall client software can have the intelligence to manage the connection.

For example, to access Napster, you must use secondary connections, as we saw earlier when configuring a protocol definition for Napster. The SecureNAT client depends on the SOCKS4 application filter to access the Napster protocol definition that we created. If the SOCKS4 application filter were disabled, the SecureNAT client would not be able to access the protocol, in spite of the fact that we had configured a protocol definition that supports access. Firewall clients do not require the application filter and can manage their own secondary connections.

While you are in the process of learning about ISA Server, it's a good idea to create a configuration that allows all protocols to all users at all times. This way, you can assess whether your basic configuration is functional. After you confirm the basic functionality of your ISA server, you can begin to tighten the screws on your security configuration.

To support this testing mode setup, let's create a protocol rule that allows access to all protocols.

Creating a Protocol Rule

To create a protocol rule, perform the following steps:

1. Open the **ISA Management** console, expand **Servers and Arrays**, and then expand **Access Policy**. Right-click **Protocol Rules**, click **New**, and then click **Rule**.
2. On the first page of the **New Protocol Rule Wizard**, enter the name of the protocol rule. In this example, call it **Allow All**. After entering the name, click **Next**.
3. On the **Rule Action** page, you have two choices (Figure 8.48):
   - **Allow** Choose Allow if you want to create a rule that will allow access to a protocol or protocols.

- **Deny** Choose Deny if you want to create a rule that will deny access to a protocol or protocols.

  For this example, we want to allow access to all protocols, so select **Allow** and click **Next**.

Figure 8.48 The Rule Action Page

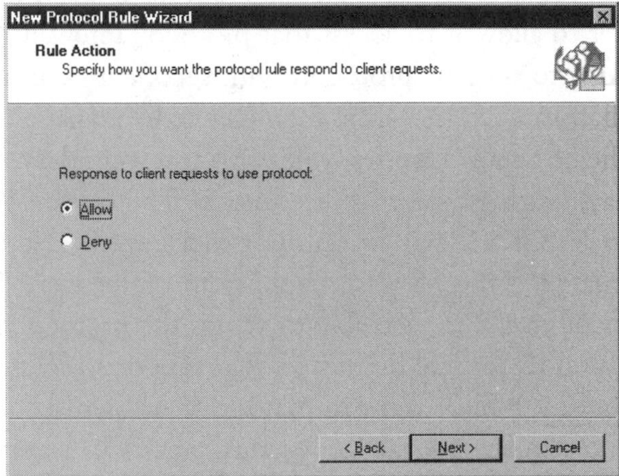

4. On the **Protocols** page, you will see the screen that appears in Figure 8.49.

Figure 8.49 The Protocols Page

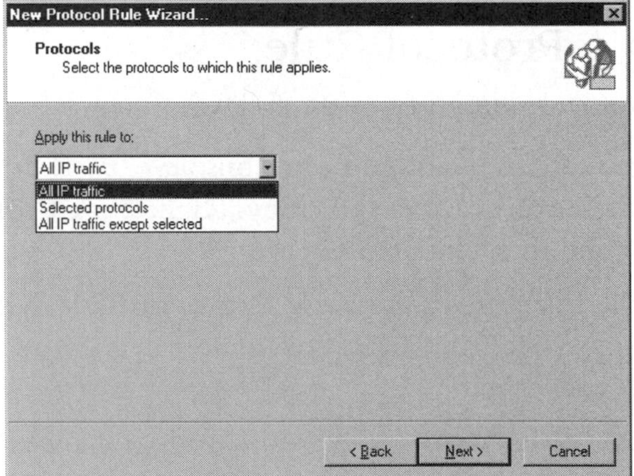

On this page you have the option to apply this rule to:

- **All IP Traffic** When you select this option, you allow all protocols to be included in the rule. Remember that when you choose All IP Traffic, only the protocols that have protocol definitions defined will be included when accessed by SecureNAT clients.
- **Selected Protocols** This option allows you to apply the rule to one or more protocols.
- **All IP Traffic except selected** This option allows you to permit all protocols *except* those you choose to include in the rule. This choice might be useful if you would like a group of employees to have access to all protocols, with the exception of Napster, NNTP, and FTP, in order to reduce the amount of inbound traffic.

For this example, select **All IP Traffic**, and click **Next**.

5. On the **Schedule** page (Figure 8.50), you can choose a schedule from your **Schedules** policy element. In this example, we want this rule to always be applied, so select the **Always** option, and click **Next**.

Figure 8.50 The Schedule Page

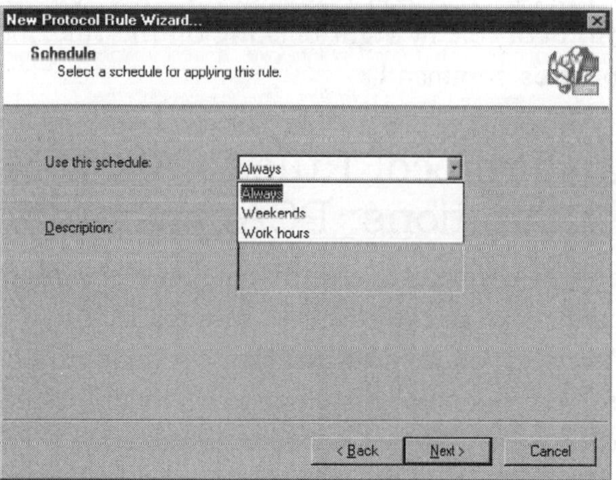

6. On the **Client Type** page, you have the following options (Figure 8.51):
   - **Any Request** This option applies the rule to all requests from all clients and client types.
   - **Specific Computers (client address sets)** This option applies the rule to a selected set of clients as defined by a client address set.

- **Specific users and groups** Use this option when you want to have this rule applied to users or groups in the forest.

  For this example, select **Any Request**, and click **Next**.

Figure 8.51 The Client Type Page

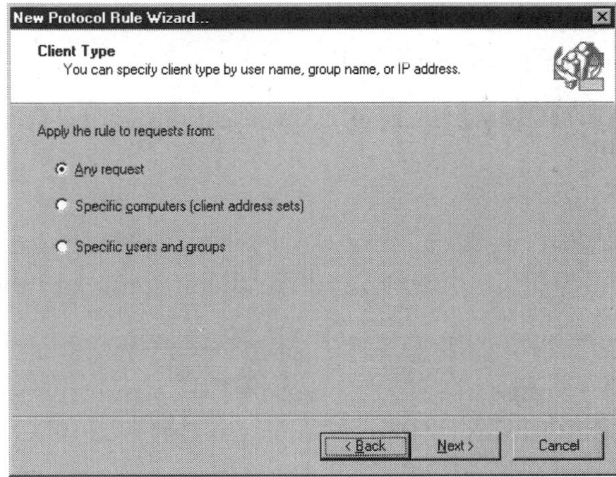

7. On the last page of the wizard, confirm your selections and click **Finish**. After the rule is added, you can access the configuration parameters of the protocol rule by right clicking on the rule and then clicking the **Properties** command.

Creating a Protocol Rule to Allow Multiple Protocol Definitions: PCAnywhere 9.x

Let's look at how to configure a rule that includes *multiple* protocol definitions. If you want to connect to an external host running PCAnywhere from a client behind an ISA server, you need to first create several protocol definitions and then configure a protocol rule that will allow access to all the protocol definitions.

Before creating the protocol rule, you must create the following protocol definitions:

TCP 5631 Outbound

TCP 5632 Outbound

UDP 5631 Send

UDP 5631 Send

Each of these is a discrete protocol definition, and each one will be included in the rule. Note that you do not need to create secondary connections, because the PCAnywhere host you call will respond to the dynamic response port created by the ISA server.

To create the rule:

1. Open the **ISA Management** console, expand **Servers and Arrays**, and then expand **Access Policy**. Right-click **Protocol Rules**, click **New**, and then click **Rule**.
2. On the first page of the **New Protocol Rule Wizard**, enter the name of the protocol rule. For this example, call it **PCAnywhere**. After entering the name, click **Next**.
3. On the **Rule Action** page, we want to allow access to these protocols, so select the **Allow** option button. Click **Next**.
4. On the **Protocols** page, select the **Selected Protocols** option, and then place a check mark in the check boxes for each of the protocol definitions you've created to support outbound access to PCAnywhere hosts (Figure 8.52). After selecting the protocol definitions, click **Next**.

Figure 8.52 Selecting the Protocol Definitions for PCAnywhere

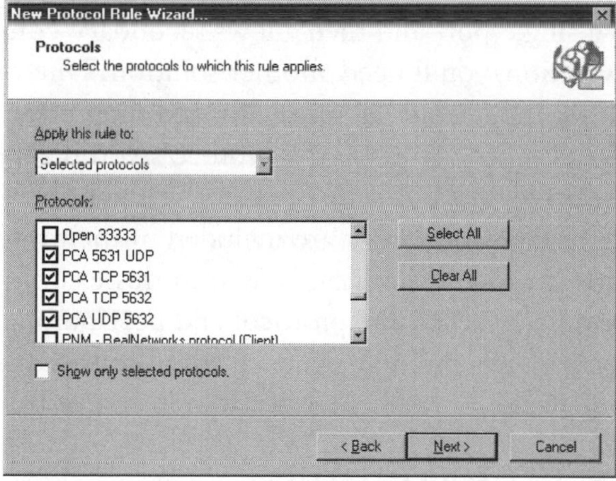

5. On the **Schedule** page, select a schedule that meets your requirement, and then click **Next**.

6. On the **Client type** page, make a selection that is appropriate for the client type that you want to have access to the external PCAnywhere clients, then click **Next**.
7. On the last page of the wizard, review the selections you've made, and click **Finish**.

This protocol will be available to both SecureNAT and firewall client computers. If you include user or group access controls, you need to use the firewall client.

Creating a Protocol Rule to Allow Access to Multiple Primary Port Connections

One issue that comes up from time to time is how to create a protocol definition or rule that will allow for a large range of port numbers to be accessed as primary connections. For example, what if you need to have ports 1025–4000 open for primary connections? You cannot create a protocol definition containing more than a single port for a primary connection. In order to allow all these port numbers to be open for a primary connection, you could create thousands of protocol definitions and then create a rule to allows these definitions. However, that option is not very feasible.

First, you should consider using another application that allows the primary connection to a single port and then allows secondary connections. But if you don't have this option, you'll need another solution. One option is to create a protocol definition that allows all protocols, and then create a protocol rule that allows access to all protocols *except* the protocols you do not want users to access. This solution is problematic for the SecureNAT client because these ISA Server clients can only use protocols that are included in the protocol definitions folder. Since no specific protocol definition is used in this example, the SecureNAT client won't be able to access the protocol and port numbers required for this protocol, which requires multiple primary connection ports be available. You need to implement the firewall client software to make this solution work.

Managing Protocol Rules

Protocol rules are not numbered, and one rule does not have a priority over the other. However, deny rules are processed *before* allow rules. When the ISA server receives a request for a particular protocol, it searches its deny rules first to see if one applies. If there is no deny rule, the server searches the allow rules for one that will allow the request. If there is no rule that will allow the request, the ISA server rejects the request.

If you want to stop using a protocol rule, you can either delete the rule or disable it. It is a good idea to disable rather than delete a rule. That way, if you need to use the rule again, you do not have to recreate it—all you need to do is enable it again.

Enterprise Array Reminder

Remember that if you are implementing an enterprise array, you might or might not be able to create protocol rules at the array level. If you are using an enterprise policy that allows array-level policies, you will be able to create protocol rules at the array level. However, you will *not* be able to create allow rules, as shown in Figure 8.53. When an enterprise policy is in effect, you can only create policies at the array level that are *more* restrictive than those implemented at the enterprise policy level. In practice, this means that you cannot create any allow rules at the array level if you have implemented an enterprise policy.

Figure 8.53 The Rule Action Page

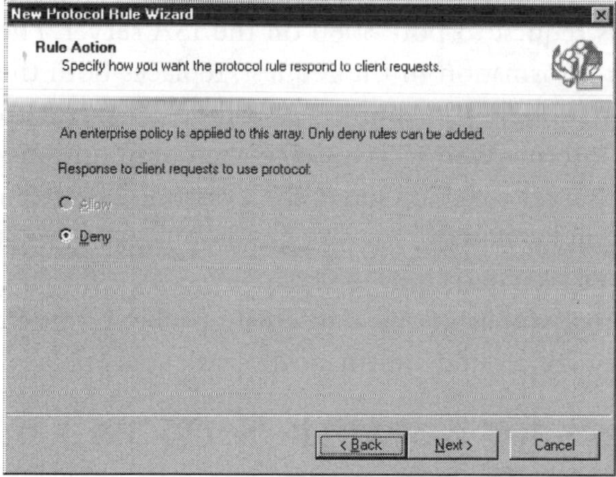

IP Packet Filters

IP packet filters are used to determine the packets that can enter and exit the external interface of the ISA server. Packet filters may be required when you enable *packet filtering* on the external interface of the ISA server. This option can be enabled locally on a stand-alone ISA server or can be enabled via the enterprise policy for an enterprise array.

You should *always* enable packet filtering when the ISA server is located at the edge of the network. Otherwise, all ports on the ISA server's external interface will be open at all times. This creates a security situation you can't defend and in which you never want to find yourself. Packet filtering is a key feature of your network security scheme when ISA Server is at the edge of your network.

We will spend more time on the issue of packet filtering in Chapter 9 in our discussion of configuring the ISA Server firewall features, since most of our concerns regarding packet filtering relate to issues of inbound access. However, a few things appropriate to the discussion of outbound access deserve mention at this time.

Dynamic Packet Filtering

ISA Server creates response ports whenever an outbound request is allowed. These dynamic response ports open only when they are needed for an allowed communication with an external server, and then they close when they are no longer required. By dynamically opening and closing these ports, you reduce the risk of having a large number of ports open on the external interface of the ISA server. Open ports can pose a security risk.

For example, suppose an internal client needs to access a Web server on the Internet. It sends its request to port 8080 on the ISA server. The ISA server then changes the header information in the request, replaces both the source IP address and the source TCP port number, and then opens that port to receive the response from the Internet Web server. Once the communication between the client and the Web server has completed, the port on the external interface used for this exchange will be closed. This process eliminates a potential vector of attack by an Internet intruder.

Keep in mind that you *do not* have to create packet filters for these dynamic response ports. They are created automatically for clients behind the ISA server.

Packet Filters for Network Services Located on the ISA Server

Dynamic packet filtering is *not* available for services and applications running on the ISA server itself. For example, you might want to use a newsreader or Web browser, send or receive SMTP, receive POP3 mail, resolve DNS names, or run an FTP or Web server directly on the external interface or the ISA server. Since the ISA server is *not* an ISA client, you must configure packet filters on the external interface to allow applications running on the ISA server to work correctly. By default, the following packet filters are installed and enabled on the ISA server:

- DNS filter
- ICMP outbound
- ICMP ping response (in)
- ICMP source quench
- ICMP timeout in
- ICMP unreachable in

The DNS filter is used to allow the ISA server to resolve DNS queries. The ISA server performs a proxy DNS service for both firewall and Web proxy clients. Therefore, a packet filter is provided that allows outbound access for DNS queries from the external interface of the ISA server. The ICMP filters are used by ISA Server to send and receive ICMP messages that are required to assess network status and error conditions. The ICMP outbound filter allows *all* types and codes of ICMP messages to leave the external interface of the ISA server. The ICMP ping response (in) filter allows the ISA server to receive ICMP echo response messages in reply to pings sent from the ISA server's external interface. The ICMP source quench, ICMP timeout, and ICMP unreachable filters allow the ISA server to receive responses from routers informing it of various network error conditions. If you want to use applications or services other than those included with the default filters, you must create your own packet filters.

SECURITY ALERT!

The default ICMP filters will not allow you to ping the external interface of the ISA server from a remote host. In order to ping from a remote host, you need to enable the ICMP query filter. Note that when you ping the external interface of the ISA server from an internal SecureNAT client, it appears that the external interface is able to respond to ICMP echo requests, even if the ICMP query filter is not enabled. However, if you ping the same interface from an external client, the ping will fail.

For security reasons, we strongly recommend against enabling the inbound ICMP query request filter.

Examples of Custom Packet Filters Supporting Applications on the ISA Server

Let's look at two examples demonstrating how you would create packet filters to support popular applications. In this section, we'll look at packet filters for:

- Supporting a Web browser on the ISA Server
- Supporting a terminal server on the ISA Server

If you want to use the Web browser on the ISA server, you have two options:

- Create a packet filter to allow outbound access to port 80
- Make the Web browser a Web proxy client

The best solution to this problem is to make the Web browser a Web proxy client. When configuring the browser as a Web proxy client, you should use the internal IP address of the ISA server. Do not use the server name, because the ISA server will try to resolve the name using the DNS server configured on its external interface. This likely will not work, since the public DNS server will not have a host mapping for the *internal* interface of the ISA server.

The problem with this solution is that it doesn't seem to work on ISA servers using dial-up connections. If you are using an analog, ISDN, or PPPoE dial-up connection, making the browser a Web proxy client does not seem to work. If you use a dedicated (permanent) connection (*not* dedicated ISDN) for the external interface, you will be able to use this method. If you cannot or do not want to set the browser as a Web proxy client, you can create a packet filter to allow outbound access. In the packet filter, you would use the following parameters:

Protocol: TCP

Direction: Outbound

Local Port: Dynamic (ports 1025-5000)

Remote Port: Fixed Port

Remote port number: 80

This allows outbound requests to the Web server's port 80 and opens a response port in the dynamic response port range.

Packet filters for other services follow a similar pattern. Suppose you have Terminal Services running in remote administration mode on the ISA server. You want to make the terminal server available so that you can administer it over the Internet. You can create a packet filter such as the following:

Protocol: TCP

Direction: Inbound

Local Port: Fixed Port

Local port number: 3389

Remote port: All ports

Although you can do this to make the terminal server available on the external interface of the ISA Server computer, we strongly recommend against doing so. The Terminal Service port is a well-known port number, and leaving this port number open using a static packet filter could open you up to exploits aimed against Microsoft Terminal Server.

Enabling PPTP Clients Outbound Access to VPN Servers

You can configure SecureNAT clients to call external VPN servers. In order to do this, right-click the **IP Packet Filters** node in the left pane of the **ISA Management** console, click **Properties**, and then click the **PPTP** tab. You will see the screen that appears in Figure 8.54.

Figure 8.54 The PPTP Tab

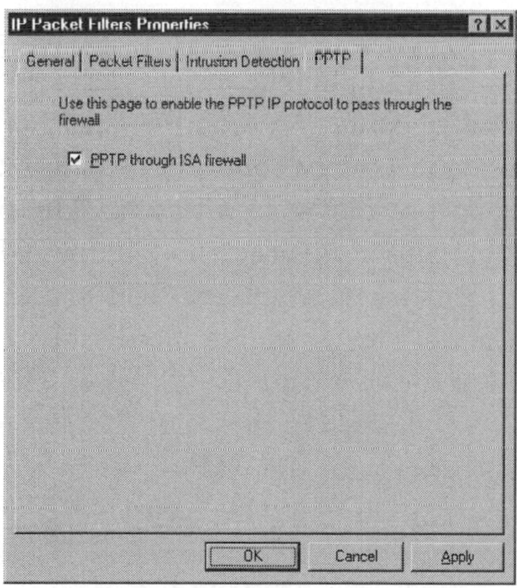

After you place a check mark in the check box for **PPTP through ISA Firewall**, a packet filter will be created. The name of the filter is **SecureNAT PPTP**. Note that you cannot use this packet filter to make outbound PPTP calls if your computer is a firewall client. If your machine is currently a firewall client, you can disable the firewall client and then configure a default gateway that routes to the internal interface of the ISA server. If there are any active firewall sessions for your computer, you will not be able to make the PPTP call. You can wait for the session to time out, or you can force the session to disconnect via the **ISA Management** console.

Configuring Application Filters That Affect Outbound Access

ISA Server includes a group of application filters that listen to inbound and outbound connections and can influence communications intercepted by the application filters. These filters are registered with the Firewall Service and therefore are dependent on the Firewall Service. Application filters are not available for ISA servers that are installed in Web proxy (cache mode) only. The built-in application filters can examine and influence both inbound and outbound access. In this section, we focus on the application filters that affect outbound access. Filters that mainly influence inbound traffic are covered Chapter 9 on configuring ISA Server's firewall features.

FTP Access Filter

The FTP access filter provides a full range of FTP services to SecureNAT clients. This filter manages secondary connections on the behalf of SecureNAT clients and makes it possible to use secondary connections without having to create protocol definitions that support secondary connections. The FTP access filter works for both internal clients attempting to access an external FTP server and for external clients attempting to access an internal FTP server.

Note that this application filter provides functionality for FTP clients that send a PORT command to the destination FTP server. The application filter intercepts the information contained in the PORT command and dynamically opens the required back channels for the FTP server to send back the requested data. Without the FTP application filter, the SecureNAT client using a standard FTP client application will not be able to access an FTP server.

For example, Internet Explorer sends FTP requests by issuing PORT commands to an FTP server. If the FTP access filter is enabled, this process works fine. If the filter is not enabled, you will see something like the screen that appears in Figure 8.55.

Figure 8.55 PORT Command Failure with FTP Filter Disabled

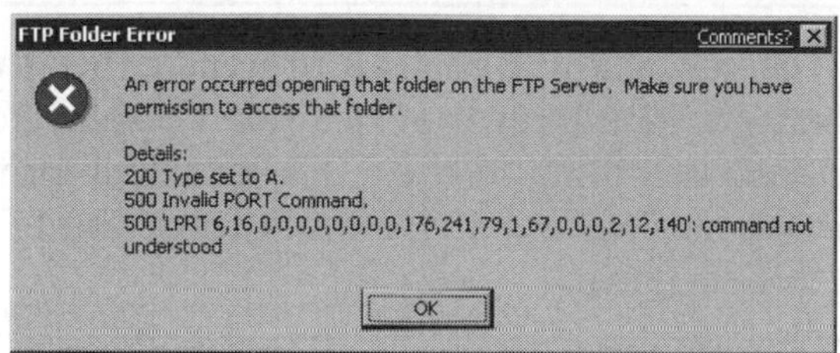

You can change the default behavior of Internet Explorer by performing the following steps:

1. Open Internet Explorer, click the **Tools** menu, and then click the **Internet Options** command.
2. Click the **Advanced** tab. Remove the check mark from the check box for **Enable folder view for FTP sites**.
3. Click **OK**, and then close the Web browser. When you open it again it will act as a **PASV** mode FTP client.

NOTE

The command-line FTP client included with Windows NT 4.0 and Windows 2000 also uses PORT commands. Although you can enter the **QUOTE PASV** command while in the command line FTP application, doing so will *not* force the client to use PASV mode. You can confirm this by using the **debug** command while in the FTP client and then issuing the **ls** command after trying to change to PASV mode.

The FTP application filter is *not* required for FTP clients configured to use PASV mode. PASV mode FTP does not require that the ISA server in front of the FTP client open new back channels from the FTP server for inbound data. Since the FTP client initiates all connections with the FTP server, the FTP server never has to initiate any non-ACK connections with the ISA server.

SECURITY ALERT!

If you have FTP clients sitting behind a firewall other than ISA server and they try to access an FTP server that has been published by an ISA server, all PORT commands will fail and the FTP clients will not be able to connect to the published FTP server. You must force the FTP clients to use PASV mode in this scenario.

The FTP access filter installs several protocol definitions. These include:

- FTP
- FTP Download Only
- FTP Server

You can use these protocol definitions in protocol rules to allow you granular control over the type of FTP access to give to users. For example, you might want users to be able to download files via FTP, but you might not want them to upload files. In this case, you can grant access to the **FTP Download Only** protocol. The FTP filter is enabled by default. If you want to disable the filter, perform the following steps:

1. Open the **ISA Management** console, expand **Servers and Arrays**, and then **Extensions**. Click the **Application Filters** node in the left pane.
2. In the right pane, double-click the **FTP Access Filter**. To disable the filter, remove the check mark from the **Enable this filter** check box.

HTTP Redirector Filter

The HTTP redirector filter provides SecureNAT and firewall clients access to the services provided by the Web Proxy Service. Most important, it allows firewall and SecureNAT clients the ability to take advantage of the Web cache, which is a feature of the Web Proxy Service.

You can control the behavior of the HTTP redirector filter by performing the following steps:

1. Open the **ISA Management** console; expand **Servers and Arrays** and then **Extensions**. Click the **Application Filters** node in the left pane.

2. In the right pane, double-click the **HTTP Redirector Filter**. This opens the **HTTP Redirector Filter Properties** dialog box. Click the **Options** tab. You will see the screen that appears in Figure 8.56.

Figure 8.56 The HTTP Redirector Filter Properties Dialog Box

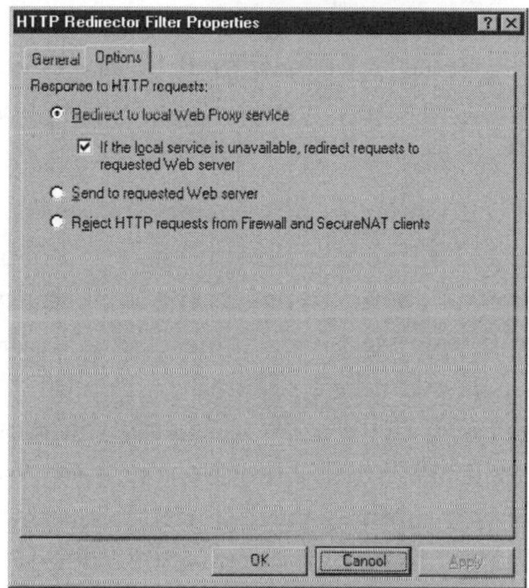

You have the following options available:

- **Redirect to local Web Proxy Service** Choose this option if you want SecureNAT and firewall clients to have their HTTP requests redirected to the Web Proxy Service. Once the requests are redirected, the clients will be able to take advantage of the Web Cache. This is the default setting. Check the **If the local service is unavailable, redirect requests to requested Web Server** option if you want the SecureNAT and firewall client requests to be sent directly to the Internet server when the Web Proxy Service is disabled. If the request bypasses the Web Proxy Service, the clients will be able to access no objects in cache, and any objects obtained will not be placed in cache while the Web Proxy Service is unavailable.
- **Send to requested Web server** Choose this option if you never want SecureNAT and firewall clients to access the Web Proxy Service for HTTP requests. In this case, the clients will never have access to the Web cache, and none of the objects they request will ever be put into the Web cache. This option might be helpful if you

have SecureNAT and firewall clients that are not configured as Web proxy clients but you still want to force authentication. In this case, the Firewall Service will authenticate the clients.

- **Reject HTTP requests from Firewall and SecureNAT clients** This option prevents SecureNAT and firewall clients from accessing any HTTP content. When you select this option, SecureNAT and firewall clients must have their browsers configured so that they become Web proxy clients if you want them to be able to access HTTP content.

As we talked about earlier in this chapter, there are some authentication issues related to using the HTTP redirector filter. If you enable the filter and allow SecureNAT and firewall clients to access the Web Proxy Service, no authentication information will be passed from these clients to the Web Proxy Service. Therefore, you *must* have in place site and content and protocol rules that will allow *anonymous* access. If there is no such rule, the request from the SecureNAT and firewall client will fail. You will *not* be presented with an authentication dialog box to allow you to enter your credentials.

In practice, this is an issue only for firewall clients. SecureNAT clients cannot be authenticated. For example, suppose you created a rule that lets everyone access all sites and another rule that denies Larry User (luser) access to a particular site via HTTP. Larry is using a firewall client computer. What do you think will happen when Larry tries to access the site? The answer is that he will be allowed access because the first rule allowed everybody (anonymous) access. Anonymous access rules for HTTP requests are always processed first.

Since SecureNAT and firewall client computers do not pass credentials up to the Web Proxy Service, user names for Web access are not included in the Web Proxy Service log files. In fact, even when you configure the Web browser on a SecureNAT or firewall client computer to be a Web proxy client, user information will not be included in the log files if the Web proxy client is able to access Web and FTP sites via an anonymous access rule. When you look at the **Sessions** node contents, you will see the username listed as **anonymous**. Remember that the anonymous access rules are evaluated first, *before* any deny rules are evaluated.

You can get around this problem by forcing authentication for all outbound access requests processed by the Web Proxy Service. In order to do this, you must perform the following steps:

1. In the **ISA Management** console, right-click the server name, and click **Properties**.
2. Click the **Outgoing Web Requests** tab (Figure 8.57).

Figure 8.57 The Outgoing Web Requests Tab

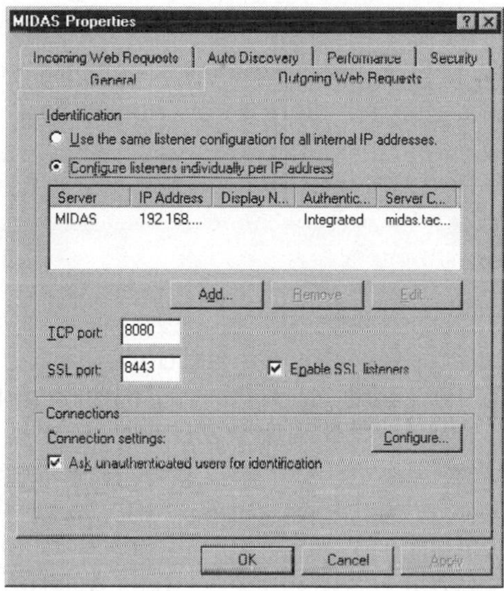

3. On the Outgoing Web Requests tab, place a check mark in the check box for **Ask unauthenticated users for identification**.
4. Click **OK**. You will be asked if you want to restart the Web Proxy Service. Say yes to this request and wait a few moments for the Web Proxy Service to restart.

Now when a request is allowed via an anonymous access rule, the Web proxy client will send user information to the Web Proxy Service, even though it is not required to do so by any of the rules. After making this change, you will have user information included in your log files, and user information will also appear in the **Sessions** node for Web Proxy Service connections.

This fixes the problem of obtaining user information for Web proxy clients, but it totally breaks all Web access for machines configured as SecureNAT or firewall clients that do not have their browsers configured as Web proxy clients (with the default HTTP redirector filter setting). The reason is that even if an anonymous access rule allows access, the Web Proxy Service will still ask for identification. Because the HTTP redirector doesn't pass this information, you will be denied access, in spite of an anonymous access rule being in place.

If you do choose to force authentication for Web proxy clients, it's a good idea to use integrated authentication. This authentication method allows clients to send their credentials transparently. If you choose basic authentication, users will be asked to provide credentials in a pop-up dialog box.

If you are in an environment that requires a high level of accountability for Web access, the best HTTP redirector filter option is to reject HTTP requests from SecureNAT and firewall clients. This option forces you to configure all the browsers as Web proxy clients and allows you the highest level of logging and access control.

NOTE

If you want to access a Hotmail account via Outlook Express from any type of ISA Server client, you must not force authentication for the Web Proxy Service. The reason is that Outlook Express uses HTTP to access the account and thus has its requests processed by the Web Proxy Service. The problem is that Outlook Express (up to version 5.5) will send your Hotmail credentials, not your domain credentials, to the Web Proxy Service. Unless your Hotmail credentials (username and password) are the same as your domain credentials, your access will be denied and you will not be able to access your Hotmail account.

SOCKS Filter

ISA Server includes a SOCKS, version 4, application filter. This filter allows you to run SOCKS 4 applications behind ISA Server. SOCKS 5 applications are not supported. However, a SOCKS 5 application filter is included in the SDK on the ISA Server CD-ROM.

The only configuration option available on the SOCKS 4 filter is the port number on which the filter listens. The default port is port 1080. To change this value, perform the following steps:

1. Open the **ISA Management** console, expand **Servers and Arrays** and then **Extensions**. Click the **Application Filters** node in the left pane.

2. In the right pane, double-click **SOCKS V4 Filter**. This opens the **SOCKS V4 Filter Properties** dialog box. Click the **Options** tab. You will see the screen that appears in Figure 8.58.
3. Type in an alternate port number, then click **OK**.

Figure 8.58 The SOCKS V4 Filter Options Tab

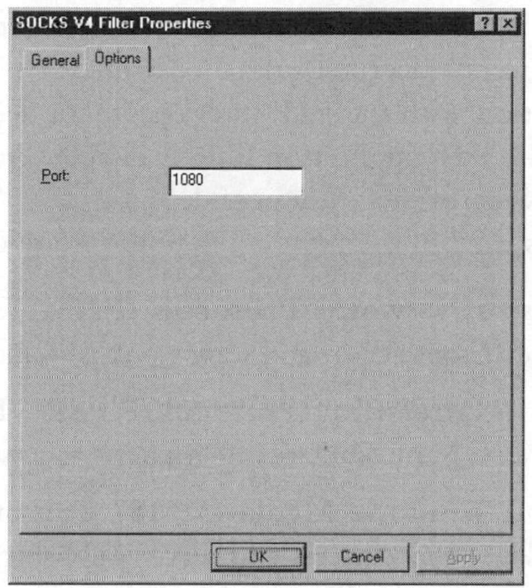

A popular SOCKS 4 application is Napster. If your computer is configured as a SecureNAT client, you must figure create a protocol definition for Napster and then create a site and content rule and a protocol rule to allow clients access to the Napster protocol definition. Then, in the configuration properties dialog box on Napster, set it to use the SOCKS 4 proxy, type in the IP address of the internal interface of the ISA server, and tell it to use port 1080 (or an alternate port if you have changed the SOCKS V4 filter settings).

Streaming Media Filter

The streaming media filter allows you to make multimedia protocols available to your ISA Server clients. The client can be internal computer behind the ISA server or an external client accessing a Windows Media Services server that has been published to the Internet.

This filter installs the following protocol definitions:

- Client PNM: RealNetworks Protocol

- Server PNM: RealNetworks Protocol
- Client RTSP
- Server RTSP
- Client MMS: Windows Media
- Server MMS: Windows Media

These protocol definitions are dependent on the streaming media filter. If you disable the streaming media filter, you also disable these protocol definitions. This is unlike the situation with the FTP filter's protocol definitions, which are still available even if the FTP application filter is disabled. You can control access via protocol rules to each of these protocol definitions.

The acronyms used in the protocol definitions are defined as:

- **Progressive Networks Protocols (PNM)** This protocol allows RealPlayer client access and server publishing.
- **Real Time Streaming Protocol (RTSP)** This protocol allows RealPlayer G2 and QuickTime 4 client access and server publishing.
- **Microsoft Windows Media (MMS)** This protocol allows Windows Media Player client access and server publishing.

Live Stream Splitting

Live stream splitting allows a single connection to a streaming media event to be shared among multiple users in an organization. Don't confuse this with *caching* of streaming media events, because that is not what live stream splitting is all about. Rather, live stream splitting allows a single connection to service all users who access a streaming media resource, rather than having each user create his or her own connection to the resource.

Splitting the media stream in this manner reduces the amount of bandwidth required to deliver the stream. For example, suppose Debi tunes in to a conference on law enforcement and Internet technologies delivered via a Windows Media server and the connection required 128Kbps of bandwidth for acceptable quality on the user side. About a minute later, Sean remembers that he was supposed to watch and listen to the conference as well, so he tunes in to the event. Without stream splitting, he would create a second connection to the Windows Media server delivering the event, thus requiring another 128Kbps of bandwidth for his connection. Now his and Debi's connections are consuming a total of 256Kbps of bandwidth on the external interface—or at least they are trying to do so.

With live stream splitting turned on, Sean's connection will consume no extra bandwidth because it will be able to take advantage of the connection Debi has already established. This significantly reduces the amount of bandwidth consumed on the external interface. The benefits are even more profound as you increase the number of users accessing the event.

To configure the streaming media filter, perform the following steps:

1. Open the **ISA Management** console, and expand **Servers and Arrays** and then **Extensions**. Click the **Application Filters** node in the left pane.
2. In the right pane, double-click **Streaming Media Filter**. This opens the **Streaming Media Filter Properties** dialog box. Click the **Live Stream Splitting** tab. You will see the screen that appears in Figure 8.59.

Figure 8.59 The Streaming Media Filter Live Stream Splitting Tab

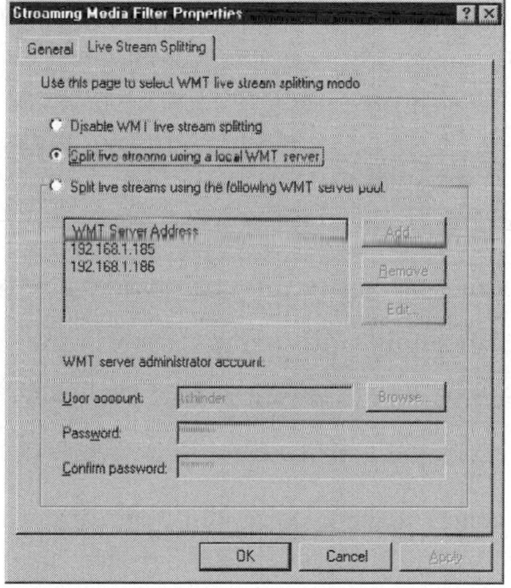

On this page you have the following options:

- **Disable WMT live stream splitting** Select this option if you do not want to use live stream splitting. You will still have access to the protocols installed by the streaming media filter.
- **Split live streams using a local WMT server** If you select this option, Windows Media Server must be installed on the ISA server. Use this option if you have a single ISA server.

- **Split live streams using the following WMT server pool** Use this option if you are running an enterprise array and have multiple Windows Media servers located on the internal network. You will need to add the IP address of each of the internal servers and include a **WMT server administrator account** that is good on each of the servers.

3. Click **OK**. You will be offered the chance to restart the Firewall Service; select that option and click **OK** again and the configuration changes will be made after a few moments.

Understanding and Configuring the Web Proxy Cache

When the ISA server is installed in either Cache or Integrated mode, the Web Proxy Service is installed. The Web Proxy Service includes the Web caching facility. This feature allows the ISA server to cache HTTP and FTP (and Gopher) objects so that they can be accessed via the cache after the first request for the object is made. Web caching is one of the most common reasons for implementing a proxy server such as ISA Server. There are multiple advantages to using the Web proxy caching facility:

- Caching can reduce the total bandwidth used on the external interface.
- Caching can significantly reduce access times for popular content.
- Active caching allows popular Web objects to be refreshed automatically.
- Caching can reduce processor and network utilization at peak usage times.

All these advantages make a compelling argument for implementing a Web caching solution for your enterprise. ISA Server's caching mechanism is superior to that found in Proxy Server 2.0. Cached files are now stored in a single file where objects can be more rapidly searched and retrieved. ISA Server also can place virtually all of the cached elements into RAM, depending on how much memory is installed on the server. Retrieving cached objects from RAM greatly increases the speed at which Web objects can be retrieved.

Because the Web cache is a component of the Web Proxy Service, it is available only when ISA Server has been configured in Cache only or Integrated mode. If you install ISA Server in Firewall mode, the Web Proxy Service is not installed and therefore the Web cache won't be available. The Web cache can be configured to meet your organization's requirements. In order to meet those requirements, you'll need to know how to configure the Web cache and understand the meaning and implications of your configuration.

Cache Configuration Elements

The Web proxy cache stores and retrieves Web objects based on how you configure the caching properties on the ISA server. The Properties sheets where you make configuration changes include:

- HTTP Caching
- FTP Caching
- Active Caching
- Advanced Caching

Each one of these sheets can be accessed by right-clicking the **Cache Configuration** node in the left pane and then clicking the **Properties** button.

Configuring HTTP Caching

Figure 8.60 shows the **HTTP** tab in the **Cache Configuration Properties** dialog box. On the **HTTP** tab, you can configure HTTP caching. Your options include:

- **Enable HTTP Caching** To enable the Web proxy cache, place a check mark in the check box for **Enable HTTP Caching**. If you do not check this box, the Web proxy cache will not function.
- **Unless source specifies expiration, update object in cache statement** Under this option, you have the following choices:
  - **Frequently (Expire immediately)** When you select this option, objects placed in the cache will expire immediately, unless there is a notation in the HTTP header that includes the expiration date of the object. If there is no expiration statement in the HTTP header for the object, the ISA server will not return the object from cache when subsequent requests for the object are made.
  - **Normally** When you select this option, the ISA server will expire the object that does not have an expiration date in such a way as to balance the amount of bandwidth required on the external interface of the ISA server. This means that these objects will be returned

from cache for a period of time and then updated. The exact values are listed in the grayed-out text boxes in the **Set Time to Live (TTL) of object in cache to** frame.

- **Less Frequently** When you select this option, ISA Server will expire objects from cache after a longer period of time that you would see if you had used the **Normally** option. This option will reduce the amount of bandwidth consumed on the external interface of the ISA server because objects in cache will be returned to users for a longer period of time before they are updated. The exact values are listed in the grayed-out text boxes in the **Set Time to Live (TTL) of object in cache to** frame.

Figure 8.60 Configuring HTTP Caching

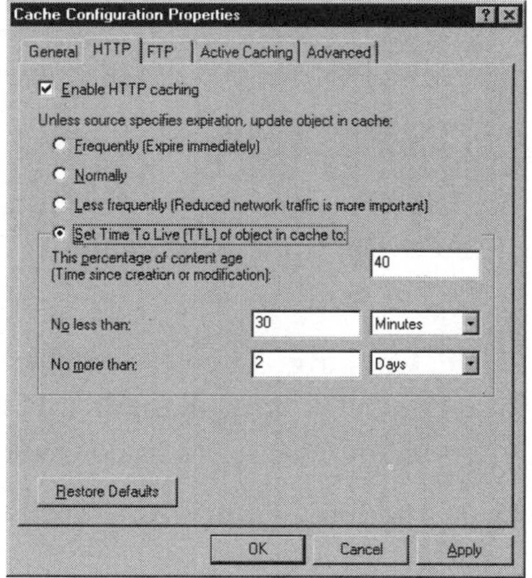

- **Set Time To Live (TTL) of object in cache to** Under this option, you have the following choices:
  - **This percentage of content age** Enter a value that will represent how long an object should be returned from cache, depending on its content age. This value is a percentage based on the modification date included in the HTTP header and the date and time when the object was placed in the cache.

    For example, suppose that the object has a modification time of 12:00 noon today, and it is placed in the Web proxy cache at 6:00 PM. If you set the value to 50 percent, the object will be returned from cache until 9:00 PM. After that, the ISA server will forward the request to the Internet Web server to update the object in cache.

Note that, like the other options, this option applies only if no HTTP header denotes an expiration date.

- **No less than** While you can set a percentage, you can also set hard-coded limits on the time the object stays in cache. You can select a minimum amount of time by including a number and the unit of time here.
- **No more than** Enter a number and unit of time to set a maximum amount of time the object with an expiration date will be kept in cache.

Configuring FTP Caching

Figure 8.61 shows the **FTP** tab in the **Cache Configuration Properties** dialog box. On the FTP caching page, you configure how long you want FTP objects received by the Web Proxy Service to remain in cache. Keep in mind that FTP objects via a dedicated FTP program *will not* be placed in the Web proxy cache.

Figure 8.61 The FTP Caching Page

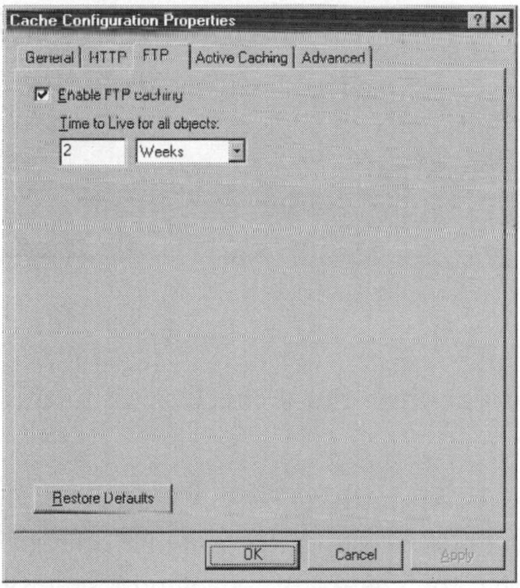

To enable FTP caching, place a check mark in the check box for **Enable FTP Caching**. To configure how long FTP objects should remain in the cache, enter a value and a unit in the text box and drop-down list box, respectively.

Remember that FTP objects can take up quite a bit of space in the cache, so configure this option judiciously.

Configuring Active Caching

The **Active Caching** tab of the **Cache Configuration Properties** dialog box appears in Figure 8.62. You enable and configure active caching on the **Active Caching** page. When active caching is enabled, the ISA Server automatically refreshes the most popular objects retrieved from the Web cache. Users retrieving popular objects will have an improved Web experience since fresh versions of these objects will be in cache before anyone actually requests the site again.

Figure 8.62 The Active Caching Page

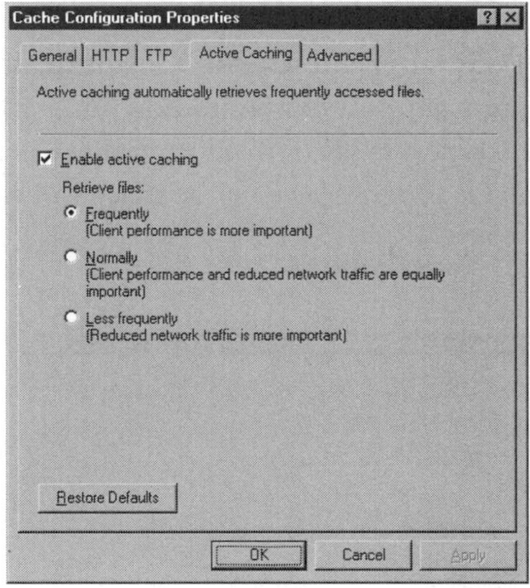

The choices are:

- **Enable active caching** Put a check mark in this check box to enable active caching.
- **Retrieve Files Frequently** The ISA server will update the cache more frequently. This option ensures that popular objects will be refreshed automatically and that the chance of retrieving a stale object is lower than if you were to select one of the other options. The downside is that more bandwidth will be consumed on the external interface, leading to less available bandwidth for users who need to obtain objects not in cache.

- **Normally** Select this option if you want the cache to be refreshed automatically but not as frequently as if you had selected the **Frequently** option.
- **Less Frequently** Select this option if you want the cache to be refresh automatically but not as often as if you had selected the **Frequently** or the **Normally** options.

Note that the less frequently the cache is refreshed, the more bandwidth is available on the external interface for users not receiving cached objects.

Active caching can have a negative effect on your bottom line if you pay for bandwidth that you actually use. The active-caching mechanism makes an assessment of the popular pages and retrieves them in advance. There is no guarantee that these pages will remain popular, however. A user might never access them again. Therefore, you could be wasting bandwidth on pages that would otherwise never be accessed again.

Undocumented ISA Server

We have often wondered what exactly these active caching options mean. The algorithm used to determine when actively cached pages should be refreshed is undocumented. However, CPU cycles play a role, and active caching is carried out when the CPU is not "busy." This means that most active cache requests are held during off-peak hours, which should minimize the amount of contention with users trying to access noncached content.

Optimal Cache Performance Configuration

Most organizations want to take advantage of active caching. To optimize the performance of your mixed active and passive caching solution, you should configure the passive caching configuration (through the **HTTP** tab) to update objects **Less frequently** and the active-caching configuration (through the **Active Caching** tab) to retrieve the files **Frequently**. The combination of caching parameters will reduce the amount of bandwidth used for refreshing pages while still frequently updating popular pages. The overall effect is that the caching mechanism uses less bandwidth on the external interface.

Configuring Advanced Caching Options

Figure 8.63 shows the content of the **Advanced** tab in the **Cache Configuration Properties** dialog box.

Figure 8.63 The Advanced Caching Configuration Page

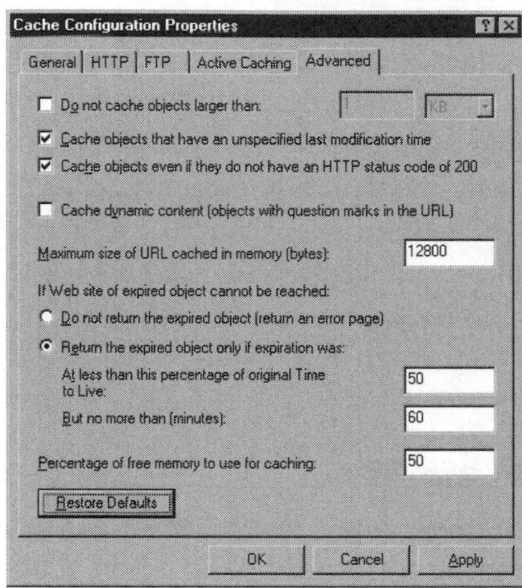

On the **Advanced** caching page, you can configure some of the advanced caching options:

- **Do not cache objects larger than** Here you can tell ISA Server to limit the size of objects placed in the Web cache. Note that in the initial release of ISA Server, if you tried to change this value to use more than 9999KB, you got an error message. Limiting the size of cached objects allows you to store more objects in your Web cache.
- **Cache objects that have an unspecified modification time** Select this option if you want ISA Server to cache objects with an unspecified modification time. It is the job of the Webmaster for a particular Web server to put an expiration time on content delivered by the Web server. If this option is selected, the ISA server will cache objects that do not contain expiration time information. The ISA server will then decide how long to keep the object in cache.
- **Cache objects even if they do not have a HTTP status code of 200** Select this option if you want to cache objects that have an HTTP

status code other than 200. This setting allows you to cache pages that return codes that essentially communicate that the Web page is not available. If you select this option, *negative caching* will be enabled. You should be careful about caching negative results, because if there is a temporary problem with a Web site, users will continue to receive the error message, even after the site is up again.

- **Cache dynamic content (objects with question marks in the URL)** Select this option if you want the ISA server to cache objects that have dynamic content. This is a good option to select if you access static databases such as TechNet searches. However, this setting can lead to receiving outdated information if the results of a query return different values because the database is updated frequently with different values being returned to the client after entering the same query.
- **Maximum size of URL cached in memory (bytes)** Use this option to configure the maximum size of a URL cached in memory. The default value is 12.8Kb, which allows a larger number of objects to be placed in RAM. If the server has an excess of RAM that you can dedicate to the cache, consider increasing this value to allow larger objects to stay in the RAM cache.

Under **If Web site of expired object cannot be reached**, you have the following options:

- **Do not return the expired object (return an error page)** Select this option if you do not want expired objects returned to the users. When this option is selected, the ISA server will return an error message when it is not able to contact the Web server to refresh the expired object. Select this option if you do *not* want users to access expired content.
- **Return the expired object only if expiration was** Under this option, you have the following choices:
    - **At less than this percentage of the original Time to Live** Configure a percentage in the text box. This option allows expired pages to be returned to users, even if the Web server containing the page cannot be contacted. The default value is 50 percent. Therefore, if the TTL on the object were 12 hours, the page would still be returned from cache for up to 6 hours.

- **But no more (than minutes)** Figure a value in number of minutes in the text box. This setting allows you to put hard constraints on how long the object can be returned from cache. For example, if the TTL on an object is 12 hours and you set it to return objects for up to 50 percent of the TTL, it would return expired pages to users for up to 6 hours. However, the default setting is to limit the time to **60 minutes**. You can change the value here.
- **Percentage of free memory to use for caching** Type in a percentage of free memory to use for caching. This value determines how much RAM you want to dedicate to the Web cache. If the machine is a dedicated caching server, set this value high. If you are running other services on the same machine, you might want to reduce this value so that more memory is available to other services running on the server. Note that only "free memory" is dedicated to the cache, rather than allowing you to configure a set value. This allows the ISA server to dump Web objects into the disk cache when other processes require memory. However, the process of releasing memory for other processes takes up processor cycles and can have a negative performance impact.

Scheduled Content Downloads

The Scheduled Content Download Service allows you to configure content to be downloaded automatically to the Web cache so that it is available to users before anyone even accesses the sites. Typically, you would schedule content to be downloaded at times of low network usage to minimize the impact on performance during working hours. By scheduling content downloads, you can make information available to your users, even when a mission-critical server becomes unavailable during the day. The caching settings you configure for your scheduled downloads will override the settings you've made for the Web cache for other content.

To configure a scheduled content download, perform the following steps:

1. Open the **ISA Management** console, expand your server or array, and then expand the **Cache Configuration** node. Right-click the **Schedule Content Download** node, click **New**, and then click **Job**.
2. In this example, let's say we want to download the contents of **Syngress.com**. In the first page of the wizard, we need to give a name to this job. Call it **Syngress Web Site**, and click **Next**.

3. The **Start Time** page appears, as shown in Figure 8.64. On this page you want to configure a date and time when this job should begin. This page configures when the first job will complete. You will configure subsequent downloads on a later page in the wizard. Select a date and time, and click **Next**.

   Figure 8.64 The Start Time Page

   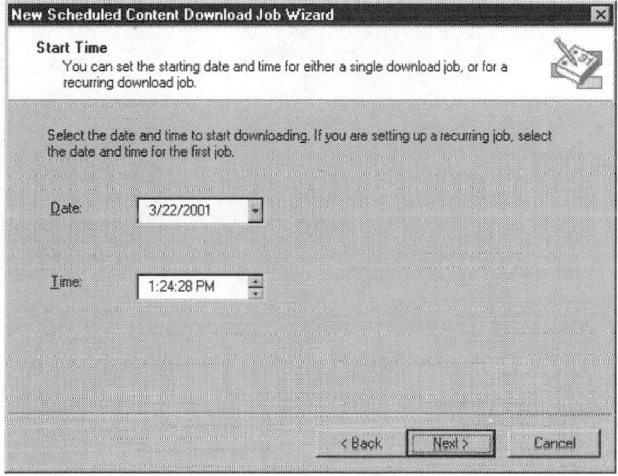

4. The **Frequency** page appears, as shown in Figure 8.65. On the **Frequency** page you configure how you want the job to be repeated. The options are:
   - **Once** This option causes the download to be performed once at the time you configured on the previous page. The download will not occur again.
   - **Daily** This option causes the job to repeat every day at the time you configured on the previous page.
   - **Weekly on** This option causes the job to take place on the days of the week you select by clicking the check box of each day you require. If a site is not updated on the weekend, do not update the pages on those days.

   For this example, select Monday through Friday, and click **Next**.

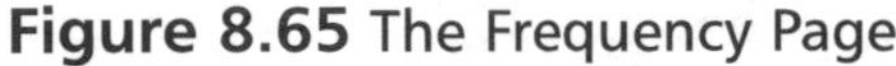

Figure 8.65 The Frequency Page

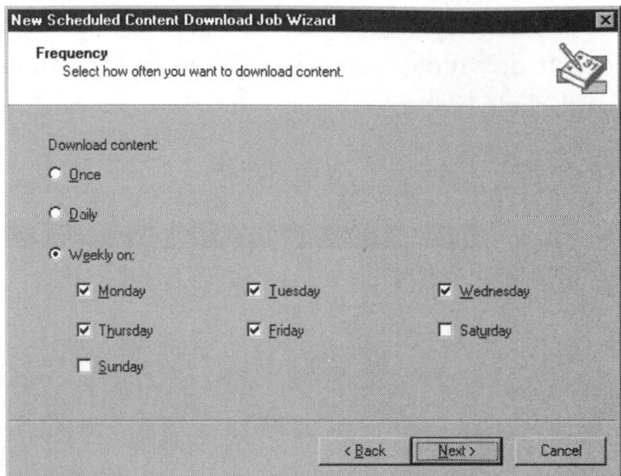

5. The **Content Page** appears, as shown in Figure 8.66. On the content page, you tell ISA Server what site you want downloaded. You have the following options:

   - **Download content from this URL** Type in the URL for the site you want to download. This can be an entire site or a subdirectory contained within the site.
   - **Download** Under this option, you have the following choices:
     - **Content only from URL domain (not site to which it links)** Choose this option to download only content from links within the same site. If the pages contain links to other domains, that content will not be downloaded. This can save a lot of time and bandwidth as well as space in the Web cache.
     - **Cache dynamic content** This option allows you to cache dynamic content that contains "?" in the URL. Note that this setting will override the setting you configured for the **Cache Properties** dialog box. However, it only overrides those settings for content obtained through this download job.

   In this example, type the URL **http://www.syngress.com** and allow dynamic content to be downloaded and restrict content to the Syngress.com domain. Click **Next**.

Figure 8.66 The Content Page

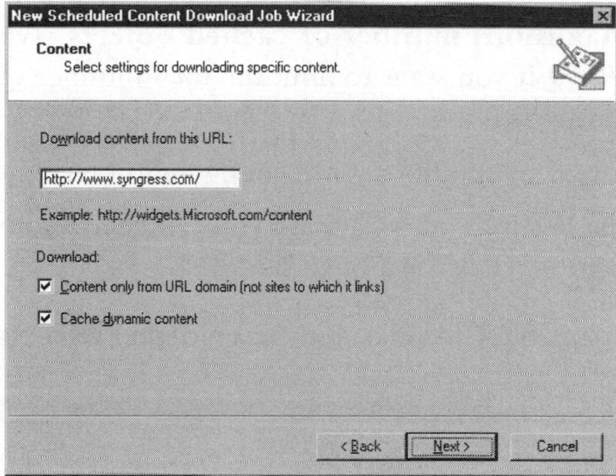

6. The **Links and Downloaded Objects** page appears, as shown in Figure 8.67. On this page you configure the TTL on downloaded objects and how many links you want cached. You have the following options:

   Under **TTL**, you have the following options:

   - **Always override objects TTL** This option allows you to override the TTL on objects downloaded through this job. If the object contains expiration information, it will be overridden with the value you configure on this page.
   - **Override TTL if not defined** If no expiration information is contained in the objects headers, you can override the TTL configured in the **Cache Properties** page by selecting this option.
   - **Mark downloaded objects with a new TTL of** In this text box you type in a hard-coded number of minutes you want objects retrieved by this job to set their TTLs. This overrides both the expiration information in the HTTP header and the settings in the **Cache Properties** dialog box.

   Under **Links depth**, you have the following options:

   - **Cache up to maximum links depth of** If you want to limit the number of pages deep you want the job to fetch, select this option and type in the number of links.

- **No limit on maximum depth** Select this option if you do not want to limit the depth of the links you want to fetch.
- **Maximum number of cached objects** Type in a number up to **99999** if you want to limit the total number of objects retrieved during this job.

  After making the desired configuration changes, click **Next**.

7. On the last page of the wizard you can check your configuration. If all looks good, click the **Finish** button.

Figure 8.67 The Links and Downloaded Objects Page

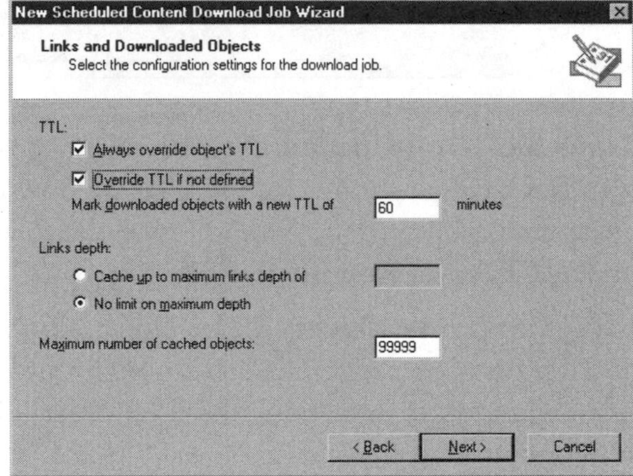

After the job is complete, it will show up in the right pane of the console. You can make changes to an existing downloaded job by double-clicking the entry in the right pane. You can **Delete** or **Disable** a job by right-clicking it and then selecting the appropriate command.

Summary

In this chapter, we covered many subjects related to outbound access controls. One of the first issues you need to address is how to control access to external resources. Allowing unfettered access to external resources can have severe negative consequences on available bandwidth and on the legal health of your organization.

You learned how to configure your server to support outbound access and how the Network Configuration Setting fit into the equation. Firewall and Web proxy routing allow you to control how request from SecureNAT and firewall clients are handled by the ISA server and allow you to control what servers are responsible for what requests.

After configuring the server to support outbound access, you can begin the process of configuring an outbound access policy. Access policies are configured using rules, in particular site and content and protocol rules. IP packet filters are also sometimes used to control outbound access.

Before site and content and protocol rules can be created, you need to create the policy elements to support the rules. Policy elements are used to define things such as destination sets and protocols that can be used in rules. After the policy elements are complete, you can create rules based on them.

Site and content and protocol rules are used to control both outbound and inbound access. Inbound access rules are more commonly referred to as *publishing rules*. For an outbound access request to be allowed, there must be both a site and content rule *and* a protocol rule to support the request. You can configure a rule that allows access to all protocols, but for SecureNAT clients this will only include protocols that have protocol definitions on the ISA server.

Application filters are used to examine traffic moving through the ISA server. Examples of application filters that affect outbound access include the FTP access application filter and the HTTP redirector filter. Application filters include protocol definitions that are used by the filter. Some of the protocol definitions used by application filters will no longer work if you disable the filter.

Finally, we covered the Web proxy cache and how to configure the cache to meet the needs of your organization. Web caching can improve performance and reduce access times for popular Web objects. The Scheduled Content Download Service allows you to build on the features provided by the Web cache and makes it possible for you to provide content to your users before any user actually accesses the content.

Solutions Fast Track

Configuring the Server for Outbound Access

☑ Several elements determine how outbound requests for Internet resources are handled. These elements can be broken down roughly into two groups: Outbound Web protocol requests, and Outbound "everything else."

☑ You can configure the amount of server memory and other resources dedicated to servicing Web requests via the **Performance** page.

☑ When you configure the **Performance tuning** slider bar to support more users per day, you dedicate more of the system resources to the ISA Server services.

Network Configuration Settings

☑ ISA Server network configuration settings that influence outbound access controls include the following: routing SecureNAT and firewall client requests, routing Web Proxy Service requests, passing outbound PPTP requests from internal clients, the local address table (LAT), and the local domain table (LDT).

☑ When firewall clients send their requests to the ISA server, the requests can be routed directly to the Internet via the *primary connection* on the ISA server, or you can configure the Firewall Service on the ISA server to forward the request to another ISA server.

☑ The most common application of routing rules is to support *Web proxy chaining.* Web proxy chains can connect ISA servers located at different sites or LAN segments in a hierarchical fashion so that downstream ISA servers can take advantage of the cache contents of upstream ISA servers.

☑ You can route Web proxy requests sent from clients to an ISA server to a Squid server and take advantage of the access controls configured on the ISA server.

☑ ISA Server supports outbound PPTP sessions between an internal network client behind an ISA server and a PPTP server located on an external network.

- ☑ The ISA server uses the *local address table (LAT)* to define the IP addresses that are internal and those that are external.
- ☑ ISA Server uses the routing table to assess where to send packets based on their destination network IDs.
- ☑ The *local domain table (LDT)* contains a list of local domains that is downloaded by firewall clients on a regular basis.

Creating Secure Outbound Access Policy

- ☑ ISA Server rules involved with outbound access are grouped into *access policies*. There are three categories of access policy: site and content rules, protocol rules, and IP packet filters.
- ☑ *Bandwidth priorities* allow you to define communications to give prioritized bandwidth to different types of communications.
- ☑ *Destination sets* allow you to create rules that are based on a particular destination. A destination can be defined by an IP address, a group of IP addresses, a computer name, a fully qualified domain name, an entire domain, or a subfolder on a computer within a domain.
- ☑ *Client address sets* are the flip side of destination sets. You can group clients together by *IP address ranges* and then control access via these client address sets.
- ☑ *Protocol definitions* allow you to create policies based on Application layer protocols.
- ☑ *Application filters* can install their own protocol definitions, and some application filters use protocol definitions included with ISA Server.
- ☑ *Content groups* allow you to control outbound access based on content contained in Web pages or FTP sites.
- ☑ *Bandwidth rules* build on the bandwidth priorities you created when configuring policy elements.
- ☑ *Protocol rules* determine the TCP/UDP protocols that network clients can access. Protocol rules can be configured to allow primary connections for either inbound or outbound requests.

Configuring Application Filters That Affect Outbound Access

- ☑ ISA Server includes a group of application filters that listen to inbound and outbound connections and can influence communications intercepted by the application filters.
- ☑ The HTTP redirector filter provides SecureNAT and firewall clients access to the services provided by the Web Proxy Service.
- ☑ ISA Server includes a SOCKS, version 4, application filter. This filter allows you to run SOCKS 4 applications behind ISA Server.
- ☑ The streaming media filter allows you to make multimedia protocols available to your ISA Server clients.
- ☑ *Live stream splitting* allows a single connection to a streaming media event to be shared among multiple users in an organization.

Understanding and Configuring the Web Proxy Cache

- ☑ When the ISA server is installed in either Cache or Integrated mode, the Web Proxy Service is installed. The Web Proxy Service includes the Web caching facility.
- ☑ The Web proxy cache stores and retrieves Web objects based on how you configure the caching properties on the ISA server.
- ☑ To optimize the performance of your mixed active and passive caching solution, you should configure the passive caching configuration (through the **HTTP** tab) to update objects **Less frequently** and the active-caching configuration (through the **Active Caching** tab) to retrieve the files **Frequently**.
- ☑ The Scheduled Content Download Service allows you to configure content to be downloaded automatically to the Web cache so that it is available to users before anyone even accesses the sites.

Frequently Asked Questions

The following Frequently Asked Questions, answered by the authors of this book, are designed to both measure your understanding of the concepts presented in this chapter and to assist you with real-life implementation of these concepts. To have your questions about this chapter answered by the author, browse to **www.syngress.com/solutions** and click on the **"Ask the Author"** form.

Q: I have configured my SecureNAT client to use a protocol rule that allows "all protocols," but I cannot access Napster. Why is this happening?

A: Remember that SecureNAT clients can access only protocols that are included in the list of protocol definitions, even when you enable an "all protocols allowed" configuration. Firewall clients do not suffer from this limitation; therefore, you do not need to configure a separate protocol definition for each protocol when allowing access to all protocols for firewall clients.

Q: I have many users who want to access external PPTP servers on the Internet. However, I want a way to limit the users who can access PPTP servers. How can I do this?

A: Unfortunately, you cannot control who accesses PPTP servers after you have enabled the SecureNAT outbound PPTP access packet filters. Protocol rules are limited to controlling access for TCP/UDP-based protocols and therefore cannot control access to General Routing Encapsulation protocol (GRE, IP protocol 47). Once you enable the filter, all users will be able to call out through PPTP.

Q: I want to prevent users from gaining access to .MP3 files from the Napster site. Is there an easy way to do this?

A: Yes. Configure a site and content rule that prevents downloading of .MP3 files. If you are interested in blocking *only* .MP3 files, you can create a new content group in the Policy Elements node and then use this content group to create the site and content rule to limit the download of .MP3s.

Q: I want to control access based on users and groups, but I do not want to install the firewall client software on any of the machines. Is there a way I can do that?

A: Sort of. SecureNAT clients cannot send credentials to the Firewall Service, but you can configure the machines as Web proxy clients and force authentication. In this way, you can require that users authenticate to the Web Proxy Service before accessing Web content.

Chapter 9

Configuring ISA Server for Inbound Access

Solutions in this chapter:

- Configuring ISA Server Packet Filtering
- Application Filters That Affect Inbound Access
- Designing Perimeter Networks

☑ Summary

☑ Solutions Fast Track

☑ Frequently Asked Questions

Introduction

In Chapter 8, we focused on how to configure an ISA server to allow for outbound access and how to configure outbound access controls. In this chapter, we look at access control from the other end: how to control inbound access to the internal network through the ISA server. One of the most exciting improvements Microsoft has made with ISA Server over Proxy Server 2.0 is the new product's ability to function as a full-fledged firewall, offering filtering at the packet, circuit, and application levels. This functionality gives administrators flexibility in designing a configuration that will provide administrators with the exact desired degree of control over traffic that is allowed to enter the local network.

Configuring ISA Server Packet Filtering

Packet filtering is the process of examining the TCP and IP header information to assess whether a packet should be allowed to enter or leave the external interface of the ISA server. With ISA Server, you can choose to enable or disable packet filtering. We recommend that you enable packet filtering on the ISA server to ensure the highest level of security.

NOTE

Manually created packet filters are *static;* that is, they open or close ports and leave them that way. *Dynamic packet filtering* is done using access policy or publishing rules.

How Packet Filtering Works

When packet filtering is enabled, only packets for which a filter has been configured are allowed to pass through the external interface of the ISA server. If you don't have a packet filter in place to allow a particular packet through the ISA server, the packet will be dropped. If there is a packet filter, the header information in the packet must match parameters in a packet filter rule before the packet will be accepted and passed through the ISA server.

Default Packet Filters

ISA Server includes packet filters that are enabled by default and that allow the ISA server to ping remote clients, resolve Internet host names via DNS, and receive network information from remote routers via ICMP. Note that these default filters do not automatically allow internal computers to ping or resolve host names, and they do not allow external computers to ping the ext ernal interface of the ISA server. In order to allow an internal client to ping external resources, the internal client must be configured as a SecureNAT client and IP routing must be enabled on the ISA server.

When Packet Filtering Is Disabled

If packet filtering is not enabled, the ISA server's external interface listens on all ports that have running services on the ISA Server computer. The default installation of Windows 2000 includes many network services that open ports that could allow an intruder to attack the ISA server and potentially gain valuable information about your internal network, if not actually access the network itself. When packet filtering is enabled, all these ports will be inaccessible from the external interface. Only ports that you explicitly open through a static packet filter, through a publishing rule, or dynamically will be available.

NOTE

Although packet filtering disables access to service ports on the external interface, it has *no* effect on the internal interface. You cannot use ISA Server to filter packets on the internal interface. If you are interested in filtering on the internal interface, you can use host-based packet filtering via the **Advanced** options in the TCP/IP Properties configuration dialog box, or you can configure packet filtering on the internal interface using RRAS.

Static versus Dynamic Packet Filtering

Static packet filters allow you to permanently open or close access to packets of your choice. Note that packet filters are not limited to TCP/UDP port filtering. You can filter for packets of various IP protocols (ICMP, GRE, etc.) as well using the IP protocol number for the appropriate ICMP packet type.

ISA Server also supports *dynamic packet filtering*. This type of packet filtering allows the ISA server to open and close ports on the external interface on an "as-needed" basis. This temporary opening and closing of ports reduces the risk of attack, because the ports are not left open permanently and because the ports accept responses from a server to which a request was sent. If a server that is not the one to which the request was sent tries to answer to that port, the access will fail. This type of filtering is also known as *stateful packet filtering*.

Dynamic packet filters allow for outbound access when you create rules. For example, when you create a protocol rule that allows outbound access for HTTP requests, you do *not* need to create a static packet filter that allows outbound requests to port 80. The dynamic packet-filtering mechanism will allow access to outbound port 80, and it opens a response port to which the Web server can respond. Once the ISA server and the destination Web server have completed their interaction, the ISA server closes the response port and does not allow outbound access to port 80 unless another request comes through that the rule allows.

In the same fashion, when you publish services on the private network or on a DMZ segment, a port is statically opened for the service on the external interface of the ISA server to receive the request, and it dynamically opens outbound ports on the external interface so that it can send the response to the external computer making the request.

When to Manually Create Packet Filters

Although in most cases Microsoft recommends that you use publishing rules to allow external clients access to internal resources, there are three primary situations in which you must use packet filters:

- If you have published servers that are located in a DMZ, or perimeter, network (also referred to as a *screened subnet*)
- If you need to allow access to protocols other than TCP or UDP
- If you are using applications or services on the ISA Server computer itself and those applications or services need to listen on the Internet

The only way to allow inbound and outbound access to resources on a perimeter network is using packet filters. There are no built-in packet filters that allow access to a perimeter network, so each one must be created manually.

Packet filters must also be created if you want to allow access to non-TCP/UDP protocols. Examples of these include:

- Generic Routing Encapsulation (GRE or IP Protocol 47), used by PPTP
- All ICMP protocols

In order for ISA Server to accept inbound or outbound messages on its external interface for these non-TCP/UDP protocols, you must create a packet filter to allow access.

Finally, all applications and services on the ISA server itself must have packet filters to support them. These services on the ISA server are not exposed to the same access policy as internal network clients. Therefore, you must create a packet filter to support applications such as POP3, SMTP, and NNTP clients or servers if you want to use these on the ISA server.

TIP

You can configure packet filters if you have installed ISA Server in firewall or integrated mode. Static packet filters are not available if ISA is installed in caching mode. Caching-only ISA Servers are still able to create dynamic packet filters for inbound and outbound requests.

Enabling Packet Filtering

To enable packet filtering on your ISA server, follow these steps:

1. Open the **ISA Management** console, and under the **Server or Array name** in the left console tree, expand the **Access Policy** node, then right-click **IP Packet Filters**. Click the **Properties** command.
2. In the **IP Packet Filter Properties** dialog box (Figure 9.1), put a check mark in the check box for **Enable packet filtering**.
3. Click **OK**.

You can later disable packet filtering, if you want, by unchecking the box. However, note that if packet filtering is forced by the enterprise policy that applies to the array, you will *not* be able to disable packet filtering.

Creating Packet Filters

Packet filters are created with the *New Packet Filter Wizard*. Follow these steps to create a new packet filter:

Figure 9.1 The IP Packet Filters Properties Dialog Box

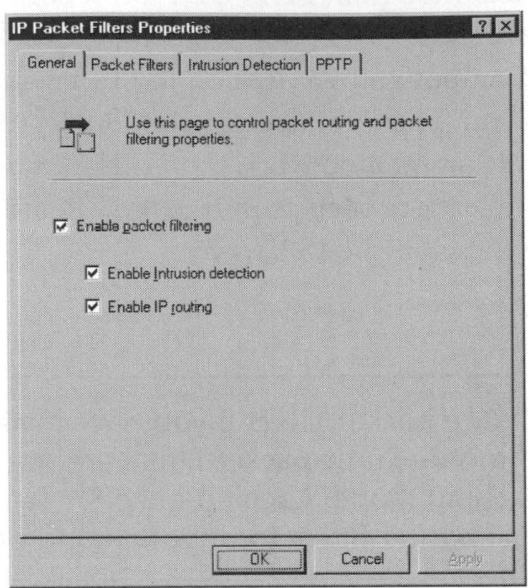

1. Open the **ISA Management** console and expand the **Access Policy** node. Right-click **IP Packet Filters**, click **New**, and then click the **Filter** command.
2. This set of actions starts the **New IP Packet Filter Wizard**. In this example, we'll create a packet filter that allows access to outbound port 80. This will allow us to use the Web browser on the ISA Server computer to access Web sites. Call this filter **HTTP-Outbound**. Click **Next**.
3. On the **Filter Mode** page, select the **Allow packet transmission**, as shown in Figure 9.2. You also have the option to **Block Packet Transmission**. Click **Next**.

NOTE

Block filters are processed *before* allow filters. Thus, if you have both a block and an allow filter for a particular protocol, the block filter takes precedence. Block filters also override dynamic packet filters. This means that if you have a block filter, for example, for HTTP, you cannot use a publishing rule to publish an internal Web server. Block filters are useful for refining your security; a common example is to block SMTP connections from known spam sites.

Figure 9.2 The Filter Mode Page

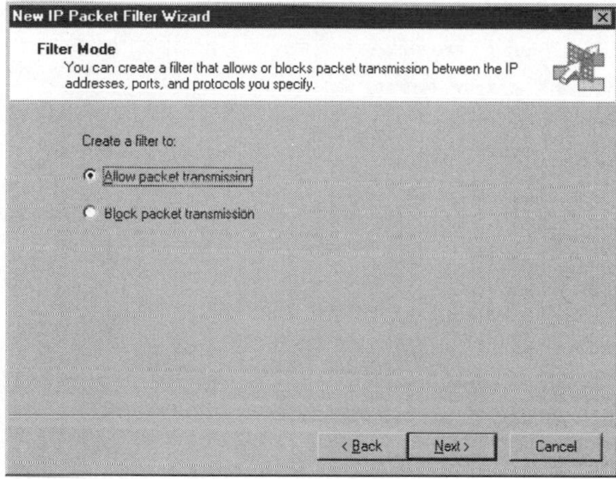

4. On the **Filter Type** page, select the **Custom** option, as shown in Figure 9.3. Note that there is a Predefined Filter for **HTTP Server (port 80)** that is grayed out in the **Predefined** drop-down list box. This filter allows *inbound* requests to port 80 on the ISA server, not outbound requests. Click **Next**.

Figure 9.3 The Filter Type Page

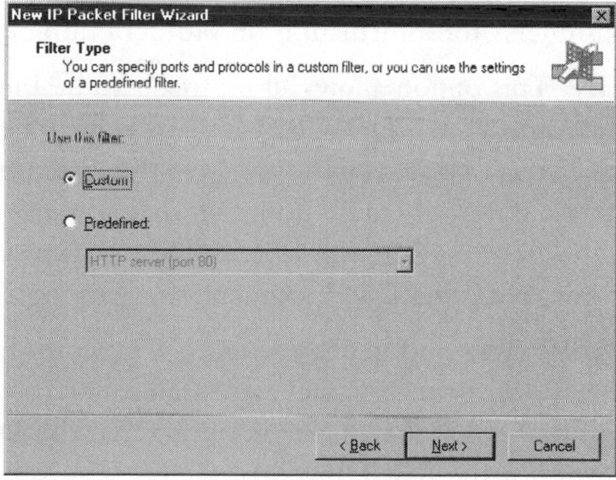

5. The **Filter Settings** page appears as shown in Figure 9.4.

Figure 9.4 The Filter Settings Page

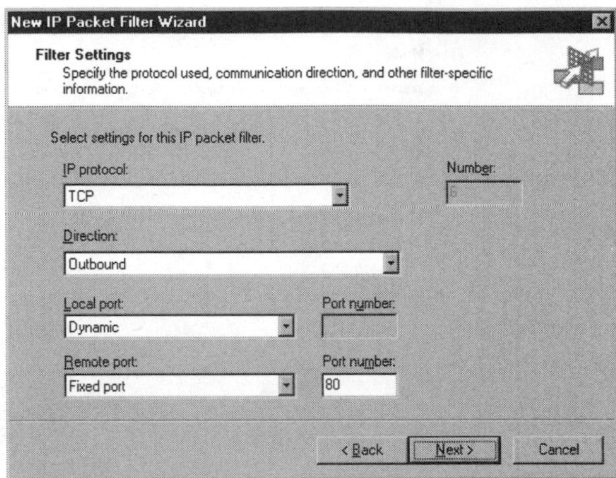

You have a number of options on this page:

- **IP Protocol** In the **IP Protocol** drop-down list box, you have the following choices:
  - **Custom Protocol** This option allows you to configure a packet filter for any IP protocol number. For example, IGMP uses IP protocol number 2. You could create a filter specifying IP protocol 2 to allow IGMP. See the sidebar entitled "Protocol Identification Numbers" for information on protocol numbers.
  - **Any** This option allows all protocols to be included in the filter, including TCP, UDP, ICMP, and any other IP protocols. When you select this option, you do not have the option to select local and dynamic ports, because it implies that all ports will be open inbound and outbound. As we'll discuss later, if you plan to create a filter to allow access to a DMZ segment, the **Any** option does not work.
  - **ICMP** This option allows you to configure packet filters for the ICMP protocol types and codes. When you select this option, you will be offered the chance to configured the **Direction**, **Type**, and **Code** for the ICMP protocol filter.
  - **TCP** Use this option to configure TCP protocols to which you want to give inbound or outbound access.

- **UDP** Select this option to configure UDP protocols to which you want to give inbound and outbound access.
- **Direction** Depending on the protocol you choose, you could have the following options:
  - **Both** The filter will control primary connections for both inbound and outbound access.
  - **Inbound** The filter will define the local port to be used to allow an external computer access.
  - **Outbound** The filter will define the remote port to be used to initiate the connection.
  - **Receive only** The filter will define the local port to be used to receive UDP messages.
  - **Send only** The filter will define the remote port to be used to initiate UDP messages.
  - **Receive Send** The filter will define the primary UDP inbound connection and remote response port.
  - **Send Receive** The filter will define the primary UDP outbound connection and local response port.
- **Number** Type in the protocol number you want to use. This option is available if you choose **Custom** for your IP protocol.
- **Local port** You'll have the following options for **Local Port**:
  - **All Ports** This option allows all local ports to be available.
  - **Fixed Port** This option allows you to define a fixed port number.
  - **Dynamic Port** This option allows ports 1025–5000 to be available as local ports used in the filter.
- **Remote port** You'll have the following options for **Remote Port**:
  - **All Ports** This option allows all ports on the remote machine to be used in the filter.
- **Fixed Port** This option allows you to define a particular port on the remote computer.

In this example, we define the filter settings as follows:

IP Protocol: TCP

Direction: Outbound

Local Port: Dynamic

Remote Port: Fixed port

Port Number: 80

Click **Next**.

6. The **Local Computer** page appears, as shown in Figure 9.5

Figure 9.5 The Local Computer Page

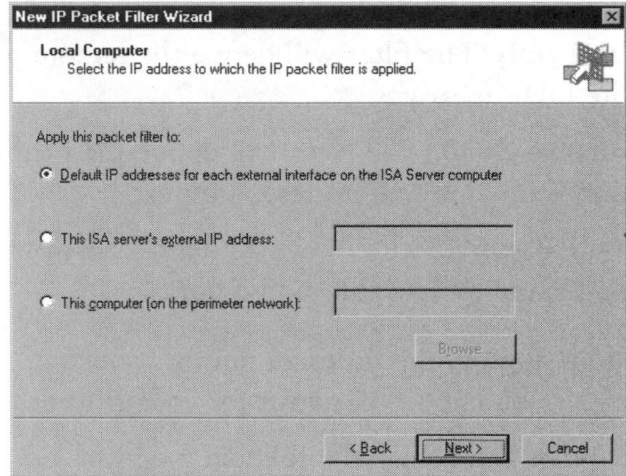

On this page you have the following options:

- **Default IP addresses for each external interface on the ISA Server computer:** This option automatically applies the filter to the *default IP address* on all the external interfaces. The default IP address is the top-most listed IP address bound to the network interface. If you have bound multiple IP addresses to an interface, this selection will apply the filter to the top selection only.
- **This ISA server's external IP address:** Select this option to designate a single IP address on the external interface to which this filter is applied. If you have only a single interface with a single IP address bound to it, you can use the first option rather than typing the IP address.

TIP

To determine which IP address is the default, in **Settings | Network and Dialup Connections,** select the desired interface, right-click it, and choose **Properties.** On the **General** tab, click the **Properties** button, and double-click **Internet Protocol (TCP/IP).** On the TCP/IP Properties sheet, click the **Advanced** button, choose the **IP Settings** tab, and observe the IP address at the top of the list.

- **This computer (on the perimeter network):** This option allows you to "publish" services and control access to services on your perimeter network. Services on the perimeter network are not controlled by Web or server publishing rules, because machines on the perimeter network are not included on the LAT. In order to control access to perimeter network computers, you need to configure packet filters. We will cover this option in more detail later in this chapter when we discuss perimeter network configurations.

For this example, select the **Default IP addresses for each external interface on the ISA Server computer**, since we have only a single interface with a single IP address bound to it. Click **Next.**

7. The **Remote Computers** page appears, as shown in Figure 9.6.

Figure 9.6 The Remote Computers Page

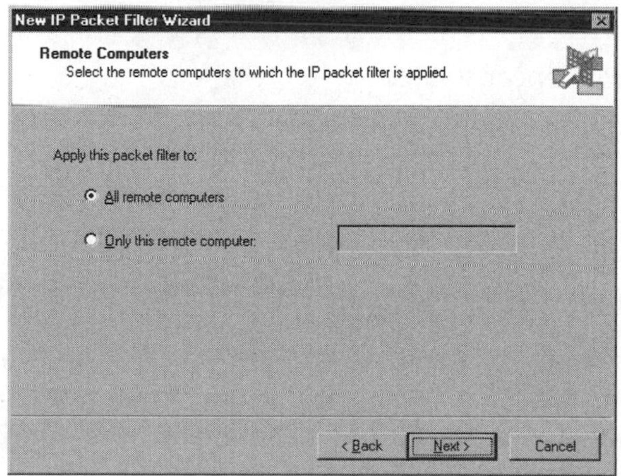

On this page your choices are:

- **All remote computers** Choose this option if you want the filter to apply to all remote computers that attempt to access the machine.
- **Only this remote computer** Select this option if you want the packet filter to apply to a single remote computer. For example, suppose we were configuring a packet filter to allow inbound access to a machine on our perimeter network, and we only want a certain partner to be able to access the machine. We could put in the address of that partner's proxy in the remote computer text box. This would allow only requests that come from our partner's proxy to access our site.

For this example, select **All remote computers**, and click **Next**.

8. On the last page of the wizard, you can review a summary of the choices you've made. If all looks good, click **Finish** to create the packet filter.

Configuring & Implementing...

Protocol Identification Numbers

Each protocol is associated with a protocol ID number. The following are the IDs for some of the more commonly used protocols:

Internet Control Message Protocol (ICMP):	1
Internet Group Management Protocol (IGMP):	2
IP/IP encapsulated	4
Transmission Control Protocol (TCP)	6
User Datagram Protocol (UDP)	17
Reservation Protocol (RSVP)	46
Generic Routing Encapsulation (GRE)	47

These protocol numbers are assigned by the Internet Assigned Numbers Authority (IANA) and are used to identify the next level protocol in the Protocol field of the IPv4 header (in IPv6, this field is called Next Header). A more complete listing can be found at www.isi.edu/in-notes/iana/assignments/protocol-numbers.

Managing Packet Filters

After creating a packet filter, at any time you can double-click the filter in the right details pane of the ISA Server MMC when **Servers and Array | Access Policy | IP Packet Filters** is highlighted and access its **Filter Properties** dialog box. Here you can view or make changes to the configuration of the packet filter.

The **General** tab allows you to change the name of the filter and add a description.

The **Filter Type** tab (Figure 9.7) allows you to change the characteristics of the filter (the protocol, direction, local port, and remote port).

Figure 9.7 The Filter Type Tab

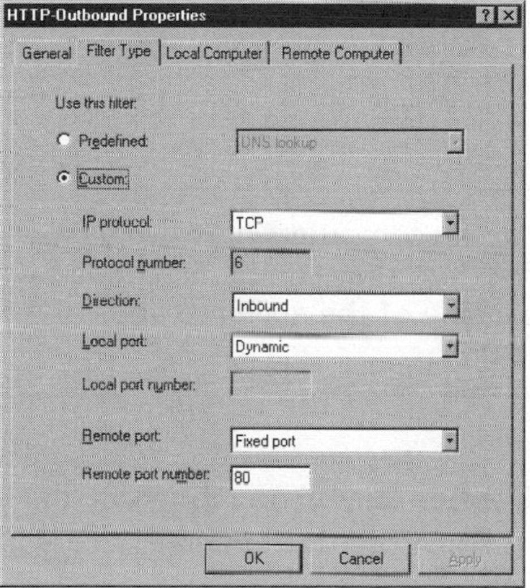

On the **Local Computer** tab (Figure 9.8), you can change the interface to which the filter applies. Note that this tab also gives you an option that was not available in the wizard. In addition to configuring a single computer on the perimeter network, you have the option **These computers (on the perimeter network)**. This option allows you to have the filter apply to a range of computers as defined by their network IDs.

Figure 9.8 The Local Computer Tab

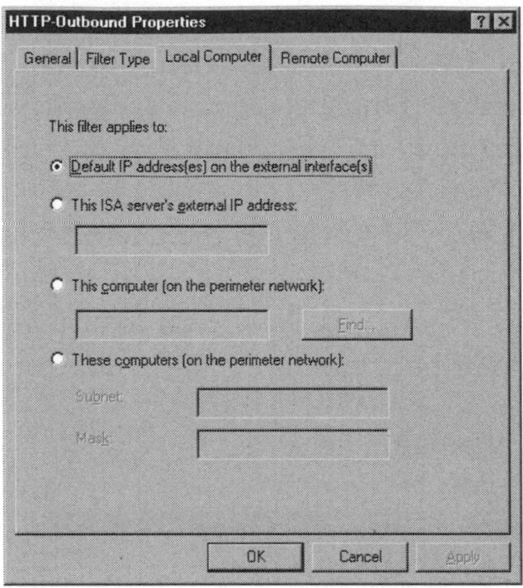

TIP

The IP addresses of the computers on your perimeter network should be carefully planned so that they can be described by a classless "supernet" mask to take advantage of the ability to apply the filter to a range of computers on the DMZ.

On the **Remote Computer** tab, you can specify the remote computers to which this filter applies. Again, note the option labeled **This range of computers**, which allows you to apply the filter to a range of remote computers rather than being limited to applying it to a single computer, as you were limited by the wizard.

NOTE

If you no longer want to use a packet filter, you can right-click it and select either the **Disable** or the **Delete** commands. If you think you might want to use it again later, select the **Disable** command.

Supporting Applications on the ISA Server

If you've tried to run applications such as a mail program or Internet Explorer on the ISA server itself, you probably have discovered that they didn't work and wondered why. The reason is that applications running on the ISA server are not run through the rules engine. Therefore, the only way to get them to work is to create packet filters.

If you want to make Internet Explorer or any other browser work on ISA Server, you actually have two options:

- You can make the browser a Web Proxy client.
- You can open a packet filter that will allow port 80 in the outbound direction.

The preferred method is to make the browser a Web proxy client, because this doesn't leave open access to port 80 outbound and therefore is more secure. However, sometimes you need to open a packet filter instead.

For example, Internet Explorer seems to have a problem being a Web proxy client on ISA servers that use dial-up connections. It is interesting to note that other browsers, such as Opera, do not have this problem and do work as Web proxy clients, even when dial-up connections are used on the ISA server.

Some examples of packet filters you might want to create on the ISA server and information for configuring them are shown in Table 9.1.

Table 9.1 Packet Filters for Applications and Services Running on ISA Server

Application or Service	Packet Filter Configuration
Web browser	IP protocol: TCP Direction: Outbound Local port: Dynamic Remote port: Fixed port Remote port number: 80
POP3 mail client	IP protocol: TCP Direction: Outbound Local port: Dynamic Remote port: Fixed port Remote port number: 110

Continued

Table 9.1 Continued

Application or Service	Packet Filter Configuration
SMTP mail client	IP protocol: TCP Direction: Outbound Local port: Dynamic Remote port: Fixed Port Remote port number: 25
NNTP client	IP protocol: TCP Direction: Outbound Local port: Dynamic Remote port: Fixed Port Remote port number: 119
TZO client	IP protocol: TCP Direction: Outbound Local port: Dynamic Remote port: All Ports Remote port number: 21331
Terminal server	IP protocol: TCP Direction: Inbound Local port: Fixed port Local port number: 3389 Remote port: All ports
POP3, SMTP, and NNTP server	Same packet filter configuration, except that you switch the local port and remote port settings.

SECURITY ALERT!

Table 9.1 includes the information for using applications on the ISA server. However, it is highly recommended that the ISA server itself should be dedicated to running ISA and should run few, if any, other applications. Although there could be situations in which you need to run one of these applications or services on the ISA server, we strongly advise that you consider purchasing additional machines or using other machines on the network to run applications. By no means should you ever try to run all of these applications and services simultaneously on an ISA server.

Publishing Services on Perimeter Networks Using Packet Filters

As we mentioned earlier in the packet filter example, you can "publish" services on a perimeter network using packet filters. This type of publishing is different from the type of publishing you use when publishing services on the internal network. In order to make services on the perimeter network available to external clients, you must create packet filters to make them accessible.

NOTE

It is important to understand that packet filtering is the *only* way to publish services on the perimeter network.

In a sense, you are not really *publishing* these servers, because external clients and the servers on the perimeter network are not run through the ISA Server rules engine. All the ISA server does is route the allowed packets to and from the perimeter network. In essence, ISA Server is acting as a stateful packet filter. For example, suppose you want to make a Web server available on the perimeter network. To do this, perform the following steps:

1. Open the **ISA Management** console and expand the **Access Policy** node. Right-click **IP Packet Filters**, click **New**, and then click the **Filter** command.
2. On the first page, give the packet filter a name (such as **HTTP on DMZ**) and click **Next**.
3. On the **Filter Mode** page, select the **Allow packet transmission** and click **Next**.
4. On the **Filter Type** page (Figure 9.9), select the **Predefined** option, then click the down arrow in the drop-down list box and select the **HTTP server (port 80)** option. Click **Next**.
5. On the **Local Computer** page, select the option labeled **This computer (on the perimeter network)**, and type in the IP address of the machine on the perimeter network.

Figure 9.9 The Filter Type Page

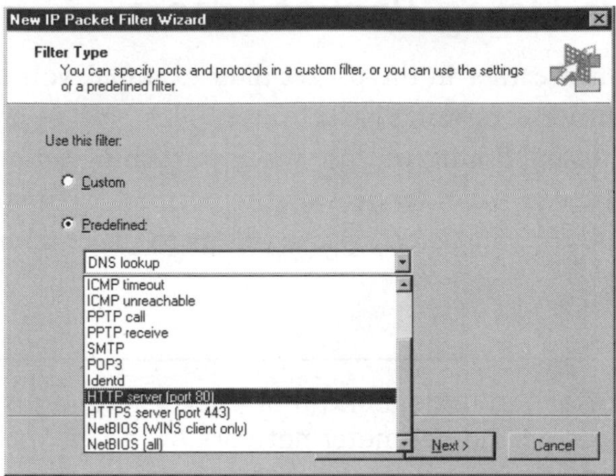

Figure 9.10 The Local Computer Dialog Box

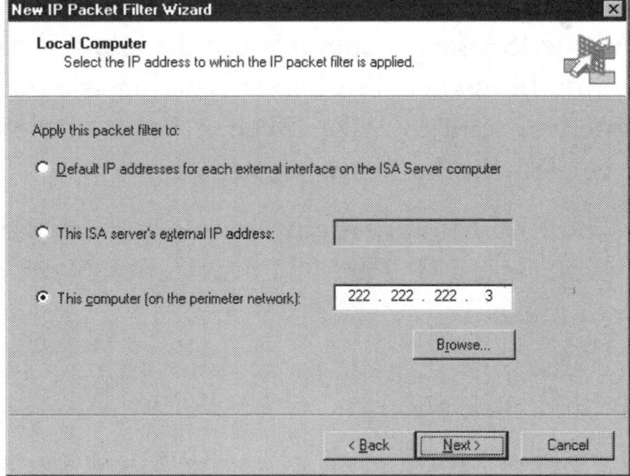

6. On the **Remote Computers** page, make the appropriate selection, depending on the purpose of your Web server. Click **Next**.
7. On the final page, review your choices and click **Finish**.

We'll go into more detail regarding configuring perimeter networks later in this chapter.

Packet Filtering Options

Several packet-filtering related options are available to you when you right-click the **IP Packet Filters** node and click **Properties**. When you do so, you'll see the **IP Packet Filters** dialog box, as shown in Figure 9.11.

Figure 9.11 The General Tab in the IP Packet Filters Dialog Box

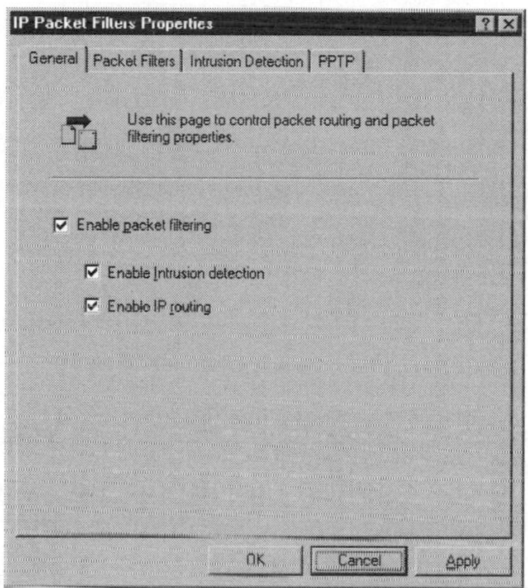

On the **General** tab of the **IP Packet Filters** dialog box, you are offered the opportunity to enable or disable packet filtering. You also have the option to **Enable Intrusion detection** and to **Enable IP routing**.

Routing between Public and Private Networks

The **Enable IP routing** option is an interesting one. It gets a little confusing when you think about routing packets from an internal network to an external, public network, since those packets aren't exactly routed (that's why the private IP addresses are referred to as being nonroutable on the Internet). Instead, those packets are translated. However, Microsoft defines NAT as a routing protocol, so this might explain the company's concept of routing between a private and public network.

Although you can't actually route (with a big "R") packets between a private and public network, the **Enable IP routing** option does have some practical significance for hosts located behind the NAT. When this option is enabled, internal clients have access to non-TCP/UDP protocols, such as ICMP and GRE (used by PPTP).

There is an important implication when packets are "routed" to and from the external network. The Web Proxy Service, in general, is responsible for the "Web protocols" (FTP, HTTP, HTTPS, and Gopher); the Firewall Service handles all other TCP/UDP-based protocols. Neither the Web Proxy Service nor the Firewall Service handles protocols that do not fit into these categories. Therefore, PPTP and ICMP requests are not subject to rules configured on the ISA server and are not exposed to the rules engine. This explains why you cannot exert access controls over who has outbound access to these "routed" protocols.

IP routing is important when you want to use a trihomed ISA Server computer with the third interface connected to a perimeter network. In this example, the ISA server routes packets from the external network to the perimeter network and back to the Internet, only applying packet filtering rules in the processes. In a sense, ISA Server is acting as a packet-filtering router.

NOTE

Enabling IP routing can result in significant improvements in SecureNAT client performance because it allows communications to go through the kernel mode data pump. For more information on this topic, check out http://support.microsoft.com (Q279347), "Enable IP Routing on ISA Server to Increase Performance."

Pre-sales questions sometime come up regarding whether you can implement ISA Server and connect it only to a DMZ segment using public IP addresses. Besides the fact that you must have at least a single entry in the LAT, it doesn't make sense to purchase ISA Server for this purpose. If all you require is a packet-filtering router, you can take advantage of the Windows 2000 Routing and Remote Access Service. RRAS allows you to configure packet filters that work in the same way as the packet-filtering feature included with ISA Server. The only difference is that RRAS does not include wizards that walk you through the process of creating the filter.

Packet Filtering/Routing Scenarios

Let's look at some of the combinations of packet filtering and routing and their implications.

Packet Filtering Disabled and IP Routing Enabled

This is a very insecure configuration. If you have a DMZ segment, IP routing must be enabled. If packet filtering is disabled, all traffic will move into and out of the DMZ, with no inspection by the ISA server. When packet filtering is disabled, you cannot create and use packet filters to control access to the DMZ network.

When packet filtering is disabled, the external interface of the ISA server will listen on all service ports that have running services, including the NetBIOS ports. Ideally, you will configure your ISA server as a good bastion host and disable all dangerous services. However, sometimes you may forget about a service running in the background and not disable it. Packet filtering helps you in this situation because, when it is enabled, the service port will not be opened until you expressly created a packet filter to support it.

Packet Filtering Enabled without IP Routing

This setup blocks all inbound packets for which there isn't an explicit packet filter. The exceptions to this rule are packets responding to a dynamically opened response port. This configuration is useful if:

- All you require is outbound access to TCP and UDP protocols.
- You do not plan to use a trihomed perimeter network configuration.
- You do not plan to use ICMP, which relies on this configuration for internal S-NAT clients.

NOTE

Ever wonder why you need to enable IP routing to reach a perimeter network when you are using a trihomed DMZ setup, whereas you don't need to enable IP routing in a back-to-back ISA Server setup with a perimeter network between the two ISA servers? The reason is that there must be at least one entry in the LAT. When the perimeter network is the only "internal" network, as in the case of the back-to-back ISA Server configuration, the perimeter network is in the LAT, and therefore the ISA Server Firewall Service will handle the routing.

Packet Filtering Enabled with IP Routing Enabled

This setup, with both packet filtering and IP routing enabled, allows you to route non-TCP/UDP packets from the private network to the Internet and also allows you to configure a trihomed perimeter network.

Packet Filtering and IP Routing Disabled

With both packet filtering and IP routing disabled, no packet filter rules are applied to the external interface, non-TCP/UDP cannot be routed to and from the internal network, and you cannot create a trihomed perimeter network.

This setup is appropriate when the external interface is connected to a trusted network, such as your internal network's backbone. You would also use this kind of configuration when you are using a back-to-back ISA Server configuration for a perimeter network. The ISA Server on the inside of a back-to-back configuration could have both packet filter and IP routing disabled. The advantage to this setup is that ISA Server performance is enhanced because no rules are applied to inbound packets at the packet level, and thus the overhead of processing packet filtering rules is avoided.

The Packet Filters Tab

When you click on the **Packet Filters** tab, you see the screen appears in Figure 9.12.

Figure 9.12 The Packet Filters Tab

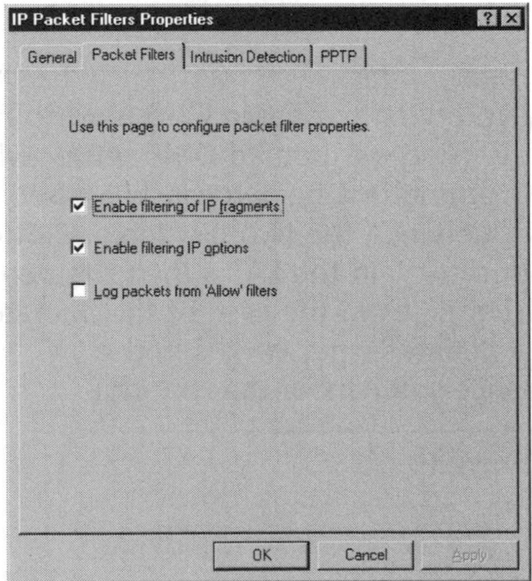

Here you have three options:

- Enable filtering of IP fragments
- Enable filtering IP options
- Log packets from "Allow" filters

The **Enable filtering of IP fragments** option allows you to reject fragmented IP datagrams. This option prevents the successful execution of certain exploits that take advantage of the fact that only fragment 0 in a fragmented IP datagram includes the original IP header information. If you do not filter IP fragments, the ISA server will pass the fragments without inspecting them, because it will base its decision on the header information in packet 0. Exploits that take advantage of packet fragmentation can be configured to exclude a fragment 0 and then reassemble a malicious packet on the destination server, effectively bypassing the packet-filtering mechanism.

NOTE

If you enable filtering of IP fragments, some multimedia connections might not work properly. You will not be able to establish a connection, or performance will be significantly degraded.

The **Enable filtering of IP options** selection prevents packets that have entries in the **options** field of the IP datagram from being passed by the ISA server. Some exploits take advantage of the options field, the most problematic one being the *source route* option. The source routing option can allow the attacker to configure a bogus alternative route for return packets.

The **Log packets from "Allow" filters** option allows you to log the packets that are allowed to pass through the ISA server. By default, there is no logging of allowed packets.

NOTE

Enabling logging of allowed packets is very processor and disk intensive. You should configure this option only when you are troubleshooting a packet-filtering problem or are performing intrusion-response activities.

Enabling Intrusion Detection

When you click the **Intrusion Detection** tab, you will see the dialog box that appears in Figure 9.13.

Figure 9.13 The Intrusion Detection Tab

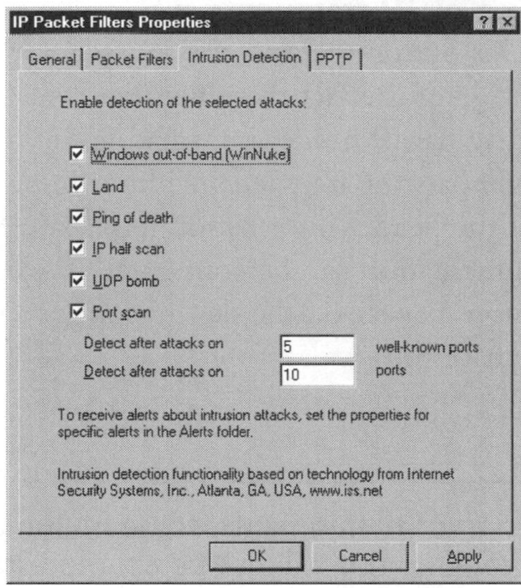

Packet filtering must be enabled in order to enable intrusion detection. ISA Server can be configured to detect a limited number of intrusion types. When you enable intrusion detection, a detected intrusion will be logged and can be viewed in the **Event Viewer**. However, if you want to be alerted at the time an intrusion occurs, you must configure an alert. For details on ISA Server intrusion detection, refer back to Chapter 3.

NOTE

You cannot configure intrusion detection when the server is installed in caching-only mode. Intrusion detection is available only in firewall or integrated mode.

Application Filters That Affect Inbound Access

In Chapter 8, we covered some of the application filters that affect primarily outbound access. There are other filters that exert the primary influence on inbound access. These application filters include:

- The DNS intrusion detection filter
- The FTP access filter
- The H.323 filter
- The POP intrusion detection filter
- The RPC filter
- The SMTP filter

Some of these filters, like those discussed in Chapter 8, can have an influence on outbound access as well as inbound access.

All of the application filters can be accessed by following these steps:

1. Expand the **Extensions** node in the left pane.
2. Click the **Application Filters** node.
3. To see the properties of any of the filters, identify the filter of interest in the right pane, and then double-click it (or alternately, right-click and select **Properties**).

DNS Intrusion Detection Filter

When you double-click the **DNS intrusion detection filter**, you will see the Properties dialog box for the filter, as shown in Figure 9.14.

The **General** tab allows you to enable and disable the filter. The **Attacks** tab allows you to configure the attack types you would like the filter to intercept.

The **DNS host name overflow** and the **DNS length overflow** attacks are buffer overflow attacks. If an intruder is able to create a buffer overflow condition, he or she might be able to create a denial of service or even obtain elevated privileges under the auspices of the service that was attacked.

The **DNS zone transfer from privileged port (1-1024)** and the **DNS zone transfer from high ports (above 1024)** search for zone transfer requests from hosts from low or high ports. You do not want external users to perform zone transfers from internal servers, because this can allow the attacker to get important knowledge about your internal naming system and IP infrastructure.

Figure 9.14 The DNS Intrusion Detection Filter Dialog Box

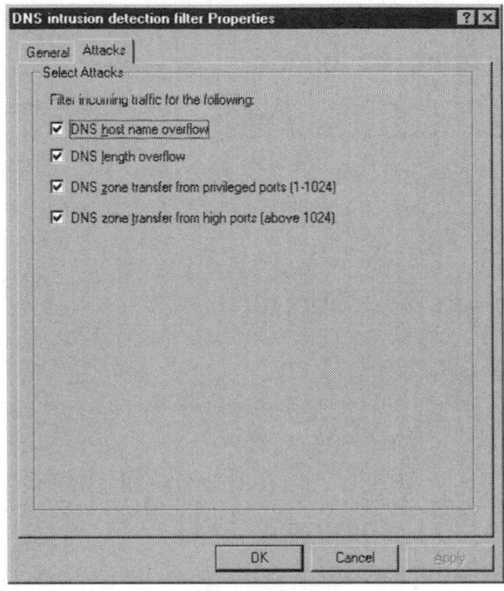

Configuring the H.323 Filter

When you double-click the **H.323 Filter** node in the left pane of the ISA Management console, you are presented with the Filter Properties dialog box, shown in Figure 9.15.

Figure 9.15 The H.323 Filter Properties Dialog Box

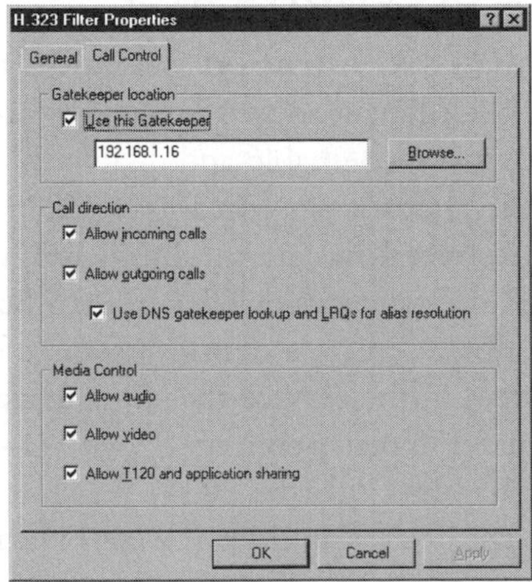

You have several options in this dialog box:

- **Use this Gatekeeper** Type in the name or IP address of the server that will act as your H.323 gatekeeper. This machine can be the ISA server or any server on your internal network. If you are using the H.323 gatekeeper on the ISA server, make sure to configure it with the IP address of the *internal* interface of the ISA server. Furthermore, if the gatekeeper is on the ISA server, do not use the name of the ISA server, because that will cause it to try to resolve the name using the DNS server address on the external interface of the ISA server. An Internet DNS server will not be able to resolve the name of the internal interface of the ISA server.
- **Allow incoming calls** Enable this option to allow incoming calls to the H.323 gateway.
- **Allow outgoing calls** Enable this option to allow outgoing calls through the H.323 gatekeeper.
- **Use DNS gatekeeper lookup and LRQs for alias resolution** This option specifies that DNS does not query for H.323 gatekeepers on the Internet. Only type A endpoint, proxy SRV, and proxy TXT queries will be made.
- **Allow audio** Allows audio data to pass through the H.323 gatekeeper.
- **Allow video** Allows video to pass through the H.323 gatekeeper.
- **All T120 and application sharing** Allows T120 communications and application sharing through applications such as Microsoft NetMeeting.

POP Intrusion Detection Filter

When this filter is enabled, ISA Server checks and filters for POP3 buffer overflow attacks. A buffer overflow occurs when an attacker floods a field with more characters than it is designed to accommodate. In some cases, these extra characters can be run as executable code, when the overflow overwrites memory past the end of the allocated buffer. This overwriting allows the attacker to gain unauthorized access to the computer and perhaps the network.

RPC Filter

The RPC filter, when enabled, allows you to publish internal servers that use RPC communications. RPC, or *remote procedure call,* is a message-passing mechanism that allows a distributed application to call services that are available on various computers on a network. It is used during remote administration of computers.

The filter adds two protocols:

- Any RPC (server)
- Exchange RPC (server)

The protocol rules installed by the RPC filter can be used when you configure server publishing rules.

SMTP Filter

SMTP is a member of the TCP/IP protocol suite, used for exchanging e-mail across the Internet. The SMTP filter can intercept all inbound messages to port 25 on the ISA Server computer and apply rules to the information contained in SMTP messages. This filter can be configured to detect buffer overflow messages and to screen SMTP content for attachments, users and domains, and keywords.

TIP

In order for the content inspection component to work correctly, you must install and configure the **Message Screener** add-on component.

The SMTP filter properties dialog box includes five tabs:

- The **General** tab
- The **Attachments** tab
- The **Users/Domains** tab
- The **Keywords** tab
- The **SMTP Commands** tab

The General Tab

The **General** tab allows you to enable or disable the SMTP filter.

The Attachments Tab

The **Attachments** tab, shown in Figure 9.16, is used for filtering e-mail attachments based on the file extension of the attachment. For example, if you want to filter all attachments containing Visual Basic scripts, select the .VBS extension. You can then specify the action that should be taken in regard to the message with the attachment.

Figure 9.16 The Attachments Tab

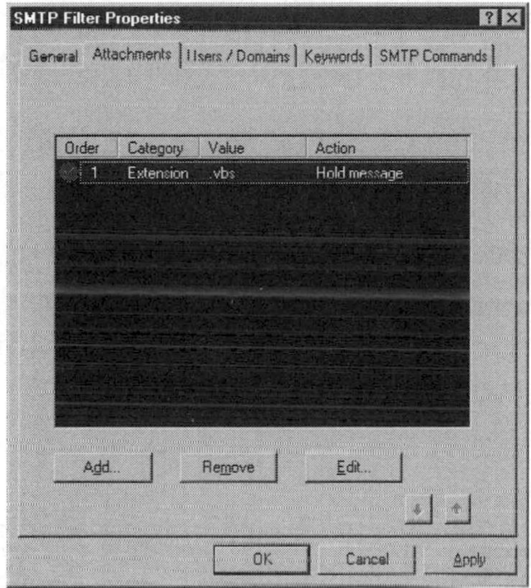

On this tab you can configure a list of attachments on which you want the Message Screener to take an action. To add an attachment to the list, click the **Add** button. You will see the screen that appears in Figure 9.17. Put a check mark in the check box for **Enable attachment rule** to enable the rule.

Figure 9.17 The Mail Attachment Rule

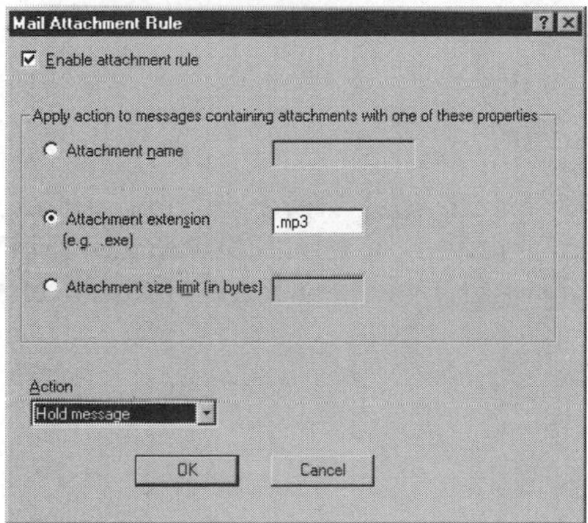

In the **Apply action to messages containing attachments with one of these properties** frame, you have the following options:

- **Attachment name** Type in the name of the attachment in the text box.
- **Attachment extension** Type in the file extension.
- Attachment size limit (in bytes) Type in a value in bytes.

In the **Action** drop-down list box, you have the following choices:

- **Hold Message** The IIS SMTP Server will hold the message in the **BADMAIL** folder.
- **Delete Message** The message will be deleted.
- **Forward message to** If you select this option, you will be presented with a text box into which you can type the e-mail address of someone to whom you want the message forwarded.

Designing & Planning...

Attachment Types You Might Want to Filter

File types commonly considered "dangerous" include those with the following extensions:

.EXE (executable)

.CMD (command)

.BAT (batch file)

.VBS (Visual Basic Script)

.JS (Java script)

In addition, be aware that Word documents and other Microsoft Office files can contain macros, which are executable code, and hypertext documents (.HTM, .HTML) can have embedded scripts or applets that can contain malicious code.

The Users/Domains Tab

On the **Users/Domains** tab, you can configure mail accounts and domains that should be blocked from the SMTP server (Figure 9.18).

Figure 9.18 The Users/Domains Tab

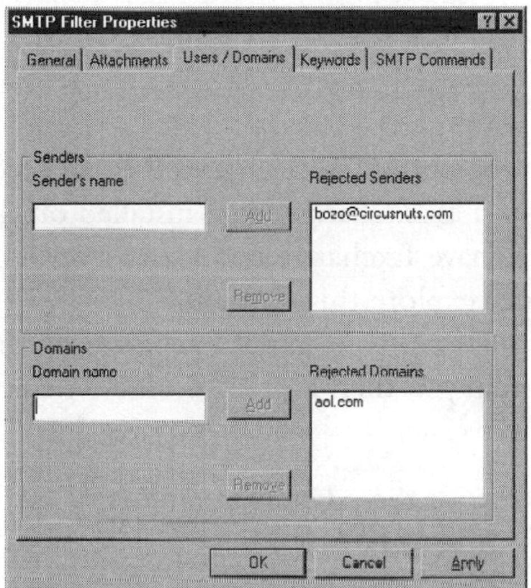

In the **Sender's name** text box, type in the e-mail addresses of individual senders whose mail you want to block. After typing the names, click the **Add** button.

In the **Domain name** text box, type in the domain names for e-mail domains for which you want to block mail. After typing the domain names, click the **Add** button.

Configuring the SMTP Message Screener

The configuration interface for the **SMTP Filter** actually allows you to configure both the SMTP filter and the SMTP Message Screener. These two entities, the filter and the Message Screener, are separate entities. The SMTP message filter is installed by default on the ISA server, the Message Screener is consider an add-on application and is not installed by default.

The SMTP filter, when enabled, can be used to filter mail by **Users/Domains** and by **SMTP Commands**. To enable this functionality, all you have to do is enable the SMTP filter, which is disabled by default.

The **Message Screener** takes a good deal of configuration outside of manipulating the properties in the **SMTP Filter Properties** dialog box. First decide how to design your network to support the Message Screener; after you've decided on a design, the next step is to configure the Message Screener to work with your internal SMTP servers.

First, decide on which of the following you want the mail server installed:

- The ISA Server
- The internal network

Although you have the option to configure the Message Screener to work with an e-mail server such as Exchange 2000 installed on the ISA server, it is poor security practice to have Exchange and ISA Server on the same computer, and therefore we will not explore this option.

The preferred solution then is to install Exchange on the internal network. After making this decision, you then have to decide where to install the Message Screener:

- On the ISA server at the edge of the network
- On an internal IIS SMTP server

For the same reasons that you do not want to install Exchange on the ISA server, you also do not want to install IIS SMTP Server on the ISA server. It is a poor security configuration for a bastion host, and therefore we will not cover this option in this book.

NOTE

This book covers the most conservative approach to using the SMTP message filter, but this isn't the only way to design a message filter solution. Look for the authors' future white papers covering these alternate methods of implementing the SMTP message filter.

Note that the message filter must be installed on a machine that is running the IIS 5.0 SMTP Service. Do not try to install the message filter on a machine that is running another version of SMTP. It will not work.

The next decision you have to make is where to install the Message Screener in relation to the corporate mail server. You can:

- Install the Message Screener on the same machine as the mail server
- Install the Message Screener on a machine separate from the mail server

We prefer to install the Message Screener on a machine separate from the corporate mail server. Even though installing the Message Screener on the mail server is possible, we've had the best success with installing it on a separate installation of the IIS SMTP Service.

In the following example of installing and configuring the Message Screener, we made the following decisions about the network design:

- The ISA server is on the edge of the network and has the SMTP filter installed and enabled.
- There is a machine that has the IIS 5.0 SMTP Service running and the Message Screener installed on that machine.
- The internal mail server is an Exchange Server configured to not allow relay to other domains.

Perform the following steps to enable the Message Screener to screen incoming messages for attachments and keywords:

1. On the ISA server, enable the SMTP filter by right-clicking the filter and clicking the **Enable** command.
2. Go to the machine on your internal network and install the ISA Server Message Screener. If you have the CD-ROM, put it into the CD drive and let it autorun. If you do not have the CD but do have the installation files somewhere on the network, click the **ISAautorun.exe** file to bring up the installation screen.
3. Start the installation of ISA Server. When the dialog box appears that allows you to choose the components to install, choose the **Custom** option. Remove the check mark from the **ISA Services** check box. Click the **Administration Tools** option, and click **Change Option**. Place a check mark in the **ISA Management** check box, and remove the check mark from the **H.323 Gatekeeper Administration Tool** check box. Click **OK**.
4. Place a check mark in the **Add-in Services** check box, and click **Change Option**. Remove the check mark from the check box for **Install H.323 Gatekeeper Service**, and place a check mark in the check box for **Message Screener**. Click **OK**. Then click **Continue**.

5. Setup will install the Message Screener on the system, which will be used by IIS 5.0. Restart the computer after installing the Message Screener.
6. In IIS 5.0, create a **Remote Domain** to support your incoming messages. Open the **Internet Services Manager** from the **Administrative Tools** menu.
7. Expand the **Default SMTP Virtual Server** and right-click the **Domains** node. Click the **New** command, and then click **Domain**.
8. The **New SMTP Domain Wizard** appears (Figure 9.19). Select the **Remote** option, then click **Next**.

Figure 9.19 The New SMTP Domain Wizard

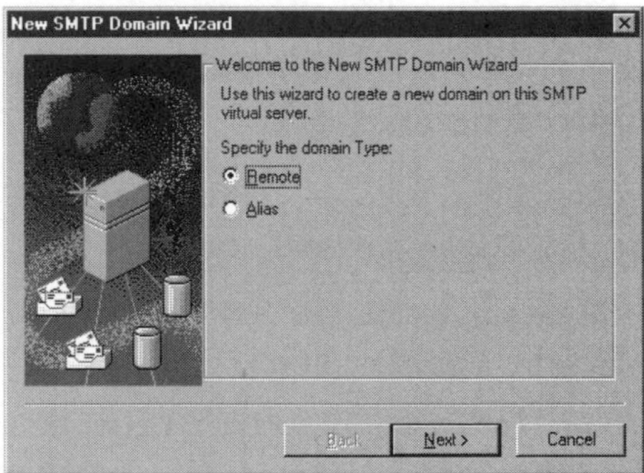

9. On the **Select Domain Name** page (Figure 9.20), type in the domain name for which your mail server will accept mail. For example, we want the IIS 5.0 SMTP server to accept mail sent to **tacteam.net** only. Messages destined for any other domain will be rejected. This setup will prevent spammers from using your SMTP server to send mail to other domains. After entering your domain, click **Next**.
10. Double-click your new remote domain, and you'll see something like what appears in Figure 9.21. Select the **Forward all mail to smart host** option button, then type in the IP address of your internal mail server, surrounded by straight brackets, as shown in the figure. Click **Apply**, and then click **OK**.
11. Stop the SMTP service and start it again.

Figure 9.20 The Select Domain Name Page

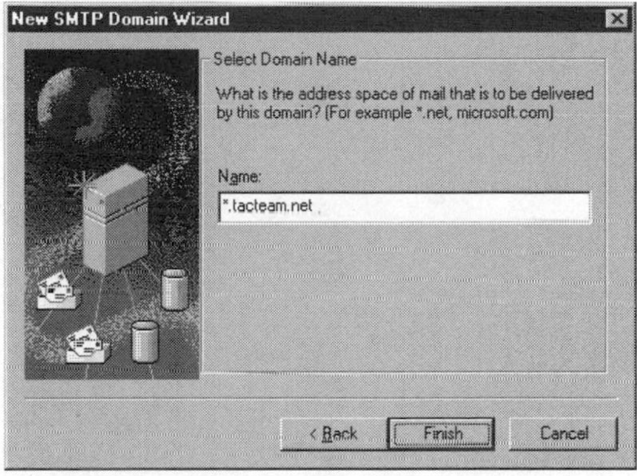

Figure 9.21 The Remote Domain Properties Dialog Box

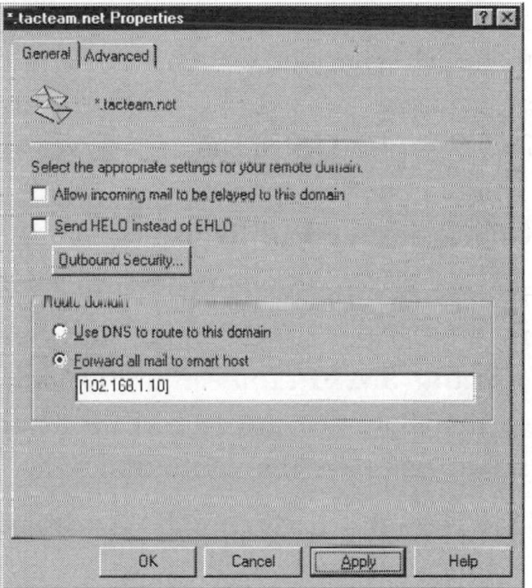

12. After completing the SMTP Server configuration, search the CD-ROM for the file **SMTPCred.exe**. Copy that file to your hard disk, and then double-click it. You will see the screen that appears in Figure 9.22.

    Type in the name of the **ISA Server**. You can leave the default time period that the remote server uses to retrieve settings, or you can change it from the default period of every 5 minutes. There's no compelling reason to change it. For the authentication data, enter a username/domain and password that has administrator access to the SMTP server. ISA Server will use these credentials to communicate with the SMTP Server.

    After entering the appropriate information, click **OK**.

Figure 9.22 The SMTPCred Tool

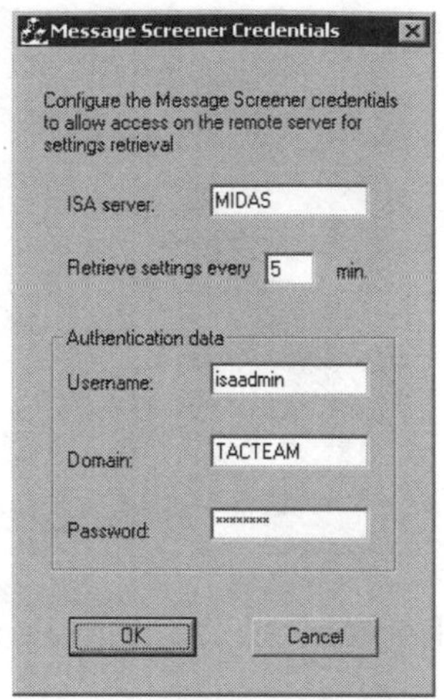

13. Now that the Message Screener has been installed and the credentials have been set using the SMTPCred tool, you can publish the internal IIS 5.0 SMTP server. Go to the ISA server and open the **ISA Management** console, expand your server or array, expand publishing, and right-click **Server Publishing**. Click the **Secure Mail Server**.
14. Go through the **Secure Mail Publishing Wizard**. (For details on using this wizard, see Chapter 10.) On the **Mail Services Selection** page, select **Incoming SMTP**. You can use Default or SSL Authentication**.** You can choose the allow **Outgoing SMTP** if you want, but in this example, the mail server will have the responsibility for sending out e-mail.
15. On the **ISA Server's External IP Address**, type in the external IP address that the ISA server will use to listen for incoming mail. On the **Internal Mail Server** page, type in the IP address of the internal IIS 5.0 SMTP server. After the wizard has completed, a publishing rule will appear to allow the ISA server to accept messages on behalf of the internal IIS 5.0 SMTP server.
16. The ISA server communicates with the Message Screener using DCOM. In order for these communications to take place, you need to configure its behavior using the **dcomcnfg.exe** properties dialog box. To open this program, click the **Start** button, click the **Run** command, type **dcomcnfg.exe** in the text box, and then click **OK**.

17. You will see the screen that appears in Figure 9.23. In the **Applications** tab, click the **VendorData** class, and then click the **Properties** button.

Figure 9.23 The Distributed COM Configuration Properties Dialog Box

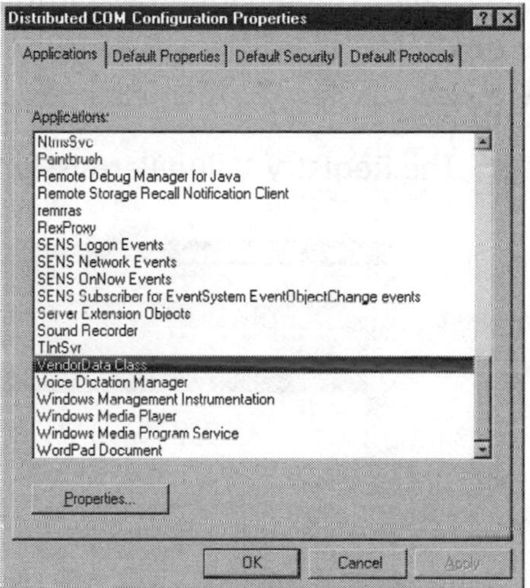

18. The **VendorData Class Properties** page appears, as in Figure 9.24. On the **Security** tab, select the **Use custom access permissions** option button. In addition, select the **Use custom launch permissions** option button. Finally, select the **Use custom configuration permissions** option button.

Figure 9.24 The VendorData Class Properties Page

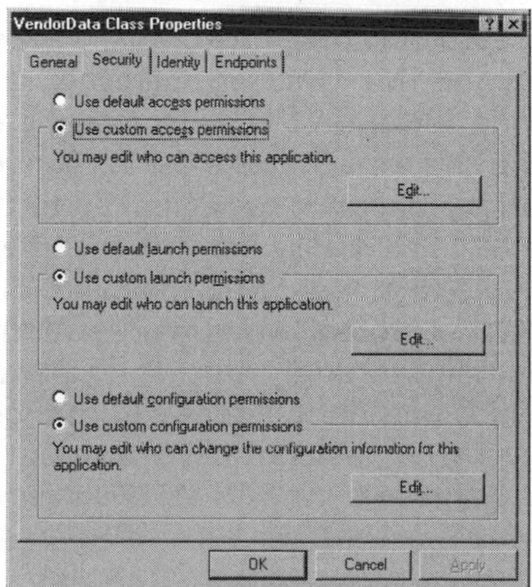

19. For each of these settings, click the **Edit** button. For example, after clicking the **Edit** button for **Use custom access permissions**, you will see the **Registry Value Permissions** dialog box, as shown in Figure 9.25.

    For each of the configuration permissions, you should add the **Everyone** group by clicking the **Add** button and selecting the **Everyone** group. Click **OK**, then click **Apply**, and then click **OK**.

Figure 9.25 The Registry Value Permissions Dialog Box

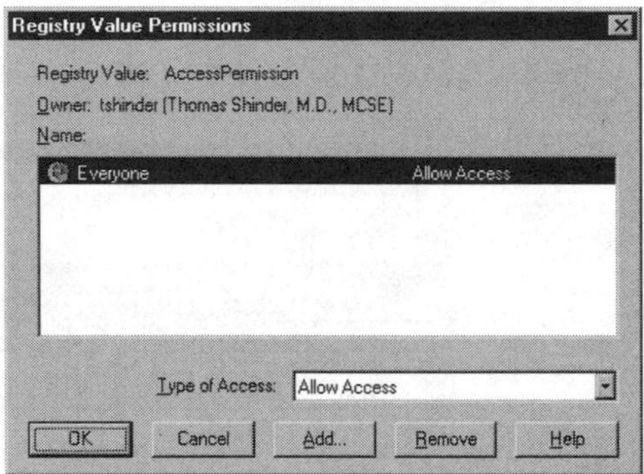

20. Restart the ISA server. After the server is restarted, click the **Sessions** node in the left pane to confirm that there is an active firewall session with the internal IIS 5.0 SMTP server.

Security Alert!

This example represents only one of many possible scenarios in which you can deploy the SMTP Message Screener. Other scenarios include having Exchange Server on the ISA server and running the Message Screener on the same machine as the Exchange server. Note that with this configuration, inbound mail is limited to the mail domain you configured in the IIS 5.0 SMTP server, and the internal Exchange (or other) mail server is able to accept SMTP messages destined for all domains. The IIS SMTP server protects your mail server from spammers trying to spam other domains through your server, because it drops messages destined for domains outside the ones you configure on the IIS 5.0 SMTP server. External SMTP messages *never* arrive at the internal mail server without being handled by the IIS SMTP server.

Designing Perimeter Networks

A *perimeter network*, also called a DMZ, is a security zone where all hosts on the network have public IP addresses. ISA Server supports perimeter network configuration by placing the perimeter network segment on a third interface on the ISA server or by placing the perimeter network between two ISA servers. You also have the option of mixing ISA Server with another firewall product in the back-to-back perimeter network configuration.

Perimeter networks allow you to publish servers without needing to change your IP addressing scheme or DNS server configuration. Requests into and out of a perimeter network are routed by the ISA server rather than being translated, as they are when servers are contained within an internal network.

Another advantage of using perimeter networks is that Internet traffic never enters your internal network. All Internet traffic can be segregated by placing all servers that receive requests from the Internet on a perimeter network. This has beneficial security implications. If an intruder is able to break into a server on the perimeter network, he or she does not automatically have access to your internal network. The reason for this is that the perimeter is just another untrusted network to machines on the internal network.

When you partition your Internet traffic on the perimeter network, you also reduce the amount of bandwidth required on the internal network used up by Internet users accessing resources on Web servers. However, we should point out that you can accomplish this by routing your internal network scheme in such a way that prevents Internet traffic from impacting your internal network's available bandwidth.

Limitations of Perimeter Networks

While placing servers such as E-mail, FTP, and Web on a perimeter network does have some advantages, there are some significant disadvantages to using perimeter network configurations with ISA Server:

- You cannot use Web or Server Publishing Rules to publish servers.
- All access into and out of the perimeter network is controlled by static packet filters.
- Packet filters access control is limited to an IP address or a subnet.
- Configuring communications between perimeter network hosts and the internal network is cumbersome.

Because communications between the perimeter network are not run through the ISA Server rules engine, you must use packet filters to control access to servers on the perimeter network. As you have seen, access control using packet filters is somewhat limited. When using the wizard to create the packet filter, you can configure a **Remote Host** entry for a single IP address. After creating the packet filter you can open the **Properties** dialog box for the filter and include an entire subnet. However, you *cannot* use Client Address Sets to control access.

Controlling communications between internal network clients and hosts on the perimeter network can be somewhat challenging. Since the hosts on the perimeter network are treated like any other untrusted external network host, you must create publishing rules for the services on the internal network in order for the perimeter network hosts to communicate with the internal clients.

This might present a problem in the rare event that you might need to publish a NetBIOS dependent server on the internal network. An example might be a SQL server that is not using SQL authentication. However, in this instance, you can configure it to use SQL authentication and obviate the need for NetBIOS. Another example might be an ISA server that is a member of a Windows NT 4.0 domain which requires NetBIOS communications for authentication.

One way to work around this is to configure the perimeter network host to use a VPN connection to the internal network client. By using a VPN connection, the nature of the communications between the perimeter network hosts and the internal networks hosts are not exposed even if security is breached and an intruder is able to install sniffing software on a perimeter network server.

Perimeter Network Configurations

Two types of perimeter network configurations are popular with ISA Server:

- Tri-homed ISA Server
- Back-to-Back ISA Servers

Let's take a closer look at each of these perimeter network configurations.

Back-to-Back ISA Server Perimeter Networks

A back-to-back perimeter network consists of two ISA server computers:

- An ISA server directly connected to the Internet.
- An ISA server connected to the internal network.

The ISA server connected to the Internet can be considered the "external" ISA server and the ISA server connected to the internal network can be considered the "internal" ISA server.

Figure 9.26 shows how you might configure such a back-to-back perimeter network.

Figure 9.26 Back-to-Back Perimeter Network Configuration

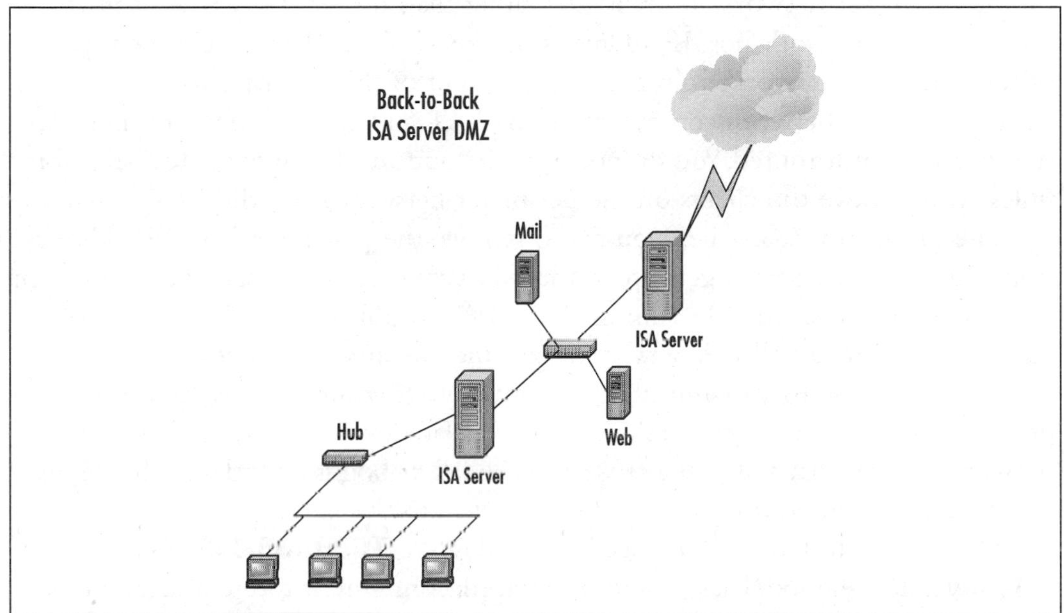

When configuring a back-to-back perimeter network, you need to do the following:

1. On the *external* ISA server, place the IP addresses of the hosts on the perimeter network in the LAT.
2. Use Server and Web Publishing Rules on the *external* ISA server to make servers on the perimeter network available to external clients.
3. On the *internal* ISA server, include only the internal network IP addresses in the LAT. *Do not* put the perimeter network IP addresses in the LAT of the *internal* ISA server.
4. Use Server and Web Publishing Rules to allow perimeter network hosts to communicate with internal network clients.

If you notice something a little funny here, then you have been paying attention. Remember we said that you must use packet filters to publish services on a perimeter network? If that is true, then why are we now saying that you can use Publishing Rules to allow access to resources on the back-to-back perimeter network?

The reason is that when you configure a perimeter network in this way, without doing anything else, communications between Internet clients and hosts on the perimeter network are translated rather than routed. By virtue of placing the perimeter network host IP addresses on the LAT, you have made them part of the "internal" network, from the vantage point of the *external* ISA server. All communications between computers on the LAT and external network hosts are translated and not routed. You do not have the option of changing this behavior unless you remove the clients on the perimeter network from the LAT.

The problem is that when you try to remove the perimeter host IP addresses from the LAT, ISA Server gets upset. You will get an error message indicating that there must be at least one IP address in the LAT. You'll see the same error message if you try to install ISA Server and not include any IP addresses in the LAT.

There is a way to work around this situation. If you do not want your perimeter network communications to be translated, you have to add another network adapter that will support what we'll call a "bogus" interface. The bogus interface will be used for the IP address to put into the LAT.

You can create such an interface by installing the **Microsoft Loopback Adapter**. After the loopback adapter is installed, configure it to use a private IP address such as 192.168.254.1. After installing the loopback adapter, you can then remove the perimeter network addresses from the LAT. The will allow you to route, rather than translate, communications between the perimeter network and the external network. At this point you will need to configure packet filters to support communications between the external network and the perimeter network.

If you do choose to add a third interface on the external ISA server to support routing packets to the perimeter network in a back-to-back configuration, you will also need to make the following changes:

1. On the *external* ISA Server enable **IP routing**.
2. On the *external* ISA Server enable **packet filtering**.

Keep in mind that with this kind of configuration, services can be published *only by using packet filters*. You will not be able to use Server and Web Publishing Rules.

SECURITY ALERT!

Note that while you can configure your back-to-back network to route packets through the ISA Server, this is not the preferred configuration. Remember that the purpose of the perimeter network is isolate your internal network from Internet traffic. You are able to accomplish this even when the traffic moving to and from the perimeter network is translated. Given that the server publishing method is more secure, you should consider this the preferred method of publishing services on the back-to-back perimeter network.

Tri-homed ISA Server Perimeter Networks

A tri-homed perimeter network configuration has the internal network interface and the perimeter network interface directly connected to the same ISA server. In this case, a single standalone ISA server or an ISA server array member is used to connect all three interfaces.

As we noted previously, this is the only configuration in which you can route packets to the perimeter network rather than translating them. In fact, the workaround we came up with creates a tri-homed ISA server although, in the above example, the third interface to the internal network was a "dummy" interface.

A tri-homed ISA server configuration would look something like what is seen in Figure 9.27.

When configuring a tri-homed ISA server, perform the following steps:

1. Install an interface with a public IP address that is directly connected to the Internet.
2. Install a second interface with a public IP address that will be used for the perimeter network.
3. Install a third interface that will be used for the private network.
4. Place only the private network IP addresses in the LAT. *Do not* place the perimeter network IP addresses into the LAT.
5. Enable IP routing.
6. Enable packet filtering.

Figure 9.27 A Tri-homed ISA Server

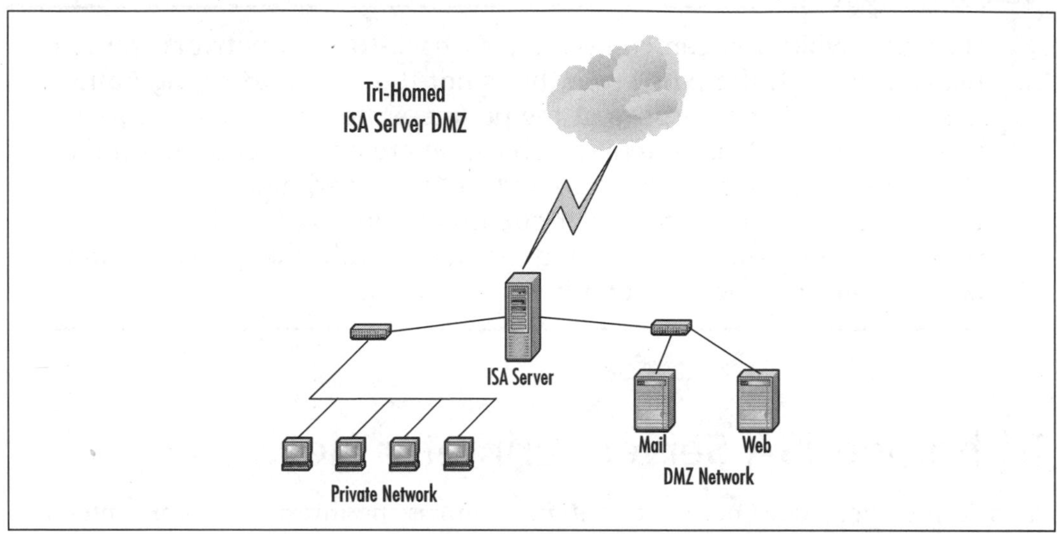

To publish resources on the perimeter network, you will need to use packet filters. There are not many reasons to publish servers in a tri-homed DMZ configuration. Server and Web Publishing offer a lot more features and are a more secure configuration. The one instance where publishing servers on a perimeter network might be useful is when you wish to publish an FTP server on an alternate port number. If you try to create a Protocol Definition and and a Server Publishing Rule that allows inbound access to an alternate port number to a FTP server, it will fail. While you could make the FTP server a Firewall Client and then create a **wspcfg.ini** file to support the alternate port, it is better to put the FTP server on a perimeter network that does not perform translation. The external clients will be able to access the FTP server on the perimeter network through the alternate port number.

Publishing Services on a Perimeter Network

When using packet filters to publish servers on a perimeter network, you have to be mindful of all required communications that must move into and out of the perimeter network. For example, suppose you want to publish a Web server on the perimeter network. You would need to configure a packet filter that allowed inbound access to port 80 to the perimeter network. To do this, perform the following steps:

1. Right click on the **IP Packet Filters** node in the left pane, click **New**, and then click **Filter**.
2. On the **Welcome** page, give the filter a name, and click **Next**.
3. On the **Filter Mode** page, select the **Allow packet transmission** option, and click **Next**.
4. On the **Filter Type** page, select the **HTTP servers (port 80)** predefined packet filter, and click **Next**.
5. On the **Local Computer** page, select the **This computer (on the perimeter network)**option button, and type in the IP address of the Web server on the perimeter network. Then click **Next**.
6. On the **Remote Computers** page, select the **All remote computers** or the **Only this remote computer**, and then type in the IP address of the remote computer. If you need to allow a group of remote computers, you can configure a subnet of computers to allow access. This option is available after you have completed the wizard. Click **Next**.
7. After reviewing your selections, click **Finish**.
8. Double click on the packet filter you created, and click on the **Remote Computer** tab. Note that you have the options to apply the filter to a single remote computer or a range of computers. In addition, if you click on the **Local Computer** tab, you can allow packets through to the entire subnet, or to a group of computers denoted by a network ID and subnet mask.

What if you need to provide access to a Web server on the perimeter network to more than one client, or to several groups of clients? It's clear that you cannot do this by creating a single packet filter because you only have the option to control access by **Remote Computer** by specifying a single IP address or subnet. There are likely to be many occasions where you would like to limit access to a select few computers or subnets, but a single filter won't accomplish the task.

You can solve this problem by creating multiple packet filters for port 80. Each packet filter will be searched by the ISA server to allow access from the appropriate client. Therefore, if you created one packet filter that allowed for inbound port 80 from remote hosts 222.222.222.0/24, you can create a second packet filter that would allow access from 111.111.111.0/24. All hosts from both network IDs would then have access to port 80 on the perimeter network client.

After the server is published by the packet filter, inbound requests to port 80 to that perimeter network host will be allowed. The ISA server will automatically allow the response to the external host by opening a dynamic packet filter.

If your perimeter network hosts need access to name resolution services, you will need to configure a packet filter that allows DNS queries outbound from the perimeter network. It's very common for administrators to forget about name services for the perimeter network. We recommend that the first packet filter you create for the perimeter network be one that allows DNS queries.

Publishing FTP Servers on a Perimeter Network

Publishing FTP servers on the perimeter network presents a special challenge. The reason is that there are two types of FTP clients that may connect to your FTP server. The two types of FTP server connections you might want to support on the perimeter network are:

- PASV servers (passive mode)
- Standard servers

To create a packet filter to support FTP servers to work with PASV mode FTP clients, you need to create a packet filter with the following specifications:

FTP Server – PASV

Protocol: TCP

Direction: Both

Local Port: Dynamic (Ports 1025-5000)

Remote Port: Any

To create a packet filter to support FTP servers to work with standard FTP clients (that send **PORT** commands), you need to create two packet filters:

FTP Server – Inbound

Protocol: TCP

Direction: Inbound

Local Port: 21

Remote Port: All Ports

FTP Server – Outbound

Protocol: TCP

Direction: BOTH

Local Port: 20

Remote Port: All Ports

Enabling Communication between Perimeter Hosts and the Internal Network

As we mentioned earlier, servers on the perimeter network are considered external, untrusted network hosts. In order to allow machines on the perimeter network to initiate communications with those on the internal network, you will need to publish those servers on the internal network. Perimeter network hosts will access the published servers as would any other external network client.

The main difference in the publishing of the internal server is that instead of allowing all hosts on the external network to communicate with the internal server, you will just let the server on the perimeter network communicate with it. If you require multiple servers on the internal network to communicate with an internal server, you can take advantage of Client Address Sets and include the perimeter network servers in a Client Address Set that you would use in your publishing rule.

For example, suppose you need your Web server on the perimeter network to communicate with a SQL server on the internal network. You can use the Microsoft SQL Server Protocol Definition to create the rule. After publishing the internal SQL Server, the Web server on the perimeter network will be able to initate an inbound connection to the private network to the published server.

If the Web server, or any other server on the perimeter network, needs to resolve names on the internal network, you will need to publish the internal DNS server and allow the servers on the perimeter network to access this server. This can get tricky because if the server on the perimeter network needs to resolve both internal and external host names, there's no way for you to get the server to "switch" what server it uses to resolve names.

Therefore, consider having the perimeter network host always use the internal DNS server and then configure the internal DNS server to use a Forwarder that can resolve Internet names. The internal DNS server then will be able to resolve the external host names for the perimeter network server.

Remember, only allow the perimeter network servers access to the internal DNS server. You do not want to publish the internal network's DNS server to all other external network users.

Bastion Host Considerations

A *bastion host* is a machine that interacts with the Internet and protects your internal resources. There are actually a number of definitions for bastion host. For example, your ISA server that directly connects to the Internet is a bastion host. Another example of a bastion host is the Web or E-mail server you put on the perimeter network. What all of these machines have in common is that they directly interact with computers on the external network. Servers on the internal network are not bastion hosts because the ISA server mediates all communications between the internal servers and the Internet clients.

The purpose of the bastion host is to protect your internal network. While some security experts feel that the bastion host should be considered a form of "sacrificial lamb," many others feel that the bastion host should be the most secure machine under your control.

When Windows 2000 is installed, as a lot of services are installed by default, any service running on the bastion host provides a potential vector for attack by an intruder. The key to good bastion host configuration is to remove all services and applications that are not required in order for the bastion host to do its job.

And here lies the rub. The job of the ISA server acting as a bastion host is to protect the internal network and provide sophisticated packet filtering routing to servers on perimeter networks. The job of the ISA server acting as bastion host is *not* to run Exchange 2000 or SQL 2000 or any other memory, disk, or network intensive application. These applications tend to be mission critical, and in the event of a break-in, the ISA server and whatever else is on it will be the first to be destroyed or compromised.

Therefore, we strongly recommend that you do not install any other server application on the ISA server acting as bastion host. However, if you are implementing the ISA server as a Caching-only server on the edge of a departmental network connecting to the corporate backbone then you may consider such a configuration.

Configuring the Windows 2000 Bastion Host

When configuring the Windows 2000 machine that runs ISA server as a bastion host, the first thing you should do is disable the *Client for Microsoft Networks*. However, if you are running IIS on the ISA server machine, you should not do this because IIS will not start if you disable the Client for Microsoft Networks. Otherwise, be sure to disable this service on each network adapter.

Another networking feature that is not required on the ISA server is the NetBIOS interface. You can disable the NetBIOS interface from the **Advanced TCP/IP** dialog box. However, this only disables attaching to Windows shares through the NetBIOS interface. Windows 2000 features a new way to access SMB shares through a method called *direct hosting*. This method uses DNS for name resolution, and shares are connected to via TCP Port 445. In order to prevent an intruder from attaching to a share via direct hosting, you need to disable the **nbt.sys** (the NetBIOS over TCP/IP driver). To do this, perform the following steps:

1. Right click on the **My Computer** object on the desktop, and click **Manage**.
2. Click on the **Device Manager** node in the left pane. Then click the **View** menu, and click **Show Hidden Devices**.
3. Right click on the **NetBIOS over Tcip** node in the right pane, and click **Disable**.

This procedure will disable connecting to SMB shares on the ISA Server.

Disabling Services

Now it's time to take a sledge hammer to the machine. What we want to do here is disable all services that are not absolutely required. The point is to run only the absolutely required services. To begin, open the **Services** applet from the **Adminsitrative Tools** menu. After the **Services** applet is opened, disable all services except the following:

- Terminal Server
- DNS Client
- Event Log
- Logical Disk Manager
- Network Connections
- Plug and Play
- Protected Storage
- Remote Procedure Call

- RunAs Service
- Security Account Manager
- Task Scheduler
- Windows Management Instrumentation
- Windows Management Instrumentation Driver Extensions
- Windows Media Services (if you are running live stream splitting) Including the Monitor service, Program service, Station service, and Unicast service
- Windows Time Service
- System Event Notification
- Routing and Remote Access Service (unless you are using VPN)
- QoS RSVP
- Performance Logs and Alerts
- Microsoft Web Proxy
- Microsoft Scheduled Content Download Service
- Microsoft ISA Server Server Control
- Microsoft Identd Simulation Service
- Microsoft H.323 Gatekeeper
- Microsoft Firewall
- COM+ Event System
- Remote Access Connection Manager
- Telephony

You may be able to get away with fewer services, and you may require more. After making the changes, reboot the system. If the system does not boot, then reboot and enter the Last Known Good configuration and check the Event Log to see what service has stalled the reboot. If the system is able to start, but something doesn't work correctly, check the Event Log to assess what the problem might be.

Summary

In this chapter, we covered some important concepts in inbound access control. Packet filters are used to control ingress and egress through the external interface. Application filters can be used to affect the flow of information through the ISA server to the internal network.

You learned the difference between static packet filtering and dynamic—or *stateful*—packet filtering, and you found out when and how to create manual packet filters.

We discussed "routing" between public and private networks and the implications of various packet-filtering and IP-routing scenarios that you might encounter on a Windows network on which ISA Server is deployed.

You learned how you can run applications and services on your ISA server (and received a strong suggestion that you dedicate a machine to running ISA and run few, if any, other applications on that machine). We also discussed how to use the built-in intrusion detection functionality of ISA, and finally, we gave you some tips on how to best design a DMZ, or perimeter network, using ISA Server.

In the next chapter, you will find out how to publish servers and services to the Internet.

Solutions Fast Track

Configuring ISA Server Packet Filtering

☑ *Packet filtering* is the process of examining the TCP and IP header information to assess whether a packet should be allowed to enter or leave the external interface of the ISA server.

☑ When packet filtering is enabled, only packets for which a filter has been configured are allowed to pass through the external interface of the ISA server.

☑ Static packet filters allow you to permanently open or close access to packets of your choice.

☑ Packet filtering must be enabled in order to enable intrusion detection. ISA Server can be configured to detect a limited number of intrusion types.

Application Filters That Affect Inbound Access

- ☑ The RPC filter, when enabled, allows you to publish internal servers that use RPC communications. RPC, or *remote procedure call,* is message-passing mechanism that allows a distributed application to call services that are available on various computers on a network.
- ☑ SMTP is a member of the TCP/IP protocol suite, used for exchanging e-mail across the Internet.

Designing Perimeter Networks

- ☑ A *perimeter network* is a security zone where all hosts on the network have public IP addresses.
- ☑ A tri-homed perimeter network configuration has the internal network interface and the perimeter network interface directly connected to the same ISA server.
- ☑ Publishing FTP servers on the perimeter network presents a special challenge. The reason is that there are two types of FTP clients that may connect to your FTP server: PASV servers, and Standard servers.
- ☑ A *bastion host* is a machine that interacts with the Internet and protects your internal resources.

Frequently Asked Questions

The following Frequently Asked Questions, answered by the authors of this book, are designed to both measure your understanding of the concepts presented in this chapter and to assist you with real-life implementation of these concepts. To have your questions about this chapter answered by the author, browse to **www.syngress.com/solutions** and click on the **"Ask the Author"** form.

Q: How can I allow an internal client to ping an external address?

A: In order for an internal client to ping an external IP address, you must configure the client as a SecureNAT client and enable IP routing on the ISA server. Note that you do not need to disable the Firewall Client software to do this. All you need is to configure a default gateway that routes to the internal interface of the ISA server, and it will be able to ping external hosts.

Q: I want to be able to ping internal clients from a computer on the Internet. However, when I enable IP routing and configure the ICMP Ping Query filters, it does not work. Why is this?

A: You cannot ping clients on the internal network from the Internet or from any external network. The reason is that external clients can only access internal clients when the internal clients have been published. In essence, you would have to make the internal clients a "ping server." However, the Server Publishing Rules only support TCP and UDP protocols, so you cannot even create such a server.

Q: How can I filter attachments on inbound e-mail?

A: Enable and configure the SMTP filter, then install and configure the Message Screener. Remember that the Message Screener needs to be installed on a computer running IIS 5.0. The preferred configuration is to place the Message Screener on an IIS server on the internal network.

Q: How can I allow internal clients to use PPTP to access external VPN servers?

A: Enable the SecureNAT PPTP packet filter. Keep in mind that once the PPTP filter is enabled, *all* computers on the network will have access to this filter.

The reason is that you can only create access controls for TCP and UDP based protocols. Since PPTP uses GRE, you cannot place access controls over this protocol.

Q: I would like to attach a modem to my computer that already has an external interface and use it for a backup route for both inbound and outbound access. Can I do that?

A: No. ISA Server was designed, for security reasons, to have a single external network access point. If you want to use the modem for a backup route, install a second ISA server and configure it as backup to the main ISA erver.

Chapter 10

Publishing Services to the Internet

Solutions in this chapter:

- Types of Publishing
- Web Server Publishing
- Publishing Services
- The H.323 Gatekeeper Service
- Virtual Private Networking

☑ Summary

☑ Solutions Fast Track

☑ Frequently Asked Questions

Introduction

In this chapter, we'll move our attention to making services on the internal network available to external network users. Typically, these external network users will be on the Internet.

The process of making services on the internal network available to external network users is known as *publishing*. When you publish content on the private network, ISA Server handles all inbound requests from external clients, and forwards those requests to the appropriate server on the internal network.

Publishing services on the internal network allows you to maintain publicly available services on the internal network in a safe manner, because external users never directly connect to machines on the internal network. All requests are mediated by the ISA server, and only requests that you have configured to allow to be forwarded are sent to the published servers. The ISA server drops all other requests for internal network resources.

Types of Publishing

When we talk about publishing resources, we refer to making resources located on a private network, using private network IDs, available to users on an external network. The process of publishing services involves the use of wizards built into ISA Server to complete the publishing process.

The are three methods of publishing services:

- Web publishing
- Server publishing
- DMZ server publishing

Each wizard allows you to publish services in a slightly different manner, and each method of publishing allows you to achieve different goals. When publishing services on a DMZ segment, you will not use a wizard, but will be able to create static packet filters to support publishing services on the DMZ segment.

Web Publishing

Web Publishing Wizards allow you to publish content contained on your internal Web servers. Services that can be published via Web publishing include:

- HTTP

- HTTPS
- FTP

The Web Publishing Wizards simplify the process of making these services available to external users. The wizards can also allow you to *redirect* requests on alternate ports on the internal server. This type of port redirection allows you to publish multiple Web sites on a single internal Web server by having each site listen on a different port number.

In addition to port redirection, the Web Publishing Wizard allows you to perform protocol redirection. For example, a user can request http://exeter.tacteam.net, and the ISA server will redirect the request to the internal Web server as an FTP request, even though the user's request was for an HTTP object. The ISA server fetches the file from the internal FTP site and returns the file to the external user.

Web publishing is mediated by the Web Proxy Service and uses the Web Proxy Service's Incoming Web Requests Listener to intercept requests from external hosts.

Rules are applied to incoming requests to published servers. You can configure a Web publishing rule to limit inbound access to a select group of IP addresses or users/groups. This allows you to fine-tune access to internal Web resources.

Server Publishing

The Server Publishing Wizard allows you to publish services on the internal network. In order to do so, there must be a *protocol definition* to support that service. After a protocol definition is defined for inbound access, the Server Publishing Wizard can use that definition to publish a server on the internal network using that protocol.

For example, you might want to publish an internal terminal server. To do this, you need a protocol definition allowing inbound access to the Terminal Services port. After creating the protocol definition for Terminal Services, you can use the Server Publishing Wizard to make that server available to external network users.

Inbound requests handled by server publishing rules are *not* processed by the Web Proxy Service; they are handled by the Firewall Service. This introduces a few limitations to what you can do with server publishing compared to what you can do with Web publishing.

For example, you can publish multiple internal Web sites, and the ISA server will listen for requests for all those sites on the same Web Proxy Service

Incoming Web Requests Listener port (which by default is TCP port 80). Server publishing does not allow multiple services to listen on the same external port number.

Let's look at an example to illustrate this problem. If you publish an internal terminal server on TCP port 3389 on the external interface of the ISA server, that port can be used only once per IP address bound to the external interface of the ISA server, and for only the single server published on that port. If you wanted to publish a second terminal server, you would have to create a protocol definition that used an alternate port, and then configure the terminal server to listen on the alternate port. Another alternative is to bind multiple IP addresses to the external interface(s).

The requests for services published through via server publishing are also subject to rules. However, your control over who can access internal services is less robust than what is available for Web publishing, since you can only limit access by client address sets (IP address). Web publishing allows you to control access through client address sets and users/groups.

Publishing Services on a Perimeter Network

When making services available on a perimeter network, the requests are handled a bit differently. Since inbound requests to the perimeter network are actually routed to machines on the perimeter network, they are not able to take advantage of the features provided by the Firewall Service such as application-aware protocol filters that allow management of complex protocols. You need to configure filters for each port required for inbound and outbound access through the perimeter network.

For example, when you publish an FTP server on the *internal* network using server publishing, the FTP application filter listens to the traffic, dynamically opens ports on the ISA server, and allows negotiation of the appropriate ports. However, this is *not* available with publishing services on the perimeter network, because the application filter is bypassed.

Another issue with publishing services on a perimeter network relates to complex protocols requiring secondary connections. When you publish a server on the internal network using the Server Publishing Wizard, you include the server protocol definition required to publish the server. The protocol definition can include secondary connections required by the protocol. Since you cannot use protocol definitions to publish services on a perimeter network, you must configure packet filters individually to meet the requirements of your protocol.

Web Server Publishing

The Web Publishing Wizard makes the process of publishing an internal Web server very easy. The wizard will walk you through the process of choosing the internal Web server and the ports you want to use on it. Once the Web publishing rule is created, you can begin to use it immediately.

NOTE

Administrators sometimes feel that the wizard is *too* easy, and feel compelled to create packet filters to support their publishing efforts. Don't do this! You do not need to create packet filters to support your publishing rules; the publishing rule will handle the opening and closing of ports as needed.

However, before you can be assured that your Web publishing rules will work, you have to make some preparations in your network infrastructure.

Preparing to Publish

Prior to publishing Web sites, you have to make sure a few infrastructure issues are correctly addressed. In order for things to go smoothly, you need to consider the following:

- DNS entries
- Destination sets
- ISA client configuration
- ISA Server Incoming Web Requests Listener configuration

Let's look at each of these and see how to get them set up so that our Web publishing rules work correctly.

DNS Entries

Users on the Internet will access your published Web sites via fully qualified domain names (FQDNs), such as www.isaserver.org. The FQDN must be resolved to an IP address before the user can connect to your site. To accomplish this name resolution, a DNS server must contain the appropriate resource records. For Web sites, there should be a host or CNAME record in a publicly available DNS server that points to your site. The address in the record will be for an IP address on the external interface of the ISA server.

You will likely have your DNS entries handled by your ISP. However, you do have the option of hosting your own public DNS servers. If you are managing your own public DNS servers, you must supply two servers that are authoritative for your zone (although some people cheat and report two IP addresses bound on the same server).

You will need to include a Host (A) entry for the internal Web server you wish to publish. For example, if you are managing your own DNS, and have a zone for "domain.com," you must create a Host (A) record for "www" within that zone file. This way, external users will be able to access your internal Web server using www.domain.com as the address.

TIP

You can make your site accessible by multiple names, such as ftp.domain.com, www.domain.com, and mail.domain.com. You can enter multiple Host (A) entries; one for each host name, or you can make a single Host (A) entry and use CNAME (alias) records for the other names. The CNAME approach is a bit easier to manage if you change the IP address of the server from time to time.

Alternatively, you could forget about DNS entries, and make everyone connect to your Web site via an IP address on the external interface of the ISA server. While this is doable, most people can hardly remember their own telephone number, much less a 12-digit IP address. As it stands with ISA Server, using IP addresses in destination sets used for inbound access to the external interface of the ISA server doesn't work.

DNS Client/Server Infrastructure

In order for your publishing rules to work, make sure you have your DNS client/server infrastructure in place. Remember, your published servers are SecureNAT clients of the ISA server.

ISA Server DNS Client Infrastructure

The DNS infrastructure must be in place to support name resolution requests, both for internal resources and resources contained on the Internet. This is one of the most common pitfalls we encounter when working with new ISA Server administrators.

First, you need to understand how the ISA server clients handle name resolution. SecureNAT clients must perform their own name resolution; the ISA server will *not* resolve requests on the behalf of a SecureNAT client. You must configure each SecureNAT client with the IP address of a DNS server to send queries for host name resolution.

Firewall clients allow the ISA server to resolve requests on their behalf. This is referred to as *DNS proxy*. After the ISA server resolves the name, it sends the name back to the firewall client, and then the firewall client issues the request for the resource.

When ISA Server performs this DNS proxy function, its uses the DNS server configured on its *external* interface. This is great for resolving host names located on the Internet, but it falls down badly when you also need to resolve names on the internal network. To get around this problem, be sure to configure the local domain table with the domain name(s) included on your internal network. The ISA server will not resolve any domain included in the local domain table. For these local domains, the ISA server will allow the firewall client to resolve the requests. This means that you need to configure the firewall clients with an IP address of an internal DNS server to resolve local domain names. Note that the local domain table is used only by firewall clients.

Web proxy clients query DNS in the same way as firewall clients, they allow the ISA server to do the work for them. However, since the Web proxy clients do not use the local domain table, you must use another method to allow them to resolve FQDNs that reside on the local network. In this case, you can configure the browsers individually, using the **Advanced** settings in the browser **Connections** dialog box. A better way to solve this problem is to go to the **Client Configuration** node in the **ISA Management** console, and use the **Web Browser Properties Direct Access** tab to configure the domain names that are considered local.

DNS Server Infrastructure

The external DNS server must be set up with the appropriate resource records, so that requests from external clients can be resolved to the external interface of the ISA server. As we've mentioned, you can have the ISP handle this for you, or you can do it yourself.

If you choose to host your own DNS, you will have publish the DNS server using server publishing rules. The server publishing rules should be configured to allow both DNS queries and DNS zone transfers (if you required these). The internal DNS server should be set up as a SecureNAT client, and it must have permissions to use the DNS query and zone transfer protocols.

You can put both your internal and your external zones on the internal DNS server, but we strongly discourage this approach. If, for some reason, your publicly available internal DNS server is compromised, you do not want the intruder to gain information about your internal network. It is best to put the public DNS server on a machine separate from your private DNS.

If you wish to use internal host names when configuring your rules, you must be sure that the internal interface of the ISA server is configured with the IP address of your private DNS server. Your internal DNS server should be configured with all your internal domains, and it should be configured to use a forwarder on the Internet to resolve external host names.

Destination Sets

Once the DNS entries have been made, you can start configuring destination sets for your site. A destination set is used by ISA server to identify which site the external user requests. Remember, when working with destination sets and publishing, you are looking at it from the vantage point of the external user, not the internal user. The destination for the external user is going to the FQDN of your site that can be resolved by a publicly available DNS server.

I point this out because often administrators will configure a destination set that uses the name of the *internal* server, and try to use that in the Web publishing rule. For example, we want to publish a Web site on our internal network. The server's name on the internal network is *webserver.internaldomain.net*. The administrator then creates a destination set for the site that includes the name *webserver.internaldomain.net* , and uses that in the publishing rule.

The problem with this is that the DNS entry for *webserver.externaldomain.com* is the one we want users to use when connecting to our published server. If you create a publishing rule using a destination set with the internal name of the server, it will not work, because the request sent by the user is for the external domain name of the published server.

To see how this works, let's look at an example. The internal server we want to publish will answer to the names ftp.domain.com, mail.domain.com, and www.domain.com. We can create a single destination set that contains all three of these destinations. Then we can use this destination set in our publishing rules.

1. Open the **ISA Management** console, and expand the **Servers and Arrays** node. Then expand the **Policy Elements** node.

2. Right-click on the **Destination Sets** node, click the **New** command and then click **Set**.
3. You'll be presented with the **New Destination Set** dialog box as it appears in Figure 10.1.

Figure 10.1 The New Destination Set Dialog Box

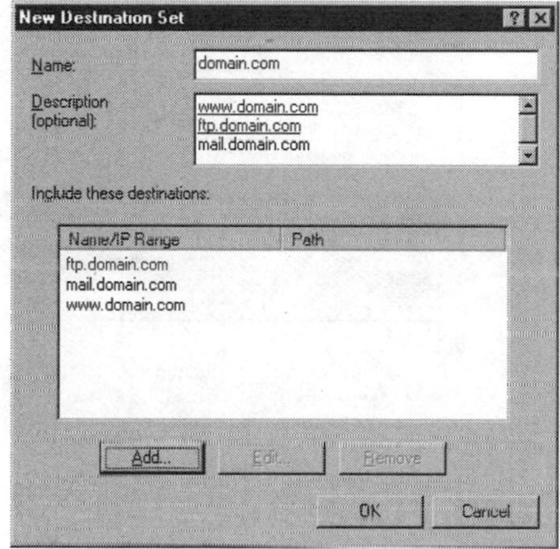

4. Enter the name of the destination set in the **Name** text box. Enter a description for the destination set in the **Description (optional)** text box. You should put each destination you plan to enter in this destination set in the **Description** text box. This will make it easier for you to figure out what the destination set is pointing to when you configure your publishing rules. The reason for this is that the description information will appear in the wizards, making it easy for you to figure out exactly what sites the destination set references.
5. To add a new destination to the set, click the **Add** button. You will see the **Add/Edit** destination dialog box as seen in Figure 10.2.
6. In the **Add/Edit Destination** dialog box, type in the **FQDN** for your site in the **Destination** text box. Note that you can use an asterisk as a wild card to represent all the host names in a domain. After entering the FQDN, click **OK**.

After creating the destination set, it will appear in the right pane of the ISA Management console. When the ISA server receives a request for one of these destinations, it will examine the headers in the request and see if it has the destination listed in the header that matches a name included in a destination set for a published server.

Figure 10.2 The Add/Edit Destination Dialog Box

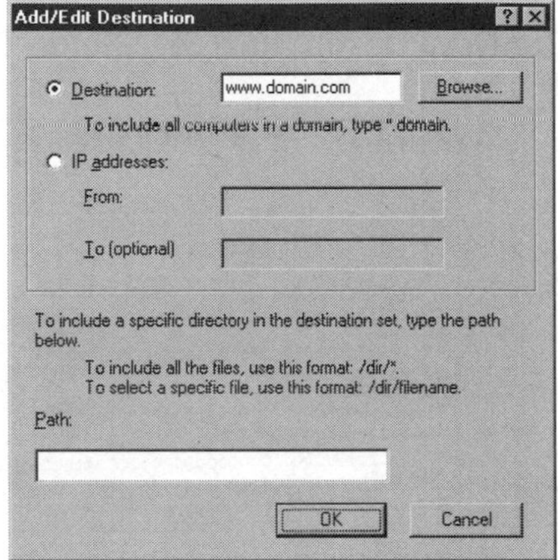

ISA Client Configuration

You should configure the published server as a SecureNAT client. This departs from how Proxy Server 2.0 did server publishing. In Proxy Server 2.0, the only way you could publish a server was to make the server a Winsock proxy client, and then hammer away at a wspcfg.ini file. ISA Server allows you to escape that pain (in most instances) by configuring published servers as SecureNAT clients.

SecureNAT client configuration is easy; the only thing you need to do is set the default gateway on the published server to an address that routes Internet-bound requests to the internal interface of the ISA server. If the published server is on the same logical network as the internal interface of the ISA server, you can set the default gateway to be the IP address of the internal interface of the ISA server.

If the published server is on a logical network ID remote from the internal network interface of the ISA server, then you must configure the default gateway on the published server to be a router interface that will route packets destined for the Internet to the internal interface of the ISA server.

When working with a routed network, make sure the routing table on the ISA server is configured properly before even setting up ISA Server. Remember that packets need to know the path from the ISA server to all subnets on the internal network, and all the subnets need to know the path to the internal interface of the ISA server.

In order for the ISA server to know the paths to the internal network IDs, you must configure the routing table on the ISA server with the appropriate gateway address(es) for each of the internal network IDs. You must configure the routing table, because you cannot configure a default gateway on the internal interface. Windows 2000 supports a single network adapter with a default gateway, and that adapter must be the external interface of the ISA server.

An alternative to configuring the routing table manually would be to implement a routing protocol on your network. In this case, a simple routing protocol such as the Routing Information Protocol (RIP), can share routing information with other router interfaces on the network that listen for RIP broadcast announcements. For large and more complex networks, you might consider using OSPF (Open Shortest Path First), which is supported by Windows 2000 RRAS.

Some published servers may not work correctly using SecureNAT. You'll see this if you plan on publishing certain Internet-enabled multiplayer games. In this case, you'll need to configure the server as a firewall client, and then configure a wspcfg.ini file on that server. If that sounds too painful, you can place the game server on a DMZ segment, and create packet filters to allow the required ports.

Configuring the Inbound Web Requests Listener

The ISA server listens for incoming Web requests on what is called the Incoming Web Requests *Listener*. By default, the Incoming Web Requests Listener uses port 80 on the external interface of the ISA server. You can change this if you like, but then everyone who needs to connect to your Web site will have to include the alternate port number in his or her request.

If you want to make your site easy to access, don't change the default listener port setting. Note that the requests accepted by the Incoming Web Requests Listener are intercepted by the Web Proxy Service. The Web Proxy Service handles all inbound HTTP requests directed to the listener's port number.

You can configure the ISA Server Incoming Web Requests Listener to use the same configuration for all IP addresses on the external interface, or you can configure each external IP address individually. The latter configuration expands the flexibility you have when publishing Web sites, especially if you want to use SSL. You will have to add the inbound listener for the IP address(es) on which you want the ISA server to listen.

To configure the Incoming Web Requests Listener, perform the following steps:

1. Open the **ISA Server Management** console, expand the **Servers and Arrays** node, and then right-click on your server. If you are running an

array, right-click on the array name. Then click the **Properties** command. In the dialog box that appears, click the **Incoming Web Requests** tab. You will see something like what appears in Figure 10.3.

Figure 10.3 The Incoming Web Requests Tab

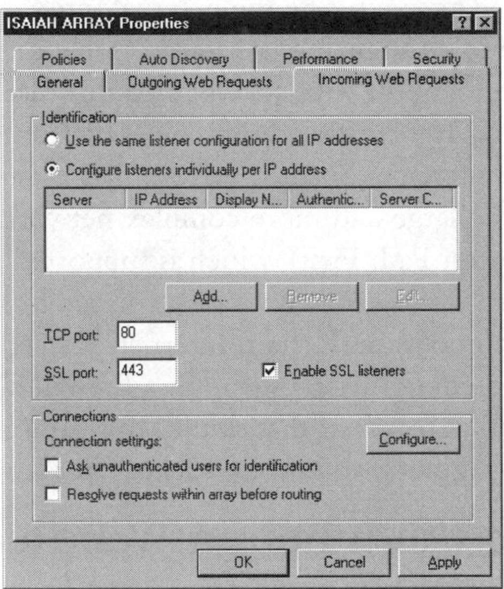

2. On the **Incoming Web Requests** page, you can make the configuration changes on your inbound Web Requests Listener. Note that there are two options: **Use the same listener configuration for all IP addresses**, and **Configure listeners individually per IP address.** If you have multiple IP addresses bound to the external interface, you should configure the listeners separately. We like to configure the listeners separately even if we have a single IP address, because it give me a better idea of what's going on.

   One situation in which it's a good idea to use the **Use the same listener configuration for all IP addresses** is if you have a dial-up connection. Although server publishing rules will break each time your IP address changes, you can prevent your Web publishing rules from breaking by selecting this option. If you were to configure Web listeners individually, the listener address would change each time the dial-up connection is established and your Web listener would not be functional.

3. Select the **Configure listeners individually per IP addresses**, and then click the **Add** button. That brings up the **Add/Edit** Listeners dialog box shown in Figure 10.4.

Figure 10.4 The Add/Edit Listeners Dialog Box

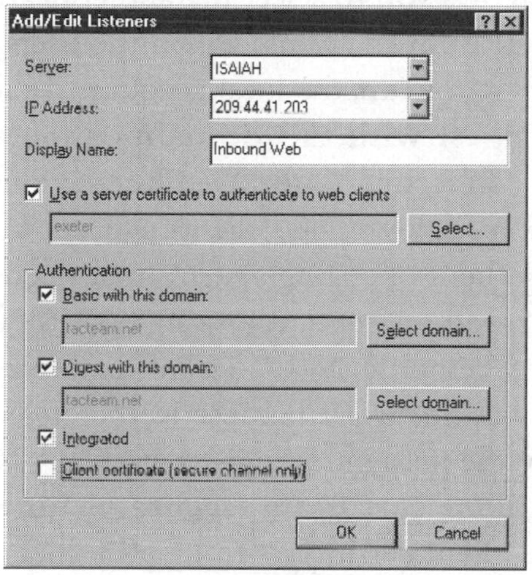

In the **Server** drop-down list box, select the server that you want to configure.

In the **IP Address** drop-down list box, choose the IP address you wish to assign to this listener.

The **Display Name** text box allows you to type in a friendly name for this listener, which will appear on the **Incoming Web Requests** page.

The **Use a server certificate to authenticate to Web clients** allows you to configure this listener with a certificate that can be used when publishing secure Web sites. Note that only a single certificate can be configured per listener. This means that you must use the same certificate for all the Web sites published through this listener. We'll talk more about this issue when we discuss secure Web site publishing.

The **Authentication** frame contains four choices:

- Basic with this domain
- Digest with this domain
- Integrated
- Client certificate (secure channel only)

These choices determine what type of authentication will be accepted by the Listener if you decide on forced authentication.

The **Basic with this domain** option allows users to use clear-text usernames and passwords to authenticate with the listener. Use this if your clients are not using Internet Explorer 4.0 or later. The **Select domain** allows you to select the authentication domain. You must provide a single domain against which the users will authenticate. If you do not specify a domain, the local accounts database will be used.

The **Digest with this domain** option allows digest authentication by clients connecting to this Web listener. Digest authentication is only available to Windows 2000 clients. Do not use this option if you have downlevel client operating systems that need to authenticate.

Integrated authentication can use either Kerberos or NT Challenge/Response. Note that in passthrough authentication scenarios, Kerberos will not work, because Kerberos requires that the client be able to identify the authenticating server.

The **Client certificate (secure channel only)** option allow clients to provide client certificates to identify themselves and authenticate. Select this option if you have clients that have been configured with client certificates to access a secure site and you have a Public Key Infrastructure (PKI) in place.

Note that all of these authentication options pertain to authenticating *with the ISA server*; they *do not* pertain to authenticating against the Web site itself. If you have configured authentication for the Web site, you will have to enter credentials again to access the site.

If you do configure authentication at the Web site, remember that ISA server will only pass *basic* and *anonymous* credentials. You will not be able to use Digest or Integrated authentication *at the Web site*.

4. Click **OK**, and you'll see something similar to Figure 10.5.
5. You should now see the new listener in the list box.

   In the **TCP Port** text box, you can change the port number used by the listeners. Note that this setting applies to *all* listeners, not just the one you selected in the box above. You cannot use a different listener port number for each specific listener; this setting is a global one.

   If you want to force authentication before accessing *any* internal Web site, put a check mark in the check box for **Ask unauthenticated users for identification**. Note that this is also a global option and cannot be configured on a per-listener basis.

Figure 10.5 The Incoming Web Requests Tab

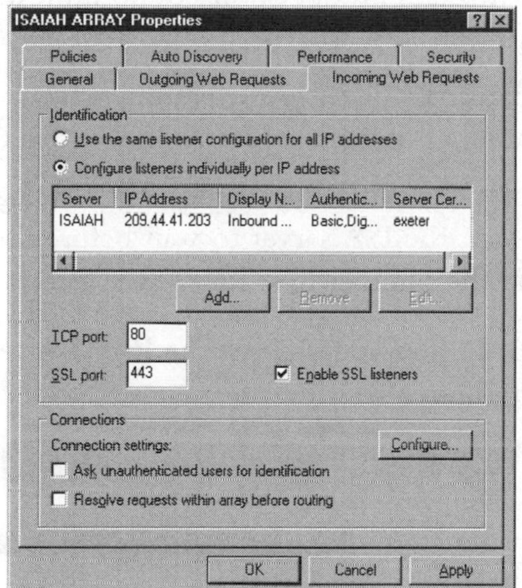

The **Resolve requests within array before routing** option forces the inbound request to be resolved in the array before forwarding to an internal Web site. This option enables CARP for inbound Web requests. Generally, its *not* a good idea to enable CARP for inbound Web requests, because it will reduce perceived performance on the user's end, and increase the amount of traffic on the internal interfaces of the servers in the array as the request is resolved within the array.

6. The **Configure** button allows you to set a couple of connection settings. When you click the **Configure** button, you'll see what appears in Figure 10.6.

Figure 10.6 The Connection Settings Dialog Box

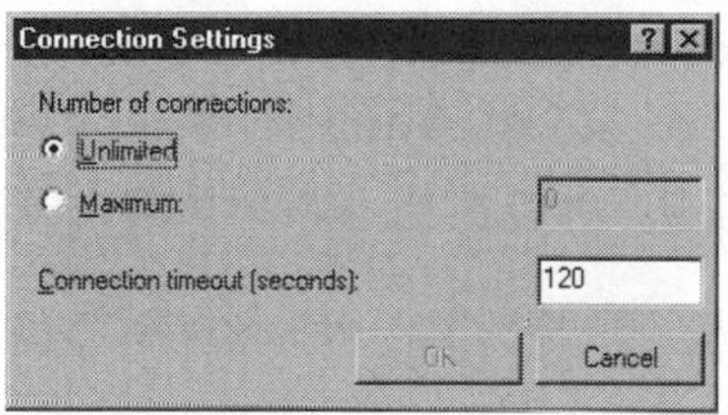

You have two options for the **Number of connections**:

- **Unlimited** This option places no limit on the number of inbound connections.
- **Maximum** When you select this option, you can place a limit on the number of simultaneous connections to the Web listeners
- **Connection timeout (seconds)** Configure the number of seconds you want the ISA server to wait before dropping idle connections by typing the number of seconds into the text box.

7. Click **Apply**, and you will see the **ISA Server Warning** text box shown in Figure 10.7.

Figure 10.7 The ISA Server Warning Dialog Box

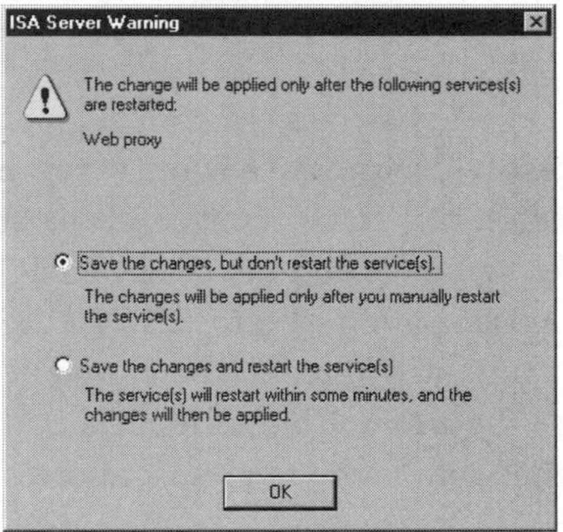

8. If you want the ISA server to restart the service, choose the **Save the changes and restart the service(s)** option. If you want to restart the service yourself, choose the **Save the changes, but don't restart the services(s)** option. We like to select the latter option, because when you let the ISA server do it for you, it might take awhile before the server actually gets around to doing it. When you do it yourself, you know exactly when the service is restarted.

After you complete the preparatory work, you're ready to publish your Web site.

Web Publishing Walkthrough—Basic Web Publishing

In this walkthrough, we'll do some basic publishing of an internal Web site. This will allow you to understanding the basics of Web publishing and expose you to the interface. After you understand these basics, we'll go through some more complex or unusual configurations.

1. In the **ISA Management** console, expand your computer or array name, and then expand the **Publishing** node in the left pane. Right-click on the **Web Publishing Rules** node. Click **New**, and then **Rule**.
2. In the first page of the wizard, type in a name for this rule. We'll call this one *Exeter Web*. Click **Next**.
3. The Destination Sets page appears as shown in Figure 10.8.

   In this example, we selected the **Specified destination set** option in the **Apply this rule to** drop-down list box. When you select this option, the **Name** drop-down list box appears. You can choose from the list of all the destination sets you've created. We'll select the **Exeter** destination set, which includes the FQDN **exeter.isa.tzo.com**. Click **Next**.

Figure 10.8 The Destination Sets Page

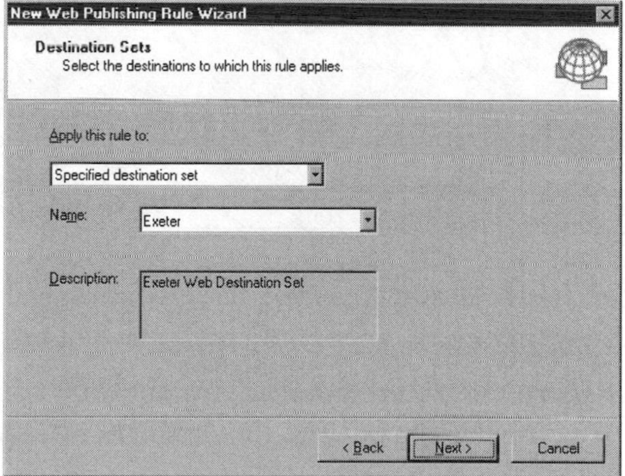

4. The **Client Type** page appears as shown in Figure 10.9.
   You have three options:

   - **Any request** This option allows anybody access to the internal server.
   - **Specific computers (client address sets)** This option allows computers, identified by the IP addresses in a client address set, access to the Web site.
   - **Specific users and groups** This option allows you to control access to the Web site via users and groups. Authentication will need to be enabled on the external interface of the ISA server in order to limit access by account.

   In this example, we'll select **Any request**, and then click **Next**.

Figure 10.9 The Client Type Page

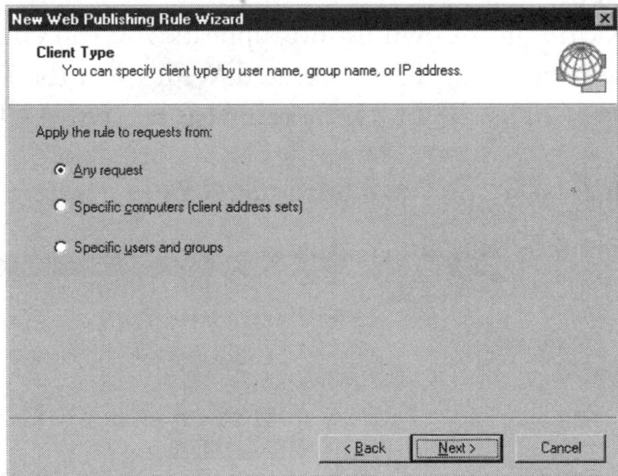

5. On the **Rule Action** page, you'll see what appears in Figure 10.10.
   There are several important configuration settings on this page:

   - **Discard the request** Select this option if you want requests sent to the computer(s) named in the destination set to be dropped.
   - **Redirect the request to this internal Web server (name or IP address)** Select this option if you want to publish the internal Web server. In the text box, you can type in either the IP address or the computer name of the internal computer. If you use the computer

Figure 10.10 The Rule Action Page

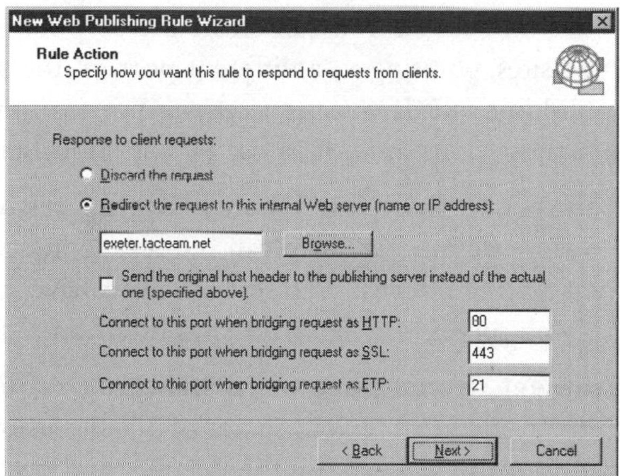

name, be sure that the internal interface of the ISA server is configured with either a WINS or DNS server that can resolve the name. You can use the **Browse** button to find the server on the internal network.

- **Send the original host header to the publishing server instead of the actual one (specified above)** This option allows the ISA server to send the original host header to the internal server, rather than the actual host header. In this example, the actual host header would be *exeter.tacteam.net*, since that is the name of the internal server, and the ISA server in the process of forwarding the request would include the server's internal name to complete the request. However, if you are using host headers to publish multiple sites on an internal server and you have mapped all those sites to an external IP address on the ISA server, you want to preserve the original header. The reason is that you want the FQDN in the original request to be forwarded to the internal server, so that the Web server can process the header and direct it to the appropriate web. Enable this option if you need to preserve the original host header to send to the internal Web server. Enable this for OWA publishing.
- **Connect to this port when bridging request as HTTP** This option allows you to use alternate ports on the internal Web server. Some Web admins like to create Web sites on different ports, rather

than using host headers. For example, you can create a Web site that listens on port 80, another that listens on port 81, and another that listens on port 82. You can create a Web publishing rule for each of these sites, pointing to a different port on the same server in each publishing rule. If you use alternate ports on the Web server, make sure those ports are not in use by any other service.

- **Connect to this port when bridging request as SSL** You have the same option here. You can redirect requests to use different SSL ports on the internal Web server. If you have multiple SSL sites on the Web server, you can have sites listen on a different port.
- **Connect to this port when bridging request as FTP** You can redirect ports to the Web server's FTP site using this option.

  In this example, we'll use the defaults, and click **Next**.

6. You can review your choices on the last page of the wizard. If all looks well, click **Finish**.

After you create the rule, wait a minute or two for the ISA server to incorporate the rule into its policy set. After the short wait, try to connect to the Web site using the FQDN included in the destination set that you used to create the rule. You should be redirected to the internal Web site!

Undocumented ISA Server

You should test your configuration from a machine on an external network. If you try to access the published server from a machine on the internal network, the request *may* fail, even though it works perfectly when accessed from an external computer.

Publishing a Web Site on the ISA Server

Publishing a Web site located on the ISA server creates some problems that you need to address before you begin publishing. By default, IIS wants to use port 80 to listen for inbound Web requests. The problem is that the ISA server's Web Proxy Service uses port 80 to listen for inbound Web requests. You cannot have both the ISA server and the IIS WWW Service listening on the same port.

To solve this problem, you should configure IIS to listen *only* on the internal interface of the ISA server. This prevents conflict with the Web Proxy Service's Incoming Web Requests Listener. However, if you publish autoconfiguration information on the internal interface of the ISA server, it will use port 80 by default.

You could change the port number that ISA server uses to listen for autoconfiguration requests and try to make it work that way. From our experience with ISA Server, it does not seem to want to work on the internal interface's port 80. This may be a problem related to the configurations we have worked with, but we have never been able to publish a Web site on port 80 of the internal interface, in spite of the documentation saying this is possible. If you wish to try this option, be sure to test it thoroughly before putting it into production, and let us know about your success!

Before publishing a Web site located on the ISA server, you first need to change the IP address and listening port number that IIS uses to listen for inbound Web requests.

Readying IIS for Publishing

To ready IIS for publishing:

1. Open the **Internet Services Manager** from the **Administrative Tools** menu.
2. Right-click on **Default Web Site**, and then click the **Properties** command. Click on the **Web Site** tab. You'll see what appears in Figure 10.11.

Figure 10.11 The Default Web Site Properties Dialog Box

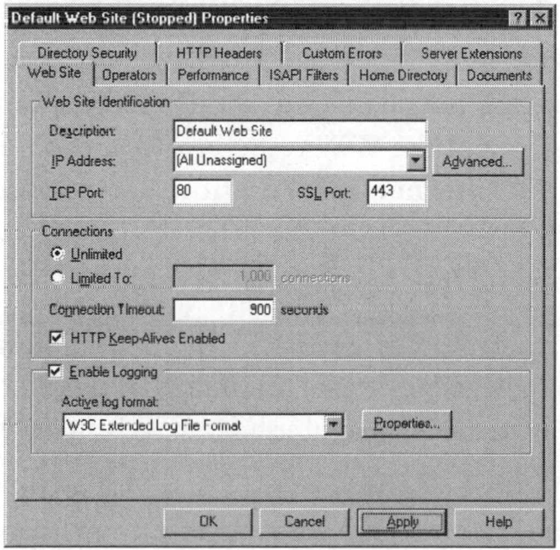

3. In the **IP Address** drop-down list box, click the **down-arrow** and select the IP address of your internal interface. In the **TCP Port** text box, type in a port number that is not already in use. You can determine which ports are already in use by opening a command prompt and typing **netstat –na**. This will list all currently open ports. Note that ports listening on 0.0.0.0 are listening on *all* interfaces. You'll be fairly safe if you use a high number port, because relatively few of those are used by Windows network services. But make sure first! For a list of reserved ports, see www.isi.edu/in-notes/iana/assignments/port-numbers.

   After making your changes, you should see something similar to Figure 10.12.

Figure 10.12 Default Web Site Properties Web Site Tab

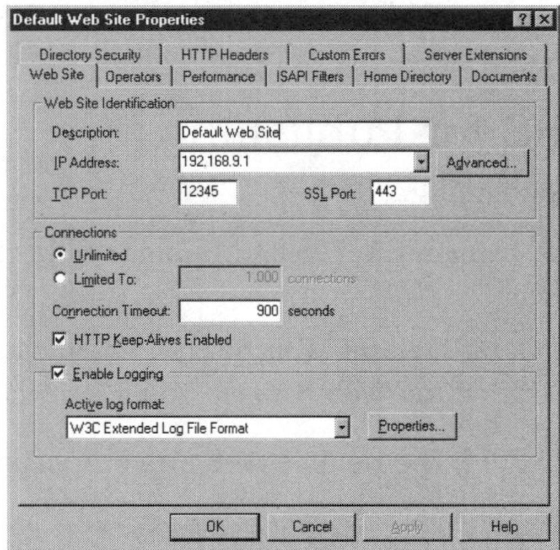

4. After making the changes to the IP Address and TCP Port number, stop, and then restart the WWW Service. You can do this via the control buttons in the **Internet Information Services** console.

Creating the Publishing Rule

Now that IIS is ready, we can get to the job of publishing our Web site. To create a Web publishing rule, we can take advantage of the Web Publishing Wizard. Perform the following steps to publish your Web site.

1. Open the **ISA Management** console, expand the **Servers and Arrays** node, and then expand your server or array name.

2. Expand the **Publishing** node, and then right-click on the **Web Publishing Rules** node. Click **New**, and then **Rule**. This will start the Web Publishing Wizard.

   On the first page of the wizard, type in the name of the rule, as we've done in Figure 10.13.

Figure 10.13 The Web Publishing Rule Wizard Welcome Page

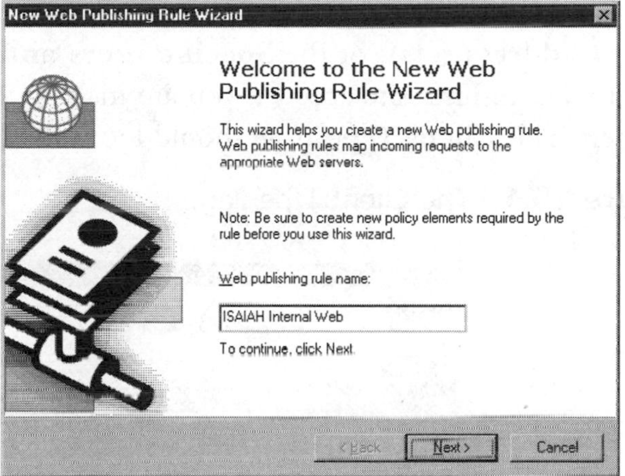

3. Click **Next**. On the **Destination Sets** page, Select the **Specified destination set** option, and then select the name of the destination set that you want to use for this publishing rule. You will see something similar to Figure 10.14.

Figure 10.14 The Destination Sets Page

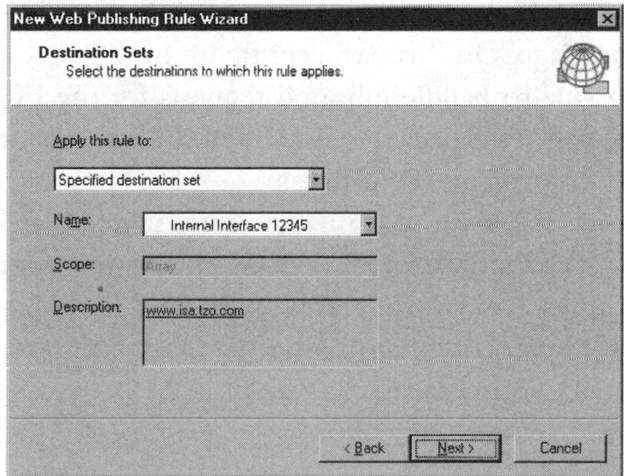

4. Note that I have included in the **Description** of the destination set the FQDN used to access the published Web site. It's always a good idea to include the FQDNs used in the destination set in the description box. That way, you'll know exactly what FQDNs are used when you configure your publishing rules. Click **Next**.
5. This takes you to the **Client Type** page. If you want everybody in the world to be able to access the Web site, select the **Any request** option. If you want to limit who can access the site, select **Specific computer (client address sets)**, or the **Specific users and groups** option. You might want to limit site access if you are making it available only to partners. The **Client Type** page should look like Figure 10.15.

Figure 10.15 The Client Type Page

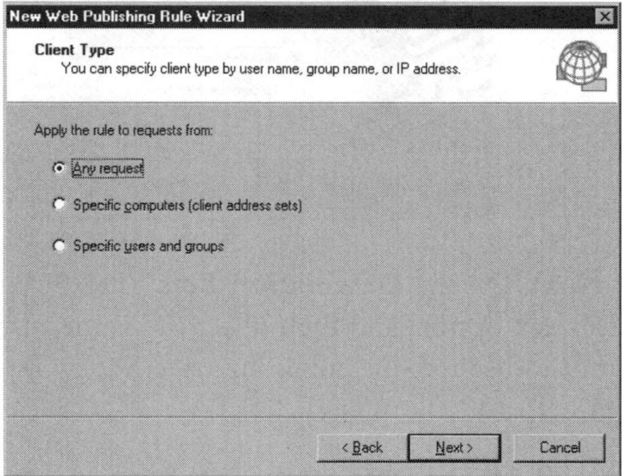

6. After configuring the client type, click **Next**. This takes you to the **Rule Action** page. On this page, configure how you want ISA Server's publishing rule to handle inbound requests for the FQDNs included in the destination set. Select the **Redirect the request to this internal Web server (name or IP address)**.

   Note that if you use a name, rather than an IP address, the internal interface of the ISA server must be configured with a DNS server address that can resolve the name. You might be able to get away with the NetBIOS name resolution sequence, but don't tempt fate. Make sure your internal DNS infrastructure is in place before working with ISA Server.

Change the port number in the text box for **Connect to this port when bridging request as HTTP** to the port number that you configured in IIS for the Web site. You can change the other options if you made changes to the other ports in IIS. The dialog box should look like Figure 10.16.

Figure 10.16 The Rule Action Page

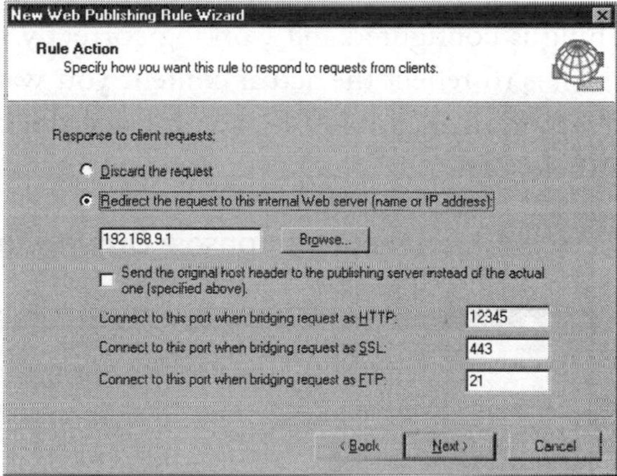

7. You can confirm your settings on the last page of the wizard. If all looks good, click **Finish**.

   Now, when we type in the URL http://www.isa.tzo.com, we see the screen shown in Figure 10.17.

Figure 10.17 Connecting to the Web Site

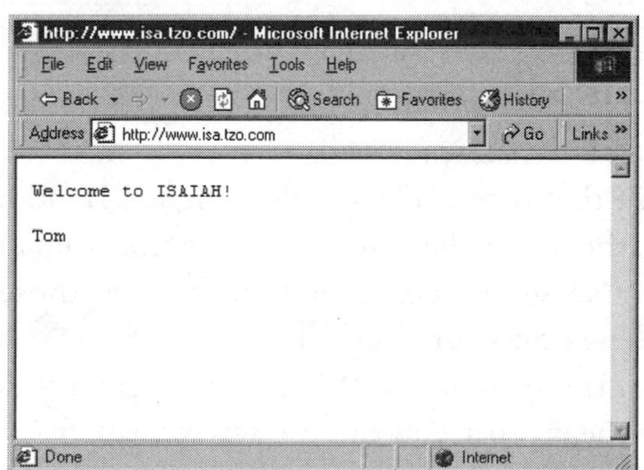

Note that I've changed the default page. This helps you know what Web site and server are accessed. Changing the default page to give server identification information is a good idea if you're working with a number of publishing rules and servers and you need to get a grip on "which is which." If you find yourself configuring a number of publishing rules during the same session, it's easy to get things mixed up and configure the same publishing rule twice. You'll be able to easily identify your errors if you change the default page to contain identifying information during your tests.

After everything is configured and working correctly, change the default page on your IIS Web sites to reflect the actual content you want to present to the public or your partners. In Figure 10.18, you can see the connection request in the ISA Management console.

Figure 10.18 The ISA Management Console Displaying Current Web Sessions

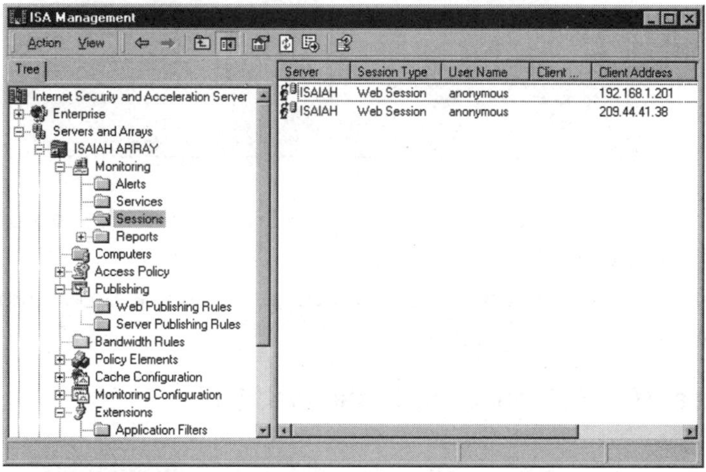

In this example, the domain name for the published server is isa.tzo.com. TZO allows you to dynamically register your domain name if you have an external interface that uses a dynamically assigned IP address. Each time your IP address changes, the TZO client software registers your new IP address with the TZO dynamic DNS server. This is quite helpful for those of you with DHCP-assigned IP addresses on your external interface.

Another cool thing about TZO is that it assigns a wildcard entry for your host name. That means that you can use www, mail, ftp, nntp, or any other host name you want, and it will resolve to the external IP address of your ISA server. Note that if you wish to use the TZO service, you will have to create a packet filter to support the service on the ISA server.

For more information about TZO and its dynamic DNS service, check out: www.tzo.com.

Undocumented ISA Server

You must configure a packet filter for the TZO client software to work correctly. Remember that all applications on the ISA server that require external network access require static packet filters. The packet filter settings are:

Filter type: Custom
IP protocol: TCP
Direction: Outbound
Local port: Dynamic
Remote port: Fixed Port
Remote port number: 21331

Web Publishing through Protocol Redirection

ISA Server web publishing rules allow you to redirect HTTP requests as other protocols. For example, suppose you want to make life easy for Internet users to access files on your FTP server. You don't want to them to have to type **FTP** in the URL of their Web browser or use dedicated FTP programs, but you still want them to use their browsers to access your FTP site on the internal network.

This can be accomplished by changing how the ISA server *bridges* requests to the internal server. Note that when you first create the Web publishing rule, you can configure the port number that a connection can be bridged to on the internal server, but you cannot change the protocol itself. That is, after you complete the wizard, the request will be bridged as an HTTP request.

To change this, double-click on the rule you created, and click on the **Bridging** tab. You'll see what appears in Figure 10.19.

To redirect an HTTP request as an FTP request to the internal FTP server, you would select the **FTP requests** option in the **Redirect HTTP requests as:** frame. The default setting in this frame is to redirect HTTP requests as **HTTP requests**. You also have the option to redirect HTTP requests as **SSL requests (establish a secure channel to the site)**. If you choose this option, "open" and SSL-protected HTTP sessions between the external client and the ISA server's external interface will be protected by SSL when the request is forwarded over the internal network to the published ISA server.

Figure 10.19 The Web Publishing Rule Properties Bridging Tab

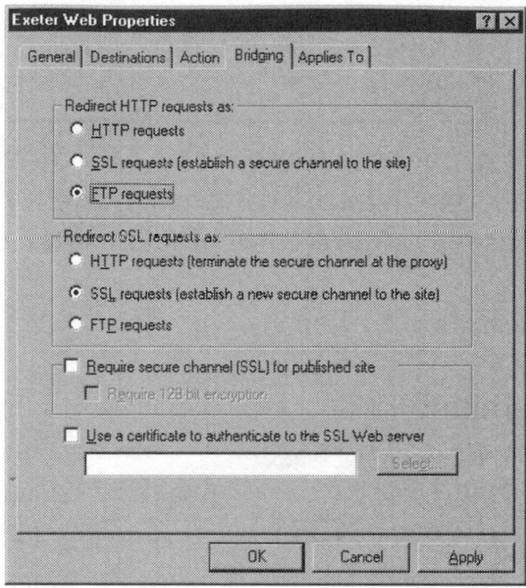

Note that you can still publish your internal FTP server using server publishing rules. By publishing the server in both ways, unsophisticated users can access the site via HTTP, and other users can still run FTP client applications to access the FTP server.

After changing the bridging properties to allow HTTP requests to be bridged as FTP requests, go to your browser and issue an HTTP to the site that you've bridged. You should see something similar to Figure 10.20.

Figure 10.20 HTTP Redirected as FTP Request

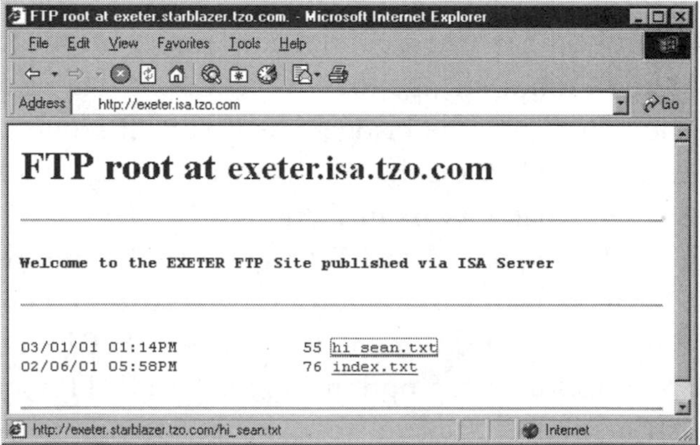

This type of protocol redirection makes life a little easier for your technology-challenged users.

There is even a more profound advantage to using this type of protocol redirection. The FTP protocol is limited to using basic authentication to secure sites. Basic authentication sends username and passwords in free text and therefore isn't very secure. By publishing an FTP site using the Web Publishing Wizard, you can use Windows authentication for inbound HTTP requests and encrypt sessions with SSL. Using this method, you can take an inherently insecure protocol and make it as secure as possible.

NOTE

Whether you choose to use alternate authentication or not, HTTP has more overhead than FTP; therefore, file transfer performance will not be as good as using the FTP protocol.

Creative Publishing Using Destination Sets

Destination sets allow you a great deal of flexibility in your Web publishing solutions. For example, you can use a path statement in a publishing rule to redirect a request to a particular server on the internal network.

Suppose you want users who type in the URL http://isa.tzo.com/database to be redirected to the /database/ folder on an internal server named EXETER. To do this, you would create a destination set that included the FQDN isa.tzo.com and the path /database/*. The asterisk ensures that access to all the files in the /database folder is available. Such a configuration would look like Figure 10.21.

After configuring the destination set, you would use it in your publishing rule. Note that there is another destination set on this server that includes the FQDN isa.tzo.com, but does not include the path, and that destination set was used to publish a Web site on the internal interface of the ISA server. However, with our new destination set, which includes that path, any request for isa.tzo.com/database will be forwarded to *a different server* on the internal network.

Figure 10.21 The Add/Edit Destination Dialog Box with Path Statement

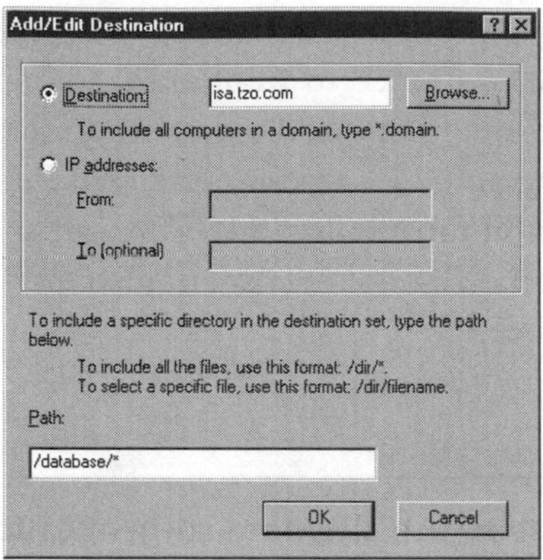

To configure the rule, perform the following steps:

1. Open the **ISA Management** console, expand your server or array name, and then expand the **Publishing** node. Right-click on the **Web Publishing Rules** node, click **New**, and then click **Rule**.
2. Name the rule in the **Welcome** dialog box, and click **Next**.
3. On the **Destination Sets** page, set the specified destination set that includes your *path* statement, and then click **Next**.
4. On the **Client Type** page, select the client type appropriate for your publishing needs. Then click **Next**.
5. On the **Rule Action** page, type in the IP address or FQDN of the internal server, and click **Next**.
6. On the last page, confirm your settings, and click **Finish**.

Now type the URL to point to the site included in the Destination Set with the path, and you'll see the page delivered from the server you published (Figure 10.22).

While you can use path statements to forward requests for a particular FQDN to different servers on the internal network, you *cannot* use a path statement to forward requests to the *Web root* of these servers.

For example, suppose you wanted to create a destination set that included the settings shown in Figure 10.23.

Figure 10.22 The Request Is Directed to the Published Server

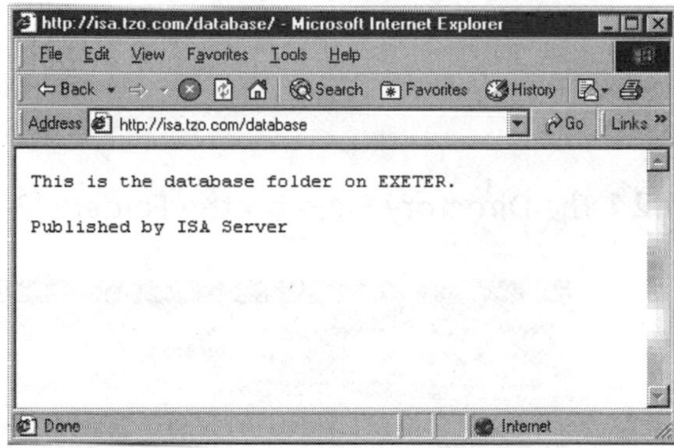

Figure 10.23 Destination Set for Internal Server

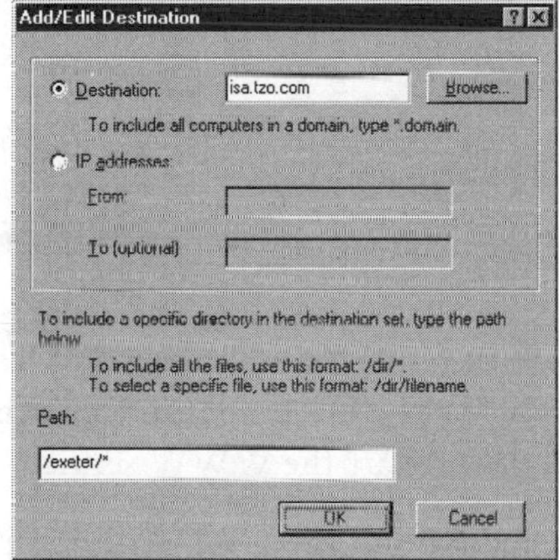

We would like to use this destination to publish the internal server EXETER, so that when users type in the URL http://isa.tzo.com/exeter, they will be forwarded to the *root* of Exeter's Default Web. While it might sound like you can do this, it will not work.

In order to accomplish the feat, you must make configuration changes on the IIS server. You can use the destination set, but you must redirect the subdirectory on the IIS server to forward requests to the root.

To redirect the requests from a particular folder on the IIS server, perform the following steps:

1. Open the **Internet Services Manager** from the **Administrative Tools** menu. This will open the **Internet Information Services** console.

2. Right-click the folder you want redirected. In this case, we want to redirect the folder **exeter** to the root of the default Web site on the same machine. Click **Properties**.
3. You should see the Properties dialog box for the folder as shown in Figure 10.24.

Figure 10.24 The Directory Page on the Folder's Properties Sheet

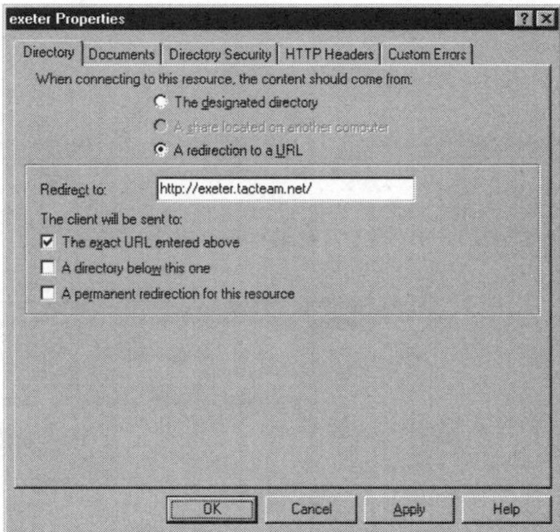

4. On the **Directory** tab, select the option for **A redirection to a URL**, and then select **The exact URL entered above** check box. Click **Apply**, **OK**, and then restart the WWW service.

Go to a Web browser and type in the URL with the path. You'll find that the request is redirected to the root of the Web (Figure 10.25). Note that on Windows 2000 machines, IIS 5.0 uses the **Under Construction** page as the default Web page (until you change it).

Secure Web Site Publishing

ISA Server supports secure Web site publishing using SSL. There are a number of ways to secure the connection between the external network clients and the internal Web site, including:

- Terminating the secure connection at the ISA server
- Bridging secure connections as SSL requests
- Server publishing a secure Web site

Figure 10.25 The Request Is Forwarded to the Root of Exeter's Default Web

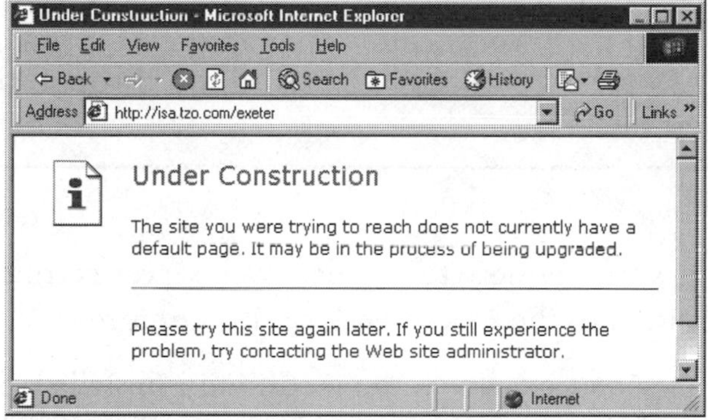

Terminating the Secure Connection at the ISA Server

When you wish to publish a secure Web site via ISA Server, you can create a secure SSL connection that terminates on the external interface of the ISA server. Once the ISA server establishes the secure connection with the external client, it can then forward the request to the internal server as an HTTP request. By requiring security only for the communications over the public Internet, you reduce the overhead required to create a second secure connection to the internal Web server.

In order to configure ISA Server to accept SSL connections on its external interface, you must install the server certificate for the internal Web server onto the ISA server. Let's look at how to do this before learning how to publish a secure Web site.

Exporting and Importing a Certificate into the ISA Server Certificate Store

You can use your own certificates created by the Microsoft Certificate Server, or you can obtain a certificate from a trusted third party such as VeriSign or Thawte. If you plan to use the site for employees or partners, you can use the Microsoft certificates you create, but if you plan to run a public Web site, you will need to obtain a certificate from a third party.

SECURITY ALERT!

If you use a third-party certificate, install that certificate on the internal Web server. After the certificate is installed, go through the export procedure described next.

In this example, we'll see how to export a Web server certificate and then import that certificate into the ISA server's certificate store.

1. At the Web server on which the certificate is installed, open an MMC by clicking **Run** and typing **mmc** in the test box. Click **OK**.
2. In the empty MMC, click the **Console** menu, and then click **Add/Remove Snap-in**. In the **Add/Remove Snap-in** dialog box, click **Add**.
3. In the **Add Standalone Snap-in** dialog box, select the **Certificates** snap-in, and then click **Add**.
4. The **Certificates Snap-in Wizard** appears. Choose the **Computer account** option, and then click **Next**.
5. On the **Select Computer** page, select the **Local computer: (the computer this console is running on)**, and click **Finish**.
6. Click **Close** on the **Add Standalone Snap-in** dialog box, and then click **OK** on the **Add/Remove Snap-in** dialog box.
7. In the console with the **certificates** snap-in loaded, expand the **Certificates (Local Computer)** node in the left pane, and then expand the **Personal** node. Click on the **Certificates** node and you should see something similar to Figure 10.26.
8. In this example, we'll right-click on the **CONSTELLATION** certificate (which is used for the default Web site) and then click **All Tasks**. From the fly-out menu, click **Export**.
9. This opens the **Certificate Export Wizard**. Click **Next** to move to the **Export Private Key** page. On this page, select the **Yes, export the private key** option, and click **Next**.
10. In the **Export File Format** page, select the **Personal Information Exchange – PKCS #12 (.PFX)** option, and then place a check mark

in the **Enable Strong protection (requires IE 5.0, NT 4.0 SP4 or above)** if you wish to support only IE 5.0 or above. Otherwise, clear this check box. Click **Next**.

Figure 10.26 Certificate Installed on the Local Computer

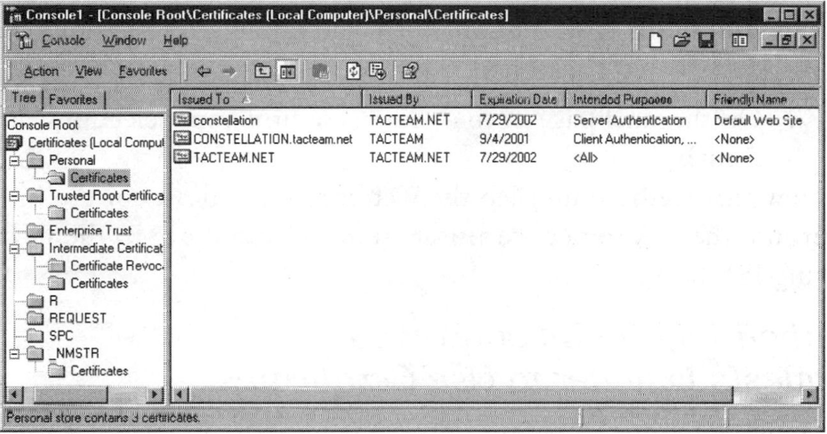

11. On the **Password** page, type a password, confirm the password, and then click **Next**.
12. On the **File to Export** page, type in the complete path to the location where you want the certificate to be stored (you need to type in the filename, but not the extension). Click **Next**.
13. On the last page, confirm your selections, and click **Finish**. If it works, you'll see a dialog box that says **The export was successful**. Click **OK**.
14. Copy the certificate to a floppy disk, and delete the original from the hard disk location where it was saved.

With floppy disk in hand, go to the ISA server computer and put it in the floppy drive. Then perform the following steps:

1. Perform steps 1 through 7 from the previous example. This will create a **Certificates** console on the ISA server that you can use to import the certificate.
2. Right-click on the **Certificates** node in the left pane, and click **All Tasks**. From the fly-out menu, click **Import**.
3. This opens the **Certificate Import Wizard**. Click **Next** to continue.

4. On the **File to Import** page, click **Browse** and find your certificate file. Click on it, and click **Open**. Click **Next** to continue.
5. On the **Password** page, type in the password you used when you exported the certificate. Click **Next**.
6. On the **Certificate Store** page, select the **Place all certificates in the following store** option. The default should be **Personal**; accept the default, and click **Next**.
7. On the final page of the wizard, confirm your selections, and click **Finish**.

Now that we have installed the Web server certificate for the internal Web server into the ISA server's certificate store, we can move to the next step of configuring ISA Server to use it.

Configuring the Inbound Web Requests Listener to Use Certificates

To configure the Incoming Web Requests Listener, perform the following steps:

1. Open the **ISA Management** console, and right-click on your server or array. Click **Properties**.
2. Click on the **Incoming Web Requests** tab. If you need to add a new interface to listen for requests for the internal server, click **Add** and the interface. If the interface is already there, click on the interface you want the certificate to be associated with, and click **Edit**.
3. In the **Add/Edit Listeners** dialog box, put a check mark in the check box for **Use a server certificate to authenticate to Web clients**. Then click **Select** to select the certificate.
4. You should see something similar to Figure 10.27. In the list of certificates, select the certificate that you just imported, and click **OK**.
5. You will see the certificate name in text box on the **Add/Edit Listeners** page. Click **OK**.
6. On the **Incoming Web Requests** page, be sure to put a check mark in the check box for **Enable SSL listeners**. Click **Apply**. When the **ISA Server Warning** dialog box appears, select the **Save the changes and restart the service(s)** option to restart the **Web Proxy** service. Click **OK**.
7. Click **OK** to close the **Properties** dialog box.

Figure 10.27 The Select Certificate Dialog Box

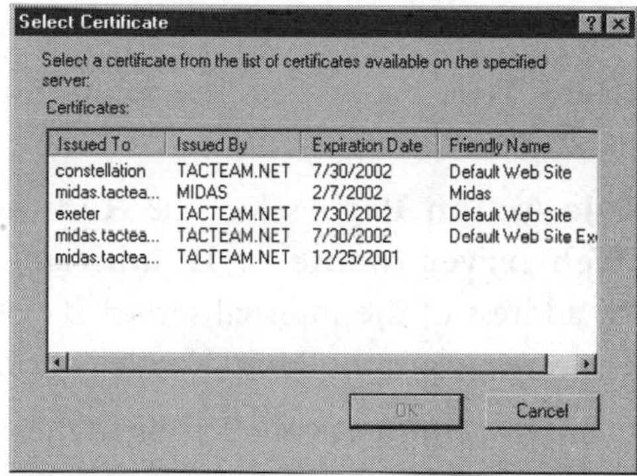

The internal server's certificate is now attached to the Incoming Web Requests Listener.

SECURITY ALERT!

You can only attach a single certificate to a particular Web listener. This limits you to publishing a single secure server per Web listener interface. If you need to publish other servers that require their own server certificates, you will need to attach those to another listener, which will require another IP address available on the external interface of the ISA server. The IP address can be bound to the same interface, or you can add another interface and bind the IP address(es) to that.

Publishing the Secure Web Site

When publishing a secure Web site, you probably do not want to make the entire site secure; instead, you want to make selected directories on the site secure. This prevents you from incurring the overhead of securing directories that do not contain secure content.

Perform the following steps to publish a secure Web site:

1. Open the **ISA Management** console, expand your server or array name, and then expand the **Publishing** node in the left pane. Right-click on **Web Publishing Rules**, click **New**, and then **Rule**.
2. On the first page, type in the name of the rules; then click **Next**.

3. On the **Destination Sets** page, select the **Specified destination set** option, then select the destination set that contains the FQDN and the path that external users will use to access the site. Click **Next**.
4. On the **Client Type** page, select the appropriate client type that fits your needs, and then click **Next**.
5. On the **Rule Action Page**, select the **Redirect the request to this internal Web server (name or IP address)** option, and type in the name or IP address of the internal server. If you need to send a host header, be sure to select the Host Header option, and then click **Next**.
6. On the final page, confirm your settings, and click **Finish**.
7. Double-click on the rules you just created to open the **Properties** dialog box for the rule. Click on the **Bridging** tab. You will see what appears in Figure 10.28.

Figure 10.28 The Bridging Tab of the Publishing Rule Dialog Box

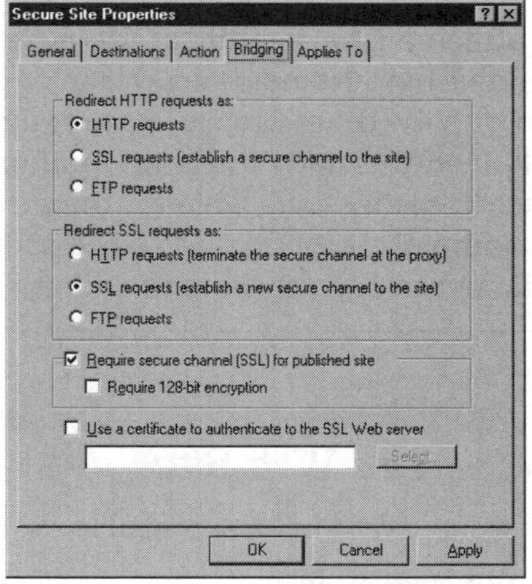

Even though you have installed the certificate on the Incoming Web Requests Listener, it will only be used when the rule requires the use of the certificate. In order to force SSL for this rule, you need to put a check mark in the check box for **Require secure channel (SSL) for published site**. If you need high encryption, select the **Require 128-bit encryption** option.

8. Click **Apply**, and then click **OK**.

Now go to your browser, type **http://www.domain.com/secure**, and replace the FQDN and the directory name with those included in your destination set. You will see what appears in Figure 10.29.

Figure 10.29 Error Message When Using HTTP

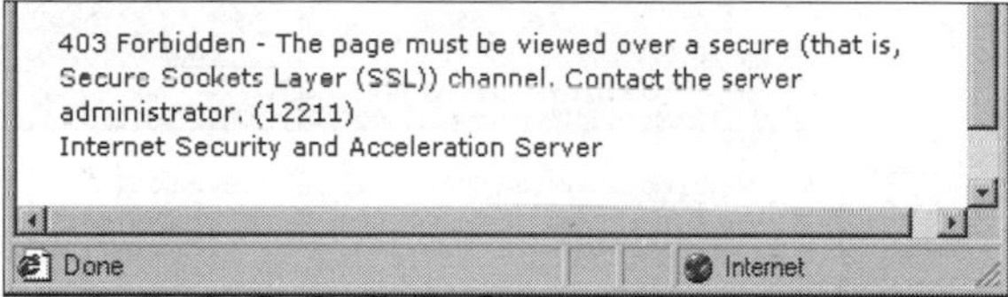

This error appears because we required SSL on the connection to the site managed by this rule. In order to issue an SSL request, you must use HTTPS in the URL.

If you using a certificate from a Microsoft Certificate Server, and the name of the site doesn't match the name of the certificate, then you'll see the message shown in Figure 10.30.

Figure 10.30 Security Alert Dialog Box

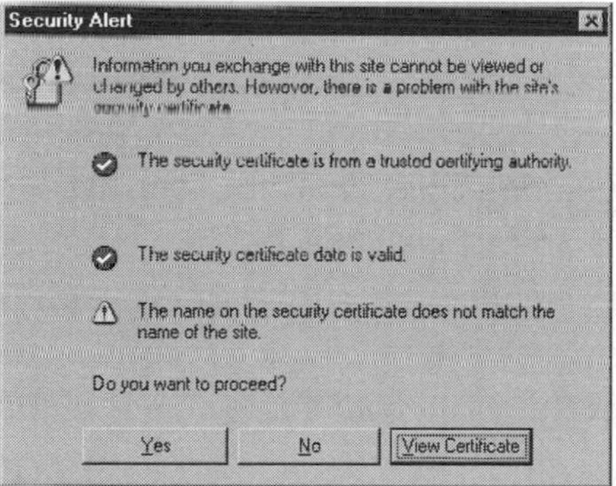

Note that the certificate comes from a trusted certifying authority, because the machine accessing the site is in the same domain as the certifying authority. You can get past this by clicking **Yes**. When you do, you'll see success, as seen in Figure 10.31.

The warning **The name on the security certificate does not match the name of the site** appears because the certificate name was for **constellation**, but we typed in the URL **constellation.isa.tzo.com**. In order to make the warning go away, you need to obtain a certificate with the same name that users will use to access the site. In addition, you must enable the **original host header** to be sent to the internal Web server.

Figure 10.31 Successful Access to Secure Web Site

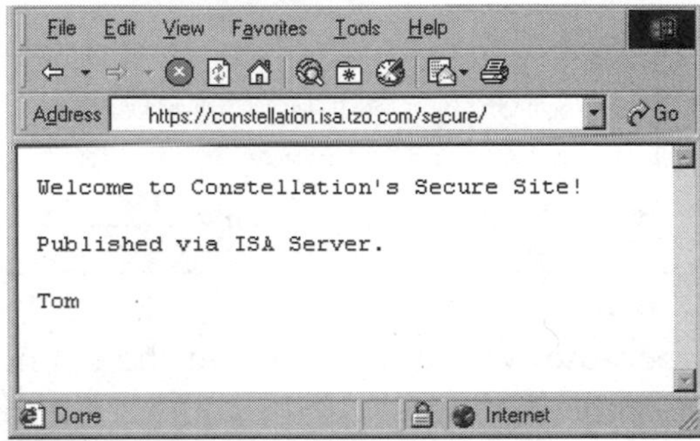

Bridging Secure Connections as SSL Requests

While the best performance solution is to terminate the secure connection at the ISA server and have it forwarded to the internal Web server as an HTTP request, there may be times when you wish to have a secure connection between the ISA server and the internal Web server. This could be the case if you don't have complete control over the internal network infrastructure between the external ISA server and the internal network; for example, if you were using a Web hosting company or an application service provider (ASP). This issue becomes problematic in the sense that if you don't have control over the network infrastructure, you probably won't have control over the ISA server configuration.

However, if you can convince the third party, or even if you have control over the network itself, you might wish to create a second secure channel to the internal server. Note that this is a *second* channel, not a continuation of the first encrypted link.

In order to configure the rule to negotiate a second secure channel with the internal Web server, you have to make a change in how the internal connection is bridged. Double-click on your Web publishing rule, and click on the **Bridging** tab. You will see what appears in Figure 10.32.

Notice in the **Redirect SSL requests as** frame, we have selected the **SSL requests (establish a new secure channel to the site)** option. This rule requires that the first connection be protected by SSL, because we selected the **Require secure channel (SSL) for published site** option. Now that we have redirected SSL requests as SSL requests to the internal server, the communication is protected end to end by SSL.

Figure 10.32 The Bridging Tab in the Web Publishing Rule Properties Dialog Box

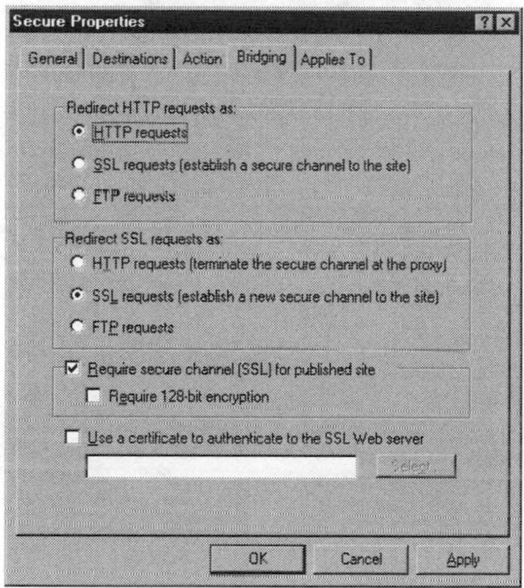

In order to force SSL on the destination Web site, you must configure IIS 5.0 to require security for the site or folder that requires the security. To force SSL on a folder on IIS, perform the following steps:

1. Open the **Internet Information Services** console from the **Administrative Tools** menu.
2. Right-click on the folder in the Web site tree that you want to secure, and click **Properties**.
3. Click on the **Directory Security** tab. You should see what appears in Figure 10.33.

   There are three buttons in the **Secure communications** frame:

   - **Server Certificate** This button is grayed out, because this machine has a server certificate. If you do not yet have a certificate installed on the server, the button will be available. You can click the button to create a request to obtain a certificate for your site.
   - **View Certificate** This option allows you to see the contents of your server certificate.
   - **Edit** This button allows you to configure security based on this certificate.

   Click **Edit**.

Figure 10.33 The Directory Security Tab

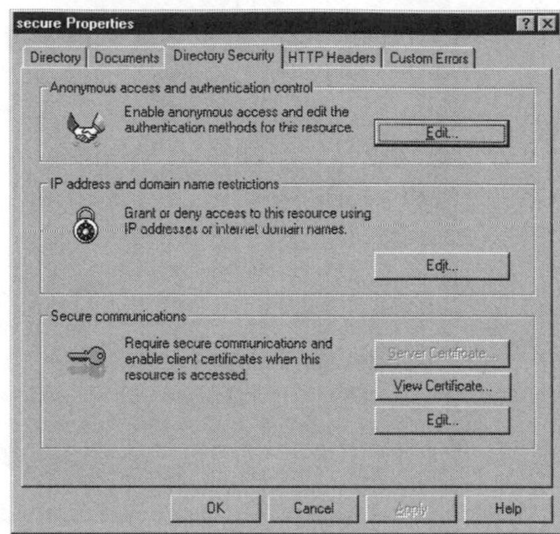

4. After clicking **Edit**, the **Secure Communications** dialog box appears as shown in Figure 10.34.

Figure 10.34 The Secure Communications Dialog Box

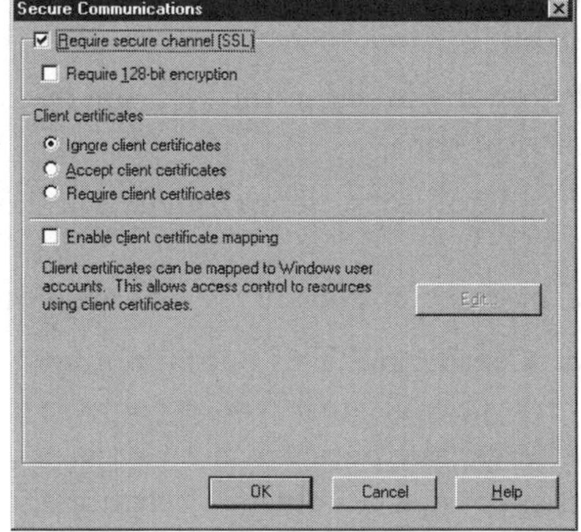

Put a check mark in the check box for **Require secure channel (SSL)**. This will require the ISA server to establish a second secure channel with the internal Web server in order to access this resource.

5. Click **OK**. Then click **Apply**, and then click **OK**. Although not always required, it's a good idea to stop and restart the Web site.

SECURITY ALERT!

If you wish to have security between the internal interface of the ISA server and the internal Web server and not be bothered with SSL and certificates, you can using IPSec. The IPSec protocol is completely transparent to all applications and is very easily implemented. You can configure the ISA server to use the **Client (respond only)** IPSec policy, and configure the internal server to use the **Server (require security)** policy. Using IPSec allows you to secure all communications between the ISA server and the internal Web server and you do not need to configure security separately for each site. IPSec can be very processor intensive and can have an adverse effect on performance. However, many network cards are available that can offload IPSec calculations onto the NIC and away from the system processor.

Publishing a Secure Web Site via Server Publishing Rules

Another way to publish a secure Web site is to use server publishing rules rather than Web publishing rules. You would publish the internal server using a protocol definition for port 443. There are some drawbacks to this approach, and it is not recommended. We'll go through an example of how to do this in the next section, *Publishing Services*.

Publishing Services

You can publish virtually any service running on your internal network using server publishing rules. Server publishing takes advantage of protocol definitions you've created for inbound access to server services. Unlike Web publishing, server publishing rules do *not* use the Web Proxy Service; they are mediated by the Firewall Service only.

Servers published by server publishing rules are configured as SecureNAT clients, which makes setup quite easy. Once the server is configured as a SecureNAT client, you can create the protocol definition and server publishing rule on the ISA server, and you're ready to go.

A wizard walks you though the process of publishing services on the internal network. Note that the procedure for publishing services on a perimeter network involves using packet filters, rather than using the Server Publishing Wizard.

Limitations of Server Publishing Rules

Server publishing allows you to publish services that cannot be made available by using the Web Publishing Wizard or static packet filters. However, server publishing does have some limitations:

- You can publish a particular service only once per IP address.
- You cannot redirect port numbers.
- You cannot bind an external IP address to an internal IP address.
- Server publishing bypasses the Web Proxy Service.
- SecureNAT will not work for all server publishing scenarios.
- You cannot use destination sets for server publishing rules.

You Can Publish a Service Only Once

When a service on the internal network is published via server publishing rules, the port number (for that interface) assigned to the server is dedicated to that rule. If you wanted to publish a second server providing the same service on the same port, it will not work unless you publish it using another external IP address.

For example, suppose you want to publish an internal mail server, *mail-1*. You would publish that server using the Server Publishing Rules Wizard. After publishing the server, the ISA server will listen on port 25 for inbound SMTP messages. However, if you try to publish a second server (on the same external IP address), say *mail-2* on the internal network, you will see what is shown in Figure 10.35.

Figure 10.35 ISA Error Dialog Box

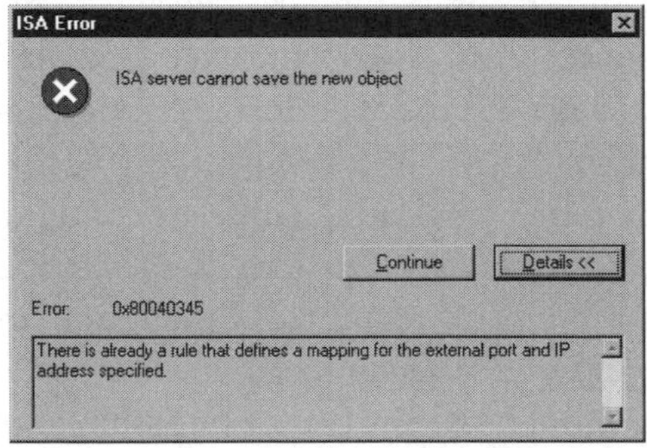

If you need to publish a second mail server using the same external IP address, you will need to configure a protocol definition and a server publishing rule that will allow the inbound SMTP messages to arrive at an alternate port number. The clients will also need to be configured to send to the alternate port number.

You Cannot Redirect Ports

Port redirection is a feature of the Windows 2000 RRAS NAT Service. Using this feature, you can forward a message received at one port number on the external interface of the ISA server to a different port number on the internal server.

For example, suppose you created a server publishing rule for a second mail server, so that SMTP messages sent to the ISA server for this published server are accepted on port 2525. You would like messages received on that port to be forwarded to the internal server's port 25. With the Windows 2000 RRAS NAT, you can do this; however, with ISA Server, you cannot do this. The message must be forwarded to the *same* port number on the internal server with which it was received on the ISA server.

Never fear, though. The next version of ISA Server will likely support this feature. Now we have something to look forward to!

You Cannot Bind a Particular External Address to an Internal IP Address

With the Windows 2000 RRAS NAT service, you can configure a pool of IP addresses that the NAT service can use. From this pool, you can choose to "bind" one of the external addresses to a specific internal IP address. Some applications might require that a different IP address be associated with each instance of that application. You can get around this problem by binding different IP addresses on the external server to different machines on the internal network,.

However, you do not have this option with ISA Server. The ISA NAT protocol driver does not allow you to bind an particular address on the external interface to machines on the internal network.

Server Publishing Bypasses the Web Proxy Service

This is not really a limitation of server publishing, since you can accomplish publishing Web sites using the Web Publishing Wizard. However, some administrators feel the need to publish internal Web sites via server publishing. If you choose to do this, you will not be able to take advantage of the Web proxy cache located on the ISA server, and all inbound requests for Web objects will be fetched from the internal server, rather than the Web cache on the ISA server. This will increase the amount of traffic on the internal network, and increase the load on the internal Web server.

It is highly recommended that you use the Web Publishing Wizard if you wish to publish Web protocols.

SecureNAT Does Not Work for All Published Servers

While making internal servers SecureNAT clients to support server publishing rules appears to be almost a panacea, it won't always work. Some server services require to you create wspcfg.ini files to bind ports on the external interface of the ISA server before the particular service works properly. If you find that using protocol definitions and protocol rules does not work in a particular server publishing scenario, you might try configuring a machine to be a firewall client with a wspcfg.ini to support the firewall client configuration.

You Cannot Use Destination Sets in Server Publishing Rules

While Web publishing rules can use destination sets to determine what internal server to forward incoming Web requests, server publishing rules do not use destination sets. The Web Proxy Service allows you to publish multiple servers on the internal network, all of which can published through the ISA server on the Web proxy's external listener port 80.

However, because server publishing rules only allow a single server to be published on a particular port, there isn't any need for destination sets. The external listener can only be used for a single internal server, and therefore does not need to make any forwarding decisions based on the destination address that might be included in a destination set.

Preparing for Server Publishing

Just as with Web publishing, you need to prepare your environment for server publishing. Most of the preparatory elements are the same, but there are some minor differences. Things you need to consider include:

- Creating protocol definitions
- Configure the ISA client
- Creating client address sets

Protocol Definitions

In order to publish services on the internal network, there must be a protocol definition defined to support the server publishing rule. ISA Server comes with several server protocol definitions right out of the box, so you may find that you do not need to create new ones. However, if you are publishing a server for which there is no built-in server protocol, you will need to create one.

You are already familiar with the procedure on how to create protocol definitions that allow internal clients access to internal resources. Creating protocol definitions to allow external clients inbound access works the same way, except that the initial connection is configured as inbound.

UNDOCUMENTED ISA SERVER

Server protocol definitions are defined as protocol definitions that have their primary connection set for inbound requests.

ISA Client Configuration

Most of your published servers will be configured as SecureNAT clients. To configure the internal server as a SecureNAT client, you need to assign the server a default gateway that can route to the internal interface of the ISA server. On a simple, nonrouted network, this will be the IP address of the internal interface of the ISA server. On more complex, routed networks, you will assign a default gateway that can route Internet-bound messages to the internal interface of the ISA server.

Client Address Sets

Unlike Web publishing rules that allow you to control inbound access via users/groups, the only inbound access control you can exert at the level of the ISA server is via IP addresses. IP addresses are configured in client address sets, which you can use to limit access to a particular internal server through a server publishing rule. If you plan to control inbound access through a server publishing rule, be sure to configure your client address sets first.

Server Publishing Walkthrough—Basic Server Publishing

To see how server publishing works, let's go through a basic server-publishing scenario. In this example, you want to publish a news server on your internal network. There is a built-in NNTP protocol definition, so we will not need to create a custom protocol definition. We will allow all users access to the internal news server.

Perform the following steps to publish an internal news server:

1. Open the **ISA Management** console, expand your server or array name, and then expand the **Publishing** node in the left pane.
2. Right-click the **Server Publishing Rules** node in the left pane, then click **New**, and then click **Rule**.
3. On the first page of the wizard (Figure 10.36), type in the name of the rule. In this example, we'll call it **Internal NNTP Server**. Click **Next**.

Figure 10.36 The New Server Publishing Rule Welcome Page

4. On the **Address Mapping** page, you'll see something similar to Figure 10.37.

   On this page, enter the IP address of the internal server and the IP address on the external interface of the ISA server that you want to

Figure 10.37 The Address Mapping Page

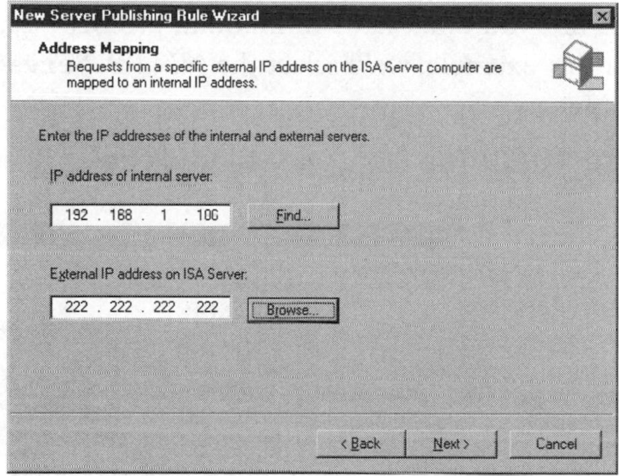

receive inbound NNTP requests from external clients. When you click **Browse**, a list of all the available external IP addresses on the ISA server will appear, and you can choose from that list. If you know the name of the internal server, but don't recall its IP address, click **Find**. After you do so, you will see what appears in Figure 10.38.

Figure 10.38 The Find Internal IP Address Dialog Box

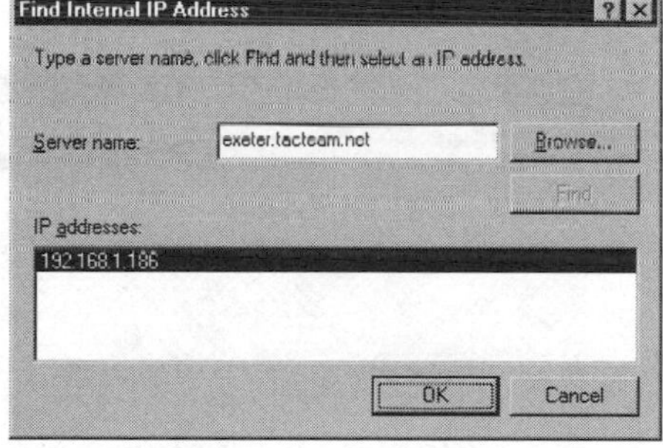

Type in the name of the server in the **Server name** text box, and then click **Find**. In the **IP addresses** box, you'll see the IP address of the server if the ISA server can find it. Note that the ISA server uses the DNS settings on its internal interface to resolve the name. Click **OK** to close this dialog box. Click **Next**.

5. On the **Protocol Settings** page (Figure 10.39), select the **NNTP Server** protocol by click the down-arrow under **Apply the rule to**

this protocol. Note that the wizard only displays protocols that allow the initial connection for inbound access. If you don't see the protocol on the list, you don't have an inbound protocol definition for it.

In this example, we'll select the **NNTP Server** protocol, and then click **Next**.

Figure 10.39 The Protocol Settings Page

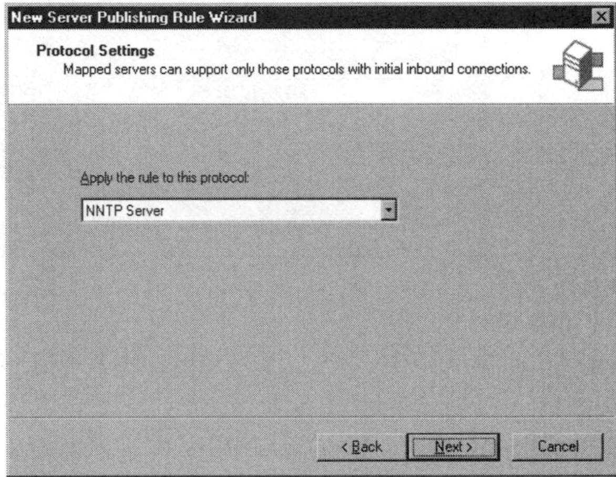

6. The **Client Type** page appears as shown in Figure 10.40.

Figure 10.40 The Client Type Page

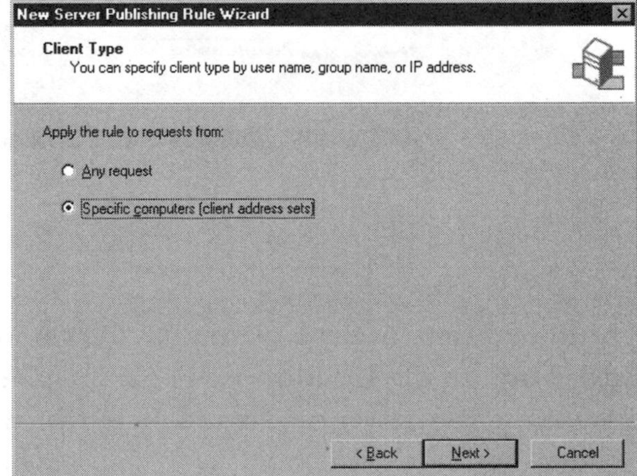

The **Any request** option allows everyone to access the published server.

The **Specific computers (client address sets)** option allows you to limit access to the published server via client address sets. If you choose this option, the following page will allow you to select client address sets to limit access.

In this walkthrough, we'll select the **Any request** option, and click **Next**.

7. On the last page of the wizard, confirm your settings, and then click **Finish**.

   Note that if you have an NNTP server running on the ISA server, it will bind to port 119 on the external interface. Be sure to disable any IIS 5.0-related services. Note that if you have an IIS NNTP server it will bind to *all* interfaces on the ISA server, even if you have configured it to bind to only the internal interface. If you do not disable the IIS NNTP Service, you will see in the Event viewer what appears in Figure 10.41.

Figure 10.41 Server Publishing Failure

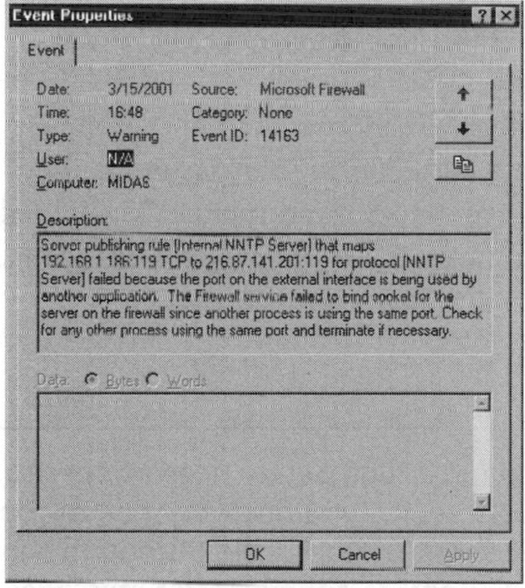

NOTE

When publishing a service using the server publishing rules, the publishing rule does all the work. You do not need to, and should not, configure a packet filter to support the server publishing rule.

Secure Mail Server Publishing

ISA Server includes a special wizard that can guide you through the process of publishing a mail server. The Secure Mail Publishing Wizard allows you to publish multiple mail-related protocols at once. It also takes care of creating the appropriate protocol rules and client address sets to make the publishing of the server possible.

UNDOCUMENTED ISA SERVER

A smart host is a mail server configured to resolve e-mail domains through DNS. If you wish to avoid the overhead of having your own e-mail server resolve the MX records for e-mail domains, you can configure your internal server to use a smart host. All outbound SMTP messages received by the internal server are sent directly to the smart host, and therefore reduce both the overhead on the mail server and DNS query traffic through the ISA server.

Mail server publishing supports all types of mail servers, including Exchange 5.5 and Exchange 2000. Non-Microsoft SMTP mail servers are also supported, such as Lotus Notes.

Keep in mind that you must make the appropriate preparatory changes to your network infrastructure to support secure mail publishing. One issue that often is forgotten is the DNS infrastructure. Many mail servers are configured to support DNS resolution of MX records so that they can route mail themselves, rather than sending the mail to a *smart host*.

NOTE

When an Exchange 2000 Server needs to perform its own DNS queries to an external DNS server, you need to open outbound access to TCP port 53 by configuring a protocol rule. Although this port is typically used for zone transfers (because zone transfer messages do not fit into a single UDP packet), Exchange Server appears to perform DNS queries by sending its requests via TCP.

If your internal server needs to use DNS to resolve mail domain names itself in order to route the mail, you will either need to configure an internal DNS server to use a forwarder, or configure the mail server with the address of an external DNS server that can resolve these names. Note that the ISA server will *not* resolve the names on the behalf of the mail server, since it will be configured as a SecureNAT client.

To publish a mail server, perform the following steps:

1. Open the **ISA Management** console, expand your server or array, and then expand the **Publishing** node. Right-click on the **Server Publishing Rules** node, and click **Secure Mail Server**.
2. The **Mail Services Selection** dialog box appears as shown in Figure 10.42.

Figure 10.42 The Mail Services Selection Dialog Box

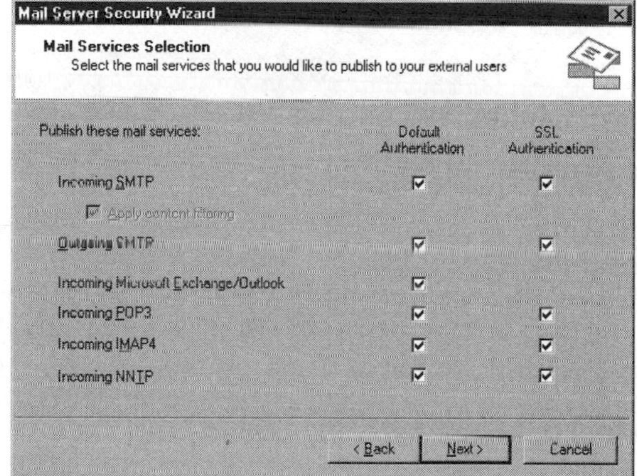

In this dialog box, you select the mail services you want to publish. You have the choice of enabling **Default Authentication** or **SSL Authentication**. Different rules will be created to support the type of authentication method you select.

Note that we have selected all the services for demonstration purposes only. We do not recommend the **Incoming Microsoft Exchange/Outlook** protocol, because this opens NetBIOS and RPC ports, which can present a security risk. If you have external clients that need to connect to an internal Exchange server, they should establish a VPN connection with the ISA server.

3. In the **ISA Server's External IP address** page, type in the IP address of the external interface that you want the ISA server to listen on for the published mail server. Then click **Next**.
4. You have two choices on the **Internal Mail Server** page (Figure 10.43).

Figure 10.43 The Internal Mail Server Page

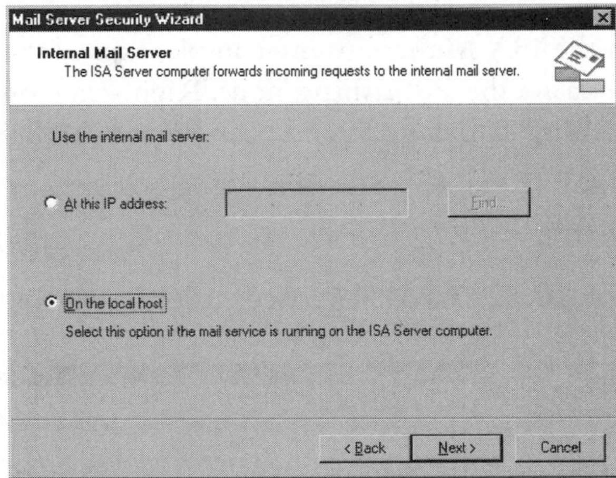

- Choose the **At this IP address** to publish a server on the internal network.
- Choose the **On the local host** option if the mail server is running on the ISA server itself. If you do choose this option, you will see two warning dialog boxes (Figures 10.44 and 10.45).

Figure 10.44 RPC Warning Dialog Box

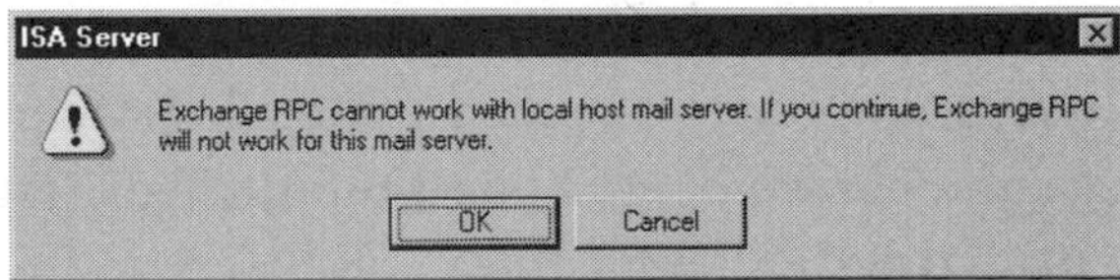

Figure 10.45 The Message Screener Warning Dialog Box

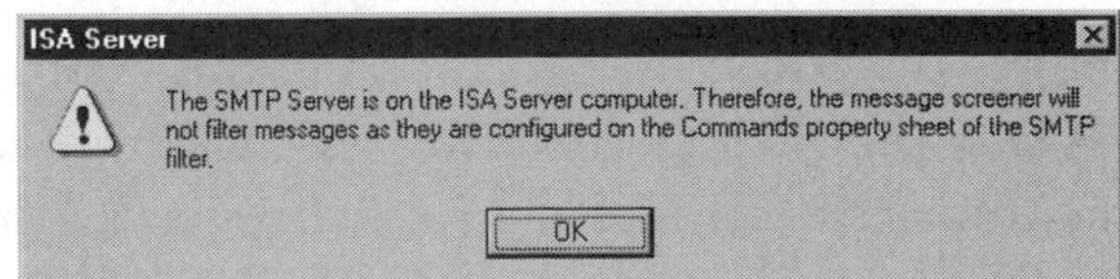

Note that the second warning will only appear if you have enabled the Message Screener option in the second page of the wizard. For a detailed discussion of the Message Screener, see Chapter 9.

When you configure the wizard to use the mail server on the local host, the wizard will create a series of static packet filters to allow the server to listen to the selected services on the external interface of the ISA server. It *does not* publish the internal interface of the ISA server. In order to do that, you would need to select the **At this IP address** option.

In this example, we'll select the **At this IP address** option, type in the IP address of the server on the internal network, and click **Next**.

5. On the last page of the wizard, review your settings, and click **Finish**. After you finish, you'll see a number of new Server Publishing Rules, as shown in Figure 10.46.

Figure 10.46 New Server Publishing Rules Created by the Mail Wizard

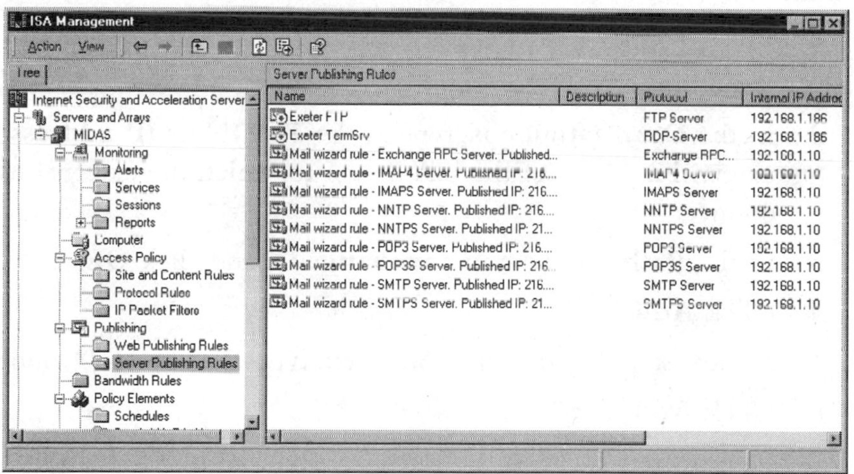

These rules are used by the Firewall Service to determine whether inbound access for these protocols is allowed. The wizard did *not* create static packet filters, because the server rules open the appropriate ports to listen for inbound requests.

Generally, you should publish SMTP servers on the internal network, and not on the ISA server. Remember that any services on the ISA server take up memory, processor cycles, and can be potential vectors of attack. The only time you might want to consider publishing the SMTP service on the ISA server is when you want to take advantage of the message screener for both inbound and outbound messages. However, as we discussed in the previous chapter, it's often easier to get the message screener working when you publish the SMTP service on the internal network.

Configuring ISA Server to Support Outlook Web Access

Outlook Web Access (OWA) allows users to access their Exchange mailboxes by using a Web browser. Since this feature is dependent on IIS, you must have IIS installed on the Exchange server you wish to publish. After the Web server is installed and OWA is configured through the Exchange setup routine, you can then publish the Web server to provide access to the Exchange message store via the browser interface.

However, before you publish the internal Web server that provides access to the Exchange message store, you have to create a new destination set to support publishing OWA. To create the destination set, perform the following steps:

1. Go to **Policy Elements** and create a new **Destination Set**. Call it something like **OWA**.
2. In the **Destination** box, type in the **FQDN** or **IP address** of the external interface of the ISA Server to which the external users will connect.
3. In the **Path** box, type in **/exchange/***, and click **OK**.
4. Click **Add**.
5. Repeat step 2, and in the **Path** box, type **/exchweb/***, and click **OK**.
6. Click **Add**.
7. Repeat step 2, and in the **Path** box, type **/public/***, and click **OK**.
8. When you are finished, the properties of the destination set should look like Figure 10.47. After the destination set is completed, click **OK**.

After the destination set is configured, you can use it in the Web publishing rule used to publish the OWA server. Perform the following steps to publish the server:

1. Right-click **Web Publishing Rule**, select **New**, and then **Rule**.
2. Name the rule something like **Outlook Web Access**, and click **Next**.

Figure 10.47 The OWA Destination Set

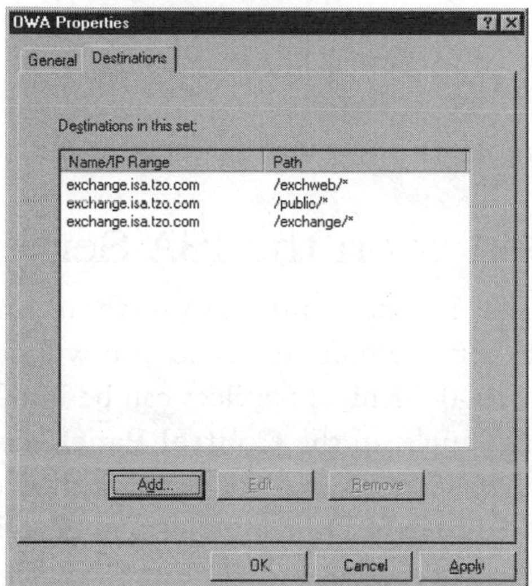

3. Using the drop-down list box, select the **OWA** destination set. Click **Next**.
4. On the **Client Type** page, select the **Any request** option, and click **Next**.
5. Select **Redirect the request to this internal Web Server (name or IP address)**, and put in either the name or the IP address of the server running OWA.
6. Check the **Send the original header to publishing server instead of the actual one (specified above)** box. Click **Next**.
7. Click **Finish**.

If you wish to secure access to OWA folders, use the secure publishing methods discussed earlier in this chapter.

Publishing a Terminal Server

One nice thing you can do with server publishing is to make terminal servers located on the internal network available to external users. Terminal Services can be used by administrators to manage an administrative mode terminal server, and to provide access to business applications when the terminal server is running in application mode.

There are two primary scenarios with which you might have to deal when publishing Terminal Services:

- Making the terminal server on the ISA server available for remote management
- Making an internal terminal server available for application usage

Terminal Server on the ISA Server

You can run Terminal Services on the ISA server to simplify your remote management of the ISA server. Before doing so, you will need to install Terminal Services. Windows 2000 Terminal Services can be installed via the **Add/ Remove Programs** applet in the **Control Panel**. Remember that when you install the Terminal Services on the ISA server, it should be installed in **Remote Administration Mode** only. Do *not* install it in **Application Server Mode**.

After Terminal Services are installed on the ISA server, you need to decide how you want to make them available. There are two options:

- Make the terminal server available through the *external* interface of the ISA server
- Make the terminal server available through the *internal* interface of the ISA server

If you wish to make the terminal server available through the external interface, you only need to create a packet filter to do so. The packet filter allows access control via remote IP address configuration.

You can also make the terminal server available only through the internal IP address of the ISA server. Then you would publish the terminal server to make it available to external administrators. The advantage of publishing a terminal server's internal interface is that you have a little more control over inbound access. While packet filters only allow you to configure the remote computer setting as a single IP address or a range of IP addresses, you can take advantage of client address sets when configuring access control over inbound connections to the published terminal server.

By default, terminal servers will listen on all adapters on TCP port 3389. If you plan to publish the terminal server through the internal interface of the ISA server, you should disable it from listening on the external interface.

To change the listener address on the terminal server, perform these steps:

1. From the **Administrative Tools** menu, open the **Terminal Services Configuration** application.
2. In the **Terminal Services Configuration** console, click on the **Connections** node. In the right pane, you should have a connection listed as **RDP-Tcp**. Right-click on the connection, and click **Properties**.
3. On the **RDP-Tcp Properties** dialog box, click on the **Network Adapter** tab. You will see something like what appears in Figure 10.48. In this dialog box, you can select the adapter you want the terminal server to listen on. Choose your internal adapter from the list, and click **OK**.

Figure 10.48 The Network Adapter Tab on the RDP-Tcp Properties Page

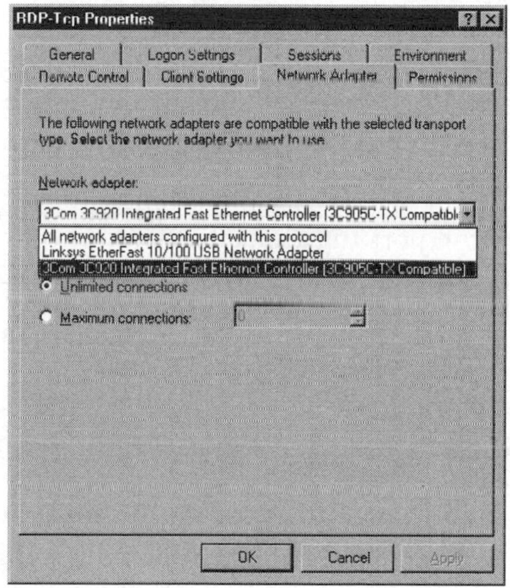

Now that Terminal Services is configured, you need to configure a protocol definition that will allow inbound access to the Remote Desktop Protocol (RDP).

Terminal Server on the Internal Network and on the ISA Server

Publishing a terminal server on the internal network works the same way as publishing the internal interface of the ISA server. In fact, it's the exact same thing, since the internal interface is on the internal network.

However, whenever you want to publish a terminal server on the internal network, *and* have a terminal server on the ISA server, you have to make some changes to accommodate the limitations of server publishing. Remember, only a single server can listen on a particular port number on a particular IP address on the external interface of the ISA server. In order to allow for publishing of an internal server that's easy for external users to access, you need to change the port number used by the terminal server located on the ISA server.

This is the preferred solution, because you don't need to make any changes on the Terminal Services client that your users use to access the terminal server. The only changes that need to be made are on the terminal server located on the ISA server and the Terminal Services client used by administrators requiring access.

Change the terminal server listening ports by performing the following steps:

1. Run **Regedt32**, and go to this key:

   ```
   HKEY_LOCAL_MACHINE\System\CurrentControlSet\Control\
   TerminalServer\Wds\Repwd\Tds\Tcp
   ```

   Find the **PortNumber** subkey, and notice the value of 0xd3d, which is hex for (3389). Modify the port number in Hex, and save the new value.

2. To change the port for a specific connection on the terminal server, begin with **Regedt32** and go to this key:

   ```
   HKEY_LOCAL_MACHINE\System\CurrentControlSet\Control\
   TerminalServer\WinStations\"connection"
   ```

3. Where **connection** is the name of the Terminal Services connection.

The next step is to change the port the Terminal Services client uses to connect to the terminal server. Perform the following steps:

1. Open **Client Connection Manager**.
2. On the **File** menu, click **New Connection**, and then create the new connection. After running the wizard, you should have a new connection listed there.
3. Making sure that the new connection is highlighted, and in the **File** menu, click **Export**. Save it as **name.cns**, with the name being the name you want to use for the connection.

4. Edit the **.cns** file using Notepad changing **Server Port=3389** to **Server Port=xxxx**, where **xxxx** is the new port that you specified on the terminal server.
5. Now import the file back into **Client Connection Manager**. You may be prompted to overwrite the current one, if it has the same name. Go ahead and overwrite it. You now have a client that has the correct port settings to match your changed terminal server settings.

NOTE

When using the TSAC client, you cannot change the port number used by the Terminal Services client. If you use the TSAC client, you will also have to publish the internal Web server on which the TSAC server-side components are located.

Terminal Services Security Considerations

Allowing Terminal Services access through the ISA server greatly enhances the accessibility to your internal network. However, there are some significant security risks when exposing Terminal Services to the Internet. The Terminal Services port number 3389 is sure to be a favorite for hackers everywhere. If hackers can get into a terminal server configured in remote administration mode, they literally have the keys to the Mint, and will be able to wreak whatever havoc they like on your network.

If you are going to make the ISA Server Terminal Service available to Internet-based admins, you need to bolster the security on that server. The best method would be to require a VPN connection to that server, and then establish a Terminal Services connection once your VPN link is established. The VPN will secure all data running through the tunnel, preventing access to any sensitive data.

Whether or not you choose to use a VPN, you should configure Terminal Services to use the highest level of encryption when connecting to Internet hosts. You can configure Terminal Services encryption by doing the following:

1. Open the **Terminal Services Configuration** application from the **Administrative Tools** menu.
2. Click the **Connections** node in the left pane, right-click on the **RDP-Tcp** node in the right pane, and click **Properties**.

3. Click on the **General** tab. You will see what appears in Figure 10.49. In the **Encryption** frame, click the **down-arrow** for the drop-down list box for **Encryption Level**. Select the **High** option.

Figure 10.49 The RDP-Tcp Properties Dialog Box

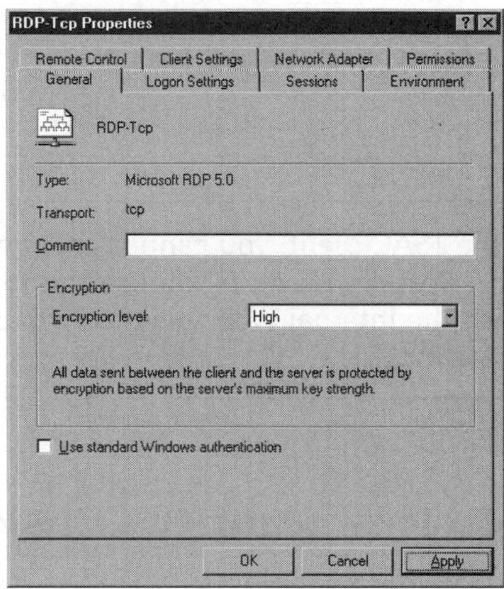

4. Click **Apply**, and then click **OK**.

Publishing a Web Server Using Server Publishing

Why would you want to publish a server using the Server Publishing Wizard? We have already gone over some of the limitations of using the server publishing method compared to what you can do with Web publishing. However, a couple of issues may lead you to consider using server publishing for a Web site:

- To obtain usage data in the IIS server logs
- To configure SSL on the internal Web server, and bypass configuring the certificate on the external interface of the ISA server

The first issue points out the fact that when you publish a Web server using the Web Publishing Wizard, the user data and page access information is *not* stored in the IIS server log files. Since access to published servers is through the Web Proxy Service on the ISA server, all this information is found in the Web

Proxy Service logs. You can use a third-party tool to parse the information in the logs and extract the relevant information. However, some people would like to have the information remain on the IIS server.

The limitation of publishing a Web server using server publishing rules is that you bypass the Web Proxy Service, and if you use port 80 for the server publishing rule, that port will no longer be available on that IP address. You will also have to change the port number used for the Web Proxy Service, which means that the default HTTP port will not be available to publish any other Web servers on your internal network on that IP address.

NOTE

Server publishing rules dedicate a port on a particular IP address. If you have multiple IP addresses, you can use a port once per IP address for a server publishing rule. For example, if you have 222.222.222.222 and 111.111.111.111 bound to the external interface, you can publish one Web server on port 80 on the first address, and another Web server on port 80 on the second address. Note that when you use port 80 in server publishing rules, you may need to reconfigure the Web Proxy Inbound Web Requests Listener. You will not be able to use the **Use the same listener configuration for all IP addresses** if you want the listener to use port 80. However, you can still use the Web Proxy Service Listener on port 80 on *IP addresses not used to publish port 80 in server publishing rules*.

If you wish to use server publishing to publish an internal Web server, perform the following steps:

1. Create a protocol definition, call it **Published HTTP Server** or something similar. Allow inbound TCP 80, and secondary connections for outbound 1025-65534. One would think that this step would not be required, but from our testing, it appears that you do need to configure the secondary connections.
2. Create a protocol rule allowing the use of the **Published HTTP Server** protocol definition.
3. Create a server publishing rule using the **HTTP Server** protocol definition, and point it to your internal server. Note that if you look in the **Alerts** node of the **ISA Server console** or if you look in the **Event**

Viewer, you'll see that the server publishing rule has failed. The reason is that the Web Proxy listener is using port 80.

4. Go to your **Incoming Web Requests Listener**, and change the listening port to something other than port 80; for example, 9999.
5. Restart the Firewall and Web Proxy Services. Wait about a minute for them to complete restarting. If you don't want to waste time guessing when the ISA server will choose to restart the service for you, restart the Web Proxy Service manually.
6. Connect to the internal Web site via the FQDN or IP address that points to the external interface or your ISA server.
7. Check the log file on the internal Web server to make sure the IP address of the external client is there.

NOTE

Another effect of bypassing the Web Proxy Service for Web publishing is that you will not be able to take advantage of the Web proxy cache for inbound connections. This will increase the amount of traffic on the internal network and load on the internal Web server.

The H.323 Gatekeeper Service

The H.323 Gatekeeper Service allows H.323-aware applications to communicate with each other over an intranet or over the Internet. Using an application such as Microsoft NetMeeting, you can carry on audio and videoconferences with other users.

For those of you accustomed to using NetMeeting by directly connecting to other computers on the Internet, you will need to rethink how you use NetMeeting to take advantage of the H.323 Gatekeeper Service. The reason for this is that the H.323 Gatekeeper Service was designed with the following configurations in mind:

- Gatekeeper-to-gatekeeper calling
- Host-to-host calling on an intranet
- IP-network-to-PSTN-gateway calling

In this section, we'll focus on the first two designs, and leave the last to our Cisco compatriots versed in VoIP and related technologies.

You can still call external machines on the Internet if you know the IP address of that computer. If the machine does not have a static IP address, but uses a dynamic DNS registration method such as TZO, you can dial up external hosts directly connected to the Internet through an FQDN.

One of the biggest differences between using NetMeeting from behind the ISA server H.323 gateway and how you might have used it in the past with a plain NAT solution is that you can no longer register with ILS servers on the Internet (including the external interface of the ISA server) and have full functionality. The reason is that when your internal host registers with an ILS server, its internal private IP address is registered, rather than the public IP address of the NAT server. This is the case even when the ILS server is located on the ISA server itself.

The result is that you can no longer use NetMeeting to call users on Internet ILS servers. If you require this feature, do not enable the H.323 gatekeeper.

NetMeeting clients on the internal network should be configured to use the internal interface of the ISA server as their gatekeeper. When the NetMeeting clients are configured to use the gatekeeper, user information is stored in the registration database, and you can see information about the registered clients in the ISA Management console. These clients dynamically register user information with the gatekeeper, and the registrations are removed automatically when the client is shut down.

To configure the NetMeeting client to use the gatekeeper, perform the following steps:

1. Open **NetMeeting**. Click on the **Tools** menu, and then click **Options**. You will see something like Figure 10.50.
2. In the **Options** dialog box, click **Advanced Calling**. You will see what appears in Figure 10.51. In the **Advanced Calling Options** dialog box, you have the following options:
   - **Use a gatekeeper to place calls** Since we want to use the ISA server's H.323 gatekeeper to place calls, you need to enter the computer name or the IP address of the internal interface on which the H.323 gatekeeper listens. If you use a computer name, make sure you have the DNS infrastructure that can resolve the name.

Figure 10.50 The NetMeeting Options Dialog Box

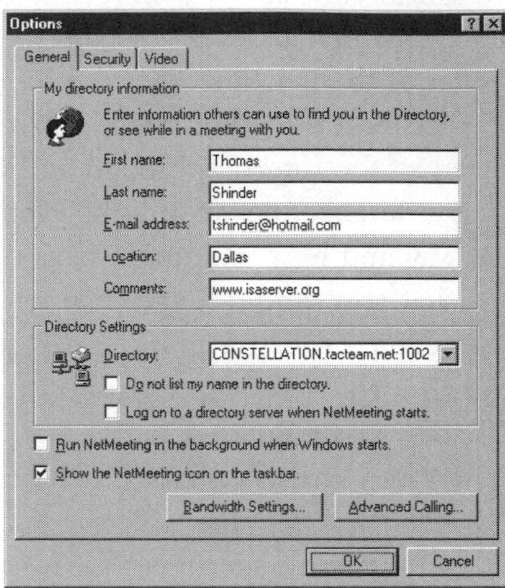

Figure 10.51 The Advanced Calling Options Dialog Box

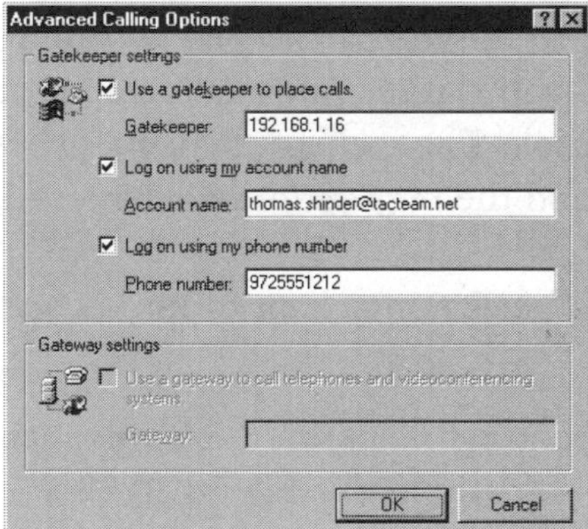

- **Log on using my account name** Select this option if you would like to register an e-mail address or username with the gatekeeper. Users on networks behind an H.323 gatekeeper will be able to call other networks behind an H.323 gatekeeper by using an e-mail address. Note that you *cannot* use an e-mail address to call a NetMeeting host if both the hosts are not behind a gatekeeper. For example, if a user running NetMeeting on his personal computer wants to call you by the e-mail address you registered with the gatekeeper, it will not work, because the external NetMeeting user is not behind a gatekeeper.

- **Log on using my phone number** Type in a telephone number you want to have registered with the gatekeeper. This number should contain *only numbers*, and should not contain letters, dashes, spaces, or anything other than numbers. External users can call you by using the telephone number you register with the gatekeeper. Even users who are directly connected to the Internet and are not behind an H.323 gatekeeper can call you using your telephone number if they configure their NetMeeting to use the external interface of the ISA server as their gateway.

3. Click **OK**, and then click **OK** again. You'll see a little icon in the lower-right corner of the NetMeeting application that looks like two terminals. If you let your mouse pointer rest over it, it should say "logged onto gatekeeper."
4. Go to the **ISA Management** console. Assuming that you've installed the optional H.323 Gatekeeper Service, expand the **H.323 Gatekeepers** node in the left pane, expand your server name, and click on the **Active Terminals** node. You should see something like what appears in Figure 10.52.

   Note that both the account name and the telephone number of the NetMeeting client is registered with the gatekeeper. Note that the Type column states that the registration is dynamic. When the NetMeeting client is closed, the registration will be dynamically removed from the list.

Figure 10.52 The Active Terminals Node

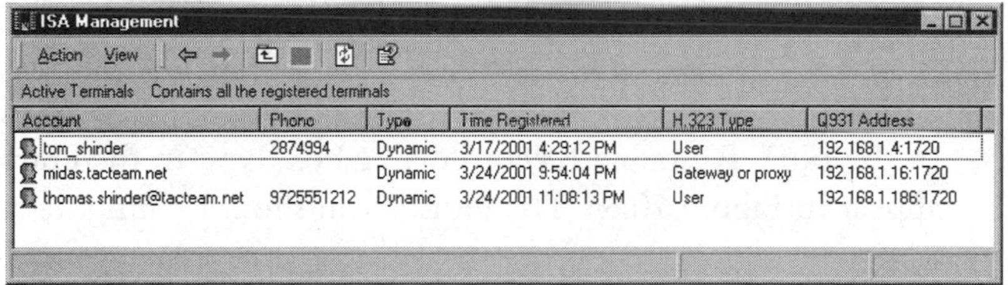

Gatekeeper-to-Gatekeeper Calling

As mentioned earlier, the H.323 Gatekeeper Service was designed to optimize the benefits of LAN-to-LAN calls. When each LAN has a gatekeeper and NetMeeting clients registered with their respective gatekeepers, users can call

NetMeeting clients on other networks by using either an e-mail address or a telephone number.

Calling by e-mail address is actually the easiest way to do this, because you do not need to set up any routing rules on the ISA server to support calling by e-mail address—all that is required is a Q931 resource record entry for your domain. The DNS entry needs to be on a publicly available DNS server. The type of entry is an SRV record called the *Q931 address record*.

To configure the Q931 address record for your domain on a Windows 2000 DNS server, perform the following steps:

1. Open the **DNS** console, and right-click on your domain. Click **Other New Records**.
2. In the **Resource Record Type** dialog box (Figure 10.53), click the **SRV** record type, and then click **Create Record**.

Figure 10.53 The Resource Record Type Dialog Box

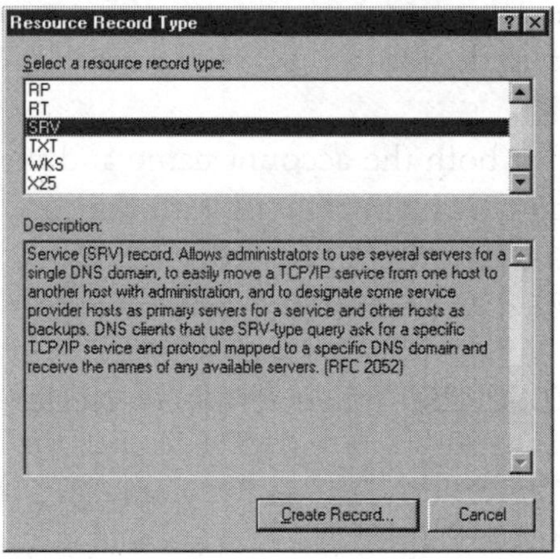

3. In the New Resource Record dialog box, type in the entries as they appear in Figure 10.54. The entries you should configure are:

   Service = _q931

   Protocol = _tcp

   Port number = 1720

   Host offering this service: [the name of your ISA server's external interface]

   Click **OK** to create the record.

Figure 10.54 The New Resource Record Dialog Box

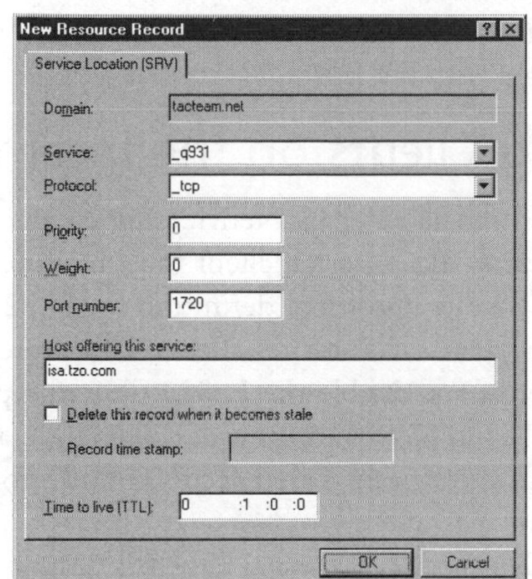

After each network using the H.323 gatekeeper has registered its Q931 address in the DNS, all a user on the internal network needs to do is call the other user by his e-mail address. Note that unlike the ILS server method, there is no way for the caller to search the registrations on the gatekeeper. The caller must know the address of the person he or she wants to call, and it is the sole responsibility of each user to configure NetMeeting with the correct information so that it is properly entered into the registration database.

Hosts on networks behind gatekeepers can also call hosts on other networks behind gatekeepers using a telephone number. However, routing rules must be in place to support these types of calls, since there is no centralized database such as DNS or ILS to support locating hosts using telephone numbers. However, routing rules can be configured using prefixes for other networks that will direct the call to the appropriate remote gateway. We will discuss routing rules later in this section.

ILS Servers

NetMeeting clients can be configured to use ILS servers on the internal network, and call other internal NetMeeting clients registered with the ILS server. However, a NetMeeting client cannot register with both an ILS server and an H.323 gatekeeper. Registering with an ILS server is not a recommended configuration, because external users will never be able to call users on the private network through an ILS server.

However, external clients can register with an internal ILS server. Internal clients can then call external users through ILS. The gatekeeper will manage conversations between the internal client and the external client. External users can dynamically register with the ILS

NetMeeting Clients on the Internet

Internal machines can call external NetMeeting clients that are directly connected to the Internet. The internal client must have permissions to use the H.323 protocol. There is a protocol definition for H.323 that you can use in protocol rules to allow access to Internet clients. This protocol definition is installed by the H.323 filter. If you disable the H.323 filter, the protocol definition will be unavailable. Both SecureNAT and firewall clients have access to this protocol, and you can implement user/group-based access controls for the protocol if you are using firewall client machines.

NetMeeting clients on the internal network cannot call an external NetMeeting client that is directly connected to the Internet by calling a telephone number or e-mail address. Calling by telephone number or e-mail address is only available when the destination NetMeeting client is behind an H.323 gatekeeper.

External NetMeeting clients directly connected to the Internet can have static registrations for them entered into the registration database. However, the client must have a static IP address, because static entries do not support using FQDNs for entering the Q931 IP address information. If you do create a static entry, you can use a telephone number to call the external NetMeeting client. One way around this problem is to create a routing rule that directs calls to the address for the static user to the registration database.

External NetMeeting clients directly connected to the Internet can call internal NetMeeting clients that are behind the H.323 gatekeeper. The external client must be configured to use the ISA server's external interface as its gateway to the internal network that it wants to call.

Perform the following steps to configure the external NetMeeting client to use the external interface of the ISA server as its gateway:

1. Open **NetMeeting**. Click on the **Tools** menu, and then click **Options**. You will see something like Figure 10.55.
2. In the **Options** dialog box, click **Advanced Calling**. You will see what appears in Figure 10.56.

   Place a check mark in the check box for **Use a gateway to call telephones and videoconferencing systems**, and type in the IP

Figure 10.55 The NetMeeting Options Dialog Box

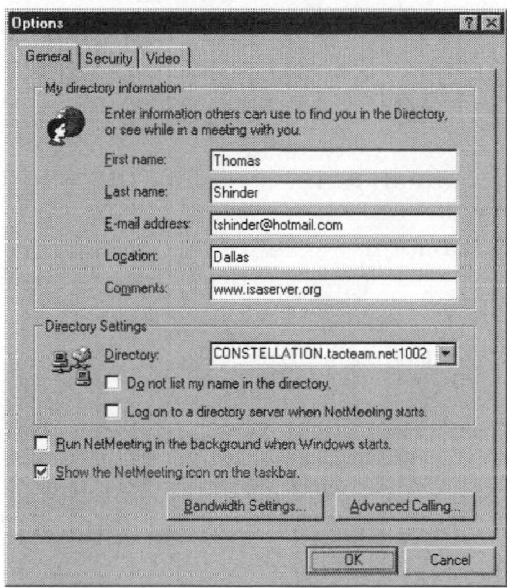

Figure 10.56 The Advanced Calling Options Dialog Box

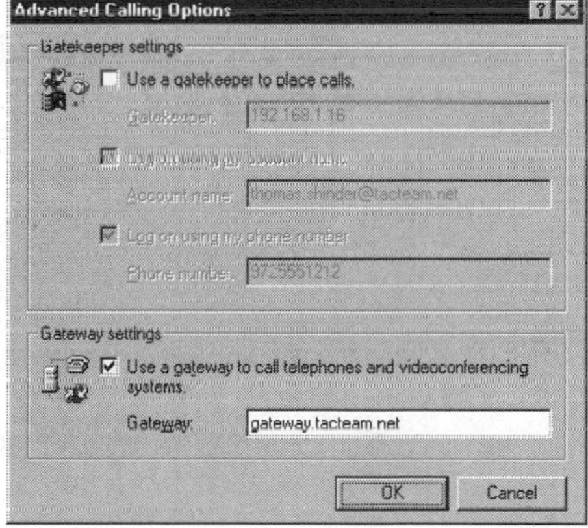

address or the FQDN that resolves to the external interface of the ISA server.

3. Click **OK**, and then click **OK** again. The NetMeeting client can now call an internal user behind the gatekeeper by using the internal user's telephone number.

A common misconception we've heard is that its possible for an external client on the Internet to dynamically register with the gatekeeper. Sometimes it appears that the client actually does register with the gatekeeper, but the connection is quickly lost or simply does not work. It is not possible for the external NetMeeting client on the Internet to dynamically register with the gatekeeper, so don't even try it.

Configuring the Gatekeeper

There are just a few basic steps to configure the gatekeeper:

- Creating destinations
- Creating phone number rules
- Creating e-mail rules
- Creating IP address rules

Destinations are used in the routing rules. After the destination is created, it is used in the routing rule so that the ISA server knows where to send the request.

Creating Destinations

To create a new destination, perform the following steps:

1. Open the **ISA Management** console, expand your server or array, and then expand the **H.323 Gatekeepers** node. Expand your server, and finally expand the **Call routing** node. Right-click on the **Destinations** node, and click **Add destination**.
2. The **New Destination Wizard** appears. Click **Next** to continue.
3. The **Destination Type** page appears, as seen in Figure 10.57.

Figure 10.57 The Destination Type Page

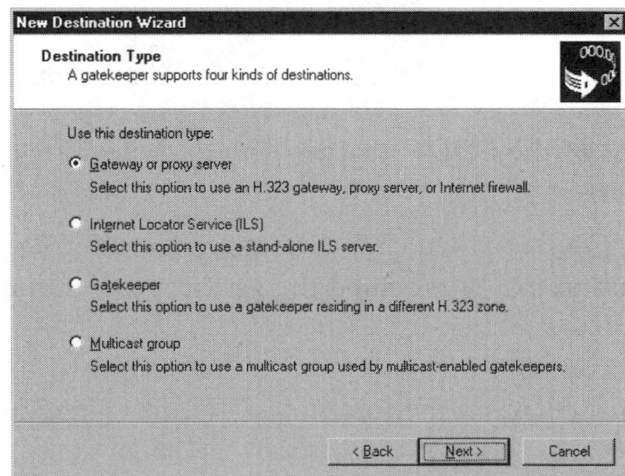

From the **Destination Type** page, you can create one of the following destination types:

- **Gateway or proxy server** This is the address of an H.323 gateway. If you wish to call NetMeeting clients on other networks, you can configure a gateway for the ISA server to route the request. You use this gateway destination in a routing rule so that the ISA server knows where to send requests for an e-mail address, telephone number or IP address.
- **Internet Locator Service (ILS)** Create an ILS destination if you want to route calls to an internal ILS server. Do not configure an ILS destination for ILS servers on the Internet.
- **Gatekeeper** While a single gatekeeper can handle up to 50,000 registrations, larger environments may wish to partition their internal client registration database. If you do so, you should configure a gatekeeper destination that can be used in rules to search for clients registered with those gatekeepers. For example, you might have all clients with the prefix 999 register with one gatekeeper, and have all clients with the prefix 888 register with another gatekeeper. Then you can create routing rules so that calls with a particular prefix are routed to the appropriate gatekeeper.
- **Multicast group** All gatekeepers listen on the multicast address 224.0.1.41. If you have a large network and do not want to configure routing rules for multiple gatekeepers, you can configure a multicast destination to search all gatekeepers on the LAN.

  Select a **Destination**, and click **Next**.

4. The **Destination Name or Address** page appears as shown in Figure 10.58. In the **Destination name or address**, type in the FQDN or IP address associated with the destination you are configuring. Click **Next**.
5. On the **Destination Description** page, type in a short description for the destination, and then click **Next**.
6. The last page lists your selections. If it looks good, click **Finish**.

One you have created your destination, you can then create routing rules and use the destination in the rule.

Figure 10.58 The Destination Name or Address Page

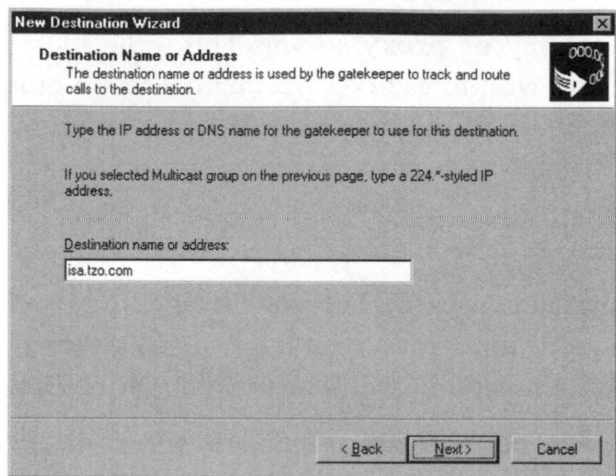

Call Routing Rules

There are three types of call routing rules:

- Phone number rules
- E-mail address rules
- IP address rules

Let's look at each type and how they are configured.

Phone Number Rules

Phone number rules can be used to route requests based on telephone number strings. These are helpful if you plan to implement multiple H.323 gatekeepers in your organization, and partition client registrations based on prefixes. For example, all machines with prefix 999 would register with one H.323 gatekeeper, and all machines with prefix 888 would register with another H.323 gatekeeper. If all numbers in your company use the same prefix, you can configure a routing rule that will direct the request to a local registration database..

Phone number rules can also be implemented if you plan to call other organizations. For example, another organization could use a prefix of 972 for all its clients. In this case, you can create a phone number rule to direct requests with that prefix to the other organization's gateway. You can even configure a routing rule that allows you to configure custom prefixes that will route calls to remote networks, even when the remote network does not use a standardized prefix system in their telephone number scheme.

If your company uses an IP-to-PSTN gateway, you can implement a routing rule that forwards all requests destined for a POTS network to a specific gateway device that handles these requests.

To create a phone number routing rule, perform the following steps:

1. Open the **ISA Management** console, expand your server or array, expand the **H.323 Gatekeepers** node, and expand the **Call routing** node. Right-click on the **Phone number rules** node, and click **Add routing rule**.
2. The **Welcome** page for the **New Routing Rule Wizard** appears. Click **Next** to continue.
3. The **Name and Description** page appears. Type in a name for this rule, and a short description that will let you know what this rule is used for. Click **Next**.
4. The **Prefix or Phone Number** page appears as in Figure 10.59. On this page, type in a prefix or entire telephone number that will trigger this routing rule. For example, the prefix 973 might be used by all NetMeeting clients in the south office, which is connected to the Internet by an H.323 gatekeeper. You can also enter a single telephone number here, and route requests for that particular number. If you choose to enter the entire telephone number, remove the check mark from the **Route all phone numbers using this prefix** check box. Click **Next** to continue.

Figure 10.59 The Prefix or Phone Number Page

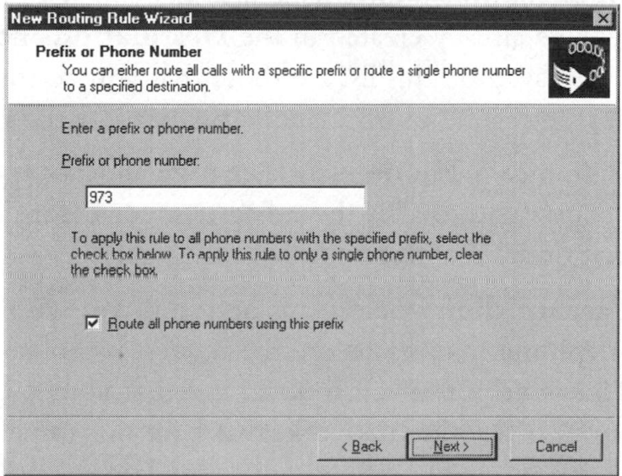

5. The **Destination Type** page appears as shown in Figure 10.60. On this page, select the type of destination that the request for the telephone number or prefix should be directed. In this case, we entered a prefix that should route numbers to another division of the company that is behind another H.323 gatekeeper connected to the Internet. Therefore, we will direct these requests to a **Gateway or proxy server**.

   Note that only options for phone number rules are available. If a particular destination type can't be used to route a telephone number, it won't be available as you can see in Figure 10.60.

   Click **Next** to continue.

Figure 10.60 The Destination Type Page

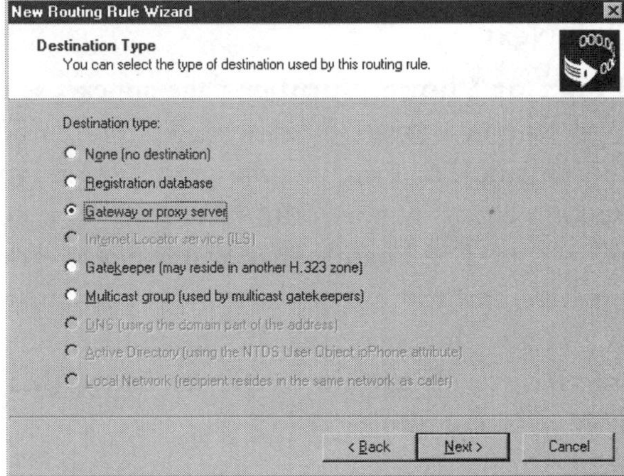

6. The **Destination Name** page presents you with a list of **Destinations** that you've already created in the **Destinations** node. The only destinations displayed on this list are those that you configured as gateways or proxies. Select the appropriate destination for the rule, and click **Next**.
7. The **Change a Phone Number** page appears as in Figure 10.61. This page allows you to alter the called number before it is actually sent to its destination. The options you have include:
   - **Discard digits** Select this option if you wish to discard digits in the telephone number before the request is sent to its final destination. This is helpful if you want to institute your own routing scheme to connect to other networks that have not implemented their own prefix-oriented numbering system. For example, suppose you have

Figure 10.61 The Change a Phone Number Page

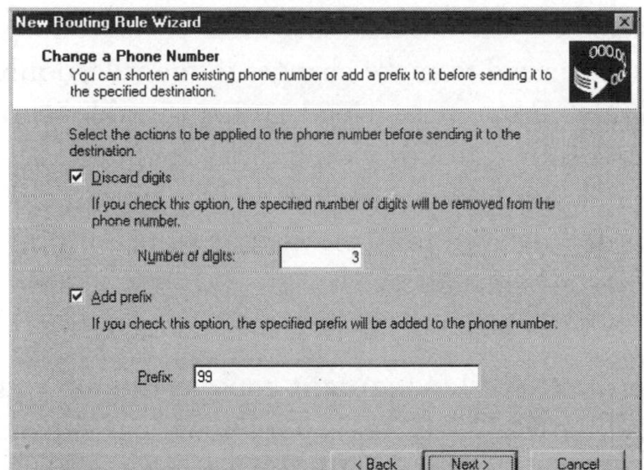

two partners that have H.323 gateways. Neither partner has implemented a numbering scheme that allows you to use the prefix to route properly to his or her gateway. In this case, you can tell your employees to use the prefix 111 to dial one company, and 222 to dial another company. Then, when one of your employees calls a number such as 2222875252, the gatekeeper will strip off the 222 because we told it to remove the first three digits. After removing the digits, the request for the remaining portion of the number will be routed to the destination gateway.

- **Add prefix** Choose this option if you wish to add a prefix to numbers. This might be helpful if the destination network uses a specific prefix in its number, and you wish to have the gatekeeper add these numbers before sending the request.

  Click **Next** to continue.

8. The **Routing Rule Metric** page appears. You can enter a metric value that will be used to determine the most favored route for a particular request. Using a metric allows you to order rules and make available multiple paths for a single request, while allowing you to determine the best path.

   Click **Next** to continue.

9. On the last page of the wizard, click **Finish** to complete the rule.

The rule will appear in the left pane of the ISA Management console. Note that there is a default rule called Local, which will route all requests to the local registration database if there is no other number that can specifically route the request. If you ever need to make changes to the rule, double-click on it and it will open the rule's Properties dialog box. E-mail address routing rules are configured in a manner similar to how you created the phone number routing rule. Note that if the destination e-mail domain has a Q931 record in a publicly available DNS, you do not need to implement an e-mail routing rule to support connections made by e-mail address.

To create an e-mail address routing rule, perform the following steps:

1. Open the **ISA Management** console, expand your server or array, expand the **H.323 Gatekeepers** node, and expand the **Call routing** node. Right-click on the **Phone number rules** node, and click **Add routing rule**.
2. The Welcome page for the **New Routing Rule Wizard** appears. Click **Next** to continue.
3. The **Name and Description** page appears. Type in a name for this rule, and a short description that will let you know what this rule is used for. Click **Next**.
4. The **Domain Name Suffix** page appears as shown in Figure 10.62.

   Enter the **domain name suffix** for the e-mail rule. If you wish the rule to route a particular address, remove the check mark from the **Route all e-mail addresses that include this general DNS domain name**. Click **Next**.

Figure 10.62 Domain Name Suffix

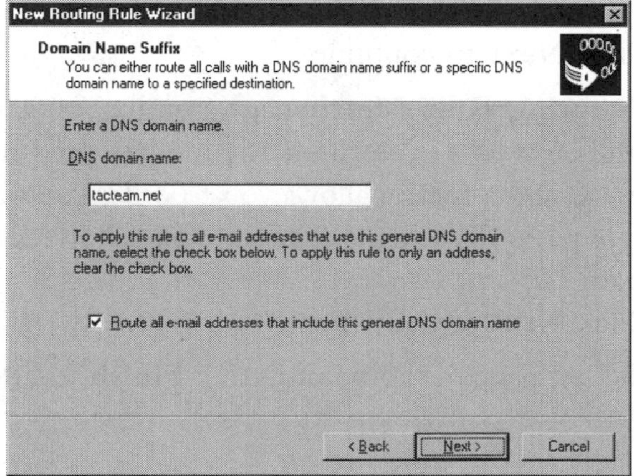

Figure 10.63 The Destination Type Page

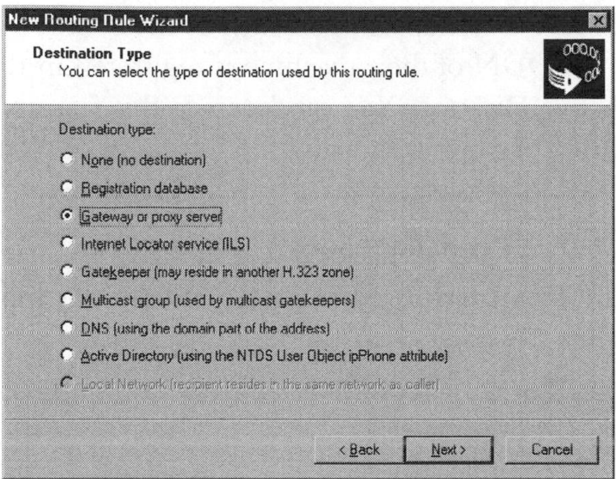

5. The **Destination Type** page appears as shown in Figure 10.63.

   On the **Destination Type** page, you can choose from a number of destination types, some of which we haven't covered yet. The "other" destination types include:

   - **None** This would be your "black-hole" route.
   - **Registration database** Requests for NetMeeting clients already registered with the H.323 gatekeeper can be sent to the registration database. You can see these entries in the Active Terminals list. Listings in the registration database have a TTL of six minutes (by default). At the end of the TTL, the gatekeeper will inform the NetMeeting client that its registration is about to be dropped, and that it should renew it. If it is not renewed, the registration is dropped from the database. Note that the database does *not* enforce uniqueness. If two registrations have the same value, calls will be routed to the most recent registration.
   - **DNS (using the domain part of the address)** Use this to specify an *internal* DNS server to resolve the domain name in e-mail rules. Note that you do not need to configure a DNS destination for external domains, because the external interface of the ISA server will attempt to resolve names automatically through its external interface.

- **Active Directory (using the NTDS User Object ipPhone attribute)** When users log on to a Windows 2000 domain and use a TAPI-aware application such as the Windows 2000 Phone Dialer, the FQDN of their machine is registered in the Users account in the Active Directory. You can leverage this feature of the Active Directory by configuring the routing rule to use the Active Directory to search for the user's location on the internal network.

  Click **Next** to continue.

6. On the **Destination Name** page, choose the appropriate Destination, and click **Next**.
7. On the **Routing Rule Metric** page, configure a metric for this rule, and click **Next**.
8. On the last page of the wizard, click **Finish** to complete the rule.

IP Address Routing Rules

IP address routing rules work in the same way that the other rules work. However, in this case, the caller uses the destination IP address to make the call. When an ISA server receives the request to call a particular IP address, it will search though the IP address rules to see if there is a destination to which the request should be routed. If one is found, it will forward the request to the appropriate destination.

Generally, users will not call each other by IP address, since most internal networks use DHCP, which makes calling by IP address problematic.

To create an IP address routing rule, perform the following steps:

1. Open the **ISA Management** console, expand your server or array, expand the **H.323 Gatekeepers** node, and expand the **Call routing** node. Right-click on the **Phone number rules** node, and click **Add routing rule**.
2. The Welcome page for the **New Routing Rule Wizard** appears. Click **Next** to continue.
3. The **Name and Description** page appears. Type in a name for this rule, and a short description that will let you know what this rule is used for. Click **Next**.
4. In the **IP Address Pattern** page, type in the IP address or network ID and subnet mask, and click **Next**.

5. On the **Destination Type** page, select the appropriate destination, and click **Next**.
6. On the **Destination Name** page, select the appropriate destination, and click **Next**.
7. On the **Routing Rule Metric** page, enter the appropriate metric, and click **Next**.
8. On the last page of the wizard, click **Finish** to complete the rule.

Managing the Gatekeeper

There are relatively few housekeeping and setup procedures for the H.323 Gatekeeper Service once it's installed. However, you should be aware of a few options.

Right-click on your server name list under the **H.323 Gatekeepers**, and click **Properties**. You will see the Properties dialog box shown in Figure 10.64.

Figure 10.64 The H.323 Server Properties Dialog Box

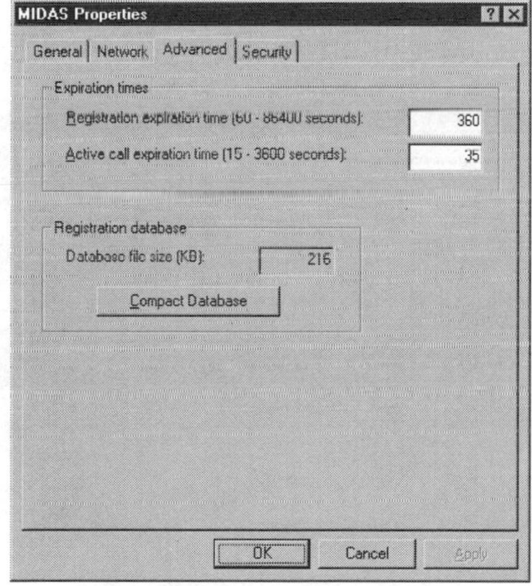

There are four tabs:

- General
- Network
- Advanced
- Security

The General tab contains information about your version of ISA Server, and provides a space for you to enter a description of the gatekeeper.

The Network tab allows you to select the interfaces you wish the gatekeeper to use. Since external users cannot register with the gatekeeper, you should uncheck any boxes that contain IP addresses for the external interface of the ISA server.

The Advanced tab allows you configure expiration times for entries in the registration database and an active call expiration time. The former setting determines how long a NetMeeting client can remain in the registration database before renewing its registration, and the latter determines how long an active call can be idle before being removed from the active calls list.

The Security tab allows you to set security on this object.

Another housekeeping duty you can perform on the H.323 gatekeeper is to create *static entries* in the registration database. Right-click on the **Active Terminals** node in the left pane, and then click on the **Register static user** entry. You will see the **Welcome** page for **the Register Static User Wizard**. Click **Next** to continue.

The **Static User Information** dialog box appears as shown in Figure 10.65.

Figure 10.65 The Static User Information Page

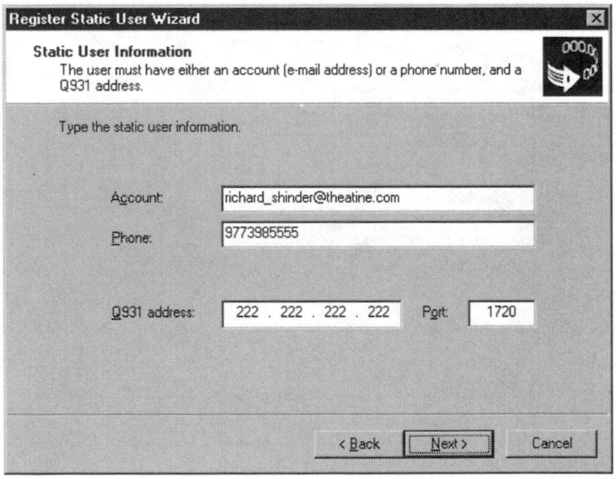

Register Static User Wizard

Static User Information
The user must have either an account (e-mail address) or a phone number, and a Q931 address.

Type the static user information.

Account: richard_shinder@theatine.com
Phone: 9773985555

Q931 address: 222 . 222 . 222 . 222 Port: 1720

< Back | Next > | Cancel

Enter an Account name, a Phone number, and an IP address for the user. Note that you cannot enter an FQDN for a static entry, so the user must have a static IP address in order to register. This type of entry is useful for users who have NetMeeting running and are directly connected to the Internet. Your internal users can call the account name or the telephone number. When the call is made, the ISA server will forward the call request to the IP address and port number you enter here. Do not change the port number if you want to call a NetMeeting client. Click **Next** to continue.

On the last page of the Wizard, click **Finish** to create the static registration.

NOTE

This discussion on the H.323 Gatekeeper Service was aimed at getting you up and running with the H.323 gatekeeper. Once you are comfortable with using the gatekeeper and have configured it by creating destinations and basic routing rules, you might want to check out more information about how the H.323 Gatekeeper Service works. The ISA Server Help File contains information on how rules are processed and has definitions for the various address types. We strongly recommend that you review this information once you are comfortable with the H.323 gatekeeper. Also, look for us to post white papers on this subject and others in the future.

Virtual Private Networking

ISA Server supports virtual private networking by allowing inbound access to the ISA server by VPN clients, and by configuring ISA Server in a gateway-to-gateway configuration. There are wizards built into ISA Server that make the process of configuring inbound VPN very easy, and they greatly simplify the process of configuring a gate-to-gateway ISA server VPN solution.

The Routing and Remote Access Service (RRAS) is required in order to configure the VPN server components on the ISA server. This is one instance when you want to have RRAS enabled. However, the ISA server VPN wizards take care of the process of enabling and configuring the ISA server to support your VPN configuration. There is no need for you to manually configure any component of the VPN through RRAS.

Configuring VPN Client Access

If you want to allow external VPN clients to dial in to the ISA server, you can use the VPN Client Wizard to allow inbound access.

Perform the following steps to allow inbound access:

1. Open the **ISA Management** console, expand your server or array, and then right-click on the **Network Configuration** node in the left pane. Click on the **Allow VPN client connections** command.
2. The Welcome page of the ISA Server Virtual Private Network Configuration Wizard appears. Click **Next** to continue.
3. The last page of the Wizard informs you that packet filters have been configured to support VPN access. Click **Details**, and you'll see something like what appears in Figure 10.66.

Figure 10.66 The VPN Server Summary Dialog Box

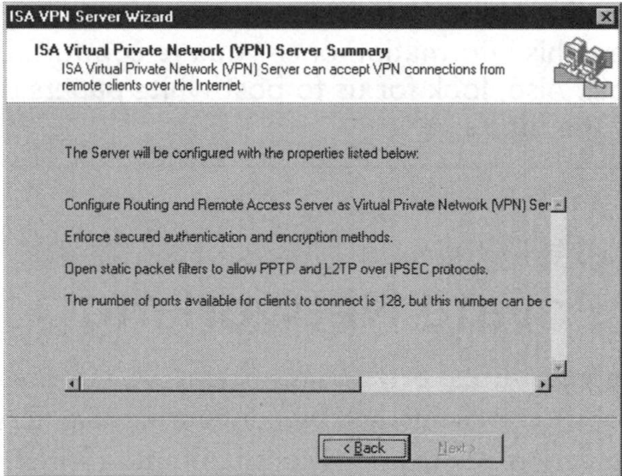

4. The dialog box informs you that the RRAS server will be configured as a VPN server. The ports listening for VPN connections will enforce secured authentication and encryption. Static packet filters will be opened on the ISA server to support both PPTP/MPPE and L2TP/IPSec connections, and the number of ports opened (for each protocol) will be 128. You can change this if you like via the RRAS console.
5. Click **Back**, and click **Finish**. If the RRAS is not enabled, the wizard will enable and configure it. If RRAS has already been enabled, it will restart the service.

NOTE

When you configure ISA Server to be a VPN server through the VPN Wizard, RRAS will not show the change in the number of ports configured. The number of ports is configured directly in the Registry. However, if you restart the server, the number of ports will show up correctly in the RRAS console.

Gateway-to-Gateway VPN Configuration

ISA Server makes it easy to configure a gateway-to-gateway solution using ISA Server at each end of the VPN. Included are Local VPN Server and Remote VPN Server Wizards. You run the Local VPN wizard on a machine that will initiate outbound connections to a remote machine. You can also configure the wizard to allow calls to be initiated at both ends of the VPN connection.

For example, say you have a branch office that needs to connect to the main office through a VPN connection. You would run the Local VPN wizard at the branch office, and then run the Remote VPN Wizard at the main office.

Configuring the Local VPN

To configure the Local VPN connection, perform the following steps:

1. Open the **ISA Management** console, expand the server or array, and then right-click on the **Network Configuration** node. Click **Set up Local ISA Server VPN Server**.
2. The **Welcome** page of the wizard appears. Click **Next** to continue.
3. The **ISA Virtual Private Network (VPN) Identification** page appears, as in Figure 10.67.

   Type in a name to describe the local network, and type in another name to describe the remote network. Note that each name must be less than 10 characters. Click **Next**.
4. On the **ISA Virtual Private Network (VPN) Protocol** page, you'll see what appears in Figure 10.68. On this page, you choose the VPN protocol you want to use:
   - Use L2TP over IPSec
   - Use PPTP
   - Use L2TP over IPSec, if available; otherwise, use PPTP

Figure 10.67 The ISA Virtual Private Network (VPN) Identification Page

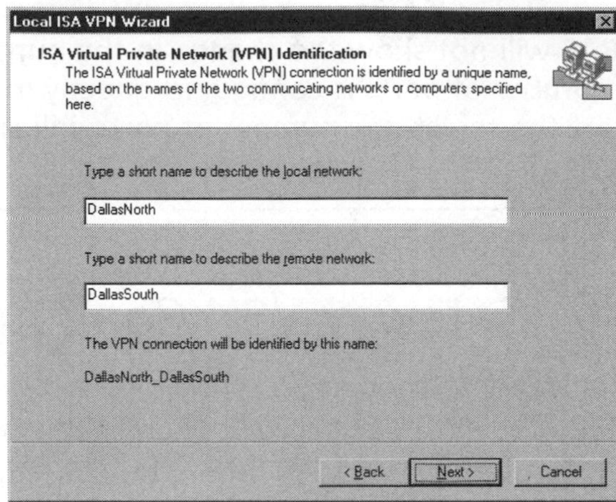

In this example, we'll choose the option that lets us use both protocols. Then click **Next**.

Figure 10.68 The ISA Virtual Private Network (VPN) Protocol Page

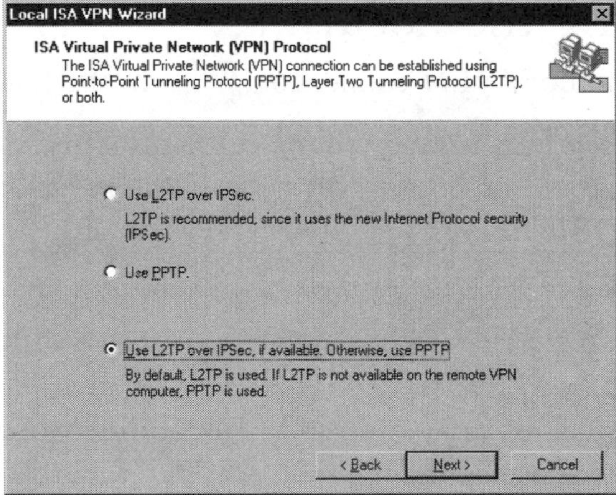

5. The **Two-way Communication Page** appears as in Figure 10.69. On this page, you can configure the wizard to create a connection that allows call initiation from both the local and the remote VPN servers.

   Select **Both the local and remote ISA VPN computers can initiate communication** if you want bidirectional call initiation.

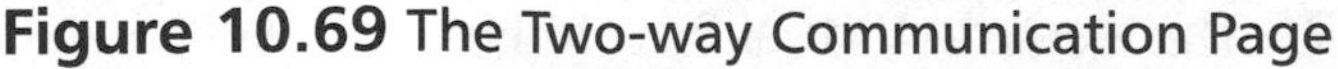

Figure 10.69 The Two-way Communication Page

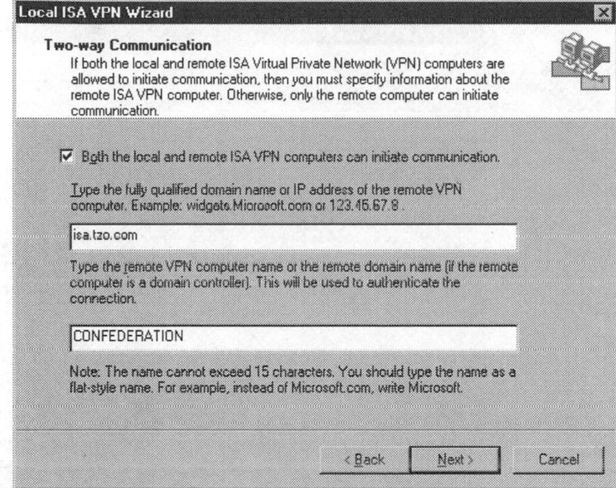

In the **Type the fully qualified domain name or IP address of the remote VPN computer** text box, type in either the FQDN or IP address of the remote computer. This entry is used to locate the remote computer.

In the **Type the remote VPN computer name or the remote domain name** text box, type in the computer name if the machine is a stand-alone or member server. If the destination computer is a domain controller, use the NetBIOS name for the domain. Do not enter the FQDN for the remote domain.

After entering the information on this page, click **Next**.

6. The **Remote Virtual Private Network (VPN) Network** page appears as in Figure 10.70. On this page, enter a range of IP addresses included on the remote network. This entry is used to create a static route that can be used to route calls to the remote network through a VPN demand-dial interface. Be sure to include all the network IDs on the remote network. Click **Add** to add more IP address ranges. If you need to remove a range, select the range, and click **Remove**.

   After entering in your IP address ranges, click **Next**.

7. The **Local Virtual Private Network (VPN) Network** page appears as in Figure 10.71.

Figure 10.70 The Remote Virtual Private Network (VPN) Network Page

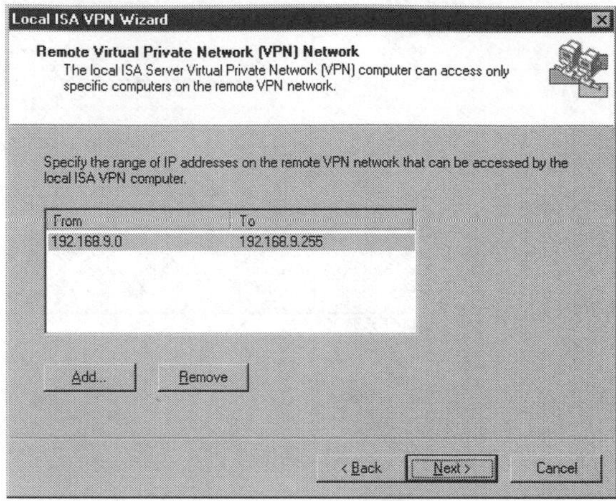

Figure 10.71 The Local Virtual Private Network (VPN) Network

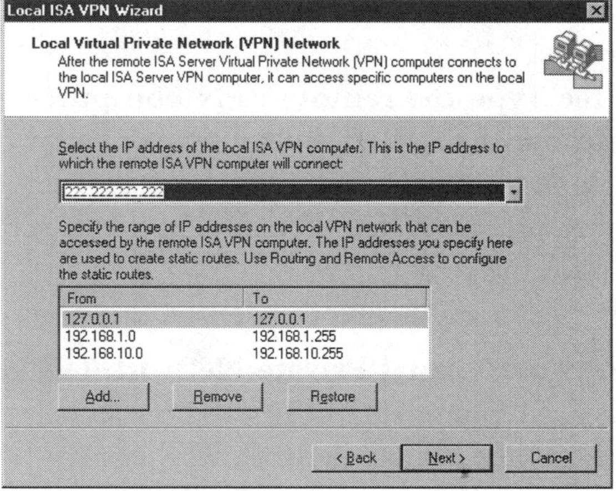

On this page, you tell the wizard what network IDs or ranges of IP addresses are on the local network. This will allow the wizard to configure the remote computer with static routing table entries that will route packets to these IP addresses through a virtual demand-dial interface on the remote computer to the local network. Make sure that you enter all the ranges of IP addresses that you want the remote network to access.

Note that there is a route for IP address 127.0.0.1. This is included because these entries are drawn from the local routing table. You do not want this address to be routed, so be sure to click on this **loopback** entry, and click **Remove** before going to the next page. You can add more IP address ranges by clicking **Add**, and remove existing ones by clicking **Remove**. If you accidentally remove a range, and want to get it back, click **Restore**.

After you are finished adding the local address ranges, click **Next**.

8. The **ISA Server VPN Configuration File** page appears as in Figure 10.72. On this page, enter the name of the .vpc file the wizard will create. You will use this file on the remote VPN server to configure the remote VPN server settings. Enter a password, and confirm the password.

   After entering this information, click **Next**.

Figure 10.72 The ISA VPN Computer Configuration File Page

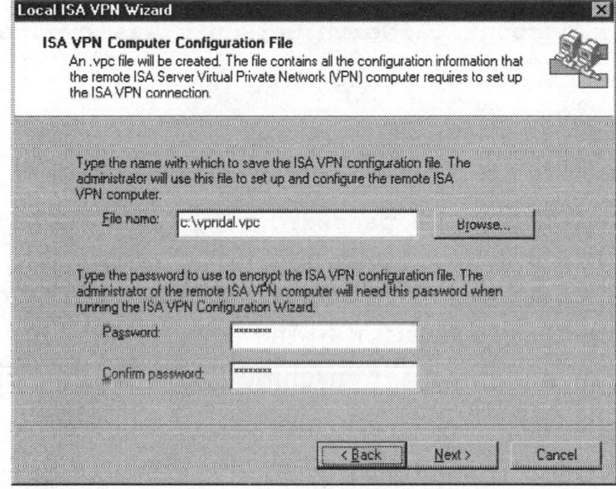

9. The last page of the wizard allows you to review your settings. Click **Details**. You'll see text similar to the following describing your configuration:

```
ISA Server Virtual Private Network (VPN) connection identification:
      DalNorth_DalSouth will be created on this router.
      DalSouth_DalNorth will be written to file.
VPN protocol type:
      Use L2TP over IPSec, if available. Otherwise, use PPTP.
Destination address of the remote ISA Server computer:
      isa.tzo.com
Dial-out credentials used to connect to remote computer running
ISA Server:
```

```
        User account: DalSouth_DalNorth.
        Domain name: CONFEDERATION.
Remote Network IP addresses range:
        192.168.9.0 - 192.168.9.255.
Remote ISA computer configuration:
        IP address of this machine: 222.222.222.222.
        Local Network IP addresses range:
                192.168.1.0 - 192.168.1.255.
                192.168.10.0 - 192.168.10.255.
The configuration file created for the remote ISA Servercomputer:
        c:\vpndal.vpc
Dial-in credentials created:
        The user account DalNorth_DalSouth was created on this computer,
        with the password set to never expire.
        Note:
        A strong password was generated for the user account.
        Changes made to the password will need to be applied to the
        dial-on-demand credentials of the remote computer.
```

Note that in addition to the demand-dial interface, a user account has been created on the machine that will allow the remote router to dial in to the local machine. When you run the wizard on the remote machine, a user account will also be created on that machine to allow the local machine to dial in using the virtual routing interface.

10. After reviewing the configuration, click **Back**, and then click **Finish**.

You can open the Routing and Remote Access console to see that a new static route has been added, as well as a new demand-dial interface that will be used to access the destination network included in the static route.

Configuring the Remote VPN

After you have completed the Local VPN Wizard and created the .vpc file, copy the file to a floppy disk, or e-mail it to the remote site. Once the file is available at the remote site, you can begin to create the VPN interface on the remote computer to complete the gateway-to-gateway VPN configuration.

Perform the following steps on the remote VPN server:

1. Open the **ISA Management** console, expand your server or array, and right-click on the **Network Configuration** node in the left pane. Click **Set Up Remote ISA VPN Server**.
2. You will see the Welcome page as shown in Figure 10.73. Click **Next** to continue.

Figure 10.73 The Remote ISA Server VPN Configuration Welcome Page

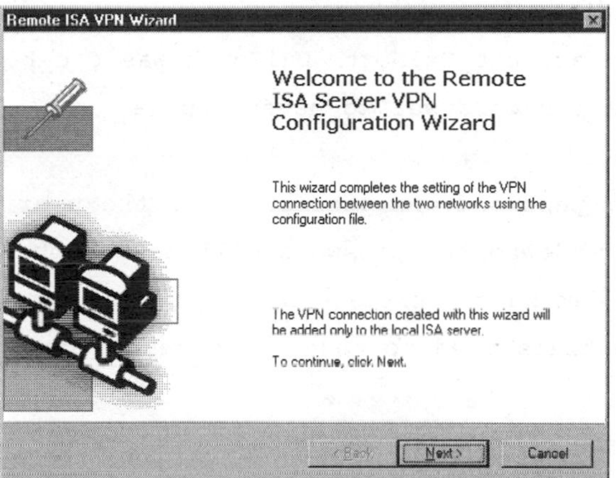

3. The **ISA VPN Computer Configuration File** page appears as in Figure 10.74. On this page, enter the path to the .vpc file that you've created. You can click **Browse** to find the file on the hard disk or floppy. Enter the same password as you used when you created the file. Click **Next**.

Figure 10.74 The ISA VPN Computer Configuration File Page

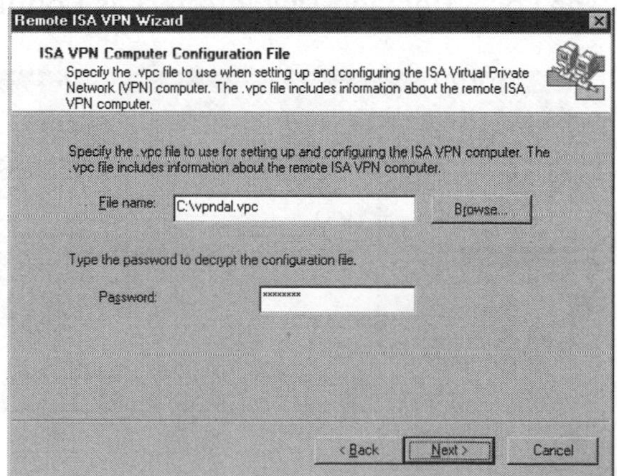

4. On the last page of the wizard, you can review the settings by clicking **Details**. You will see something like what appears here:

```
Configuration read from file:
ISA Server Virtual Private Network (VPN) connection identification:
      DalSouth_DalNorth will be created on this router.
Destination address of the remote ISA Server computer:
      222.222.222.222
Dial-in credentials created:
      The user account DalNorth_DalSouth was created on this computer,
      with the password set to never expire.
      Note:
      A strong password was generated for the user account.
      Changes made to the password will need to be applied to the
      dial-on-demand credentials of the remote computer.
Dial-out credentials used to connect to remote computer running
ISA Server:
     User account: DalNorth_DalSouth.
```

Testing the Configuration

After running the wizard on both the local and remote computers, open the RRAS console on the local computer, and then initiate a call from a machine on the local network to the remote network by requesting a resource on the remote network. Your RRAS Routing Interfaces node will show that the Demand-dial interface has connected, as shown in Figure 10.75.

Figure 10.75 The Local Demand-Dial Interface Is Connected

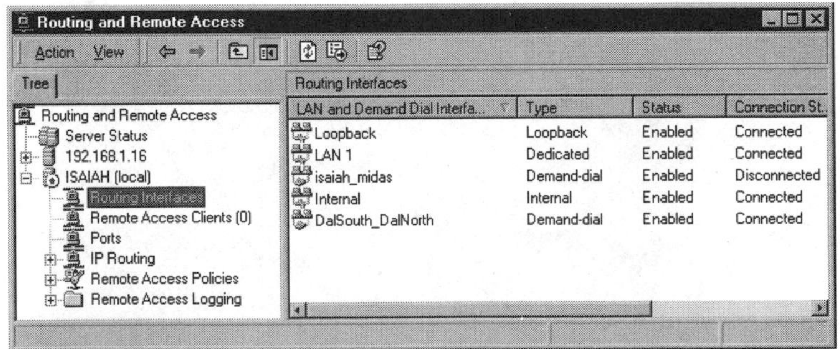

Click on the **Port** node in the RRAS console, and you'll see the status of the VPN port as **Active**, as shown in Figure 10.76.

Figure 10.76 The VPN Port Is Active

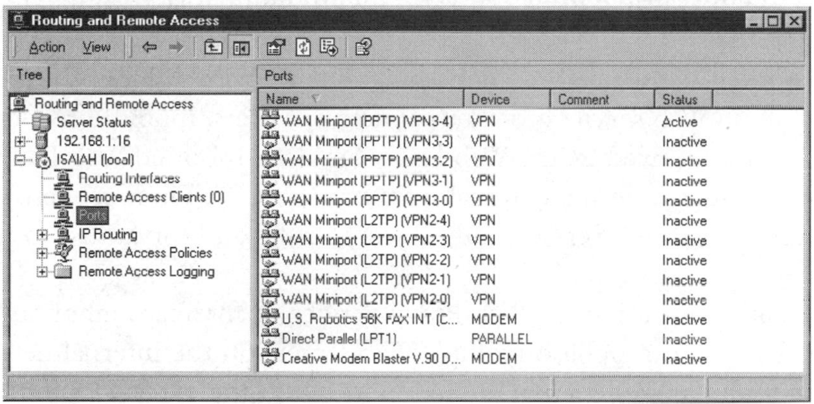

To view the static routes created to access the remote network, click on the **Static Routes** node in the RRAS console, and you'll see something like what appears in Figure 10.77.

Figure 10.77 The Static Routes Node in the RRAS Console

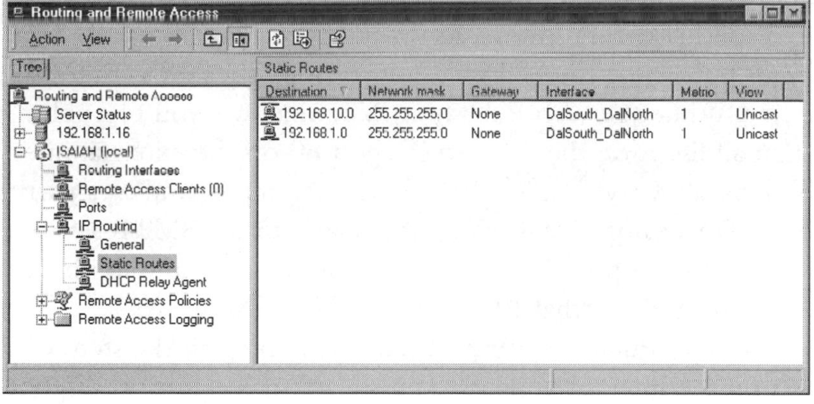

Summary

In this chapter, you learned about publishing services to external network users. By publishing services, you can maintain services on your internal network, and safely make them available to external users with minimal risk from external intruders.

We first discussed secure Web publishing. The Web Publishing Wizard makes it easy to publish Web services to external network users. Inbound requests for Web services are received by the Web Proxy Service's Inbound Web Requests Listener, which listens on the external interface's port 80. These requests are processed by the Web Proxy Service, and subject to rules and forwarded to internal servers.

The advantage of using the Web Proxy Service to intercept inbound Web requests is that you can publish multiple Web servers on the internal network. You can publish multiple Web servers through port 80 on the external interface of the ISA server, because the Web proxy server can read the destination Web site address in the request, and compare that information to the Web publishing rules. If a destination set in one of those rules contains an entry that matches the request, it will be forwarded to the internal Web server.

We then discussed server publishing. The Server Publishing Wizards allow you to publish servers on the internal network based on protocol definitions. If there is a protocol definition that allows the primary connection for inbound access, then you can use the definition in a server publishing rule.

The server publishing method isn't quite as sophisticated as the Web publishing method. While the Web Publishing Wizard allows you to publish multiple Web sites that all listen on the ISA server's port 80 on the external interface, server publishing allows you to publish a single service bound to a particular port per IP address. For example, after you publish an internal SMTP server, that server will be bound to port 25, and you will not be able to publish any other mail servers on port 25 on that IP address.

The Secure Mail Publishing Wizard walks you through the steps of publishing a mail server on the internal network. The wizard makes it easy to select the appropriate mail-related protocols, and automatically configures the protocol rules required to publish the internal mail server. The wizard also supports enabling message screening for mail coming in to, and out of, the internal network.

In this chapter, we reviewed some of the features of the H.323 gatekeeper. You learned that the H.323 Gatekeeper Service is comprised of two important components: the gatekeeper and the gateway. The gatekeeper makes decisions regarding routing of requests, and then the gateway component forwards those requests. For inbound connections, the gateway receives the requests, and then forwards them to the gatekeeper for resolution of internal network hosts.

The gatekeeper allows for audio/visual and text messages to be shared between computers using H.323-compliant applications such as Microsoft NetMeeting. You saw that clients using NetMeeting behind the gatekeeper should configure the NetMeeting application to use the gatekeeper's internal interface. External clients that are not behind a gatekeeper should configure their NetMeeting application to use a gateway that is the external interface of an ISA server computer.

The H.323 gatekeeper was designed with a gatekeeper-to-gatekeeper design in mind. When you have such a setup, the gatekeeper can easily connect to the destination gateway based on routing rules, and internal clients on both sides can connection to internal clients on the other side of a gatekeeper. This is in contrast to the fact that you cannot have a NetMeeting client that is directly connected to the Internet initiate inbound calls to an internal NetMeeting host behind the gatekeeper.

Finally, you saw how to configure ISA Server as a VPN server to allow inbound calls from VPN clients, and how to configure a gateway-to-gateway ISA server VPN solution. The configuration of VPNs is easy using the VPN wizards included with ISA Server.

A wizard allows you to enable inbound VPN client calls using PPTP/MPPE and L2TP/IPSec. After running the wizard, VPN clients anywhere on the Internet can initiate inbound calls to the ISA VPN server. The clients will be assigned an IP address that is valid on the destination remote network, and will be able to access resources on the network depending on how you configured the server.

When you use the wizards to create a gateway-to-gateway solution, you actually run two VPN Wizards: the Local VPN and the Remote VPN. The Local VPN Wizard is run on the network that will initiate inbound calls. The Remote VPN Wizard configures the VPN server that will receive the calls from the machine configured with the Local VPN Wizard. The wizards create demand-dial VPN interfaces and static routes that use the demand-dial interfaces to reach the remote network. The wizards allow you to create a one-way VPN call initiation, or you can choose a two-way call initiation so that both the local and remote VPN servers can initiate outbound calls to the other VPN server.

Solutions Fast Track

Types of Publishing

- ☑ The process of publishing services involves the use of wizards built into ISA Server to complete the publishing process.
- ☑ Web Publishing Wizards allow you to publish content contained on your internal Web servers. Services that can be published via Web publishing include: HTTP, HTTPS, and FTP.
- ☑ The Server Publishing Wizard allows you to publish services on the internal network. In order to do so, there must be a *protocol definition* to support that service.
- ☑ When you publish a server on the internal network using the Server Publishing Wizard, you include the server protocol definition required to publish the server.

Web Server Publishing

- ☑ The Web Publishing Wizard makes the process of publishing an internal Web server very easy. The wizard will walk you through the process of choosing the internal Web server and the ports you want to use on it.
- ☑ Users on the Internet will access your published Web sites via fully qualified domain names (FQDNs), such as www.isaserver.org.
- ☑ In order for your publishing rules to work, make sure you have your DNS client/server infrastructure in place. Remember, your published servers are SecureNAT clients of the ISA server.
- ☑ Firewall clients allow the ISA server to resolve requests on their behalf. This is referred to as *DNS proxy*.
- ☑ When working with a routed network, make sure the routing table on the ISA server is configured properly before even setting up ISA Server.
- ☑ Before publishing a Web site located on the ISA server, you first need to change the IP address and listening port number that IIS uses to listen for inbound Web requests.

- ☑ ISA Server web publishing rules allow you to redirect HTTP requests as other protocols.
- ☑ Destination sets allow you a great deal of flexibility in your Web publishing solutions. For example, you can use a path statement in a publishing rule to redirect a request to a particular server on the internal network.
- ☑ ISA Server supports secure Web site publishing using SSL.
- ☑ Another way to publish a secure Web site is to use server publishing rules rather than Web publishing rules. You would publish the internal server using a protocol definition for port 443.

Publishing Services

- ☑ You can publish virtually any service running on your internal network using server publishing rules. Server publishing takes advantage of protocol definitions you've created for inbound access to server services.
- ☑ When a service on the internal network is published via server publishing rules, the port number (for that interface) assigned to the server is dedicated to that rule.
- ☑ Port redirection is a feature of the Windows 2000 RRAS NAT Service. Using this feature, you can forward a message received at one port number on the external interface of the ISA server to a different port number on the internal server.
- ☑ It is highly recommended that you use the Web Publishing Wizard if you wish to publish Web protocols.
- ☑ In order to publish services on the internal network, there must be a protocol definition defined to support the server publishing rule.
- ☑ Most of your published servers will be configured as SecureNAT clients.
- ☑ ISA Server includes a special wizard that can guide you through the process of publishing a mail server. The Secure Mail Publishing Wizard allows you to publish multiple mail-related protocols at once.
- ☑ Outlook Web Access (OWA) allows users to access their Exchange mailboxes by using a Web browser.

- ☑ Publishing a terminal server on the internal network works the same way as publishing the internal interface of the ISA server.

The H.323 Gatekeeper Service

- ☑ The H.323 Gatekeeper Service allows H.323-aware applications to communicate with each other over an intranet or over the Internet.
- ☑ The H.323 Gatekeeper Service was designed to optimize the benefits of LAN-to-LAN calls. When each LAN has a gatekeeper and NetMeeting clients registered with their respective gatekeepers, users can call NetMeeting clients on other networks by using either an e-mail address or a telephone number.
- ☑ NetMeeting clients can be configured to use ILS servers on the internal network, and call other internal NetMeeting clients registered with the ILS server.
- ☑ Phone number rules can be used to route requests based on telephone number strings. These are helpful if you plan to implement multiple H.323 gatekeepers in your organization, and partition client registrations based on prefixes.

Virtual Private Networking

- ☑ ISA Server supports virtual private networking by allowing inbound access to the ISA server by VPN clients, and by configuring ISA Server in a gateway-to-gateway configuration.
- ☑ The Routing and Remote Access Service (RRAS) is required in order to configure the VPN server components on the ISA server.
- ☑ If you want to allow external VPN clients to dial in to the ISA server, you can use the VPN Client Wizard to allow inbound access.

Frequently Asked Questions

The following Frequently Asked Questions, answered by the authors of this book, are designed to both measure your understanding of the concepts presented in this chapter and to assist you with real-life implementation of these concepts. To have your questions about this chapter answered by the author, browse to **www.syngress.com/solutions** and click on the **"Ask the Author"** form.

Q: Can I publish multiple Web sites using a single IP address on the external interface of the ISA server?

A: Yes. You need to configure a destination set that includes an FQDN for each of your sites, and then have an entry in a publicly available DNS server for each site. The DNS should resolve your names to the external interface of the ISA server. After creating the DNS entries and the destination sets, use the destination sets to publish your Web sites.

Q: I want to publish an internal FTP site, but I also want to require authentication to access the site. Is there any way I can do this with ISA Server?

A: Yes. You can configure a Web publishing rule for your FTP site. After you create the rule, redirect the inbound HTTP requests so that the ISA server sends an FTP request to the internal server. When creating the rule, require authentication. In this way, you can publish an FTP server and use authenticated access at the same time.

Q: The IIS logs do not show information about which external users are accessing my Web sites on my internal Web server. I would like to get that information on the IIS server, and not have to parse the Web Proxy Service logs to get user information. I would also like to install my server certificate on the internal Web server, and not have to install it on the ISA server. Is there any way I can do this?

A: Yes, but at the cost of some functionality. You can have your user information recorded in the IIS logs, and install your certificate on the internal server and allow SSL connections directly to the server if you use server publishing. In order to do this, you must change the port the Inbound Web Requests Listener uses, and then create a publishing rule using the HTTP (server) protocol definition. You would then create a second publishing rule using a protocol definition that allows inbound access to TCP port 443. The drawback of using server publishing for your Web sites is that you bypass the Web Proxy Service; therefore, you can only publish a single Web server on the internal network using the default HTTP port, TCP 80.

Q: Can I publish an internal terminal server that is using the Terminal Services Advanced Client?

A: Yes. However, you must publish both the terminal server using a protocol definition that allows inbound access to TCP port 3389, and you must also publish the Web site that contains the TSAC server extensions. Note that when you publish a Terminal Service to be used by TSAC, you cannot change the port number on which the terminal server listens, and you cannot change the port to which the client will make its requests.

Q: I have published an internal mail server. Inbound mail seems to come in fine, but the outbound mail received by the internal mail server seems to get stuck in the queue. I have my mail server configured to resolve domain names for outbound mail, and I do not use a smart host. What might be the problem?

A: That fact that inbound mail comes in indicates that the DNS is functioning properly on the Internet, so that external servers are able to send mail to the external interface of your ISA server. However, the problem with sending mail out is probably related to the internal mail server not being able to access a DNS server that can resolve domain names to properly route the mail. The best solution is to configure an internal DNS server that can use a forwarder on the Internet to resolve Internet names. Make sure that there is a protocol rule that will allow outbound DNS queries for the DNS server, and make sure the DNS server is a SecureNAT client.

Q: I am trying to publish a multiplayer game server that requires multiple primary and secondary connections. I have configured the server as a SecureNAT client, but the games do not seem to work correctly. What can I do to fix this?

A: Some services cannot be published properly when the internal server is configured as a SecureNAT client. In order to allow such services to operate properly, you will need to configure a wspcfg.ini file on the internal server that will allow you to bind the appropriate ports on the external interface of the ISA server. You will also have to configure the internal server as a firewall client. This server publishing configuration is the same as you would have done with Proxy Server 2.0.

Q: I am using NetMeeting, and want to connect to an ILS server on the Internet. My NetMeeting client is behind an H.323 gatekeeper. When I check the directory, I see my information there, but I can't communicate with other users on the same ILS server. What is the problem?

A: When you have an internal NetMeeting client register on an Internet ILS server, it registers your internal, private IP address on the server; therefore, no one on the Internet can contact you. You could put an ILS server on the internal network and allow external users to register with that server. However, they will not be able to initiate any calls, although you will be able to call them.

Q: I would like to use e-mail addresses to contact a user through NetMeeting. How can I do this?

A: There are two ways you can contact a user using an e-mail address. In both instances, the NetMeeting client you are using to call from must be behind the H.323 gateway. First, you could configure a routing rule. This routing rule would route all e-mail destined for *@domain.com* to be sent to a gateway that you have configured in the list of destinations on the ISA server H.323 Gatekeeper Service. The destination would need to be running an H.323 gateway as well. Another option allows you to avoid configuring a routing rule. In this case, the destination domain would have a Q931 record in its DNS, in the form of *_q931._tcp.domain.com*. The gatekeeper will be able to resolve the address and send the call request to the destination gateway.

Chapter 11

Optimizing, Customizing, Integrating, and Backing Up ISA Server

Solutions in this chapter:

- Optimizing ISA Server Performance
- Customizing ISA Server
- Integrating ISA Server with Other Services
- Backing Up and Restoring the ISA Configuration

☑ Summary

☑ Solutions Fast Track

☑ Frequently Asked Questions

Introduction

In the preceding chapters, you've learned about what ISA Server is and how it works, how it fits into your network security plan, some tips on planning and deploying it in your organization, basic management techniques, how to configure inbound and outbound access, and how to use the publishing features and VPN support.

With the information we've covered so far, you should be able to install and set up an ISA solution. However, you still might not be getting the best possible performance out of your ISA server(s). There is a difference between "getting it to work" and "getting it to work at peak efficiency." In this chapter, we turn to performance issues and explore ways of optimizing ISA Server to enjoy all its benefits without negatively impacting your overall network performance.

We'll talk about bandwidth, load balancing, and scalability issues as well as application compatibility and how you can use the ISA Server SDK to customize ISA to fit your network's needs or use third-party add-ons to provide even more functionality in specific areas.

This chapter also discusses how ISA "gets along" (or doesn't get along) with other services. You will learn how to ensure that ISA peacefully coexists with Active Directory, RRAS, IIS, and IPSec, along with how you can best integrate your ISA servers into an existing Windows 2000 or NT 4.0 network environment.

Optimizing ISA Server Performance

The word *performance* has different meanings to different people. To some, computer hardware or software performance refers solely to speed—how fast a computer can complete a specified task or operation, usually measured by some *benchmark test.*

NOTE

A *benchmark* is a reference point or set of reference points against which something can be compared. This point or points can be list of performance criteria a product is expected to meet, a set of conditions by which a product is measured, or a known product to which other products are compared.

A more generic definition of *performance* includes the total effectiveness of the computer's actions, taking into account such factors as availability, individual response time, cost effectiveness, and throughput.

NOTE

To understand the difference between *speed* and *throughput,* consider the task of downloading a file over a modem connection. The connection *speed* of 50Kbps refers to the rate at which a signal travels. The *throughput* refers to the actual amount of data which can be transferred across the link in a given time period. If many data packets are dropped or damaged, the throughput could be less than the speed. On the other hand, by using *data compression* technologies, you can achieve a throughput that is higher than the actual modem speed so that with a 50Kbps connection, you might be able to get a throughput of 100Kbps or more.

Optimizing performance involves finding a way to make all components of a system work together smoothly with the smallest possible amount of delay or downtime. As with any other computing component, the struggle to achieve and maintain optimum performance from your ISA server is a never-ending one.

Hardware specifications and condition, software configuration, and interaction with other networking components combine to determine the speed and efficiency with which your ISA servers do their jobs. In some cases, ISA's performance will be affected not only by the ISA Server software settings but also by other factors unique to your network's topology and configuration.

You should assess performance issues in the context of:

- The server's hardware resources (especially RAM and processor)
- Other services and applications running on the server
- The network's physical limitations (speed supported by NICs, hubs, switches, and cabling)
- Network protocols and services that could limit performance
- Actual performance needs of your network

Before you can optimize the performance of an ISA Server—or any other system component—you must first be able to do two things:

- Establish criteria for what constitutes unsatisfactory, acceptable, or excellent performance.
- Have a way to objectively measure your system's performance to determine whether it meets your established criteria.

The process of defining acceptable criteria is referred to as *establishing a baseline.* Then you measure your network's performance by *monitoring* over a set period of time, and you compare the results to your baseline.

In the next section, we examine how to establish a performance baseline and how to use performance-monitoring tools such as the ISA Server Performance Monitor to gather information about the performance of individual components.

Establishing a Baseline and Monitoring Performance

A key factor in any performance-monitoring program is to establish a baseline. This is done by collecting information at intervals, averaged over a period of time when the network is performing normally. If you gather this information at different times of day over a period of weeks or even months, you will be able to ascertain the characteristics of normal network traffic patterns.

How Baselines Are Used

Baseline measurements are used to perform *trend analysis,* which is a fancy term for comparing performance measurements to your historical values in order to spot patterns or trends from which you can project future performance expectations or determine future needs.

Baselining is an important element of *performance management* and *performance tuning.*

NOTE

It might seem logical to perform your data collections at a time when the network is experiencing low usage, such as at night or on weekends. However, if you limit your information gathering to these times, you will not be able to get an idea of accurate traffic patterns. You must gather your data at different times—low usage, peak usage, and average usage—in order to establish a true baseline.

The component values to be measured are sometimes referred to as *metrics.* A metric is a measurement of a specific characteristic or component of a system's or software program's performance or efficiency. A separate baseline will be associated with each metric.

Defining Threshold Values

Creating the baseline gives you a road map of the normal patterns for your network's performance. After you have this guideline, you can set *threshold values,* which are measured values at which performance becomes unacceptable. Depending on what component is being measured, you may set *rising threshold values, falling threshold values,* or both. A rising threshold indicates a measurable point that, when exceeded, indicates unsatisfactory performance. A falling threshold is the opposite; it indicates a value that, when measurements fall below it, indicates unsatisfactory performance. Threshold values should be set based on the baseline data.

ISA Server's performance alerts can be set to recognize when a threshold value is passed and do one or more of the following:

- Log an entry to the application event log
- Send a network message
- Start a performance data log
- Run a specified program

Threshold values might have to be adjusted on a periodic basis as you continue to collect and analyze data. It is important to set threshold values appropriately. If the values are set too high (for rising values) or low (for falling values), you will not be notified of performance events in time to prevent an impact on your network's productivity. If values are set too low (for rising values) or high (for falling values), there will be too many notifications; administrators could be overwhelmed with messages and, like the boy who cried "wolf" in the old fairy tale, the notifications could soon come to be ignored.

The first decision to make in creating a performance-monitoring and tuning program is how you plan to collect the necessary data. Although third-party monitoring tools are available, Microsoft has provided a built-in solution that will meet many of your needs in monitoring the performance of your system as a whole and your ISA Server installation in particular. In the next section, we look at the Windows 2000 Performance console, which includes the System Monitor tool and the Performance Logs and Alerts. Then we look at the special implementation of Performance that is installed with ISA Server.

Using the Performance Monitor Tools

Windows 2000 provides the Performance MMC with all versions of the operating system. Performance has two components:

- **System Monitor** This component is used to gather measurements of performance and activity in real time and view the data in graph, histogram, or report format.
- **Performance Logs and Alerts** This component is used to record collected data to be viewed later and to set alerts to notify you or perform a specified task when a particular performance counter falls above or below the threshold you have set.

The Windows 2000 Performance MMC is accessed via the **Start | Programs | Administrative Tools** menu or by typing **perfmon.exe** at the command line. When you install ISA Server, a new icon is placed in the **Start | Programs | Microsoft ISA Server** menu. This icon opens the ISA Server Performance Monitor, shown in Figure 11.1, which is an implementation of the Windows 2000 System Monitor that includes a set of ISA performance counters as default objects.

Figure 11.1 The ISA Server Performance Monitor Includes a Set of ISA Server-Specific Default Counters

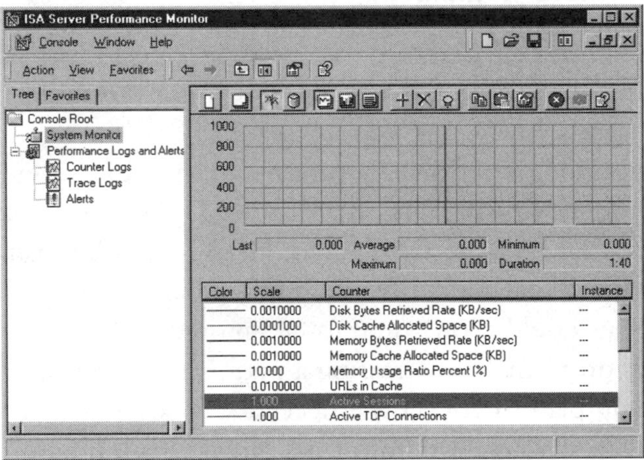

The ISA Server Performance Monitor also allows you to add monitoring of other Windows 2000 components included in System Monitor (such as processor, memory, server service, TCP, the browser service, and many more) along with the ISA object counters.

If you are familiar with the Windows 2000 System Monitor (which replaced the Performance Monitor tool in Windows NT 4.0), you will find the ISA Server Performance Monitor very easy to navigate. By default, measurements are shown in *graph view* (which can be changed, as we discuss in the next section), with the line graph for each counter shown in a different color.

Undocumented ISA

When you install ISA Server on a Windows 2000 machine, the ISA Server object counters are also added to the Windows 2000 System Monitor's list of counters that can be monitored. The advantage of the ISA Performance Monitor is that common ISA objects do not have to be individually added for monitoring but are monitored by default.

Customizing the View and Appearance of the System Monitor

Data collected by the System Monitor can be presented in one of three ways:

- **Graph (also called a chart)** Data is shown as one or more line graphs, as shown in Figure 11.1
- **Histogram** Data is presented as one or more bar charts.
- **Report** Data is summarized and presented as text information.

The line graph works best when you need to see immediate fluctuations in measurements in real time, because it traces the "peaks" and "valleys" over a period of time. The histogram is good for comparing the values of one counter to those of another at a given point in time. The report view gives you the exact numbers to work with in a form that is easy to understand at a glance. The histogram view is shown in Figure 11.2.

Figure 11.2 In a Histogram View, Data Is Presented as a Set of Bar Charts

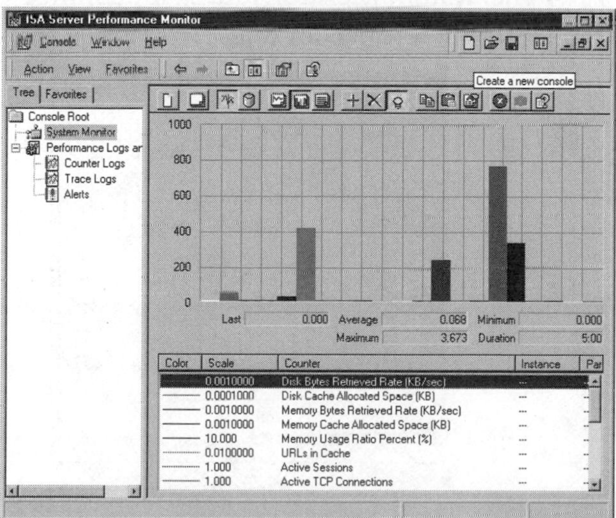

The report view is often the most useful for precise analysis of performance data, although perhaps less visually compelling. An example of the report view is shown in Figure 11.3.

Figure 11.3 Report View Summarizes Data and Presents It in Text Format

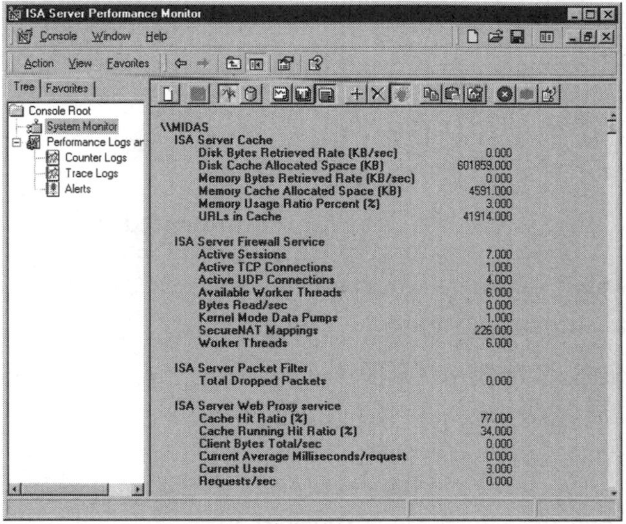

You can change the view in one of two ways:

- Click the appropriate icon from the toolbar.
- Select the view in the **General** tab of the System Monitor **Properties** sheet. The **General** tab of the Properties sheet is shown in Figure 11.4.

Figure 11.4 The System Monitor Tool's Appearance Can Be Customized Using the Properties Sheet

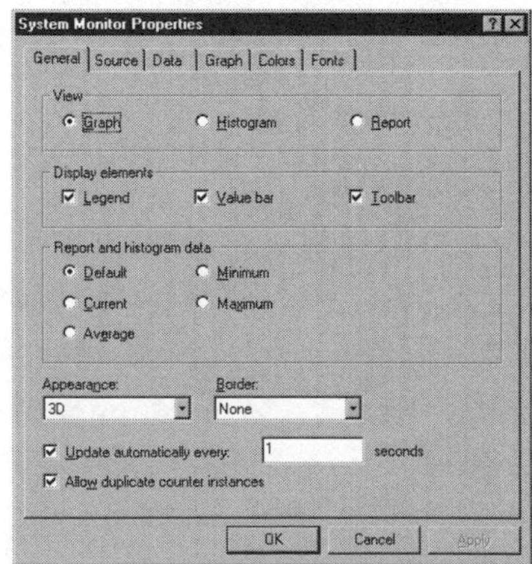

NOTE

When you right-click **System Monitor** in the left console pane, you will see a selection called **Properties**; however, this choice will *not* open the System Monitor Properties sheet referenced here, nor will selecting **Properties** on the **Action** menu. Use the **Properties** icon in the toolbar to open the **Properties** sheet that allows you to configure these settings.

In addition to changing the view for display of data, the **General** tab allows you to:

- Select the display elements that will be shown. (By default, the legend, value bar and toolbar are all displayed. To hide one or more, uncheck its box.)
- Select the way data will displayed in Report or Histogram view. (The Default value is the current value for activity being measured at that time, or the average for logged activity.) In Graph view, all these values are shown in the value bar beneath the chart.
- Select a 3-D or flat appearance. (3-D is the default.)
- Select whether to show a fixed single border or no border. (None is the default.)
- Select whether to update the display automatically, and if so, how often. (In seconds; default is one second).
- Select whether to allow duplicate counter instances to run simultaneously (by default, this is allowed.)

Additional tabs on the properties sheet allow you to do the following:

- **Source tab** Specify whether the source of the data displayed on the System Monitor is to be current (real-time) activity or data from a log file (for which you can enter the path or browse). If you select a log file, you can also specify a time range within the file if you don't want to display the data for the entire time over which the log was recorded.
- **Data tab** Allows you to add or remove counters from the display, specify the color assigned to each counter in the graph, and set the width and style of the graph line that represents each counter.

- **Graph tab** Allows you to create a customized graph with an identifying title, select which elements to show (vertical grid, horizontal grid, vertical scale numbers), and set maximum and minimum values for the vertical scale.
- **Colors tab** Allows you to customize the colors used for the grid, time bar, background, and foreground, as well as the system colors (menu bar, title bars, borders, scrollbars, and other system elements).
- **Fonts tab** Allows you to specify font style and size for the display. The selected font will be applied to all text in the System Monitor display and will be used for the text in the Report view.

System Monitor Components

The Windows 2000 System Monitor and the ISA Server Performance Monitor work in an identical manner, using the following components:

- **Performance object** This is a resource or service that can be monitored (for example, ISA Server Packet Filter and ISA Server Cache are two performance objects that can be monitored).
- **Performance counter** This is a collection of data items associated with a performance object, for which the monitor can measure a value that corresponds to a particular aspect of the object's performance (for example, Total Dropped Packets and Total Logging Packets Lost are two performance counters associated with the ISA Server Packet Filter performance object).

NOTE

It is possible for an object counter to have more than one *instance.* For example, if you are monitoring processor performance and the machine has multiple processors, you can have an instance of each processor object counter for each of the processors.

The Default Performance Counters

The ISA Server Performance Monitor console differs from the Windows 2000 System Monitor in that it already has a set of default performance counters configured. Monitoring of these counters starts when you open the Performance

Monitor. Let's take a look at each of these default counters (descriptions of these counters are also found in the ISA Server Help files, which often provide more detailed information than is available using the **Explain** button).

The following are Firewall Service counters:

- **Active Sessions** This counter counts the number of active sessions for the Firewall Service. By comparing this counter at both peak and off-peak times, you can determine ISA Server usage patterns.
- **Active TCP Connections** This counts the total number of active TCP connections.
- **Active UDP Connections** This counts the total number of active UDP connections.
- **SecureNAT Mappings** This Firewall Service counter tracks the number of mappings created by secure network address translation (SecureNAT).

The following are Web Proxy Service counters:

- **Cache Hit Ratio (%)** This counter measures the relationship between two other Web proxy counters—**Total Cache Fetches** as a percentage of **Total Successful Requests**. This counter value, together with the value of **Cache Running Hit Ratio**, indicates how effectively the cache is performing. A high percentage for these counters indicates that a high level of requests is being serviced from the cache, meaning faster response times. A zero counter means caching is not enabled. A low counter can signal a configuration problem.
- **Cache Running Hit Ratio (%)** This counter measures the number of requests served from the cache as a percentage of total successful requests serviced. This is the same as the ratio measured by **Cache Hit Ratio (%)**. The difference between the two is that **Cache Running Hit Ratio (%)** measures the ratio for the last 10,000 requests serviced, and **Cache Hit Ratio (%)** measures the ratio since the last time that the Web proxy service was started.
- **Client Bytes Total/Sec** This counter presents the sum of two other counters, **Client Bytes Sent/Sec** and **Client Bytes Received/Sec**, for a total rate for all bytes transferred between the ISA Server computer and Web proxy clients.
- **Current Average Milliseconds/Request** This counter displays the average amount of time that it takes ISA Server to process a request. A

low number indicates a faster response. A high number that remains high over a period of time indicates that ISA Server is working at maximum capacity, and you might need to add another server to the configuration.

- **Current Users** This counter shows how many clients are currently running the Web proxy service. You can monitor this counter at peak and off-peak times to determine server usage.
- **Requests/Sec** This counter indicates the rate of incoming requests made to the Web proxy service. A high value means that more ISA Server resources are required to service incoming requests.

The following are cache performance counters:

- **Disk Cache Allocated Space (KB)** This counter measures how much space is being used by the disk cache. (This will be equal to or less than the amount of space you have configured for the disk cache.)
- **Max URLs Cached** This counter presents the maximum number of URLs that have been stored in the cache.
- **Memory Cache Allocated Space (KB)** This counter measures how much space is being used by the memory cache.
- **Memory Usage Ratio Percent (%)** This counter calculates the ratio between the number of cache fetches from the memory cache and the total number of cache fetches. A high percentage could mean that you need to allocate more available memory resources to the cache. A low number could mean that some of the memory resources allocated to cache could be better used for other purposes.
- **URL Commit Rate (URL/Sec)** This counter measures the speed at which URLs are written to the cache. Note that if this rate is comparable to the value of another ISA Server cache counter, **Disk Failure Rate (Fail/Sec)**, a high proportion of attempts to write to the cache are failing, which might be due to a problem with cache configuration.
- **URLs in Cache** This counter measures the current number of URLs that are in the cache.

The following is a packet filter counter:

- **Total Dropped Packets** Displays the total number of packets that were dropped or filtered, for whatever reason.

Other ISA Performance Counters

The following performance objects are added to System Monitor when you install ISA Server:

- Bandwidth Control Performance Counters
- Cache Performance Counters
- Firewall Service Performance Counters
- Web Proxy Service Performance Counters
- Packet Filter Performance Counters
- H.323 Performance Counters

Let's take a look at the counters associated with each.

- **Bandwidth control performance counters** Five performance counters are associated with the bandwidth control object:
  1. **Actual Inbound Bandwidth** Measures the actual inbound bandwidth in bytes per second.
  2. **Actual Outbound Bandwidth** Measures the actual outbound bandwidth in bytes per second.
  3. **Assigned Connections** Counts the number of connections with an assigned bandwidth priority.
  4. **Assigned Inbound Bandwidth** Measures the assigned inbound bandwidth in bytes per second.
  5. **Assigned Outbound Bandwidth** Measures the assigned outbound bandwidth in bytes per second.

- **Cache performance counters** Twenty-two performance counters are associated with the ISA Cache performance object:
  1. **Active Refresh Bytes Rate (KB/Sec)** Measures the rate at which bytes of data are retrieved from the Internet to actively refresh popular URLs in the cache. This will relate to the configuration set for active caching.
  2. **Active URL Refresh Rate (URL/Sec)** Measures the rate at which popular cached URLs are actively refreshed from the Internet. This will relate to the configuration set for active caching.

3. **Disk Bytes Retrieve Rate (KB/Sec)** Measures the rate at which "bytes of data" are retrieved from the disk cache.
4. **Disk Cache Allocated Space (KB)** See the description under default counters.
5. **Disk Content Write Rate (Writes/Sec)** Measures the number of writes per second to the disk cache for the purpose of writing URL content to the cache disk.
6. **Disk Failure Rate (Fail/Sec)** Measures the number of input/output (I/O) failures per second. (An I/O failure occurs when ISA Server fails to read from or write to the disk cache.) A large number of I/O failures can indicate problems with disk cache.
7. **Disk URL Retrieve Rate (URL/Sec)** Measures how many URLs are sent to clients from the disk cache in 1 second and can be used to evaluate the performance of the disk cache.
8. **Max URLs Cached** See the description under default counters.
9. **Memory Bytes Retrieved Rate (KB/Sec)** Measures the rate at which bytes of data are retrieved from the memory cache.
10. **Memory Cache Allocated Space (KB)** See the description under default counters.
11. **Memory URL Retrieve Rate (URL/Sec)** Measures how many URLs are sent to clients from the memory cache in 1 second.
12. **Memory Usage Ratio Percent (%)** See the description under default counters.
13. **Total Actively Refreshed URLs** Shows the cumulative number of popular URLs in the cache that have been actively refreshed from the Internet.
14. **Total Bytes Actively Refreshed (KB)** Displays the total number of bytes that have been retrieved from the Internet to actively refresh popular URLs in the cache.
15. **Total Disk Bytes Retrieved (KB)** Measures the cumulative number of disk bytes that have been retrieved from the disk cache. If you add the value of this counter to that of **Total Memory Bytes Retrieved (KB)**, you will have the total number of bytes retrieved from the cache.

16. **Total Disk Failures** Measures the number of times that the Web proxy service failed to read from or write to the disk cache due to an I/O failure.
17. **Total Disk URLs Retrieved** Measures the cumulative number of URLs that have been retrieved from the disk cache. You can calculate the total number of URLs retrieved from cache by adding the value of this counter to that of **Total Memory URLs Retrieved**.
18. **Total Memory Bytes Retrieved** Measures the cumulative number of memory bytes that have been retrieved from the memory cache in response to client requests to the cache. A low value here could mean that memory resources allocated to the cache are not being used efficiently. A high number could mean that additional memory resources need to be allocated to the cache.
19. **Total Memory URLs Retrieved** Measures the cumulative number of URLs that have been retrieved from the memory cache in response to client requests to the cache.
20. **Total URLs Cached** Measures the cumulative number of URLs that have been stored in the cache. A low number might mean the cache size is too small.
21. **URL Commit Rate (URL/Sec)** See description under default counters.
22. **URLs in Cache** See the description under default counters.

- **Firewall Service performance counters** Twenty-five performance counters are associated with the Firewall Service object:
  1. **Accepting TCP Connections** Shows the number of connection objects that wait for a TCP connection from firewall clients.
  2. **Active Sessions** See the description under default counters.
  3. **Active TCP Connections** See the description under default counters.
  4. **Active UDP Connections** See the description under default counters.
  5. **Available Worker Threads** Shows the number of firewall work threads that are available or waiting in the completion port queue.
  6. **Back-Connecting TCP Connections** Shows the total number of TCP connections awaiting an inbound connect call to complete.

These connections are placed by the Firewall Service to a client after accepting a connection from the Internet on a listening socket.

7. **Bytes Read/Sec** Shows the number of bytes per second read by the data pump.
8. **Bytes Written/Sec** Shows the number of bytes per second written to the data pump.
9. **Connecting TCP Connections** Shows the total number of TCP connections that are awaiting completion between the Firewall Service and remote computers.
10. **DNS Cache Entries** Displays the current number of DNS domain name entries that are cached because of Firewall Service activity.
11. **DNS Cache Flushes** Shows the total number of times the DNS cache has been cleared by the Firewall Service.
12. **DNS Cache Hits** Shows the total number of times a DNS domain name was located in the DNS cache by the Firewall Service.
13. **DNS Cache Hits %** Calculates the percentage of DNS names serviced by the DNS cache from the total number of DNS entries retrieved by the Firewall Service.
14. **DNS Retrievals** Shows the total number of DNS names that the Firewall Service has retrieved.
15. **Failed DNS Resolutions** Shows the number of failed **gethostbyname** and **gethostbyaddr** API calls from the Firewall Service.
16. **Kernel Mode Data Pumps** Displays the number of kernel mode data pumps that have been created by the Firewall Service.
17. **Listening TCP Connections** Shows the number of connection objects that are waiting for TCP connections from remote Internet computers.
18. **Memory Allocation Failures** Shows the number of memory allocation errors.
19. **Non-connected UDP Mappings** Displays the number of mappings that are available for UDP connections.
20. **Pending DNS Resolutions** Displays the number of **gethostbyname** and **gethostbyaddr** API calls that have been made by the Firewall Service and are awaiting resolution.
21. **SecureNAT Mappings** See the description under default counters.

22. **Successful DNS Resolutions** Displays the number of **gethostbyname** and **gethostbyaddr** API calls that have been successfully resolved.
23. **TCP Bytes Transferred/Sec by Kernel Mode Data Pump** Shows the number of TCP bytes that have been transferred by the kernel mode data pump each second.
24. **UDP Bytes Transferred/Sec by Kernel Mode Data Pump** Shows the number of UDP bytes that have been transferred by the kernel mode data pump each second.
25. **Worker Threads** Displays the number of firewall worker threads that are currently active.

- **Web Proxy Service performance counters** Fifty-one performance counters are associated with the Web Proxy Service performance object:
  1. **Array Bytes Received/Sec (Enterprise)** Monitors the rate at which bytes of data are received from other ISA servers within an array.
  2. **Array Bytes Sent/Sec (Enterprise)** Monitors the rate at which bytes of data are sent to other ISA servers within an array.
  3. **Array Bytes Total/Sec (Enterprise)** Displays the sum reached by adding the **Array Bytes Sent/Sec** and **Array Bytes Received/Sec**, to give you the total rate for all bytes of data that are transferred between this ISA server and other array members.
  4. **Cache Hit Ratio (%)** See the description under default counters.
  5. **Cache Running Hit Ratio (%)** See the description under default counters.
  6. **Client Bytes Received/Sec** Calculates the rate at which bytes of data are received from Web proxy clients. If this rate is consistently slow, a delay could be occurring in the servicing of requests.
  7. **Client Bytes Sent/Sec** Calculates the rate at which bytes of data are set to Web proxy clients. As previously stated, a consistently slow rate could signal a delay in request servicing.
  8. **Client Bytes Total/Sec** See the description under default counters.
  9. **Current Array Fetches Average (Milliseconds/Request)** Displays the mean number of milliseconds required for servicing a

Web proxy client request that has to be fetched through another member of the array (not including SSL tunnel requests).

10. **Current Average Milliseconds/Request:** See the description under default counters.
11. **Current Cache Fetches Average (Milliseconds/Request)** Displays the time, in mean number of milliseconds, that it takes to service a Web proxy client request from the cache (not including SSL tunnel requests).
12. **Current Direct Fetches Average (Milliseconds/Request)** Displays the time, in mean number of milliseconds, that it takes to service a Web proxy client request directly to the Web server or upstream proxy server (not including SSL tunnel requests).
13. **Current Users** See the description under default counters.
14. **DNS Cache Entries** Displays the number of DNS name entries cached by the Web Proxy Service (a high count usually means good performance, because the more entries in the cache, the fewer that require a DNS lookup, which takes additional time and resources).
15. **DNS Cache Flushes** Displays the number of times the name cache has been cleared by the Web Proxy Service.
16. **DNS Cache Hits** Displays the number of times a DNS name was found in the DNS cache by the Web Proxy Service. A low number of hits means names must be looked up, which slows performance.
17. **DNS Cache Hits (%)** Displays the percentage of DNS entries that have been resolved using cached data. A high value indicates better performance.
18. **DNS Retrievals** Displays the number of DNS names that have been retrieved by the Web Proxy Service.
19. **Failing Requests/Sec** Calculates the rate per second for Web proxy requests that result in an error. A high failure rate could mean that the connection settings for incoming Web requests are not configured properly or that there is not enough connection bandwidth to handle all the requests.
20. **FTP Requests** Displays the number of FTP requests made to the Web Proxy Service.
21. **Gopher Requests** Displays the number of Gopher requests made to the Web Proxy Service.

22. **HTTP Requests** Displays the number of HTTP requests made to the Web Proxy Service.
23. **HTTPS Sessions** Displays the number of Secure HTTP (HTTPS) sessions that have been serviced by the SSL tunnel.
24. **Maximum Users** Displays the maximum number of users connected to the Web Proxy Service at the same time.
25. **Requests/Sec** Calculates the rate of incoming requests to the Web Proxy Service. A high number could mean that you need to allocate additional ISA Server resources.
26. **Reverse Bytes Received/Sec** Calculates the rate at which bytes of data are received by the Web Proxy Services from Web publishing servers in response to incoming requests.
27. **Reverse Bytes Sent/Sec** Calculates the rate at which bytes of data are sent by the Web Proxy Services to Web publishing servers in response to incoming requests.
28. **Reverse Bytes Total/Sec** Displays the sum resulting from the addition of the two preceding counters to provide a total rate of bytes transferred between the Web Proxy Service and the Web publishing servers in response to incoming requests.
29. **Site Access Denied** Displays the number of Web sites to which the Web Proxy Service has denied access. If this number is high, you might want to re-evaluate your Web access policy.
30. **Site Access Granted** Displays the number of Web sites to which the Web Proxy Service has granted access.
31. **SNEWS Sessions** Displays the number of SNEWS sessions serviced by the SSL tunnel.
32. **SSL Client Bytes Received/Sec** Displays the rate at which SSL data is received by the Web Proxy Service from secure Web proxy clients.
33. **SSL Client Bytes Sent/Sec** Displays the rate at which SSL data is sent by the Web Proxy Service to secure Web proxy clients.
34. **SSL Client Bytes Total/Sec** Calculates the sum resulting from adding the two preceding counters to provide a total rate for all SSL bytes transferred.

35. **Thread Pool Active Sessions** Displays the number of sessions that are being actively serviced by thread pool threads.
36. **Thread Pool Failures** Displays the number of requests that have been rejected because of a full thread pool.
37. **Thread Pool Size** Displays the number of threads in the pool, representing the resources that are available for servicing client requests.
38. **Total Array Fetches (Enterprise)** Displays the number of Web proxy client requests served by requesting data from another ISA server that is a member of the array, as a result of the CARP algorithm.
39. **Total Cache Fetches** Displays the number of Web proxy client requests served from cached data.
40. **Total Failed Requests** Displays the number of requests that the Web Proxy Service has failed to process because of errors. A high value could indicate configuration problems or that the connection is too slow.
41. **Total Pending Connects** Displays the number of waiting Web Proxy Service connections.
42. **Total Requests** Displays the number of requests made to the Web Proxy Service, the result of adding the **Total Successful Requests** and **Total Failed Requests** counters.
43. **Total Reverse Fetches** Displays the number of incoming request that have been served by requesting data from Web publishing servers.
44. **Total SSL Sessions** Displays the number of SSL sessions serviced by the SSL tunnel.
45. **Total Successful Requests** Displays the number of requests made to the Web Proxy Service that have been successfully processed.
46. **Total Upstream Fetches** Displays the number of requests serviced by getting the data from the Internet or from an upstream chained proxy server.
47. **Total Users** Displays the total number of users that have connected to the Web Proxy Service over the history of the service.
48. **Unknown SSL Sessions** Displays the number of unknown SSL sessions that have been serviced by the SSL tunnel.

49. **Upstream Bytes Received/Sec** Calculates the rate at which bytes of data are received by the Web Proxy Service from servers across the Internet or upstream chained proxy servers.
50. **Upstream Bytes Sent/Sec** Calculates the rate at which bytes of data are sent by the Web Proxy Service to servers across the Internet or upstream chained proxy servers.
51. **Upstream Bytes Total/Sec** Displays the result of adding the two preceding counters to provide a total rate for bytes transferred between the Web Proxy Service and Internet or chained proxy servers.

- **Packet filter performance counters** Four performance counters are associated with the packet filter performance object:
  1. **Packets Dropped Due to Filter Denial** Displays the number of packets that are dropped because the data was rejected due to dynamic packet filtering when the default "deny all" policy is set in the ISA Server configuration.
  2. **Packets Dropped Due to Protocol Violations** Displays the number of packets that are dropped for reasons other than the default filtering rules (such as those rejected because of intrusion detection).
  3. **Total Dropped Packets** Displays the total number of packets dropped, for whatever reasons.
  4. **Total Lost Logging Packets** Displays the number of packets that cannot be logged.
- **H.323 performance counters** Only two performance counters are associated with the H.323 filter performance object:
  1. **Active H.323 Calls** Shows the number of H.323 calls that are currently active.
  2. **Total H.323 Calls** Displays the total number of H.323 calls that have been handled by the H.323 filter from the time the ISA Server was started.

Understanding ISA Performance Logs

In addition to viewing the performance data in real time using the System Monitor component of the ISA Performance Monitor, you can record this data for later viewing using the Performance Logs functionality. Logs provide administrators with a permanent record and are useful for establishing and storing baseline data. You can create logs to record the data that is collected over time and analyze it to come up with your baseline values against which subsequent performance measurements will be compared.

NOTE

You can view the performance data in real time at the same time the data is being written to a log.

Logging runs as a service, so it is not necessary for a user to be logged on to the computer for the log to be written. Logged data can be saved as comma-delimited or tab-delimited text files, which can be imported into a spreadsheet program such as Excel or a database program such as Access. Logs can also be saved in binary format, which is used for *circular logging.* Circular logging is the action of writing the log continuously to a single file, overwriting the older data when the file reaches its maximum size.

You can configure two types of logs with the ISA Server Performance Monitor. In this section, we look at how to create and configure *counter logs,* which log data using the ISA performance counters discussed in the previous section.

Designing & Planning...

What Are Trace Logs?

The second type of log that the ISA Server Performance Monitor allows you to configure is called a *trace log.* Trace logs are triggered by specific system events. A trace log records data when the specified event occurs, rather than logging at specified intervals, as counter logs do. The trace log records data that is collected by the operating system or a program or service (called the *provider)*, such as Kerberos, NetLogon, or the Active Directory Service. Trace logs are often used in troubleshooting situations.

Trace logs are configured similarly to counter logs. You will be asked to specify enabled providers and configure a filename, location, and maximum file size, as with counter logs. Trace logs can be saved as two

Continued

types: sequential or circular. Sequential logging starts a new log when the maximum file size is reached (numbering the logs to distinguish them from one another). Circular logging overwrites the older data in the single log file when the maximum size is reached.

In trace logging, data is temporarily saved to memory buffers before being written to the log file. You can set a buffer size and minimum and maximum number of buffers, and you can specify that data be transferred from the buffers to the log file at specific intervals. (The default setting is to transfer the data to the file only when the buffers are full.)

Trace log output is interpreted by a parsing tool, which can be created by developers using the APIs available on the Microsoft Web site.

To create a counter log, follow these steps:

1. In the left console pane of the ISA Performance Monitor MMC, expand **Performance Logs and Alerts** and right-click **Counter Logs**, and then select **New Log Settings**.
2. You will be asked to provide a name for the new log. Type in your log name.
3. On the **General** tab of the New Log Properties sheet, you must add at least one counter to be logged. You can then set the interval at which the data should be sampled, as shown in Figure 11.5. (The default interval is every 15 seconds, but you can set intervals in seconds, minutes, hours, or days.)

Figure 11.5 Add at Least One Counter to Be Logged to the File

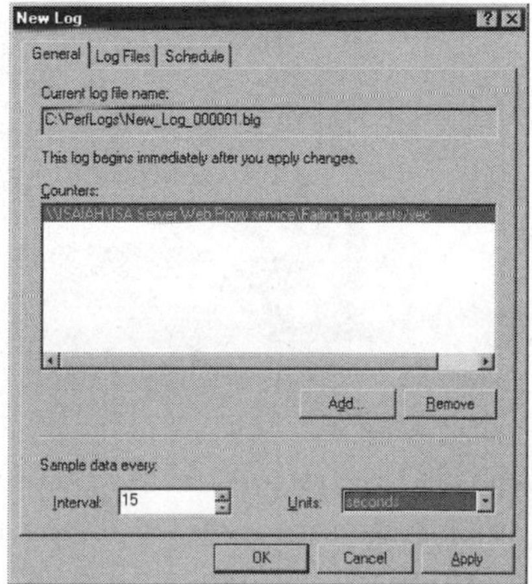

4. On the **Log Files** tab, you can set the location and filename for the log file, and if you want, you can specify that the log filename end with the date, selecting the date format (i.e., month/day/hour, month/day/hour/minute, year/day, year/month, year/month/day, or year/month/day/hour). You can also specify the use of a numeric sequence (default) and where to start numbering the log files (the default is 1). This is used to distinguish between multiple logs with the same name logged at different times or days.
5. Also on the **Log Files** tab, select the file type in which the file will be saved. Your choices are:
   - Text File CSV (comma-delimited text)
   - Text File TSV (tab-delimited text)
   - Binary File
   - Binary Circular File

   Binary files are saved with the .BLG extension.
6. Finally, at the bottom of the **Log Files** sheet, you can allow log files to grow to the maximum limit, or you can set a maximum size for the file in kilobytes (if you choose to set a specific limit, the default is 1000KB), as shown in Figure 11.6.

Figure 11.6 Use the Log Files Tab to Set Filename, Location, and Other File Properties

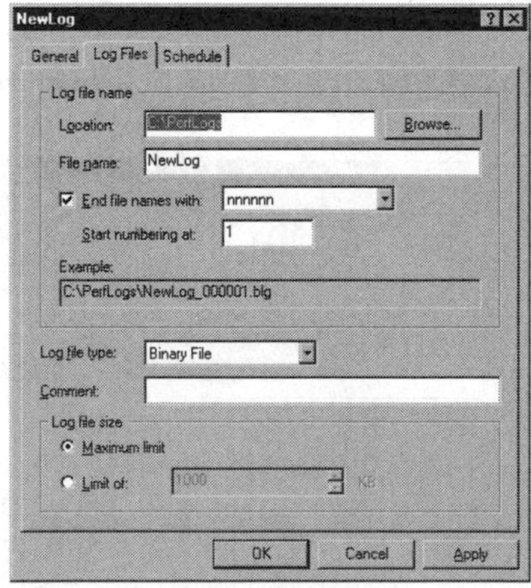

7. The last tab, labeled **Schedule**, is used to set the start and stop times for logging if you choose not to start and stop the logging manually (which is the default setting). If you set times, you can also specify what happens

when a log file is closed—whether to start a new log file and whether to run a program (which you specify), as shown in Figure 11.7.

Figure 11.7 Use the Schedule Tab to Define Start and Stop Times for Logging

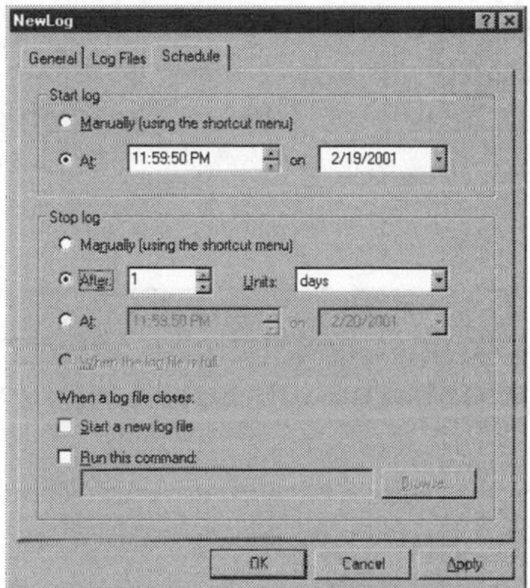

8. Click **OK** when you finish configuring the log file properties, and the new file will appear in the right details pane when you select **Counter Logs** in the left console. You can change the configuration by right-clicking it and selecting **Properties**, or you can stop the logging activity by selecting **Stop** in the right context menu. To view the log, access it in the location you specified for it to be saved. (Use a text editor such as Notepad to view the raw data in the .CSV or .TSV files, or import the file into a spreadsheet or database for viewing.)

Configuring & Implementing...

Permissions and Rights Required for Logging

To create and use logging, you must have the appropriate permissions. In order to create a new log or make changes to an existing log configuration, you need to have Full Control permission to the Registry key **HKEY_LOCAL_MACHINE\SYSTEM\CurrentControlSet\Services\Sysmon Log\Log\Queries**. Members of the Administrators group have Full Control Permission for this key by default, but if you need to give a user permission to create or change log files and you do not want to grant

Continued

other administrative privileges, you can use the **Security** menu in the Registry editing tool **Regedt32.exe** to do so. As always, exercise caution when editing the Registry.

You also need to have the right to start or configure services on the Windows 2000 computer in order to run the service that runs in the background when you configure a log file. Again, members of the Administrators group already have this right by default. You can give users this right via Windows 2000 Group Policy.

NOTE

It is a good idea to specify a limit for the log file size; otherwise, the log file can grow until you run out of disk space, interfering with other operations.

Setting ISA Performance Alerts

Although you can monitor whether and when your performance thresholds are reached by enabling logging and reviewing the performance logs, in many instances it is important for an administrator to be made immediately aware when the threshold value has been reached. This is the case, for example, if a critical service fails or if free disk space reaches a low level that could threaten normal operations of the server. You can use alerts to notify administrators so that the problem can be addressed immediately and unpleasant consequences prevented.

Performance alerts can be set to perform a selected action when a performance counter reaches the defined threshold value.

SECURITY ALERT!

Don't confuse the performance alerts, which are configured on performance counters via the ISA Performance Monitor MMC, with the ISA Server alerts that are triggered by designated ISA events and conditions and are configured via the ISA Server Management console. The latter were discussed in Chapter 6.

To configure a performance alert, right-click **Alerts** under **Performance Logs and Alerts** in the left console pane of the ISA Server Performance Monitor MMC. The first step in creating a new alert is to assign it a name. You'll note that there is no wizard to walk you through the process, as there was when you configured ISA Server alerts. Instead, you will configure the performance alert via a three-page Properties sheet.

On the **General** tab, shown in Figure 11.8, you can optionally enter a comment to further identify the alert. You then must add one or more counters that will be monitored for triggering of the alert.

Figure 11.8 Counters to Be Monitored for Triggering of a Performance Alert Are Added via the General Tab of the Alert Properties Sheet

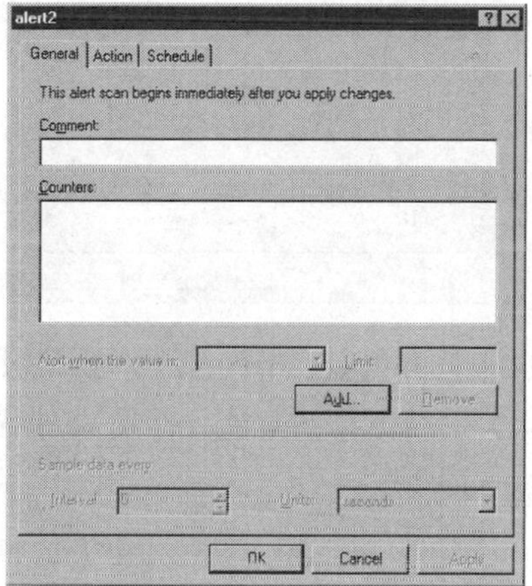

To add a counter, click the **Add** button, and select:

- Whether to use local computer counters or those on another computer (in which case, you must specify the UNC path for the computer to be monitored)
- The performance object to be monitored
- The counter(s) to be monitored (or you can select to monitor all counters for that object)

Once you have selected an object and counter(s) to be monitored, you need to configure the threshold value as well as how often data should be sampled, as shown in Figure 11.9.

As you can see in the figure, you can set the alert to be triggered when the value is either over or under a specified limit. In our example, illustrated by Figure 11.9, we have elected to monitor the Active Sessions counter for the ISA Server Firewall Service performance object. We have set the alert to be triggered when the threshold value (the number of active sessions) is *over* the limit of 100.

The data sample interval has been left at the default setting: sample data every 5 seconds. This value can be set in seconds, minutes, hours, or days.

Figure 11.9 After Adding Counters, You Must Define the Threshold and Data Sample Interval

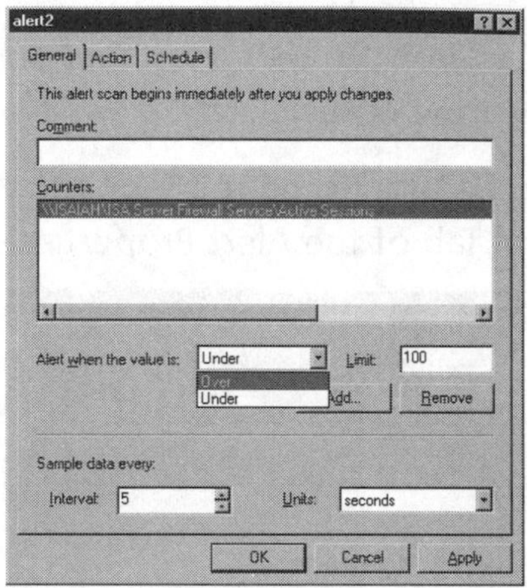

Next, you must specify on the **Action** tab of the Properties sheet the action that should take place when the alert is triggered. As shown in Figure 11.10, you can select one or more of the following:

- Log an entry to the Application event log (accessed via Event Viewer).
- Send a network message to a specified computer or user account (you must enter the name of the account).
- Start a performance data log.
- Run a program, such as a script or batch file (you can enter the path or browse for the program file).

Figure 11.10 You Can Select One or More Actions to Be Taken When the Alert Is Triggered

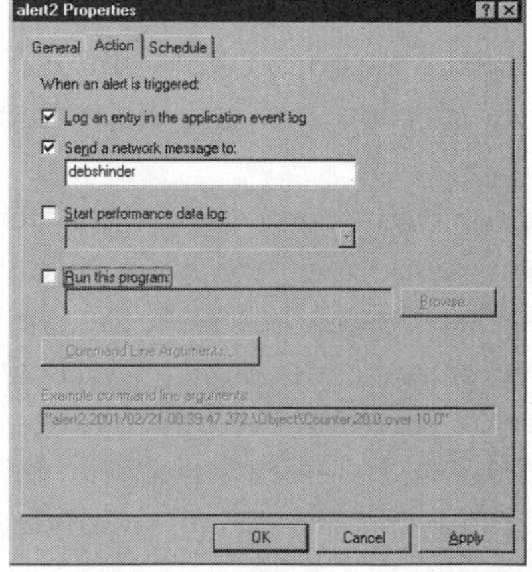

If you choose to run a program, you can specify one or more of the following command-line arguments:

- Single argument string
- Date/time
- Measured value
- Alert name
- Counter name
- Limit value
- Text message

On the **Schedule** tab, you can set a time to start and stop the scan, or you can choose to start and stop it manually using the shortcut menu. By checking the check box shown in Figure 11.11, you can also specify that when a scan finishes, a new scan should be started.

Figure 11.11 You Can Use the Schedule Tab to Schedule the Scan to Start and Stop at a Specified Time and Elect to Start a New Scan When One Finishes

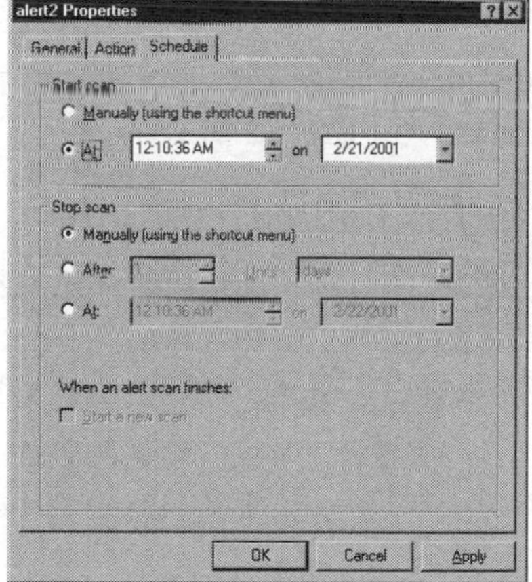

After you have finished configuring the alert, it will appear in the right details pane in the ISA Server Performance Monitor MMC when you select **Alerts** in the left console pane. If you elect to send a message to your user account or computer account when the alert is triggered, you will receive a message, as shown in Figure 11.12.

Note that the Windows Messenger Service is used for sending notifications. In order for alert notifications to be received, the Messenger Service must be running on the recipient's computer as well as the ISA Server.

Figure 11.12 A Network Message Is Sent to the Specified Account When the Alert Is Triggered

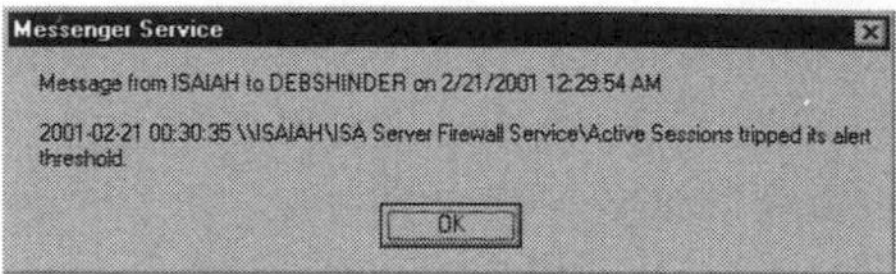

Addressing Common Performance Issues

In this section, we look at a few of the common performance issues related to ISA Server and what you can do to prevent them and/or to address them if they do occur on your network. Specifically, we discuss:

- Network bandwidth issues
- Load-balancing issues
- Cache configuration issues

We also show you how you can edit the Windows 2000 Registry to tune your ISA Server performance settings.

Addressing Network Bandwidth Issues

Network bandwidth usage is dependent on several factors: available bandwidth, number of users, type of usage, and timing of usage.

Performance Tuning for User Capacity

You can set the array properties to automatically optimize performance based on the number of users per day. To do so, right-click the name of the array in the left console pane of the ISA Management MMC, and select **Properties**. Select the **Performance** tab on the Properties sheet, as shown in Figure 11.13.

Set the slider to one of the following settings, as appropriate for your organization:

- Fewer than 100
- Fewer than 1000
- More than 1000

Performance will be tuned for all the servers in the array in accordance with the setting.

Figure 11.13 ISA Automatically Optimizes Performance Based on Number of Users per Day

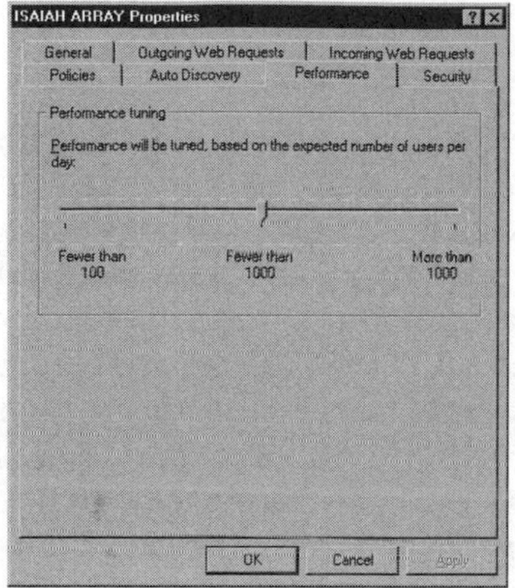

Determining Effective Bandwidth

The *effective bandwidth* is defined by Microsoft as the actual bandwidth for a specific connectivity device such as a modem or ISDN terminal adapter, or the total effective network bandwidth.

To determine the effective bandwidth, you should find out the maximum effective bandwidth for all the connections on the ISA server or array. For a dial-up device, the effective bandwidth will vary depending on several factors:

- Maximum rated speed of the device (for example, a 56K analog modem or a 128K ISDN terminal adapter).
- Maximum speed of the port to which the device is connected, for external modems and TAs; this speed is based on the UART chip and the limitations on port speed set in Windows (see the sidebar).
- Line condition; analog phone lines that are "dirty" (in other words, that have a high degree of noise or interference) will not support the top speeds attainable by your modem and port.
- Data compression allows actual throughput to exceed the top supported speed.

Configuring & Implementing...

Serial Port Speed Settings

The *universal asynchronous receiver-transmitter (UART) chip* built into the motherboard or serial port card handles serial communications between the computer and an external modem or other serial device. Internal devices have their own UART chips built into their circuit boards. The UART chip limits the amount of data that can be transferred through the port. A high-speed UART (16650) will enable faster communications. Some manufacturers make super high-speed or enhanced serial ports (ESPs) that have a large buffer to increase data flow.

However, the speed of the hardware device doesn't matter if the software caps the speed at which the serial port can communicate. Windows 2000 allows you to set the port speed, using the **General** tab on the modem's Properties sheet. You can select a maximum port speed from 300bps to 115,200bps. In order to change this setting, you must be logged on with administrative privileges.

Setting Effective Bandwidth Limits

You can specify an effective bandwidth for a dial-up device by following these steps:

1. Under the server or array name in the left console pane of the ISA Management MMC, expand **Policy Elements** and click **Dial-up Entries**.
2. In the right details pane, right-click the dial-up entry pane for which you want to specify an effective bandwidth.
3. Click **Enable bandwidth control** on the **Bandwidth** tab.
4. Enter the desired effective bandwidth in kilobits per second (for all devices in the array) in the **Effective Bandwidth** field, as shown in Figure 11.14.

You can also set effective bandwidth for a network card in a similar way. To do so, right-click **Bandwidth rules** in the left console pane, select **Properties**, and choose **Enable bandwidth control** on the **General** tab. You can then enter the desired bandwidth in kilobits per second in the **Effective bandwidth** field.

Figure 11.14 Enable Bandwidth Control and Set Effective Bandwidth for a Dial-up Entry

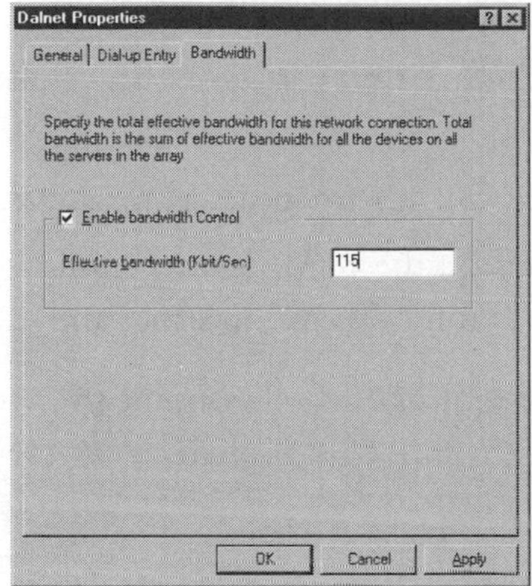

Configuring & Implementing...

About Bandwidth Control and Effective Bandwidth

The purpose of the bandwidth control feature in ISA Server can be confusing. The name might seem to imply that it allows you to allocate a specific amount of bandwidth to a specific user, group, or application. In fact, ISA bandwidth control does not limit how much bandwidth can be used; rather, it uses the Windows 2000 QoS packet-scheduling service to set *priorities* on network connections. Connections that have associated bandwidth rules will be scheduled ahead of those without associated rules (default priority connections).

In order to set bandwidth rules, bandwidth control must be enabled. Effective bandwidth is the actual bandwidth for the specified device. ISA uses your specifications in the effective bandwidth field on the **Bandwidth** tab of the Properties sheet to determine the actual bandwidth that will be assigned, taking into account the bandwidth priority that is specified for the rule.

When determining effective bandwidth for a modem, you must consider several factors:

- Speed of the modem
- Compression
- Phone-line condition

For frame relay connections, the ISP will determine the maximum effective bandwidth. Bandwidth is set in the same way as for a network card.

The steps in setting effective bandwidth are:

1. Determine the maximum bandwidth of all the connections on the ISA Server.
2. Monitor performance for peak-hour activity and generate reports.
3. Analyze, based on the reports, how much bandwidth is actually allocated for all requests (on both the internal and external cards).

When ISA Server returns cached content to a computer on the internal LAN, bandwidth rules will not be applied.

NOTE

Configure the effective bandwidth, specifying the minimum bandwidth (the *lowest maximum*) available for all devices on the ISA Server. For example, if the effective bandwidth for the modem is 56Kbps, that is the value that should be configured for the effective bandwidth, even though another device (such as the internal network card) has a higher effective bandwidth.

Addressing Load-Balancing Issues

Load balancing refers to a method of spreading the processing workload across multiple machines, for better performance and fault tolerance. ISA Server allows you to configure the load factor by dividing the ISA tasks among members of an array. Windows 2000 Advanced and Datacenter Server include a feature called *Network Load Balancing,* or NLB, to enhance availability and performance for mission-critical servers. NLB is a means of *clustering* multiple computers running TCP/IP, allowing the group of computers to be addressed by the same cluster IP addresses. The NLB service distributes incoming client requests across the cluster of computers. You can configure the *load weight* of each server or distribute the load equally among all servers in the cluster.

In this section, we discuss:

- How to configure the load factor in an ISA Server using CARP
- Interaction between ISA Server and Windows NLB

NOTE

Prior to the release of Windows 2000, Microsoft called the Network Load Balancing service *Windows Load Balancing,* or WLB.

Configuring the Load Factor in an ISA Server Using CARP

When the Cache Array Routing Protocol (CARP) is enabled on an ISA Server computer, you can configure the servers in the array so that they have different loads by setting the *load factor.* Why would you want to do this? All servers are not created equal, and if some of your servers have larger hard disks, for example, you might want those servers to handle a larger amount of the cache load. Changing the load factor increases or decreases the proportion of the load for a specific ISA server.

To configure the load factor, select the **Computers** container object in the left console pane of the ISA Management MMC. In the right details pane, you will see a list of the servers that belong to the array. Right-click the name of the server for which you want to configure the load factor, and select **Properties**. Select the **Array Membership** tab, as shown in Figure 11.15.

Figure 11.15 The Load Factor Is Configured on the Array Membership Tab of the Computer's Properties Sheet

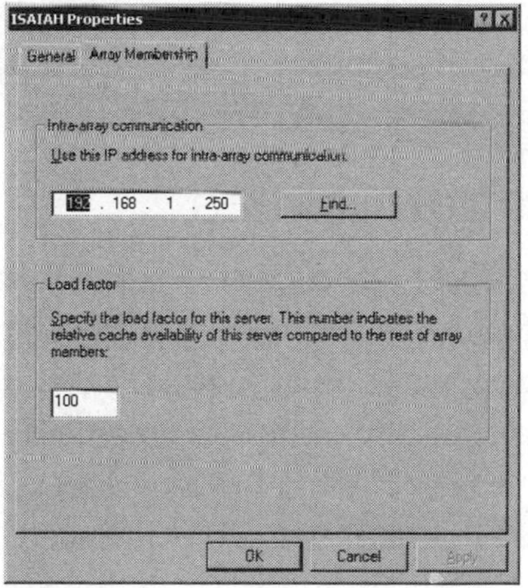

In the **Load Factor** field, specify a value relative to the other array members. The value should be between 0 and 100. A load factor of 0 would prevent this computer from handling any of the load.

NOTE

By default, CARP is enabled for outgoing Web requests and is disabled for incoming requests. You learned how to configure CARP in Chapter 8. The load factor configuration is a global setting; that is, it cannot be set separately for incoming and outgoing requests but is applied to the requests for which CARP is enabled.

ISA Server and Windows 2000 Network Load Balancing

If you are using Windows 2000 NLB on your network, you should not enable CARP on incoming Web requests. The reason for this is that the load-balancing driver will determine to which server the requests should be directed and route each request to one of the servers in the array.

External clients will not have the autoconfiguration script, so they can't perform resolution themselves. Thus, it is more efficient, from a performance standpoint, to have CARP disabled for external (incoming) requests, because it will result in the eventual caching of the Web objects on each of the servers.

Note that, for internal clients, the autoconfiguration script performs basically the same task as NLB; the Web proxy client has a list of all members of the array, and if the first doesn't respond, it tries another. This system provides fault tolerance. The firewall client, however, doesn't have the array information, so NLB is useful for fault tolerance.

ISA Server's load-balancing support enhances its scalability, making it especially suitable for use with large, high-traffic Web sites.

Cache Configuration Issues

Performance—specifically, Web performance—is the purpose of ISA Server's caching functionality. Performance can be improved by properly configuring the cache settings. In this section, we look at how you can improve performance by configuring RAM caching and how access to frequently used objects can be improved by configuring active caching. We also discuss how performance is impacted by the hard disk on which the cache is stored.

Improving Performance by Configuring RAM Caching

Because RAM is faster than hard disk speeds, objects that are cached in RAM can be retrieved faster than those that are cached on the disk. ISA Server caches objects in both locations; by default, objects that are less than 12,800 bytes in size are cached in RAM as well as being cached on the hard disk. If an object is larger than this, it is only cached to the disk.

If your ISA server has a large amount of RAM, you can improve performance by increasing the maximum size for objects that can be cached in RAM. To do so, right-click **Cache Configuration** in the ISA Management MMC's left console pane, and select **Properties**.

Select the **Advanced** tab on the Properties sheet. In the field labeled **Maximum size of URL cached in memory**, enter a new size in bytes (see Figure 11.16). You can also change the percentage of free memory that can be used for caching.

Figure 11.16 You Can Increase Performance by Increasing the Size of Objects That Can Be Cached in RAM

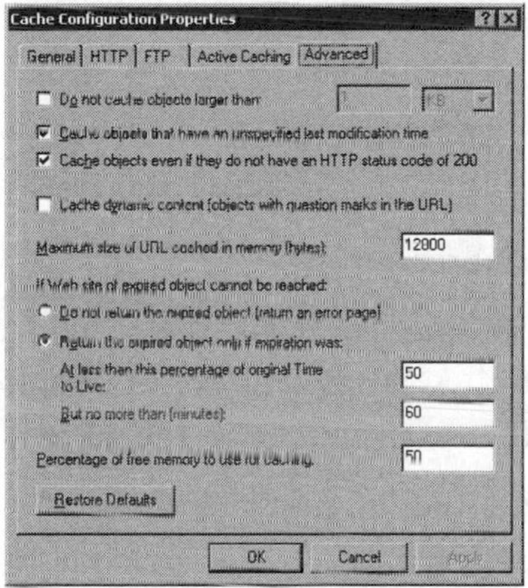

Improving Performance by Configuring Active Caching

Active caching is a means of speeding up access to files that are accessed frequently, by automatically refreshing the content of such objects when they are soon to expire. ISA automatically goes out onto the Internet and retrieves these objects based on the active caching settings. Active caching improves clients' Web performance, and because it works at off-peak hours when network activity is low, when properly configured it should not cause a hit on overall network performance. Microsoft allows you to configure settings in accordance with those factors that are most important in your situation.

One issue to consider is freshness of objects in cache. If an object is in cache and its TTL hasn't expired, the client will get the cached object and not the page on the Web site, which might have changed. The need for the most current content must be balanced against the desire for higher performance.

To enable active caching, select the **Active Caching** tab on the Cache Configuration Properties sheet and check the check box (by default, active caching is disabled), as shown in Figure 11.17.

Figure 11.17 Active Caching Balances Client Web Performance against Network Traffic

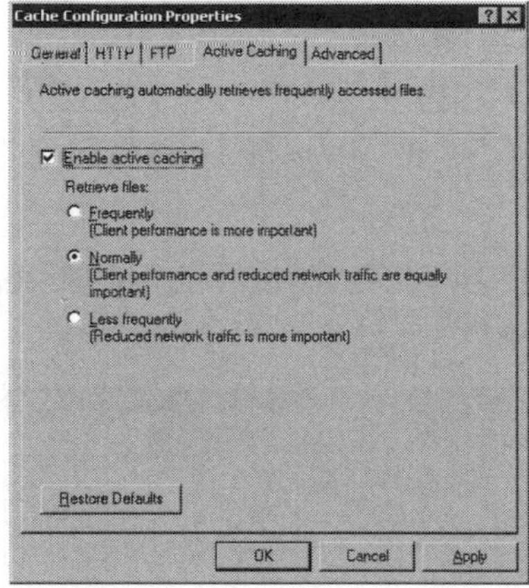

You can choose one of three settings:

- **Frequently** All the most popular objects will be downloaded to the cache regularly, so they are not allowed to expire. This makes it more likely that a client request will be in the cache.
- **Normally** Objects will be updated frequently, but network performance is also considered.
- **Less Frequently** Some popular objects will be cached automatically; however, network load/performance will be given top priority.

If client Web performance is most important, choose the first setting. The second (Normally) is the default setting.

Performance Issues Associated with Passive Caching Settings

The settings on the **HTTP** tab control passive caching behavior. These settings allow you to control the expiration of objects in cache. You can select from three standard settings:

- Frequently (objects expire immediately)
- Normally
- Less frequently

A fourth option is to set a specific TTL for objects in cache. The settings you select here can adversely impact performance in conjunction with the settings you have configured for active caching. For example, the worst possible combination of settings for cache performance would be to select **Less frequently** on the Active caching page and **Frequently** on the HTTP page. In this case, the TTL for objects in the cache will expire immediately, but the automatic update of objects by active caching will occur on a less frequent basis. Thus ISA Server will have to go out on the Internet to retrieve objects requested by clients rather than being able to return them from cache.

NOTE

Configuring the cache settings is discussed in more detail in Chapter 8.

Improving Performance by Cache Drive Configuration

You are prompted, during the installation of ISA Server in cache or integrated mode, to select the disk partition(s) on the local computer on which the cache will be stored. This partition must be formatted in NTFS.

For best performance, the cache should be stored on a physical disk that is fast and a different disk from those on which the Windows 2000 operating system and the ISA Server software are installed.

NOTE

Disk speed is indicated by *seek time* in milliseconds (for example, 9ms; a lower number indicates a faster disk) and *rpm* (for example, 7200rpm; a higher number indicates a faster disk). SCSI disks are generally faster than IDE disks.

By default, the installation program sets a default cache size of 100MB on the largest NTFS partition on the computer. You can configure the cache drive(s) by expanding the **Cache Configuration** object in the left console pane of the ISA Server Management MMC, selecting **Drives**, and double-clicking the server name in the right details pane. This sequence displays the server's drives Properties sheet, shown in Figure 11.18.

You need to know which drive letter represents a partition on which of your physical disks in order to choose the best location for the cache. You also need to know where your <systemroot> directory is located and to which disk ISA Server was installed.

Figure 11.18 You Can Change the Cache Drive Settings for Better Performance

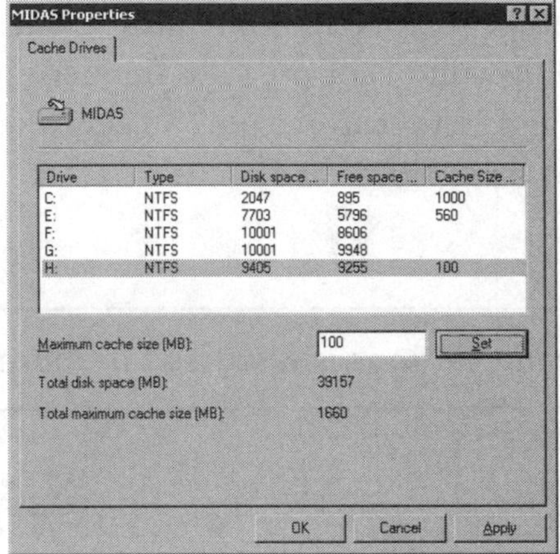

NOTE

The ISA Server cache can only be assigned to partitions that have designated drive letters, although Windows 2000 allows you to format a partition without a drive letter and mount it to an NTFS folder.

Editing the Windows 2000 Registry to Tune ISA Performance Settings

Several settings can be used to fine-tune performance that cannot be configured via the ISA interface. Changing these settings requires that you edit the Windows 2000 Registry.

SECURITY ALERT!

It is always imperative that you exercise caution when making any changes to the Registry. Incorrectly editing the Registry can create serious problems or even render your system unbootable. It is wise to back up valuable data prior to modifying the Registry.

To make these changes, you can use either of two Registry editing tools provided with Windows 2000: **Regedit** or **Regedt32**. You can start either one by typing its name at the **Run** prompt.

The Registry keys that you can edit to tune the performance of your ISA Server are located in the HKEY_LOCAL_MACHINE\System\CurrentControlSet\Services path, shown in Figure 11.19.

Figure 11.19 The Registry Keys Used to Tune ISA Performance Are Found Under HKEY_LOCAL_MACHINE\System\CurrentControlSet\Services

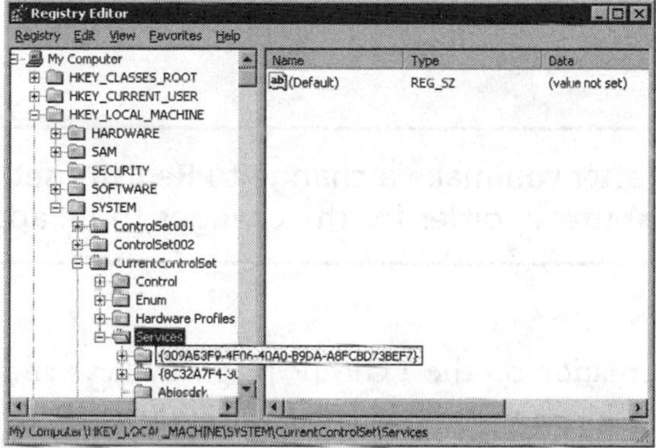

The following keys can be configured for ISA performance optimization:

- **\W3Proxy\Parameters\OutstandAccept** The value set for this key controls the number of accepted pending connections before new connection requests are rejected. A high value minimizes the number of rejected connection requests.
- **\Tcpip\Parameters\MaxUserPort** The value set in this key controls the number of TCP/IP ports that can be allocated by a client making a connection request. Setting the value to 0000ffff in hexidecimal (65,535 in decimal) sets the range for client port numbers to the maximum.

The following keys can be added (**Edit | New | Key** in the Registry Editor menu) and configured for optimum performance:

- **\W3PCache\Parameters\TZPersistIntervalThreshold** This key can be used to set a maximum time interval in minutes that will be lost when cache is recovered after the W3Proxy service is stopped unexpectedly.
- **\W3Cache\Parameters\RecoveryMruSizeThreshold** You can use this key to set a time interval in minutes in which the content cached will be recovered first from the time the W3Proxy service is stopped unexpectedly.

- **\W3Proxy\Parameters\MaxClientSession** You can use this key to control the size of the pool for the client session object. A client session object will be freed and its memory returned to system memory management only if the pool has a number of objects that exceeds this value. Freeing objects is time consuming, so you can cause objects to be freed less frequently by setting this key to a high value.
- **\Tcpip\Parameters\TcpTimedWaitDelay** This value sets a time interval in seconds that will pass before a socket is reused for a new connection.

NOTE

In most cases, after you make a change to Registry settings, you must restart the computer in order for the changes to be applied.

For general information on the TCP/IP Registry keys and what they do, see the Microsoft white paper entitled *MS Windows 2000 TCP/IP Implementation Details* on the Microsoft Web site at www.microsoft.com/technet/win2000/win2ksrv/technote/tcpipimp.asp.

There are also a number of Web sites that provide information on how to tweak Registry settings to provide for higher performance with cable modems and DSL connections.

Some vendors provide optimization software that can be used to change these settings using a friendly interface. For example, Accelerate 2000 (www.webroot.com) helps you optimize MTU and other TCP/IP settings for maximum connection speed.

Customizing ISA Server

ISA Server's functionality can be enhanced in several ways. Microsoft provides the ISA Server Software Developer's Kit (SDK), which allows developers to extend ISA by creating components that are built on or that work with ISA Server. Several third-party software vendors have already developed add-on products that add flexibility to the ISA product. In this section, we take a look at the SDK and a few of the available third-party add-ons.

Using the ISA Server Software Developer's Kit

The ISA Server SDK is a comprehensive collection of development tools and sample scripts that can be used to build new, custom features that enhance ISA's firewall, caching, and management functionality.

The SDK comes with the ISA Server software. It includes full API documentation as well as useful sample extensions such as management tools, application and Web filters, and user interface extensions.

Administration Scripts

Administration scripts can simplify and automate administrative tasks. Developers can create custom administration scripts, or administrators can use the sample scripts included with the SDK.

Sample Administration Scripts

Sample administration scripts provided with the ISA SDK include:

- **Add_Dod** A VBScript sample that demonstrates how to add a new Dialup Entry and set the Dialup Entry Credentials.
- **AdditionalKey** A VBScript script that demonstrates how to change an additional key.
- **AddLATEntry** A VBScript script that demonstrates how to add an IP range to a LAT.
- **AddScheduledContentDownload** A VBScript that receives an array name, a URL, and a job name and adds a scheduled content download job.
- **ApplicationFilterList** A script that prompts the user to enter an array, then lists the application filters of the selected array.
- **CacheSettings** A script that prompts the user to enter the name of an array, then displays the cache settings of that array.
- **ConstructLAT** A script that demonstrates how to construct the LAT of an array based on its NICs.
- **DisableScheduledContentDownloads** A VBScript that disables all prefetcher jobs on Monday and Wednesday on a given array.
- **Enterprise_Destination** A VBScript that adds a new destination set to the Enterprise, sets the array policy to use Array and Enterprise Policies,

and configures the new rule to use the Enterprise destination. (Can be run only by an enterprise administrator.)

- **FetchUrl** A VBScript script that causes the Web proxy to fetch an object and store it in the Web proxy's cache. The cached object can be stored under a different name than the source object.
- **ListServers** A script that lists all the servers in a given array through the name property of the FPCArray object.
- **FindScheduledContentDownload** A VBScript that receives an array name and a URL and checks to see if any job includes that URL.
- **SetUpstreamRouting** A VBScript script that demonstrates how to set up upstream routing to another server using the RoutingRules collection and the RouteEntity object.
- **ShowAllProtocolRules** A script that lists all the protocol rules of an array by looping through the PrxProtocolRules collection.
- **ShowAllRoutingRules** A VBScript script that lists all the routing rules of an array by looping through the RoutingRules collection. The script also lists whether or not each routing rule is enabled or disabled and the action that the rule follows.
- **StaticFilter** A VBScript script that demonstrates how to add a static packet filter that allows NTP communication from the ISA server to the Internet.

Running Administration Scripts

You can run the sample scripts simply by double-clicking the script name in the sdk\samples\admin\Scripts directory, located on the ISA Server CD. You can also run a script by typing its full path at the **Run** prompt.

Some scripts might prompt you to enter information before performing their tasks. For example, when you run the CacheSettings script, you will be asked to enter an array name (or you can leave the field blank and click **OK** to specify the first array listed in the ISA Server management console), as shown in Figure 11.20.

Figure 11.20 The CacheSettings Script Prompts You to Specify an Array Name

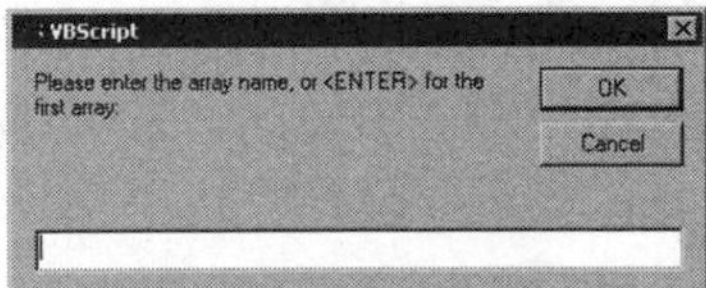

When you enter the information or click OK, the script will run and display its results, as shown in Figure 11.21.

Figure 11.21 The Script Runs and Displays the Results

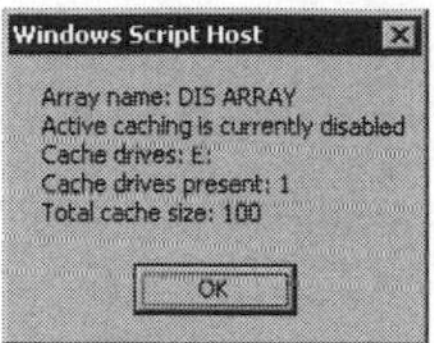

NOTE

Some of the sample admin scripts are provided in both Visual Basic Script (VBS) and Java Script (JS) versions; others are provided only in VBS.

Sample Filters

In addition to the sample scripts, Microsoft has provided in the SDK a number of sample filters to demonstrate how to create firewall, Web, and application filters. A readme.txt file is supplied with each sample filter, an example of which is shown in Figure 11.22.

Figure 11.22 Each Sample Filter Includes a Readme File That Provides More Information

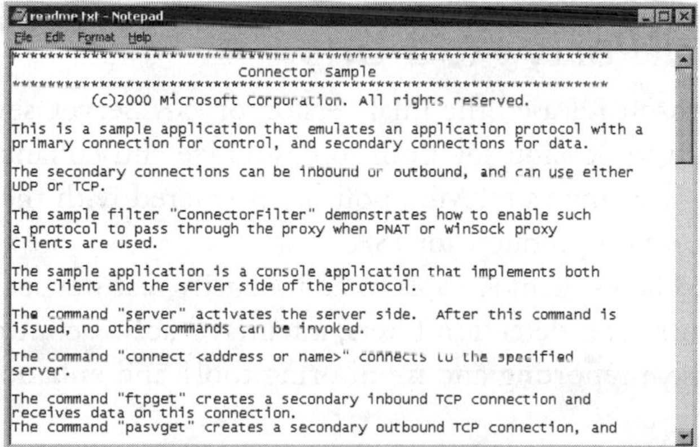

readme.txt - Notepad

File Edit Format Help

Connector Sample

(c)2000 Microsoft Corporation. All rights reserved.

This is a sample application that emulates an application protocol with a primary connection for control, and secondary connections for data.

The secondary connections can be inbound or outbound, and can use either UDP or TCP.

The sample filter "ConnectorFilter" demonstrates how to enable such a protocol to pass through the proxy when PNAT or WinSock proxy clients are used.

The sample application is a console application that implements both the client and the server side of the protocol.

The command "server" activates the server side. After this command is issued, no other commands can be invoked.

The command "connect <address or name>" connects to the specified server.

The command "ftpget" creates a secondary inbound TCP connection and receives data on this connection.
The command "pasvget" creates a secondary outbound TCP connection, and

The readme.txt file provides additional information about the filter and the purpose of each file included in the sample. The following are descriptions of included sample filters:

- **Connector** A console application that emulates an application protocol with a primary connection for control and secondary connections for data. The secondary connections can be inbound or outbound and can use either UDP or TCP.
- **ConnectorFilter** Enables a complex protocol that requires secondary connections on random ports and makes it possible for the Connector sample to work through Microsoft Proxy for PNAT clients and WinSock clients.
- **DbgDump** Registers for notifications on all possible events and installs data filters on all connections, then outputs information about the events to the debugger.
- **ExeBlock** Demonstrates the use of data filters and hooking into the proxy thread pool.
- **ServerSplit** Demonstrates the use of connection emulation for inbound connections.
- **SMTPFltr** Captures and analyzes data sent by external clients using the SMTP protocol. The proxy attaches a new instance of the data filter to every inbound port 25 TCP session. The filter can be configured to look for a particular string in the SMTP message.
- **SOCKS 4/4a** Demonstrates the use of SOCKS protocol version 4/4A.
- **SOCKS 5** Demonstrates the use of the SOCKS 5 protocol.

Using Third-Party Add-ons

Even before Microsoft released the final version of ISA Server, several third-party vendors had begun to develop solutions to customize and enhance ISA's features and functionality. In many cases, Microsoft has partnered with these companies to provide complementary products for ISA.

Third-party add-ons include tools to add security features such as virus scanning, additional intrusion detection filters, integrated access control solutions, more comprehensive reporting and monitoring tools, and enhancements to simplify administrative tasks.

Types of Add-on Programs

The available add-on tools can generally be categorized as follows:

- Administration and management tools

- Reporting tools
- Monitoring tools
- Content security tools
- Access control tools
- Intrusion detection tools
- Network protocol tools

In many cases, a vendor provides one tool that incorporates two or more of these functions. Most tools provide a user-friendly graphical interface. For example, GFI LANguard, shown in Figure 11.23, creates a custom console that includes the ISA Management snap-in along with the LANguard configuration tools. It links into ISA Server as an ISAPI extension so that alerting and reporting functions of ISA are integrated.

Figure 11.23 GFI LANguard Is a Third-Party Add-on That Creates a Custom Console, Which Includes the ISA Management Snap-in

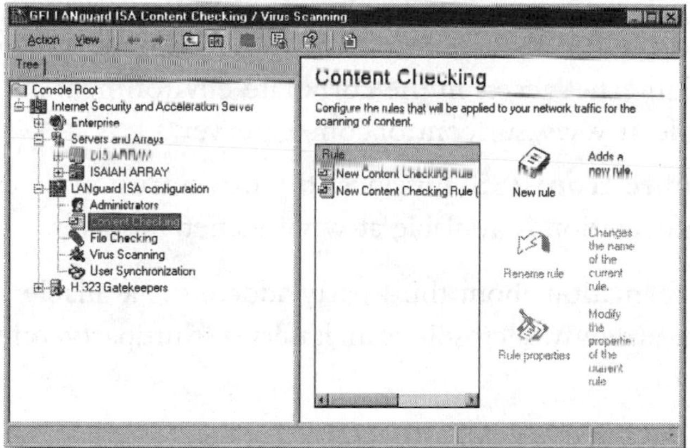

Some of the features of LANguard include virus protection (scanning of HTTP and FTP files) with automatic virus signature updates, monitoring of Internet usage (including notification to administrators when users access undesirable sites or blocking users from accessing those sites) based on keywords in the URL or Web page. Word macros can be automatically removed from communications, and potentially dangerous file types (executables, Word documents, and the like) can be "quarantined." LANguard can even verify that a file is of the type that its extension indicates (for example, it can verify that a file with the .AVI extension is in fact a video file). LANguard offers very granular control; the program retrieves a list of users and groups from your network and allows you to specify particular users when you create a rule.

Overview of Available Add-on Programs

Other add-on programs provide functionalities similar to those of LANguard. Some of the add-ons that are available or will soon be available include:

- **btPatrol from Burst Technology** A real-time monitoring tool. More information is available at www.burstek.com/isaserver.
- **LANguard from GFI** Content filtering and antivirus protection. More information is available at www.gfi.com/isaserver.
- **WebTrends firewall suite** Analyzes ISA Server activity and generates custom reports. More information is available at www.webtrends.com/isaserver.
- **SmartFilter for ISA from Secure Computing** Allows you to control Internet access in a manner tailored to your network's needs. More information is available at www.securecomputing.com/isaserver.
- **AppManager for ISA Server from NetIQ** Monitors ISA modules and services. More information is available at www.netiq.com/isaserver.
- **SuperScout for ISA Server from SurfControl** Enhances management of Internet access in the corporate environment. More information is available at www.surfcontrol.com/isaserver/.
- **RealSecure from ISS** Enhances the ISA intrusion detection filters. More information is available at www.iss.net/isaserver.

Additional information about third-party add-ons is available on the Microsoft Website at www.microsoft.com/isaserver/thirdparty/offerings.htm and at www.isaserver.org.

Integrating ISA Server with Other Services

ISA Server software does not operate in a vacuum; it must interoperate with other services and applications on the computer and on your network. In this section, we take a look at some common interoperability and integration issues. Specifically, we examine how ISA works in conjunction with:

- Windows 2000 Active Directory Services
- Windows 2000 Routing and Remote Access Services (RRAS)
- Internet Information Server (IIS)

- The IP Security protocol (IPSec)
- Windows NT 4.0 domains

It is also important to be aware of those services with which ISA Server *cannot* peacefully coexist. For example, you cannot use Internet Connection Sharing or the Windows 2000 Network Address Translation (NAT) functions to provide Internet connectivity on a computer that is running ISA Server. ISA replaces ICS/NAT, providing translation services along with security and caching.

Understanding Interoperability with Active Directory

The Windows 2000 Active Directory is a hierarchical database that is stored on Windows 2000 domain controllers. It holds information about objects on the network (users, groups, computers, printers, files, and other network resources). The Active Directory controls logon authentication, serving the same function as the Security Accounts Management (SAM) database in Windows NT. Active Directory Services provides for easy accessibility to network resources by authorized users.

Standalone versus Array Member

The way in which ISA Server interacts with the Windows 2000 Active Directory is dependent on how ISA is installed: as a standalone server or as a member of an array.

When ISA is installed as a standalone system, its configuration information is saved to the Registry on the local machine. However, if you install ISA as an array member (or promote a standalone server to array membership status), the ISA configuration information is then stored in Active Directory. This means that information will be replicated to all domain controllers in the domain. This system obviously provides a measure of fault tolerance that a standalone server does not have.

The Active Directory Schema

Active Directory is governed by a set of rules called the *schema,* which define object classes and attributes (these are called *metadata* because they describe "data about data"). The content of the schema is controlled by a single domain controller that holds the role of *schema master.*

When Windows 2000 Active Directory is installed, the schema contains a basic set of metadata. However, the schema can be extended; members of the schema administrators group can define new classes or new attributes for existing classes. The schema is also extended by some programs, which need new object classes and/or attributes in order to function.

When the first member of an ISA Server array is to be installed, you must first initialize the enterprise, as discussed in Chapter 5. This automatically makes the necessary extensions to the Active Directory schema.

NOTE

Programmers use the Active Directory Service Interfaces (ADSI), available in the Windows 2000 Software Developer's Kit, to write programs that extend the schema.

ISA Server and Domain Controllers

Although the ISA configuration is stored on the Windows 2000 domain controllers, you do *not* have to install ISA Server on a DC. It is actually preferable that the ISA computer not be a domain controller, for a couple of reasons:

- Performance of the ISA server will be improved if the computer is not a domain controller, because DC tasks require significant resources.
- Security of the domain controller is improved if you place the DC(s) *behind* the ISA server on the local network, thus allowing the ISA server to protect the DC(s) from unauthorized access.

Because Active Directory is required in order to install ISA Server as an array member, ISA servers cannot be array members in a Window NT 4.0 domain.

Understanding Interoperability with Routing and Remote Access Services

Windows 2000 Routing and Remote Access Services (RRAS) provide a collection of services that allow a Windows 2000 server to function as a full-fledged software router, forwarding IP packets from one subnet or network to another, or as a dial-up server and to create and control dial-up networking policies and virtual private networking connections across WAN links.

RRAS Components

The RRAS console allows you to configure a number of components, including:

- Enabling IP Routing to allow the server to function as a router on the local network and as a demand-dial router
- Configuring the server to assign IP addresses via DHCP or a static address pool.
- Enabling the remote access server service
- Enabling support for multilink PPP, Bandwidth Allocation Protocol (BAP), Link Control Protocol (LCP) extensions, and/or software compression
- Selecting an authentication method for remote access clients and demand-dial routers, using Windows authentication or RADIUS
- Selecting one or more authentication protocols (EAP, MS-CHAPv1 or v2, CHAP, SPAP, PAP) and allowing remote access without authentication
- Configure remote access logging properties
- Create demand-dial routing interfaces
- View remote access client connections
- Configure ports (modem, PPTP/L2TP, parallel routing)
- Add and configure routing protocols (IGMP, NAT, RIP, OSPF)
- Configure a DHCP relay agent
- Create remote access policies
- Configure static routes and view the Windows 2000 routing table

RRAS and ISA Server

RRAS can be enabled on an ISA Server computer. The ISA server can also function as a remote access server or VPN server.

However, there is one RRAS feature that is not compatible with the ISA Server software. You cannot use the NAT protocol on a server that is running ISA Server. The reason for this is that ISA Server provides its own translation service, which is more sophisticated and robust than the Windows 2000 NAT.

NOTE

Although the ISA address translation service provides sophisticated NAT functionality, some tasks that ISA's S-NAT cannot do, such as port mapping, can be done using Windows 2000's NAT.

If NAT is installed on a server on which you want to install ISA, you should delete it. The same is true of Internet Connection Sharing (ICS), a "light" form of NAT that is also included with Windows 2000 Server and is configured on a connection via the Network and Dialup Connections properties.

Understanding Interoperability with Internet Information Server

Microsoft Proxy Server required the presence of IIS in order to function. However, ISA does *not* require that IIS be installed on the ISA server, although you can install IIS on your ISA computer if you desire.

IIS Functionality

Windows 2000 Server includes IIS 5.0, and it is installed by default when you install the operating system. However, you can elect not to install it in a custom installation, or you can remove it later using the **Add/Remove Programs** applet in the Control Panel.

NOTE

IIS 5.0 will *not* be installed by default if you upgraded to Windows 2000 from Windows NT 4.0 and IIS 4.0 was not installed on the NT system.

IIS is Microsoft's Web server software, which also includes NNTP, FTP, and SMTP functionality. IIS 5.0 supports Active Server Pages (ASP); Windows Media Services (WMS), which is installed separately as a Windows component from **Add/Remove Programs**; distributed authoring and versioning; and other advanced features. IIS can be used to make documents and Web objects available over the Internet or on an intranet.

Publishing IIS to the Internet

If you do choose to install IIS on the ISA computer, there are two ways you can publish IIS to the Internet:

- Using Web publishing rules
- Using packet filters

Let's briefly look at each of these methods.

Using Web Publishing Rules

The first way to publish the Web server that runs on the ISA Server computer is by configuring Web publishing rules. Chapter 10, "Publishing Servers to the Internet," discusses in detail how Web publishing rules work. Note that you need to configure IIS not to use the ports that are used by ISA Server for outgoing and incoming Web requests (ports 8080 and 80, respectively, by default). You can also configure IIS to listen on a different IP address.

NOTE

When using Web publishing rules, you must associate the Web server with an internal IP address and change the port it uses to a different port number.

Using Packet Filters

You can allow IIS to continue using TCP port 80 to listen for Web requests if you configure an IP packet filter to map incoming requests on that port to IIS. In this case, you should ensure that ISA's autodiscovery is not set to listen on port 80. If you use this method, you should *not* create Web publishing rules to publish the Web server.

Note that this is *not* the preferred method of publishing, because it cannot take advantage of dynamic packet filtering.

NOTE

When you install ISA Server, the World Wide Web Publishing Service (w3svc) will be stopped. After you finish the installation, you should first change the port on which IIS will listen, and then restart the w3svc.

Understanding Interoperability with IPSecurity

The IP Security Protocol (IPSec) support is a new feature in Windows 2000 that was not included in Windows NT 4.0. IPSec is an Internet standard, developed by the Internet Engineering Task Force (IETF).

NOTE

IPSec specifications are defined in Request for Comments (RFC) 2401.

IPSec provides security for data as it travels across a TCP/IP network. Although there are other methods of encrypting data, IPSec enjoys a distinct advantage: It operates at the Network layer (Layer 3) of the OSI model. This means that, unlike Application layer encryption protocol uses, there is no requirement for the network applications to be IPSec aware.

IPSec uses cryptographic security services to provide for confidentiality and integrity of transmitted data and authentication of the identity of the sender.

How IPSec Works

To secure and authenticate transmissions, IPSec uses two protocols:

- **Authentication Header (AH)** AH signs the entire data packet, providing authentication and integrity but not confidentiality, because it doesn't encrypt the data. AH can be used alone when it is not necessary that the message be kept secret—only that you ensure that it cannot be modified and that the sender's identity is verified.
- **Encapsulating Security Payload (ESP)** ESP does not sign the entire packet (except in the case of tunneled data), but it does encrypt the data, providing confidentiality.

Both protocols support two modes: transport (which provides end-to-end security) and tunnel (which provides gateway-to-gateway security).

IPSec uses *Security Associations (SAs)* to establish a secure connection. An SA is a combination of policy and keys that define how data will be exchanged and protected. The Internet Security Association and Key Management Protocol (ISAKMP) is used in conjunction with the Oakley key generation protocol, in compliance with IETF standards. ISAKMP/Oakley uses a two-stage process that employs negotiated encryption and authentication algorithms, which are agreed on by the sending and receiving (or *source* and *destination)* computers.

In Windows 2000's implementation of IPSec, properties of security associations are governed by IPSec policies.

How IPSec Is Configured in Windows 2000

Windows 2000 allows you to set IPSec policies via Group Policy, which can be configured on a local machine via the **Local Security Settings** administrative tool or for a domain by editing the domain's Group Policy Object, as shown in Figure 11.24.

Figure 11.24 IPSec Policies Are Configured via Windows 2000 Group Policy

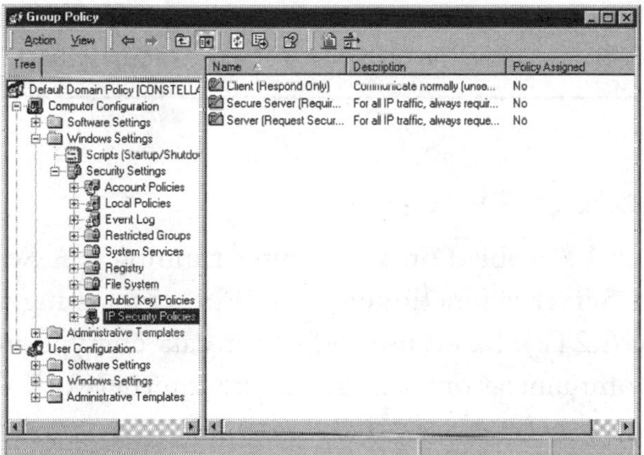

One option you have when editing the properties of an IPSec policy is to select which of the two IPSec protocols will be used. The Security Method Wizard allows you to configure the security method (Microsoft uses the term *security methods* to refer to the IPSec protocols), as shown in Figure 11.25.

Figure 11.25 You Can Select the IPSec Protocol to Be Used via the Security Method Wizard

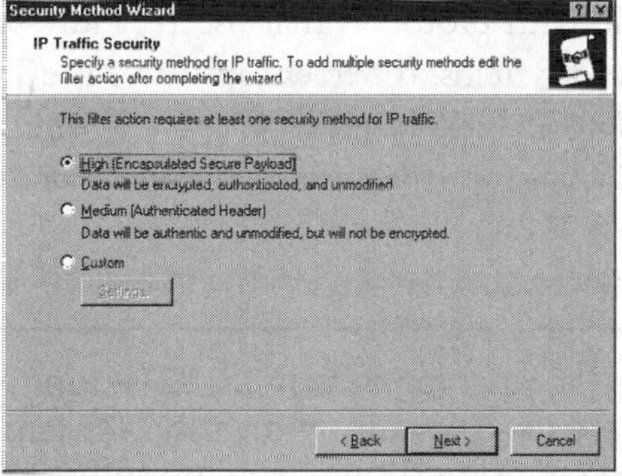

You can use ESP and AH together to provide added security if you want the data encrypted and the entire packet signed. However, you cannot specify both protocols during the Wizard process; you must edit the filter action afterward to add a second security method.

Microsoft implements IPSec in Windows 2000 via the *IPSec driver.* Let's take a look at this component.

NOTE

IPSec is a complex topic; exploring all facets of its operation is beyond the scope of this book. For more information, see RFC 2401 or *IP Security for Windows 2000 Server* on the Web at www.eu.microsoft.com/windows2000/library/howitworks/security/ip_security.asp.

IPSec and ISA Server

The IPSec driver can be enabled on a computer running ISA Server. Doing so is necessary if the ISA Server is functioning as a VPN server using the Layer 2 Tunneling Protocol (L2TP). L2TP uses IPSec for data encryption, to ensure confidentiality of the communications sent across the internetwork via the tunnel, thus making the virtual network a "private" one.

When IPSec is not enabled on the ISA server, the ISA policy determines which packets are allowed or blocked. However, if IPSec is enabled, AH and ESP protocols (which are IP protocols 30 and 51, respectively) are controlled by the IPSec driver instead of the ISA Server packet filter driver. The IPSec driver allows only valid AH and ESP traffic to enter the network.

Note that when ISA Server is configured to block IP fragments, AH and ESP fragments will be blocked along with all others, even when IPSec is enabled on the server.

NAT is incompatible with protocols that use IP addresses in fields other than the standard TCP/IP header fields. IPSec encapsulates the TCP/IP headers; thus IPSec cannot be used *through* an ISA server. IPSec can only be used to encrypt L2TP traffic using the ISA Server machine as the endpoint for a VPN.

NOTE

When IPSec is used to encrypt data in an L2TP tunnel, public key computer certificates are used for authentication. At least one computer-level certificate must be configured on each computer (VPN client or server).

Integrating an ISA Server into a Windows NT 4.0 Domain

You can install Windows 2000 Server as a standalone or member server on a computer that is a member of a Windows NT 4.0 domain. (A Windows 2000 Server *cannot* be a domain controller in an NT domain; when you promote a Windows 2000 computer to DC status, Active Directory is automatically installed and you must create or join a Windows 2000 domain.)

ISA Server can be installed *in standalone mode only* on a Windows 2000 server in an NT domain. The reason for this is that ISA arrays require Active Directory, and there is no Active Directory in an NT domain.

If you want to provide firewall protection to users who belong to an NT domain and you also want the benefits of ISA array membership (fault tolerance and distributed caching), you can set up a separate Windows 2000 domain on the same network and create a trust relationship between the new domain and the NT domain. Then you can install an ISA Server array in the new domain.

Backing Up and Restoring the ISA Configuration

Backing up important system information is a vital part of any network administrator's routine, and ISA Server includes a backup and restore feature that allows you to save and reapply configuration information in the event of a failure.

Backup Principles

You should back up the configuration each time you make any major change to the ISA server or array settings. In particular, Microsoft recommends that you make a backup of the array configuration immediately after you do any of the following:

- Modify the installation mode (firewall, caching or integrated)
- Modify the enterprise policy settings in any way
- Add, remove, or rename an ISA server or array
- Change the location or size of the cache
- Add or remove Web filters

You should also back up server-specific information on a periodic basis. This is done on each ISA Server computer. The process includes:

- Passwords
- Local Registry parameters/settings
- Cache configuration information
- Cache contents
- The H.323 Gatekeeper configuration
- Local settings for application filters
- Performance-tuning parameters
- Reports
- Log files

Backing Up and Restoring Standalone Server Configurations

You will recall that when an ISA server is installed in standalone mode, the ISA configuration settings are stored in the computer's local Registry. When you back up a standalone server, the configuration information is restored to the same standalone server.

To use the Backup feature, simply right-click the server name in the left console pane of the ISA Management MMC, and choose **Back Up** (or make the same choice on the **Action** menu while the server name is highlighted), as shown in Figure 11.26.

Figure 11.26 The ISA Management Console Provides a Tool for Backing Up Server Information

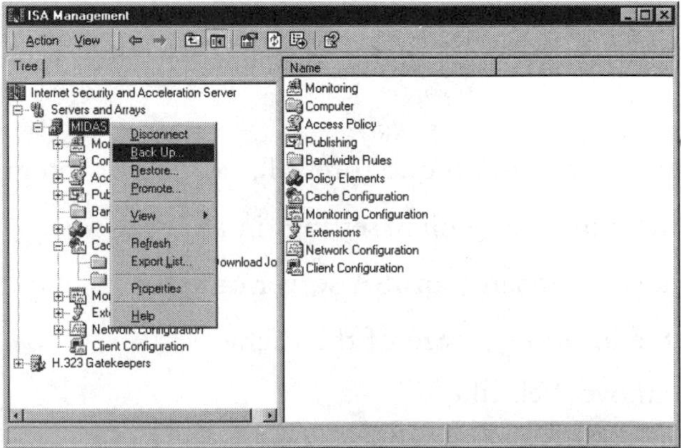

You will be prompted to enter a location where you want to store the backup confirmation information. You can type a path or browse for a location. The backup information file will be saved with a .BIF extension.

NOTE

Microsoft recommends that you always store the configuration backup on an NTFS partition for security purposes. Doing so will allow you to protect the files from unauthorized access, using NTFS permissions.

You can also enter a comment to provide more information about the backup file or to identify who made the backup, as shown in Figure 11.27.

Figure 11.27 You Can Provide an Identifying Comment for the Backup File

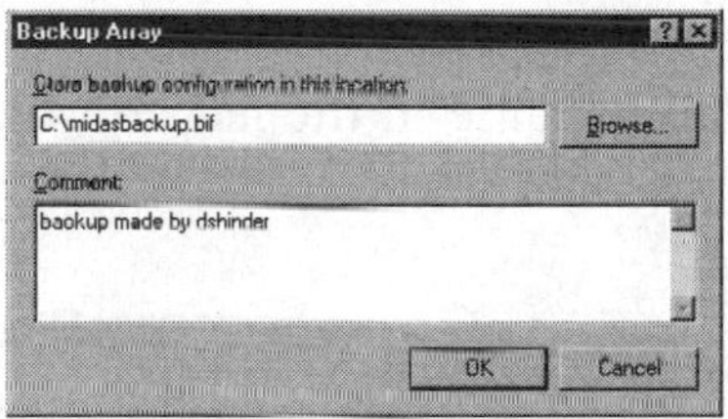

To restore the data, right-click the server name and select **Restore** from the context menu, and you will receive a warning message notifying you that the existing configuration will be replaced when you restore from a file. When you click **OK**, you will be asked to enter or browse for the path to a backup (.BIF) file.

SECURITY ALERT!

Be certain that the file you select is the most current backup of your ISA configuration. The existing configuration will be overwritten when you restore from backup. Restoring from the wrong file could have undesirable effects on your ISA server.

Backing Up and Restoring Array and Enterprise Configurations

When ISA Server is installed as an array member (even if the array has only one member), the configuration information is stored in Active Directory.

Backing Up and Restoring an Array Configuration

Backing up and restoring configuration information for an array is similar to the process for standalone devices. ISA Server backs up the array's general configuration information, including the following:

- Array policies
- Access policy rules
- Publishing rules
- Policy elements
- Alert configuration
- Cache configuration

The process for backing up the array is the same as shown for a standalone server; you right-click the array name in the left console pane, select **Back Up**, and follow the same steps.

Unexplained ISA Server Mystery

Microsoft's ISA Server documentation states that the backup files must be stored on the local computer—in other words, you cannot save them to a network location. The authors' experiments, however, indicate that it is possible to save the backups across the network and restore them from the remote location.

Some server-specific configuration information, including cache content, activity logs, reports, and effective enterprise policy, is not backed up when you back up the array. The restoration process, once again, involves selecting **Restore** from the context menu and entering a path or browsing for the backup file, as shown in Figure 11.28.

Figure 11.28 You Must Enter a Path to the File in Which You Backed Up the Array Configuration

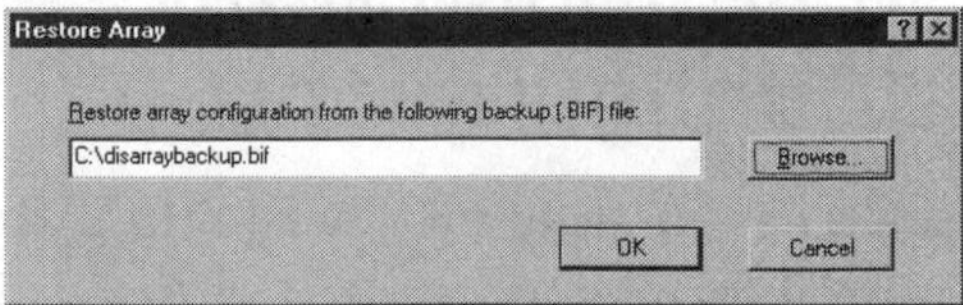

Backup file information will be displayed, as shown in Figure 11.29, so that you can ensure this is the correct file before you go ahead with the restoration process.

Figure 11.29 Backup File Information Is Displayed Prior to the Restoration

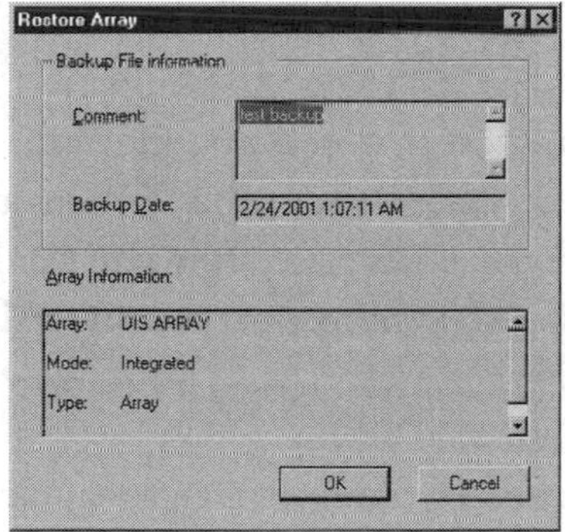

The restoration process might take a few moments. When it is completed, a message will be displayed notifying you that the array has been successfully restored.

NOTE

You cannot back up an array configuration and then restore that configuration to a different array or to a standalone server. You must restore to the same array.

Backing Up and Restoring an Enterprise Configuration

You can backup the enterprise configuration data to a separate file. Backing up the enterprise saves all enterprise-specific information. This includes enterprise-level policy elements and policies as well as information regarding which arrays in the enterprise use specific enterprise policies.

NOTE

When you back up the enterprise configuration, array-specific data will *not* be saved. You must back up the array configuration separately, as described earlier.

The enterprise configuration is stored in a file with the .BEF extension (for *backup enterprise file,* to differentiate it from the .BIF array backup files). You should back up all arrays in the enterprise after you back up the enterprise configuration, and after restoring the enterprise, you should restore all arrays. This process ensures that arrays that use enterprise policies will have the policies applied correctly.

To back up the enterprise configuration, right-click the **Enterprise** object in the left console pane of the ISA Management MMC and select **Back Up**, then follow the same steps already discussed for backing up a standalone server or an array.

NOTE

A .BEF file cannot be restored to an array, nor can a .BIF file be used to restore the enterprise.

The restoration process is the same as for a standalone server or array: Right-click the object (in this case, **Enterprise**) and select **Restore**, then select the appropriate .BEF file.

Summary

In this chapter, we addressed ways of optimizing ISA Server's performance and customizing the product to better fit the needs of your network. We discussed how ISA Server interoperates with other Windows 2000 services and applications and how to integrate a standalone ISA Server into a Windows 2000 domain. We also provided information on how to back up and restore the configuration of an ISA standalone server, an array, or the enterprise.

You learned some basic performance concepts, including how to establish and use a baseline in managing and tuning performance. We showed you how to define threshold values, and you learned that ISA Server can perform a specified action—such as logging an event, sending a network message, starting a performance data log, or running a specified program—when a threshold value is reached.

We demonstrated the use of the ISA Server Performance Monitor, which includes two components: the System Monitor and Performance Logs and Alerts. You learned to customize the view of the System Monitor and how to use the performance counters for various performance objects to determine how efficiently your ISA server is operating. You also learned to configure logs so that performance data can be saved and viewed at a later time and how to set performance alerts.

Next, we addressed some specific, common performance issues. You learned to set Performance properties based on user capacity as well as how to determine effective network bandwidth and set effective bandwidth limits for dial-up devices and network cards. We discussed load-balancing issues, and you learned how to configure the load factor in an ISA Server using CARP. The interaction of ISA Server—particularly when CARP is enabled—with Windows 2000's Network Load Balancing (NLB) was discussed, and you learned that CARP should not be used for incoming Web requests when NLB is being used on the network. You then learned how to improve performance by configuring RAM caching and that you can speed up access by enabling and configuring active caching of frequently accessed files. We also discussed cache drive configuration and its impact on performance.

You discovered that some performance settings can be made only by editing the Windows Registry, and we showed you a few specific Registry keys that can be configured to fine-tune performance.

In the next section, you learned that there are a couple of ways to customize or enhance ISA Server: by developing extensions or writing scripts using the ISA Server Software Developers Kit (SDK) and by using third-party add-on products that integrate with ISA Server.

You learned that ISA Server interoperates with many other Windows 2000 services and applications, including Active Directory, Routing and Remote Access (RRAS), Internet Information Server (IIS), and the IP Security Protocol (IPSec). You learned that some Windows 2000 services, such as ICS and NAT, are not compatible with ISA Server and should be removed when you install ISA Server on a computer.

We also discussed how to integrate a standalone ISA Server into a Windows NT 4.0 domain, and you learned that in order to function as an array member, ISA requires the Active Directory Services of a Windows 2000 domain.

The final section introduced you to the ISA Server Backup feature and showed you how to back up and restore the ISA configuration information for a standalone server, an array, and the enterprise.

We are nearing the end of the book, and by this time, you should have a good idea of the functionalities ISA Server provides and how it works. Regardless of how good a software program is, it is likely that in using it, at some point you will encounter problems of some sort. In the next (and last) chapter, we will take a look at some of the common problems that could occur as you install, configure, and use ISA Server on your network and offer some troubleshooting tips.

Solutions Fast Track

Optimizing ISA Server Performance

- ☑ A *benchmark* is a reference point or set of reference points against which something can be compared. This point or points can be list of performance criteria a product is expected to meet, a set of conditions by which a product is measured, or a known product to which other products are compared.
- ☑ Optimizing performance involves finding a way to make all components of a system work together smoothly with the smallest possible amount of delay or downtime.
- ☑ Hardware specifications and condition, software configuration, and interaction with other networking components combine to determine the speed and efficiency with which your ISA servers do their jobs.
- ☑ A key factor in any performance-monitoring program is to establish a baseline. This is done by collecting information at intervals, averaged over a period of time when the network is performing normally.

- ☑ The ISA Server Performance Monitor console differs from the Windows 2000 System Monitor in that it already has a set of default performance counters configured.
- ☑ In addition to viewing the performance data in real time using the System Monitor component of the ISA Performance Monitor, you can record this data for later viewing using the Performance Logs functionality.
- ☑ The *effective bandwidth* is defined by Microsoft as the actual bandwidth for a specific connectivity device such as a modem or ISDN terminal adapter, or the total effective network bandwidth.
- ☑ *Load balancing* refers to a method of spreading the processing workload across multiple machines, for better performance and fault tolerance.
- ☑ When the Cache Array Routing Protocol (CARP) is enabled on an ISA Server computer, you can configure the servers in the array so that they have different loads by setting the *load factor.*
- ☑ If you are using Windows 2000 NLB on your network, you should not enable CARP on incoming Web requests. The reason for this is that the load-balancing driver will determine to which server the requests should be directed and route each request to one of the servers in the array.
- ☑ Because RAM is faster than hard disk speeds, objects that are cached in RAM can be retrieved faster than those that are cached on the disk.
- ☑ *Active caching* is a means of speeding up access to files that are accessed frequently, by automatically refreshing the content of such objects when they are soon to expire.

Customizing ISA Server

- ☑ The ISA Server SDK is a comprehensive collection of development tools and sample scripts that can be used to build new, custom features that enhance ISA's firewall, caching, and management functionality. Administration scripts can simplify and automate administrative tasks. Developers can create custom administration scripts, or administrators can use the sample scripts included with the SDK.
- ☑ Even before Microsoft released the final version of ISA Server, several third-party vendors had begun to develop solutions to customize and enhance ISA's features and functionality. In many cases, Microsoft has

partnered with these companies to provide complementary products for ISA.

Integrating ISA Server with Other Services

- ☑ ISA Server software does not operate in a vacuum; it must interoperate with other services and applications on the computer and on your network.
- ☑ The Windows 2000 Active Directory is a hierarchical database that is stored on Windows 2000 domain controllers. It holds information about objects on the network (users, groups, computers, printers, files, and other network resources).
- ☑ Active Directory is governed by a set of rules called the *schema,* which define object classes and attributes (these are called *metadata* because they describe "data about data"). The content of the schema is controlled by a single domain controller that holds the role of *schema master.*
- ☑ Although the ISA configuration is stored on the Windows 2000 domain controllers, you do *not* have to install ISA Server on a DC.
- ☑ Windows 2000 Routing and Remote Access Services (RRAS) provide a collection of services that allow a Windows 2000 server to function as a full-fledged software router, forwarding IP packets from one subnet or network to another, or as a dial-up server and to create and control dial-up networking policies and virtual private networking connections across WAN links.
- ☑ RRAS can be enabled on an ISA Server computer. The ISA server can also function as a remote access server or VPN server.
- ☑ Windows 2000 Server includes IIS 5.0, and it is installed by default when you install the operating system. However, you can elect not to install it in a custom installation, or you can remove it later using the **Add/Remove Programs** applet in the Control Panel.
- ☑ The IP Security Protocol (IPSec) support is a new feature in Windows 2000 that was not included in Windows NT 4.0. IPSec is an Internet standard, developed by the Internet Engineering Task Force (IETF).
- ☑ IPSec uses *Security Associations (SAs)* to establish a secure connection. An SA is a combination of policy and keys that define how data will be exchanged and protected.

☑ You can install Windows 2000 Server as a standalone or member server on a computer that is a member of a Windows NT 4.0 domain.

Backing Up and Restoring the ISA Configuration

☑ Backing up important system information is a vital part of any network administrator's routine, and ISA Server includes a backup and restore feature that allows you to save and reapply configuration information in the event of a failure.

☑ You should back up the configuration each time you make any major change to the ISA server or array settings.

☑ Microsoft recommends that you always store the configuration backup on an NTFS partition for security purposes. Doing so will allow you to protect the files from unauthorized access, using NTFS permissions.

☑ When ISA Server is installed as an array member (even if the array has only one member), the configuration information is stored in Active Directory.

☑ You can backup the enterprise configuration data to a separate file. Backing up the enterprise saves all enterprise-specific information. This includes enterprise-level policy elements and policies as well as information regarding which arrays in the enterprise use specific enterprise policies.

Frequently Asked Questions

The following Frequently Asked Questions, answered by the authors of this book, are designed to both measure your understanding of the concepts presented in this chapter and to assist you with real-life implementation of these concepts. To have your questions about this chapter answered by the author, browse to **www.syngress.com/solutions** and click on the **"Ask the Author"** form.

Q: Do alerts send notification via email or via the Windows messenger service, or both?

A: This confusion arises from the fact that two very distinct and separate types of alerts can be configured in relation to ISA Server. The first type is an ISA alert, which you configure using the ISA Management MMC. When you configure these alerts, one of the actions that you can select to occur when a threshold value is reached is to send email to a specified recipient using a particular SMTP server. The other type of alert is a performance alert. These alerts are configured via the ISA Server Performance Monitor application, not the ISA Management console. You can specify that a performance alert send notification to a user or computer on the network. This notification uses the Windows messenger service, so that service must be running for the notification messages to be received.

Q: If I back up the enterprise, does that mean that all information is saved that is necessary to restore all my ISA Servers throughout the enterprise network, or do I have to back up something else, too?

A: Backing up the enterprise saves *only* enterprise-specific data. No array-specific data is saved, so you should back up all your arrays after backing up the enterprise. However, the array backup does not save some server-specific data, so you should back up each of your individual ISA servers' server-specific information. Finally, it is important as part of your network disaster protection plan that you back up mission-critical data on all servers, including your ISA servers, and use the Windows Backup utility (ntbackup.exe) to save system state data on a regular basis.

Q: Can I set a bandwidth limitation, such as 56Kbps, on specific users to prevent them from "hogging" the bandwidth and negatively affecting network performance?

A: In a word, no. Although ISA Server allows you to create bandwidth rules that can be applied to users or groups, these rules set bandwidth priorities; they do not allow you to limit the bandwidth usage (throttle bandwidth) for the specified users/groups. In other words, these settings determine whose packets will go through and whose will be dropped (and have to be sent again) if the bandwidth becomes saturated.

Q: My network uses a Network Address Translation program, such as Sygate or NAT32, to provide Internet connectivity to all the computers on a small internal network using only one registered public IP address. Can I install ISA Server on the computer that is connected to the Internet to add firewall protection and still use my NAT program for address translation?

A: No. ISA Server provides address translation services, which would conflict with the translation services of your third-party NAT solution. For the same reasons that you must remove the Windows 2000 NAT protocol or ICS from a computer when you install ISA Server on it, you also must remove any third-party NAT program. ISA will still allow you to provide Internet connectivity to all the computers on the LAN via a single public IP address while adding sophisticated firewall and caching functionality as well. Sygate or NAT32 is no longer needed.

Chapter 12

Troubleshooting ISA Server

Solutions in this chapter:

- Understanding Basic Troubleshooting Principles
- Troubleshooting ISA Installation and Configuration Problems
- Troubleshooting Authentication and Access Problems
- Troubleshooting ISA Client Problems
- Troubleshooting Caching, Publishing, and Services

☑ Summary

☑ Solutions Fast Track

☑ Frequently Asked Questions

Introduction

Troubleshooting refers to the process of discovering, diagnosing, and correcting problems. As with any piece of computer software, many potential problems with ISA Server can be prevented—and time spent troubleshooting thus avoided—by careful deployment planning and attention to details during installation and configuration. A classic truism says that it's easier to get it right the first time than to go back and fix it later, and this is especially true when it comes to software. One incorrect setting made inadvertently because you were in a hurry or because you didn't understand how the setting works can result in hours or days of effort later as you search for the cause of the resulting problems.

Some network administrators enjoy the challenge of the hunt. Troubleshooting *can* be fun, especially when you can do it at your leisure. Unfortunately, in the real world, we often get those "Help! It isn't working!" calls at the most inconvenient times and are under pressure to figure out what's wrong and fix it *now.*

In this chapter, we first provide you with some general troubleshooting guidelines that will help you organize your efforts and maximize the efficiency of the troubleshooting process. If you are a "born problem solver," it's likely that you already follow an effective procedure for gathering information, analyzing that information, forming hypotheses, testing your theories, and developing a plan to address the problem once you've discovered the cause. Nonetheless, it could be helpful for you to check your troubleshooting routine against our guidelines to ensure that you aren't leaving out an important step (for instance, documentation of the resolution, which can save you from having to repeat the entire process if you encounter the same problem again in a few weeks or months because you've forgotten exactly how you finally solved it the first time).

If problem solving doesn't come naturally to you, the basic principles and procedures in the first section of this chapter will give you a structure on which to build. They can also serve as a basis for checklists that will keep you on track as you make your way through the jungle of possibilities that often present themselves when a software program isn't behaving as we expect.

In the subsequent sections, we address specific problems that commonly occur in conjunction with ISA Server. These problems are divided into logical categories so that you can more easily use this chapter as a reference in the field.

Understanding Basic Troubleshooting Principles

Troubleshooting is a specialized form of problem solving. The same general problem-solving skills that work in other areas of life can also be applied to troubleshooting computer problems in general and ISA Server-related problems in particular.

Before you can solve a problem, you must first be aware of it. Some problems make themselves known immediately and dramatically (e.g., the server crashes and won't reboot). Others are more subtle (you have no idea that anything is wrong until you discover that the packets you thought were blocked are flowing freely into your network). Performance problems can be especially insidious, because the slowdown happens so gradually that no one really notices. Regardless of the problem, the first step in problem solving is always *problem recognition*. Once you've identified that you have a problem, you can get on with the business of solving it.

Some might say there are two approaches to troubleshooting:

- The hypermaniacal "sink or swim," approach of those who, having discovered that there is a problem, rush right in where angels fear to tread, working on sheer intuition and trying whatever comes to mind, hoping that one of their many experimental changes, along with the proper alignment of the planets, will "fix" what's gone wrong.
- The cool, calculated, obsessive-compulsive approach of those who cordon off the perimeter with yellow tape ("IT line—do not cross"), separate all witnesses, and interrogate each individually, bring in a team of consultants to plan a proper course of action, arm themselves with every possible diagnostic tool in the book, make sure all the manuals and reference books are on hand, painstakingly photograph every error message, and don sterile rubber gloves before touching so much as a mouse button.

In truth, the most efficient approach falls somewhere between these two extremes on the "type of troubleshooter" continuum. Although it is certainly possible to be so overly cautious that you never get started, and it is true that the "gut feeling" of an experienced IT pro most likely has a foundation in fact, it is also important that you have a plan, a standardized procedure, before you begin to make changes to the system.

A systematic set of troubleshooting guidelines that you follow in each instance will help you organize your problem-solving efforts *and* speed up the diagnostic and treatment process. In the next section, we offer some guidelines based on problem-solving strategies that have proven successful both in and outside the high-tech industry.

Troubleshooting Guidelines

Many professions exist for the purpose of solving problems of one sort or another. When people have legal problems, they call an attorney. When they have medical problems, they visit a doctor. When they have problems with their computers or the network, they turn to you—the administrator—to solve those problems. Doctors, lawyers, and other professionals learn, as part of their formal education and practical training, the importance of following a step-by-step procedure that can be applied to most problem-solving situations.

A classic example of an occupation that relies on problem-solving skills is that of the police detective (or, as he/she is more commonly called these days, the criminal investigator). A problem-solving model that is often taught to law enforcement agents is known as the *SARA method*. The acronym stands for the four phases of an investigation: scanning, analysis, response, and assessment. Physicians use a similar sequence of steps when they "investigate" patients' complaints: examination, diagnosis, treatment, and follow-up examination. When a client comes to a lawyer with legal troubles, the attorney follows a set of steps that adhere to the same principles: research, formulate a legal theory to build a case, take a legal action (such as filing a lawsuit or motion), and evaluate the effectiveness of that action.

This same basic process applies to troubleshooting problems with computer software programs such as ISA Server. In the following section, we explain each step as it applies to network administrators. We have also added a fifth step, which the other professionals also practice but which is rarely mentioned in formal problem-solving models: documentation. Police officers file reports, doctors complete medical charts, and attorneys decimate entire forests to create the mass of paperwork that document every step of the legal process. IT professionals—although not required to do so by law, as those in the other professions are—should get into the habit of thoroughly documenting troubleshooting incidents. This practice will benefit you as well as others who encounter the same problem in the future.

The Five Steps of Troubleshooting

Our systematic approach to troubleshooting involves five basic steps:

1. Information gathering

2. Analysis and planning
3. Implementation of a solution
4. Assessment of the effectiveness of the solution
5. Documentation of the incident

In the following sections, we address each of these steps individually.

Information Gathering

Before we can determine how to address a problem—or even assess what the problem is—we must gather information. Doctors do it by asking questions of their patients, observing physical signs and symptoms, and conducting lab tests. Detectives do it by interviewing witnesses, personally examining the crime scene, and gathering evidence. Attorneys do it by taking depositions, researching the facts of the case, and studying prior court decisions.

An ISA Server administrator can gather information by observing the undesirable behavior of the software, questioning users who are experiencing problems, and using common tools and utilities to monitor the server's and network's activity (see Figure 12.1).

Figure 12.1 Information Gathering Can Take Many Forms

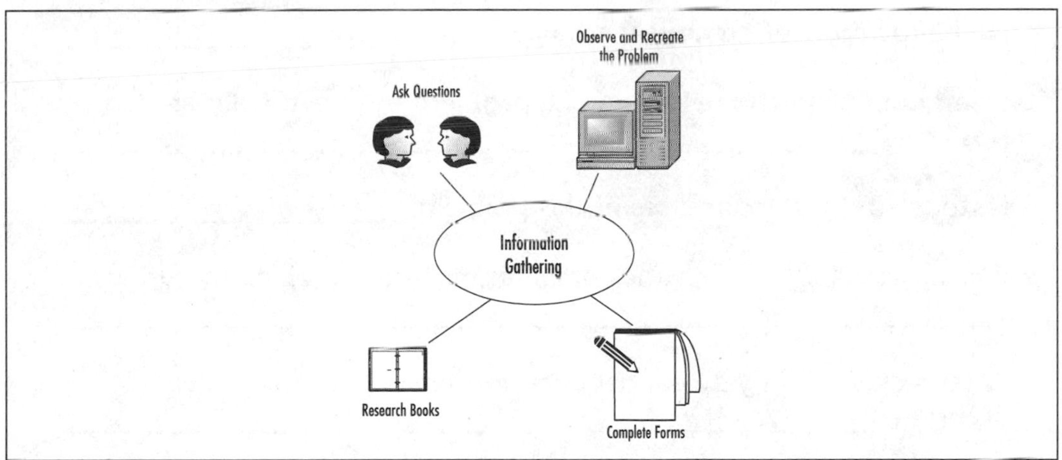

Doctors, lawyers, and criminal investigators often use preprinted *forms* to guide them in the information-gathering phase. Using a form ensures that you don't forget to ask important questions or check important settings, and it gives you a head start on the documentation process, which we address a little later in the chapter. See the sidebar for a sample troubleshooting information form. You can customize the generic form to fit your own needs.

NOTE

Of course, forms don't have to be printed on paper. Many IT shops use special software—electronic forms—to track problem diagnosis and resolution.

Configuring & Implementing...

A Sample Troubleshooting Information Form

Standard information forms help you gather information in a systematic way that makes it easy to organize and analyze. You can adapt a general network troubleshooting information form to use for ISA Server problems, or you can use the sample form shown here:

Troubleshooting Information Form

Date: **Time:**

Person reporting problem: ______________________________

Name/location of computer displaying problem: ______________

Briefly describe the nature of the problem as specifically as possible: ______________________________

History—former occurrences of this problem: __________________

Was anyone logged onto the computer when the problem occurred?

____

What task(s)—if any—were being performed when the problem occurred?______________________________

What programs and processes were running when the problem occurred? ______________________________

What error messages (if any) were displayed? _________________

Continued

Was the computer restarted?:_____? Restarted manually _____?
Automatic restart ______

If the computer was restarted, did it boot into the operating system normally? _____

If no, describe any problems, freezes, error messages, or unusual behavior upon reboot. ____

Network Connectivity information: _________________________________

TCP/IP Configuration information: __________________________________

During the information-gathering stage, you should be striving to see the "big picture." Don't fall prey to tunnel vision, in which you focus narrowly on the immediate problem and fail to see its broader ramifications. For example, if the company president is upset because he isn't able to access a specific Web site, it might seem that the only thing that matters is making him happy. Reconfiguring your site and content rules might fix the immediate problem, but be certain that you consider how the reconfiguration will impact other users. Will they now be able to access sites you wanted to block? And have you really fixed the boss's problem or only relieved it temporarily? That is, will you be called back an hour later because now he wants to go to a different site and can't?

Gathering information can be particularly challenging when the problem manifests itself at the client side. You might have to formulate your questions carefully in order to get meaningful information from users, who often are unable to describe the problem more precisely than "It doesn't work." In that case, ask specific questions such as:

- Exactly what were you attempting to do when the problem occurred?
- What error messages (if any) were displayed?
- Is anyone else experiencing the same problem?
- Were you able to perform the task (access the site, download files, etc.) previously?
- If yes, when were you last able to perform this task?
- Have you made any changes to any of the settings on the computer, installed any new software, etc.?

Log files comprise another source of information you should consult during the data-gathering stage. Both the Windows 2000 Server logs (accessed via Event Viewer) and the ISA Server logs (by default, located in the ISA Server Installation folder, in the ISALogs subfolder) can provide valuable information and a starting point for troubleshooting problems. An example of an IP Packet Filter log is shown in Figure 12.2.

Figure 12.2 ISA Log Files Can Be Useful in Troubleshooting Various Problems

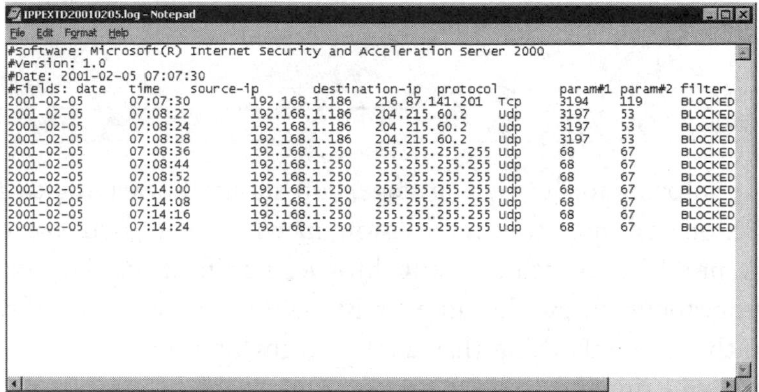


```
#Software: Microsoft(R) Internet Security and Acceleration Server 2000
#Version: 1.0
#Date: 2001-02-05 07:07:30
#Fields: date   time    source-ip      destination-ip  protocol     param#1 param#2 filter-
2001-02-05      07:07:30       192.168.1.186  216.87.141.201  Tcp     3194    119     BLOCKED
2001-02-05      07:08:22       192.168.1.186  204.215.60.2    Udp     3197    53      BLOCKED
2001-02-05      07:08:24       192.168.1.186  204.215.60.2    Udp     3197    53      BLOCKED
2001-02-05      07:08:28       192.168.1.186  204.215.60.2    Udp     3197    53      BLOCKED
2001-02-05      07:08:36       192.168.1.250  255.255.255.255 Udp     68      67      BLOCKED
2001-02-05      07:08:44       192.168.1.250  255.255.255.255 Udp     68      67      BLOCKED
2001-02-05      07:08:52       192.168.1.250  255.255.255.255 Udp     68      67      BLOCKED
2001-02-05      07:14:00       192.168.1.250  255.255.255.255 Udp     68      67      BLOCKED
2001-02-05      07:14:08       192.168.1.250  255.255.255.255 Udp     68      67      BLOCKED
2001-02-05      07:14:16       192.168.1.250  255.255.255.255 Udp     68      67      BLOCKED
2001-02-05      07:14:24       192.168.1.250  255.255.255.255 Udp     68      67      BLOCKED
```

ISA logging can be configured for the Proxy Service, Firewall Service, and Web Proxy Service, in W3extended format or ISA Server format, as discussed in Chapter 11. Performance logs can also be useful in troubleshooting performance-related problems.

Analysis

Once you've gathered all the information possible regarding the problem (including attempting to reproduce it), it's time to analyze the data. This phase is also called the *diagnostic* or the *problem isolation* phase. The first step is to sort through all the information collected and determine which is relevant and which is not.

The primary task in this phase is to look for patterns. Do the "symptoms" match something you've experienced, heard about, or read about? Organize the relevant information—on paper, on screen, or in your head—and determine which facts fit each of your possible theories as to the cause of the problem.

An important part of the analysis phase involves *prioritizing.* This includes prioritizing the problems, if there are multiple problems (and often there are). Performance problems are generally less urgent than access problems, for example. You also need to prioritize the possible solutions. Time, cost, and ease of implementation are all factors to consider. A good rule of thumb is to try the simplest, least expensive, and quickest solutions first.

Your analysis of the data will lead you to formulate a logical *plan* based on your diagnoses, possible solutions, and priorities.

Solution Implementation

Although there could be several possible solutions to a problem, you should always implement *one change at a time.* Assess the results of that change before trying something else. This will save you much grief in the long run; there is nothing more frustrating than changing several different settings, discovering that the problem has been solved, and not knowing which of your actions solved it.

Assessment

This is also called the *follow-up* stage. It is vital that you assess the results of your actions and determine whether your "fix" worked, whether it was only a temporary workaround or actually solved the problem, whether it caused other problems while correcting the original one, and what can be done in the future to prevent the problem from recurring.

Documentation

After completing your assessment, you should develop a succinct summarization of the problem, which should include:

- The reported and observed symptoms of the problem
- Causation theories and the reasoning behind them
- Corrective actions taken
- Results of those actions
- Recommendations for prevention of a recurrence of the problem

This summarization should be in written form and kept in a permanent log. You might also want to distribute copies of the report to others, such as your superiors within the company, the affected users, other members of the IT department, and so forth. Documentation is a very important but often-overlooked step in the troubleshooting process.

Troubleshooting Tips

Experienced troubleshooters develop their own ways of approaching new problems. Most "tricks of the trade" are based on what has been learned from years of trial and error. Here are five troubleshooting tips endorsed by problem solvers in many fields:

- **Precisely define the problem** This means defining the specific nature of problem. If a user reports that "The Web isn't working," you must ask precise questions to determine whether this means that he or she is unable to access any Web sites, is unable to access only certain Web sites, Web performance is slow, or something else.
- **Recreate the problem** If you can reproduce the problem, you will have valuable clues to point you in the right direction as you attempt to solve it. Once you've narrowed down exactly what the problem is, try to reproduce it from the same machine, from a different machine, using a different user account, and so on. This process will help you determine both the scope of the problem and where to look for a solution.
- **Don't get tunnel vision** Problems that appear to be related to ISA Server might actually be problems with the physical network connection, the browser software, the DNS server, or other causes. Keep an open mind and consider all possibilities.
- **Practice the art of patience** Plenty of patience is an asset in any sort of investigative work, and that's what troubleshooting is. You will undoubtedly follow many leads that end up as dead ends. It's easy to get exasperated when things are not working properly and the pressure is on. You could find yourself going over configuration settings one at a time, and it might feel like you're hunting the proverbial needle in a haystack. Don't allow frustration to cause you to skip steps; follow the systematic procedure, no matter how frustrating.
- **Use available resources** In the next section, we list some specific resources for more information on ISA Server. Even with a product that is new and relatively undocumented, the Internet has a wealth of information that is free for the taking. The trick is finding it—and separating the good advice from the not so good. Always check these resources to find out if someone else has already put in the time and effort to figure out the solution to your problem, so you won't have to "reinvent the wheel."
- **Don't be afraid to ask for help** If your patient efforts fail and you are unable to find the answer on the Web, in a book, or via mailing lists and newsgroups, ask for help directly. Even if your particular problem has never come up on a mailing list, you can post there and solicit responses. You can contact the frequent newsgroup posters privately when you're stymied. The worst they can do is *not* answer your question (and you'll be no worse off than you already were).

When you are troubleshooting network problems, it is a good idea to start at the bottom of the OSI model and work your way up. That is, consider Physical layer "culprits" first, and proceed up through the Data Link, Network, Transport, Session, presentation, and Application layers, if necessary. If there are multiple possible causes of a specific problem, first eliminate those that are easiest to correct.

NOTE

When troubleshooting network problems, always start by checking the Event Viewer and other logs. In many cases, the information that will point you in the right direction is there waiting for you.

You can also contact the authors of books on the subject—including the authors of this book. You might have a completely unique problem and we might not know the answer or have the time to spend hours trying to recreate and solve your problem if it is a complex one. On the other hand, we might have encountered the very same thing a week before, in which case we'll be perfectly happy to share our thoughts with you. Contact information is provided in the authors' biographies and on the book's Web site at www.syngress.com.

ISA Server and Windows 2000 Diagnostic Tools

The Windows 2000 operating system and the ISA Server software include a number of tools and utilities that will help you gather information for troubleshooting purposes. These tools include:

- Event Viewer logs
- Performance Monitor
- Network Monitor
- Various log files

We discussed the use of the Performance Monitor in Chapter 11 and how to use ISA Server logs in Chapter 6. In this section, we look briefly at the Event Viewer logs and the Network Monitor.

Event Viewer Logs

The Windows 2000 Event Viewer monitors application, security, and system events and records information to log files, which you can examine for clues to the causes of hardware and software problems. The Event Viewer is accessed via

Start | Programs | Administrative Tools | Event Viewer or through the Computer Management MMC.

Three basic logs are available in the Event Viewer.

- The Application log contains information about events logged by programs (for example, ISA Server). Events logged by the application are determined by the developer of the application.
- The System log contains information about events that are logged by the Windows 2000 system components, such as driver failures, failure of a system service to load, and so forth.
- The Security log records security-related events. Auditing must be enabled in order for events to be logged to the Security log. We discussed auditing in Chapter 3.

Depending on what other services you have installed on the Windows 2000 Server, there could be other logs in the Event Viewer (for example, the Directory Service log, DNS Server log, or the File Replication Service log).

The *event types* recorded depend on the log type. Event types are identified by special icons. For example, the Application log records three event types:

- **Error** Identified by a red circle with a white X, this event type indicates a significant problem that could result in loss of functionality or data.
- **Information** Identified by a white balloon with a blue *i*, this event type indicates successful completion of an operation.
- **Warning** Identified by a yellow triangle with a black exclamation point, this event type indicates a potential problem, although not as serious or imminent as events tagged as errors.

Events in the log are listed in the right detail pane of the Event Viewer. Additional information can be viewed in the event's Properties sheet, accessed by double-clicking the event. Each event is identified by an Event ID. In the Help files subsection of the next section, we discuss how to interpret ISA Server event IDs.

Network Monitor

The Windows 2000 Network Monitor is a built-in packet sniffer that can be used to capture and display frames (packets) that pass to or from the Windows 2000 server. Network Monitor can be invaluable in troubleshooting network-related problems.

NOTE

The version of Network Monitor included with Windows 2000 has limited functionality. It captures only frames sent to or from the computer on which Network Monitor is running, and it does not allow you to edit and transmit frames. Another version of Microsoft's Network Monitor provides these functions and will capture packets sent to and from all computers on the network segment. The full-featured version is included in Microsoft System Management Server (SMS).

The Network Monitor tool uses the Network Monitor driver to receive frames from a network adapter and display statistics relating to specified frames (which can be displayed according to protocol, sending/receiving computer, and other criteria).

Network Monitor's *capture filters* are configured by the administrator to specify the types of network information that should be monitored (for example, only the packets received from a particular IP address or using a specific protocol). Network Monitor's *display filters* allow you to sort data that has already been captured, to display only specified information.

Network Monitor can be used to view the packets that are sent to or from the ISA server. For example, you could monitor packets to determine what port is being used by a particular protocol or application.

ISA Server Troubleshooting Resources

As ISA Server is implemented on more and more networks, the amount of formal and informal documentation available is sure to increase. Meanwhile, there are already a number of resources (in addition to this book) to which you can turn when you need troubleshooting help. These include:

- ISA Server Help files
- Microsoft Tech Support
- Web resources
- Books and magazines
- Internet mailing lists and newsgroups

In the following sections, we discuss each of these resources in more detail.

ISA Server Help Files

The ISA Server Help files provide a wealth of information on both concepts and the how-to of configuration. The organization of the Help files makes them easy to navigate. You will find useful checklists to ensure that you don't omit important steps during installation, configuration and other tasks. The "How To…" section guides you step by step through important procedures. In the "Concepts" section, you will find background information to help you understand how various ISA components operate and interoperate. Finally, a separate "Troubleshooting" section addresses specific reported problems and what to do about them (see Figure 12.3).

Figure 12.3 ISA Server Help Files Contain a "Troubleshooting" Section

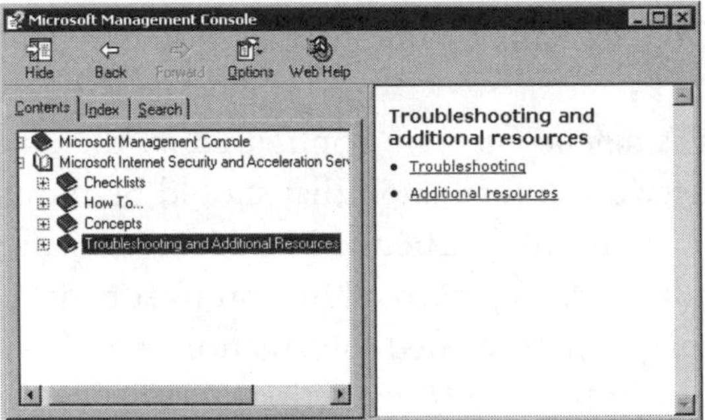

Under the "Additional Resources" heading in the Help files, you will find a glossary of terms relating to ISA Server. An especially important resource that is listed under "Additional Resources" is a list of event messages that will help you decipher those sometimes-mysterious ISA-related messages that appear in the Event Viewer logs.

Event messages are broken into the following categories:

- Alert event messages
- Bandwidth event messages
- Caching event messages
- Common service event messages
- Dial-up connection event messages
- Intrusion detection event messages
- ISA Server Control Service event messages
- ISA Server Firewall Service event messages

- ISA Server Web Proxy Service event messages
- Log event messages
- Packet filter event messages
- Server event messages

Within the categories, event messages are identified by the event ID. This ID number identifies the event type and is shown in the Event Properties sheet when you click the event (information, warning, or error) in the right pane of the Event Viewer in the Application log.

For example, in Figure 12.4, we can select an event from the right context pane. In this example, we have selected the Warning event recorded by the Microsoft Web Proxy Service at 3:01:46 PM. When you double-click the selected event, you will see its Properties sheet, as shown in Figure 12.5.

Figure 12.4 Select an Event from the Right Context Pane in the Application Log

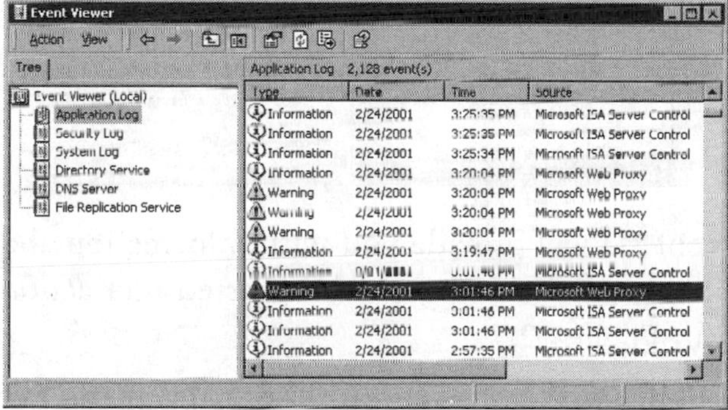

Figure 12.5 The Event's Properties Sheet Gives You a Great Deal of Information, Including the Event ID

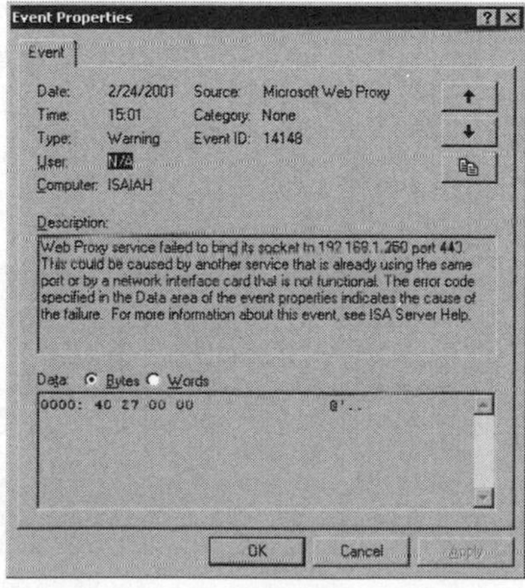

On the Properties sheet, you will see a summary of pertinent information about the event, including the date and time of occurrence, warning type, user or computer from which the event originated, source/service, category (if applicable), and the Event ID. There is also a description of the event, which refers you to the ISA Server Help file.

If we then go to the Help file and look under the event category (Web Proxy Service), we will find the ID (14148) in the list, as shown in Figure 12.6.

Figure 12.6 You Can Use the Event Category and ID to Locate the Event Message in the Help Files

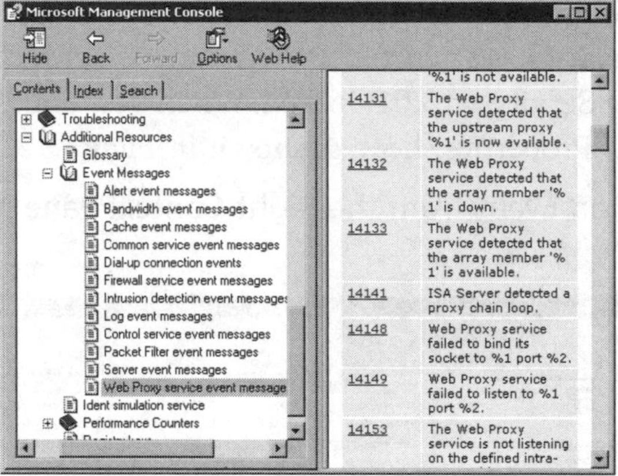

Clicking the event ID will provide you with information about the event message, an explanation of the message, and suggested user action(s) to rectify the problem, as shown in Figure 12.7.

Figure 12.7 The Help File Provides Information About the Event Message, an Explanation, and Suggested User Action(s)

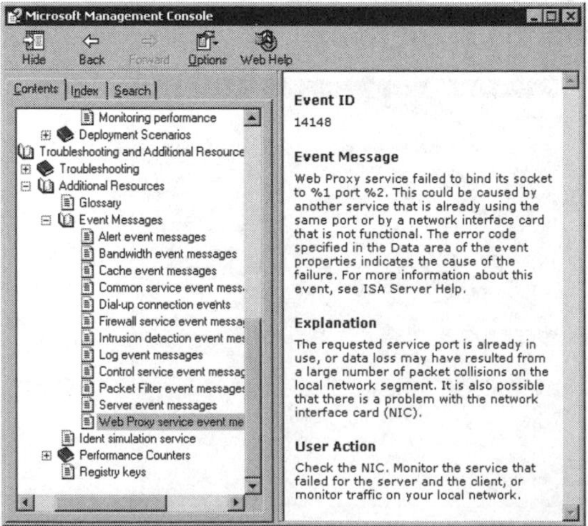

Another useful source of information included in the "Additional Resources" section is the list of all ISA performance counters and the descriptions and explanations of how each works. These are categorized according to the associated performance objects.

Finally, there is a list of Registry keys that can be modified to fine-tune ISA Server performance.

Microsoft Documentation and Technical Support

Microsoft provides a wealth of support resources on its Web site (http://support.microsoft.com/directory), where you will find two categories of available support options:

- Self-support resources
- Assisted-support information

The self-support resources include the searchable knowledge base (see Figure 12.8), which provides technical support information based on known problems and their solutions (organized as "Q" articles because of their numbering scheme; for example, Article Q257218).

Figure 12.8 The Searchable Knowledge Base Provides Technical Support Information and Self-Help Tools

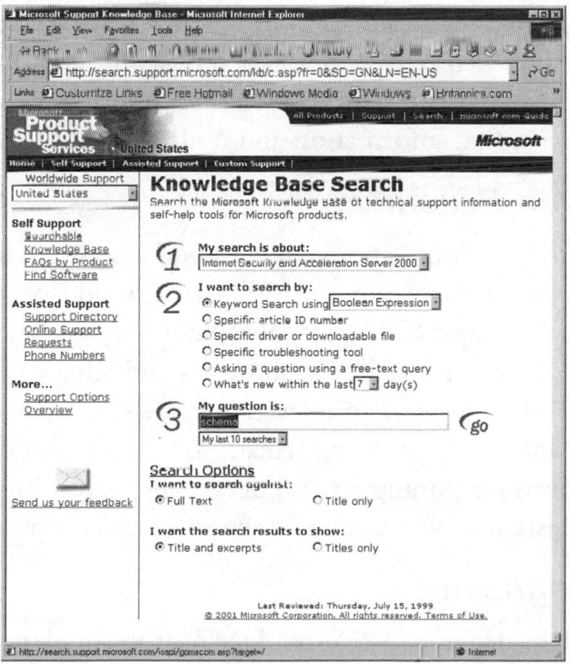

The self-support section also includes a set of lists of FAQs and a Download Center where you can find service packs, patches, and updates.

The assisted-support section provides support phone numbers and online support request forms for registered products. Additional assisted-support resources include the Microsoft Gold Certified Support Partner program, Expired Warranty options, and Microsoft Certified Partners (independent experts you can hire to provide solutions to your problems with Microsoft products).

NOTE

Professional support services do not come cheap. Telephone support from Microsoft costs $245 per incident if the product is not under warranty. Web-based support requests are $195 each. Pricing for certified partner support varies, ranging from $99 per incident and up.

Premier and Alliance support packages are available to enterprise-level businesses. More information on these offerings can be found on the Microsoft Web site.

Another excellent source of support information is TechNet Online, at www.microsoft.com/technet. Here you will find security bulletins, planning and deployment guides, white papers, and announcements of upcoming professional and training events as well as evaluation kits for new software packages.

Microsoft maintains Web resources for each of its product lines. ISA Server, as part of the .Net family, is featured on its own Web site at www.microsoft.com/isaserver. Here you will find information and updates about ISA Server issues.

Third-Party Web Resources

Third-party Web sites can come and go, but a good search engine will turn up several sites that provide information on ISA Server or add-on products that work with it. One of the best third-party Web sites is www.isaserver.org. This site features current ISA Server-related news, tutorials and advice on deploying ISA Server, ISA Server FAQs, pointers to relevant articles and books, the newest bug fixes, white papers, and certification information. The site also provides message boards and instructions for joining an ISA Server discussion list (discussed in the "Internet Mailing Lists and Newsgroups" section of this chapter).

Books and Magazines

Specific issues (such as deploying ISA in a DMZ or perimeter network or configuring ISA servers in a chained hierarchy) could be the subject of articles in popular Windows 2000-oriented technical magazines. As the use of ISA Server becomes more widespread, you will see more information about it in both print publications and online "e-zines" and tech Web sites. Here are a few of the good online sources of technical articles on Microsoft products:

www.swynk.com Microsoft-related articles and columns.

www.brainbuzz.com IT career network, certification study aids, and IT resources.

www.techrepublic.com Information site for IT professionals.

www.w2knews.com The *Sunbelt Software W2K Electronic Newsletter.*

Internet Mailing Lists and Newsgroups

One of the most diverse sources of information for current and aspiring IT professionals is Internet mailing lists. There are literally hundreds of thousands of lists, powered by automated mailing list software such as Listserv, Majordomo, and Lyris, as well as those hosted through Web-based mailing list services such as Yahoogroups.com and Topica.com. There are mailing lists devoted to almost any IT (or other) topic imaginable, including ISA Server.

The premier ISA-specific mailing list is hosted by www.isaserver.org. It is a fairly high-volume list, membership is open, and list members share their experiences installing, configuring, and using ISA Server, posting their questions and problems and assisting one another with ISA-related issues.

Those who don't want to receive the large amount of mail generated by some mailing lists might find it more convenient to subscribe to Internet newsgroups. With a newsreader such as Outlook Express, you can subscribe to as many newsgroups as you like and read the messages only when you like. There are no mail messages to clutter up your inbox.

Microsoft hosts several public newsgroups devoted to discussions of ISA Server:

- ISA Server General Support group (microsoft.public.isa)
- ISA Server Enterprise (microsoft.public.isa.enterprise)
- ISA Server newsgroup (Microsoft.public.isaserver)

The newsgroups often generate a very high volume of posts. Most newsreaders allow you to sort posts by thread (subject line) to better organize the information, as shown in Figure 12.9.

Figure 12.9 Microsoft's ISA Server Newsgroups Provide an Excellent Source of Troubleshooting Information

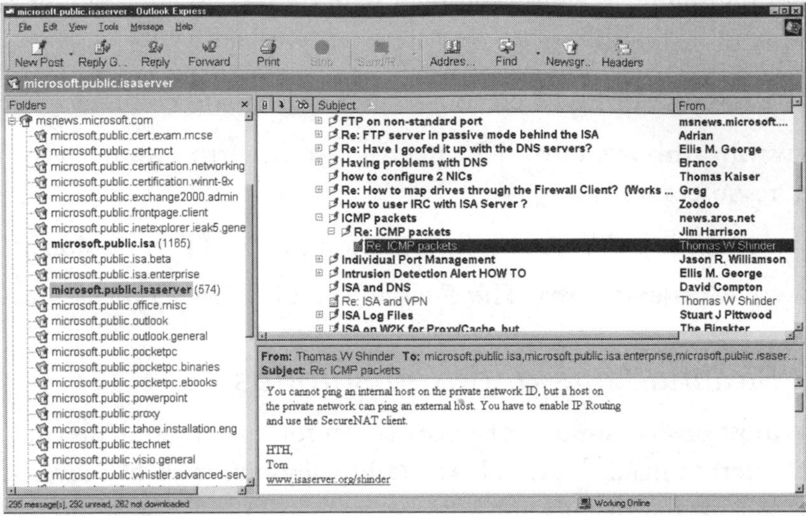

Although Microsoft does not monitor the content of its public newsgroups, they are often populated by Microsoft Most Valuable Professionals (MVPs), who provide informal leadership.

Microsoft newsgroups can be downloaded from the msnews.microsoft.com news server. You can visit http://support.microsoft.com/support/news/howto/default.asp on the Web for information about how to view the newsgroups.

Troubleshooting ISA Server Installation and Configuration Problems

Installation of ISA Server usually proceeds in a straightforward fashion. Problems during or directly following installation are often related to one of three things:

- Hardware incompatibilities
- Software incompatibilities
- Improper initial configuration

Let's look briefly at each category in the following sections.

Hardware and Software Compatibility Problems

In most cases, ISA Server works with common hardware and software configurations. In some cases, however, hardware incompatibility causes a conflict or ISA does not run properly in conjunction with another software program that is installed on the server.

ISA Server Doesn't Meet Minimum System Requirements

In order for ISA Server to function properly, the computer on which it is installed must meet the minimum hardware specifications:

- Pentium II or compatible processor running at 300MHz or above
- A member of the Windows 2000 Server family with SP1 or later
- At least 192MB (256MB recommended) of RAM
- At least 20MB of free disk space
- At least one NTFS partition
- A Windows 2000-compatible NIC connected to the internal network

If you are installing ISA Server as an array member, Active Directory must be implemented on your network. In some cases, ISA could refuse to install if the proper hardware configuration is not present. In others, ISA might appear to install successfully, even though your machine does not meet the minimum requirements. However, you might find that unusual behavior results; for example, all ISA Server services might not start if you have an insufficient amount of RAM.

You should also check the Windows 2000 Hardware Compatibility List (HCL) prior to installing Windows 2000 Server on the machine. The HCL is available on the Microsoft Web site at the following location: www.microsoft.com/hcl/default.asp.

ISA Server Exhibits Odd Behavior When Windows 2000 NAT Is Installed

If Network Address Translation (NAT) or Internet Connection Sharing (ICS) is being used on the Windows 2000 Server computer, when you install ISA Server, NAT/ICS will automatically be disabled. However, we have found that, in some cases, having NAT installed will cause continuing odd behavior on the part of the ISA Server, resulting in intermittent loss of connectivity. The solution to this problem is to delete the NAT routing protocol from the **IP Routing** section of the RRAS console tree.

NOTE

ISA Server's address translation function is also incompatible with third-party NAT solutions such as Sygate or NAT32. You should uninstall these programs from the Windows 2000 computer before installing ISA Server.

Internal Clients Are Unable to Access External Exchange Server

When you install ISA Server and your clients need to be able to use an external Exchange Server, you might find that using Outlook for e-mail does not work, although Web services function properly.

In this case, you need to add the IP address of the external Exchange Server to the LAT and install the firewall client software on the internal machines that are running Outlook. This will allow the clients' e-mail to go through.

Initial Configuration Problems

Many of the problems that occur following installation result from incorrect or incomplete configuration during the installation process or changes made to the ISA Server configuration following installation.

Unable to Renew DHCP Lease

You might find that, after upgrading from Microsoft Proxy Server or installing a fresh copy of ISA Server, you are unable to renew a lease from the DHCP Server using the **ipconfig/release** and **ipconfig/renew** commands. The only way to renew the lease is to reboot the server. This occurs even after adding a custom packet filter to allow UDP in both directions on local fixed port 68 and remote fixed port 67, as you might have done to solve this problem with Proxy Server.

NOTE

Knowing how ISA Server works—and how Windows 2000 services such as DHCP, with which it interacts, work—are the basis of solving problems of this type. For example, if you know that the lease is obtained before the packet filters are applied, you will understand why it is necessary to reboot the server to obtain a new DHCP lease.

The solution is to enable the DHCP client rule under Packet Filters, as shown in Figure 12.10. Once you enable the filter, you should be able to use the ipconfig switches to release and renew your DHCP lease.

Figure 12.10 Enable the DHCP Client Rule to Allow a Release and Renew of the DHCP Lease

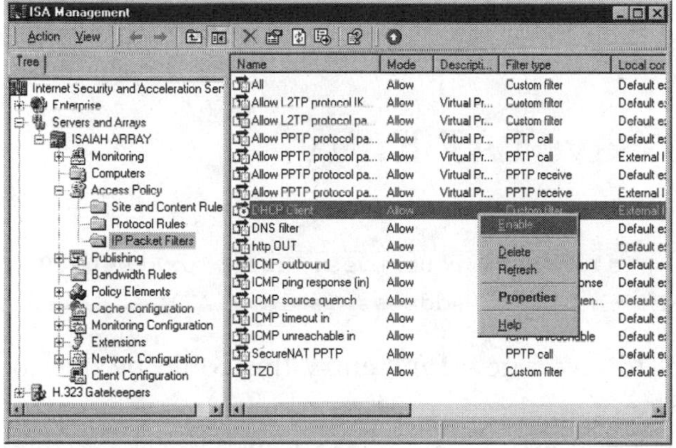

Failure of Services to Start After Completing Installation

For a couple of reasons, the ISA services might not start after installation has completed successfully. As always, check the Event Viewer for any relevant messages.

In some cases, we have noted that, if there is insufficient RAM in the server, the services might not start or might have to be started manually. Upgrading the physical memory will solve the problem if this is the cause.

If the LAT is not configured correctly and doesn't include the internal NIC (which communicates with Active Directory), the ISA Server services will not be able to start. In this case, you should first stop the ISA services (you can do this by typing **net stop mspfltext** at the command line) and then reconfigure the LAT using ISA Server Administration COM objects. An article in the ISA Server SDK, *Constructing the Local Address Table*, will instruct you in how to do this.

After you have added the appropriate entries to the LAT, you must reboot the ISA Server computer.

Inability to Join Array

You could find that it is possible to create a new array by right-clicking **Servers and Arrays** in the ISA Management MMC and selecting **New** and **Array**. This starts the New Array Wizard. You can enter a name, site, and domain location for the new array, and it will appear in the management console. However, when you install a new ISA server and attempt to join an array, you will not be able to join the new array you have created.

Our experience shows that during installation, you are given the option to join only those arrays that have at least one member. Because the array you created with the wizard contains no members, you cannot join it. You can create a new array during the installation of the first computer that will be a member of the new array, and then this array will be available to join when you install subsequent ISA servers.

Inability to Save LAT Entry

If you receive an error message:

```
ISA Server cannot save the properties. Error 0x80040340. The IP range
already exists in the Local Address Table (LAT)
```

when you attempt to save a new LAT entry, this could be due to the fact that it is an exact duplicate of an already existing address.

It is possible to overlap IP ranges in the LAT. That is, a new entry can have either a "from" address or a "to" address that already exists in the LAT, but not both.

NOTE

Although Microsoft allows overlapping LAT entries as described, it is recommended that you *not* use such entries, because doing so can result in unpredictable behavior by the ISA Server.

ISA Server Control Service Does Not Start

You could get the following error messages when you attempt to connect to an array in the ISA Management MMC:

```
ISA Error
The operation failed
Failed to connect
Error 0x8007203a
```

This happens when the LAT is not configured properly. If you have installed ISA Server Enterprise Edition as an array member and you include only the external interfaces in the LAT, the array will not be able to communicate with Active Directory on the internal Windows 2000 network. Array configuration information is stored in Active Directory when ISA Server is installed as an array member, and if ISA cannot contact Active Directory, it cannot determine its configuration.

The result is that the ISA Server Control (ISACTRL) service will not be able to start, and you will not be able to correct the LAT entries from any array member, because the ISA Management MMC will not display the current configuration.

This problem must be corrected from another computer or ISA array that is running the ISA Management MMC. The ISA management tools can be installed on any Windows 2000 computer (including Windows 2000 Professional) that is connected to the domain in which the ISA array resides.

Use the **Connect to** feature to connect to the array that has the misconfigured LAT. You will be able to access the configuration information that is stored in Active Directory and make the appropriate changes to the LAT. You need to restart the ISA Servers in the array after you make the modifications to the LAT.

For detailed, step-by-step instructions and more information about this problem, see article Q282035 in the Microsoft Knowledge Base on the Microsoft Web site.

Troubleshooting Authentication and Access Problems

One of the purposes of ISA Server is to control unauthorized access; however, improper configuration or conflicts can result in the inability of authorized users to access the resources they need. In some cases, this could be due to authentication requirements and inability of clients to be authenticated; in other cases, it could be due to the ISA configuration, browser settings, or other reasons. In the following sections, we discuss some common authentication and access problems and what to do about them.

Authentication Problems

Authentication requirements depend on the client type making the request (firewall, Web proxy, or S-NAT) and whether rules have been configured that apply to specific users and groups. When a client makes a request for a Web object, authentication information is passed to the ISA Server only if it is required, such as when the Web Proxy Service must identify the user in order for the request to be allowed.

With S-NAT clients, no authentication is involved (unless you are using the Web proxy client in conjunction with S-NAT). Only client address sets can be used to restrict outbound access.

NOTE

ISA Server can be configured to always require authentication for Web requests. To do so, you configure the array's **Outgoing Web Requests** properties by checking the option to ask unauthenticated users for identification.

HTTP requests that are made by firewall clients are treated as though they come from unauthenticated users if the filter to pass requests to the HTTP redirector is enabled. The ISA server will not ask for authentication information in this situation, so ISA is unable to pass the requests from unauthenticated users, and the request will be denied. A solution to this problem is to configure the Web proxy client (see Chapter 7 for details).

User's HTTP Request Is Sometimes Allowed, although a Site and Content Rule Denies Access

If you have configured a site and content rule that denies access to a specific user, you could find that the user's HTTP request is still allowed if the user's computer is set up as a Web proxy client and Web access is configured to allow anonymous access. If you have protocol rules that allow everyone to use all protocols, and you have site and content rules that allow everyone to access all sites, and you have an additional site and content rule that denies access to the specified user, the user might still be able to access the content.

If the computer is configured as a Web proxy client, no authentication will be required and the user will be allowed access.

If the computer is configured as a firewall client, the request will likewise be allowed because authentication will not be requested. (If non-HTTP content is requested, authentication will be required by the Firewall Service and the user's request will be denied.)

If authentication is not requested, ISA Server will not know that this is the user who is supposed to be denied access. To make the rule that applies to the specific user work in these scenarios, configure the array to ask unauthenticated users for identification, as discussed previously.

NOTE

Remember that access problems in general point to misconfiguration of permissions. This is true whether the problem is that users are unable to access resources to which they should have access or that users are being allowed to access resources that should be restricted.

Failure to Authenticate Users of Non-Microsoft Browsers

Users of Netscape or other non-Microsoft browsers might be unable to be authenticated by ISA Server. This happens because ISA can be configured to accept only Windows integrated authentication. If the client's browser cannot provide the user's credentials in NTLM format, those users will not be able to access the requested Web objects if authentication is required.

The supported authentication methods are configured in the array's incoming and outgoing Web request properties. In order to be authenticated, the client browsers must be able to use at least one of the authentication methods that ISA is configured to use.

To specify authentication methods, edit the listeners' properties, as shown in Figure 12.11.

Figure 12.11 The Authentication Method Is Configured via the Listeners' Properties Sheet for Incoming and Outgoing Web Requests

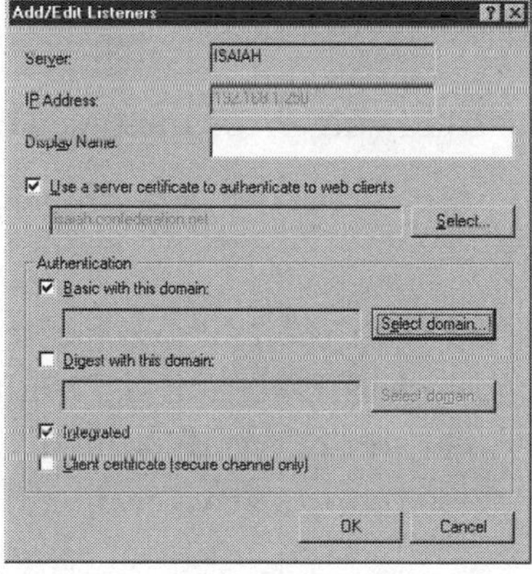

The following authentication methods can be used:

- Basic
- Digest

- Integrated Windows
- Client certificate

Microsoft Internet Explorer 5.x supports all of the above authentication methods. Some browsers might support only Basic or Digest authentication.

SECURITY ALERT!

Basic authentication transmits and receives the users' credentials as plain text. No encryption is used to protect the confidentiality of the information.

Error Message When Using Pass-Through Authentication with NTLM

Pass-through authentication could fail if you are attempting to use ISA pass-through authentication with NTLM authentication, using one of the following browsers:

- Microsoft Internet Explorer Versions 4.x or 5.x for Windows 95
- Microsoft Internet Explorer Versions 5.x for Windows 98 and 98 SE
- Microsoft Internet Explorer Versions 5.x for Windows 2000
- Microsoft Internet Explorer Versions 3.02, 4.x, and 5.x for Windows NT 4.0

This failure results in the following error message:

```
HTTP 401.2 unauthorized - Logon failed due to Authentication Failure
Internet Information Services
```

This is a problem identified with the Microsoft Internet Explorer browser software, which was corrected in MSIE Version 5.5 with Service Pack 1. The solution is to install the latest version of MSIE, which you can download from the Microsoft Internet Explorer Web site at www.microsoft.com/windows/ie.

Access Problems

Access problems include both the inability of authorized clients to access needed resources *and* the ability of unauthorized users to access resources that should not be available to them. Incorrect ISA Server configuration can result in both kinds of access problems.

Inability of Clients to Browse External Web Sites

When clients cannot access external Web sites, this can be related to one of two things:

- The ISA Server settings
- The client's browser settings

By default, ISA Server allows no communications to and from the Internet by internal clients. You must create rules to allow access. If you have just installed ISA Server and have not configured rules and your clients are unable to reach the external Web servers, this is normal ISA Server behavior. In this case, you can create protocol rules that will allow users (all users or selected users) to use the protocols and then create site and content rules to allow access to particular sites or all sites, using the protocols that are allowed by your protocol rules.

If the ISA Server settings are configured to allow client access and there is still a problem, it could be due to the client's browser settings. The proxy port must be set correctly (to 8080 if you are using the default port).

Problems with Specific Protocols or Protocol Definitions

If clients are unable to use specific protocols to communicate with the external network, you can allow the use of particular protocols in one of two ways:

- Configure IP packet filters to allow the protocols.
- Configure protocol rules to allow the protocols.

Protocol rules can be created to apply to all IP traffic, to only a specific set of protocol definitions, or to all *but* a selected set of protocols. A list of preconfigured commonly used protocol definitions is included with ISA Server, but you can also add protocol definitions.

NOTE

Protocol rules can only be applied to HTTP, Secure HTTP, Gopher, and FTP protocols when ISA Server is installed in caching mode. For detailed information on how to configure protocol rules, see Chapter 8.

Inability of Clients to PING External Hosts

A very common complaint in regard to a new deployment of ISA Server is that internal clients are not able to PING computers on the external network. The PING command is often used to send an ICMP echo request message to a host on the Internet for the purpose of testing connectivity. By default, S-NAT clients do not pass ICMP messages between internal and external computers (a process called *ICMP proxying*).

To enable this feature, you must enable IP routing. Follow these steps:

1. In the ISA Server Management MMC, expand the array or server object node for the appropriate array or server.
2. Expand the Access Policies object.
3. Right-click IP Packet Filters.
4. Select Properties.
5. On the General tab, check the Enable IP routing check box.

In addition to having IP routing enabled, there must be a packet filter that allows ICMP packets to be transmitted and received by the external network interface. The default ISA Server installation package includes filters for outbound and inbound ICMP requests. See Chapter 9 for detailed instructions on enabling and configuring packet filters.

Redirection of URL Results in Loop Condition

A *redirection loop* can occur when URL redirection is specified in the site and content rules so that when you request the URL www.aaa.com, you are redirected to www.bbb.com, which in turns redirects you back to www.aaa.com, and so forth.

This can happen if the site and content rule you have created denies all destinations. When you select **Redirect the request to an alternate URL** and set the rule to apply to all requests, client browsers will continually try to reach the original destination and be redirected to the URL specified in the rule.

There are two ways to solve this problem:

- You can create a rule that denies all destinations *except* the destination to which you want to redirect the request.
- You can choose *not* to specify a URL to which requests will be redirected when you select **Redirect the request to an alternate URL**.

Ability of Clients to Continue Using a Specific Protocol After Disabling of Rule

You could find that even after you have disabled a protocol rule, clients are still using the protocol that was allowed by the rule. This happens because disabling a protocol rule does not terminate any of the existing client sessions. Until the session has been disconnected, clients can continue to use the protocol after you disable the rule.

Experienced administrators will recognize that this is the same thing that happens when you change the permissions on a file or folder; a user who is currently logged on must log off and log back on before the change applies, because the access token that specifies the users' permissions is issued at logon.

To solve this problem, you can disconnect the current client sessions that are using the protocol. To do so, expand the server or array name in the left console tree, expand the **Monitoring** object, and expand the **Sessions** object. Then right-click the session that you want to disconnect and select **Abort Session**, as shown in Figure 12.12. Clients will not be able to use the protocols when they reconnect.

Figure 12.12 Disconnect the Sessions of Clients Who Are Using Protocols You Want to Disable

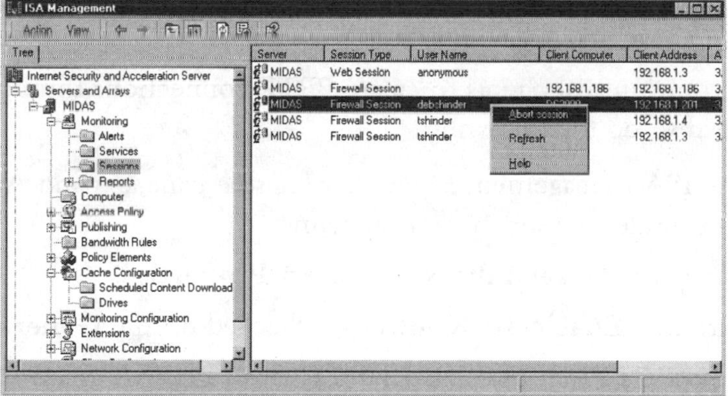

Dial-up and VPN Problems

In the following sections, we look at some common troubleshooting scenarios that involve dial-up and VPN connections.

Inability of ISA Server to Dial Out to the Internet

If the ISA server is not able to dial out to connect to the ISP, but you can dial out manually, you should check the dial-up entry's credentials. If the incorrect username and password are entered (or if the credentials are not specified), the ISP's dial-up server will not authenticate the connection and it will disconnect before a logon is established.

The properties for the dial-up entry can be edited by expanding the server or array name in the left console pane, expanding **Policy Elements**, and selecting **Dialup Entries**. In the right detail pane, right-click the dial-up entry you want to edit, and select **Properties**.

Dial-up Connection Is Dropped

A dial-up connection can be dropped because it was inadvertently disconnected. If you restart the ISA Server services, the connection should be automatically reestablished.

To restart the ISA Server services, expand the name of the server or array in the left console pane of the ISA Management MMC, expand **Monitoring**, and select **Services**. Right-click the service that you want to restart, and select **Start**.

Inability of PPTP Clients to Connect through ISA Server

If internal clients are unable to create PPTP tunnels to a destination on an external network (on the other side of the ISA server), this could be due to the fact that you have not configured a PPTP pass-through in the ISA Management MMC. By default, this option is *not* configured.

To allow your internal clients to create PPTP connections through the ISA server, you need to do the following:

1. In the ISA Management MMC left console pane, expand **Access Policy** under the server or array name.
2. Right-click **Packet Filters**, and select **Properties**.
3. Ensure that **Enable IP Routing** is checked on the **General** tab.
4. On the **PPTP** tab, check the **PPTP through ISA firewall** check box.

PPTP sessions can now be established through the ISA server by S-NAT clients. Note that you cannot establish PPTP connections using the firewall client. This is a very common problem and a good example of where one little check box can make all the difference.

Troubleshooting ISA Client Problems

Many ISA-related problems, even if they result from misconfiguration on the server side, manifest themselves on the client side. In the following sections, we discuss some common client problems and how you can resolve them. These problems include:

- Client performance problems
- Client connection problems

Let's take a look at each category.

Client Performance Problems

Performance problems at the client end are often caused by configuration problems on the ISA server. The origin of the slow client connections might vary, depending on the client type. In the next sections, we look at possible causes and fixes for slow client connections involving SecureNAT clients and firewall clients.

Slow Client Connection: SecureNAT Clients

If SecureNAT (S-NAT) connections are slow, the cause could be the result of not enabling packet filtering. You can solve this problem by enabling IP packet filtering. If IP routing is enabled (either in RRAS or in the ISA console), you should enable dynamic packet filtering.

NOTE

You will see the terms *IP routing* and *IP forwarding* used interchangeably in Microsoft and other documentation and even in different dialog boxes on Microsoft products. The meanings of the two terms are the same.

To enable packet filtering, expand the name of the server or array in the left console pane of the ISA Management MMC, expand **Access Policy**, and right-click **IP Packet Filters**; select **Properties**. Check the **Enable packet filtering** check box on the **General** tab of the Properties sheet. To enable IP routing, check the **Enable IP routing** check box on the same sheet, as shown in Figure 12.13.

Note that if IP routing is enabled via the Windows 2000 RRAS console on the ISA server, IP forwarding will be enabled, even if the check box on the Packet Filters Properties sheet is unchecked.

Figure 12.13 You Can Enable IP Packet Filtering and IP Routing to Improve S-NAT Performance

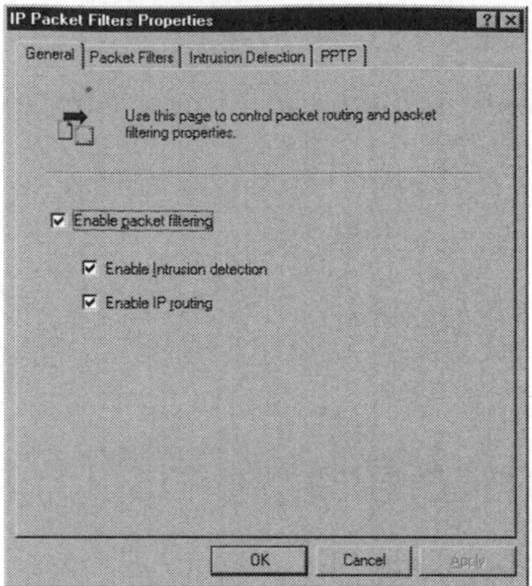

Slow Internal Connections: Firewall Clients

If the internal connections are inordinately slow for firewall clients, it might be due to the fact that clients cannot resolve local names using an external DNS server that does not have the necessary records. When the client sends requests to the DNS server, it must wait for the requests to time out before attempting to resolve the names using some other method.

The solution is to configure an internal DNS server that has records for the names and addresses of all clients on the internal network. The clients using the Firewall Service should be configured with a DNS address; all client name resolution requests will be handled by the ISA Server computer, and clients will not be delayed by waiting for a response from a DNS server that cannot resolve the internal names.

If packet filtering is enabled, you should also create an IP packet filter to use DNS Lookup. This will allow the ISA server to send DNS queries for names of external hosts on the Internet. Note that if you are using internal DNS servers that are configured as forwarders, this might not be necessary.

Client Connection Problems

Client connection problems can take many forms. The inability of clients to connect can be caused by a variety of circumstances, including misconfiguration of the client or of the ISA server. In the following sections, we look at several scenarios in which clients are unable to connect, including:

- Inability of clients to connect via modem

- Inability of SecureNAT clients to connect to the Internet
- Inability of clients to connect to external SSL sites
- Inability of SecureNAT clients to connect using computer names
- Inability of SecureNAT clients to connect to specific port due to a timeout

Inability of Clients to Connect via Modem

Client machines running the firewall client software cannot dial out directly to the Internet; this is a security feature.

To solve this problem, you must disable the firewall client. To do so, in **Start | Settings | Control Panel**, open the Firewall Client applet (shown in Figure 12.14). Uncheck the **Enable Firewall Client** check box to allow the client to dial out directly via the modem.

Figure 12.14 Disable the Firewall Client to Allow Direct Dial-out from the Machine

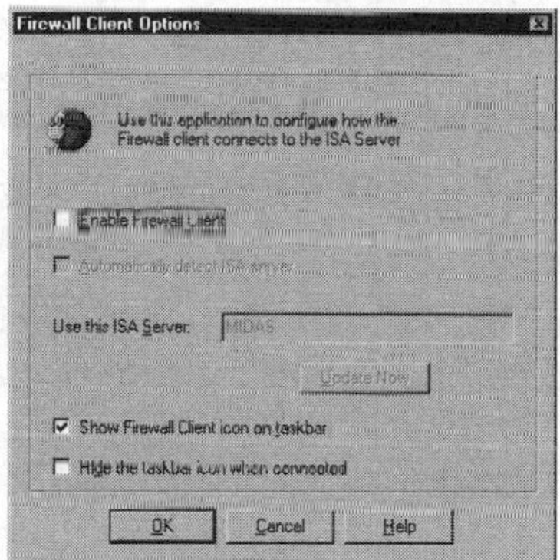

Inability of SecureNAT Clients to Connect to the Internet

SecureNAT clients will not be able to connect to the Internet through the ISA server if the client is not properly configured with the default gateway and DNS server. Check the configuration settings in the client's TCP/IP properties. See Chapter 7, "ISA Architecture and Client Configuration," for detailed information on how to configure the S-NAT client.

Inability of Clients to Connect to External SSL Sites

If a client attempts to connect to a secure site via the Web Proxy Service, the data must be encrypted end to end. This means that ISA Server must create an SSL tunnel for the traffic to pass through. Because ISA Server only allows tunnel connections on ports 443 and 563 by default, if a client tries to connect to a secure site using a different port, the connection attempt will fail.

The solution is to modify the ISA Administration COM object to allow tunneling on additional ports. The correct object to be modified is FPCTunnelPortRange. A sample VBScript for adding ports to the tunnel port range is available in the ISA SDK.

Instructions on how to modify the COM objects are available in the ISA Server SDK Help files. To access the Help files, run **help.cmd** in the **sdk** folder on the ISA Server CD-ROM.

Configuring & Implementing...

The Administration COM Objects

Component Object Model (COM) is an object-oriented programming architecture and includes a set of operating system services. COM is intended by Microsoft to allow developers to create applications in a modular, building-block process. New programs can be built by reusing existing components. Distributed COM (DCOM) adds interfaces to distribute various components of an application to different computers in a network.

The Administration COM objects in ISA Server can be used by developers working with any programming language that supports COM. Some of the objects are used for programmatic monitoring of currently running services; most are used for programmatic configuration of internal ISA settings.

Developers can extend ISA's functionality by using scripting to access and control ISA via the administration COM objects. The ISA Server SDK contains instructions on using the administration objects with Visual Basic and with C++.

Inability of SecureNAT Clients to Connect Using Computer Names

If an S-NAT client can connect to Internet sites using the IP address but is not able to connect using the "friendly" computer name, this is likely due to the fact that the client is configured to use an internal DNS server, which cannot resolve external Internet domain names.

The best solution is to configure the DNS server to forward requests to an external DNS server on the Internet. Another solution is to configure the clients to use a different DNS server that forwards name resolution requests to an external DNS server.

Inability of SecureNAT Clients to Connect to a Specific Port Due to a Timeout

S-NAT clients could experience an inability to connect to specific ports because the connection times out, even though protocol rules are set to allow "any IP traffic."

This problem can occur if the application that is attempting to connect uses multiple ports. The solution in this case, if some of the ports are determined dynamically, is to use an application filter that specifies and defines the ports.

If the application does not use multiple ports, the problem might be that the protocol is not listed in the protocol definitions. In this case, you need to define a protocol in which the specific port is the primary port.

NOTE

You cannot edit protocol definitions that are installed with application filters (they can be deleted). You can neither modify nor delete protocol definitions included with ISA Server. You can edit protocol definitions that you have created (in other words, user-defined protocol definitions).

To create a new protocol definition, right-click **Protocol Definitions** in the left console pane of the ISA Management MMC, under the **Policy Elements** object for either the array or the enterprise. Select **New** and **Protocol Definition**. This invokes the Protocol Definition Wizard, which walks you through the steps. Specify the port (along with the protocol type and direction) for the primary connection on the **Primary Connection Information** page of the wizard.

Troubleshooting Caching and Publishing Problems

In this section, we examine some common problems involving two important ISA Server functions: caching and publishing.

Caching Problems

When ISA Server is installed in caching or integrated mode, it caches objects to accelerate client access. In some cases, you might encounter problems with the caching function. In this section, we look at some common cache-related problems.

All Web Objects Not Being Cached

You might find that client access to Internet objects does not seem to enjoy any noticeable improvement with ISA Server. This could be due to the fact that your clients are commonly requesting objects that are not in the cache. ISA Server caches only the objects that meet the caching criteria you have configured.

The solution could be to adjust the cache content specifications. You can determine which HTTP objects will be cached according to several factors. To configure which content should or should not be cached, right-click **Cache Configuration** in the left console pane of the ISA Management MMC under the name of the server or array. Select **Properties**.

Select the **Advanced** tab of the Properties sheet, shown in Figure 12.15. You can make adjustments here that result in caching of more (or fewer) objects.

Figure 12.15 You Can Configure Which Content Will Be Cached Using the Cache Configuration Properties Sheet

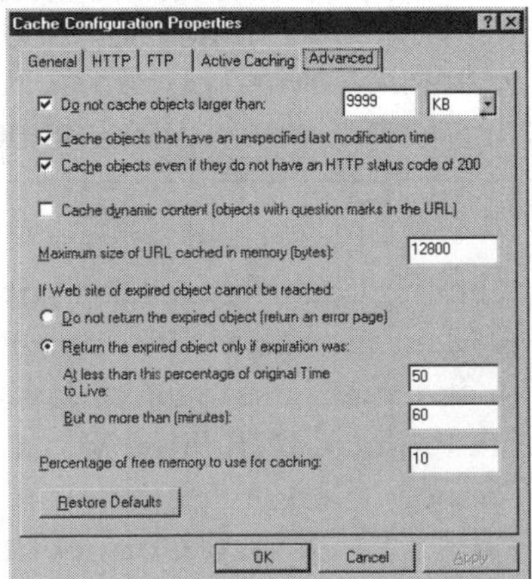

Web Proxy Service Does Not Start

If the Web Proxy Service will not start, this can be due to the fact that the cache contents file has become corrupted. The cache file is stored on a drive on which space has been allocated for this purpose.

To correct this problem, you might need to reconfigure the cache drive(s). Remember that the cache drive(s) must be formatted in NTFS. For more information about how to configure the cache drives, see Chapter 11, "Optimizing, Customizing, Integrating, and Backing Up ISA Server."

Designing & Planning...

Common HTTP Error Messages

Some of the more commonly encountered HTTP error codes include:

- **302** Redirection to a new URL. The resource has moved and the new URL is presented.
- **400** Bad request. The server did not understand the URL entered due to incorrect syntax.
- **401** Unauthorized. The user requested a document and did not provide authentication credentials.
- **403** Forbidden. Access is explicitly denied.
- **404** Not found. The document does not exist on this server.
- **500** Internal server error. The system administrator should check the error log.
- **8181** Certificate has expired (secure servers).

An HTTP 200 code indicates a successful transmission. All codes in the 3xx range indicate redirection messages; those in the 4xx range indicate client errors of some type; those in the 5xx range indicate server errors of some type. Messages in 1xx range are informational (for example, 101: switching protocols).

Publishing Problems

Publishing makes servers on the internal network available to users outside the LAN (on the other side of the ISA server). Publishing problems can involve the inability of authorized clients to access the published servers.

In this section, we look at some specific scenarios that involve publishing problems and how you can correct them.

Inability of Clients to Access Published Web Server

If clients are unable to access a published Web server and they receive a 403 ("Access Forbidden") error, this could be due to the fact that an access policy requires authentication. If no authentication method is configured for the listener, clients will not be able to authenticate, and thus access will be explicitly denied.

The solution is to configure one or more authentication methods for the listener. Clients' browsers will have to support one of the configured authentication methods in order to be authenticated. Authentication methods are configured on the **Incoming Web Requests** and **Outgoing Web Requests** tabs of the array's Properties sheet, as described earlier in this chapter.

Inability of External Clients to Send E-mail via Exchange Server

If you have external clients who need to send e-mail via an internal Exchange Server and they are unable to do so, the cause and solution could depend on how the Exchange Server is set up, either as a firewall client or a SecureNAT client.

Exchange Server Set Up as Firewall Client

If the Exchange Server is a firewall client, there could be a conflict between a server publishing rule and a firewall client configuration file.

The solution is to remove the Wspclnt.ini file from the publishing server and run the Mail Server Security Wizard. The wizard allows you to host and secure a mail server behind the ISA server and easily configures ISA rules to publish the mail services to the external users.

To run the wizard, right-click **Server publishing rules** under the **Publishing** object for the server or array. Select **Secure Mail Server**, as shown in Figure 12.16.

Details on publishing servers to the Internet and using server publishing rules are discussed in Chapter 10.

Another cause of this problem is the inability of the Exchange server to bind to the SMTP port on the ISA server due to another local or service or application on the ISA server that is binding to port 25 before the Exchange server has a chance to do so. Ensure that no other services or applications are using port 25 on the ISA server.

Figure 12.16 Use the Secure Mail Server Option to Publish a Mail Server to External Clients

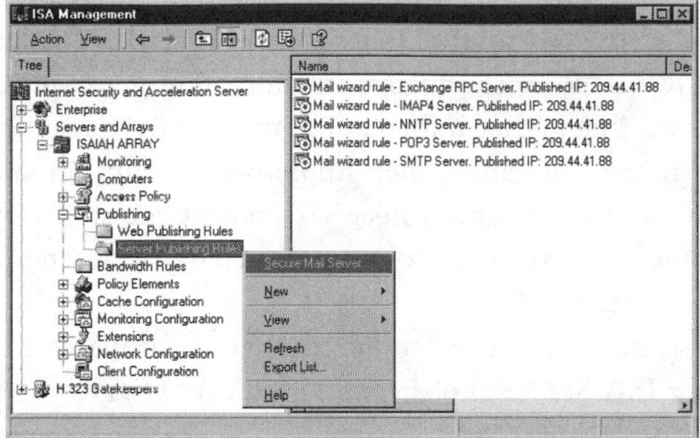

NOTE

If the connection between the ISA server and the Exchange server is broken momentarily, you need to restart the Exchange services in order for the Exchange server to bind to the appropriate ports on the ISA server.

Exchange Server Set Up as SecureNAT Client

If the Exchange server is a S-NAT client, this problem can be caused by incorrect configuration of the server publishing rules. The solution is to see that the publishing rules are configured to allow the external interface to pass SMTP traffic on port 25 and POP3 traffic on port 110 to the IP address and port of the internal Exchange server. See Chapter 10 for information on how to configure server publishing rules.

You should also check to ensure that the publishing rule is configured to apply to all Internet clients or that a client address set is specified that includes the addresses of the clients who need to use the server. Note that IP packet filtering must be enabled in order to use client address sets; if IP packet filtering is not enabled, the rule will apply to all clients.

Summary

In this chapter, we have provided you with some guidelines to help you establish a troubleshooting "style" and routine that works for you. We discussed the common procedure that is most effective in approaching any problem-solving situation, in which you first gather information, then analyze the data and come up with possible "diagnoses" or causes, then implement a solution and assess the success or failure of your actions (and if necessary, repeat the steps). Finally, you should fully document the incident to preserve what you learned from it for your own and for others' future reference.

We discussed some of the many resources that are available to help you solve problems involving ISA Server and the Windows 2000 Server operating system on which it runs. You learned about formal technical support venues; official and unofficial Web sites; where to find useful books, magazines, and online articles; and how to use mailing lists and newsgroups to cut down on the time spent "reinventing the wheel."

Next, we approached a sampling of real-life troubleshooting scenarios based on commonly reported ISA Server-related problems. You learned how to implement solutions to address problems involving ISA installation and configuration, authentication and access, client configuration, caching, publishing, and services.

This chapter and this book were written to help you master a new, complex, and exciting software product that promises to be a popular choice for corporate networks all the way up to the enterprise level, where a viable, integrated, easy-to-administer Internet security and acceleration solution is needed.

Solutions Fast Track

Understanding Basic Troubleshooting Principles

☑ Troubleshooting refers to the process of discovering, diagnosing, and correcting problems.

☑ Our systematic approach to troubleshooting involves five basic steps: information gathering, analysis and planning, implementation of a solution, assessment of the effectiveness of the solution, and documentation of the incident.

☑ Standard information forms help you gather information in a systematic way that makes it easy to organize and analyze.

- ☑ Once you've gathered all the information possible regarding the problem (including attempting to reproduce it), it's time to analyze the data. Your analysis of the data will lead you to formulate a logical *plan* based on your diagnoses, possible solutions, and priorities.
- ☑ Although there could be several possible solutions to a problem, you should always implement *one change at a time.* Assess the results of that change before trying something else.
- ☑ In the *follow-up* stage of troubleshooting, it is vital that you assess the results of your actions and determine whether your "fix" worked, whether it was only a temporary workaround or actually solved the problem, whether it caused other problems while correcting the original one, and what can be done in the future to prevent the problem from recurring.
- ☑ Always start by checking the Event Viewer and other logs. In many cases, the information that will point you in the right direction is there waiting for you.
- ☑ Five troubleshooting tips endorsed by problem solvers in many fields are precisely defining the problem; recreating the problem; avoiding tunnel vision; practicing the art of patience; using available resources; and not being afraid to ask for help.

Troubleshooting ISA Installation and Configuration Problems

- ☑ Installation of ISA Server usually proceeds in a straightforward fashion. Problems during or directly following installation are often related to one of three things: hardware incompatibilities, software incompatibilities, and improper initial configuration.
- ☑ If you are installing ISA Server as an array member, Active Directory must be implemented on your network.
- ☑ ISA Server's address translation function is also incompatible with third-party NAT solutions such as Sygate or NAT32. You should install these programs from the Windows 2000 computer before installing ISA Server.
- ☑ If you receive an error message:

```
ISA Server cannot save the properties. Error 0x80040340. The IP range
already exists in the Local Address Table (LAT)
```

when you attempt to save a new LAT entry, this could be due to the fact that it is an exact duplicate of an already existing address.

- ☑ When you install ISA Server and you need for your clients to be able to use an external Exchange server, you may find that using Microsoft Outlook for e-mail does not work, although Web services function properly. In this case, you need to add the IP address of the external Exchange server to the LAT and install the firewall client software on the internal machines that are running Outlook. This will allow the clients' e-mail to go through.

Troubleshooting Authentication and Access Problems

- ☑ ISA Server can be configured to always require authentication for Web requests. To do so, you configure the array's **Outgoing Web Requests** properties by checking the option to ask unauthenticated users for identification.
- ☑ Users of Netscape or other non-Microsoft browsers might be unable to be authenticated by ISA Server. This happens because ISA can be configured to only accept Windows integrated authentication. If the client's browser cannot provide the user's credentials in NTLM format, those users will not be able to access the requested Web objects if authentication is required.
- ☑ Access problems include both the inability of authorized clients to access needed resources *and* the ability of unauthorized users to access resources that should not be available to them. Incorrect ISA Server configuration can result in both kinds of access problems.
- ☑ If clients are unable to use specific protocols to communicate with the external network, you can allow the use of particular protocols in one of two ways: configure IP packet filters to allow the protocols, and configure protocol rules to allow the protocols.
- ☑ You might find that even after you have disabled a protocol rule, clients are still using the protocol that was allowed by the rule. This happens because disabling a protocol rule does not terminate any of the existing

client sessions. Until the session has been disconnected, clients can continue to use the protocol after you disable the rule.

- ☑ A dial-up connection might be dropped because it was inadvertently disconnected. If you restart the ISA Server services, the connection should be automatically reestablished.

Troubleshooting ISA Client Problems

- ☑ If Secure NAT (S-NAT) connections are slow, the cause might be the result of not enabling packet filtering.
- ☑ SecureNAT clients will not be able to connect to the Internet through the ISA server if the client is not properly configured with the default gateway and DNS server. Check the configuration settings in the client's TCP/IP properties.
- ☑ If the internal connections are inordinately slow for firewall clients, it could be due to the fact that clients cannot resolve local names using an external DNS server that does not have the necessary records.
- ☑ S-NAT clients may experience an inability to connect to specific ports because the connection times out, even though protocol rules are set to allow "any IP traffic."
- ☑ The Administration COM objects in ISA Server can be used by developers working with any programming language that supports COM. Some of the objects are used for programmatic monitoring of currently running services; most are used for programmatic configuration of internal ISA settings.
- ☑ If a S-NAT client can connect to Internet sites using the IP address but is not able to connect using the "friendly" computer name, this is likely due to the fact that the client is configured to use an internal DNS server, which cannot resolve external Internet domain names.

Troubleshooting Caching, Publishing, and Services

- ☑ When ISA Server is installed in caching or integrated mode, it caches objects to accelerate client access. In some cases, you might encounter problems with the caching function.

- ☑ If the Web proxy service will not start, this can be due to the fact that the cache contents file has become corrupted. The cache file is stored on a drive where space has been allocated for this purpose.
- ☑ Publishing makes servers on the internal network available to users outside the LAN (on the other side of the ISA Server). Publishing problems could involve the inability of authorized clients to access the published servers.
- ☑ If the Exchange server is a S-NAT client, this can be caused by incorrect configuration of the server publishing rules. The solution is to see that the publishing rules are configured to allow the external interface to pass SMTP traffic on port 25 and POP3 traffic on port 110 to the IP address and port of the internal Exchange server.
- ☑ If the Exchange server is a firewall client, there could be a conflict between a server publishing rule and a firewall client configuration file.

Frequently Asked Questions

The following Frequently Asked Questions, answered by the authors of this book, are designed to both measure your understanding of the concepts presented in this chapter and to assist you with real-life implementation of these concepts. To have your questions about this chapter answered by the author, browse to **www.syngress.com/solutions** and click on the **"Ask the Author"** form.

Q: Where can I find the latest updates, service packs, and new information about ISA Server?

A: The Microsoft Internet Security & Acceleration Server Web site at www.microsoft.com/isaserver/ is the first place to check for the latest information. Links to the newest documentation and downloadable software are included on this page.

Q: Where can I get an evaluation copy of ISA Server to play with, evaluate for possible deployment, and learn the product?

A: The Microsoft Web site at www.microsoft.com/isaserver/downloads/evaluationedition.htm provides a 120-day trial version of ISA Server called the Evaluation Edition. You can choose between the Standard and Enterprise editions for evaluation, and there is an upgrade version if you already have Release Candidate 1 installed. The Evaluation Edition is *not* for deployment on a production network and expires at the end of the 120-day trial period.

Q: What training is available for ISA Server?

A: Microsoft provides several online seminars, including the following:

- Microsoft Internet Security and Acceleration Server 2000 Overview
- In-Depth Look at Microsoft Internet Security and Acceleration Server
- Internet Security and Acceleration Server 2000 Web Seminar

These can be accessed from the Web site at www.microsoft.com/isaserver/trainevents/default.htm. Microsoft Official Curriculum (MOC) course 2159 provides training in installation and deployment of ISA Server with an emphasis on the enterprise. You can also find independent training programs and online courses offered by non-Microsoft certified training centers, community colleges, and private technical schools.

Appendix

ISA Server 2000 Fast Track

This Appendix wlll provide you with a quick, yet comprehensive, review of the most important concepts covered in this book.

❖ Chapter 1: Introduction to Microsoft ISA Server

What Is ISA Server?

- ☑ Internet Security and Acceleration (ISA) provides two very different sets of functionality. Consequently, some organizations use ISA primarily for its security function. For others, speeding up Web access via the acceleration function could be more important. Of course, many organizations benefit from both features.
- ☑ Proxy servers have been around for quite a while. Despite its new, somewhat esoteric name, ISA Server is a proxy server, albeit a very full-featured one.
- ☑ Proxy servers "stand in" between the computers on a LAN and those on the public network outside.
- ☑ ISA Server performs the functions of a full-featured dedicated firewall.
- ☑ The advantage of Microsoft's ISA Server is that it combines these components—proxy, NAT, and firewall—into one package. This makes it easier to deploy and administer than separate software programs and/or hardware devices.
- ☑ ISA is not only an Internet security server; it is also an Internet acceleration server. This means faster access to frequently viewed Web sites and less internetwork traffic.
- ☑ Because Web caching reduces Internet traffic, it can also reduce your bandwidth cost.
- ☑ H.323 is a standard of the International Telecommunications Union (ITU), which was approved in 1996 (version 2 was approved in 1998) to provide a foundation for audio, video, and data communications across IP-based networks such as the global Internet.
- ☑ The ISA Server Standard Edition is appropriate for small business networks (or even sophisticated home networks) and for implementation on a departmental basis in larger organizations.
- ☑ The ISA Enterprise Edition is designed for maximum scalability to the largest, high-traffic enterprise networks. Fault tolerance, centralized management, and multiple-level policy application are at the core of the Enterprise Edition's feature set.

Chapter 1 Continued

☑ ISA Servers can be installed as individual standalone servers or, if you have the Enterprise Edition

☑ A big advantage of joining multiple ISA servers in an array is the ability to manage them as one entity.

☑ Just as Proxy Server was considered a member of the Microsoft BackOffice Family, ISA Server also belongs to a new Microsoft "family," the members of which are designed to work with Windows 2000 in an enterprise environment. This group of enterprise servers is now called the Microsoft.Net family, or simply ".Net" (pronounced dot-net) servers.

☑ It is Microsoft's goal to offer, in the .Net family of servers, a group of products that can work individually or together to provide the full range of features needed in today's increasingly large and diversified network environments.

Firewall products support the filtering of messages to either allow data to pass through or prevent data from doing so, according to specified criteria.

☑ Packet filtering does most of its work at the Network Layer of the OSI networking model (equivalent to the Internetwork Layer of the DoD model), dealing with IP packets.

☑ Dynamic packet filtering provides higher security because it opens the necessary port(s) only when required for communication to take place, then closes the port immediately after the communication ends.

☑ Circuit filters restrict access on the basis of host machines (not users) by processing the information found in the TCP and UDP packet headers. This allows you to create filters that would, for example, prohibit anyone using Computer A from using FTP to access files on Computer B.

☑ The ISA firewall service works at the circuit level with most Internet applications and protocols, making them perform as though they were directly connected to the Internet.

☑ Application filtering is the most sophisticated level of filtering performed by the firewall service and is especially useful in allowing you to protect your network against specific types of attacks such as malicious SMTP commands or attempts to penetrate your local DNS servers.

☑ By definition, a SecureNAT client cannot also be a firewall client.

Chapter 1 Continued

- ☑ The firewall service on the ISA server intercepts Winsock API calls initiated by the clients and redirects those requests to the Internet computer to which they are addressed.
- ☑ If a computer is configured as a client to the ISA Server (by setting the default gateway in the computer's TCP/IP properties) and does not have the firewall client software installed, it will automatically be a SecureNAT client.
- ☑ If your network is larger and more complex and there are routers between the SecureNAT clients and the ISA Server, the default gateway settings on the clients will be configured with the IP address of the router on the local subnet.
- ☑ Certificates are digital "documents" that verify the identity of a client or server and that are issued by a trusted third party to which that identity has been satisfactorily proven.

ISA Server Features Overview

- ☑ By including a friendly interface that allows you to perform system hardening, or a lockdown of the Windows 2000 operating system on which ISA Server is running, Microsoft has made it easy to configure security appropriate to your network's needs.
- ☑ One of ISA Server's star attractions is its smooth integration with virtual private networking. A VPN is established by creating a virtual "tunnel" through the Internet to communicate securely with a private network.
- ☑ When the ISA Server is configured as a VPN server, it supports secure gateway-to-gateway communications or client-to-gateway communications over the Internet.
- ☑ An exciting feature of the ISA Server firewall service is the intrusion detection system that can actually recognize that an attack of a specific type is being attempted and can perform a predefined action when such an intrusion is identified.
- ☑ ISA as a Web caching server also offers a plethora of features designed to speed Internet access for your organization while reducing WAN link bandwidth usage.
- ☑ ISA allows computers on a LAN to access the Internet via a single modem or ISDN/DSL adapter and a single phone line, using one ISP account and

Chapter 1 Continued

requiring only one public registered IP address (either assigned permanently by the ISP or assigned dynamically by its DHCP server each time a dial-up connection is established to the ISP server).

- ☑ ISA Server uses the Microsoft Management Console (MMC) that is the cornerstone of all Windows 2000 administrative tools (and was introduced with IIS 4.0 and Microsoft Proxy Server back when NT ruled the Windows networking roost).
- ☑ Microsoft is positioning ISA Server as an extensible platform, based on the fact that developers can add to its user interface with ISA Administrator COM objects.
- ☑ Administrators who have some programming or scripting experience can use COM objects of ISA Server in scripts or VB applications to automate administration and configuration of ISA.

Who This Book Is For and What It Covers

- ☑ Microsoft has targeted ISA Server for the enterprise market, and that notion is reflected in the company's stated audience profile for the exam: Candidates are expected to have at least a year of experience operating in a medium-sized to very large networking environment (defined as 200 to 26,000 or more users and multiple physical locations) where the Windows 2000 operating system is in use.
- ☑ If you're looking for specific scenarios that address your own situation or answers to troubleshooting problems that occur in your ISA deployment, we have tried to make it easy for you to find and flip to the section of this book that you need.
- ☑ An understanding of the TCP/IP protocol stack is necessary to configuring and working with ISA Server. If you do not have previous networking experience, or come from a NetWare 4.x or earlier environment and need a review of basic TCP/IP concepts, see *Troubleshooting Windows 2000 TCP/IP*, (Syngress Publishing, 2000).

❖ Chapter 2: ISA Server in the Enterprise

Enterprise-Friendly Features

☑ Over the past several years Microsoft has made a conscious effort to penetrate the enterprise market, and we have begun to see the Windows server operating systems replace or at least take their place beside the UNIX machines and mainframes that have served this market in the past.

☑ Enterprise technologies provide ways to integrate the networking needs of an organization that has multiple divisions, functions, and/or physical locations. Microsoft defines an enterprise network as one that incorporates multiple subnets with routed LAN and WAN links.

☑ In a large business network environment, access and security are not just desirable; they are mission critical.

☑ The ability to create server arrays, which can be managed together as a single entity, is one of the features that provide fault tolerance, making ISA Server a highly reliable solution to your network's security and access acceleration needs.

☑ Scalability can be defined as the ability of a system (individual computer or network) to maintain or improve performance as size (of the application or network load) increases.

☑ Scaling up generally refers to the addition of more resources (for example, memory, processors or disks).

☑ Scaling out refers to the ability to distribute resources across multiple computer systems so that higher performance is possible even though the requirements might be greater than the capability of a single system.

☑ Windows 2000 Server can support up to four microprocessors out of the box and up to 32 processors in the OEM versions of Windows 2000 Data Center Server.

☑ The speed at which a computer can process data (by performing the necessary arithmetical calculations on the binary code) depends on the speed of its microprocessor.

☑ Load balancing refers to spreading the burden, or load, of work across servers so that no one server is overloaded.

Chapter 2 Continued

- ☑ Microsoft defines a cluster as a group of independent servers that are managed as a single system for higher availability, easier manageability, and greater scalability.
- ☑ ISA Server uses Cache Array Routing Protocol (CARP) to allow multiple ISA servers to use a single logical cache. This process is called distributed caching.

Designing Enterprise Solutions

- ☑ The trend today is toward open standard Internet services such as HTTP (Web), FTP (file transfer), SMTP/POP/IMAP (e-mail), NNTP (news), and DNS (name resolution). This is in contrast to vendor-specific services (such as Novell's file and print sharing or Microsoft's Exchange 5.x directory services).
- ☑ ISA Server is dependent on TCP/IP and cannot function without it.
- ☑ In Windows NT 4.0 networks, there was a limit on the number of security objects (user accounts, group accounts, computer accounts) that could exist in a single domain.
- ☑ Windows 2000 networks are built on the concept of domain trees, which are groups of domains that share a contiguous namespace.
- ☑ All domains in a Windows 2000 domain tree share implicit, two-way transitive trust relationships with each other.
- ☑ An NT domain must have one and only one primary domain controller (PDC), on which the master writable copy of the SAM database is stored. Windows 2000 networks can have multiple domain controllers, all of which have a writable copy of the Active Directory partition.
- ☑ In an NT network, the domain is the smallest administrative boundary, but this is not true in a Windows 2000 network where administrative authority can be delegated at the OU level.
- ☑ Because many enterprise networks span international boundaries, there is a likelihood that your network will need to be divided into multiple domains to accommodate differences in languages, currencies, and laws.
- ☑ An intranet in its simplest form is an internal, private Web. Businesses, especially large ones, have discovered the advantages of using Internet technologies such as HTTP to publish information for employees and provide a

Chapter 2 Continued

means for those within the organization to distribute information easily and inexpensively.

- ☑ An extranet is similar to an intranet in that it is a private network using Internet technology. The difference is that whereas the intranet is made accessible to internal users (employees), the extranet is made accessible to selected external users (business partners, vendors, and customers).
- ☑ An important part of ISA design and deployment planning involves estimating the expected usage, based on number of users and usage patterns, in order to determine the number of ISA servers required.
- ☑ A big advantage of installing additional ISA servers instead of merely adding processors to the existing server is the ability to group the multiple machines in arrays.
- ☑ If you have multiple ISA servers that you want to join in arrays, all members of an array must belong to the same Windows 2000 domain and to the same Active Directory site.
- ☑ Both the firewall and caching modes allow implementation of enterprise policy, but caching mode supports access policy only for HTTP.
- ☑ To install ISA Server as a standalone, you need an account that belongs to the local administrators group on the machine on which you are installing.

Planning Multiserver Arrays

- ☑ Arrays are appropriate for medium-sized and large networks, and in the enterprise environment, they offer many advantages.
- ☑ Array configuration information can be backed up using ISA Server's backup and restore feature.
- ☑ Microsoft documentation recommends that you always back up the array configuration after making significant changes to your array, such as changing installation mode, cache size or location, or enterprise policy settings, and any time you add or remove a server to or from the array or change the name of a computer that is an array member.
- ☑ Policy elements refer to properties of ISA policy rules, which can be created for your enterprise policy and for each array policy.

Chapter 2 Continued

Understanding ISA Server Licensing

- ☑ Many experience network administrators will be familiar with the licensing methods used by Microsoft for its server operating systems, Window NT and Windows 2000. In both cases, there are two options for licensing connections to the servers: 1. Purchase of an individual Client Access License (CAL) for each client machine on the network, allowing it to access as many servers on the network as desired. 2.Purchase of a set number of licenses for each server, allowing that number of clients to connect simultaneously to that particular server.
- ☑ ISA Server uses a processor-based licensing structure, which means that the cost of an ISA Server license is dependent on how many microprocessors are installed in the computer on which it runs.
- ☑ Enterprise-level organizations often need multiple licenses. For example, if you will be setting up an ISA server array (or several), you need to purchase at least one license for each machine and, if some are multiprocessor machines, more than one.
- ☑ Cost per processor also differs depending on whether you purchase the Standard or the Enterprise edition and whether you qualify for the upgrade price or must purchase the full product.
- ☑ Microsoft has announced that the processor-based licensing model used for ISA Server will also apply to other server products in the .Net family.

❖ Chapter 3: Security Concepts and Security Policies

Security Overview

- ☑ Network security solutions can be loosely divided into three categories: hardware, software, and human.

Defining Basic Security Concepts

- ☑ To protect your network resources from theft, damage, or unwanted exposure, you must understand who initiates these events, why they do it, and how they do it.

Chapter 3 Continued

- ☑ A good network security system will help you easily remove the temptations (open ports, exploitable applications) and will be as transparent to your users as possible. ISA Server, when properly configured, meets these requirements.

Addressing Security Objectives

- ☑ File servers on which sensitive data is stored and infrastructure servers that provide mission-critical services such as logon authentication and access control should be placed in a highly secure location. At a minimum, servers should be in a locked room to which only those who need to work directly with the servers have access. Keys should be distributed sparingly, and records should be kept of issuance and return.
- ☑ Don't depend on access permissions and other software security methods alone to protect your network. If a potential intruder can gain physical access to a networked computer, he or she is that much closer to accessing your valuable data or introducing a virus onto your network.
- ☑ Although switches and routers are somewhat more secure than hubs, any device through which the data passes is a point of vulnerability. Replacing hubs with switches and routers makes it more difficult for an intruder to "sniff" on your network, but it is still possible to use techniques such as *Address Resolution Protocol (ARP) spoofing.*
- ☑ Despite the many benefits of wireless technologies, they also present special problems, especially in the area of network security. Data traveling over wireless media is more vulnerable to interception than data over cabled media. Radio and microwave are known as *broadcast media.*
- ☑ According to most computer security studies, as documented in RFC 2196, actual loss (in terms of money, productivity, computer reputation, and other tangible and intangible harm) is greater for internal security breaches than for those from the outside.
- ☑ Like Windows NT, Windows 2000 provides for granular auditing of security-related events and records the information to a security log. The log can be viewed (by users with administrative privileges only) via the Windows Event Viewer.

Chapter 3 Continued

Recognizing Network Security Threats

- ☑ There are probably as many different specific motives as there are hackers, but we can break the most common intruder motivations into a few broad categories: recreation, remuneration, revenge.
- ☑ In some instances, hackers working for competitors will go "undercover" and seek a job with your company in order to steal data that they can take back to their own organizations.
- ☑ Unlike the other attack types, *social engineering* does not refer to a technological manipulation of computer hardware or software vulnerabilities and does not require much in the way of technical skills. Instead, this type of attack exploits *human* weaknesses—such as carelessness or the desire to be cooperative—to gain access to legitimate network credentials.
- ☑ Because social engineering is a human problem, not a technical problem, prevention must come primarily through education rather than technological solutions.
- ☑ Although they do not destroy or steal data as some other types of attacks do, the objective of DoS attackers is to bring down the network, denying service to its legitimate users. The purpose of a DoS attack is to render a network inaccessible by generating a type or amount of network traffic that will crash the servers, overwhelm the routers, or otherwise prevent the network's devices from functioning properly.
- ☑ *Distributed DoS (DDoS) attacks* use intermediary computers, called *agents,* on which programs called *zombies* have previously been surreptitiously installed. The hacker activates these zombie programs remotely, causing the intermediary computers (which can number in the hundreds or even thousands) to simultaneously launch the actual attack.
- ☑ The *DNS DoS attack* exploits the difference in size between a DNS query and a DNS response, in which all the network's bandwidth is tied up by bogus DNS queries. The attacker uses the DNS servers as "amplifiers" to multiply the DNS traffic.
- ☑ *Synchronization request (SYN) attacks* exploit the TCP "three-way handshake," the process by which a communications session is established between two computers. Because TCP (unlike UDP) is connection-oriented, a *session,* or

Chapter 3 Continued

direct one-to-one communication link, must be created prior to sending data. The client computer initiates the communication with the server (the computer that has the resources it wants to access).

☑ The ping-of-death attack is launched by creating an IP packet (sometimes referred to as a *killer packet*) larger than 65,536 bytes, which is the maximum allowed by the IP specification. This can cause the target system to crash, hang, or reboot. ISA allows you to specifically enable detection of ping-of-death attacks.

☑ A *worm* is a program that can travel across the network from one computer to another. Sometimes different parts of a worm run on different computers. Worms make multiple copies of themselves and spread throughout a network.

Categorizing Security Solutions

☑ Hardware security solutions come in the form of network devices. Firewalls, routers, even switches can function to provide a certain level of security.

☑ Hardware-based firewalls are often referred to as *firewall appliances.* A disadvantage of hardware-based firewalls is the proprietary nature of the software they run. Another disadvantage of many of these products, such as Cisco's highly respected PIX, is the high cost.

☑ Software security solutions cover a much broader range than hardware solutions. They include the security features built into network operating systems as well as additional security software made by Microsoft or third-party vendors.

Designing a Comprehensive Security Plan

☑ A widely accepted method for developing your network security plan is laid out in RFC 2196, *Site Security Handbook,* and attributed to Fites, et al (1989).

☑ It is important to understand that a security *plan* is not the same thing as a security *policy,* although the two words are sometimes used interchangeably.

☑ A LAN that is self-contained and has no Internet connectivity nor any modems or other outside connections does not require the degree of protection (other than physical security) that is necessary when an intruder can take many avenues "in."

Chapter 3 Continued

- ☑ The best security policy is to have as few connections from the internal network to the outside as possible and control access at those entry points (collectively called the *network perimeter*).
- ☑ An organization's management model can have a profound influence on what is or isn't acceptable in planning security for the network.
- ☑ The U.S. government provides specifications for rating network security implementations in a publication often referred to as the *Orange Book,* formally called the *Department of Defense Trusted Computer System Evaluation Criteria,* or *TCSEC.* The *Red Book,* or *Trusted Network Interpretation of the TCSEC (TNI),* explains how the TCSEC evaluation criteria are applied to computer networks.
- ☑ Best practices dictate that no one person should have complete authority or control. Besides, in an enterprise-level network, it would be difficult for any single person to handle all facets of developing and implementing the security plan.
- ☑ Best practices for password creation require that you address the following: password length and complexity, who creates the password, and forced changing of passwords.

Incorporating ISA Server in your Security Plan

- ☑ ISA Server's firewall function prevents unauthorized packets from entering your internal network. ISA also provides monitoring of intrusion attempts as well as allowing you to set alerts to notify you when intrusions occur.
- ☑ The goal of *system hardening* is to create as many barriers as possible to unauthorized persons who would try to access your network.
- ☑ *Secure Sockets Layer (SSL)* is a protocol that can be used to manage the security of Internet communications. SSL operates between HTTP at the Application layer and TCP at the Transport layer.
- ☑ *SSL tunneling* allows a client computer to create a tunnel through the ISA server to a Web server whenever the browser on a client machine requests a secure HTTP object, thus allowing the client to connect to and communicate directly with the external Web server.
- ☑ Using *SSL bridging,* ISA Server can encrypt or decrypt requests from clients and forward the requests to a Web server.

❖ Chapter 4: ISA Server Deployment Planning and Design

ISA Deployment: Planning and Designing Issues

- ☑ Prior to installing ISA Server, you need to assess hardware requirements to meet the needs of your organization's ISA Server deployment plan. An organization that has 50 network clients and chooses to utilize only the Web proxy service will have very different requirements than an organization with 30,000 network clients that wants to avail itself of all the networking services ISA Server has to offer.
- ☑ Whether you choose to install one or 100 ISA servers, each server must meet minimum hardware and software requirements.
- ☑ ISA Server must be installed on a Windows 2000 Server family computer.
- ☑ If you do not have Windows 2000 Service Pack 2 installed, you must install a pre-Service Pack 2 hotfix that is included on the CD-ROM.
- ☑ ISA Server and Windows 2000 support multiprocessor system setups.
- ☑ The number of processors determines how much you'll pay for ISA Server, because the licensing fees are based on the number of processors on the server.
- ☑ Microsoft recommends that any ISA server you deploy should have at least 256 MB of RAM to take advantage of all the product's features.
- ☑ The amount of disk space you allot to your ISA Server configuration can be quite variable. The space required for the program files will always be about 20 MB.
- ☑ You need to plan for a larger amount of disk space per user in a larger environment because there will be a wider variation in the per-user statistics.
- ☑ You should have at least two network interfaces if you plan to use the ISA server as a firewall.
- ☑ If you plan to use a perimeter network, that network can be connected to a third interface connected to the ISA Server.
- ☑ You should always disable file and print sharing for Microsoft networks on the external interface and even for the internal interface of the ISA computer.

Chapter 4 Continued

- ☑ Incorrectly configuring the LAT is a one of the quickest ways to completely disable security provided by ISA Server.

Active Directory Implementation

- ☑ If you plan to centralize configuration of your ISA servers or you want to install an array of ISA servers, you need an Active Directory domain.
- ☑ ISA servers that have all network interfaces connected to the internal network can safely be configured as members of an internal Active Directory domain.

Mission-Critical Considerations

- ☑ *Mirrored volumes* provide a method to allow all data written to one volume to be automatically copied to a second volume. Mirrored-volume configurations allow for real-time fault tolerance for the data stored on a mirrored volume.
- ☑ The major advantage of a RAID 5 volume over a mirrored volume is speed.
- ☑ In your ISA Server configuration, you should include log files, cache files, and reports on the RAID 5 array. Doing so will significantly speed ISA server performance and allow for fault tolerance for these important files. *Keep in mind that your array is fault tolerant only when all disks are in working order*
- ☑ More sophisticated (and expensive) RAID implementations allow you to keep "hot spares" online so that, in the event of a disk failure, a hot spare is introduced to the array automatically.
- ☑ The ideal network fault-tolerance solution for your external interface is to have multiple ISA Servers participating in an enterprise array on the edge of your network.
- ☑ The best way to provide for server fault tolerance is to take advantage of arrays of ISA servers when you deploy the Enterprise Edition.
- ☑ One way you can accomplish server fault tolerance is to configure a *DNS round robin* on your network. In your DNS, you assign the same host name to the IP addresses of your respective ISA servers.
- ☑ A *bastion host* is a computer that has an interface with an untrusted network. In the context of ISA Server, that untrusted network is typically the Internet.

Chapter 4 Continued

Planning the Appropriate Installation Mode

- ☑ There are three types, or *modes*, of ISA Server installation: Firewall mode, cache mode, integrated mode.
- ☑ ISA servers support virtually all ISA Server features, with the exception of the Web cache.
- ☑ A cache mode server is best placed on the internal network, in which case you can use a single interface or multiple interfaces. *Be sure that you implement some kind of firewall solution at the edge of your network to protect your internal computers from Internet intruders.*
- ☑ ISA Server Enterprise Edition can be installed as either an array member or as a standalone server.
- ☑ A critical aspect of your ISA Server design is the ISA Server *client base* you expect to support. Proxy Server 2.0 supported what were known as the *Web proxy client, WinSock proxy client*, and *SOCKS proxy client*.
- ☑ Network computers configured as Firewall Service clients are able to access all Winsock protocols.
- ☑ SecureNat clients are the simplest type of ISA client to set up, because virtually no configuration is required.
- ☑ ISA Server supports Web publishing and server publishing. By publishing servers, you are able to offer Internet clients services on your internal network. ISA Server Publishing allows you to publish services such as HTTP, NNTP, SMTP, and POP mail to users on the Internet in a secure context.

❖ Chapter 5: ISA Server Installation

Installing ISA Server on a Windows 2000 Server

- ☑ The installation files for ISA Server can be accessed via the product CD-ROM or from a network installation share point. If you are installing from a share point, make sure that the Share and NTFS permissions at the source allow you to install the program.
- ☑ If you plan to install an enterprise array, the machine onto which you install ISA Server must be a member of a domain. You also need to connect to a domain controller during the installation.

Chapter 5 Continued

- ☑ It is paramount that you configure the LAT correctly because it defines the networks that are considered internal and those that are considered external. If for some reason an external network ID finds itself on the LAT, requests from that network ID will be treated as internal network clients and will not be subjected to the same access controls applied to external network hosts.
- ☑ The H.323 Gatekeeper allows multiple inbound and outbound calls using a program such as NetMeeting to conduct voice, video, and data sessions.

Performing the Installation

- ☑ You *must* install the ISA Services. However, you can customize your selections for add-in services and administration tools.
- ☑ If you choose to install the H.323 Gatekeeper administration tool, it will place a node in your ISA Management console that will allow you to configure the H.323 Gatekeeper service.
- ☑ ISA Server listens for Web proxy server requests on port 8080 on the internal interface. This is a departure from the way Web proxy clients accessed the Proxy Server 2.0 Web Proxy Service, which they were able to access by connecting to port 80.
- ☑ You need to have Windows 2000 deployed and available if you want to make the server a member of an enterprise array.
- ☑ Before you promote a standalone server to an array member, you need to complete the *enterprise initialization*.
- ☑ ISA Server has its own management console and does not snap into the Internet Services Manager console the way Proxy Server 2.0 does. You can create your own console that includes the ISA Management standalone snap-in along with other snap-ins.

Migrating from Microsoft Proxy Server 2.0

- ☑ If you work in an organization that already has a Proxy Server 2.0 installation in place, you don't have to redo all the configuration settings that you have so carefully applied.

Chapter 5 Continued

- ☑ When you migrate your Proxy Server 2.0 configuration to Windows 2000, virtually all components of your configuration will be ferried over to ISA Server.
- ☑ Proxy Server 2.0 included the ability to access the Internet while network clients ran IPX/SPX as their transport protocol. This capability has not been extended to ISA Server.
- ☑ If you are running Proxy Server 2.0 on an IPX network, you need to upgrade the networking infrastructure to support TCP/IP prior to installing ISA Server.
- ☑ The Web Proxy Service included with ISA Server is not dependent on IIS or WWW Service configuration parameters.
- ☑ ISA Server Web proxy clients need to send their requests to TCP port 8080 on the internal interface of the ISA server (by default).
- ☑ One of the sweetest features of ISA Server is that you do not need to configure servers that you want to publish to the Internet as Winsock proxy clients.
- ☑ Proxy Server 2.0 saved the Web cache to the file system. That meant you could easily collect thousands of files that needed to be managed by the NTFS file system. ISA Server saves the cache as one file.
- ☑ If you ran the SOCKS Proxy Service and configured access rules for SOCKS proxy clients on your Proxy Server 2.0, you won't be able to configure selective rules for those clients in ISA Server.
- ☑ If you must run a Web server from the same machine running ISA, make sure that no Web sites listen on port 80 of either the internal or external interface.
- ☑ Performing the actual migration from Proxy Server 2.0 to ISA Server is relatively easy. However, if you are going to install Proxy Server 2.0 directly onto a Windows 2000 machine, you must to use a special installation file called msp2wizi.exe that can be downloaded from the Microsoft Proxy Web site at www.microsoft.com/proxy.
- ☑ When the ISA Server installation routine detects that Proxy Server 2.0 was installed on the same machine, it will tell you that an older version of ISA Server is on the machine. Well, this isn't *exactly* right, but you know what it's trying to say. When you are performing the upgrade, you must install the files into the same folder.

❖ Chapter 6: Managing ISA Sever

Understanding Integrated Administration

☑ An entire array of servers can be managed together as one entity. When the configuration of an array is changed, the desired modifications are made to every server in the array.

☑ When you install ISA Server on a Windows 2000 server, the ISA Server selection will be added to the Programs menu with two selections, ISA Management and ISA Server Performance Monitor.

☑ If you have worked with Windows 2000's Active Directory, you'll remember that a *container object* is an object in the tree inside of which other objects can reside.

☑ When you use array and enterprise policies together, array-level rules can be applied to enterprise-level policy elements. This means that when you create a policy element at the enterprise level, it appears as a selection when you create a new rule at the array level.

☑ *Routing rules* determine where Web proxy client requests are sent and apply to both incoming and outgoing Web requests.

☑ The H.323 Gatekeeper is used to allow clients to use NetMeeting and other H.323-compliant applications through the ISA server.

Performing Common Management Tasks

☑ ISA Server uses Windows 2000 discretionary access control lists (DACLs) to control access to objects and object properties.

☑ When you add an array to or remove an array from the enterprise, the information is written to the Active Directory and replicated to all domain controllers in the domain.

☑ A standalone ISA server cannot be joined to an existing array; however, after you have initialized the enterprise, you can *promote* a standalone server to create a new array of which the promoted server will be a member.

Chapter 6 Continued

Using Monitoring, Alerting, Logging, and Reporting Functions

☑ ISA Server allows real-time monitoring of all alerts that occur on any of the servers in an array.

☑ The ISA Server's alert service acts as an event filter, recognizing when events occur, determining whether configured conditions are met, and seeing that the chosen action(s) occurs in response.

☑ When your ISA servers belong to an array, logging is configured for the entire array, but log files are created on every ISA Server that is a member of the array.

Understanding Remote Administration

☑ You can connect to the network via a WAN link by dialing in to the remote access server or by connecting across the Internet through a VPN. Once the connection to the local network is established, you can remotely manage a standalone ISA server, an array, or the enterprise.

☑ Windows 2000 Server family products (Server, Advanced Server, and Datacenter Server) include terminal services as a Windows component.

☑ Terminal Services can be deployed in one of two modes: application server or remote administration.

☑ You can create installation disks containing the Terminal Services client software by running the Terminal Services Client Creator program on the terminal server.

❖ Chapter 7: ISA Architecture and Client Configuration

Understanding ISA Server Architecture

☑ Proxy Server 2.0 was built on three basic services: the Web Proxy Service, the Winsock Proxy Service, and the SOCKS Proxy Service.

Chapter 7 Continued

☑ The four components that form the foundation of the ISA Server are: the Web Proxy Service, the Firewall Service, the Network Address Translation Protocol driver, and the Scheduled Content Download Service.

☑ The Web Proxy Service (w3proxy.exe) provides and controls access to the Web protocols, which are Application layer protocols.

☑ The Web Proxy Service is implemented as the w3proxy.exe file. You can start and stop the service via the net start w3proxy.exe and the net stop w3proxy.exe commands.

☑ The Web Proxy Service is also responsible for the Web cache, which provides a mechanism that allows content retrieved from the Internet to be stored on the ISA server.

☑ The Firewall Service (fwsrv.exe) provides the same functionality to network clients as the Winsock Proxy Service did in Proxy Server 2.0.

☑ The firewall client installs a special version of the Windows Sockets (Winsock) interface. The Winsock interface is a Session layer interface and is implemented as an API.

☑ The firewall client software captures Winsock API calls and forwards them to the Firewall Service via the Firewall Service's control channel.

☑ The Network Address Translation (NAT) Protocol driver allows network clients on a network that uses a private IP addressing scheme to access the Internet.

☑ To solve the problem of Internet access for private network hosts, Windows 2000 provides the Network Address Translation Protocol, or NAT. This protocol allows private network clients to send requests to the NAT server rather then directly to the Internet host.

☑ ISA Server takes advantage of the NAT Protocol driver included with Windows 2000 and extends its functionality so that it is able to work with the other ISA Server services.

☑ The Scheduled Content Download Service provides ISA Server a mechanism to automatically download Web content from sites you want to have available on the ISA server before a user actually makes a request for the content.

Chapter 7 Continued

- ☑ All requests, regardless of whether they are from SecureNAT, firewall, or Web proxy clients, must pass though the ISA server's packet filters.
- ☑ HTTP requests issued by a Web proxy client, or a SecureNAT or firewall client with the HTTP redirector enabled, can also be subjected to a custom set of Application layer filters known collectively as Web filters.

Installing and Configuring ISA Server Clients

- ☑ The SecureNAT service provides virtually transparent proxy services for your network clients.
- ☑ Whether you install a DNS server on your internal network or configure your SecureNAT clients to use a DNS server on the Internet, you must have site and content as well as protocol rules in place that will allow your SecureNAT clients to query an external DNS server.
- ☑ If you choose to implement a single, centralized DHCP server, you must configure multiple scopes to service all network IDs that have DHCP clients.
- ☑ In order to ping an external client, the ISA Server must be configured to allow IP Routing.
- ☑ The firewall client installation file can also be accessed via a Web page, but the Web installation information files must be manually moved to a directory in the Internet Information Server WWW service accessible hierarchy.
- ☑ If you have Mac, UNIX, or other non-Microsoft operating systems on the network, you will not be able to install the firewall client and therefore will not be able to take advantage of the complete range of protocols provided by the firewall client.
- ☑ You should not configure servers that are published to the Internet to use the firewall client.
- ☑ When you use the software deployment tools in the Windows 2000 Group Policy objects, you'll typically have an organizational unit (OU) or a set of OUs to which you will make the software available.
- ☑ The firewall client supports a process known as autodiscovery, in which the firewall client is able to query either a DHCP server via a DHCPINFORM message or directly query a DNS server via a DNS query for the name wpad.<domain_name>.

Chapter 7 Continued

- ☑ The most compelling reason to use DHCP, rather than DNS, when configuring your wpad entries is that DCHP allows you a more granular approach to assigning your ISA servers to the network clients.
- ☑ ISA Server allows you to publish servers by configuring them as SecureNAT clients, therefore virtually obviating the need to set up the published servers as firewall (Winsock) clients.
- ☑ A Web proxy client is a CERN-compliant Web browser or other application that can be configured to send requests to the Web Proxy Service on the ISA server.
- ☑ When the Web proxy client is configured to support autodiscovery, it can take advantage of a wpad entry contained in either a DHCP or DNS server.

❖ Chapter 8: Configuring ISA Server for Outbound Access

Configuring the Server for Outbound Access

- ☑ Several elements determine how outbound requests for Internet resources are handled. These elements can be broken down roughly into two groups: Outbound Web protocol requests, and Outbound "everything else."
- ☑ You can configure the amount of server memory and other resources dedicated to servicing Web requests via the **Performance** page.
- ☑ When you configure the **Performance tuning** slider bar to support more users per day, you dedicate more of the system resources to the ISA Server services.

Network Configuration Settings

- ☑ ISA Server network configuration settings that influence outbound access controls include the following: routing SecureNAT and firewall client requests, routing Web Proxy Service requests, passing outbound PPTP requests from internal clients, the local address table (LAT), and the local domain table (LDT).

Chapter 8 Continued

- ☑ When firewall clients send their requests to the ISA server, the requests can be routed directly to the Internet via the *primary connection* on the ISA server, or you can configure the Firewall Service on the ISA server to forward the request to another ISA server.
- ☑ The most common application of routing rules is to support *Web proxy chaining.* Web proxy chains can connect ISA servers located at different sites or LAN segments in a hierarchical fashion so that downstream ISA servers can take advantage of the cache contents of upstream ISA servers.
- ☑ You can route Web proxy requests sent from clients to an ISA server to a Squid server and take advantage of the access controls configured on the ISA server.
- ☑ ISA Server supports outbound PPTP sessions between an internal network client behind an ISA server and a PPTP server located on an external network.
- ☑ The ISA server uses the *local address table (LAT)* to define the IP addresses that are internal and those that are external.
- ☑ ISA Server uses the routing table to assess where to send packets based on their destination network IDs.
- ☑ The *local domain table (LDT)* contains a list of local domains that is downloaded by firewall clients on a regular basis.

Creating Secure Outbound Access Policy

- ☑ ISA Server rules involved with outbound access are grouped into *access policies.* There are three categories of access policy: site and content rules, protocol rules, and IP packet filters.
- ☑ *Bandwidth priorities* allow you to define communications to give prioritized bandwidth to different types of communications.
- ☑ *Destination sets* allow you to create rules that are based on a particular destination. A destination can be defined by an IP address, a group of IP addresses, a computer name, a fully qualified domain name, an entire domain, or a subfolder on a computer within a domain.

Chapter 8 Continued

☑ *Client address sets* are the flip side of destination sets. You can group clients together by *IP address ranges* and then control access via these client address sets.

☑ *Protocol definitions* allow you to create policies based on Application layer protocols.

☑ *Application filters* can install their own protocol definitions, and some application filters use protocol definitions included with ISA Server.

☑ *Content groups* allow you to control outbound access based on content contained in Web pages or FTP sites.

☑ *Bandwidth rules* build on the bandwidth priorities you created when configuring policy elements.

☑ *Protocol rules* determine the TCP/UDP protocols that network clients can access. Protocol rules can be configured to allow primary connections for either inbound or outbound requests.

Configuring Application Filters That Affect Outbound Access

☑ ISA Server includes a group of application filters that listen to inbound and outbound connections and can influence communications intercepted by the application filters.

☑ The HTTP redirector filter provides SecureNAT and firewall clients access to the services provided by the Web Proxy Service.

☑ ISA Server includes a SOCKS, version 4, application filter. This filter allows you to run SOCKS 4 applications behind ISA Server.

☑ The streaming media filter allows you to make multimedia protocols available to your ISA Server clients.

☑ *Live stream splitting* allows a single connection to a streaming media event to be shared among multiple users in an organization.

Chapter 8 Continued

Understanding and Configuring the Web Proxy Cache

☑ When the ISA server is installed in either Cache or Integrated mode, the Web Proxy Service is installed. The Web Proxy Service includes the Web caching facility.

☑ The Web proxy cache stores and retrieves Web objects based on how you configure the caching properties on the ISA server.

☑ To optimize the performance of your mixed active and passive caching solution, you should configure the passive caching configuration (through the **HTTP** tab) to update objects **Less frequently** and the active-caching configuration (through the **Active Caching** tab) to retrieve the files **Frequently**.

☑ The Scheduled Content Download Service allows you to configure content to be downloaded automatically to the Web cache so that it is available to users before anyone even accesses the sites.

❖ Chapter 9: Configuring ISA Server for Inbound Asscess

Configuring ISA Server Packet Filtering

☑ *Packet filtering* is the process of examining the TCP and IP header information to assess whether a packet should be allowed to enter or leave the external interface of the ISA server.

☑ When packet filtering is enabled, only packets for which a filter has been configured are allowed to pass through the external interface of the ISA server.

☑ Static packet filters allow you to permanently open or close access to packets of your choice.

☑ Packet filtering must be enabled in order to enable intrusion detection. ISA Server can be configured to detect a limited number of intrusion types.

Chapter 9 Continued

Application Filters That Affect Inbound Access

- ☑ The RPC filter, when enabled, allows you to publish internal servers that use RPC communications. RPC, or *remote procedure call,* is message-passing mechanism that allows a distributed application to call services that are available on various computers on a network.
- ☑ SMTP is a member of the TCP/IP protocol suite, used for exchanging e-mail across the Internet.

Designing Perimeter Networks

- ☑ A *perimeter network* is a security zone where all hosts on the network have public IP addresses.
- ☑ A tri-homed perimeter network configuration has the internal network interface and the perimeter network interface directly connected to the same ISA server.
- ☑ Publishing FTP servers on the perimeter network presents a special challenge. The reason is that there are two types of FTP clients that may connect to your FTP server: PASV servers, and Standard servers.
- ☑ A *bastion host* is a machine that interacts with the Internet and protects your internal resources.

❖ Chapter 10: Publishing Servers to the Internet

Types of Publishing

- ☑ The process of publishing services involves the use of wizards built into ISA Server to complete the publishing process.
- ☑ Web Publishing Wizards allow you to publish content contained on your internal Web servers. Services that can be published via Web publishing include: HTTP, HTTPS, and FTP.
- ☑ The Server Publishing Wizard allows you to publish services on the internal network. In order to do so, there must be a *protocol definition* to support that service.

Chapter 10 Continued

- ☑ When you publish a server on the internal network using the Server Publishing Wizard, you include the server protocol definition required to publish the server.

Web Server Publishing

- ☑ The Web Publishing Wizard makes the process of publishing an internal Web server very easy. The wizard will walk you through the process of choosing the internal Web server and the ports you want to use on it.
- ☑ Users on the Internet will access your published Web sites via fully qualified domain names (FQDNs), such as www.isaserver.org.
- ☑ In order for your publishing rules to work, make sure you have your DNS client/server infrastructure in place. Remember, your published servers are SecureNAT clients of the ISA server.
- ☑ Firewall clients allow the ISA server to resolve requests on their behalf. This is referred to as *DNS proxy*.
- ☑ When working with a routed network, make sure the routing table on the ISA server is configured properly before even setting up ISA Server.
- ☑ Before publishing a Web site located on the ISA server, you first need to change the IP address and listening port number that IIS uses to listen for inbound Web requests.
- ☑ ISA Server web publishing rules allow you to redirect HTTP requests as other protocols.
- ☑ Destination sets allow you a great deal of flexibility in your Web publishing solutions. For example, you can use a path statement in a publishing rule to redirect a request to a particular server on the internal network.
- ☑ ISA Server supports secure Web site publishing using SSL.
- ☑ Another way to publish a secure Web site is to use server publishing rules rather than Web publishing rules. You would publish the internal server using a protocol definition for port 443.

Chapter 10 Continued

Publishing Services

- ☑ You can publish virtually any service running on your internal network using server publishing rules. Server publishing takes advantage of protocol definitions you've created for inbound access to server services.
- ☑ When a service on the internal network is published via server publishing rules, the port number (for that interface) assigned to the server is dedicated to that rule.
- ☑ Port redirection is a feature of the Windows 2000 RRAS NAT Service. Using this feature, you can forward a message received at one port number on the external interface of the ISA server to a different port number on the internal server.
- ☑ It is highly recommended that you use the Web Publishing Wizard if you wish to publish Web protocols.
- ☑ In order to publish services on the internal network, there must be a protocol definition defined to support the server publishing rule.
- ☑ Most of your published servers will be configured as SecureNAT clients.
- ☑ ISA Server includes a special wizard that can guide you through the process of publishing a mail server. The Secure Mail Publishing Wizard allows you to publish multiple mail-related protocols at once.
- ☑ Outlook Web Access (OWA) allows users to access their Exchange mailboxes by using a Web browser.
- ☑ Publishing a terminal server on the internal network works the same way as publishing the internal interface of the ISA server.

The H.323 Gatekeeper Service

- ☑ The H.323 Gatekeeper Service allows H.323-aware applications to communicate with each other over an intranet or over the Internet.
- ☑ The H.323 Gatekeeper Service was designed to optimize the benefits of LAN-to-LAN calls. When each LAN has a gatekeeper and NetMeeting clients registered with their respective gatekeepers, users can call NetMeeting clients on other networks by using either an e-mail address or a telephone number.

Chapter 10 Continued

- ☑ NetMeeting clients can be configured to use ILS servers on the internal network, and call other internal NetMeeting clients registered with the ILS server.
- ☑ Phone number rules can be used to route requests based on telephone number strings. These are helpful if you plan to implement multiple H.323 gatekeepers in your organization, and partition client registrations based on prefixes.

Virtual Private Networking

- ☑ ISA Server supports virtual private networking by allowing inbound access to the ISA server by VPN clients, and by configuring ISA Server in a gateway-to-gateway configuration.
- ☑ The Routing and Remote Access Service (RRAS) is required in order to configure the VPN server components on the ISA server.
- ☑ If you want to allow external VPN clients to dial in to the ISA server, you can use the VPN Client Wizard to allow inbound access.

❖ Chapter 11: Optimizing, Customizing, Integrating, and Backing Up ISA Server

Optimizing ISA Server Performance

- ☑ A *benchmark* is a reference point or set of reference points against which something can be compared. This point or points can be list of performance criteria a product is expected to meet, a set of conditions by which a product is measured, or a known product to which other products are compared.
- ☑ Optimizing performance involves finding a way to make all components of a system work together smoothly with the smallest possible amount of delay or downtime.
- ☑ Hardware specifications and condition, software configuration, and interaction with other networking components combine to determine the speed and efficiency with which your ISA servers do their jobs.

Chapter 11 Continued

- ☑ A key factor in any performance-monitoring program is to establish a baseline. This is done by collecting information at intervals, averaged over a period of time when the network is performing normally.
- ☑ The ISA Server Performance Monitor console differs from the Windows 2000 System Monitor in that it already has a set of default performance counters configured.
- ☑ In addition to viewing the performance data in real time using the System Monitor component of the ISA Performance Monitor, you can record this data for later viewing using the Performance Logs functionality.
- ☑ The *effective bandwidth* is defined by Microsoft as the actual bandwidth for a specific connectivity device such as a modem or ISDN terminal adapter, or the total effective network bandwidth.
- ☑ *Load balancing* refers to a method of spreading the processing workload across multiple machines, for better performance and fault tolerance.
- ☑ When the Cache Array Routing Protocol (CARP) is enabled on an ISA Server computer, you can configure the servers in the array so that they have different loads by setting the *load factor.*
- ☑ If you are using Windows 2000 NLB on your network, you should not enable CARP on incoming Web requests. The reason for this is that the load-balancing driver will determine to which server the requests should be directed and route each request to one of the servers in the array.
- ☑ Because RAM is faster than hard disk speeds, objects that are cached in RAM can be retrieved faster than those that are cached on the disk.
- ☑ *Active caching* is a means of speeding up access to files that are accessed frequently, by automatically refreshing the content of such objects when they are soon to expire.

Customizing ISA Server

- ☑ The ISA Server SDK is a comprehensive collection of development tools and sample scripts that can be used to build new, custom features that enhance ISA's firewall, caching, and management functionality. Administration scripts can simplify and automate administrative tasks.

Chapter 11 Continued

Developers can create custom administration scripts, or administrators can use the sample scripts included with the SDK.

- ☑ Even before Microsoft released the final version of ISA Server, several third-party vendors had begun to develop solutions to customize and enhance ISA's features and functionality. In many cases, Microsoft has partnered with these companies to provide complementary products for ISA.

Integrating ISA Server with Other Services

- ☑ ISA Server software does not operate in a vacuum; it must interoperate with other services and applications on the computer and on your network.
- ☑ The Windows 2000 Active Directory is a hierarchical database that is stored on Windows 2000 domain controllers. It holds information about objects on the network (users, groups, computers, printers, files, and other network resources).
- ☑ Active Directory is governed by a set of rules called the *schema,* which define object classes and attributes (these are called *metadata* because they describe "data about data"). The content of the schema is controlled by a single domain controller that holds the role of *schema master.*
- ☑ Although the ISA configuration is stored on the Windows 2000 domain controllers, you do *not* have to install ISA Server on a DC.
- ☑ Windows 2000 Routing and Remote Access Services (RRAS) provide a collection of services that allow a Windows 2000 server to function as a full-fledged software router, forwarding IP packets from one subnet or network to another, or as a dial-up server and to create and control dial-up networking policies and virtual private networking connections across WAN links.
- ☑ RRAS can be enabled on an ISA Server computer. The ISA server can also function as a remote access server or VPN server.
- ☑ Windows 2000 Server includes IIS 5.0, and it is installed by default when you install the operating system. However, you can elect not to install it in a custom installation, or you can remove it later using the **Add/Remove Programs** applet in the Control Panel.

Chapter 11 Continued

- ☑ The IP Security Protocol (IPSec) support is a new feature in Windows 2000 that was not included in Windows NT 4.0. IPSec is an Internet standard, developed by the Internet Engineering Task Force (IETF).
- ☑ IPSec uses *Security Associations (SAs)* to establish a secure connection. An SA is a combination of policy and keys that define how data will be exchanged and protected.
- ☑ You can install Windows 2000 Server as a standalone or member server on a computer that is a member of a Windows NT 4.0 domain.

Backing Up and Restoring the ISA Configuration

- ☑ Backing up important system information is a vital part of any network administrator's routine, and ISA Server includes a backup and restore feature that allows you to save and reapply configuration information in the event of a failure.
- ☑ You should back up the configuration each time you make any major change to the ISA server or array settings.
- ☑ Microsoft recommends that you always store the configuration backup on an NTFS partition for security purposes. Doing so will allow you to protect the files from unauthorized access, using NTFS permissions.
- ☑ When ISA Server is installed as an array member (even if the array has only one member), the configuration information is stored in Active Directory.
- ☑ You can backup the enterprise configuration data to a separate file. Backing up the enterprise saves all enterprise-specific information. This includes enterprise-level policy elements and policies as well as information regarding which arrays in the enterprise use specific enterprise policies.

❖ Chapter 12: Troubleshooting ISA Server

Understanding Basic Troubleshooting Principles

- ☑ Troubleshooting refers to the process of discovering, diagnosing, and correcting problems.

Chapter 12 Continued

- ☑ Our systematic approach to troubleshooting involves five basic steps: information gathering, analysis and planning, implementation of a solution, assessment of the effectiveness of the solution, and documentation of the incident.
- ☑ Standard information forms help you gather information in a systematic way that makes it easy to organize and analyze.
- ☑ Once you've gathered all the information possible regarding the problem (including attempting to reproduce it), it's time to analyze the data. Your analysis of the data will lead you to formulate a logical *plan* based on your diagnoses, possible solutions, and priorities.
- ☑ Although there could be several possible solutions to a problem, you should always implement *one change at a time.* Assess the results of that change before trying something else.
- ☑ In the *follow-up* stage of troubleshooting, it is vital that you assess the results of your actions and determine whether your "fix" worked, whether it was only a temporary workaround or actually solved the problem, whether it caused other problems while correcting the original one, and what can be done in the future to prevent the problem from recurring.
- ☑ Always start by checking the Event Viewer and other logs. In many cases, the information that will point you in the right direction is there waiting for you.
- ☑ Five troubleshooting tips endorsed by problem solvers in many fields are precisely defining the problem; recreating the problem; avoiding tunnel vision; practicing the art of patience; using available resources; and not being afraid to ask for help.

Troubleshooting ISA Installation and Configuration Problems

- ☑ Installation of ISA Server usually proceeds in a straightforward fashion. Problems during or directly following installation are often related to one of three things: hardware incompatibilities, software incompatibilities, and improper initial configuration.
- ☑ If you are installing ISA Server as an array member, Active Directory must be implemented on your network.

Chapter 12 Continued

- ☑ ISA Server's address translation function is also incompatible with third-party NAT solutions such as Sygate or NAT32. You should install these programs from the Windows 2000 computer before installing ISA Server.
- ☑ If you receive an error message:

```
ISA Server cannot save the properties. Error 0x80040340. The IP
range already exists in the Local Address Table (LAT)
```

  when you attempt to save a new LAT entry, this could be due to the fact that it is an exact duplicate of an already existing address.
- ☑ When you install ISA Server and you need for your clients to be able to use an external Exchange server, you may find that using Microsoft Outlook for e-mail does not work, although Web services function properly. In this case, you need to add the IP address of the external Exchange server to the LAT and install the firewall client software on the internal machines that are running Outlook. This will allow the clients' e-mail to go through.

Troubleshooting Authentication and Access Problems

- ☑ ISA Server can be configured to always require authentication for Web requests. To do so, you configure the array's **Outgoing Web Requests** properties by checking the option to ask unauthenticated users for identification.
- ☑ Users of Netscape or other non-Microsoft browsers might be unable to be authenticated by ISA Server. This happens because ISA can be configured to only accept Windows integrated authentication. If the client's browser cannot provide the user's credentials in NTLM format, those users will not be able to access the requested Web objects if authentication is required.
- ☑ Access problems include both the inability of authorized clients to access needed resources *and* the ability of unauthorized users to access resources that should not be available to them. Incorrect ISA Server configuration can result in both kinds of access problems.
- ☑ If clients are unable to use specific protocols to communicate with the external network, you can allow the use of particular protocols in one of two ways: configure IP packet filters to allow the protocols, and configure protocol rules to allow the protocols.

Chapter 12 Continued

- ☑ You might find that even after you have disabled a protocol rule, clients are still using the protocol that was allowed by the rule. This happens because disabling a protocol rule does not terminate any of the existing client sessions. Until the session has been disconnected, clients can continue to use the protocol after you disable the rule.
- ☑ A dial-up connection might be dropped because it was inadvertently disconnected. If you restart the ISA Server services, the connection should be automatically reestablished.

Troubleshooting ISA Client Problems

- ☑ If Secure NAT (S-NAT) connections are slow, the cause might be the result of not enabling packet filtering.
- ☑ SecureNAT clients will not be able to connect to the Internet through the ISA server if the client is not properly configured with the default gateway and DNS server. Check the configuration settings in the client's TCP/IP properties.
- ☑ If the internal connections are inordinately slow for firewall clients, it could be due to the fact that clients cannot resolve local names using an external DNS server that does not have the necessary records.
- ☑ S-NAT clients may experience an inability to connect to specific ports because the connection times out, even though protocol rules are set to allow "any IP traffic."
- ☑ The Administration COM objects in ISA Server can be used by developers working with any programming language that supports COM. Some of the objects are used for programmatic monitoring of currently running services; most are used for programmatic configuration of internal ISA settings.
- ☑ If a S-NAT client can connect to Internet sites using the IP address but is not able to connect using the "friendly" computer name, this is likely due to the fact that the client is configured to use an internal DNS server, which cannot resolve external Internet domain names.

Chapter 12 Continued

Troubleshooting Caching, Publishing, and Services

- ☑ When ISA Server is installed in caching or integrated mode, it caches objects to accelerate client access. In some cases, you might encounter problems with the caching function.
- ☑ If the Web proxy service will not start, this can be due to the fact that the cache contents file has become corrupted. The cache file is stored on a drive where space has been allocated for this purpose.
- ☑ Publishing makes servers on the internal network available to users outside the LAN (on the other side of the ISA Server). Publishing problems could involve the inability of authorized clients to access the published servers.
- ☑ If the Exchange server is a S-NAT client, this can be caused by incorrect configuration of the server publishing rules. The solution is to see that the publishing rules are configured to allow the external interface to pass SMTP traffic on port 25 and POP3 traffic on port 110 to the IP address and port of the internal Exchange server.
- ☑ If the Exchange server is a firewall client, there could be a conflict between a server publishing rule and a firewall client configuration file.

Index

A

B

C

D

E

F

G

H

I

J

K

L

M

N

O

P

S

T

U

V

X

Z

The Global Knowledge Advantage

Global Knowledge has a global delivery system for its products and services. The company has 28 subsidiaries, and offers its programs through a total of 60+ locations. No other vendor can provide consistent services across a geographic area this large. Global Knowledge is the largest independent information technology education provider, offering programs on a variety of platforms. This enables our multi-platform and multi-national customers to obtain all of their programs from a single vendor. The company has developed the unique CompetusTM Framework software tool and methodology which can quickly reconfigure courseware to the proficiency level of a student on an interactive basis. Combined with self-paced and on-line programs, this technology can reduce the time required for training by prescribing content in only the deficient skills areas. The company has fully automated every aspect of the education process, from registration and follow-up, to "just-in-time" production of courseware. Global Knowledge through its Enterprise Services Consultancy, can customize programs and products to suit the needs of an individual customer.

Global Knowledge Classroom Education Programs

The backbone of our delivery options is classroom-based education. Our modern, well-equipped facilities staffed with the finest instructors offer programs in a wide variety of information technology topics, many of which lead to professional certifications.

Custom Learning Solutions

This delivery option has been created for companies and governments that value customized learning solutions. For them, our consultancy-based approach of developing targeted education solutions is most effective at helping them meet specific objectives.

Self-Paced and Multimedia Products

This delivery option offers self-paced program titles in interactive CD-ROM, videotape and audio tape programs. In addition, we offer custom development of interactive multimedia courseware to customers and partners. Call us at 1-888-427-4228.

Electronic Delivery of Training

Our network-based training service delivers efficient competency-based, interactive training via the World Wide Web and organizational intranets. This leading-edge delivery option provides a custom learning path and "just-in-time" training for maximum convenience to students.

Global Knowledge Courses Available

Microsoft

- Windows 2000 Deployment Strategies
- Introduction to Directory Services
- Windows 2000 Client Administration
- Windows 2000 Server
- Windows 2000 Update
- MCSE Bootcamp
- Microsoft Networking Essentials
- Windows NT 4.0 Workstation
- Windows NT 4.0 Server
- Windows NT Troubleshooting
- Windows NT 4.0 Security
- Windows 2000 Security
- Introduction to Microsoft Web Tools

Management Skills

- Project Management for IT Professionals
- Microsoft Project Workshop
- Management Skills for IT Professionals

Network Fundamentals

- Understanding Computer Networks
- Telecommunications Fundamentals I
- Telecommunications Fundamentals II
- Understanding Networking Fundamentals
- Upgrading and Repairing PCs
- DOS/Windows A+ Preparation
- Network Cabling Systems

WAN Networking and Telephony

- Building Broadband Networks
- Frame Relay Internetworking
- Converging Voice and Data Networks
- Introduction to Voice Over IP
- Understanding Digital Subscriber Line (xDSL)

Internetworking

- ATM Essentials
- ATM Internetworking
- ATM Troubleshooting
- Understanding Networking Protocols
- Internetworking Routers and Switches
- Network Troubleshooting
- Internetworking with TCP/IP
- Troubleshooting TCP/IP Networks
- Network Management
- Network Security Administration
- Virtual Private Networks
- Storage Area Networks
- Cisco OSPF Design and Configuration
- Cisco Border Gateway Protocol (BGP) Configuration

Web Site Management and Development

- Advanced Web Site Design
- Introduction to XML
- Building a Web Site
- Introduction to JavaScript
- Web Development Fundamentals
- Introduction to Web Databases

PERL, UNIX, and Linux

- PERL Scripting
- PERL with CGI for the Web
- UNIX Level I
- UNIX Level II
- Introduction to Linux for New Users
- Linux Installation, Configuration, and Maintenance

Authorized Vendor Training

Red Hat

- Introduction to Red Hat Linux
- Red Hat Linux Systems Administration
- Red Hat Linux Network and Security Administration
- RHCE Rapid Track Certification

Cisco Systems

- Interconnecting Cisco Network Devices
- Advanced Cisco Router Configuration
- Installation and Maintenance of Cisco Routers
- Cisco Internetwork Troubleshooting
- Designing Cisco Networks
- Cisco Internetwork Design
- Configuring Cisco Catalyst Switches
- Cisco Campus ATM Solutions
- Cisco Voice Over Frame Relay, ATM, and IP
- Configuring for Selsius IP Phones
- Building Cisco Remote Access Networks
- Managing Cisco Network Security
- Cisco Enterprise Management Solutions

Nortel Networks

- Nortel Networks Accelerated Router Configuration
- Nortel Networks Advanced IP Routing
- Nortel Networks WAN Protocols
- Nortel Networks Frame Switching
- Nortel Networks Accelar 1000
- Comprehensive Configuration
- Nortel Networks Centillion Switching
- Network Management with Optivity for Windows

Oracle Training

- Introduction to Oracle8 and PL/SQL
- Oracle8 Database Administration

Custom Corporate Network Training

Train on Cutting Edge Technology

We can bring the best in skill-based training to your facility to create a real-world hands-on training experience. Global Knowledge has invested millions of dollars in network hardware and software to train our students on the same equipment they will work with on the job. Our relationships with vendors allow us to incorporate the latest equipment and platforms into your on-site labs.

Maximize Your Training Budget

Global Knowledge provides experienced instructors, comprehensive course materials, and all the networking equipment needed to deliver high quality training. You provide the students; we provide the knowledge.

Avoid Travel Expenses

On-site courses allow you to schedule technical training at your convenience, saving time, expense, and the opportunity cost of travel away from the workplace.

Discuss Confidential Topics

Private on-site training permits the open discussion of sensitive issues such as security, access, and network design. We can work with your existing network's proprietary files while demonstrating the latest technologies.

Customize Course Content

Global Knowledge can tailor your courses to include the technologies and the topics which have the greatest impact on your business. We can complement your internal training efforts or provide a total solution to your training needs.

Corporate Pass

The Corporate Pass Discount Program rewards our best network training customers with preferred pricing on public courses, discounts on multimedia training packages, and an array of career planning services.

Global Knowledge Training Lifecycle

Supporting the Dynamic and Specialized Training Requirements of Information Technology Professionals:

- Define Profile
- Assess Skills
- Design Training
- Deliver Training
- Test Knowledge
- Update Profile
- Use New Skills

Global Knowledge

Global Knowledge programs are developed and presented by industry professionals with "real-world" experience. Designed to help professionals meet today's interconnectivity and interoperability challenges, most of our programs feature hands-on labs that incorporate state-of-the-art communication components and equipment.

ON-SITE TEAM TRAINING

Bring Global Knowledge's powerful training programs to your company. At Global Knowledge, we will custom design courses to meet your specific network requirements. Call (919)-461-8686 for more information.

YOUR GUARANTEE

Global Knowledge believes its courses offer the best possible training in this field. If during the first day you are not satisfied and wish to withdraw from the course, simply notify the instructor, return all course materials and receive a 100% refund.

REGISTRATION INFORMATION

In the US:
call: (888) 762–4442
fax: (919) 469–7070
visit our Web site:
www.globalknowledge.com

LICENSE AGREEMENT

THIS PRODUCT (THE "PRODUCT") CONTAINS PROPRIETARY SOFTWARE, DATA AND INFORMATION (INCLUDING DOCUMENTATION) OWNED BY SYNGRESS PUBLISHING, INC. ("SYNGRESS") AND ITS LICENSORS. YOUR RIGHT TO USE THE PRODUCT IS GOVERNED BY THE TERMS AND CONDITIONS OF THIS AGREEMENT.

LICENSE: Throughout this License Agreement, "you" shall mean either the individual or the entity whose agent opens this package. You are granted a limited, non-exclusive and non-transferable license to use the Product subject to the following terms:

(i) If you have licensed a single user version of the Product, the Product may only be used on a single computer (i.e., a single CPU). If you licensed and paid the fee applicable to a local area network or wide area network version of the Product, you are subject to the terms of the following subparagraph (ii).

(ii) If you have licensed a local area network version, you may use the Product on unlimited workstations located in one single building selected by you that is served by such local area network. If you have licensed a wide area network version, you may use the Product on unlimited workstations located in multiple buildings on the same site selected by you that is served by such wide area network; provided, however, that any building will not be considered located in the same site if it is more than five (5) miles away from any building included in such site. In addition, you may only use a local area or wide area network version of the Product on one single server. If you wish to use the Product on more than one server, you must obtain written authorization from Syngress and pay additional fees.

(iii) You may make one copy of the Product for back-up purposes only and you must maintain an accurate record as to the location of the back-up at all times.

PROPRIETARY RIGHTS; RESTRICTIONS ON USE AND TRANSFER: All rights (including patent and copyright) in and to the Product are owned by Syngress and its licensors. You are the owner of the enclosed disc on which the Product is recorded. You may not use, copy, decompile, disassemble, reverse engineer, modify, reproduce, create derivative works, transmit, distribute, sublicense, store in a database or retrieval system of any kind, rent or transfer the Product, or any portion thereof, in any form or by any means (including electronically or otherwise) except as expressly provided for in this License Agreement. You must reproduce the copyright notices, trademark notices, legends and logos of Syngress and its licensors that appear on the Product on the back-up copy of the Product which you are permitted to make hereunder. All rights in the Product not expressly granted herein are reserved by Syngress and its licensors.

TERM: This License Agreement is effective until terminated. It will terminate if you fail to comply with any term or condition of this License Agreement. Upon termination, you are obligated to return to Syngress the Product together with all copies thereof and to purge and destroy all copies of the Product included in any and all systems, servers and facilities.

DISCLAIMER OF WARRANTY: THE PRODUCT AND THE BACK-UP COPY OF THE PRODUCT ARE LICENSED "AS IS". SYNGRESS, ITS LICENSORS AND THE AUTHORS MAKE NO WARRANTIES, EXPRESS OR IMPLIED, AS TO RESULTS TO BE OBTAINED BY ANY PERSON OR ENTITY FROM USE OF THE PRODUCT AND/OR ANY INFORMATION OR DATA INCLUDED THEREIN. SYNGRESS, ITS LICENSORS AND THE AUTHORS MAKE NO EXPRESS OR IMPLIED WARRANTIES OF MERCHANTABILITY OR FITNESS FOR A PARTICULAR PURPOSE OR USE WITH RESPECT TO THE PRODUCT AND/OR ANY INFORMATION OR DATA INCLUDED THEREIN. IN ADDITION, SYNGRESS, ITS LICENSORS AND THE AUTHORS MAKE NO WARRANTY REGARDING THE ACCURACY, ADEQUACY OR COMPLETENESS OF THE PRODUCT AND/OR ANY INFORMATION OR DATA INCLUDED THEREIN. NEITHER SYNGRESS, ANY OF ITS LICENSORS, NOR THE AUTHORS WARRANT THAT THE FUNCTIONS CONTAINED IN THE PRODUCT WILL MEET YOUR REQUIREMENTS OR THAT THE OPERATION OF THE PRODUCT WILL BE UNINTERRUPTED OR ERROR FREE. YOU ASSUME THE ENTIRE RISK WITH RESPECT TO THE QUALITY AND PERFORMANCE OF THE PRODUCT.

LIMITED WARRANTY FOR DISC: To the original licensee only, Syngress warrants that the enclosed disc on which the Product is recorded is free from defects in materials and workmanship under normal use and service for a period of ninety (90) days from the date of purchase. In the event of a defect in the disc covered by the foregoing warranty, Syngress will replace the disc.

LIMITATION OF LIABILITY: NEITHER SYNGRESS, ITS LICENSORS NOR THE AUTHORS SHALL BE LIABLE FOR ANY INDIRECT, INCIDENTAL, SPECIAL, PUNITIVE, CONSEQUENTIAL OR SIMILAR DAMAGES, SUCH AS BUT NOT LIMITED TO, LOSS OF ANTICIPATED PROFITS OR BENEFITS, RESULTING FROM THE USE OR INABILITY TO USE THE PRODUCT EVEN IF ANY OF THEM HAS BEEN ADVISED OF THE POSSIBILITY OF SUCH DAMAGES. THIS LIMITATION OF LIABILITY SHALL APPLY TO ANY CLAIM OR CAUSE WHATSOEVER WHETHER SUCH CLAIM OR CAUSE ARISES IN CONTRACT, TORT, OR OTHERWISE. Some states do not allow the exclusion or limitation of indirect, special or consequential damages, so the above limitation may not apply to you.

U.S. GOVERNMENT RESTRICTED RIGHTS. If the Product is acquired by or for the U.S. Government then it is provided with Restricted Rights. Use, duplication or disclosure by the U.S. Government is subject to the restrictions set forth in FAR 52.227-19. The contractor/manufacturer is Syngress Publishing, Inc. at 800 Hingham Street, Rockland, MA 02370.

GENERAL: This License Agreement constitutes the entire agreement between the parties relating to the Product. The terms of any Purchase Order shall have no effect on the terms of this License Agreement. Failure of Syngress to insist at any time on strict compliance with this License Agreement shall not constitute a waiver of any rights under this License Agreement. This License Agreement shall be construed and governed in accordance with the laws of the State of New York. If any provision of this License Agreement is held to be contrary to law, that provision will be enforced to the maximum extent permissible and the remaining provisions will remain in full force and effect.

***If you do not agree, please return this product to the place of purchase for a refund.**

Syngress Publishing's Sweepstake Terms

OFFICIAL RULES - NO PURCHASE NECESSARY

1) TIMING

The contest (the "Contest") begins March 1, 2001 at 9:00 a.m. EST and ends November 30, 2001 at 11:59 p.m. EST (the "Entry Period"). You must enter the contest during the Entry Period.

2) THE PRIZES

Three (3) prizes will be awarded: (a) a Sony DVD Player ("1st Prize"); (b) a Palm Pilot V ("2nd Prize"); and (c) a Rio MP3 Player ("3rd Prize"). One of each prize will be awarded. The approximate retail value of the three prizes is as follows: (a) the Sony DVD Player is approximately $595; (b) the Palm Pilot V is approximately $399; and (c) the Rio MP3 Player is approximately $299.

Sponsors make no warranty, guaranty or representation of any kind concerning any prize. Prize values are subject to change.

3) ELIGIBILITY REQUIREMENTS

No purchase is necessary. Contest is void in Puerto Rico, and where prohibited by law. Employees of Syngress Publishing, Inc. (the "Sponsor") and their affiliates, subsidiaries, officers, agents or any other person or entity directly associated with the contest (the "Contest Entities") and the immediate family members and/or persons living in the same household as such persons are not eligible to enter the Contest.

This contest is open only to people that meet the following requirements:

- legal residents of the United States
- Must be at least 21 years of age or older at the time of winning
- Must own a major credit card

4) HOW TO ENTER: No purchase is necessary to enter. Contestants can enter by mail (see below) or may enter on the Syngress website located at: www.syngress.com/sweepstake.html. ONLY ONE ENTRY PER PERSON OR E-MAIL ADDRESS PER HOUSEHOLD WILL BE ACCEPTED.

No purchase is necessary to enter. To enter by mail, print your name, address, daytime telephone number, email address and age. Mail this in a hand-addressed envelope to: **Syngress Publishing Contest, Syngress Publishing, Inc., 800 Hingham Street, Rockland, MA 02370**. All mail entries must be postmarked before November 15, 2001.

Sponsor assumes no responsibility for lost, late, or misdirected entries or for any computer, online, telephone, or human error or technical malfunctions that may occur. Incomplete mail entries are void. All entries become the property of Sponsor and will not be returned.

If a prize notification or prize is returned to Sponsor or its fulfillment companies as undeliverable for any reason, it will be awarded to an alternate. If necessary, due to unavailability, a prize of equal or great value will be awarded at the discretion of the Sponsor. Prizes are not transferable, assignable or redeemable for cash.

By entering the Contest on the Sponsor Internet site, you may occasionally receive promotion announcements from Sponsor through e-mail. If you no longer wish to receive these e-mails, you may cease your participation in such promotions by sending an e-mail to promotions@syngress.com with your First Name, Last Name, and your e-mail address.

5) WINNER SELECTION/DEADLINE DATES: Random drawings will be conducted by the Sponsor from among all eligible entries. Odds of winning the prize depend on the number of eligible entries received. The first drawing will be for the winner of the 1st Prize, then a drawing will be held from all remaining eligible entries for the winner of the 2nd Prize and finally a drawing will be held from all remaining eligible entries for the winner of the 3rd Prize. These drawings will occur on December 1, 2001, at the offices of Syngress Publishing, Inc., 800 Hingham Street, Rockland, MA 02370. The decisions by the Sponsor shall be final and binding in all respects.

6) GENERAL CONDITIONS: Contest entrants agree to be bound by the terms of these official rules. The laws of the Commonwealth of Massachusetts and the United States govern this Contest, and the state and federal courts located in Suffolk and Middlesex Counties in the Commonwealth of Massachusetts shall be the sole jurisdiction for any disputes related to the Contest. All federal, state, and local laws and regulations apply. Winners will be notified via e-mail and/or U.S. Mail within two (2) weeks of prize drawing. Winners will be required to execute and return an Affidavit of Eligibility and Release of Liability and where legal, Publicity Release within 14 days following the date of issuance of notification. Non-compliance within this time period or return of any prize/prize notification as undeliverable may result in disqualification and selection of an alternate winner. Acceptance of prize constitutes permission for Sponsor to use winner's name and likeness for advertising and promotional purposes without additional compensation unless prohibited by law. BY ENTERING, PARTICIPANTS RELEASE AND HOLD HARMLESS SYNGRESS PUBLISHING, INC., AND ITS RESPECTIVE PARENT CORPORATIONS, SUBSIDIARIES, AFFILIATES, DIRECTORS, OFFICERS, PRIZE SUPPLIERS, EMPLOYEES AND AGENTS FROM ANY AND ALL LIABILITY OR ANY INJURIES, LOSS OR DAMAGE OF ANY KIND ARISING FROM OR IN CONNECTION WITH THE CONTEST OR ACCEPTANCE OR USE OF THE PRIZES WON.

7) INTERNET: If for any reason this contest is not capable of running as planned due to infection by computer virus, bugs, tampering, unauthorized intervention, fraud, technical failures, or any other causes beyond the control of the Sponsor which corrupt or affect the administration, security, fairness, integrity, or proper conduct of this contest, the Sponsor reserves the right, at its sole discretion, to disqualify any individual who tampers with the entry process, and to cancel, terminate, modify, or suspend the online portion of the contest. The Sponsor assumes no responsibility for any error, omission, interruption, deletion, defect, delay in operation or transmission, communications line failure, theft or destruction or unauthorized access to, or alteration of, entries. Sponsor is not responsible for any problems or technical malfunction of any telephone network or telephone lines, computer on-line systems, servers, or providers, computer equipment, software, failure of any e-mail or entry to be received by Sponsor on account of technical problems, human error or traffic congestion on the Internet or at any Web site, or any combination thereof, including any injury or damage to participant's or any other person's computer relating to or resulting from participation in the Contest or downloading any materials in the Contest. CAUTION: ANY ATTEMPT TO DELIBERATELY DAMAGE ANY WEB SITE OR UNDERMINE THE LEGITIMATE OPERATION OF THE CONTEST IS A VIOLATION OF CRIMINAL AND CIVIL LAWS AND SHOULD SUCH AN ATTEMPT BE MADE, SPONSOR RESERVES THE RIGHT TO SEEK DAMAGES OR OTHER REMEDIES FROM ANY SUCH PERSON (S) RESPONSIBLE FOR THE ATTEMPT TO THE FULLEST EXTENT PERMITTED BY LAW. In the event of a dispute as to the identity of a winner based on an e-mail address, the winning entry will be declared made by the authorized account holder of the e-mail address submitted at time of entry. "Authorized account holder" is defined as the natural person who is assigned to an e-mail address by an Internet access provider, on-line service provider, or other organization (e.g., business, educational, institution, etc.) that is responsible for assigning e-mail addresses for the domain associated with the submitted e-mail address.

8) WHO WON: Winners who enter on the web site will be notified by e-mail and winners who had entered via mail will be notified by mail. The winners will also be posted on our web site. Alternatively, to receive the names of the winners please send a self addressed stamped envelope to: Syngress Publishing Contest, care of Syngress Publishing, Inc., 800 Hingham Street, Rockland, MA 02370.

The Sponsor of this sweepstakes is Syngress Publishing, Inc., 800 Hingham Street, Rockland, MA 02370.